THE LIFE AND LETTERS OF WILLIAM SHARP AND "FIONA MACLEOD" VOL. II

The Life and Letters of William Sharp and "Fiona Macleod"

VOLUME II: 1895–1899

William F. Halloran

https://www.openbookpublishers.com

ISBN Paperback: 978-1-78374-869-3
ISBN Hardback: 978-1-78374-870-9
ISBN Digital (PDF): 978-1-78374-871-6
ISBN Digital ebook (epub): 978-1-78374-872-3
ISBN Digital ebook (mobi): 978-1-78374-873-0
ISBN Digital (XML): 978-1-78374-874-7
DOI: 10.11647/OBP.0196

Cover image: "Mr William Sharp: from a photograph by Frederick Hollyer: *The Chap-book*, September 15, 1894", Wikimedia, Public Domain, https://commons.wikimedia.org/wiki/File:William_Sharp_1894.jpg#/media/File:William_Sharp_1894.jpg
Cover design: Anna Gatti.

To the memory of
Noel and Rosemarie Sharp
and
Esther Mona Harvey

Contents

Acknowledgements

William Sharp's wife and first cousin, Elizabeth Amelia Sharp, became his literary executor when he died in 1905. Upon her death in 1932, the executorship passed to her brother, Robert Farquharson Sharp. When he passed away in 1945, that role fell to his son, Noel Farquharson Sharp, who, like his father, was a keeper of printed books in the British Museum. When he died in 1978, the executorship fell to his wife, Rosemarie Sharp, who lived until 2011 when it passed to her son, Robin Sharp.

I am heavily indebted to Noel and Rosemarie Sharp for their assistance and friendship. They granted me permission to publish William Sharp's writings and shared their memories of his relatives and friends. I am especially grateful to Noel Sharp for introducing me in 1963 to Edith Wingate Rinder's daughter, Esther Mona Harvey, a remarkably talented woman whose friendship lasted until her death in 1993. Her recollections of her mother, who played a crucial role in the lives of William and Elizabeth Sharp, were invaluable.

Through many years of my involvement with an obscure and complex man named William Sharp, my wife — Mary Helen Griffin Halloran — has been endlessly patient, encouraging and supportive. This work has benefited greatly from her editorial skills.

I am also grateful to a succession of English graduate students at the University of Wisconsin–Milwaukee who assisted me in transcribing and annotating William Sharp's letters: Edward Bednar, Ann Anderson Allen, Richard Nanian, and Trevor Russell. Without the support I received from the College of Letters and Science and the Graduate School of the University of Wisconsin–Milwaukee this project would not have seen the light of day.

The Appendix lists the institutions that have made copies of their Sharp/Macleod letters available and granted permission to transcribe, edit, and include them in this volume. It also lists the letters held by each institution. Without these libraries, their benefactors, and their competent staffs, a project of this sort — which has stretched over half a century — would have been impossible.

Finally, this project would not have come to fruition had it not been for Warwick Gould, Emeritus Professor and Founding Director of the Institute for English Studies at the University of London. It was he who supported the first iteration of the Sharp letters as a website supported by the Institute, and it was he who suggested Open Book Publishers as a possible location for an expanded edition of *The Life and Letters of William Sharp and Fiona Macleod*. His support and friendship have been a beacon of light.

This is the second volume of a three-volume work which presents Sharp's life from 1895 through 1899. The first volume rages from 1855, the year of his birth, through 1894; and the third from 1900 through 1905, the year of his death.

Introduction[1]

William Sharp was born in Paisley, near Glasgow, in 1855. His father, a successful merchant, moved his family to Glasgow in 1867; his mother, Katherine Brooks, was the daughter of the Swedish Vice Consul in Glasgow. A talented, adventurous boy who read voraciously, he spent summers with his family in the Inner Hebrides where he developed a strong attachment to the land and the people. In the summer of 1863, his paternal aunt brought her children from London to vacation with their cousins. Months short of his eighth birthday, Sharp formed a bond with one of those cousins, Elizabeth Sharp, a bright girl who shared many of his enthusiasms. Their meeting led eventually to their engagement (in 1875) and their marriage (in 1884).

After finishing school at the Glasgow Academy in 1871, Sharp studied literature for two years at Glasgow University, an experience that fed his desire to become a writer. Following his father's sudden death in August 1876, he fell ill and sailed to Australia to recover his health and look for suitable work. Finding none, he enjoyed a warm and adventurous summer and returned in June 1877 to London where he spent several weeks with Elizabeth and her friends. A year later he settled in London and began to establish himself as a poet, journalist, and editor. Through Elizabeth's contacts and those he made among writers, including Dante Gabriel Rossetti, he became by the end of the 1880s a well-established figure in the literary and intellectual life of the city. During this decade he published biographical studies of Rossetti, Percy Bysshe Shelley, and Robert Browning; three books of poetry; two novels; many articles and reviews; and several editions of other writers. None of those publications brought the recognition he sought. By 1890 he had accumulated enough money to reduce his editing and reviewing and devote more time to poetry and prose.

    https://doi.org/10.11647/OBP.0196.09

That autumn he and Elizabeth went to Heidelberg for several weeks and then to Italy for the winter. In January, Edith Wingate Rinder, a beautiful young woman and the wife of Frank Rinder, accompanied her cousin by marriage, Mona Caird, a close girlhood friend of Elizabeth, on a three-week visit to Rome. There Edith spent many hours exploring the city and surrounding area with Sharp, who fell deeply in love with her. Inspired by the joy he felt in her presence and the warmth and beauty of the country, Sharp wrote and printed privately in Italy a slim book of poems, *Sospiri di Roma*, that exceeded in quality those he had written previously.

After returning to England in the spring of 1891 and under the influence of his continuing relationship with Edith, Sharp began writing a prose romance set in western Scotland. When he found a publisher (Frank Murray in Derby) for *Pharais, A Romance of the Isles,* he decided to issue it pseudonymously as the work of Fiona Macleod. In choosing a female pseudonym, Sharp signaled his belief that romance flowed from the repressed feminine side of his nature. The pseudonym also reflected the importance of Edith in the novel's composition and substance. Their relationship is mirrored in the work's depiction of a love affair doomed to failure. Finally, it disguised his authorship from London critics who, he feared, would not treat it seriously if it appeared as the work of the prosaic William Sharp.

Pharais changed the course of Sharp's life. Along with *The Mountain Lovers*, another west of Scotland romance that followed in 1895, it attracted enthusiastic readers and favorable notices. When it became apparent that his fictional author had struck a sympathetic chord with the reading public and the books were bringing in money, Sharp proceeded to invent a life for Fiona Macleod and project her personality through her publications and letters. In letters signed William Sharp, he began promoting the writings of Fiona and adding touches to her character. He sometimes functioned as her agent. To some, he asserted she was his cousin, and he implied to a few intimate friends they were lovers. In molding the persona of Fiona Macleod and sustaining it for a decade, Sharp drew upon the three women he knew best: Elizabeth, his wife and first cousin; Edith Rinder, with whom he had developed a deep bond; and Elizabeth's friend and Edith's cousin, Mona Caird, a powerful and independent woman married to a wealthy Scottish

Laird. He enlisted his sister Mary Sharp, who lived with their mother in Edinburgh, to provide the Fiona handwriting. His drafts of Fiona Macleod letters went to her for copying and mailing from Edinburgh.

For a decade before his death in 1905, he conducted through his publications and correspondence a double literary life. As Fiona, he produced poems and stories which, in their romantic content, settings, characters, and mystical aura, reflected the spirit of the time, attracted a wide readership, and became the principal literary achievement of the Scottish Celtic Renaissance. As Sharp, he continued reviewing and editing and tried his hand at several novels. As Fiona's chief advocate and protector, he deflected requests for interviews by insisting on her desire for privacy. If it became known that he was Fiona, critics would dismiss the writings as deceptive and inauthentic. Destroying the fiction of her being a real woman, moreover, would block his creativity and deprive him of needed income. So he persisted and maintained the double life until he died. He refused to disclose his authorship even to the Prime Minister of England in order to obtain a much-needed Civil List pension. The popular writings of Fiona Macleod may have obtained Parliament's approval, but not those of the journeyman William Sharp.

Sharp's rugged good looks and exuberant manner obscured the fact that he had been ill since childhood. Scarlet fever in his youth and rheumatic fever as a young man damaged his heart. In his forties, diabetes set in, and attacks increased in frequency and seriousness. Given his declining health after the turn of the century, though interrupted by occasional bursts of exuberant creativity, his death in December 1905 was not a surprise to his family and close friends. It occurred while he and Elizabeth were staying with Alexander Nelson Hood, the Duke of Bronte, at his Castello Maniace on the slopes of Mount Etna in Sicily. Sharp is buried there in the estate's Protestant Cemetery, where a large Celtic cross marks his grave.

Structure of the Volume

LIFE

The introductions to each chapter constitute a chronological biography that draws upon the letters and places them in context. The focus is on Sharp's life; his writings are discussed only as they shed light on his daily comings and goings, his beliefs, his values, and his physical and mental condition. The letters reveal more than has previously been known about William Sharp, and he emerges from them as a unique individual who was talented, ambitious, determined to succeed as a writer, and aware of his shortcomings. He was immersed in the cross-currents of ideas and in the artistic and social movements of the last two decades of the nineteenth century in Great Britain and continental Europe. He participated in spiritualist efforts to affirm the existence of some form of life after death, and he embraced new ideas about the place of women in society, the constraints of marriage, the fluidity of gender identity, and the complexity of the human psyche. Those issues and many others are addressed in his letters and, often indirectly, in his writings. The Life sections of *Life and Letters* are not a comprehensive biography, but they are intended to provide, with the letters, the basis for more comprehensive studies of his life and work. They may also be of interest to scholars studying other individuals of the period and the issues in which they were involved.

LETTERS

Most of the letters transcribed, dated, and annotated were made available to the editor by libraries and private collectors throughout the world. They are of interest for what they reveal about Sharp, his correspondents, and the topics he addressed. He knew and corresponded with many influential writers, among them Dante Gabriel Rossetti, Walter Pater, George Meredith, Thomas Hardy, and William Butler Yeats. He wrote extensively as William Sharp and as Fiona Macleod to the firms that published his books and to the editors of magazines, journals, and newspapers for which he wrote essays and reviews. Individuals interested in literary and publishing activities in Great Britain and the United States in the 1880s and 1890s may find the letters useful.

The Fiona Macleod letters contributed significantly to Sharp's ability to maintain the fiction of her independent identity. When claims that he was the author emerged in print, he countered by pointing to the different handwriting. He also used the letters to move Fiona from place to place to avoid meetings with avid readers and skeptical journalists. Given her constant travels, it was convenient for her letters to be sent from and received at the address of a good friend she often visited in Edinburgh. It was the address of Sharp's mother and his sister Mary, who supplied the handwriting for Fiona and who was always on guard against visitors seeking her.

Sharp also used the letters to create and mold the person or, more accurately, the persona of Fiona Macleod. Exercising his imagination and literary skills, he entered the consciousness of an imaginary woman and projected her convincingly to her correspondents. She was well-educated and steeped in Celtic lore. She was well-traveled and well-fixed. She had the good fortune to be sometimes the daughter and other times the wife — there were inconsistencies — of a wealthy Scotsman who owned a yacht that could whisk her away on a moment's notice to the western isles, Iceland, or Scandinavia. She was shy and reclusive, but also firm in her decisions, formal in her manner, and resolved not to let herself be taken advantage of by publishers or diverted from her writing by newspaper reporters or suitors. She also had a sharp tongue which she exercised in correspondence when her privacy or integrity was in danger. She was particularly harsh in chastising those brash enough to suggest she was William Sharp.

The poems and stories Sharp published as Fiona Macleod exceed in quality and popularity those he wrote as William Sharp, but Fiona Macleod herself was his most impressive achievement. Her personality emerges in many stories that describe the people she met and the places she visited, and in dedications and prefatory notes in her books, but it is in the letters that Sharp brought her fully into being. Speaking directly as Fiona, he crafted her distinct personality. Initially a lark, she became a financial necessity. Enjoying the deception, he soon became entranced by the woman he was creating. He continued to embellish his creation to the point he could claim and sometimes believe she was a separate person inhabiting his body. His fictional creation became the perfect means for expressing a strand of his being that had its origin in his childhood summers in Scotland's Inner Hebrides. Cast in this light, the character who emerges in the Fiona letters and other writings is one of the most compelling and provocative literary creations of the 1890s.

FORMAT

The letters are divided chronologically into Chapters, and each Chapter begins with a biographical introduction. The letters have a uniform format:

> Line one contains the name of the recipient and the date of composition. For undated letters, a date derived from a postmark, internal evidence, or context provided by other letters is placed in brackets. A question mark precedes questionable dates as [January ?12, 1892].

> Line two states the place where the letter was written or from which it was mailed. Vertical marks denote line divisions in the original.

> Line three contains the salutation if one exists.

> Lines four and following contain the body of the letter with Sharp's paragraphing preserved where it can be determined.

> Following the body, a single line contains the complimentary close and signature separated by a vertical mark if the close and signature are separate lines in the original.

> If the original contains postscripts, they follow the signature.

The form of the original manuscript and its location follow each letter in a separate line at lower left. When a letter has been transcribed from a printed source, that source is indicated. Most letters have been transcribed from the manuscripts or photocopies of the manuscripts provided by institutions and individuals. Their locations are identified, but any previous printings, with a few exceptions, are not identified.

Obvious errors of spelling are silently corrected. Errors of punctuation and grammar are corrected only when necessary to attain clarity of the author's presumed intention. Notes on margins marked as inserts are placed within the body of the text at the point of intended insertion. Postscripts on margins follow the main body and signature. Every effort has been made to attain a balance between authenticity and readability. Sharp and his sister Mary sometimes omitted the comma after the salutation, and that inconsistency has been preserved in transcribing the letters.

The notes explain or clarify references. Given the multitude of people, places, literary and artistic works, and events mentioned in the letters, the process of annotation required editorial judgment about what is too much and what is not enough.

ABBREVIATIONS

Letters to Yeats	*Letters to W. B. Yeats*, Vols. I and II, ed. Richard Finnernan, George Mills Harper, and William M. Murphy (New York: Columbia University Press, 1977)
E. A. S.	Elizabeth A. Sharp
E. C. S.	Edmund Clarence Stedman
E. W. R.	Edith Wingate Rinder
F. M.	Fiona Macleod
W. S.	William Sharp
Memoir	*William Sharp (Fiona Macleod): A Memoir*, compiled by his wife, Elizabeth A. Sharp (New York: Duffield & Co., 1910)
Middle Years	Katherine Tynan Hinkson, *The Middle Years* (Boston: Houghton Mifflin, 1917)
Romantic '90s	Richard Le Gallienne, *The Romantic '90s* (New York: G. P. Putnam's Sons, 1926)

These abbreviations describe the form of the original letter:

AD	autograph draft
ALS	autograph signed letter
ACS	autograph lettercard signed
APS	autograph postcard signed
TL	typed letter
TLS	typed letter signed

Chapter Twelve

Life: January–June, 1895

In January 1895 William Sharp wrote to a friend: "London, I do not like, though I feel its magnetic charm, or sorcery. I suffer here. The gloom, the streets, the obtrusion and intrusion of people, all conspire against thought, dream, true living." The city was "a vast reservoir of all the evils of civilised life with a climate which makes me inclined to believe that Dante came here instead of to Hades." Elizabeth said "the noise and confused magnetism of the great City weighed disastrously" on her husband. "The strain of the two kinds of work he was attempting to do, the immediate pressure of the imaginative work [by which she meant the work of Fiona Macleod] became unbearable, 'the call of the sea,' imperative" (*Memoir*, p. 242). To alleviate the crisis, the Sharps went to Ventnor on the Isle of Wight on January 6. Before they left, Sharp managed to write several letters. On January 1, he wrote to the editor of a Scottish paper recommending the publication of an article Frank Rinder had written about the Scottish poet Robert Fergusson, who died prematurely at the age of twenty-four in 1774. Rinder was an "able and promising young writer." In fact, he was thirty-two — only seven years younger than Sharp — and was married to the woman Sharp loved.

On January 2 Sharp attended the funeral of Christina Rossetti and proposed to Horace Scudder, editor of the *Atlantic Monthly*, an article about her similar to that which he wrote on Walter Pater in the December issue of *Atlantic Monthly*. Scudder accepted the suggestion, and Sharp's "Some Reminiscences of Christina Rossetti" appeared in the July issue. He also asked Scudder if he would like an article on "The Celtic Renaissance," which was a subject that was "becoming recognized as one of profound interest and indeed of paramount significance." He was

   https://doi.org/10.11647/OBP.0196.01

"a specialist in old and contemporary Scots-Irish Celtic literature," and he would, of course, restrict himself to "the Celtic *spirit*: not to what is written in Scottish Gaelic or Irish Gaelic." The new "Celtic movement in Ireland & Scotland, & in a less degree in Wales, is, in a word, of vital importance." Sharp wanted to be part of that movement, and he hoped Fiona Macleod would be its dominant literary voice in Scotland.

On the other hand, in a letter to Catherine Janvier on January 5 he said he resented "too close identification" with the "so-called Celtic renaissance." His work, if it were to survive, "must be beautiful in itself." The main purpose of this letter was to tell Mrs. Janvier he was Fiona Macleod. He had no choice since she had recalled for him an August 1893 letter in which he said he was writing a romance called *Pharais*. Now he had to trust her to preserve his secret, which was known by only one or two others in Britain. He went on to say the book came from the "core of my heart," and was "the beginning of my true work." As he wrote it, his pen was "dipped in the ichor of my life." More hopeful than accurate, he claimed the book had "reached people more than I dreamt of as likely" and "created a new movement" in Scotland. In England, it was hailed as a "work of genius" by the likes of George Meredith, Grant Allen, H. D. Traill, and Theodore Watts. It was "ignored in some quarters, abused in others, and unheeded by 'the general reader,'" but Sharp was nonetheless "deeply glad with its reception."

Mrs. Janvier's curiosity about how Sharp came upon the name "Fiona Macleod" elicited his clearest explanation of its origin:

> The name was born naturally: (of course I had associations with the name Macleod.) It, Fiona, is very rare now. Most Highlanders would tell you it was extinct — even as the diminutive of Fionnaghal (Flora). But it is not. It is an old Celtic name (meaning "a fair maid") still occasionally to be found. I know a little girl, the daughter of a Highland clergyman, who is called Fiona.

He could not say more about *Pharais* without telling her about his whole life, but one day he would confide "some of the strange old mysteries of earlier days I have part learned, part divined, and other things of the spirit." As Fiona Macleod he could write out of his heart in a way he could not do as William Sharp. Neither could he do so were he the woman Fiona Macleod was supposed to be "unless veiled in scrupulous anonymity." He continued:

This rapt sense of oneness with nature, this cosmic ecstasy and elation, this wayfaring along the extreme verges of the common world, all this is so wrought up with the romance of life that I could not bring myself to expression by my outer self, insistent and tyrannical as that need is…. My truest self, the self who is below all other selves, and my most intimate life and joys and sufferings, thoughts, emotions, and dreams, must find expression, yet I cannot save in this hidden way.

This explanation of his adoption of the pseudonym reproduced in part by Elizabeth Sharp in the *Memoir* is one of his most extensive and forthright. There is no mention of supernatural beings or of a separate person speaking through him, but simply a recognition of multiple personalities, or "selves," within the single human being. The most basic of those he experienced could be expressed only by the adoption of the feminine pseudonym and by projecting a separate identity for a feminine hidden self. That the deeper self is female raises important questions concerning what is now called *gender identity*. These questions have plagued the reputation of William Sharp since his pseudonym was revealed upon his death in 1905. They have arisen earlier in this work, and will arise again later. Here it is enough to observe that possible answers to these questions lie in his recognition and the recognition of many of his contemporaries that men and women had the potential for multiple personalities, with different personalities achieving dominance at various stages of their lives.

The Sharps met Anna and Patrick Geddes in the fall of 1894, and the couple figured prominently in their lives as 1895 unfolded. There arose between Sharp and Geddes, according to Elizabeth,

a friendship with far-reaching results for "Fiona Macleod" […] Both were idealists, keen students of life and nature; cosmopolitan in outlook and interest, they were also ardent Celts who believed in the necessity of preserving the finer subtle qualities and the spiritual heritage of their race against the encroaching predominance of materialistic ideas and aims of the day (*Memoir*, pp. 248–49).

The Geddes lived in Dundee, where he was Professor of Botany at University College, and they were also active in the intellectual and social life of Edinburgh where, in 1887, Geddes established Scotland's first student hostel and a summer school of arts, letters, and science. The summer school continued every August until 1899 and attracted students and scholars from Great Britain and the Continent. In 1894 he transformed a town mansion known as "Laird of Cockpen," located near the Castle on the Edinburgh High Street, into the Outlook Tower, where he established the first "sociological laboratory" in the world. Best known for the camera obscura in its tower in which one can view a panorama of the city of Edinburgh, the building became the locus of the Scottish version of the Celtic Revival, and Geddes became the dominant figure in that revival. He fostered the movement as a means of furthering his ambition to restore Edinburgh as a major center of learning in Europe. The Celtic Renaissance article Sharp offered Horace Scudder for the *Atlantic Monthly* was one of a series of lectures Geddes asked Sharp to deliver in his Summer School in August, 1895. The lectures, as we will see, had an unfortunate result, but the invitation initiated a friendship between the two men and opened the way for significant contributions to the Celtic movement by Sharp as an editor and Fiona Macleod as a writer.

Fig. 1. Sir Patrick Geddes (1854–1932). Photograph by Lafayette, 30 December 1931. © National Portrait Gallery, London. Some rights reserved.

From Ventnor on January 10, Sharp asked Anna Geddes if she was surprised when her husband told her "W. S. and Fiona Macleod are one in the same person." Since the Fiona writings were his "Celtic" credentials for taking part in the publishing firm Geddes was organizing, he had confided in Geddes and given him permission to share the secret with his wife. Sharp's purpose in writing to Anna was to emphasize the need for "absolute preservation of the secret." He had sent her a letter from Fiona, written in Fiona's handwriting, before she was apprised of Fiona's true identity. Now he wrote in his own handwriting and signed the letter, curiously, "Fiona Macleod and William Sharp." This is a unique instance of the double signature in a letter and of the Fiona Macleod signature in a letter written in Sharp's hand. Signing both names and asserting that W. S. and F. M. are one in the same implies the presence of two personalities in the same body. Sharp was trying to find a means of defining and describing the psychological phenomena he was experiencing. It is no wonder Elizabeth believed her husband's frequent ailments were exacerbated by the strain of being two people, of appearing to the world as William Sharp while experiencing insights and feelings that found an adequate means of expression only through the female persona.

On January 15 Sharp wrote again to Patrick Geddes from Ventnor to say he thought he should go to Edinburgh to discuss details of the publishing firm and "Celtic matters." They would be able to accomplish more in a day than in "months of correspondence." The Sharps were returning to London on January 18 and would be fully occupied through the weekend, but he might be able to get away on January 21 and spend the next two days in Edinburgh. He could ill afford the trip, but it seemed a necessity. Geddes replied he would come to London for the meeting, and Sharp wrote on January 21 to say he would keep the afternoon and evenings of January 29, 30, and 31 entirely free to talk with Geddes. The Sharp's flat had only one bedroom, but he would arrange with a nearby friend — probably Mona Caird — a place for him to stay.

In his response to Sharp's January 15 letter, Geddes suggested Sharp consider moving to Edinburgh to play a leading role in the publishing firm and avoid extensive travel back and forth between London and Edinburgh. In his January 21 letter Sharp said he found the idea tempting: "I have a profound & chronic distaste for London & London life and a nostalgia for the north." The chief drawback of a move would be financial as a good deal of his income derived from reviewing London art exhibits and works of literature. Editors were less likely to ask for reviews beyond the London postal zone "partly on account of late transmissions & early return of proofs." He doubted there was "publishing, secretarial, tutorial, or other work in Edinburgh that, without more expenditure of time and energy than I now give to my reviewing, would ensure me say £300 & leave me time for my own particular work." In addition to the financial disadvantage of a permanent move to Edinburgh, the Sharps had "a great number of acquaintances and some dear friends" in London, and the city was a great meeting place, a "bazaar of fortunate & smiling chances." Sharp mentioned his interest in "the Stage" and his "ambitions in that direction — &, I may add, Music, which is one of my wife's chief joys." He didn't see how he could "throw up Fogtown — at present." Perhaps he could have "rooms in Edinburgh (or the flat in Ramsey Gardens we want to take if possible [...] and come & go a good deal: in fact, if the publishing idea develops, & you entrust me with a responsible part in it, I would need to be in Edinburgh for one week & perhaps two weeks in each month." On the other hand, if his work for the Geddes publishing firm were to develop to the point where he could receive a guaranteed salary of £300 per year, the move might be possible as he would be glad to drop all his "miscellaneous pen-work."

Having addressed his own situation and availability to take part in the new publishing venture, Sharp turned to the proposed firm and described at some length how he thought it should develop. "The effort," he wrote, "should be to produce at first certain books of as pronounced a character as possible — books of significance so to say: so that the Firm be known at once for a certain distinction." To help the firm get a good start, he suggested "a little Fortnightly," like *The Chap-Book* Stone and Kimball was publishing in Chicago. Selling for only two pence, it was "attractive in itself and a splendid advt. of their wares." He had given Geddes an issue of *The Chap-Book* that featured his photograph and an article publicizing the American edition of his *Vistas.* The fortnightly would require careful editing and handling, and Sharp would be glad to undertake it. Here, Geddes inserted "Agreed" on the letter. Sharp's suggestion was the genesis of *The Evergreen: A Northern Seasonal,* a more elaborate publication, the first issue of which appeared in the spring of 1895.

Sharp went on to say the firm should engage in "no haphazard publishing at first": "There might be, to start with, a biological book by

A. Thomson: a sociological or other work by yourself: 'A New Synthesis of Art' or other work by myself [...] a Celtic romance by Fiona Macleod [...] (for it is on Celtic lines, I think, the most development will take place first)." He estimated the firm would need an initial outlay of about £1,000; authors would be paid on a royalty system. As for his own involvement,

> If you intend me to be the literary "boss" in the firm (tho' perhaps I mistake your intent!) I would give my best thought, care, & experience to making the venture a success in every way, & ultimately a potent factor in the development of Scotland & of Edr [Edinburgh] in particular. Of course, my editorial experiences, & far-reaching literary connections, would stand me in good stead: & in a year or so we could have a varied and potent "staff."

Sharp was thinking very grandly as he continued, "If I were lity. 'boss,' as I say, one effort would be to centralise in Edinburgh all the Celtic work now being done by Scottish, Irish, and Welsh writers." Capital would be needed to "grease the wheels" and then "patience" and "wise discretion." Here Geddes again wrote, "Agreed." There is always room at the "top of the tree," Sharp asserted, and "We are too enthusiastic, too determined, not to get to that top if it be possible, as I firmly believe it is, and as I know you do." To this statement, Geddes gave his final blessing: "Quite so. Full speed ahead!" Sharp concluded by apologizing for writing "so scrappy and unsatisfactory a note," but said the writing of it moved him out of his "depression & 'doleful dumps.'" This letter must have provided the basis for their discussion in London as Geddes noted his agreement with many of Sharp's suggestions and moved ahead with them without involving Sharp. He must have sensed Sharp's inability to stay focused for long on the practical details of management.

In early February 1895, Sharp was putting the finishing touches on the second Fiona Macleod romance, *The Mountain Lovers*, which John Lane published in the summer. He was also writing Fiona Macleod stories for a volume called *The Sin-Eater and Other Tales* which was published in November of 1895 by the Geddes firm in Edinburgh and by Stone and Kimball in Chicago. He was corresponding with Herbert Stone as Fiona about that volume and other possible Fiona publications and as William Sharp about a collection of short stories entitled *The Gypsy Christ and Other Tales* which Stone and Kimball published, also in

1895. The combination of writing fiction and arranging for publications negatively affected Sharp's health. Elizabeth Sharp recalled an incident that brought home to her the seriousness of his condition.

> A telegram had come. I took it to his study. I could get no answer. I knocked, louder, then louder, — at last he opened the door with a curiously dazed look in his face. I explained. He answered, "Ah, I could not hear you for the sound of the waves!" It was the first indication to me, in words, of what troubled him (*Memoir*, pp. 242–43).

He was troubled by "the noise and confused magnetism of the great City" and his estrangement from the sea. Since there were no waves to be heard in London, he soon left for the West of Scotland.

In a February 13 letter to Herbert Stone, Sharp reported that he was going to Edinburgh at the weekend where he would see Fiona Macleod. On February 18 he would go to Corrie on the western island of Arran. He described his arrival in a letter to Elizabeth the next day:

> It was a most glorious sail from Ardrossan. The sea was a sheet of blue and purple washed with gold. Arran rose like a dream of beauty. I was the sole passenger in the steamer, for the whole island! What made the drive of six miles more beautiful than ever was the extraordinary, fantastic beauty of the frozen waterfalls and burns caught as it were in the leap. Sometimes these immense icicles hung straight and long, like a Druid's beard: sometimes in wrought sheets of gold, or magic columns and spaces of crystal. Sweet it was to smell the pine and the heather and bracken, and the salt weed upon the shore. The touch of dream was upon everything, from the silent hills to the brooding herons by the shore.

"In that exquisite solitude," he continued, "I felt a deep exaltation grow. The flowing of the air of the hills laved the parched shores of my heart." Arran brought a dramatic improvement in his mental condition, and the sea and the quiet majesty of the cold landscape released his creative impulses. The William Sharp who wrote this letter was deeply hidden from the world of London editing and publishing. He wrote vividly, compellingly, directly, and with no invocation of a feminine persona.

Years later, Sharp retold the story of this 1895 visit to Arran in an essay called "Earth, Fire, and Water" which appeared in Fiona Macleod's *The Divine Adventure: Iona; By Sundown Shores* (1900). After repeating several tales about men who were called to the sea by hearing the sound of waves, the narrator continued:

I have myself in lesser degree, known this irresistible longing. I am not fond of towns, but some years ago I had to spend a winter in a great city. It was all-important to me not to leave during January; and in one way I was not ill-pleased, for it was a wild winter. But one night I woke, hearing a rushing sound in the street — the sound of water. I would have thought no more of it, had I not recognized the troubled noise of the tide, and the sucking and lapsing of the flow in weedy hollows. I rose and looked out. It was moonlight, and there was no water. When, after sleepless hours, I rose in the grey morning I heard the splash of waves. All that day and the next I heard the continual noise of waves. I could not write or read; at last I could not rest. On the afternoon of the third day the waves dashed up against the house. I said what I could to my friends and left by the night train. In the morning we (for a kinswoman was with me) stood on the Greenock Pier waiting for the Hebridean steamer, the Clansman, and before long were landed on an island, almost the nearest we could reach, and one that I loved well. We had to be landed some miles from the place I wanted to go, and it was a long and cold journey. The innumerable little waterfalls hung in icicles among the mosses, ferns, and white birches on the roadside. Before we reached our destination, we saw a wonderful sight. From three great mountains, their flanks flushed with faint rose, their peaks white and solemn, vast columns of white smoke ascended. It was as though volcanic fires had once again broken their long stillness. Then we saw what it was: the north wind (unheard, unfelt, where we stood) blew a hurricane against the other side of the peaks, and, striking up the leagues of hard snow, drove it upward like smoke, till the columns rose gigantic and hung between the silence of the white peaks and the silence of the stars.

That night, with the sea breaking less than a score yards from where I lay, I slept, though for three nights I had not been able to sleep. When I woke, my trouble was gone.

The word painting of this passage is precise and moving; it illustrates the beauty Sharp could achieve when he dropped his defenses and wrote from his heart. In this passage he recalls the peace that came to him in February 1895 when he escaped from London to the Isle of Arran. The incident itself and his description of it in the letter to his wife had germinated and evolved into a striking and controlled passage of poetic prose. Does Fiona Macleod, the supposed author of "Earth, Fire and Water," enter the picture? The short answer is no. While there are subtle efforts to feminize the narrative voice earlier and later in the essay, none appear in this passage.

Elizabeth directly addressed the issue: "Although the essay is written over the signature of 'Fiona Macleod' and belongs to that particular phase of work, nevertheless it is obviously 'William Sharp' who *tells* the story, for the 'we' who stood on the pier at Greenock is himself in his dual capacity; his 'kinswoman' is his other self." Sharp sometimes believed — and often encouraged his wife to believe — he was two separate people, one male and one female. In the 20 February letter of 1895, after telling Elizabeth he was alone on the ferry to Arran, he wrote, "There is something of a strange excitement in the knowledge that two people are here: so intimate and yet so far-off. For it is with me as though Fiona were asleep in another room. I catch myself listening for her step sometimes, for the sudden opening of a door. It is unawaredly that she whispers to me. I am eager to see what she will do — particularly in *The Mountain Lovers*. It seems passing strange to be here with her alone at last." It was one thing to be William Sharp and Fiona Macleod, two people in one body, and in full control of both. It was quite another to claim to have no control over a second self that flourished within him. The implied separation of his creative imagination is unique and remarkable.

When Sharp objectified the Fiona persona as a separate person entirely free of control by the man the world knew as William Sharp, he was often describing not simply a creature of his imagination but a real person. The kinswoman who accompanied him to Arran in mid-winter 1895, stood on the pier with him, and was sleeping in the next room, may have been not the imaginary woman, Fiona Macleod, but the woman he loved, Edith Wingate Rinder. Ever kind and generous, Elizabeth wrote of Mrs. Rinder:

> Because of her beauty, her strong sense of life and of the joy of life; because of her keen intuitions and mental alertness, her personality stood for him as a symbol of the heroic women of Greek and Celtic days, a symbol that, as he expressed it, unlocked new doors in his mind and put him "in touch with ancestral memories" of his race.

Sharp wrote to his wife of Edith Rinder in 1896: "to her I owe my development as 'Fiona Macleod,' [...] without her there would have been no Fiona Macleod" (*Memoir*, p. 222).

One can speculate endlessly about the psychological interaction between Sharp and Edith that enabled him to produce the writings of Fiona Macleod, but it is impossible to define it precisely. It shifted over time, and even the Sharps, who described it variously, failed to understand it. Near the end of 1895, in writing to his friend Sir George Douglas, for example, Sharp called Fiona Macleod a "puzzling literary entity." The previous January, we recall, he told Catherine Janvier, "My truest self, the self who is below all other selves, and my most intimate life and joys and sufferings, thoughts, emotions and dreams, *must* find expression, yet I cannot save in this hidden way." We know Sharp and Edith were deeply in love for many years. It was she who enabled him to drop his defenses, release his deepest "self," exercise most fully his creative imagination. He claimed he could become Fiona Macleod — and thus write most easily as Fiona Macleod — only when he and Edith were alone together. It sometimes appears he was using his need to be away from the city, his need for solitude, as an excuse to be alone with Edith. The build-up of frustration that preceded his escape to the West of Scotland in February 1895 and again in June of that year may have been, at least partially, a build-up of sexual tension. The sense of relief and renewal in his February 20 letter to Elizabeth and later in a June 4 letter to Geddes is palpable.

By March third, Sharp was back in London writing again to Geddes, this time with a detailed proposal for a quarterly which would be used as a vehicle for stories, articles, poems and visual art and as a means of advertising the firm's other publications. He had in mind "a thoroughly representative Anglo-Celtic 'quarterly'" that would be "well-supported" in all the big towns of Great Britain and America and draw "Anglo-Celtic writers to look to Edinburgh." He enclosed a draft of what he thought the first number should contain and volunteered to be its editor (with the help of his wife). Drawing on his London connections, he would assemble a strong list of contributors, and he envisioned the quarterly as "a valuable record" of the entire Celtic Revival. The quarterly would be entitled "The Celtic World." Rather than naming an editor, it should say only: "Published by Patrick Geddes and Colleagues" or "Edited and Published in Edinburgh." He outlined a possible Table of Contents for a "Summer Number" that included items by the most notable Irish, English, Welsh, and Scottish Celticists: W. B. Yeats, Ernest Rhys, Patrick Geddes, Katherine Tynan, George Russell (AE), and, of course, Fiona Macleod among them, and a Frontispiece and Celtic Ornament by John Duncan. Sharp was planning expansively.

Geddes took the idea of a quarterly issued as a book and implemented it quickly and more restrictively. He ignored Sharp's offer of himself as editor, began correspondence with T. Fisher Unwin in London to arrange for distribution, and produced not a summer issue, as suggested by Sharp, but a Spring issue called simply *The Evergreen: A Northern Seasonal.* This would be followed, in accordance with Sharp's suggestion, by Summer, Fall and Winter issues. Geddes asked William Macdonald, an aspiring poet, to assemble and oversee the publication of the volume. The volume began with a seven-page "Proem" signed by Macdonald and J. Arthur Thomson, a biologist and a friend of Geddes which clearly set forth Patrick Geddes's ideas for reforming not only Edinburgh's Old Town, but the industrialized cities of Britain and the world. It equated the decadence that pervades literature and the arts with the decay of cities and asserted there were signs of a New Birth "against the background of Decadence."

> The music of the coming Renascence is heard so far only in "broken snatches," but in these snatches four chords are sounded, which we would fain carry in our hearts — That faith may be had still in the friendliness of fellows; that the love of country is not a lost cause; that the love of women is the way of life; and that in the eternal newness of every Child is an undying promise for the Race.

In those words, one hears the distinctive voice of Patrick Geddes filtered through the voice of the aspiring poet William Macdonald.

The content of the Spring volume was divided into four sections: "Spring in Nature," "Spring in Life," "Spring in the World," and "Spring in the North." Each story, poem, and essay touches on the theme of renewal. The authors are not the luminaries of the larger Celtic renaissance proposed by Sharp, but Scots largely unknown today — except, of course, Patrick Geddes, who contributed two essays ("Life and its Science" and "The Scots Renascence"), and William Sharp, who contributed one short poem under his own name and two poems and a story ("The Anointed Man") as Fiona Macleod. Celtic designed Headpieces and Tailpieces appear throughout the volume which was printed by Constable in Edinburgh on fine paper. Some copies were produced with tan leather bindings and a full-page design on the front cover embossed in green. There are several full-page drawings, the finest by John Duncan, the principal visual artist of the Scottish revival, one of which ("Apollo's School-Days") shows the influence of Aubrey Beardsley.

Fig. 2. "Apollo's School Days," John Duncan, in *The Evergreen: A Northern Seasonal, The Book of Spring* (Edinburgh: Patrick Geddes and Colleagues, 1895). Photograph by William F. Halloran (2020) of his copy formerly owned by Lady Mears, Patrick Geddes' daughter.

In a letter to Geddes dated May 15, Sharp said he liked much of what was in the Spring volume, but some of it lacked "distinctiveness as well as distinction." It was promising and with "careful piloting" should "come to stay." He read Geddes's two contributions "with particular interest and pleasure, not only with the affection of a friend but with the sangfroid of a critic." The poetry in the volume, including that of Fiona Macleod, did not seem as good as the prose. The editorial control, he wrote, "must be more exigent." And the illustrations, he thought, perilously weak: "With the exception of Duncan's "Apollo's School Days" & some of the head-pieces, there is not a drawing [...] which is not crude in draughtsmanship and in design — or in one or two instances frankly meaningless!" He thought John Duncan's "Anima Celtica" weakly imitative and lacking in any redeeming features. Sharp judged this kind of work as "the mere dross and debris of the 'fin-de Siècle' ebb," stating that it had "the same effect on one's optic nerves as a scraping nail has on one's auditory ditto." He expected much adverse criticism of the volume because of its art; "the Yellow Book drawings are at least clever if ultra-fin-de-Siècle, while the majority of these of *The Evergreen* are fin-de-Siècle without being clever." Perhaps he was too severe in his criticism, but he felt so strongly "that a really valuable & significant future awaits the 'Evergreen' if it preserve & develop its best, in literature & art, & disengage itself from what is amateurish, that it seems worthwhile to be severely exigent."

The second volume of *The Evergreen* appeared in the fall of 1895, the third (Summer) and the fourth (Winter) in 1896. Though Sharp was not named editor, his critique had the effect of improving the quality of the later volumes. In a note called "Envoy" at the close of the fourth volume Patrick Geddes and W. Macdonald announced the end of the first series and declared the need to take some seasons off before producing a second series. Since the publication was without an editor and invited authors were free to contribute as they wished, *The Evergreen* reflected Geddes's effort to create an artistic commune in the Outlook Tower and its surrounding buildings, in which writers, visual artists, and scientists would live together happily stimulating each other's creativity. According to the "Envoy," the artists and scientists now recognized the need to go off on their own and do their own work before coming together in a new synthesis. *The Evergreen* was not revived.

Fig. 3. The Outlook Tower, Castlehill, Edinburgh. Photograph by Kim Traynor (2013), Wikimedia, CC BY-SA 3.0, https://commons.wikimedia.org/wiki/ File:Outlook_Tower,_Castlehill,_Edinburgh.JPG#/media/File:Outlook_ Tower,_Castlehill,_Edinburgh.JPG

In early April Sharp wrote a long letter to Herbert Stone complaining that he had not received the proof sheets for *The Gypsy Christ* though they had been promised in February. Moreover, Fiona Macleod was upset for not having heard from him about the agreement to publish an American edition of *Pharais*. Sharp was beginning to have doubts that Stone and Kimball would be a reliable American publisher of his books. It was an early sign that stresses had begun to develop between the two young publishers. In fact, Melville Stone — Herbert's father and the publisher of the *Chicago Daily News* — who supported the publishing venture was beginning to wonder if it would develop into a viable business.

In mid-April Sharp went to Paris to cover a salon for the *Glasgow Herald*. Back in London on April 27, he apologized to Geddes for not having time in Paris to look up Thomas Barclay, a Scottish barrister specializing in international law, and ask him to support Geddes's scheme to create a Franco-Scottish College somewhere in France. He promised to contact Barclay when he was back in Paris on May 5, this time with his wife, to review another salon.

Prior to the second Paris visit, he wrote another long letter to Geddes (April 29) that described an elaborate plan for the Geddes's firm's book publications. He planned to be in Scotland around May 20 and would stay with the Geddes in Dundee for a few days to confer "about the publishing business." The two men had come to an arrangement, perhaps during Geddes's late January visit to London, for Sharp to oversee the publication of books, and his April 29 letter was filled with proposals for them to discuss in person. Sharp thought that a volume of short stories by Fiona Macleod (*The Sin-Eater and Other Stories*) should be one of the firm's "start-off books." He explained that short stories of the kind were in demand at that time, and its sales should be helped by the appearance of Fiona's second romance, *The Mountain Lovers*, in June. Geddes must have had Sharp's letter on hand when the two met in Dundee as Geddes noted in its margin "Press for July" and then "Agreed 23/5/5/ for the Autumn."

Lyra Celtica would also be ready for publication in the fall. Though Sharp was the primary editor of the volume, he wrote on April 29 that its editor of record will be not F. M. or W. S., but Elizabeth Sharp. This was advisable "for several reasons (one among them, the inclusion of F. M.'s runes & Celtic lyrics)." Sharp, however, would write a "critical introductory essay (as distinct from an ordinary preface)." This book, "though mainly Scottish-Celtic and Irish Celtic," would contain "representative pieces by Breton (trs), Cornish, & Welsh, & Manx poets." Sharp suggested that the firm's first book be an "R. L. S. volume" — that is, a volume either about or by Robert Louis Stevenson — followed by a romance composed by "a well-known Man." Here Geddes wrote in the margin "Mrs. Mona Caird — Agreed 23/5/5." Though not a man, Mona Caird was well-known as an advocate for the rights of women, especially for granting women equal legal rights within the marriage contract. Geddes's marginal note raises the interesting prospect that Mona Caird, who, in 1894, had published her ground-breaking novel, *The Daughters of Danaus*, was working on or had in mind a romance. Neither the Stevenson book nor a Mona Caird romance was published by the Geddes firm. Sharp also proposed a series of short books of fiction, perhaps called "The Evergreen Series," and a "Cosmopolitan Series" containing translations of works by "foreign authors of marked power & distinction in the 'new movement' — a vague phrase that really means little save the onward wave of the human mind." He listed no fewer than fourteen authors from six countries, including the United States. Finally, he thought it best to leave until 1896 the publication of a book called *The Literary Ideal*, which would contain the lectures he planned to deliver in August in Geddes's Summer School. Geddes wisely wrote in the margin "Discuss in August," as he wanted to see the lectures before agreeing to publish them.

Though few of the ideas proposed in this letter materialized, Sharp served briefly as Manager of Patrick Geddes and Colleagues and, when that proved impracticable, as its Literary Adviser. Under his guidance the firm produced several beautifully designed books — authored by William Sharp, his wife, and his friends — that rival in design and format those published by established firms in London and Dublin for the Irish contingent of the Celtic Revival. Under Sharp's guidance, the firm became the principal vehicle for publishing his own writings under the guise of Fiona Macleod, who became, according to an article in *The Irish Independent*, "the most remarkable figure in the Scottish Celtic Renascence." *The Sin-Eater and Other Tales* appeared in the fall of 1895 and *The Washer of the Ford* in 1896. Also, in 1896, the firm issued Fiona's *From the Hills of Dream* (1896), a collection of poems that was published in multiple editions. In 1897, when Sharp was no longer Literary Director, the firm issued Fiona's *Songs and Tales of St. Columba and His Age* and *The Shorter Stories of Fiona Macleod*, a rearrangement and reissue in three inexpensive paper-covered volumes of the stories published in *The Sin-Eater* and *The Washer of the Ford*. *Lyra Celtica* and the first two Fiona Macleod books appeared in a series Sharp called "The Celtic Library."

Lyra Celtica was the firm's most successful publication, with several editions published, beginning in 1896. As proposed in Sharp's April letter, it was compiled and edited by Elizabeth Sharp, with a lengthy introduction and copious notes written by Sharp. The series also included, in 1896, *The Fiddler of Carne: A North Sea Winter's Tale*, a Welsh romance set in the late eighteenth century by Sharp's friend Ernest Rhys, and, in 1897, *The Shadow of Arvor; Legendary Romances and Folk-Tales of Brittany*, translated and retold by none other than Edith Wingate Rinder. The binding of the latter volume was among the most beautiful of the series.

Fig. 4. *The Shadow of Arvor: Legendary Romances and Folk-Tales of Brittany*, Translated and Retold by Edith Wingate Rinder (Edinburgh: Patrick Geddes & Colleagues, 1897). Printed by W. H. White and Co. Ltd., Edinburgh Riverside Press. Photograph by William F. Halloran (2019).

The Rhys and Rinder books exemplify Sharp's desire to have the firm represent more than Scottish Gaeldom by introducing tales from Wales and Brittany. Neither Patrick Geddes nor William Sharp were well organized businessmen, and the firm soon descended into financial insolvency. Sharp's efforts to sustain the writing and publication of his dual-authorship, his frequent bouts of ill-health and depression, and his inability to remain for long in one place placed a strain on his relationship with the individuals Geddes enlisted to try to save the firm. Geddes was endlessly patient with Sharp and concerned with his well-being. Their close friendship produced a great deal in a brief period, but the strain ultimately became too great, and they gradually parted ways, with Geddes's interests expanding into town planning on a grand scale.

Sharp went to York on May 18, spent two nights there with his friend George Cotterell, editor of the *Yorkshire Herald*, and visited the Geddes home in Dundee on May 20. On May 23, he left for a long weekend of relaxation in the West of Scotland. During their brief visit Geddes became concerned about the state of Sharp's physical and mental well-being. He wrote to Elizabeth Sharp to ask her opinion about her husband's health and to propose the possibility of the publishing firm providing him a stipend for the work he would do. This would also enable him to spend less time on reviewing, and more time on his poetry and fiction. In a late May response, Elizabeth expressed her deep appreciation for Geddes's concern and generosity. She was thankful to have someone else who "sees how he is expending health and strength — and encroaching on his reserve — in work of a kind he ought not to do." She continued:

> Like you, I have a great belief in the future of W. S. and Fiona M., and I am equally persuaded that he must give up the fretting hack-work in order to give his real work its chance. But it is so difficult to make him do so; he grows nervous, and, I regret to say, chiefly on my account. But I feel sure, that now, your kind interest in him, and thought for him will do more [than] anything else to make him, not only feel, but act on our advice — which coincides. You are indeed a most valuable ally.

It was a relief for her "to see that there is a friend who understands Will and sees his persistent overwork and delicacy." She would discuss Geddes's offers with her husband when he returned to London and put him into "his doctor's hands" to deal with the weakness in his back, which was the result of overwork. She assured Geddes of her interest in all the "schemes" he and her husband were discussing and hoped she might be allowed "to share in a little of the work."

Shortly after he returned to London on May 29 and heard from Elizabeth about the letter from Geddes, Sharp expressed his gratitude to Geddes for his "solicitude about his health and welfare." "You are truly," he wrote, "a good & loyal comrade as well as a dear friend." He promised to ponder all Geddes's "arguments and advice," but he was sorry Geddes had written "so exigently" about his health, especially about his back, as he had hoped not to worry Elizabeth about that "passing trouble". He then launched into a lengthy description of his days in the West:

I had the most glorious weather in the West and had a true sun-bath every day. Friday, Saty, Sunday, & Monday last I spent at one of my favourite remote places on Loch Fyne in Western Argyll. There I lived mentally, spiritually, & physically (excuse the unscientific specifications!) in rainbow-gold. All day from sunrise to midnight I was on the higher mountain slopes, or in the pine-woods (full of continuous solemn music with the north wind), or on the sea. On Sunday forenoon I rowed across (2 miles or so) to the uninhabitable rocky solitudes opposite (South of Ceann More) — went for a long glorious swim of about an hour! — lay naked in the sunlight below a pine on a mossy crag, & dreamed pagan dreams, & fell asleep, & had a wonderful vision of woodland lives unknown of men, and of a beautiful Child God, of which you will hear something from Fiona in due time — & wakened two hours later, still sun-bathed, tanned & burnt & midge-bitten — then another swim — then rowed across the loch again &, after tea etc., away up to the summit of a hill set against a marvellous vision of mountains & peaks & lofty ranges, which I have baptised with a Gaelic name meaning the Hill of the Beauty of the World — then watched the sunglow till 10 p.m. & came down thro' the dewy heather to the pinewoods, where I climbed into the branches of a great red brother & lay awhile listening to the wind, with its old-world wonder-song of the pines, & watching the moon sail upward.

While his physical and mental state doubtless was improved by this brief interlude, the main impetus of the letter is to convince Geddes that he was well enough to undertake work for the publishing firm, and well enough to prepare the lectures he promised to deliver for Geddes's Summer School in August:

I have come away with a sense of the sunflood through & through me: of magic rhythms and hints: of secret voices and cadences haunting-sweet: & with the almost passionate health & eagerness of that young Norse god who in sheer extravagance of joy wove the rainbows into a garland for the moment's mountain he made out of falling worlds.

All this, Sharp asserts, "means [that] I am well". He thanks God "for life — for a swift pulse & red blood — and fever in the heart and brain," and states his intention to "be good, & to lecture, & to publish, & behave, & always love Mrs. Geddes & yourself." Much of this is overblown, but it nonetheless again illustrates Sharp's determination to recover quickly from frequent bouts of illness and depression. The overt "Paganism" of his account and his promise to behave raise the possibility that he was not alone in this restorative interlude. Though he remained well enough through June to do a good deal of work, his recovery, as usual, was only temporary.

Letters: January–June, 1895

To a friend [January 1, 1895][1]

... London I do not like, though I feel its magnetic charm, or sorcery. I suffer here. The gloom, the streets, the obtrusion and intrusion of people, all conspire against thought, dream, true living. It is a vast reservoir of all the evils of civilised life with a climate which makes me inclined to believe that Dante came here instead of to Hades... .

Memoir, p. 242

To Dr. Ward, January 1, 1895

Rutland House | Greencroft Gardens | So. Hampstead | 1: Jan: '95

Dear Dr. Ward,

I send this line introducing to you my friend Mr. Frank Rinder, an able & promising young writer. Everyone is now talking of Stevenson's recent utterance — and among these none is more interesting than that about "Mr. Robin," as he called his poetic forerunner, Robert Fergusson.[2] Fergusson's poetry, & still more his short and tragic life — ill-starred as that of his contemporary Chatterton — fascinated Stevenson, & certainly his stirring words (read at the Burns Club) have done much to create a keen interest in this pioneer of Burns & Tannahill.[3]

Mr. Frank Rinder has written an excellent & authoritarian account of the poet — and at my suggestion is to submit his MS to you, as it seems to me likely to appeal to the readers of your ever fresh & welcome paper. (Please keep room for me, once in a way? Etc?)

I hope you & yours, & all friends in common, are well.

With Cordial New Year wishes | Sincerely yours | William Sharp

ALS Princeton University

To Horace Scudder, January 2, 1895

Rutland House, | Greencroft Gardens, | So. Hampstead. |
2nd January 1895

My dear Horace Scudder,

Frederick Shields and I have just come back from the funeral of Christina Rossetti — who, I have no doubt you will agree with us, may well be regarded as our foremost woman poet since Mrs. Browning. We have been talking, too, of our friend of oversea: and about his delightful book on "Childhood in Lit: and Art":[4] and both wishing that you could see the wonderful work that is now being done by Shields in the building near Tyburn Gate that is to be called, and is to be, a House of Rest. The opportunity is one that has never really come to an English painter before: and Shields is unquestionably, now in his noble maturity, just the man.

I do not know if you would care to have another article by me at present: but I would much like to write for you a paper of the "Walter Pater" kind (about which I have had several gratifying letters from America and elsewhere) on Christina Rossetti.[5] I knew her intimately, and of late years was one of the few who saw anything of her. She had a strange personality — & I think the story of her life, of her relationships with Dante Gabriel Rossetti, and iterary record — with a critical estimate and some illuminative quotations — would be of wide interest both in this country and in America: in America particularly, if it be true what I have heard, that there she is the most widely read of all modern English poets. An old friend who knew her when she was a girl (in the *Germ6* days) has given me some interesting details, & of course I know William Michael Rossetti. I may add that during the last week or two of Rossetti's life, I stayed with him at Birchington, with Miss Christina Rossetti as fellow-guest: & that I could give some interesting reminiscences.

Kindly let me hear from you by return.

My other proposal is in connection with a lecture which I have been invited to give at University Hall in Edinburgh next Special Summer Session (August) — on *"The Celtic Renaissance"*, a subject which is becoming recognised as one of profound interest and indeed of paramount significance. I need hardly say I should not be asked to do this were I not a specialist in old and contemporary Scots-Irish Celtic literature. But of course I restrict myself to the Celtic *spirit*: not to what is written in Scottish Gaelic or Irish Gaelic. The new Celtic movement in Ireland & Scotland, & in a less degree in Wales, is, in a word, of vital importance.

My other lectures (these chosen by myself) are to be on "The Relations of Nature and Poetry", "The Ideals of Art", and "The Literary Ideal". The last named will also be the first essay in, or Introduction to, a volume of critical studies which I hope to publish this year under that title, *"The Literary Ideal".*[7]

But I mention "The Celtic Renaissance" as most likely to suit you.

My kind remembrances & best wishes for 1895 to Mrs. and Miss Scudder, and as for yourself you know that you have the friendliest regard of

Yours Cordially, | William Sharp

ALS Harvard University, Houghton Library

To Catherine Janvier, January 5, 1895

London, January 5, 1895

Early tomorrow morning I leave for the Isle of Wight for a fortnight... . I hope to send you a letter from the beautiful place by the sea where we are going to. It will be a letter from Fiona Macleod.

Yes, *Pharais* is mine. It is a book out of my heart, out of the core of my heart. I wrote it with the pen dipped in the ichor of my life. It has reached people more than I dreamt of as likely. In Scotland especially it has stirred and created a new movement. Here, men like George Meredith, Grant Allen, H. D. Traill, and Theodore Watts hailed it as a "work of genius." Ignored in some quarters, abused in others, and unheeded by "the general reader," it has yet had a reception that has made me deeply glad. It is the beginning of my true work. Only one or two know I am "Fiona Macleod." Let you and my dear T. A. J.[8] preserve my secret. I trust you.

You will find more of me in *Pharais* than in anything I have written. Let me add that you will find *The Mountain Lovers*, at which I am now writing when I can, more elemental still, while simpler... . By blood I am part Celt, and partly so by upbringing, by Spirit wholly so... . One day I will tell you of some of the strange old mysteries of earlier days I have part learned, part divined, and other things of the spirit. You can understand how I cannot do my true work, in this accursed London...

... I resent too close identification with the so-called Celtic renaissance. If my work is to depend solely on its Gaelic connection, then let it go, as go it must. My work must be beautiful in itself — Beauty is a Queen and must be served as a Queen... . You have asked me once or twice about F. M., why I took her name: and how and when she came to write Pharais. It is too complex to tell you just now. The name was born naturally: (of course I had associations with the name Macleod.) It, Fiona, is very rare now. Most Highlanders would tell you it was extinct — even as the diminutive of Fionnaghal (Flora). But it is not. It is an old Celtic name (meaning "a fair maid") still occasionally to be found. I know a little girl, the daughter of a Highland clergyman, who is called Fiona. All my work is so intimately wrought with my own experiences that I cannot tell you about *Pharais*, etc., without telling you my whole life.

... I can write out my heart in a way I could not do as William Sharp, and indeed I could not do so if I were the woman Fiona Macleod is supposed to be, unless veiled in scrupulous anonymity...

This rapt sense of oneness with nature, this *cosmic ecstasy* and elation, this wayfaring along the extreme verges of the common world, all this is so wrought up with the romance of life that I could not bring myself to expression by my outer self, insistent and tyrannical as that need is... . My truest self, the self who is below all other selves, and my most intimate life and joys and sufferings, thoughts, emotions and dreams, must find expression, yet I cannot save in this hidden way.

Memoir, pp. 226–27

To Patrick Geddes, [January 10, 1895]

[Croft House | House | Hambrough Road | Ventnor][9]

In a few days now I expect to have the long delayed copies of the new American edition of my *Vistas*, & to send one to you.

But now enough about myself. You, I hope are well: with your busy brain as alert and hopeful & observant as usual. I often think of you, cher ami.

On some other occasion I must write to you about the papers & pamphlets of your own which you gave me. In all, a remarkable power of distinctive thought is evident: in those that deal with art there is not only forcible and admirable writing but unusual *flair*. My wife begs to be most cordially remembered to you — & to thank you — for all your kindness in the matter of the Nit. of Amyl Capsules etc. etc.[10]

We shall be here for about a week yet: but must be in London again by the afternoon of Friday the 18th.

Do let me hear from you.

> Your comrade in many things & Your friend in all | William Sharp

Please if practicable write to me (& give me as long a letter as you can spare) by return: if impracticable, send me at least a P/C of acknowledgment. Letter writing is a great strain for me just now — & I don't want to have to write this note a third time! So I'd like to know you've received it!!

ALS National Library of Scotland

To Anna Geddes, January 10, 1895

Croft House | Hambrough Road | <u>Ventnor</u> | 10/1/95

Dear Mrs. Geddes,

I have just written a long letter to that unduly silent spouse of yours: and now enclose a brief line to you.

I have not been very well of late, though now greatly better: mainly from overwork. So, a week or so ago my wife & I came here, at the doctor's suggestion, for a short spell of comparative rest, & for the sea-air, quiet, & long "sleeps". We'll remain in the Isle of Wight (at above address) for about a week yet, but must be home again in South Hampstead by the afternoon of Friday next, 18th.

I often think of you and Geddes: and always with a glow of pleasure, and, if you will allow me to say so, of affection. My wife, who liked you both so much, now says she is quite in love with both of you!

Well, were you very surprised when Geddes told you that W. S. and Fiona Macleod are one and the same person? I could not resist the temptation to write to you, as F. M., in response to your kind letter: indeed, courtesy prompted this, then, and in the circumstances. Still, I did not mean to leave you long in the misunderstanding, of course.

I need hardly say I have every confidence in you as well as in him, as to the absolute preservation of my secret: even if the subject, by any hazard, come up in conversation any time.

I wished to pay you a little act of homage & esteem: & so got a little album (with Celtic designs) from Iona, and filled it with MS. excerpts from *Pharais* & other unpubd. writings, specially for you. I sent it to you just before Xmas: but I fear my little Celtic offering is gone to No-Man's-Land. If so, you must take the will for the deed, and believe that you are held in friendship & esteem by two of your sincerest well wishers

Fiona Macleod | and William Sharp

P.S. My wife is going to write to you someday soon. She looks forward with keen pleasure to next August.

ALS National Library of Scotland

To Patrick Geddes, [January 15, 1895][11]

Croft House, Hambrough Road, Ventnor. |
Tuesday afternoon

My dear Geddes,

I hope that by this time you are under less strain of work and that "Bhean Gath-greine" and the little gathain-greine* are well. Bhean Gath-Greine is right to be in bed, and resting: but I trust that the actual need is now over. Please thank her for the welcome little supplementary note I had this morning: and in telling her that I am glad she likes that volume of stories I so strongly recommended to you both, add that the author *is* a Scot, from Perthshire, and I think from near Perth, though his name is not Ian Maclaren. He is a man of middle age, and is a clergyman of a Scot's church in Liverpool.

*Anglice: "Lady Sunbeam and the little Beam-lets!"

Later

Well I took up the pen to answer your letter in detail, but I find it difficult to be succinct and adequately explanatory in so complicated a matter.

The long and short of it is that I think, just before I settle down again, I had better take a run up to Edinburgh to talk this and other questions over with you. We could do more thus (in the matter of publishing, Celtic matters, etc.) in a day than we could manage in a month by correspondence: and at present any writing about details tires me very much: or writing of any kind, except in the morning: though I am ever so much better. Certainly I can ill afford to do this, as things are: but there are two economies to consider, and I think I choose the wiser in deciding to go to Edinburgh to see you. (I can also take notes for the Celtic school of ornament article etc.)

Friday and Saturday & Sunday of this week are fully preoccupied. But I might be able to get away on Monday morning. Could you put me up that night? I daresay I'll stay in Edinburgh over Tuesday & Wednesday, but I could go to my mother's on those days. (In fact, it must be on these days or not at all just now.)

I am taking for granted that you will not be at Dundee — and that you will be able to spare the time to talk things over. (I have neither time nor health to spare just now for meeting other people.)

If this reach you tomorrow (Wednesday) evening, will you kindly write by return. If not till Thursday, then address to me at the Grosvenor Club, New Bond St, London: marked "Not to be forwarded." We leave here early on Friday morning: but my art-work will prevent my getting home till about 9 or 10 p.m.

Perhaps the little "rune" overleaf will suit you for *"The Evergreen."*

Ever yours, | William Sharp

ALS National Library of Scotland

To Patrick Geddes, [January 21, 1895]

Monday[12]

My dear Geddes,

We are very sorry indeed to hear of the illness of your very little boy, but hope it will now run its course swiftly and mildly. Our sympathies are with you both. It is probably hard upon Mrs. Geddes, after the children having been so long from home, & now the girlet having to be sent away.

I am too pressed to write letters today, and yet I cannot do anything else, feeling as "down" as though I had that infernal influenza again — tho' I think it is more the low swing of the pendulum. However, proofs and revision of typed MSS etc. are ready to hand, and must be gone on with.

Well, as things are, it would suit better if you came to us next Tuesday. You will not mind having to sleep away from here will you: i.e. as our guest, but in a room in another house, somewhere near? I'll get one for you as near as possible, and you can look upon my study as your own: & of course you'll have all your meals with us, consistently with your wishes or arrangements. For alas, in our small flat there is no spare room.

Let me hear from you soon [and also] because I wish to keep myself as free as possible for you. At present, I am free (or have freed myself) on Tuesday, Wednesday, Thursday: i.e. as regards afternoon and evening freedom — for I am too much in arrears just now not to have to utilise the morning hours (say till 12). Perhaps one day you would care to come for a ramble in the country near: — Milton's and Matthew Arnold's country. (Chalfont St. Giles & Chemis).

I am sure you are right about Edinburgh versus London. I have a profound & chronic distaste for London & London life: and a nostalgia for the north. The chief drawback to any change is the problem as to some surety in income (here chiefly derived from art-work, which would be lost to me & to my wife, worth about £250, as a regular thing, but increased by occasional art-work in the magazine etc.) — Thus a considerable part of my reviewing would be lost, owing to the growing habit with editors not to send review-books beyond the London postal area (partly on account of late transmission & early return of proofs).

Again, London is a great meeting-place, a "bazaar of fortunate & smiling chances": then, we have a great number of acquaintances and some dear friends: and, finally, there is my interest in the Stage, & my ambitions in that direction — &, I may add, Music, which is one of my wife's chief joys. However, partial residence in London, or frequency of visitation, could be placed to the other side.

As you will understand, the point is mainly one of means of subsistence. In other words, is there publishing, secretarial, tutorial, or other work in Edinburgh that, without more expenditure of time and energy than I now give to my art work and reviewing, would ensure me say £300 & leave me time for my own particular work. I doubt it.

On the other hand, I would in some ways be glad to stop all this miscellaneous pen-work. I feel I am wasting time, and opportunities, myself. If I were free from it, I could devote more of my time to making a name for myself in fiction and the drama: & once I could depend on that kind of pen-work, I should be independent of London.

On the whole then, I don't see how I could throw up Fogtown — at present. What I would like to do would be to have rooms in Edinburgh (or the flat in Ramsey Gardens we want to take if possible — and about which we'll speak to you when you come) and come & go a good deal: in fact, if the publishing idea develops,[13] & you entrust me with a responsible part in it, I would need to be in Edinburgh one week & perhaps two weeks in each month.

Àpropos of publishing — the effort should be to produce at first certain books of as pronounced a character as possible — books of significance so to say: so that the Firm be known at once for a certain distinction. Again, it will be financially important that the publications should be as varied as practicable: i.e. fiction and belles lettres as well as science, philosophy, etc. Among ourselves (Arthur Thomson, you, Fiona Macleod, W. S. etc.) we could start well: and by loyally seeking the common good as well as looking to our own interests (i.e. not letting our own interests be the primary determining factors in our procedure). I am convinced we should maintain & speedily develop that good start — among the highly advisable things to do would be the production of a little Fortnightly like that *Chap Book* I gave you (the one with [an] article on myself, and photo — you remember?) — which would be at once attractive and a splendid advt. It might be brought out in the same way, and at the same price 2^{d}. [Here Geddes has written: "Why not 3^{d}?"] The C.B.[14] was originally started by Stone & Kimball as an artistic & worthy advt. of their wares — but speedily attained a circulation of 10,000 copies each fortnightly issue — & now sells out 12,500 each issue. It would require careful editing & handling: — & I should be glad to undertake it. [Here Geddes has written: "Agreed"] It would be paying in itself — & would attract wide notice to the publications.

There might be, to start with, a biological book by A. Thomson:[15] a sociological or other work by yourself: "A New Synthesis of Art" or other work by myself, or perhaps "Ernest Hello: A Study" or my wife's "The Spirit of Man" (being a translation of *L'Homme* of Hello): a Celtic romance by Fiona Macleod: some other Celtic book, in prose or verse (for it is on Celtic lines, I think, the most development will take place first): a vol. of striking short stories: if possible, a really striking and original novel. These could be printed, bound, & advertised, & distributed on an outlay (carefully administered) varying from £500 to £750: or including the Edinburgh Chap Book, & extra & unforeseen expense, & extra advertising, etc. at say £1,000. As to payments to authors: that wd. need to be on a royalty system. There would need to be no haphazard publishing at first: & especially in the choice of what to begin with fiction, great judgment would need to be exercised. If you intend me to be the literary "boss" in the firm (tho' perhaps I mistake your intent!) I would give my best thought, care, & experience to making the venture a success in every way, & ultimately a potent factor in the development of Scotland & of Edr.[16] in particular. Of course my editorial experiences, & far-reaching literary connections, would stand me in good stead: & in a year or so we could have a varied and potent "staff". If I were lity. "boss," as I say, one effort would be to centralise in Edinburgh all the Celtic work now being done by Scottish, Irish, and Welsh writers.

It is a question of capital, of "greasing the wheels pro tem" and of patience & wise discretion [Here Geddes wrote: "Agreed"].

There is, as has been wisely said, always room — at the top of the tree!

We are too enthusiastic, too determined, not to get to that top if it be possible, as I firmly believe it is, and as I know you do. [Here Geddes wrote: "Quite so. Full speed ahead!"].

However, these & all other relevant matters I must leave over now till we meet. Let me have a line from you to say if you will come to us on Tuesday. You know how welcome you will be.

My wife sends her affectionate sympathy to Mrs. Geddes — to whom also mine, with all cordial greetings.

Forgive so scrappy & unsatisfactory a note: the writing of which, however, has moved me out of my depression & "doleful dumps".

À Vous, Cher ami et Confrère, | W. S.

ALS National Library of Scotland

To Professor William Knight,[17] January 30, 1895

15, Greencroft Gardens | South Hampstead | 30/1/95

My dear Sir

I have been ill — and have just returned from Ventnor. I am under very great pressure, now — &, moreover, must do as little extra work as possible.

But at the earliest moment I can spare I will see if I have any material that can serve your aim.

Yours very truly, | William Sharp

Professor Wm. Knight LL. D.

ACS Pierpont Morgan Library

To Herbert S. Stone, January 31, [1895]

9. Upper Coltbridge Terrace | Murrayfield. | Midlothian | Jan. 31st

My dear Sir

I thank you for your courteous and friendly note, and am glad to inform you that I am now quite recovered.

I am glad you are so much interested in my stories. By the way, just as I was writing to you the acceptance of your terms, I was urgently "approached" by a publisher: so I am glad you were able to make a definite proposal, as otherwise I should have accepted the rather tempting offer made me here. I hope, and venture to believe, you will be pleased with "The Sin-Eater" volume.[18] The three or four I have read or shown to qualified judges have been praised so very highly that I am confirmed in my own opinion that some of the best I can do is here. The book, I am hopeful, will attract attention in both countries. (If I could get out of my engagement with "The Mountain Lovers" I would do so — for I should much like the three romances, *Pharais*, *The Mountain Lovers*, and *The Herdsman*,[19] to be published by one firm: but I fear this is not practicable. However, it may yet be arranged that you issue it in America.)

By the way, you have not written as to what I am to do about *Pharais*. Kindly let me know by return if possible, as another and rather important proposal has been made me. Since recovery from my nondescript illness (overwrought nerves from insomnia, and influenza, and from being — *pro: tem:* — in a town, and away from the sea of the west) I had first, because of priority of the commission and of my promise, to finish the section of the volume (to be called, probably, *Celtic Sorrows*) which was commissioned by the editor of *Harper's Magazine*, on the head of "Pharais." This section of seven to ten short pieces will probably be called "From the Hebrid Isles": and is, if possible, to appear in 1895: so I understand at least. The MSS. went off yesterday.[20]

You may be sure I will not needlessly delay a day in transmission of *"The Sin-Eater* etc" For my own part as well, I am most anxious that, if practicable, this book should be brought out this Spring, or, at latest, early summer. Kindly oblige me by letting me know by return if this is your intention: if you are too busy to write at once upon other matters please send me the briefest line about this and *Pharais*, as I have consequent arrangements to make.

The names of the *longest* stories are "The Sin-Eater" — "The Judgment o' God" — The Ninth Wave" — "The Annointed Man" — "The Dark Mile of Achnacarry" — "The Bandruidh" — "The Ransom" — and "The Seven Hunters". They are now being typed, (more than half are done) and will then have a final revision. I dare not *promise* to let you have the book before the end of February: but if I can I will. These stories wear me very much in writing: sometimes even in the rewriting of [?]revision.

I was actually ill for weeks after *Pharais*!! This, no doubt, is a foolish weakness of

Yours very sincerely | Fiona Macleod

P.S. My cousin, Mr. William Sharp, has sent me some "Chap-Books" to look at. What delightful little periodicals they are: so charmingly got up: and extremely interesting. In particular, I have read Mr. Bliss Carman's Critical Articles with vivid interest, the more so as I admire greatly what I have seen of his poetry.

In his letter, Mr. W. S. in allusion to the number for Oct. 15. (Mr. W. Kennedy's story), incidentally says something about "how pleasant it would be if I printed" in a Chap-Book number, either the opening section of *The Mountain Lovers* (which would stand by itself, as it is of the nature of a prologue and is mainly an intimate revelation of the evolution of night from dusk to dawn on a remote mountain solitude) or else the three Iona tales in *The Sin-Eater*, — "The Judgment o'God", "The Ninth Wave", and the strange tale of St. Columba days "Deirthrê Anguifera" (which, by the way, I now think of calling "The Idolaters".)

This, he says, "would — with a portrait — doubtless be welcome."

But I gather from his words that this is a mere remark of his, and not suggested by you?

If by any chance, a special number were made, I take it for granted a financial arrangement would be come to first.

Perhaps a better plan would be the expression of "the Idolaters" ("Deirthrê Anguifera") into a longer story (i.e. for appearance in the Chap-Book only) with more of St. Columba and Oran and the early life (700 years before Chaucer!). But all this may be "the blue smoke of the village out of sight."

My mention of the matter at all may be presumptuous. If so, pray put the matter aside, and think no more of it.

F. M.

ALS Stanford University

To Herbert Stuart Stone, February 1, 1895

Rutland House | Greencroft Gardens | So. Hampstead, London | 1st Feby /95

Dear Mr. Stone

I have been asked to write an article for the *Fortnightly Review* on the "Younger Transatlantic Poets"[21]: & would be much obliged if you would (i.e. if you care to) send me a copy severally of Geo. Santayana's "Sonnets", Gilbert Parker's book of verse, and Hamlin Garland's "Prairie Songs"[22] — and indeed anything new you have published lately that you think well of. Of course I will allude to you as publisher — & indeed will have something to say about "Stone & Kimball" and the new movement.

Why don't you reprint the first 2 vols. of *The Chap-Book*. Surely it wd. pay you to do so, and wd. gratify many here as well as in the U.S.A. You will be glad to hear that the *Green Tree Vistas* is much admired. By the way, your delightful posters have created quite a flutter. I have just had an eager request for one from J. Pennell[23]: who had seen one somewhere.

I suppose I shall be hearing from you shortly about the "Gypsy Christ"etc.

Do you ever see *The Realm*? If so, you will find an article by me on Pater's *Greek Studies* in last week's issue, which may interest you: as you like my "Atlantic Monthly" article on W.P.[24] Do you know Addington Symonds's work well? I have a long review of him in the *Academy* this week.[25]

With cordial regards,

Sincerely yours, | William Sharp

P.S. I suppose you won't be here till after March at earliest. Please let me know when next you write.

ALS Huntington Library

To Horace Scudder, February 2, 1895

Rutland House | Greencroft Gardens | So. Hampstead | N.W. | 2/2/95

My dear Horace Scudder,

Many thanks for your letter — and for your friendly suggestions. As to the latter, I'll write to you later. I hope to send "Christina Rossetti"[26] by next mail (Wednesday 6th). I want to interpolate a few extra particulars as to early days (from William Rossetti). She was not only a poet of rare distinction, but a woman, representative of the fine flower of Christianity, one of the white-souled of the world.

Despite the pressure of books, I have at last got the Ed. of the *Academy* to agree to have an article upon your "Childhood".[27] I hope to write it end of next week. Herewith I send you a "leader" of mine from this week's *Academy* on J. Addington Symonds — whom I knew and liked well, though I have had to say some plain things in my causeriè.[28]

At home, I had done up a copy of last week's *Realm* (with an article by myself on Pater's *Greek Studies*, which I thought you might care to see) — and also a copy of the new edition of my *Vistas*, which please accept from me with my cordial regard: but I have come away without them (I write this at the Grosvenor Club) & so they must wait over till next mall.

Shields[29] sends you "his brotherly love": & says you will be welcomed with open arms. It will be a great pleasure to him, and myself, and many others, to see you here. (But don't come in August or Septr!)

Cordially Yours, | William Sharp

ALS Harvard University, Houghton Library

To Stone and Kimball, [early February, 1895]

Rutland House | Greenscroft Gardens | So. Hampstead | *London*

Dear Sirs,

Herewith my Postal order for Renewal of my Subscription to "The Chap Book."

Please note in your address-book that the penultimate address is not *Homestead* but *So. Hampstead*.

Yours faithfully | William Sharp

P.S. I think I subscribed for the 3rd. vol. (*Verlaine*) in the *Green Tree Library*:[30] but if so I have never recd. it.

ALS Huntington Library

To Herbert Stuart Stone, February 13, 1895

Rutland House | Greencroft Gardens | South Hampstead, London | 13/2/95

Dear Mr. Stone,

Thanks for your letter of acceptance of my terms, in the matter of "The Gypsy Christ" — proofs (& "copy" of the G. C.) of which I await in due course.

I am not so wedded to "The Rape of the Sabines" as to insist on its inclusion against your will. It will do just as well in another volume, *The Daughters of Vengeance*,[31] which I may have ready for publication next winter. So do as you wish. I will loyally accept your decision. If you would rather exclude that story, do so. I send you two others, instead. In any case I would like "The Lady in Hosea" to go in. I have not had time to reread and consider "The Graven Image": you can do so, and include or exclude as you think best. So that the volume could now stand (with or without "The Second Shadow"):

I. The Gypsy Christ | II. Madge o' the Pool | III. The Coward | IV. A Venetian Idyl | V.? ["The Second Shadow" — or "The Graven Image"]? | VI. Fröken Bergliot | VII. The Lady in Hosea.[32]

What bitter weather! I trust it is better with you. (I go to Edinburgh for a few days this week-end, & hope to see Miss Fiona Macleod, who is staying near: and very busy with the revision of the volume she is doing for you. It is the strongest thing she has done, I think.)[33]

My cordial regards, | Sincerely yours, | William Sharp

By this mail I am also sending a commissioned article (for the *Atlantic Monthly*) of "Reminiscences of Christina Rossetti," which I wd. like you to read on appearance.

P.S. You will already have got my letter about *Vistas*, with which all my friends (as well I) are charmed.

ALS Huntington Library

To Elizabeth A. Sharp, February 20, 1895

Corrie, Isle of Arran, | 20:2:1895.

... You will have had my telegram of my safe arrival here. There was no snow to speak of along the road from Brodick (for no steamer comes here) — so I had neither to ride nor sail as threatened: indeed, owing to the keen frost (which has made the snow like powder) there is none on the mountains except in the hollows, though the summits and flanks are crystal white with a thin veil of frozen snow.

It was a most glorious sail from Ardrossan. The sea was a sheet of blue and purple washed with gold. Arran rose above all like a dream of beauty.

I was the sole passenger in the steamer, for the whole island! What made the drive of six miles more beautiful than ever was the extraordinary fantastic beauty of the frozen waterfalls and burns caught as it were in the leap. Sometimes these immense icicles hung straight and long, like a Druid's beard: sometimes in wrought sheets of gold, or magic columns and spaces of crystal. Sweet it was to smell the pine and the heather and bracken and the salt weed upon the shore. The touch of dream was upon everything, from the silent hills to the brooding herons by the shore.

After a cup of tea, I wandered up the heights behind. In these vast solitudes peace and joy came hand in hand to meet me. The extreme loneliness, especially when I was out of sight of the sea at last, and could hear no more the calling of the tide, and only the sough of the wind, was like balm. Ah, those eloquent silences: the deep pain-joy of utter isolation: the shadowy glooms and darkness and mystery of night-fall among the mountains.

In that exquisite solitude I felt a deep exaltation grow. The flowing of the air of the hills laved the parched shores of my heart... .

There is something of a strange excitement in the knowledge that two people are here: so intimate and yet so far-off. For it is with me as though Fiona were asleep in another room. I catch myself listening for her step sometimes, for the sudden opening of a door. It is unawaredly that she whispers to me. I am eager to see what she will do — particularly in The *Mountain Lovers*. It seems passing strange to be here with her alone at last... .

Memoir, pp. 243–44

To Patrick Geddes, March 3, 1895

Rutland House | Greencroft Gardens | South Hampstead | London |
Sunday 3rd March/95

My dear Geddes,

When I saw you last, and again when I wrote to you yesterday, I quite forgot to communicate to you my scheme for a thoroughly representative Anglo-Celtic "quarterly"[34] — broadly speaking, about the size & on the technical lines of "The (new) Evergreen". It would, I think, be well supported in all the big towns of Scotland and Ireland, and (in England) in Newcastle and London, & doubtless elsewhere, & of course in Wales: also, most certainly, in America (particularly in the Teuto-Celtic New England States and the North). In addition to this, it wd. greatly help our Publishing firm, & aid in drawing Anglo-Celtic writers to look to Edinburgh. I think 2s/6 net would be best, as price. I send you [a] partially drawn out scheme: for your approval, examination, & comments. Tho' I am willing to be Editor (with my wife's help) — I think it best that the Editorial indication should be either | Published by Patrick Geddes and Colleagues |or simply Edited and Published in Edinburgh. I could, I know, soon get a very strong list — & the quarterly would become a valuable record. It is quite easy to see why foregoing Celtic mags. have spelt failure or relative failure. I have studied this point carefully: (& would take up only the best lines of "The Highland Monthly", the defunct "Celtic Mag.," etc.).

Please give the matter your careful consideration (Time-bills, eh?) & let me hear from you in due course.

Yours ever | William Sharp

You have a most thorough ally (in all you urged upon me) in my wife. We both foresee (in the fulness of time) — Edinburgh! in a broad sense, i.e. she takes greatly to the whole publishing idea, & I foresee how she may prove of great service, & well worth her time-bills!

N.B. "The Hill of God" by F. M. in the first no. wd. be an account ("from a relative") of the sacrificial episode I told you about.

PROSPECTUS

Vol. I No. I July to September 1895. Quarterly | 2/6 Net.

The Celtic World

Published By Patrick Geddes & Colleagues

(or else) Edited and Published in Edinburgh

July August September

Summer Number

Frontispiece	By John Duncan
1. The Celtic Renaissance	A Prologue (Editorial)
2. The Word Anglo-Celtic	A Note "
3. Anglo-Celtic Magazines	"
4. The late Professor Blackie	By Prof. MacDonald
5. The Hill of God	By Fiona Macleod
6. A Poem	By W. B. Yeats
7. The Hill-Way	By Ernest Rhys
8. The House of Rest. A Forecast	By Patrick Geddes
9. A Poem	By Moira O'Neill or Katherine Tynan
10. Three Hebridean Folk-Hymns	By A. Carmichael
11. Celtic Ornament	By John Duncan or ?
12. Standish O'Grady's Historical Romance	By –
13. Anima Celtica	By "A. E."

Notes

Names of Some of the Earliest Contributors

(If possible) George Meredith & the older writers like Geo. Macdonald and Robt Buchanan, Douglas Hyde & Prof. Rhys, Grant Allen etc., as well as the younger men.

In the Second Quarterly Number (Oct–Dec.) will appear the first installment of "The Celtic Wonderland" and Stories, Poems, Episodes, Articles, Critical-papers, Folk-Lore, etc.

By Douglas Hyde, George Russell, W. B. Yeats, Fiona Macleod, Moira O'Neill, Dr. Donald Macleod, Robert Buchanan, George Macdonald, Grant Allen, W. Macdonald, Ian Maclaren, and other Irish, Scottish, Welsh, Manx, Cornish, & Breton writers.

With a Frontispiece by P. MacGillivray *or* by T. Hope Mclauchlan or Photogravure of *Evensong*, by Macaulay Stevenson

ALS National Library of Scotland

To J. Stanley Little, March 21, 1895[35]

21/Mch/95

My dear Boy

The beginning of a long & happy & prosperous time has, I am sure, dawned for you. All happiness & luck be yours. Be good to her, for she is worthy of it: and both of you enjoy to the full what nature has been good enough to supply you with.

In all ways, happiness and weal!

Your friend, | William Sharp

ALS Princeton University

To Edmund Clarence Stedman, March 30, 1895

Rutland House, | Greencroft Gardens, | So. Hampstead. | 30/Mch/95

My dear Stedman

I know you will be glad to meet the bearer of this note, Mr. John Lane, whose name will be familiar to you as that of one of our most distinguished publishers. It seems hardly necessary to add that he is himself an able and discriminating student of literature, the friend of many of the *beaux esprits* of the day, and himself a good fellow. I know you will welcome him to your hospitable abode: & if you can give him any advice or introduce him to any one whom he wants particularly to meet, you will not only be obliging Mr. Lane but also

Yours affectionately, | William Sharp

Edmund Clarence Stedman Esq

ALS Princeton University

To Mrs. Henry Mills Alden, [*April, 1895*]

... And now I write in Sussex[36] — in my ears the cries of the lambs, the cawing of rooks, the song of a labourer sowing seed, instead of the harsh summons of the muezzin, the call of the water-carrier in Tunis, the bark of the jackal on the Desert, the barbaric chant of the Hasebircheaters of Constantine. It seems almost incredible at times.

Yes it is all equally beautiful. Life is life everywhere. Here, in placid England, as in the austere South, as in the grey savage North, there is a diurnal banquet of joy. Everywhere this indescribable, alluring, haunting, lovely seduction of Beauty.

How I wish, dear Mrs. Alden, that you could be here just now — it is all so Spring-essential. But of course it will be as lovely in New Jersey. I wish, though, I could send you some of our yellow primrose glory, a breath of an old English cottage-garden, with its mignonette and wallflowers.

It is, just now, — though the malcontents say it is too warm, & that 6 weeks of unbroken weather & cloudless skies is serious — so unspeakably lovely. It is all a joy of green tress, green hedges, cowslip'd fields, daffodil pastures, — blossoms of apple, pear, quince, plum, and cherry all like blown surf suddenly suspended in the warm blue air — larks in rapture, the cuckoo and the wood-dove calling, calling, through the noontide, birds everywhere in the trees, the hedgerows, and by the brook — a song of Spring begun by the Black-cap at sunrise, sustained through the drowsy afternoon by the thrush, & now just lifted with an exquisite preliminary thrill when at the edge of o'dark the nightingale calls from the thickets of jasmine and elder.

Have you the delight in words that I know the author of "God in His World"[37] has so keenly? If so, you will rejoice in an almost unknown West-Country word for twilight which I have just learned — unknown save in remote parts of Devon & Cornwall. "Twilight" is lovely: "The Gloaming" is lovelier and sweeter: but is there something solemn, almost Biblically austere & noble about "The Dim-Sea" (the dimsee as pronounced).

How I hope this Spring will bring you healing and peace and joy. Will you let me send you my "love"? Alden already has it, and my deep admiration: and you know, you two are one. Let me slightly alter Bacon's beautiful saying; "The soul of the twin-soul is the Beauty of the World".

Cordially Yours, | William Sharp

ALS University of Delaware Library

To Herbert S. Stone, April 6, 1895

Rutland House | Greencroft Gardens | South Hampstead N.W. |
London | 6th April 1895

Dear Mr. Stone,

I admit that I am much put about by the long silence on your part: and, I may add, I have had two or three letters of late from Miss Macleod to the same effect, so displeased, indeed, is she that she wrote to me the other day to say that she would prefer to make other arrangements, particularly as she is much pressed by publishers here. It really does seem too much of a good thing that urgent letters should be allowed to be unanswered, and this quite apart from the apparent discourtesy. I wrote to Miss Macleod to say that I was sure no actual discourtesy was intended — and that probably you had been or were ill; to which she naturally enough replied that someone could have sent a reply to the specific enquiry she wrote on the 2nd of February, with a request for an answer by return.

Well, about "The Gypsy Christ"? For some time past I have been looking to every mail to bring me the promised proofs, and also the MS. of the titular story for revision. In the first place, I had particularly specified my wish, & understood that you entirely shared it, for early spring issue of the book: but here is April, and no proofs come, and apparently no arrangements made! Had I foreseen this I should, of course, have made other arrangements. There is now no mail due till the 9th — & I can only hope that at last I shall hear from you. In your letter of January 28th, formally agreeing to my terms, you say that you will go ahead with the composition at once: & that you will dispatch the MS. of the G.C. itself by registered post. These proofs, you say, will be sent "in the course of two or three weeks". If they had been sent in two or three weeks I might have received them by the end of February. Now the first week in April is over, and no word of them — nor, for that matter, of "The Tower of Silence", concerning which you say (28th January) — "I shall write regarding this within the week."

Leaving aside other considerations, this delay is very inconvenient for me in the matter of proof-revision etc. In a life as busy [as] mine, with chronically more work on hand that I can well get through, it is impossible to manage things aright unless matters are conducted on both sides (in each instance) in a prompt and businesslike way. As soon as I received your letter of Jany 28th, I made corresponding arrangements: so that I should be comparatively free at the time I could reasonably expect Proofs. Financially & for every other reason I hoped to see the book out in early Spring: but for this reason, also, trusted for early proofs, namely that April & May are my two busiest months, and every hour has to be discounted. At the end of April or early in May I have to go to Paris for the Salons: & proofs and revision at that time will be a difficulty and inconvenience added to existing difficulties & inconveniences.

I trust that an early post now will bring communication from you: but if not I must beg of you to write to me without delay, & explicitly.

As for Miss Macleod — I am not quite sure what to advise her: but from what she writes to me I think her best plan would be to arrange with someone here. She says, & rightly, she will not send any MS. to you till she has an explicit reply and that in any case she now holds herself free to come to any arrangement that suits her. She was pleased by your first letter, but your extraordinary silence of late has both annoyed and offended her.

And now apart from business let me express my hope that you are not or have not been ill: and that matters go well with you. When do you intend to come over here?

By the way, I gave John Lane a line of introduction to you. Lane, I may add, is going to issue Miss Macleod's new book, *"The Mountain Lovers"*. As it will be in the Keynotes series it is not likely he will offer it to you first — tho' Miss M. wrote expressly asking him to do so if possible.

Forgive me for saying that if we are to have any business relations in the future, I make it an indispensable condition that this kind of treatment does not recur. I am glad, however, to feel sure that it is due to pressure and inexperience: & certainly look forward with pleasure to a chat over business & other matters when you come to London.[38]

Yours very truly | William Sharp

ALS New York Public Library, Berg Collection

To Patrick Geddes, April 27, 1895

Rutland House, | Greencroft Gardens. | So. Hampstead. |
Saty 27th April/95

My dear Geddes,

Owing to the press of work and engagements it was impossible for me to see Mr. Barclay[39] àpropos of the Franco-Scottish College scheme (a most alluring and I should think inevitably fruitful one) — but I hope to do so when I return to Paris, on the 5th May for the Old Salon etc. My wife will go with me to Paris this time, & we'll be there for 3 or 4 days at any rate. By the way, when I was at the Douane on my outward journey I met Mrs. Traquair[40] on her way to a brief holiday in Rome.

W. Macdonald[41] does not seem to have come to a bed of roses. Work which he had looked upon as fairly assured has not "come off" — & he writes to me to see what I can do or suggest. He seems to have become impatient over the Evergreen: for, àpropos, he writes: "I got tired waiting, & came to the conclusion that the book would never appear until one or two artists had been taken back to the nursery & locked up there."

I'll write to you a publishing and book-anticipatory communication on Monday. Too seedy today, having caught a bad facial chill in the passage and being unable to go out owing to an inflamed jaw (an abscess I fear) — and bad facial neuralgia: together keeping me in considerable pain and discomfort.

As to Campbell Irons[42] — yes, I wholly agree to all you say as politic & advisable every way.

I am afraid it will be quite impracticable for me to get to Paris at Whitsuntide. But I *hope* to see you before then: Of this more when I write on Monday.

Love to you and yours | William Sharp

ALS National Library of Scotland

To Patrick Geddes, April 29, 1895

Rutland House, | Greencroft Gardens, | So. Hampstead. | Monday 29/4/95

My dear Geddes

I forget if I told you how seedy I was on Saturday when I wrote to you. At any rate, by the afternoon I was in high fever, with inflammation of the jaw, & severe frontal & optic-nerve neuralgia — an infernal form of influenza (complicated with an abscess somewhere, generally in the ear, but in my case at the top of the left jaw) which attacks many people here just now, & has just laid low my doctor (Dr. Moir of whom I spoke to you) & our other reserve "medico". I had a pretty bad time of it on Saturday night, almost delirious: & all Sunday: but today am greatly better, and hope to be up and about tomorrow, though of course I won't get out till next day and then only if fine and warm.

I think I told you that my wife and I go to Paris for our art-work at this coming week-end (on Sunday probably) & will be away for 5 or 6 days. I don't know where we'll stay, probably at the "Continental" — but in any case I'll try to see Mr. Barclay.[43] Perhaps, if writing, you will kindly mention this to him, in case he knows nothing of me, and takes me for what Rabelais calls somewhere "a villain cut-throat Scot", a man to be hurried off the premises!"

I'll do my best to get north soon after my return from Paris etc. about the 12th — i.e. to get north on or about the 20th. I want to talk over "publishing business" for one thing: and perhaps I could see Mr. Campbell Irons & Branford[44] and some others. Yes, by all means let us have Mr. C. Irons as ally and client.

Meanwhile, as I must be making certain arrangements, please let me know if you will be at Dundee on or about the 20th. of May — & when it is your intention to leave for Paris. (I am afraid there is now no chance of my getting over at Whitsuntide.) And are you sure it will still be quite convenient for Mrs. Geddes & yourself to put me up at Dundee, as you kindly suggested.

(1) For the late *autumn* of 1895, I'll do what I can to place the vol. of stories by Fiona Macleod (*The Sin-Eater: and Other Stories*) with "Patrick Geddes & Colleagues."[45] So far, I am free of the arrangement with Stone and Kimball, I *think*: for as they were not up to time with their undertaking I wrote about 3 weeks ago to break off with them as regards the British edn. I have not definitely heard from them yet in response to my ultimatum — but the strong chances are that I shall now be able to make this one of our start-off books — of which I shall be glad from the publisher's standpoint, as short stories of the kind are in demand just now, and as "The Mountain Lovers" (to be out in June) will give a fillip to F. M.'s growing public. I am afraid that, as author, the arrangement may not be so much to my advantage — but, after all, the reverse is possible, & in the long run may even prove much the better: but in any case I am willing to make this arrangement if I can.[46] The book is practically ready, and will reach a wider audience than either *Pharais* or *The Mountain Lovers*, I fancy. Certainly some of the strongest work I have ever done is in it.

(2) *Lyra Celtica* will also be ready, & will be a valuable and suggestive vol. Two-thirds of it is in shape already: indeed it is more the long critical "weighing" & rejecting & adding that has now to be done. It will have the additional value of being representative, for though mainly Scottish-Celtic and Irish Celtic, there are representative pieces by Breton (trs), Cornish, & Welsh, & Manx poets. Can you give me the name of a Welsh poet you spoke of to me at Arran? But please note that L/C will be edited *not* by F. M. or by W. S. but by my wife. This is advisable for several reasons (one among them, the inclusion of F. M.'s runes & Celtic lyrics), & also because she is well known by her critical anthologies, & was recently commissioned to do the important "Musa Catholica" for Elkin Mathews.[47] If, however, any critical introductory essay (as distinct from an ordinary preface) is considered advisable it will be written (& signed) by me.

(3) The R. L. S. volume will, I presume, be the first actual issue? (apart from *The Evergreen* & *A Scottish College*).[48]

(4) "Life of Croll" could come out. Also "Heredity" if ready.[49] ("The Literary Ideal" by W. S. ought, I think, to stand over till beginning 1896 — but, if wished particularly, *might* be available for issue say in mid-October or November of this year)[50]

(5) We must have some "romance" of a kind likely to be popular. If possible, some well-known man: but what is more important is a really *modern* romance, full of life & movement.[51]

(6) What about a series of short books of fiction — as that is so much the vogue at present: — books of about 30,000 words, or say from a minimum of 25,000 to a max. of 35,000. It might be called *"The Evergreen Series"*: or, say, the "Cosmopolitan" Series.[52]

(7) Àpropos of the last named, I think a good bid for public favour would be occasional vols by foreign authors of marked power & distinction in the "new movement" — a vague phrase that really means little save the onward wave of the human mind: men like the Scandinavians, Jonas Lie & Ola Hansson (Swede), Southerners like the Italians Gabriele d'Annunzio, Antonio Fagazzaro, Matilde Serao, or the Spaniard José Echegaray,

Germans like Hermann Sudermann, Frenchmen like Anatole France, J. H. Rosny, etc., Belgians like Geo. Eekhoud (Flemish), Lemonnier, and others, and the notable Americans among the younger generation, above all of [sic] Hamlin Garland.[53]

This either in a "Cosmopolitan Series", or to be worked into the other. I am strongly in favour of some translations from the contemporary fiction of countries near us, & that are in touch with this country — notably Belgium. The Flemish & Walloon side of B. (tho' now familiar to thousands) is little touched in book-form or translation. Good translations of such (past) masters as Henri Conscience or (living) as G. Eeckhoud would take.

As soon as things are settled on a business footing, I'll put affairs *en train*. I have already talked to some able writers & translators — but of course can commission or advise nothing as yet. Send me a word, too, about this idea of representative translations.

Meanwhile let me know what you think — & also about your being at Dundee at the date named and when you leave for Paris.

Love to you and yours.

W. S.

ALS National Library of Scotland

To Robert Murray Gilchrist, April 30, 1895

Rutland House | Greencroft Gardens | So. Hampstead | 30th April/95

My dear Boy

How goes the world with you? I hope you are well, & that the pen has been busy, and happily. I have been much away this year — twice for a long time in Scotland (once in the Western Isles), and in France. I go to Paris again this week-end but expect to be in London again by the 12th. A few days later I'll likely be in Scotland for 10 days or so. When are we to meet again? When I look back upon this last year, it seems to me as though life were a fever indeed. I am not tired of life — which is more wonderful & fascinating than ever: but sometimes now I am tired of living. In a vague way you know something of the tragic issues which underlie the surface-calms of my life stream. Well, tragedy or high comedy — for low farce to men like ourselves is impossible — or tragi-comedy or inscrutable irony, it is all a dream.

"*The Mountain Lovers*," the successor to Fiona Macleod's "*Pharais*," is now in the printer's hands, & ought to be out from a month to 5 weeks hence. It is to be published by John Lane.

Are you coming south this June? I hope so. My cordial regards to your mother & kind remembrances to your sisters — nor, or course, omit my greetings to Garfitt. As for yourself you [know] that I am

Your Affectionate friend | William Sharp

ALS Sheffield City Archives

To J. Stanley Little, May 10, 1895[54]

Paris: Friday Night

Dear S.

We are to return tomorrow after a very pleasant but rather too extravagant time in Paris. (This is my second visit to Paris within the last 3 weeks.) I shall, however, be in town for 3 or 4 days only — as I wish to go to Scotland for a fortnight or so. I hope you and "Madame" are both flourishing, and bear in mind my favourite adage "Be good, and you will be happy".

Yours ever | W. S.

ACS Princeton University

To Patrick Geddes, May 15, 1895

Rutland House, | Greencroft Gardens, | So. Hampstead. | 15th May 1895

My dear Geddes,

I am glad we are to meet so soon, and I am much looking forward to Monday evening, to see you & Deò-grein again.[55] As I explained to her in my note of yesterday, I shall arrive by the North British train due at Tay Bridge at 6:10. If it stop at Esplanade Station, I'll get out there. I leave here on Saturday, as I have to be in York on Saturday evening, & shall remain there with my friend George Cotterell[56] till Monday morning (address, if needed, 3 Grosvenor Terrace, York) when I leave at 10.

I have thought out a good deal about publishing schemes — and so we'll have lots to discuss if you can spare me the time. For the moment, however, I need not go into so these, as we are to meet so soon. For the same reason, indeed, I'll reserve detailed mention of "The Evergreen". Much of it I like, but some of it seems to me to lack in distinctiveness as well as distinction. In the main, however, it is a most promising and interesting production. With careful piloting it ought "to come to stay". We must all do what we can to make it as scrupulously near to the highest attainable standard as is practicable. Your own writing therein I have read with particular interest & pleasure, not only with the affection of a friend but with the sangfroid of a critic. The poetry, including that of Miss Fiona Macleod does not seem to me to be so good in its kind as is the best of the prose in *its* kind. That also is a point where the editorial control must be more exigent.

But the real and I fear perilous weakness is in the illustrations. With the exception of Duncan's[57] "Apollo's School Days" & some of the head-pieces, there is not a drawing (Cadenhead's[58] and Wall's[59] "cuts" are distinct from those I am referring to) which is not crude in draughtsmanship and in design — or in one or two instances frankly meaningless! (I mean from the standpoint of art, which, as you know, is as exigent in its demand for an adequate & convincing raison-d'être, as the Art of Poetry is for adequate rhythmic motive). In the latter category, I include a muddled, badly composed, & ill drawn "Natura Naturans" by Robert Burns[60] (his "Casket" is better, but shows little sense of rhythmic balance or movement in the composition) — but, in particular, a really deplorable plate, "Anima Celtica", by Duncan. It is weakly imitative to start with, & in my judgment has not a redeeming quality. Aubrey Beardsley[61] may be a depraved & decadent artist — but at least he is an artist & original: but work of this kind is the mere dross and débris of the "fin-de-Siècle" ebb. I am afraid that even the most casual critic will notice the bad drawing throughout — which has the same effect on one's optic nerves as a scraping nail has on one's auditory ditto. (On the other hand, though it lacks firmness in touch, i.e. surety, Duncan's head-piece to "The Norland Wind" is at once appropriate & winsome). In a word, I anticipate much adverse artistic criticism on the ground that the Yellow Book[62] drawings are at least clever if ultra fin-de-Siècle, while the majority of these of *The Evergreen* are fin-de-Siècle without being clever.

Probably, I am too severe a critic here — & in any case I'll be glad if I'm a false prophet. But I feel so strongly that a really valuable & significant future awaits the "Evergreen" if it preserve & develop its best, in literature & art, & disengage itself from what is amateurish, that it seems worthwhile to be severely exigent.

The binding & get-up are very novel & attractive, & the type & setting are in Constable's[63] best style. Altogether, it is a promising start for "Patrick Geddes &Colleagues". There is the real breath of earnest life in it — & that is a saving grace indeed. Well, *Skoal* to it, & to its projectors and contributors, & to all our fellowship!

I had a long talk in Paris with Mr. Barclay (whose name is *Thomas* not *William*, as you had in your notes & typed letters from him) about the Scots College. As you will know by this time, there is not now to be any Whitsuntide meeting in Paris: but, later, in London, and also, I understand, in Edinburgh.

Of this, again, more when we meet.

Till Monday evening then, auf wiedersehen — |
Affectionately Your Friend | William Sharp

"Porporsia Celtica" is better now than he was, though till yesterday he was very "down" indeed. No doubt the heat & London atmosphere had something to do with it. He made his will, poor thing, one day: which affected him so much that he got better![64]

ALS National Library of Scotland

To Robert Murray Gilchrist, [May 16?, 1895][65]

till middle of next week | c/o Prof. Patrick Geddes |
17 Westfield Place | Dundee

After the 22nd | to | 9 Upper Coltbridge Terrace |
Murrayfield | Midlothian |
(letter address only)

My dear Gilchrist

Herewith I send you a pipe — though I fear it may not suit you. "Pipes" are as "Kittle Cattle" as hats or umbrellas, & each man has his own fancy. But if the accompanying article would never make for a smoker's paradise, send it back to me — & I'll get another. It pleased me, your asking for it. May it make you think of me sometimes.

Don't overwork into apathy: that is the dangerous hole to get into. Overwork to a certain strain on the nerves, if you will — even till Heaven one moment & Hell the next seem near — but stop short of a dull apathy in the act of composition, a dull apathy in the sense of atmosphere. Then, body, and nerves, and brain, crave for a path of silence: for sleep.

I doubt if it will be possible for me to see you on my way back (somewhere about Whitsuntide, probably a day or two later rather than earlier) — but I'll let you know.

Why did you not let me know you were in London, when on your way to or from Paris? I am sorry at that.

I do hope your work is to your satisfaction, i.e. as much as it ever is to anyone who really cares for his work. Work, my dear Boy, with sunshine in your heart, and the sunrise air in your brain and a moonlight imagination. You will do big things some day.

I am glad you are going over to Cartledge.[66] It will be better for you every way I shd. think.

Ever yrs affectly | William Sharp

ALS Sheffield City Archives

To Patrick Geddes, [late May, 1895]

74. Upper Grosvenor Terrace | Tunbridge Wells | Sunday.

Dear Professor Geddes[67]

First let me say that I read your letter — which reached me yesterday — with feelings of unmixed relief and thankfulness. I cannot express to you how grateful I feel for your loving friendship for my husband and for all the care and thought you and Mrs. Geddes have given him. I am *thankful* that there is someone else than myself who sees how he is expending health and strength — and encroaching on his reserve — in work of a kind he ought not to do. Like you, I have a great belief in the future of W. S. and Fiona M. and I am equally persuaded that he *must* give up the fretting hack-work in order to give his real work its chance. But it is so difficult to make him do so; he grows nervous, and, I regret to say, chiefly on my account. But I feel sure, that now, your kind interest in him, and thought for him will do more [than] any thing else to make him, not only feel, but act on our advice — which coincides. You are indeed a most valuable ally.

And, indeed, I do not know what to say concerning the kind proposals in the latter half of your letter. I feel deeply touched by and grateful for the genuine friendship which prompted them. I think the very knowledge of such an offer will suffice to give Will peace of mind to work in greater belief in himself and in the future of his work. I think it will give him the confidence he lacks when he seizes nervously the first piece of work that offers. I see that little by little he begins to believe what I say about him; & feel sure your letter to me — so full of generous solicitude and help — will do the rest. I, too, promise to remind him to let you know if at any time an advance from the publishing account would save him from pot-boiling temptations; I will be only too glad to do it — glad, too, to feel that the responsibility concerning him — which I feel to be heavy sometimes — is thus lessened. That statement sounds very selfish, now I reread it; but I do not mean to be selfish. I mean it is a relief to me to see that there is a friend who understands Will, and sees his persistent overwork and delicacy. With regard to the other offer in your letter, Friend, I feel overwhelmed, and can say nothing. But I will show your letter to Will when we meet. I think he, like myself, will feel so encouraged by the kindly thought that prompted the suggestion, that the desired *sense* of rest and freedom from worry will thus be attained.

I intend to have him put into his doctor's hands as soon as he returns, in the hope that the weakness in Will's back may [be] bettered. It is the result of overwork; but a symptom not to be disregarded.

I feel this note is very inadequate in its attempt to say how I appreciate your friendship shown in your letter. But words do not come readily to me, alas! Believe that I feel it deeply; also that I look forward with delight to August,[68] when I shall have a chance of knowing you and Mrs. Geddes still better than I do now.

Will has, I know, told you how much I am interested in all the schemes; and how I hope I may be allowed to share in a little of the work.

With cordial greetings to Mrs. Geddes and yourself,

Gratefully and sincerely yours, | Elizabeth A. Sharp

ALS National Library of Scotland

To Robert Murray Gilchrist, [May 28, 1895]

Murrayfield | Midlothain | (Tuesday)[69]

I return to London Tomorrow (Wednesday)

My dear Gilchrist,

Alas, the visit is impracticable this time — but may be made about the end of July possibly, if you are to be at Cartledge then. I (& my wife) have to be in Edinburgh all August — where, at University Hall, I have to give a course of ten lectures on *"Life & Art."* Then in all September we'll be at a remote & beautiful place in the West Highland, Tigh-na-Bruaich in the Kyles of Bute.

I have just come here (Murrayfield) from a most beautiful place, near Lock Fyne in Argyle. There, the Lord be praised, for a few days I have been swung across the frontiers of ordinary life into an existence of rainbows & moonlight & endless, impossible, hauntingly beautiful horizons. Now the dream is over — but the rainbow gold of it is for life! Don't you think you could manage a week or so at Tigh-na-Bruich in September? There is a pleasant inn, where you could doubtless have comfortable & moderate accommodation (or a cheap lodging somewhere) & we could see something of each other.

My best remembrances to your mother & sisters, & know me ever your affectionate friend.

William Sharp

ALS Sheffield City Archives

To Patrick Geddes, June 4, 1895

4 June 95

I am grateful to you for all your solicitude about my health and welfare, cher ami. You are truly a good & loyal comrade as well as a dear friend.

As to "working the constituency": yes, I'll do what I can. If possible I'll come to Edinburgh a little before the beginning of August. Thanks for the summarized conversation with MacCormick.[70] Be assured that all your arguments & advice have been, are being, & will be loyally pondered by me. My wife is touched & pleased by a letter you have written to her. I have not seen it, & can do no more than infer: but while I gladly accept the friendly intent as further proof of your affectionate friendship I am sorry you wrote exigently about my health — & particularly about my back. I was eager that she should know nothing of a passing trouble — partly due to over strain & partly no doubt rheumatic.

I am now not only ever so much better, but full of energy & ardour. I had the most *glorious* weather in the West, and had a true sun-bath every day. Friday, Saty, Sunday, & Monday last I spent at one of my favourite remote places on Loch Fyne in Western Argyll. There I lived mentally, spiritually, & physically (excuse the unscientific specifications!) in rainbow-gold. All day from sunrise to midnight I was on the higher mountain slopes, or in the pine-woods (full of continuous solemn music with the north wind), or on the sea. On Sunday forenoon I rowed across (2 miles or so) to the uninhabitable rocky solitudes opposite (South of Ceann More) — went for a long glorious swim of about an hour! — lay naked in the sunlight below a pine on a mossy crag, & dreamed pagan dreams, & fell asleep, & had a wonderful vision of woodland lives unknown of men, and of a beautiful Child God, of which you will hear something from Fiona in due time — & wakened two hours later, still sun-bathed, tanned & burnt & midge-bitten — then another swim — then rowed across the loch again &, after tea etc., away up to the summit of a hill set against a marvellous vision of mountains & peaks & lofty ranges, which I have baptised with a Gaelic name meaning the Hill of the Beauty of the World — then watched the sunglow till 10 p.m. & came down thro' the dewy heather to the pinewoods, where I climbed into the branches of a great red brother & lay awhile listening to the wind, with its old-world wonder-song of the pines, & watching the moon sail upward.

I have come away with a sense of the sunflood through & through me: of magic rhythms and hints: of secret voices and cadences haunting-sweet: & with the almost passionate health & eagerness of that young Norse god who in sheer extravagance of joy wove the rainbows into a garland for the moment's mountain he made out of falling worlds.

All which dithyrambic exultation means I am well. I thank the Gods for life — for a swift pulse & red blood — and fever in the heart and brain —

and

But I'm going to be good, & to lecture, & to publish, & behave, & always love Mrs. Geddes & yourself –

W. S.

ALS National Library of Scotland

To Frederick Shields, June 24, 1895

Rutland House | Greencroft Gardens | So. Hampstead | 24:6:95

My dear Shields

I want to introduce to you my friend, Mr. MacKenzie Bell (an intimate friend, also, of two whom you hold dear — our Dear Christina Rossetti, & Theodore Watts).

I want to do this, partly because Mr. MacKenzie Bell is anxious to make the acquaintance of one whose work he admires so much: partly that you, too, may meet a poet & man of letters and what is best of all a good fellow: & partly that he may chat to you about Christina Rossetti whose life (or rather a monograph on whose life-work — with some biographical detail) he has been commissioned to write.

With Greetings, | Ever yours affectionately, | William Sharp

ALS Yale University

To Herbert Stuart Stone, [late June, 1895]

9. Upper Coltbridge Terrace | Murrayfield

Dear Mr. Stone

I thank you for your letter — the suggestions in which I endorse and will abide by. Yes: "*The Washer of the Ford*"[71] may stand over till February: a decision I should probably have come to even if you and Mr. Sharp (from whom I heard by the same post) had not urged it.

It will be all the better for keeping, and for the opportunities of close and repeated revision. There are in particular two things in this book ("Muime Chriosd" and "The Washer of the Ford") which I think will attract more attention than anything I have done.

As to *Pharais*. Yes, I will abide loyally by my undertaking to give you first option in America of all my books. Please send me a line to say when you wish my revised and slightly altered (for copyright) copy to be delivered to you. Will it do if you receive it in Chicago before the end of August? If, however, you wish it earlier you can have it.

In writing about this, please add if the letter of terms as to "The Sin-Eater" volume still holds. I have not the letter at hand, but the undertaking was a 15% royalty on the published price of each copy sold. Kindly add if you confirm this: i.e., for America. I will send you duplicate typed copy (ready for press) by or before the end of July. As I told you, the book will be issued here by Patrick Geddes and Colleagues early in October: of course, the exact date will be fixt by mutual agreement later. The present stipulation on the part of P.G. & Colleagues is that I send in "The Sin-Eater" complete by or before end of July, when it will at once be sent to the printers, to be ready for issue in (say) first week of October.

I hope you will please me by accepting from me a copy of *The Mountain Lovers* on its shortly forthcoming publication by Mr. Lane, (who now awaits only a cable from Messrs. Roberts Bros. of Boston, who are printing the book in America.

Believe me, | Yours very truly, | Fiona Macleod

ALS Pierpont Morgan Library

Chapter Thirteen

Life: July–December, 1895

For the first three weeks of July, Sharp was "wildly busy" in London, writing and negotiating with Herbert Stone about American editions of The Gypsy Christ and Other Tales (by W. S.) and Pharais and The Sin-Eater (by F. M.). He told Stone that his arrangement with Elkin Mathews specified Stone and Kimble had the right to publish another collection by Sharp, Ecce Puella and Other Prose Imaginings, in America, and the book was issued simultaneously by the two publishers in November. On July 5, he and Elizabeth went to Hindhead in Haslemere, Surrey to spend the weekend with the Grant Allens — which Sharp, in a letter to J. Stanley Little, called "a brief respite." In a letter thanking Mrs. Allen for a very enjoyable time, Sharp assured her she need not be concerned about a rumor floating through London involving her husband and a "literary Parisian." Sharp must have mentioned the rumor during the weekend since he was anxious to assure Mrs. Allen it would soon pass. Most people, he wrote, knew Allen had been in Paris not with a French woman named Belloc, but with his wife. Sharp's focus on this rumor is notable given the likelihood that he himself was recently in Paris with a woman who was not his wife.

In an interesting postscript, Sharp declared the publisher John Lane "should be careful how he speaks," and advised Allen "not to give himself away." Having received the manuscript of Allen's *The Woman Who Did* and agreed to publish it, Lane let it be known Allen was its author. Allen intended to publish the novel pseudonymously, and Sharp advised him to stick with that intent despite Lane's indiscretion. When the novel appeared several months later, its author was Grant Allen. The book attracted a great deal of attention, positive and negative, and made its author both famous and infamous. Soon after it appeared, Victoria

© William F. Halloran, CC BY 4.0   https://doi.org/10.11647/OBP.0196.02

Fig. 5. "The Croft," Grant Allen's House in Hindhead, Haslemere, Surrey (1906).
© The Francis Frith Collection, https://www.francisfrith.com/hindhead/
hindhead-grant-allen-s-house-1906_55569

Crosse produced *The Woman Who Didn't*, and Mrs. Lovett Cameron produced *The Man Who Didn't*. The woman in one and the man in the other adhered closely to the norms of Victorian society. Allen's woman believed women should throw off the shackles of male dominance and assert their equal rights, views shared by Sharp. In recommending Allen publish pseudonymously, Sharp knew the book would generate a good deal of outrage. The novel has recently emerged from obscurity as an important contribution to the *fin de siècle* feminist movement known as the "New Woman." The Paris rumor, Sharp's concern about Lane's indiscretion, and the negative response to Allen's novel offer a glimpse of the self-reflective and interconnected London publishing scene in the 1890s.

Allen shared Sharp's interest in authorial deception. He published several books as the work of invented males, and in 1897 he issued *The Type-Writer Girl* as the work of a woman, Olive Pratt Rayner. By that time, he knew Fiona Macleod was William Sharp, and Sharp's use of a female pseudonym may have encouraged him to follow suit. In 1895, however, Sharp worried Allen might learn the truth and not keep the secret. Writing to Allen on July 15 as Fiona, he made a "small request." If Allen intended to write anything about her *Mountain Lovers*, she hoped he would "not hint playfully at any other authorship having suggested itself." She continued, "And, sure, it will be a pleasure to me if you will be as scrupulous with Mr. Meredith or anyone else, in private, as in public, if chance should ever bring my insignificant self into any chit-chat." Sharp was especially concerned that George Meredith not be apprised of Fiona's identity. He had praised her work and Sharp thought he might lose his friendship if he discovered Sharp had deceived him. Fiona ended her letter by telling Allen she looked forward to meeting him "when she came south in late Autumn." Sharp may have planned to take Edith Rinder, posing as Fiona, to meet Allen, just as he would take her to meet Meredith.

Sharp was also worried about finding time to prepare the lectures he promised for Patrick Geddes's Summer School in August, "over 70,000 words to write in 10 days or so." On July 13, he found time to go down to the Burford Bridge Hotel in Surrey for a dinner meeting of the Omar Khayyam Club, an organization of literary figures dedicated to the pleasures of good wine and food. Many important writers, including Grant Allen, attended, chief among them George Meredith who was the guest of honor (*Memoir*, p. 246). He was lured to the dinner by his friend Edward Clodd, the club's president, and arrived only for the dessert course. Clodd welcomed him "in a charming and eloquent speech not devoid of pathos," and Meredith, overcoming his famed reticence about speaking in public, responded graciously and wittily. After attending this dinner as a guest, Edward Clodd recommended Sharp for membership in the Club, and he joined in November.

In a letter dated July 15, Sharp told Richard Le Gallienne, who was living near Allen and Meredith in Surrey, that he was sorry to have missed him at the Omar dinner, since he needed to talk with him. Le Gallienne could not meet that week, and Sharp could not meet the following week. He was leaving London and would not return until October, by which time Le Gallienne would be in America. Since Le Gallienne missed the Omar dinner and a meeting was impossible, Sharp made the point he had hoped to make in person: "Yes, my boy, be just to Miss Macleod. Anything you can say for her will be gratefully appreciated, but she as well as her worthy cousin [Sharp himself] earnestly hope for no more confusion respecting her actual authorship of *The Mountain Lovers* etc., publicly or privately." Having concluded, through textual comparison, that Fiona Macleod was William Sharp, Le Gallienne had already shared his opinion with Grant Allen, who remained skeptical. Sharp was especially hopeful that Le Gallienne would not share it with Meredith, who had just sent Fiona a letter of praise and encouragement. "He knows she is my cousin," Sharp wrote, "but, I hope, will never be 'put about' by hearing any other rumors." Wherever the fires might arise, Sharp tried to contain, if not extinguish, them.

The Sharps planned to spend August in Edinburgh to take part in Patrick Geddes's Summer School, and then continue on to the Kyles of Bute in Argyll for September. On the July 13 Sharp told Murray Gilchrist that he would like to pay him a visit on his way to Scotland in approximately ten days. When Geddes learned that Sharp was coming north in advance of his wife, he proposed a hiking trip. Sharp declined, saying he could "see no one for the week I shall be 'hanging about.'" Until the end of July, he would be in Edinburgh only intermittently. Thereafter he would be available to talk with Geddes about *The Evergreen* and other publications of the new firm. On July 18 Sharp told Gilchrist that he was unable to leave London until the morning of July 22 and that he had to be in Edinburgh that evening. Because of this, he would be unable to visit Gilchrist Gilchrist in Homesfield on the way north. On July 20, before he left London, Sharp wrote a heartfelt letter to Annie Alden, whose mother (the wife of Henry Mills Alden) had recently died after a long and debilitating illness. While visiting the Aldens in Metuchen, New Jersey during his visit to America in 1891, he developed a sincere affection for the family. His letter to Annie reveals a good deal about his conception of the afterlife and, indeed, life: "I am sure that there are some people who go through life as white spirits clothed with the accident of the body — rather than, as most of us, as human beings animated by a spirit — and that she was one of these." In the afterlife, Sharp asserts, her spirit had been released from the confines of her body. At the age of nearly forty, Sharp had settled on a realm of disembodied spirits as a means of coping with evolutionary theories that undermined Biblical teachings. Sharp must have told the Aldens he was Fiona, since, after expressing his hope that Annie would enjoy the copy of Fiona's *The*

Mountain Lovers he sent to her father, he asked her to preserve the secret of her identity.

A clue to Sharp's whereabouts after he went to Scotland alone on July 22 appears in a late July letter from Fiona to Grant Allen thanking him for his favorable review of *The Mountain Lovers* in the *Westminster Review*. As he passed through Edinburgh, Sharp had his sister copy this letter into the Fiona hand with a "temporary" return address of 144 North St. | St. Andrews | Fife, (now a shopping area across the street from the University), and Sharp mailed it from there. In the letter, Fiona says she is visiting friends in St. Andrews and that her cousin Will Sharp is "coming to spend the weekend" with her — "or I with him, I should say, as I am to be his guest, at almost the only Celtic place we know of on this too 'dour' shoreland of Fife." From later correspondence, we know that Edith Rinder was vacationing in or near St. Andrews until late August, when she left for Brittany to collect folklore. Sharp's insistence on being alone that week, and his claim that Fiona was visiting him in St. Andrews, suggests he was using a rendezvous with Fiona as a cover for one with Edith. As the years went by, Sharp claimed Fiona as his cousin, and sometimes he implied they were romantically involved, though both were married to another. Fiona's movements as portrayed by Sharp in correspondence and conversations often modeled those of Edith. When Edith was in Scotland, Fiona was there; when Edith was abroad, so was Fiona; when Edith was with him, Fiona was with him. This tracking was a convenient way for Sharp to remember Fiona's whereabouts. It also signaled his predisposition to conflate the two women, one real and the other imagined.

In an early August note to Stanley Little, Sharp said his lectures were going well but they had "told upon" him heavily, and he was "far from well." According to Elizabeth, while he was delivering the first of ten scheduled lectures on "Life & Art" at Geddes's Summer School, Sharp "was seized with a severe heart attack and all his notes fell to the ground. It was with the greatest effort that he was able to bring the lecture to a close: and he realized that he must not attempt to continue the course; the risk was too great" (*Memoir*, p. 251). The plural in the letter to Little implies more than one lecture was delivered, but that seems not to have been the case. At the end of August, he informed Herbert Stone that he had not been at all well, "the strain of lecturing" had been too great.

As much as he liked to sketch out the topic of lectures, Sharp was less successful in forming his notes into a coherent narrative, and delivering a lecture provoked great anxiety. The "heart attack" was probably an attack of angina brought on by nervous apprehension. Whatever the case, he quickly repaired across the Firth of Forth to recuperate at the Pettycur Inn in Kinghorn where Edith Rinder could visit from St. Andrews. Elizabeth stayed on in Ramsay Gardens "to keep open house for the entertainment of the students."

Fig. 6. Ramsay Gardens from Princess Street, Edinburgh. Photograph by David Monniaux (2005), Wikimedia, CC BY-SA 3.0, https://commons.wikimedia. org/w/index.php?curid=228032#/media/File:Edinburgh_old_town_ dsc06355.jpg

Sharp's illness did not prevent him from continuing his correspondence with Herbert Stone in August. Two letters dated August 12, one from Fiona and one from Sharp, illustrate his careful manipulation of the duplicity. In the Sharp letter, with a Ramsey Gardens return address, he informed Stone that "Miss Macleod" was staying with him and Elizabeth for a day or two to hear his lectures, "particularly that on The Celtic Renascence." This was the fifth lecture of the ten he had planned to give, and, if Elizabeth's recollection was correct, he did not get beyond the first. But having Fiona with him at Ramsey Gardens at the halfway point of his planned lectures explains why he was able to add a brief note of his own to Fiona's letter of the same day. The simultaneity of the two letters was possible because Sharp's sister Mary was close by in Murrayfield to supply the Fiona handwriting.

In an August 30 letter to Stone, Sharp reported that Edith Rinder had entered the Ramsay Gardens milieu: during the previous week, he wrote, they had "a short visit from Mrs. Wingate Rinder." He reports that she had been staying in Fifeshire during August, and she was leaving the next day for Brittany "to work up Breton legends and folklore." Sharp was sure Stone would be pleased with her Belgian book, *The Massacre of the Innocents and other Tales by Belgian Writers*, which Stone published in 1896. To publicize the book, he offered to write "a short article on the Belgian Renascence" for Stone's *Chap-Book*. There followed one of Sharp's more curious stratagems. Edith, he wrote, was "Miss Macleod's most intimate woman-friend" and the "dedicatee of *Pharais*." She was certainly Sharp's "most intimate woman friend," and he did indeed dedicate *Pharais* to her. Having equated himself with the imagined Fiona, he went on to say Edith and Fiona had been "staying together recently and (I believe) writing or planning something to do together." The phrasing reinforces the likelihood of Edith's presence at the Pettycur Inn. After broaching the possibility of joint authorship, Sharp quickly dismissed it — "that, from what I know of Miss F. M., will never come off, as she is far too essentially F. M. to work in harness with anyone." The underlying import is that Edith is not Fiona; nor is she collaborating with Fiona. Rather, Edith is translating and editing continental stories and folktales, including those of Celtic Brittany. By sharing these details of the Sharp | Macleod | Rinder triangle with Stone, Sharp reinforced the separate identity of Fiona. The three were good friends and compatriots in the Celtic cause, but quite independent of each other.

Sharp's careful manipulation of people's locations was not limited to Edinburgh. He and Elizabeth had taken a cottage with his mother and sisters for September in the west of Scotland, and in his August 30 letter to Stone Sharp said he was leaving the next day for Tigh-Na-Bruaich in the Kyles of Bute, in Argyll. A postscript to Fiona's August 12 letter informed Stone that throughout September her address would be "c/o Mrs. William Sharp [not Mr.] | Woodside | Tigh-Na-Bruaich | Kyles of Bute | Argyll | Scotland." After bringing Fiona to Ramsey

Gardens in mid-August, he had arranged for her to stay with him in the West during September. More correspondence with Stone about his publication of Fiona's *Sin-Eater* and *Pharais* would be necessary, and sister Mary would be on hand to supply the requisite handwriting. This sort of manipulation of Fiona's whereabouts was a fact of Sharp's life for the next decade, until his death in 1905. It was necessary to sustain the fiction of Fiona's separate existence, and Sharp enjoyed orchestrating the complexities.

In mid-September, the Sharps were joined in the Kyles of Bute by Elizabeth's mother, travelling from London. On September 18 Sharp told Stone their party was breaking up the next day, but he and Elizabeth would stay on till the end of the month. By September 26, however, the plans had changed. Sharp had to take his mother-in-law back to London, he wrote to Gilchrist, "as she is prostrated by a telegram from abroad saying that her son has suddenly developed a malignant cancer and is dying — so rapidly that he must give up hope of coming home." This turn of events disrupted his plans to spend "three days in Edinburgh on important business: my day and night in York: & my two days with you," but he assured Gilchrist he would stop to visit in late October when he would be returning to Edinburgh.

On September 27, William and Elizabeth, with her mother, left the Kyles of Bute for Edinburgh, where Sharp posted a long birthday letter to E. C. Stedman. Stedman should receive from Stone and Kimball "on or about the 8th" — Stedman's birthday — a copy of *The Gypsy Christ*. He had hoped to send a book of "prose imaginings," *Ecce Puella*, but Elkin Mathews had delayed publication until late October. Stedman would also soon receive from Stone and Kimball as a special present a copy of the American edition of *The Sin-Eater* by his cousin Fiona Macleod, who "is now admitted," Sharp said, "to be the head of the Scots-Celtic movement — as W. B. Yeats is of the Irish-Celtic." The British edition of *The Sin-Eater,* which was to be published in Edinburgh, "is novel & beautiful as a piece of book-making — though I say it, who am responsible for its type, paper, binding, & general format! For (apart from *The Evergreen*) it is the first publication of the new Edinburgh firm, 'Patrick Geddes & Colleagues,' of which I am chief literary partner." The books published by the Geddes firm in 1895–1896 are, indeed, beautiful examples of bookmaking, and Sharp did play a significant role in their design. That he also played a critical role in their content is clear enough, for they were all written by Fiona Macleod (*The Sin-Eater, The Washer of the Ford,* and *From the Hills of Dream*), by his wife (*Lyra Celtica,* with a lengthy introduction by her husband), and by his close friends Edith Rinder (*The Shadow of Arvor*) and Ernest Rhys (*The Fiddler of Carne*).

Fig. 7. Fiona Macleod, *The Sin-Eater and Other Tales* (Edinburgh: Patrick Geddes & Colleagues, 1895). Photograph by William F. Halloran (2019).

From Edinburgh on 28 September, Sharp sent Stone an article on the Belgian Renaissance for publication in *The Chap-Book.* Sharp told Stone that it would not be necessary to send Mrs. Rinder proofs of her *Massacre of the Innocents and Other Tales,* since she was anxious for it to appear. As it turned out, those translations of stories by twelve Belgian writers was not published until 1896 in Stone's Green Tree Library series. The book took its title from its first story, "The Massacre of the Innocents," by Maurice Maeterlinck, whose dramas had established his substantial reputation. In her introduction, Edith said Maeterlinck was amazed she had unearthed his only published prose tale from "an obscure and long since defunct French periodical where it made its first appearance before anyone had heard a word concerning its author."

Sharp wanted to issue works by W. S. and F. M. at about the same time "in part to sustain what reputation belonged to his older Literary self, and in part to help preserve the younger literary self's incognito" (*Memoir*, p. 251). To counterbalance the publication of Fiona's *Sin-Eater* by the Geddes firm in October 1895, Sharp produced two books by W. S. One was *The Gypsy Christ and Other Tales*, which Stone and Kimball published in Chicago as the first in their "Carnation Series." The volume's first story, which provided its name, drew upon Sharp's experience as an adolescent with a band of gypsies in Scotland, and on a recent encounter while walking with Murray Gilchrist on the moors of Derbyshire. When the book was published in England by Archibald Constable and Co. in 1897, it was named after the volume's second story: *Madge o' the Pool: The Gypsy Christ and Other Tales*.

Sharp dedicated a second book, *Ecce Puella and Other Prose Imaginings* (published by Elkin Mathews in London on November 1) to his friend George Cotterell, editor of the *Yorkshire Herald*. Not one to pass up dedicatory possibilities, he ascribed each of the book's sketches to a close female friend. The title piece, "Ecce Puella," a revised and condensed rendition of "Fair Women in Painting and Prose," which Sharp wrote for P. G. Hamerton's *Portfolio of Artistic Monographs* in 1894, celebrates the beauty of women. Dedicated "To the Woman of Thirty," it begins with a quotation by H. P. Siwaarmill, an anagram of William Sharp: "*A Dream of Fair Women*: Every man dreams his dream. With some it happens early in the teens. It fades with some, during the twenties. With others it endures, vivid and beautiful under grey hairs, till it glorifies the grave." Sharp's dream of a fair woman endured and became a reality in the person of Edith Rinder — the dedicatee — who, in 1895, was a "Woman of Thirty."

The second piece in the book, "Fragments from the Lost Journals of Piero di Cosimo," is one of Sharp's attempts to produce a prose version of Robert Browning's "dramatic monologues." Cosimo, an Italian Renaissance painter, records in old age his failure to measure up to the promise of his youth. Sharp dedicated this piece to E. A. S. — Elizabeth Amelia Sharp — who introduced him to the paintings of Cosimo and his more accomplished contemporaries. The next piece — "The Birth, Death, and Resurrection of a Tear" — is dedicated "To A. C." whose identity is still a mystery. She must have been a woman of great beauty, since the narrator elaborately parallels the course of his unrequited love for her with the course of a tear which falls down "the lovely sunbrown cheek no bloom of any 'sun'd September apricock' could outvie." Next, "The Sister of Compassion," is dedicated "To A. M. C." — Alice Mona Caird — Elizabeth's "dear friend" (*Memoir*, p. 252). The woman of the title is "so wrought by the tragic pain of the weak and helpless" that she laid down her life in order that she might be "a messenger of that tardy redemption which man must make in spirit and deed for the incalculable wrong which he had done to that sacred thing he most values — Life." Mrs. Caird was a well-known spokeswoman not only for the rights of women but also for the animal rights movement in the 1890s. The first-person narrator, a stand-in for Sharp, "loves and honors" her as Sharp surely did since she supplied shelter and sustenance for the Sharps whenever they were in need.

The next piece, "The Hill-Wind," resembles the impressionistic prose poems Sharp was writing as Fiona Macleod, and he dedicated it to F. M. Personified as a beautiful woman, the Hill-Wind sees the "whiteness of her limbs beneath the tremulous arrowy leaves and the thick clusters of scarlet and vermillion berries" as she descends to become the bride of the Sea-Wind. The image of red berries against the white flesh recalls Sharp's "Swimmer of Nemi" in *Sospiri di Roma,* the volume of poems he published in Italy in 1891. Since he associated that poem with the birth of Fiona Macleod, the dedication to Fiona is fitting, but the overwrought description of the forest through which the winds blow contrasts sharply with the restrained language of the poem. "Love in a Mist," the final piece in the volume, is dedicated "To a Midsummer Memory." In this poem, "Love" is a young Cupid who spends a good deal of time examining a beautiful forest in search of something to do. He comes upon a handsome man and a beautiful woman who provide an opportunity to carry out his designed function; he shoots each with an arrow. He is concerned as they appear to fall in agony, but he soon realizes "they were not dead or even dying, but merely kissing and fondling each other, and this too in the most insensate fashion." Sharp's memory of this encounter, one supposes with the woman of thirty who was his dedicatee in the first essay, enabled him to end a book dedicated to the women in his life with a note of titillation for his female readers. *Ecce Puella* thus constitutes a further example of Sharp's preoccupation with women.

In a series of letters to Murray Gilchrist in the fall of 1895, Sharp revealed his deeply conflicted state of mind. His unfulfilled promises to visit caused Gilchrist to wonder if a rift had developed. From Argyle on September 26, addressing Gilchrist as "My dear boy," he wrote, "*Of course*, my dear fellow, there is no 'shadow of a shadow of hill or sea,' as they say here, between us. At all times I bear you in affectionate remembrance: and then, we are comrades." He was sorry Gilchrist's year was filled with "mischances and misadventures." His own year had such extremes of "light and shade' that it was no wonder his friends noted the progressive greying of his hair. To further allay Gilchrist's concern, he closed the letter: "to you, my dear friend & comrade, my love, sympathy, & affectionate heed." With the letter, he sent a set of proofs of the "Tragic Landscapes" section of Fiona's *Sin-Eater* and asked Gilchrist, who knew the Fiona secret, what he thought of the three prose poems. He especially wanted to know what Gilchrist thought of the third piece — "Summer Sleep" — which Gilchrist would know was

> an exact transcript of — Phenice Croft at Rudgwick, and that the three men are — you, Garfitt, and myself. I cannot explain aright: you must read into what you read. The most tragic & momentous epoch of my life followed that visit of yours to Phenice Croft, & is, so far, indissolubly linked with that day I met you, and that time.

Published as the work of Fiona Macleod, the "Summer Sleep" section of "Tragic Landscapes" recounts an incident that occurred when Gilchrist and Garfitt were staying with Sharp at Phenice Croft in 1894. As discussed at some length in Chapter Eleven of Volume 1, Sharp wanted Gilchrist to read that section carefully and recognize its hidden meaning.

Shortly after returning to London, Sharp wrote another letter to Gilchrist to say he would spend a day with him between the October 13 and October 19. He was disappointed by Gilchrist's failure, in his note of acknowledgement, to say what he thought of "Tragic Landscapes." He would elicit Gilchrist's thoughts when they met in person. Sharp returned to Edinburgh on October 12 without stopping to see Gilchrist, and, on October 14, he asked Gilchrist by what means he could go from York to his house in Derbyshire when he returned to London at the weekend. Two days later, he told Gilchrist he was ill with a diarrheic weakness, and wondered if Gilchrist could meet him on Friday 18 after

9:00 p.m. at the Station Hotel in York where he would spend that night and where Gilchrist would be his guest. The meeting did not take place.

On November first, Sharp wrote again to Gilchrist thanking him for a letter praising *The Sin-Eater*. Grateful for Gilchrist's favorable opinion, he remained unsatisfied by what he did not say in his "little message." He wanted to know what Gilchrist felt and thought about the entire book which, he wrote, "is full of myself, of my life — more than any (save one other than myself) can ever know." Edith Rinder, as we shall see, must have been the only one other than himself who knew *The Sin-Eater* was full of his life. That he would make Gilchrist the third to know shows Sharp considered him an intimate friend and trusted him to preserve the secret. He continued with a deeper confession: "I am in the valley of Deep Shadow just now. Great suffering, of a kind that must not be shown, has led me stumbling and blindfold among morasses and quicksands. I see the shining of my star — and so have hope still, and courage. But, while I stumble on, I suffer." The language implies a deep depression.

What, we must wonder, had Sharp embedded in *The Sin-Eater* that he hoped Gilchrist would uncover? The tales in the first section — "The Sin-Eater," "The Ninth Wave," and "The Judgment of God" — each tell the story of a man who commits an infraction of the norms of the Gaelic islands and ends up naked and consumed by the sea. In his depressed state, Sharp must have identified with these poor bedraggled men. In each of the volume's final three stories — "The Daughter of the Sun," "The Birdeen," and "Silk o' the Kine" — Sharp, disguised as Fiona, described a beautiful woman. In the first, she is Ethlenn "with her tall, lithe, slim figure, her dark-brown dusky hair, her gloaming eyes, her delicate features, with, above all, her radiant expression of joyous life." In the second, the Birdeen, or baby girl, grows into a young lady who is

> tall and slim, with a flower-like way wither: the way of the flower in the sunlight, of the wave on the sea, of the tree-top in the wind. Her changing hazel eyes, now grey-green, now dusked with sea-gloom or a violet shadowiness; her wonderful arched eye brows, dark so that they seemed black; the beautiful bonnie face of her, wither mobile mouth and white flawless teeth; the ears that lay against the tangle of her sun-brown shadowed hair, like pink shells on a drift of seaweed; the exquisite poise of head and neck and body.

In the third, Eilidh was the "most beautiful woman of her time." Because of her "soft, white beauty, for all the burning brown of her by the sun and wind, she was also called Silk o' the Kine." She slays the man the King forces her to marry and joins Isla, the man she loves. They shed their clothes and swim out "together against the sun and were never seen again by any of their kin or race." Sharp hoped Gilchrest, reading deeply, would recognize that in each of these stories of female beauty, intense love, and inevitable tragedy, Sharp was telling the story of his troubled relationship with Edith Rinder, which he had described to Gilchrist when they met at Phenice Croft. He concluded the November first letter with a dramatic appeal to Gilchrist: he needed his help, and he needed it "just now."

That plea reached its apotheosis in a late December letter, where he recalled for Gilchrist the "tragic issues" underlying his despair:

> To me, 1896 comes with a gauntleted hand. It will be a hard fight against the squadrons of Destiny (for I hear the trampling of an obscure foe and menacing vague cries) — but perhaps I may — for a time, and that is the utmost each of us can expect — emerge victor. What a bitter strange mystery fate is! You know, dimly and in part, out of what tragic pain and amid what tragic issues I wrote "Summersleep," the third of the "Tragic Landscapes"? Well, every environment is changed, and circumstances are different, and yet the same two human souls are once more whelmed in the same disastrous tides & have once more to struggle blindly against what seems a baffling doom.

The imagery recalls that of the "Silk o' the Kine," but Sharp and Edith could not shed their responsibilities and swim out "together against the sun," never to be seen again "by any of their kin or race." Sharp was "wrought by overwork, anxiety, and the endless flame of life," and he needed to have a long talk with Gilchrist. He was in financial trouble due to the indisposition of his wife, who had to leave England for the three winter months in Italy. He asked again if *The Sin-Eater* "wore" with Gilchrist. He wished Gilchrist would write a long letter, not "one of his usual notelets." He would be thankful if he could leap over "the black gulf of January" and be "safe on the shores of February."

Over-dramatized, but with a ring of truth, the letter is a long cry of desperation and a plea for help. It ends with an "offering" to Gilchrist, a "specially bound proof-revise copy of his last book: *Ecce Puella:*

And Other Prose Imaginings." The volume's extensive ruminations on beautiful women were unlikely to interest Gilchrist, but the intensity of Sharp's adoration might drive home the seriousness of his dilemma. The letter raises Gilchrist to the status of a secular priest whose receipt of an offering might elicit an absolution, a way forward. It is not clear how Sharp thought Gilchrist could help, but he must have thought the restrictions placed on Gilchrist's relationship with Garfitt resembled those on his relationship with Edith (see below). Gilchrist's experience may have produced insights that would alleviate Sharp's depression. But Gilchrist's writings offer another clue to the intense language of Sharp's appeal for help and to his repeated requests for Gilchrist's response to Fiona's "Summer Sleep" in which Sharp saw and feared the "Gates of Hell."

In his writings and his conversations with Sharp, Gilchrist was drawn to speculating about the dark mysteries embedded in the human psyche. Hugh Walpole, in his *The Apple Trees: Four Reminiscences* (Waltham Saint Lawrence, Berskhire: Golden Cockerel Press, 1932), described a visit to Gilchrist (pp. 42–51):

> So dark was the house that we lived for most of the day in candle-light. [...] He liked candles and Elizabethan thickness of atmosphere and, if possible, the rain beating on the leaded windows. [...] He liked to sit in the low heavily-beamed room and, as the candles flickered in the old silver candlesticks, and read aloud some of his favorite pieces from his writings.

In their introduction to a selection of Gilchrist's tales (R. Murray Gilchrist, *The Baselisk and Other Tales of Dread*, (Ashcroft, British Columbia: Ash Tree Press, 2003), pp. ix–xvi), John Pelan and Christopher Roden wrote:

> The themes of madness and doomed love echo through the majority of his stories and in rare instances where his protagonists survive their encounters with the supernatural, it is a close call, and we know that they will carry the psychic scars left by their encounter with the Otherworldly for ever more. Gilchrist's tales are High Tragedy; stories with an air of the morbid and grim, compressed into vignettes of just a few thousand words.

Sharp was especially interested in Gilchrist's response to *The Sin-Eater* because he saw in Gilchrist's tales of "doomed love" and "psychic scars" a reflection of those he was writing as Fiona Macleod, and he thought their author's view of the world resembled his own.

Pelan and Roden also describe the "duality of Gilchrist," as shown by his shift in the late 1890s from "ornately crafted fantasies" to "deftly limned sketches of the Peakland District," from horror stories to local color. "It has been posited" they continue, "that Gilchrist abandoned the realm of the fantastic due to concerns for his own safety following the arrest of Oscar Wilde." Pedan and Roden, however, reject that view. While they agree that Gilchrist, as "a homosexual living in homophobic times," "had reason to be concerned," their analysis of the full scope of his writings indicates that Gilchrist turned to "charming travel books and mainstream novels" primarily because he recognized a change in the literary market and decided to produce writings that would sell.

In addition to the duality in his writing, Gilchrist, like Sharp, experienced a further, more basic splitting of self. Though he was living with George Garfitt (see Endnote 55, Chapter 10, Volume 1) in a homosexual relationship, to those outside the relationship its nature remained obscure. Less flamboyant than Wilde, Gilchrist was not averse to distinctive role-playing. In *Eyam — The "Milton" of Robert Murray Gilchrist* [a small pamphlet of unknown date written by a resident of Eyam and available locally], Clarence Daniel recalled his father saying Gilchrist attended church services wearing "a cassock and girdle, as though it indicated membership of some religious order," while another villager said that Gilchrist was "a huge man, full of tricksy humor, who could rattle off anything on a piano and surprise the stranger with the sweetness of a tenor voice coming from his massive frame." With occasional lapses, Gilchrist projected a distinctive but decidedly masculine image to the world. Sharp also projected that image while secretly wondering if he was more a woman than a man. Gender identity is not openly addressed in Sharp's letters to Gilchrist, but it is clearly a subtext. The confidential tone and confessional content of Sharp's letters suggest they shared while together their concerns about dual identities and gender fluidity. Gilchrist must have been surprised, if not perplexed, by the desperation projected in Sharp's letters, but he must also have recognized similarities in their circumstances. Several qualities that Sharp observed in Gilchrist likely prompted Sharp to pursue an intimate relationship with the younger man in the hope that

Gilchrist might provide him with some solace, and a path of escape of depression: the fascination, expressed by Gilchrist in his writings, with the supernatural and the psychic traumas lurking below accepted patterns of behavior; the dark atmosphere of the large old house he shared with his mother and sister; his unconventional relationship with Garfitt who shared his bleak section of the manse; and the periodic emergence of a softer, "tricksy" self.

Sharp seems not to have desired or needed a sexual relationship with another man, but he had a compelling need for a male friend to whom he could confide his deepest feelings. That need appeared to be rooted in his emotional distance from his father during his childhood, and in his father's early death, which prevented a healing of the breach. In the late 1870s and 1880s, Sharp confided in John Elder, the brother of Elizabeth Sharp's close friend, Adelaide Elder. They met just before Elder immigrated to New Zealand for reasons of health, and the record of their relationship, which ended abruptly in Elder's premature death, is preserved in Sharp's letters. Dante Gabriel Rossetti adopted Sharp as an acolyte in the early 1880s, and Sharp became a willing supplicant. Recently discovered letters to Hall Caine show how Caine became Sharp's confidant when Rossetti died in 1882. In the early 1890s, Sharp developed a close friendship with J. Stanley Little, whom he remained friends with for many years, and who informed the Sharps they could let Phenice Croft, and who lived nearby in West Sussex. When he met Gilchrist in 1894, Sharp, sensing their compatibility and the comparability of their circumstances, adopted him first as a confidant and then a confessor.

Sharp met his first cousin, Elizabeth Amelia Sharp, a well-educated girl from London, when they were children, and they became engaged when they were twenty. She became his companion, his mentor, and his confidant, and remained such until he died. In his mid-life, he met, and came to depend on, the beautiful and brilliant Edith Rinder. The "needs and desires, interests and friends" of the Fiona Macleod side of his "nature," which was "deepening and becoming dominant," needed her presence. It was she who enabled him to summon and objectify his female self. "Without her," he said, "there would have been no 'Fiona Macleod'" (*Memoir*, p. 222). He came to love her; he needed to be with her; and several Sharp sonnets in the National Library of Scotland suggest his despair was deepened by the circumstances that prevented them from having a child. A passage in Elizabeth's *Memoir* (p. 292) offers further insight into the state of mind that caused Sharp to reach out in despair to Gilchrist:

> The production of the Fiona Macleod work was accomplished at a heavy cost to the author as that side of his nature deepened and became dominant. The strain upon his energies was excessive: not only from the necessity of giving expression to the two sides of his nature; but because of his desire, that, while under the cloak of secrecy F. M. should develop and grow, the reputation of William Sharp should at the same time be maintained. Moreover, each of the two natures had its own needs and desires, interests, and friends. The needs of each were not always harmonious one with the other but created a complex condition that led to a severe nervous collapse.

Here Elizabeth addressed her husband's condition in 1898, although the problem had surfaced four years earlier when he tried to come to terms with the effects on his psyche of his creation of a female persona who gradually assumed a separate identity.

To the extent that Sharp identified Edith with the woman he experienced in himself, one might say one part of his nature had fallen in love with another — that, like Narcissus, he had fallen in love with himself. In November 1880, when he was twenty-five years old, he unabashedly declared this love to John Elder: "Don't despise me when I say that in some things I am more a woman than a man — and when my heart is touched strongly I lavish more love upon the one who does so than I have perhaps any right to expect returned; and then I have so few friends that when I do find one I am ever jealous of his or her absence." This sentence should be read in the broader historical context of Tennyson's relationship with Arthur Henry Hallam, Matthew Arnold's with Arthur Hugh Clough, and many similar relationships between men in nineteenth-century Britain. In this case, however, Sharp was seriously attempting to come to terms with his gender identity: sometimes he identified as a man, and other times as a woman. The norms of his society, however, dictated that he be one or the other, not both.

Despite his mental anguish, Sharp continued writing and negotiating with Stone and Kimball about the publication of his *Gypsy Christ* and

Fiona's *Pharais* and *Sin-Eater*. Annoyed by the firm's delays in sending proofs and checks, he was unaware of the managerial and financial problems that soon led to its dissolution. At the end of December, Sharp wrote to Sir George Douglas, a family friend in Scotland who had guessed the Fiona Macleod writings were the work of William Sharp. He admitted the truth and asked Douglas to refrain from telling anyone. He also spoke of Fiona as though she were a separate person. He included several lines about the role of Edith Rinder in the emergence of Fiona Macleod, and then crossed them out as "too personal." Sharp's characterization of Fiona Macleod in this letter as a "puzzling literary entity" is both apt and revealing of the limits to his understanding of the phenomenon with which he was living. In his response to Sharp's letter (*Memoir*, pp. 253–34), Douglas obliged him by speaking of Miss Macleod as a separate person, but said he detected her "mystical tendency" in the poems Sharp wrote in the early 1880s. He insightfully implied that Fiona had been there all along. In Sharp's letter to Douglas, there is no hint of the troubled state of mind expressed so forcefully in his letters to Gilchrist.

He told Douglas that Elizabeth's doctor had ordered her to spend the three winter months in a warm climate, but only with Gilchrist did he share his worries about the strain this development placed on their finances. Far more worrying, however, was his state of mind. "Two human souls," he wrote in his December letter to Gilchrist, "struggle blindly against what seems a baffling doom." He and Edith were bound together in a hopeless love. In the story entitled "Daughter of the Sun" in *The Sin-Eater*, the narrator states: "We have all our dreams of impossible love. Somewhere, sometimes, the impossible happens. Then a man and a woman know that oblivious rapture of love [...] the ecstasy of the life of dream paramount over the ordinary human gladness of the life of actuality." For Sharp, the impossible had happened, but the fact that he and Edith could not live together and build a family was tearing him apart. One cannot help but wonder if Elizabeth's decision to spend three months in Italy was motivated, at least in part, by her desire to remove herself from what seemed a hopeless situation and give her husband and Edith time and space to work matters out for themselves.

1895 saw the launching of the Geddes publishing firm in Edinburgh with Sharp in control of its literary affairs; the appearance from the

Geddes firm of *The Evergreen*; the publication in London of Fiona's *The Mountain Lovers* and Sharp's *Ecce Puella*; the publication in Edinburgh of Fiona's *The Sin-Eater*; and the publication in the United States of Sharp's *Vistas* and *The Gypsy Christ*, and Fiona's *Pharais* and *The Sin-Eater*. It is not surprising that this level of productivity under two names, his extensive negotiations with publishers, his responsibilities with the Geddes firm, and the frustrations and fears in his personal life had, by the end of the year, taken a heavy toll on Sharp's physical and mental well-being.

Letters: July–December, 1895

To J. Stanley Little, July 5, 1895

Rutland House | Greencroft Gardens | So. Hampstead | 5/7/95

My dear Stanley

Just a hurried line (as I am off to stay overnight with the Grant Allens)[1] to say that if you can do anything — as, I remember, you did so well before — for my cousin & dear friend, Miss Fiona Macleod's new book, I hope you will generously do so. It is called "The Mountain Lovers", & will be published on Tuesday next by John Lane, in the Keynotes series.

"Pharais" — Miss F. M.'s first book, you will recollect — made a great impression, & has made her name well known in America as well as here.

I am wildly busy — literally working from 12 to 14 hours daily. Thankful for a brief respite. I have also all my lectures to prepare yet — over 70,000 words to write in 10 days or so![2]

Affectionate greetings to you and la sposa — | Will

P.S. I have directed Lane to send you a copy direct. I hope he'll do so.

ALS Princeton University

To J. Stanley Little, July 9, 1895[3]

Thanks, old man.

I am indeed distressed to hear of your serious anxieties. I do hope things will get better than at the moment they appear. No man has worked more steadfastly, more courageously, & in every way worthily: & you do deserve to have your shares of the spoils of Egypt. One good big spoil came to you with "la belle Maud" — & that *must* bring good fortune with it.[4]

If good wishes could smooth your way, you would simply slide!

Ever yours affectly, | Will

ACS Princeton University

To Herbert Stuart Stone, [July 9?, 1895][5]

Ecce Puella | And Other Prose Imaginings.[6]

I. Ecce Puella. | II. The Lost Journal of Piero di Cosimo. | III. The Birth, Death, & Resurrection of a Tear. | IV. The Sister of Compassion | V. The Hill Wind | VI. Love in a Mist

All are fantasies of one kind or another — Nos. 3, 4, & 5 quite short, especially 4 and 5. Of the reprints, No. II was much noted 2 or 3 years ago when it appeared in two nos. of *The Scottish Art Review*.[7] I like it one of my best prose things. No. I is a condensed version of the successful monograph on "Fair Women" I wrote to commission of P. G. Hamerton for Seeley & Co.[8] It has I think, verve. No. 6, is a narrative-fantasy on "Young Love": and appeared with illustrations in *Good Words*.[9]

I told E. Mathews (who suggested someone, I forget whom, but I think Copeland and Day)[10] that I had virtually promised that so far as I am concerned I must give you the first offer of all my books for America. He said he wd. write to you. I have signed my E. & A.[11] rights with him — on this condition.

So, I hope you may be able to issue it there.

All the more reason for the G/C[12] to come out, as arranged, at the beginning of October.

I do hope you are having a good time, but not overtiring yourself. When do you leave Paris — & when are you to be here again?

It is an awful rush here just now.

Cordial greetings, amico mio, | Yours sincerely, | William Sharp

P.S. I note by the evening paper that my cousin Miss Macleod's new book is out — but I have not yet seen it.[13]

It is just possible I may be able to post a few more galleys today. If not, all remaining will go by next mail. Have just done up Mrs. Rinder's MS for her.[14]

P.S. By registered Book-Post goes herewith (in one packet):
    (1) The Revised Type-Copy of "The Gypsy Christ" itself
    (2) First Galleys of Proofs so far received –

namely
    last 3 galleys of "Madge o' the Pool" (7, 8, & 9)
    first 3 Galleys of "The Coward" (10, 11, & 12)
    & first 2 Galleys of "A Venetian Idyl" (16 & 17)

So that, I have not up to date recd. galleys 1 to 6 inclusive, or 13, 14, or 15

ALS Huntington Library

To George Meredith, [July 10,? 1895]

Upper Coltbridge Terrace, | Murrayfield.

Dear Sir,

Will you gratify one of your most loyal readers by the acceptance of the accompanying book?[15] Nothing helped me so much, or gave me so much enduring pleasure, as your generous message to me about my first book, *Pharais*, which you sent through my cousin, Mr. William Sharp.

Naturally, I was eager it should appeal to you — not only because I have long taken keener delight in your writings than in those of any living author, but also because you are Prince of Celtland.... .

I hope you will be able to read, and perhaps care for, *The Mountain Lovers*. It is not a story of the Isles, like *Pharais*, but of the remote hill-country in the far northwest. I know how busy you are: so do not consider it necessary to acknowledge either the book or this letter. Still, if some happy spirit move you, I need not say that even the briefest line from you would be a deep pleasure to[16]

Yours, with gratitude and homage, | Fiona Macleod

Memoir, pp. 244–45

To Mrs. Grant Allen, July 11, 1895

Rutland House | Greencroft Gardens, | So. Hampstead | 11/7/95

Dear Mrs. Allen,

(Pray excuse a pencilled line — as I have to write away from home & enroute) I am going to put a further strain upon your hospitality by asking you to give a small space on your shelves to the accompanying two recent books of mine.[17] Both are (revised & augmented) American new editions — but I have no English copies, in fact I am myself without copies of some of my books.

We did so very much enjoy our visit to Hind Head. It was a pleasure to breathe that fine air, & to stay in your more than pretty house: to meet Mr. Clodd[18] again, and to make the acquaintance of Dr. Bird[19] (who is as sweet & sunshining as a mellow day in St. Martin's Summer) — to see and hear your Nightjar! — and above all to see something of and get to know better G.A. & yourself.

He is in every sense of the term "a good fellow" — and you (let me speak *moré Scotico*) — "a bonnie winsome lassie": and it will always be a South Wind for us — as my Island-cousin would say — whenever & wherever we meet you or "Grant".

Friendship & Comradeship give something of the best that Life has to offer: and I, who already account myself rich, am now the wealthier by two new fortunes!

Chère Amie — think no more of that other matter.[20] It seems to have died a natural death. The man who told it to me admitted that it was the crudest rumour — & that he himself had contradicted it the moment he heard you were both together in Paris. Honestly, it appears to be dead

& done for. The lady's name turns out to be — Belloc! So you will at once see how the confusion came about. "Marie Belloc"[21] sounds French: that she was "a literary Parisian" was presumably inferred from the fact that she translated the De Goncourt Journals: — in a word, it is clear, how, with a heedless tongue to wag, the story grew from a shadowy ill-conditioned guess into a foolish rumour.

So set your mind at rest. (Cotton[22] has heard nothing — and he hears "everything": which is another proof.) Frankly, you & G. A. have no cause <u>now</u> to worry. "Let be," as the Aberdonian motto has it. Let me add that you have too many & loyal friends to make it possible for any foolish or cruel rumour to survive. As a matter of fact, this unfortunate affair is really moribund, & will soon be dead.

You & G.A. are built to be happy & comradely throughout life: how, indeed, could he fail to be so with one so winsome and so young in all ways always beside him — or you, with so brilliant & interesting & good a fellow.

The gods are with you — so, <u>Prosper</u>!!!

Cordially & let me say affectionately | Your friend, | William Sharp

P.S. Please tell G. A. that I have written to Stone. Also that I have written to Mr. Alden[23] of *Harper's Magazine*.

P.S. Lane[24] sh^d be more careful how he speaks. Tell G. A. (subrosa) not to give himself away. (I am referring to the MS. book in L's hands.) But this of course is strictly private.

ALS Pierpont Morgan Library

To Richard Le Gallienne, July 11, 1895

Rutland House, | Greencroft Gardens. | So. Hampstead. | 11th July. 1895

My dear Le Gallienne,

Will you be at the Omar Khayyám dinner at Burford Bridge on Saturday night?[25] I suppose it is likely, as you are a member. If so, we can have a few words as to our ability to arrange a meeting, either here or with you (for my wife is anxious to see the little one, & also your house — as well as you).

I am forwarding the cutting from tonight's *Star* to my cousin, Miss Fiona Macleod; who, I know, will be gratified by your kind words of praise for "The Mountain Lovers." I must again,

though, make a friendly protest against your inference as to her pseudonymity.[26] Please Don't! — for her sake much more than for that of

Yours ever in friendship, | William Sharp

ALS University of Texas, Austin

To Herbert Stuart Stone, [*July 12?, 1895*]

9. Upper Coltbridge Terrace | Murrayfield, Midlothian

Dear Mr. Stone

Herewith I send to you one of the first published copies of *The Mountain Lovers* which Mr. Lane has forwarded to me. I should much like to know what you think of it, when you have time to write.

With hopes that you will have a pleasant sojourn in Paris (for your address in which city I am indebted to Mr. Sharp).

Believe me | Yours Very Truly | Fiona Macleod

P.S. Shall I, when ready about the end of the month or early in August, send the retouched Pharais and the "Sin-Eater" volume (my best, I think) direct to you or to America?[27]

ALS Huntington Library

To Robert Murray Gilchrist, July 13, 1895

Rutland House | Greencroft Gardens | So. Hampstead | Saty | 13:7:95

My dear Gilchrist,

If I am to have the pleasure of a glimpse of you & your mother & sisters, on my way to Scotland (& I won't be returning till after the beginning of October) it must, alas, be a very brief one: & about the beginning of the week after next. Will you please send me a line by return to say (1) if this date (i.e. abt 23rd) will suit you & (2) how Holmesfield is to be reached from Sheffield. If I were to leave by the 10.15 from London on Tuesday morning — that is, on Tuesday the 23rd — which is due at Sheffield at 1.42 p.m. how could I get on to you? (I shd. perforce need to leave next morning.)

It is possible I may be able to leave London on Monday night — sleep at Sheffield (arriving at 2.30 am.) — & go on in the morning: but this is not likely: indeed if I can leave on Monday (22nd) at all it wd. probably be in the morning at 10.15. Even thus, I must add that my plans are still uncertain. But I would like to get a glimpse of you, if possible. I'll know definitely in a few days.

Our friend Fiona Macleod did not send you a copy of "The Mountain Lovers" as she sent one to your mother.[28] She hopes you will read it, & let me know what you think of it. It seems to me to strike a deeper & stronger note than *Pharais*.

Cordial regards to your Mother & Sisters |
Affectionately yours | William Sharp

Am just off to Surrey, where (Burford Bridge) the Omar Khayyam banquet is to be held, with George Meredith as the Presiding Genius.[29]

ALS Sheffield City Archives

To Grant Allen, [July 15? 1895][30]

Kilcreggan, Argyll | *Letter Address* | 9. Upper Coltbridge Terrace |
Murrayfield, Midlothian

Dear Mr. Grant Allen

You are very kind indeed — both to write to me, you who are so busy, and to promise to do anything you can for my book.[31] It is very good of you. Truly, it is the busiest people who find time to do what is impossible to idle folk.

But, really, you must disengage from your mind that idea of yours as to my being my cousin, Will Sharp. It makes me smile to think how surprised you will be someday. Except that we are both tall, he as a man and I as a woman, there is not even any likeness between us. I am very dark, in hair and eyes: and, what is more important, we are very different otherwise, despite our remarkable affinity in literary sentiment and expression. If you will allow me, I will send you my photograph someday.

I have just had a letter of deeply gratifying praise and recognition from Mr. George Meredith, who says he finds my work absolutely "rare and distinctive." He writes one phrase, memorable as coming from him: "Be sure that I am among those readers of yours whom you kindle."[32]

Permit me, dear Mr. Allen, to make a small request of you. If you are really going to be so kind as to say anything about my book I trust you will not hint playfully at any other authorship having suggested itself to you — or, indeed, at my name being a pseudonym. And, sure, it will be for pleasure to me if you will be as scrupulous with Mr. Meredith or anyone else, in private, as in public, if chance should ever bring my insignificant self into any chit-chat.

My name is really Fiona (i.e. Fionnaghal — of which it is the diminutive: as Maggie, Nellie, or Dair are diminutives of Margaret, Helen, or Alasdair).

Again thanking you most cordially and hoping to have the great pleasure to seeing Mrs. Allen and yourself when (as is probable) I come south in the late Autumn or sometime in November.

Sincerely and gratefully yours | Fiona Macleod

ALS Pierpont Morgan Library

To Patrick Geddes, July 15, 1895

Rutland House, | Greencroft Gardens, | So. Hampstead |
Monday 15th July:'95

My dear Geddes,

In my concurrent note to your wife, I have told her how elated I am by a letter I have had (i.e. F. M. has had) from George Meredith. He slips the laurel into Fiona's dark locks right royally, & prophesies big things of her. I know you will be glad to hear this. Also, you will be glad to know that I am in robust health again.

I am to be in Scotland next week, but shall not be in Edinburgh, save intermittently & by swallow-flights of an hour's duration at most, until the 30th or 31st. On the latter date my wife arrives — so that we shall have 3 or 4 days before the Session begins.

No, my dear fellow, gladly as I would be off with you somewhere for a day or two, it is not practicable. I can see no one for the week I shall be "hanging about." I <u>must</u> be alone for a bit.[33]

As soon as we can, though, we must have a talk about the *Evergreen*, & publishing schemes. I have enlisted the promised support of Wm. Strang,[34] the West-Country etcher & painter (the strongest living etcher, I think) & others for future *Evergreens*: & have also been prowling through several literary preserves, with fierce publisher-eyes. And done well, prospectively.

When you are in Edinburgh will you speak to Constable's[35] in connection with the Printing etc, of *The Sin-Eater* etc. It will make a book about the size of *The Mountain Lovers*, & should, I think, be got up in somewhat the same way as to type, paper, & general format. I should like to send it to the printers early in August: as it has to come out simultaneously in America & this country early in October. I'll see to its being well announced, in due time.

Lyra Celtica need not, indeed cannot, go to Press till September. Coming after *The Mountain Lovers*, I think The S/Eater will go well: & will probably attract much more attention.

My "Lectures" will be as over.[36]

"Art and Life"

I.   Life & Art: Art & Nature: Nature.

II.   Disintegration: Degeneration: Regeneration.

III.   The Return to Nature: In Art, in Literature. The Literary Outlook in England and America.

IV.   The Celtic Renascence, Ossian, Mathew Arnold, The Ancient Celtic Writers.

V.   The Celtic Renascence. Contemporary. The School of Celtic Ornament.

VI.   The Science of Criticism: What it is, what it is not. The Critical Ideal.

VII.   Ernest Hello.

VIII.   The Drama of Life, and Dramatists.

IX.   The Ideals of Art — pagan. Medieval. The Modern Ideal.

In great haste, | Ever yours, | William Sharp

ALS National Library of Scotland

To Richard Le Gallienne, July 15, 1895

Rutland House, | Greencroft Gardens, | So. Hampstead, |
Monday | 15/7/95

My dear Le Gallienne

Thanks for your note. I am sorry you were unable to get to the Omar dinner: a memorable as well as a pleasant one, because of George Meredith.

I am sorry we cannot meet this week. I wanted to have a long chat with you — for I too have missed the pleasant intimacy of old. And now, I fear, there must be a postponement until you return from America: for I leave town next Sunday or Monday for Scotland, & shall not be back until early in October, by which time you will be in the States, I suppose. (Do you know Hall Caine? He goes out to America also sometime in September.) However, my dear fellow, I am now & always your admiring confrère as well as your affectionate friend — and so a further lapse of time won't be a douche upon our cordiality when we do meet!

I suppose there is no chance of your being Grosvenor Club (Bond St) way any late afternoon this week? If so, & if I knew in advance, I could arrange that.

In one of the lectures (that on "The Return to Nature") I have to give before long in Edinburgh I lay great success on your recent poetic work, and quote the lovely "Ode to Spring" and "Tree Worship": as, in another, that on Contemp: Pessimism, I give your delightful "Animalcule on Man".[37]

I have read this last book of yours 3 or 4 times now, & with increasing appreciation and pleasure.

Yes, my boy, be just to Miss Macleod. Anything you can say for her will be gratefully appreciated, but she as well as her unworthy cousin earnestly hope for no more confusion respecting her actual authorship of "The Mountain Lovers" etc., publicly or privately.

More about her when we meet. (George Meredith has just sent to her present Argyllshire address a letter of splendid praise & encouragement. He knows that she is my cousin: but, I hope, will never be "put about" by hearing any other rumour.)

Affectionately Your Friend, | William Sharp

P.S. I shall have a book of my own to send to you early in October.[38] I'll send it to Mulberry Cottage — unless you are to be away till late in the year, in wh. case I'll get your American address from Lane.

ALS University of Texas, Austin

To Robert Murray Gilchrist, July 18, [1895]

Rutland House | Greencroft Gardens | So. Hampstead | 18ᵗʰ July

My dear Boy

I am so very sorry, but it is now impossible for me to stop on my way north. I regret this the less, however, as it would have to be a few hours visit at best: while, on my return south early in October, it will be possible for me to stay a day or two.

In a word, I must be in Edinburgh on Monday night — & as I cannot possibly leave London before Monday morning, my stopping en route is out of the question. I did warn you of this, I remember. Please, too, express my regret to your mother & sisters. But I promise, so far as it is possible to foresee, to stop with you on the way back.

I am glad you like "The Mountain Lovers." But do write to me about how you feel it, & what you think of it. You, & a few like you, constitute the sole public for whose opinion I really care. Your mother, too, has kindly promised to write: & I need hardly say that she, likewise, is one of the few I allude to. Did I tell you of the letter of splendid praise & recognition which George Meredith wrote to Miss Macleod. It is one of several, some wholly unexpected: but a letter like that of GM's remains a kind of beacon in one's life. "Be assured," he adds, "that I am among those whom you kindle." Yes: <u>to kindle</u>: <u>that</u> is what one wants to do. Elsewhere, alluding to a certain quality in the book, he says: "How rare is this! I do not know it elsewhere."

I know you will be glad.

Your affectionate friend | William Sharp

P.S. On & after Monday my address will be (for July–August) | c/o J. Oliphant Esq. | 14 Ramsey Garden | Edinburgh

ALS Sheffield City Archives

To Miss Anne Alden, July 20, [1895]

Saty July 20th

My Dear Miss Alden

I am very grateful to you for your letter — a letter full of beautiful thought & emotion, as though illumined by the light of the fair mind & spirit so recently taken from you. And indeed I am grateful, too, that you should have told me so fully the story of her last days and hours.[39] She was one of the white souls of the world — and born into new life as she is she must yet have still another resurrection — that resurrection in the minds of all who knew her, which keeps green and fresh a vivid and dear memory.

I suppose all who came in contact with her loved her, or came soon to love her. Certainly I did. And, in, truth, some mental or spiritual link seemed to unite us. It may seem to you very strange — but I have actually suffered when she had to undergo an operation or any severe stress of pain: & sometimes I could hardly bear to think of it. Again & again through the early part of this year I dreamed of her: & once I think I wrote to your father to tell him how I had a kind of vision of her, white and sunlit, walking through a shadowy wood that was all bright where she went.

I am sure that there are some people who go through life as white spirits clothed with the accident of the body — rather than, as most of us, as human beings animated by a spirit — and that she was one of these.

I am indeed glad that my little tale of "The Foster Mother of Christ"[40] reached her in time to give her pleasure.

To you, dear Miss Alden, (though I think of you as "Annie" always) I would send a copy of my new book *The Mountain Lovers* (I know you are cognizant of & will preserve my secret as to my identity with Fiona Macleod) but that I have already sent one to your father, at Metuchen. If misadventure befall that copy please let me know, & I will send another. I know it will please you to hear that George Meredith has written to Miss Macleod a letter of splendid praise & recognition, and that other letters have already made our friend Fiona very proud & glad — but glad mostly.

I go to Edinburgh in a day or two, where I have to deliver, at University Hall, ten lectures on "Life and Art". In the first and tenth I shall be reading extracts from (& thus, I hope send many readers to) "God in His World"[41.]

Please give your father my comradely love and deepest sympathy. In the book upon which he is engaged he will find not only some measure of solace, but also know that he builds his House of Dream about a fair and sacred memory.[42]

I hope, dear Miss Alden, we may meet again in a year or so: but in any case you know that I am now and always

Affectionately Your Friend | William Sharp

ALS University of Delaware Library

To Grant Allen, [?,1895]

Temporary address | 144. North St. | St. Andrews. | Fife.

Dear Mr. Grant Allen

How generous you are! If it were not for fear of what you say about my Gaelic phrases I should quote one to the effect that the wild bees that make the beautiful thoughts in your brain also leave their honey on your lips.

Your *Westminster* review has given me keen pleasure — and for everything in it, and for all the kind interest behind it, I thank you cordially.[43]

What you say about the survival of folklore as a living heritage is absolutely true — how true perhaps few know, except those who have lived among the Gaels, of their blood, and speaking the ancient language. The Celtic paganism lies profound and potent still beneath the fugitive drift of Christianity and Civilization, as the deep sea beneath the coming and going of the tides.

No one can understand the Islander and remote Albion Gael who ignores or is oblivious of the potent pagan and indeed elementally barbaric forces behind all exterior appearances. (This will be more clearly shown in my next published book, a vol. of ten Celtic tales and episodes[44] — with, I suppose, a more wide and varied outlook on life, tho' narrow at that! — than either of its predecessors.)

Your review and that of Miss (or Mrs.?) Annie MacDonell in the August *Bookman* have pleased and interested me most of all I have seen.[45] But, sure, I have no reason but for gratitude all round. Even *The Athenaeum* says some pleasant things,[46] though its critic betrays his own limited knowledge of Gaelic in his faultfinding with some of mine — for he ought to know that the signs of the genitive and aspirations vary considerably; and that the Gaelic of the Isles, for example, differs much in these and kindred minor matters from that (say) of Inverness, and still more from that of the more Anglo-Celtic districts. He objects to "Oona" and wants "Una" which is non-existent in Gaelic — unless, which may be, English people pronounce the U as Oa.

But excuse this rambling. Your review is all the more welcome to me as it comes to me during a visit to friends at St. Andrews — and to me, alas, the East Coast of Scotland is as foreign and remote in all respects as though it were Jutland or Finland.

It has also been the cause of a letter from my cousin, Will Sharp, who, in sending the *Westminster* review, adds that he is coming to spend the week-end with me — or I with him, I should say, as I am to be his guest, at almost the only Celtic place we know of on this too "dour" shoreland of Fife.

Again with thanks, dear Mr. Allen,

Believe me | Most sincerely yours | Fiona Macleod.

P. S. In his letter Mr. Sharp says (writing to me in his delightful shaky Gaelic) that "[both Grant and Nellie Allen are] clach-chreadhain." It took me some time to understand the compliment. Clach-Chreadh means "stone of clay" — i.e. Brick!

ALS Pierpont Morgan Library

To J. Stanley Little, [early August, 1895]

14 Ramsey Garden | Edinburgh

My dear Stanley

Just a hurried line (for I am far from well, and am frightfully busy) of affectionate sympathy with you from us both in your great loss, of which we hear for the first time thro' your note. It was expected, but the loss is nonetheless severe. I hope things may move better for you, later.[47]

My lectures here have been a marked success — but they have told upon me heavily.[48]

Forgive more just now, old chap.

Love from both of us to both of you, | Ever affectly yrs, | Will

ALS Princeton University

To Herbert Stuart Stone, August 12, 1895

9 Upper Coltbridge Terrace | Murrayfield |
Midlothian | 12th August. 1895.

Dear Mr. Stone,

Herewith I send, by registered Book-Post, the "copy" for *The Sin-Eater* volume. You said you would have it set up at once, so that I could see proofs (needful, with the numerous Gaelic names and words, and peculiar idioms, and for other reasons). I suppose that about 25 days must elapse in the coming and returning of these proofs?

As the book is to be published simultaneously in this country and America, early in October (if possible by the 5th) — this leaves little time. So will you kindly give immediate and urgent instructions. Also, please let me remind you that, if practicable, the proofs be sent in page, and in triplicate. I append my September letter-address at left hand top-margin [see P.S. below]. I expect to write to you by next mail with exact particulars as to publication here. (I estimate the book to be about 53,000 words.)

Also by next mail, I hope to send you the slightly amended *Pharais*, in the Green Tree Library issue. When you acknowledge this, may I ask you kindly to remit the £10 which you agreed to pay for the reprint of Pharais in the "Green Tree Library".

I wonder if you received a copy of *The Mountain Lovers* I sent to you. I forwarded it to you while you were at the Hotel Voltaire in Paris. You will be interested to hear that the book has attracted a great deal of attention, and is going well.

Please acknowledge receipt of *The Sin-Eater* by return, and state if you will be able to publish on (say) Saturday the 5th of October.

With kind regards, |Yours Sincerely | Fiona Macleod

P.S. Throughout September my address will be c/o Mrs. William Sharp | Woodside | Tigh-Na-Bruaich | Kyles of Bute | Argyll. | Scotland.[49]

ALS Newberry Library

To: Herbert S. Stone, [August 12, 1895][50]

14 Ramsay Gardens | Edinburgh

My dear Herbert

Miss Macleod is staying with us for a day or two (for my lectures — particularly that on The Celtic Renascence) — & I add this to her note, to say that the date of publicn. for her book is arranged here to be on Oct. 5th. thro' Patrick Geddes & Colleagues.

By the way, let me write a short *Chap-Book* article on the Belgian chaps, to help the book, her, & the publisher.[51]

Yours ever, | Will

I am more chagrined than I can say about the extraordinary delay with *The Gypsy Christ*. Not a sign yet of a proof. I do trust for every reason financially & otherwise, I am not to lose my Autumn pubn. as I have already lost the late Spring.

ALS Huntington Library

To Herbert S. Stone, [August 25?, 1895]

9. Upper Coltbridge Terrace | Murrayfield. | Midlothian.

Dear Mr. Stone.

Thank you for your letter of Aug. 15th.

By this time you will have received the complete "copy" of The Sin-Eater: of which I am now awaiting proofs. As I told you then, the date fixed for publication here is Saturday 5th. October.

By this mail (and even if it should miss the mail I shall post it all the same on chance — and I mention this simply because of some alteration in the mail hour, for registered packets, concerning which I am at present ignorant.) — by this mail I send you the slightly amended

"Pharais" for the Green Tree Library. Kindly oblige me by letting me have this amended copy back again: as it is the only large paper copy I have, and none other is now procurable.

If not already dispatched, would you kindly remit the sum promised on account of *Pharais*.

I think I told you in my last letter that throughout the month of September I shall be staying with Mr. and Mrs. William Sharp at Woodside Cottage | Tigh-Na-Bruaich | The Kyles of Bute | Argyll | Scotland — | after which date please address to me as usual to my Murrayfield address.

Yes, I have every reason to be deeply gratified by the success of *The Mountain Lovers*. Besides warmly sympathetic notices on all sides, there have been signed articles of a rarely emphatic kind by Mr. Grant Allen, Mr. Traill, Mr. George Cotterell, Mr. Ashcroft Noble, and others. Herewith I send you the last which has appeared by Mr. Ashcroft Noble, in *The New Age*, from which doubtless you may wish to quote: also, perhaps, this from a leader in *The Yorkshire Herald*: — "Wordsworth's beautiful suggestion of 'The light that never was on sea or land' is...[52]

ALS Huntington Library

To Herbert S. Stone, August 30, 1895

14 Ramsay Gardens | Edinburgh | 30th August 1895

My dear Herbert,

At last the long delayed proofs have reached this often blaspheming author — albeit in an incomplete form, like the abortive baby that was born the other day minus a hand and a leg. The galleys containing the first part of "Madge o' the Pool," and several other galleys later in the series, are missing, and have not, at the moment I write, yet come to hand.

To save time, I send you by this post the revised type-copy of "The Gypsy Christ" itself. Proofs of this can, of course, be revised by you, or any capable person whom you may depute:

as there will be no time to send proofs oversea. I have had no opportunity to reread this revise since I left London: so if you notice anything to delete or improve, act freely on your discretion.

I'll return by this post, also, those galleys which I can get through in time: the others will go by the next mail, three days hence.

By the way, when you remit cheque as promised (& its non-receipt happens to be very inconvenient, confound you!) — which I hope will be forthwith — please say if you have made any arrangement for the Gypsy Christ volume in this country. I never heard if you had come to an arrangement with Methuen or Lane or Mathews or anyone: as I hope you have.[53]

I think you have the fore-pages of the G.C. vol.,[54] with dedication To my Friend, Lady Colin Campbell, etc.

Glad things promise well in America. I hope the G.C. may prove a Redeemer of lost output!

"Wives in Exile" won't reach you till near the end of October, I fear. It will be a book of about 60,000 words: and is, as I explained to you, a blithe comedy of "high life," told, I hope, both with verve and picturesqueness. Of the two heroines, one, Mrs. Leonora Wester, is a beautiful American: the other, her cousin, Mrs. Helen Adair, an equally lovely Irishwoman. If you prefer it, the novel could be sent out in installments for you to set up: otherwise, it will be best to dispatch it complete. It will, I believe, be a sure "draw" — so far as it is possible to foretell.

I have not been at all well, but am now better. I found the strain of lecturing too great. Tomorrow we go to Tigh-Na-Bruaich in the Kyles of Bute, in Argyll.[55] I must have an absolute holiday (save for proofs) for at least a week or 10 days. We shall have my cousin Miss Macleod with us most of the time. I understand that her new book has duly gone to you. Personally I like *The Sin-Eater* better than either of its predecessors, and I have read nearly all its contents: though *The Mountain Lovers* has unquestionably had a remarkable reception.

Last week we had a short visit from Mrs. Wingate Rinder, who has been staying in Fifeshire during August but leaves tomorrow for Brittany, where she hopes to work up Breton legends and folk-lore. I am sure you will be pleased with her Belgian book,[56] which she has taken endless pains to make adequately representative, and has, I think, translated admirably. The difficulties in some cases were almost overpowering, for

Flemish French when obscurer than its wont is as obscure and involved as a German treatise on Simplicity!

I hope, my dear chap, you are now much better, & not overworking. Take care of yourself. Have you seen Bliss C. since your return?[57] By the way, I have not yet had the promised "proofs" from Theodore Watts[58] — but as soon as he transmits them I'll send you the Chap-Book article. Also, if you want it, a short article on the Belgian Renascence as exemplified by Mrs. E. W. R.'s book. Did I ever tell you that she is Miss Macleod's most intimate woman-friend, and that she is the dedicatee of Pharais? They have been staying together recently, and (I believe) writing or planning something to do together–though that, from what I know of Miss F. M., will never come off, as she is far too essentially F. M. to work in harness with anyone.[59]

Don't forget your promise about the photograph of yourself.

Good luck to you, my boy — Be a good man if you can, but whatever happens be a good publisher, & so earn the Blessing of your

Affectionate friend | William Sharp

I'll be at Tigh-Na-Bruaich till the end of September, then at my Hampstead address as usual.

ALS New York Public Library, Berg Collection

To Herbert S. Stone, [early September, 1895]

Woodside | Tigh-Na-Bruaich | Kyles of Bute | Argyll | Scotland

My dear Herbert

By this post I return all the proofs of "The G/Christ" vol[60] — except the missing galleys, which have never yet come to hand. These must now just be revised in the office — to my regret, particularly in the instance of the opening galleys of "Madge o' the Pool." Please don't let the printer forget my Dedica. | To my Friend | The Lady Colin Campbell.

By the last mail I sent you the G/C itself & other sets of proof.

The order of the stories is:

(1) The G/Christ (2) Madge o' the Pool (3) The Coward (4) A Venetian Idyl (5) The Graven Image (6) The Lady in Hosea (7) Fröken Bergliot.

———————

I also wrote to you last mail abt. *Wives in Exile.*

What abt. publicn. in England of the G/C vol? Did you arrange with Methuen? And if so, are they simply to bind & fresh title-page your American sheets?

E. Mathews writes that he [?has] communicated with you.

In haste, | Yours Affectly | William Sharp

P.S. My dear Herbert,

These missing proofs, & other "vaguenesses" annoy me somewhat. Believe me, my dear boy, these things tell ill. A close scrutiny at first hand is absolutely necessary. Hope you are better now,

Ever yrs. | Will

ALS Huntington Library

To Herbert Stuart Stone, September 6, [1895]

The lost proofs have at [last] turned up & I have at once revised & now send them back to you herewith. It is just possible they may reach you at the same time as the other proofs sent on Wednesday, as the steamer from the West was late owing to a gale.

I hope these & the others will reach you in good time.

By the way, in case I forget, please send the 25 gratis copies you promised me of The G.C. vol. to Rutland House etc. — marked "not to be forwarded".

William Sharp

ACS Huntington Library

To Herbert S. Stone, [*mid-September, 1895*]

9 Upper Coltbridge Terrace | Murrayfield | Midlothian

Dear Mr. Stone

Your letter of the 26th just to hand, forwarded to me by Mrs. Sharp from Tigh-Na-Bruaich, where I go the day after tomorrow.

I have sent word to Messrs. W. H. White & Co, of the Riverside Press St., Bernard's Row, Edinburgh (who are printing the book)[61] to send you revised Proofs so far as done, and to follow up with revises, which should all be ready by middle of next week. You can then, as you say, revise the American sheets from these. This will save time, of course: as well as possible miscarriage and delay here.

In accordance with your letter I have written to Messrs. Patrick Geddes & Colleagues to postpone the date of publication till Tuesday the 15th of October: but as this will be, I know, an inconvenient delay, I must beg of you not to postpone it a day later. Kindly send a line by return (to my Murrayfield address) saying if you can fix on this date, the 15th.

In great haste | Yours Sincerely | Fiona Macleod.

ALS New York Public Library, Berg Collection

To Stone and Kimball, [*mid-September 1895*][62]

Dear Sirs,

On hearing from Miss Fiona Macleod, we at once instructed Messrs. W. H. White & Co., of the Edinburgh Riverside Press, to forward to you Sigs. A. to F. (pp. 1 to 96 of text) of *The Sin-Eater*, and the remainder as the Revises are passed. There are a good many textual & other alterations from the type-written copy: so your readers will have to collate carefully.

It is now definitely arranged that the book in question is to be published on Tuesday the 15th of October — a date later than was quite convenient for us, but which we have accepted as (we understand from Miss Macleod) more suitable for you.

Yours faithfully | Patrick Geddes & Colleagues | per William Sharp
Messrs. Stone and Kimball | <u>Chicago</u>

P.S. Until after the end of October, all communications for Patrick Geddes & Colleagues to be addressed to Mr. William Sharp, Rutland House, Greencroft Gardens, So. Hampstead, London, N.W.

ALS Huntington Library

To Herbert Stuart Stone, September 18, 1895

Tigh-Na-Bruaich | The Kyles of Bute | Argyll | 18/9/95

My dear Herbert

Theodore Watts — or his printers, to him — has proved faithless. At any rate, he has not yet sent the promised advance copy, typed, or printed, of his *Poems*.

Unless I hear from you to the contrary, within 2 mails from now, that is by the beginning of next week, — my suggestion about a Chap Book paper on the leading men of the Belgian Renaissance, àpropos of Mrs. Wingate Rinder's book[63] — about which I wrote to you about a month ago or less — I'll write and send out the paper in question.

I trust that one of the two mails in question will bring me the long expected Gypsy Christ Cheque — whose non-arrival has, as it happens, seriously inconvenienced me.

I heard yesterday from Elkin Mathews that you had by cable declined my Ecce Puella volume. Is this because you did not want it, or because you have enough of W. S. on hand as it is? I thought at the time that it was a mistake as you have The G/Christ ready and Wives in Exile to handle later.[64]

By the way, will you send me the promised copies of The G/Christ, when published, to my home address as usual: Rutland House, 15

Greencroft Gardens, South Hampstead, London. When is Mrs. E. Wingate Rinder's book to be published? I see, in the latest Chap Book, you announce it as an imminent "Green Tree." Please send me an unbound copy in page, as soon as printed. By the way, the advt. is wrong abt. that book's containing C. Van Lerberghe's "drama-let."

Herewith I send you, for the Chap Book, if you care for it, & there is time, in lieu of the Watts article, my authorized translation of Charles Van Lerberghe's Les Flaireurs.[65] It is to appear in the Second Part of *The Evergreen*, which will be published about Oct. 12th–15th, but copies of which will not reach America till late in the month probably.

C. Van L. is one of the foremost younger men of the Belgian Renascence — though really only by virtue of *Les Flaireurs*, which was not only anterior to Maeterlinck but was the first thing of its kind, & had a marked influence on Maeterlinck[66] and several of the young men who rally to the flag of "La Jeune Belgigue" or "Le Coq Rouge".[67]

Our small party breaks up here tomorrow, though my wife & I do not leave till the 28th or 30th.[68] After that date, I shall be in London. Miss Macleod leaves us tomorrow also, to our regret. I was to have enclosed a note from her, but I see she has done it up separately.

In haste for our mail-steamer,

Ever yours, my dear boy, | William Sharp

ALS Huntington Library

To Patrick Geddes, [mid-September,1895]

Of course I'd look at the "Prefatory Note" again if you wish — & if there is ample time — but I did not feel free to alter what I had nothing to do with in the writing.

Editorially, I didn't care for it. But that did not warrant me in altering it, as I am not Editor but only a colleague.[69]

Hoping you will have a good time in the North.

W. S.

ACS, NLS

To Robert Murray Gilchrist, [*September 26, 1895*][70]

Tigh-Na-Bruaich | The Kyles of Bute | Argyle

My dear Boy,

Your letter has been forwarded to me here. Of course, my dear fellow, there is no "shadow of a shadow of hill or sea" as they say here, between us. At all times I bear you in affectionate remembrance: and then, we are comrades.[71]

I am sorry you have had so ill a time of it this year, and trust that it is all over now, the mischances and the misadventures. For myself I have gone through a year of such varied experiences of light and shade (both in extremes) and innumerable interblent gleams of life of all kinds, that no wonder my friends note the greying of my hair more & more, though less now than a year ago.

It has been lovely here, in this beautiful fjïord between the hills and Bute, with the open sea & the mountains of the Isle of Arran to the south. I wish you could have been here. But tomorrow I leave — though we intended to be here for a week or 10 days yet: as I have to take my mother-in-law (at present on a short visit to us) back to London, as she is prostrated by a telegram from abroad saying that her son has suddenly developed a malignant cancer and is dying — so rapidly that he must give up hope of coming home.

This has upset all our plans — including my three days in Edinburgh on important business: my day & night at York: & my two days with you. On the other hand, it is almost certain that I must go back to Edinburgh about the end of October — & on my way north shall stay with you. If, however, I do not require to go I'll still take a run to join you for a day or two, then or early in November, if you can't come south.

Fiona Macleod's new book *The Sin Eater* will soon be out (Oct. 15th) — and I think it will afford you some pleasure. Also, Stone & Kimball of Chicago are about to publish (probably in both countries simultaneously) a vol. by W. S., *The Gypsy Christ: and Other Tales.* The titular story is inspired, so far, by Eyam-surroundings. You shall have a copy of each book. In *The Sin Eater* there is a small section called *Tragic Landscapes*: wherein (or rather preeminently in the first of which) the human element is wholly insignificant and accidental. I find I have a proof of this, which you may have. You will read the third piece, "Summersleep," with mingled feelings, when you know that it is an exact transcript of — Phenice Croft at Rudgwick, and that the three men are — <u>you</u>, Garfitt, and myself. I cannot explain aright: you must read into what you read. The most tragic & momentous epoch of my life followed that visit of yours to Phenice Croft, & is, so far, indissolubly linked with that day I met you, and that time.[72]

Let me have a line from you at Rutland House | Greencroft Gardens | So. Hampstead

on (or after) Tuesday 1ˢᵗ, by which time I shall be there from Mrs. S's house.

My cordial regards to your mother & sisters, and to you, my dear friend & comrade, my love, sympathy, & affectionate heed.

Yours | William Sharp

ALS Sheffield City Archives

To Edmund Clarence Stedman, September 27, 1895

Tigh-na-Bruaich | in the Kyles of Bute | Argyll

27ᵗʰ Sept, 1895 | For the morning of the 8ᵗʰ

My dear Stedman

It is an age since I have written to you, and my conscience smites me — but, alas, never has correspondence been so difficult as during this last year, when a hundred adverse influences have combined to make me seem forgetful of my dearest friends. However, I am going to make amends, in this my new year — for a month ago I entered another "shadowy portal."[73] And now, of course, I am writing to greet *you* on the morning of *your* new year and to wish for you the beauty of the world, the music of life, fresh joy and energy to the beautiful young heart and poet's brain of which you are the royal possessor; — love, and

sympathy, and homage; health and prosperity and largesse of good, &
everything to make your life fair and sweet.

How I wish I could see you! What a lot I have to tell you that cannot
well be told in letter. My life has never been richer and deeper than
in this last year. Looking back upon it I can see scores of days going
crowned with sunshine and deathless flowers, & can hear the clapping
of the hands of innumerable rejoicing proud-eyed hours.

With you, I hope things now go well. Do not write a letter, for I love
and admire you too much to wish to lay even the pleasantest tyranny of
love upon you: but send me a P/C, or a brief line through your secretary.

The "Anthology" marches, I hope: also I trust the "Poe" goes well.
(By the way, I saw Lugné Poë, a French kinsman of E.A.P., acting in one
of Maeterlinck's dramas, when I was last in Paris. He bore a striking
resemblance to the best portrait of E.A.P.)

For myself I have been and am very busy. On or about the 8th you
ought to receive from Stone & Kimball a copy of *"The Gypsy Christ,"*
a volume of tales they commissioned. All of them have grown out of
personal experiences. The same firm is, later, to publish a "comedy in
romance" by me, called "Wives in Exile," which ought to be the most
widely successful thing I have written. Also, I had hoped to send you a
copy of a book of "Prose Imaginings" on your birthday, but *Ecce Puella*
(as it is called from the longest, & titular, piece) will not be out till late
in October.

As a special birthday gift, however, I shall post to you, in 10 days
or so, an early copy of my cousin's, Miss Fiona Macleod's, heavy
new book, *The Sin-Eater*. Doubtless you have heard of her *Pharais*
and *The Mountain Lovers*, two books which have given her a leader's
place in the Celtic Renascence which is like to prove so remarkable a
tributary to the stream of literature within the next few years. She is
now admitted to be the head of the Scots-Celtic movement — as W.
B. Yeats is of the Irish-Celtic. The new book is novel & beautiful as a
piece of book-making — though I say it, who am responsible for its
type, paper, binding, & general *format*! For (apart from *The Evergreen*)
it is the first publication of the new Edinburgh firm, "Patrick Geddes
& Colleagues," of which I am chief literary partner. At the end of *The
Sin-Eater* you will see some of our announcements. (By the way, Stone
& Kimball are issuing in October Miss Fiona Macleod's *Pharais* in

their "Green Tree Library": and Messrs. Roberts Bros. have already issued (with John Lane, here) her "Mountain Lovers" — and Harper's Magazine is to have an illustrated series of Celtic "episodes" by her in the Xmas number.)

Tell Mrs. Stedman (to whom my love, & all affectionate greetings) that the copy of the *Evergreen* I shall send in a fortnight or so is really for her. It is a beautiful production in its *format*, & she is to keep it in her drawing room for a little & show it to your literary friends as the organ of "Young Scotland."

Well, the steamer is coming round the distant promontory of this beautiful & romantic place in the West Highlands, where I have been for a month. I have to go to Edinburgh by it, where I shall post this. Two days later I shall be in London again.

Soon I hope to write again, & more fully. Meanwhile, my homageful love, dear Poet, Friend, & Comrade.

Your affectionate | William Sharp

I have a "big" book on hand — but of this more, later.

ALS *University of British Columbia Library*

To Herbert Stuart Stone, September 28, 1895

Rutland House | Greencroft Gardens | South Hampstead |
London | 28th Septr./95

My dear Herbert

Belgian Article

Herewith (from Edinburgh, where I am for a night or two, en route from the West Highlands to London) I send you the promised article for the Chap-Book, "A Note on the Belgian Renaissance," àpropos of Mrs. Wingate Rinder's admirably representative book[74]

Will you kindly direct that a dozen copies of the Chap-Book containing it be sent me?

Van Lerberghe

As to the Van Lerberghe drama-let[75] I sent to you recently, there need be no hesitation so far as the date the *Evergreen* is published. Owing to unforeseen trouble with type etc. Messrs. Patrick Geddes & Colleagues cannot issue *The Evergreen* before October 15th *at earliest*, & more probably, now, about the 20th — but certainly not before the 15th.

I have just had a letter from Mrs. Wingate Rinder from a remote place in Brittany. She asks me to decide for her, as she has no time to catch the mail (& indeed only writes a pencilled line on your letter to her of the 5th, which she had just received (25th) — as to the question of seeing proofs. As for your sake, and hers, delay would distinctly be disadvantageous, I write to say that in accordance with your suggestion, proofs of "The Massacre of the Innocents" need not be sent: so that the book may come out this Autumn.

But please, yourself, or B.C., or some true craftsman, give a glance over the proofs as well as the proof-reader's textual revision. The book had to be typed at lightning speed at the last — and there are probably many instances where a deletion or an alteration of some kind, in a word or words, might be an advantage. However, Mrs. E.W.R. certainly did her best to make it independent of further revision, so far as time & other circumstances permitted.

To save time, & enable you to get the book out earlier, I shall cable you "Essankay, Chicago" today ("Proofs unnecessary, Rinder")

Just saw the covers & end-papers for Miss Macleod's "Sin Eater," which is now printed, and ready to be issued on the 15th of Oct. as arranged. It will be a beautiful book, & ought to attract notice to the new firm.

What glorious weather we are having — though the heat-wave is becoming trying, especially in London.

Ever yours, | In haste, | William Sharp

ALS Huntington Library

To Catherine Ann Janvier, Autumn, 1895

Sometimes I am tempted to believe I am half a woman, and so far saved as I am by the hazard of chance from what a woman can be made to suffer if one let the light of the common day illuminate the avenues and vistas of her heart... .[76]

William Sharp

Memoir, pp. 227–28

To Robert Murray Gilchrist, [October 1?, 1895][77]

My dear Gilchrist

I have just returned. Thanks for your note: & I know you will be pleased to hear that I shall have to be north earlier than I anticipated, so that I shall have a day at least with you, somewhere between 13th & 19th of this month.

But of this later. (You don't say what you thought of my experiment in these *Tragic Landscapes* particularly in "The Tempest").

My cordial greetings to you & yours —

Your affectionate friend | W. S.

ALS Sheffield City Archives

To Elkin Matthews, [October] 11, [1895]

Rutland House, | Greencroft Gardens, | So. Hampstead. | Friday 11th

Dear Mr. Mathews

I thought I shd. have heard from you, as our meeting failed to come off yesterday.

If you have not already written — or your representative — please do so to me at | 9 Up. Coltbridge Terrace | Murrayfield | Edinburgh | where I shall be for a week to come from tomorrow night.

I wish to know the date of publication of *Ecce Puella*, & if any American arrangement has been made.[78]

In haste | Yours sincerely | William Sharp

ALS Private

To J. Stanley Little, [October 11?, 1895]

Rutland House | Greencroft Gardens | So. Hampstead

My dear Stanley

Just got back. Hope to see you soon: but not till next week, as I have to be off again. E. not very well — & sorrowing for sudden death of brother. Nor am I as fit as I shd. be.

Will you do what you can for Frank Rinder's charming first book, "Old World Japan."[79] I have asked that a copy be sent to you. Also, I have asked the publisher (Elkin M.) to send you for yourself a copy of a new little book of mine — "Ecce Puella & other Prose Imaginings." I hope you will like it. No other literary news, save that my cousin Miss Macleod also brings out her new book this week.[80] When I saw her in Scotland recently she told me she was going to send you a copy. If you can help it you will I know.

How are you both, — & prospects, how are they? What a drive life is — For me, I am willing to stop — or to go. But, I'm beginning to feel a little tired of this flame of life.

My love to you both, | Always your affectionate friend, | Will

ALS Princeton University

To Robert Murray Gilchrist, [October 14, 1895][81]

9 Up. Coltbridge Terrace | Murrayfield | Midlothian

Please send me by return a line to say
  (1) How I am to get to you (from York) from Sheffield tho' I fear it will be impossible for me to stay more than one night —
  (2) If, supposing I cannot manage to get to you you could come to York (as my guest there) (at the moment this seems to me likeliest)

In Great Haste | W. S.

ACS Sheffield City Archives

To Robert Murray Gilchrist, [October 16, 1895]

9 Up. Coltbridge | Murrayfield

My dear Boy

I too am far from well (at the moment, with a diarrheic weakness) — & it is as difficult, if not more so, for me to get to you, as for you to come to York.

In any case, I could not manage more than the night (with early departure next morning) — & that I do not now feel able to undertake. I am sorry, as you know — but... !

Either I must wait till business or domestic affairs take me north again (& time and opportunity permit a visit) or else I could see you in York on Friday evening. If you *can* come to the Station Hotel (as my guest there) I would suggest the late evening. I could join you from 9 p.m. till as late as the Spirit & Hotel-Hours permit! I leave Edinburgh now on Friday morning, and shall get to my friend in York about 3 p.m. or so. My address there is c/o George Cotterell Esq., 3 Grosvenor Terrace, but if you think you can come, please send me a line tomorrow (if in time for the Scotch mail for first delivery in Edinburgh) or a wire.

I miss much in not seeing again your mother, and you & yours, but I musn't play with my health just now, I find — & I have been "so harassed & driven lately" that he dreaded any avoidable fatigue.

Always your affectionate friend | William Sharp

ALS Sheffield City Archives

To Richard Garnett, October 25, 1895

Rutland House, | Greencroft Gardens, | So. Hampstead. | 25:Oct:95

My dear Garnett

You have been so infinitely serviceable a friend to me and innumerable others, that another straw cannot break your back! The straw is my friend, W. E. Garrett Fisher,[82] a brilliant young journalist & man of letters, who has just settled in London. If he should require a word of help, in any difficulty, I trust you will not grudge him that privilege. In any case I would like him to have the pleasure of meeting you — whose own literary work he knows & admires.

Mr. & Mrs. Garrett Fisher are, I think, settling in or near Bloomsbury. It is a change from Edinburgh — but, after all, all roads lead to the B.M. — as all bothering scribes come at last to R.G.!

I shall soon have a little book of prose imaginings of which to ask your acceptance. It is called *Ecce Puella*: but there is no Marie Corellian or other Satanry in it — nor do I advertise that Harems are supplied with E.P. at a reduction!

Ever Cordially Yours | William Sharp

ALS University of Texas, Austin

To _____, Fall, 1895[83]

9. Upper Coltbridge Terrace | Murrayfield | Midlothian

Dear Sir

I thank you for your letter. I have directed (through the publisher) that a copy of *The Sin-Eater* be sent to you.

Although I permitted certain personal details in *The Bookman* for September at the request of the Editor, I did not consent there and have not consented elsewhere, to reproduction of my portrait — mainly because this is a kind of publicity I don't court.

Therefore, while thanking you for your suggestion, I must beg of you to excuse me.

If you wish, I could give you a page of the original MS of one of my books for reproduction — though this seems but a poor alternative to the granting of your request.

Yours faithfully | Fiona Macleod

ALS, Princeton University

To Robert Murray Gilchrist, November 1, 1895

Rutland House | Greencroft Gardens | So. Hampstead | 1 Nov 95

My dear Comrade,

I can do no more than send you the briefest line today: & that only to thank you for your little message.

You gladden me, when you tell me that my work sinks *in profundis*. The book is full of myself, of my life — more than any (save one other than myself) can ever know.[84] But I am in the valley of Deep Shadow just now. Great suffering, of a kind that must not be shown, has led me stumbling and blindfold among morasses and quicksands. I see the shining of my star — and so have hope still, and courage. But, while I stumble on, I suffer.

Write to me about what you feel & think of "The Sin Eater" — particularly of the barbaric section, & the more intimate final section, dedicated "Ri mo Aisling" — It will help me, and I need help just now.[85]

Your loving friend | William Sharp

ALS Sheffield City Archives

To Edward Clodd,[86] November 2, 1895

Rutland House | 2nd Nov., 1895.

Dear Brother-in-Omar,

On my return from Scotland the other day I found a note informing me that I had been elected an Omarian on the nomination of your distinguished self.

My thanks, cher confrère. "A drop of my special grape to you," as Omar might say, if he were now among us with a Hibernian accent! Herewith I post to you another babe, born into this ungrateful world so recently as yesterday... . Such as it is, I hope you may like it. "Ecce Puella" itself was written at white heat — and ran in ripples off the drain: and so is probably readable.

"Fragments from The Lost Journals of Piero di Cosimo"[87] when they appeared (some few years ago) won the high praise of Pater — but perhaps their best distinction is that they took in the cocksure and leveled the omniscient. One critical wight complained that I was not literal (probably from the lack of knowledge of medieval Italian), which he clinched by the remark that he had compared my version with the original! I see that Silas Hocking has just published a book called "All men are liars." I would fain send a copy to that critic, even now. By the way, my cousin Miss Fiona Macleod wrote to me the other day for your address. I understand she wanted to send you a copy of her new book. If you got it, you should, as a folklorist, read the titular story, *The Sin-Eater*.

My wife joins with me in cordial regards, and I am

Sincerely yours, | William Sharp.

Memoir, p. 247

To Hannibal Ingalls Kimball,[88] November 8, 1895

Rutland House | Greencroft Gardens | So. Hampstead. | London | 8th Nov/95

Dear Mr. Kimball

Herewith the signed agreement. It is all clear to me save the wording in lines 10 & 11 on the first page.

If no arrangement has been made to publish the book in England simultaneously as I infer has not been done — and as I lose not only immediate profit but English Copyright by this not having been done, *which I had all along understood Mr. Stone was to see to* — I suppose I am at liberty now to bring out the book in this country, either with the same contents under a fresh title or as *The Gypsy Christ*.[89] Kindly let me have a line about "this" by return.

With kind regards, | yours very truly, | William Sharp

P.S. In the circumstances, should not the words "and in England" in 12th line, be struck out and the deletion initialed by you?

ALS Huntington Library

To [*Hannibal Ingalls Kimball*], *November 23, 1895*

9 Upper Coltbridge Terrace | Murrayfield, Midlothian | 23ʳᵈ. Nov.1895

My dear Sir

Your note of the 25ᵗʰ. Oct. duly came to hand about a fortnight ago with Contracts for "The Sin-Eater" and Memd. of agreement about *Pharais* — but I have delayed acknowledgment, as I have expected that each successive post would bring me the draft on honour for £10 (a/c *Pharais*) which you say you enclose, but which was not enclosed. Some six or seven mails have passed, and still no sign of the Draft.

I await, therefore, its receipt, either any day now, or after you write to this communication, before I send you the Note of Agreement (with a slight amendment) which you enclosed in duplicate.

Yours faithfully, | Fiona Macleod

P.S. Kindly let me have a dozen copies of *Pharais*, if now published.

The note with enclosed cheque for £10 has just reached me this moment. Will write by next mail. | F. M.

ALS Huntington Library

To [*Hannibal Ingalls Kimball*], *November 25, 1895*

9. Upper Coltbridge Terrace. | Murrayfield, Midlothian. | 25ᵗʰ.
November. /95

Dear Sir,

As stated in P/S. to my note per last mail, the delayed draft for £10 on a/c *Pharais* came to hand.

Herewith I return formal receipt, but not one of the forms you sent to me. In the first place, I am not legally describable as "Fiona Macleod of London, England" — but as "Fiona Macleod of Murrayfield,

Midlothian" — and in the next you are under some misapprehension as to the conditions of the American issue of *Pharais*. The honorarium of £10 was not to be for "the entire American rights in the book entitled *Pharais* to have and to hold for themselves and for their assigns for ever" — but for the alterations I made in that book, in order to protect you against piracy of the English edition. It is true, I have no further rights in your *Green Tree* issue of said book: but, on the other hand, neither have you the right to issue the book in any other form or price without agreement with me or my representative.

Naturally, I would not dispose of the whole American rights, and in perpetuity, for the sum of £10 — which sum in any case was not of my fixing, but Mr. Stone's offer in consideration of my making alterations which would make the reprinted American issue different here and there from the original English edition. *The Sin-Eater* contract you will have already received.

Hoping that both books — and other writings of mine — will in every way justify the confidence of your firm,

Believe me, | Yours very truly, | Fiona Macleod

P.S. I send one stamped and signed Receipt-Agreement, for you to keep. The other please endorse with your firm's signature, and kindly return to me.

ALS Huntington Library

[*November 25, 1895*][90]

Upper Coltbridge Terrace | Murrayfield | Midlothian

In consideration of 10 (Ten Pounds) Sterling to me in hand paid, the receipt of which is now acknowledged, I, Fiona Macleod, of Murrayfield, Midlothian, Scotland, do hereby assign to Messrs. Stone and Kimball, a corporation organized under the laws of Illinois, doing business principally in Chicago, Cook County, State of Illinois, U.S.A., all rights in the Green Tree Library issue of "Pharais", which book, in consideration of said honorarium, I have amended so as to safeguard the said firm's rights in said issue of "Pharais". But this with the reservation that all other rights of alteration and republication of said book remain with me, and that the said Stone and Kimball bind themselves to publish no other edition of "Pharais" than said Green Tree Library issue unless by special consent of and compact with me or my legal representative.

Fiona Macleod

ALS Huntington Library

To the Editor of Blackwood's Magazine, [late Fall, 1895]

(*Letter address.*) | 9. Upper Coltbridge Terrace | Murrayfield

Dear Sir

Will the enclosed suit you for *Blackwood's*? I must add at once (1) that I reserve my copyright, with freedom to reprint in volume form after Xmas 1895: and (2) that the American serial newspaper's rights of this story are already bought beforehand by a New York Syndicate.

The circumstances may make your acceptance of "Morag of the Glen" infeasible — but I hope not, as it would be a great pleasure to me to have one of my Celtic stories in *Blackwood's*.

I am at present in Skye, but I give the address (that of a cousin) where all my letters are sent to.

Believe me | Yours very truly | Fiona Macleod

P.S. May I beg the favour of a reply at your earliest convenience, as I have both Syndicate and Magazine applications for any work of mine I have to dispose of.

ALS National Library of Scotland

To _____, *December 11, 1895*

11th Dec/95

Dear Sir

In continuation of my letter per last mail,[91] I may add that *The Strayed Reveller* and other early poems of Matthew Arnold have now lapsed out of copyright. "The Stayed Reveller" has long been worth literally its weight in gold — so rare is it. I knew Matthew Arnold, & know his work well, & wd. gladly write upon him in this connection.

Faithfully Yours | William Sharp

ALS University of Kentucky, W. Hugh Peal Collection

To Henry Mills Alden, [December, 1895]

30 Greencroft Gardens | South Hampstead | London

My dear Alden, | and dear Miss Annie, | and dear everyone else at the home in Metuchen,

My cordial greetings for Christmastide & the coming year — from your ever affectionate & unforgetting friend.

William Sharp

who sends herewith, as a Xmas offering, his recently taken "image".

My wife though unknown, demands a share in a full half of the Love Sent!

ACS University of Delaware Library

To Sir George Douglas,[92] *December 21, 1895*

Rutland House | Greencroft Gardens | So. Hampstead | 21/Dec/95

My dear Douglas:

I send you my cordial thanks for your friendly and helpful letter — helpful because it comes from one whose trained intelligence I respect, and whose insight and swift response to any genuine keen manifestation of intellective or spiritual emotion I discovered a long time ago now — and friendly, because at once so generously sympathetic and so honest.

Yes, though Traill and some other critics (& let me say that not one of these "big guns" suspects what *you* have all along felt sure of, and which I can no longer, in fairness, keep from you, trusting you however to be scrupulous in your guarding of my secret — namely, that I *am* Fiona Macleod) — prefer its two predecessors to "The Sin-Eater," I entirely agree with you in ranking the latter as a worthier achievement — so far as it is an achievement at all: — and this I say in no false modesty, for "in finding myself" in F. M. I have lost all literary arrogance, and work now in what someone once called "a passionate humility".

Certainly, I have *wrought* it as well as been profoundly wrought *by* this development of my childhood & boyhood "*tendenz.*" The movement — to speak largely about small matters — began with "Sospiri di Roma" (with more obvious notes first struck in "The Weird of Michael Scott" & "The Death Child") and "Vistas." Then I suddenly harked back — and wrote straight out of my own life, knowledge, experience, and inner self. *Pharais* was in this sense inspirational.

Please forgive these deleted lines.[93] They contained something as to the strange complexities which underlie the puzzling literary entity, "Fiona Macleod": but, after all, were too private — though, some day, I may allude to their drift.

À propos; when a rumour got about last season that F. M. was "a man, and a well-known man of letters, it was denied by an eminent critic on the ground of "impossibility." "There is no more pronounced individuality among our living writers," he declared: "and even if F. M. were not a woman, as she almost certainly is — even her very "wildness" and strange atavistic barbarism confirming rather than dissuading me in this — she could not be any one of the possible names mentioned. If she were, it would be one of the strangest episodes in Victorian literature — and a puzzling nut to crack for the critics & psychologists of the next century."

As a matter of fact, this is the view now held apparently — and even the one or two who suspected W. S. (Grant Allen, W. B. Yeats, Garrett Fisher[94] the critic) have at last admitted they were wrong. Yeats, I believe, went so far as to say that, after careful examination, he had come to the conclusion that "it was impossible."

Well: F. M. hopes to do something that will last — better, something that will deserve to last.

I do not think "The Washer of the Ford" will please "the general reader." It is much more austere, for one thing, than anything F. M. has done — but, I think, as great an advance upon "The Sin-Eater," as that upon the others. The two books, however, that are most near her heart, will not (probably) be done (or at any rate published) for a year or two.

By the way, she has a "legendary romance" in the current *Evergreen*[95] (of course: I forgot, you must have seen this comrade to "Cobweb Hall") — and a series of illustrated Hebridean & Highland episodes, runes, etc., in the Xmas number of *Harper's*.[96]

Herewith I send you a copy of the first note from George Meredith:[97] also a digest of the press opinions to hand. Please let me have both again at your convenience.

I am extremely interested in what you say by way of critical remonstrance.[98] Very likely you are wholly right. For myself, some instinct seems to tell me you *are* right in what you say about the four "damning" words on the last page of "The Dan non Ron" — "a red irrecognisable mass", of course. Yes, I do admit it. You are right. Possibly, too, you are right about the bloodthirstiness in "Green Branches". I *think* you are wrong about the beginning of "The Ninth Wave," and I am *certain* I am right about the fittingness of the close of "The Sin-Eater".

But you are right in your attitude, & I thank you for writing to me. I will remember your warning. I wonder why the strangeness & horror of madness, and the lust of blood, are so potent factors in my imagination — when I know also the wells of tenderness and love for men, women & children, for beasts & all living things, out of which "Fiona" draws her draught of tears and pain and tragic joy.

Do you think you would care to help me by overlooking for me (next February probably) the type-duplicate, or proofs, of the "Washer of the Ford" volume? Or is this asking too much? Say frankly.

A matter that amused me at first has assumed a more tragic hue. A man (a Scottish clergyman — and a Highlander) has read & reread F. M.'s books till — he has fallen passionately in love with her!! He created an ideal "Fiona," poor chap, and has "pinned all to his passionate hope." I thought I had definitely prevented all further idea of anything of the kind, or even any correspondence — but I have had a letter from his mother, saying that her son is desperate because of my rebuff, and is dying for love of me; and she begs me to be merciful, & even if I cannot become his wife, at least to see him. She warns me, too, that she fears he will take his life, "as he has become almost distraught by his mad love for you." Then she makes a personal appeal, about her age, & her belief in & pride in him, & so forth. It may seem only amusing to you — as it did to me at first — but upon my soul I am very uncomfortable about it. After the first definite proposal of marriage (by the way, this is the second Fiona has had!) I made enquiries, & found that, wild as it all sounds, everything is "on the square." Strangely enough, a friend of mine has an estate near where my "lover" resides with his mother.

I am damnably put out about the whole affair.

Did I tell you of my wife's serious ill-health? She has to leave England for 3 months or so — & starts on the 5th Jany for central Italy. It is impossible for me to go with her, alas: but she will be with friends. We are hopeful that this complete change to a fine climate will prove wholly remedial.

Ever yours, my dear Douglas, | William Sharp

ALS Yale University

To Messrs. Stone and Kimball, December 21, 1895

Rutland House | Greencroft Gardens | South Hampstead | 21 Dec '95

Messrs. Stone & Kimball | Chicago

Dear Sirs,

If, partly by lateness in placing the book on the market and because of the great pressure of long-arranged-for books this winter season here, & for other reasons also (because of the nature of the "Gypsy Christ" story, I hear from one source — tho' that seems to me rather absurd) there is no likelihood of *The Gypsy Christ* volume being on the English market soon — I suggest that it would surely he much the best plan for you to publish it (if you have not already done so — as I infer from your advts., though I have not yet received any copy) in the States, and simply send over a certain number of copies here for sale through an agent. If you have not already issued the book, simultaneous issue would give copyright here. I have no doubt whatever that, if you do not make arrangements with your regular agents here, copies on sale would be taken by Messrs. Patrick Geddes & Colleagues of Edinburgh. Only, in that case how about advertising & other incidental expenses. For several reasons I would prefer another arrangement. Has the book been submitted to Mr. Lane?[99]

Please note
- (1) That I wrote, to commission, an article on the Belgian Renaissance, for the ChapBook — and posted it in <u>September</u> last. Its receipt was never acknowledged, nor has it appeared, nor have I heard anything about it.
- (2) I also sent to you about same date tho' a little earlier, with a letter, my translation of a short play by Charles Van Lerberghe.[100] <u>This has never been acknowledged or taken notice of in any way</u>.
- (3) At Mr. Stone's request, the recently published vol. (which I am glad to say is going very well) *Ecce Puella* was submitted to your firm, for publication in America. To this day I have never heard why it was declined, or had any word about it (save a line from Mr. Stone acknowledging a copy I sent him).

(4) Three letters of mine about these matters seem to have been ignored.

As we are, I hope, to have many dealings with each other in future, I trust such lapses of memory will no longer be a source of annoyance & loss of time.[101]

Yours faithfully | William Sharp

Will you kindly let me have the promised number of copies of *"The Gypsy Christ"* (if not already dispatched). I liked the *format* of Miss Macleod's *Sin-Eater* very much (By the way, will you please furnish me with a copy of her *Pharais* and of Mrs. Wingate Rinder's "Green Tree"?)

ALS New York Public Library, Berg Collection

To Robert Murray Gilchrist, [December 22?, 1895]

Rutland House | Greencroft Gardens | So. Hampstead

My dear Gilchrist

I hope Christmastide comes with happiness to you & yours.

To me, 1896 comes with a gauntleted hand. It will be a hard fight against the squadrons of Destiny (for I hear the trampling of an obscure foe, and menacing vague cries) — but perhaps I may — for a time, and that is the utmost each of us can expect — emerge victor. What a bitter strange mystery fate is! You know, dimly and in part, out of what tragic pain and amid what tragic issues I wrote "Summersleep," the third of the "Tragic Landscapes"? Well, every environment is changed, and circumstances are different, and yet the same two human souls are once more whelmed in the same disastrous tides, & have once more to struggle blindly against what seems a baffling doom.[102]

At least, thank God, there is <u>grip</u>.

I wish very much I could have a long talk with you. I wonder when it is to be. (In case you shd. be coming to town, note that I shall be away from London from the 4th to the 10th inclusive).

Meanwhile, I am wrought by overwork, anxiety, and the endless flame of life.

I am in financial and other trouble, too, partly because of the serious indisposition of my wife. The doctor says she must leave England for three months — so in less than a fortnight now she goes to Central Italy. It is impossible for me to get away — but she goes to a relative, & afterward with a dear friend and among friends. Perhaps you would come here for a few days, say in February?

I wish you would write to me — a long letter, not one of your usual notelets! I *need* something just now.

Does *The Sin Eater* volume wear with you? It seems to have made a profound impression on George Meredith and the few whom I particularly wanted to reach — and indeed upon many, known and unknown. It has received praise, too, in the best quarters, that makes me almost shy — for a great word has been used more than once by scrupulous critics.

I hope your mother cared for at least something in the book (you told me she was "deep" in it, & would write to me: but as I have never heard from her I fear that she has been disappointed.)

Herewith as a small Xmas offering I send you a specially bound proof-revise copy of my last book: "*Ecce Puella: And other Prose Imaginings.*" It is rather larger, & is differently bound, in the published edition.

If I could leap from now over this black gulf of January, & be safe on the shores of February, how thankful I should be! And yet — there are gulfs beyond, I know.

What are you doing? What have you done?

Write to me as comrade, and intimate friend. I have a weary feeling as tho' I had done <u>nothing</u>, & could never write a line worth reading.

My love to *you*, & Cordial Greetings to all of you.

Your friend | William Sharp

ALS Sheffield City Archives

To John S. Stuart-Glennie, December 26, 1895 [103]

Rutland House, | Greencroft Gardens, | So. Hampstead. | Dec. 26, 1895.

Dear Sir,

It has been very difficult to arrive at a conclusion as to how best to meet your wishes, and also to consider our own interests, on account of the several plans of publication specified by you.

In the first place we do not see our way to purchasing the whole or half the edition for a cash sale, as you suggest in your letter of the 15th.

It seems to me that the simplest plan is for us to undertake the publication at our own expense, and to grant you what you consider an adequate royalty on all copies sold, with a stipulation that we guarantee you the sum of fifty pounds (£50.) irrespective of possible failure of the book's sales to reach that sum in royalties. Further, I suggest that the book be published at 5/ nett (so as to aid it toward a larger sale) and that you be paid a royalty at the rate of a shilling a copy on all copies sold. In this way you are freed from all responsibility of production, guaranteed (to the extent of £50.) against non-receipt of any income from your book, and we, on our part, are not so heavily handicapped with a volume whose sales at the best cannot be large, and in the present state of the book market are highly problematical.

On hearing from you, I shall at once reply to you decisively: when, too, I shall return, with many thanks, Mr. Carmichael's ballad.[104] Let me add that the "Arthurian Localities" seem to me a work in every way worthy of republication and that I shall very gladly see it introduced to a wider public, and to a younger generation of writers,

Yours faithfully | W. S.

MS Copy National Library of Scotland

[*To Patrick Geddes, December 27, 1895*][105]

Herewith copy of letter sent yesterday to Stuart Glennie. You advised me to be as liberal as practicable — but I don't think we can do more than suggested here, do you? (He is mistaken in saying he has not heard from me since he wrote on Nov. 28th — he has heard from me twice.)

ALS National Library of Scotland

To Richard Le Gallienne, [December] 28, [1895]

Rutland House | Greencroft Gardens | So. Hampstead | *Saty 28th*

My dear Le Gallienne,

It is long since we met, & I miss our friendly intimacy. Can we not meet soon?

Is there likelihood of your being at home & disengaged tomorrow week (i.e. on Sunday the 5th) — and, if so, would it suit you if I came that evening?

If agreeable to you, this would suit me particularly — for on that forenoon I have a bad separation to go through, & would rather be with one who is at once a friend & not a relative. To be explicit: my wife's health has given way, and the doctor says her chance lies in leaving the country for some months to come. So, on Sunday, she starts for Central Italy.[106] It is, alas, impossible for me to get away also: tho', fortunately, she goes to friends — first to a relative who has a villa outside Florence, and then to a dear friend, at Frascoti, in the Alban Hills above Rome.

Please let me have a line from you by return if practicable.

Meanwhile — as always —

Your friend, | William Sharp

ALS Princeton University

To Herbert S. Stone December 30, 1895

9 Upper Coltbridge Terrace. | Murrayfield, Midlothian.

Dear Mr. Stone,

Let me begin by wishing you health, prosperity, and happiness in 1896.

Herewith I send you the *précis* of the press-opinions here about "The Sin-Eater." The latest — a long and important article in *The Daily Chronicle* — has attracted many more readers. I believe there is to be an article on the book in next week's *Academy*, or the week after.

I hope to be able to send you the completed M.S. of *The Washer of the Ford* by the end of January.[107] Messrs. Patrick Geddes & Colleagues wish to issue the book early in March. Will this suit you? Please specify a date, if you can: and kindly let me have a reply by return. May I ask you to give me £50 on date of publication, in advance of royalties?

Of late, and particularly since the issue of *The Sin-Eater*, I have had many offers as to publication: and I can easily get £50 (or more), only that I bear in mind my promise to you. If I remember rightly, our original understanding was a 15% royalty, with £25 advance on publication.

Have you forgotten your promise about sending me the 25 copies of the "Green Tree Library" edition of *Pharais*? I am eager to see the book in that form. (Mr. Lane, I understand, is about to issue a second edition of "*The Mountain Lovers*.")[108]

Bliadhua mhath ùr duit![109] and believe me,

Sincerely yours, | Fiona Macleod

30ᵗʰ December/95

The contents, as at present arranged, are

The Washer of the Ford and Other Legendary Moralities

I. The Washer of the Ford | Muime Chriosd | The Kind of the World | Joseph Macrae | Black Dougal | The Hidden Years | The Fisher of Men

II. Marlin the Wild | The Annir-Coilyä | The Swineherd | The Love of
    Hydullan | The Helot
III. The Colloquy of the Ancients |

ALS Huntington Library

Chapter Fourteen

Life: January–June, 1896

In December 1895, Elizabeth's doctor was worried about her health and recommended three months in a warm climate. During the first week of January, her husband accompanied her as far as Calais, and she went on to Florence, where she stayed for several weeks with her aunt. From there, she continued on to Rome, accompanied by her friend Mona Caird. After returning to London, Sharp wrote several letters on January 6. One informed the publisher Elkin Mathews that Elizabeth was ill and unable to continue her editing of *Musa Catholica*, an anthology of Catholic poetry. Mathews was free "to arrange with Mrs. Meynell, or Mr. Lionel Johnson, or Mrs. Katherine Tynan Hinkson, or any other Catholic poet or writer, to undertake the volume." Two other letters asked W. Scott Tebb, a physician, and Richard Garnett if he could borrow their editions of Matthew Arnold first two books to collate text for an edition of Arnold's poetry Walter Scott would publish in the Spring. Short of money, Sharp was also writing as many reviews as he could manage, and becoming yet more active in Patrick Geddes and Colleagues. That work took him to Edinburgh for four days on January 12. From there, he sent Geddes, who was teaching in Dundee, letters from several Belgian writers whose stories Edith Rinder had included in *The Massacre of the Innocents*. They thanked her for copies of the book and praised the quality of her translations. He also enclosed for Geddes a "digest of press opinions" of Fiona's *Sin-Eater*, some twelve from Scottish, Irish, and English papers and all very favorable. He wanted to assure Geddes that his work as Literary Editor was attracting attention and might restore the firm to solvency.

On January 9 Sharp met Grant and Nellie Allen at a social event in London, and they invited him for another visit to their home in

 https://doi.org/10.11647/OBP.0196.03

Hindhead, Surrey. On the next day, he wrote a note to Nellie Allen asking if Sunday, January 19 would be convenient for them. Still trying to assure her husband he was not Fiona, he added: "If I were Fiona Macleod, as Grant seems to 'hanker after believing,' I would call you *Deo-Grein*, for you are of the Sunbeam kind." After a "very fatiguing time in Edinburgh," Sharp spent the weekend of January 18 with the Allens. In a thank you note he told Nellie Allen he "had good news from Lill [...] tho' she is still very far from well." The Allens were considering a move to London, where Grant would be better able to defend and enhance his reputation. Sharp recommended strongly against a move to the "fog and gloom" of the city. If the Allens could only sleep a little better and be brave, they would know their luck and "feel inclined to throw the cat across [their] shadow for mere delight." He asked for "a pat on the head for not being obviously down" during his visit, for he "arrived at a moment of great anxiety and profound heart-sinking, & one of the telegrams was not calculated to allay either." It was a relief to "throw himself into sympathy" for the Allens. He remained worried and depressed about the personal tensions and financial problems he described to Murray Gilchrist in December. He was in "the black gulf of January" waiting for the "safe shores of February," but he managed to surface briefly over the weekend.

On January 24 he wrote what he called "a chronicle of woe" to Herbert Stone, his American publisher. In Edinburgh he had found Miss Macleod ill and unable to work, which meant *The Washer of the Ford* would not be published by the Geddes and Stone firms until May. When he returned from Edinburgh to London, he found Edith Rinder in bed with a serious infection, also unable to work. She hoped to be up and about soon but could not have the manuscript of *The Shadow of Arvor* ready until mid-March. Sharp had proposed to Stone that he undertake United States publication of Ernest Rhys' *The Fiddler of Carne* and Elizabeth Sharp's *Lyra Celtica*, both in preparation under his direction at the Geddes firm. Everything except the anthology was delayed, including Sharp's romance, *Wives in Exile*, which Stone had accepted. He told Stone he also was "far from well:" apart from "the trouble connected with Mrs. Sharp's break-down & going to Italy, & the heavy extra strain thrown on me, & having her work to do for her [...] I have been under a great strain of anxiety & suffering of another kind," about which he could only hint to Stone. Ever anxious to present an optimistic face to publishers, he closed by telling Stone the "strain" was passing. He hoped to complete *Wives in Exile* in February and receive the one-hundred pounds Stone had agreed to pay upon receiving the manuscript. Tapping all sources of money, he sent a statement to John Ross on January 28, which showed the firm owing him seventy-five pounds.

In the January 25 issue of *The Highland News,* a weekly paper published in Inverness, John Macleay published the first of a two-part article on Scottish highland writers entitled "A Highland Novelist." He praised Fiona Macleod's first three books and called on other Highlanders to follow her lead. It is to be hoped, he said, that "Miss Macleod is but the first in a movement which shall bring the Highlands into line with the great band of young Irish writers who are at present attracting so much attention in the literary world." In the next issue of *The Highland News* (February 1), under a section entitled "The Highlands in Literature: A Symposium," Macleay printed letters dated January 28 from William Sharp and Fiona Macleod. In the Sharp letter, he refuted the notion that the Gaelic language was disappearing:

> In Scotland at this moment there are estimated to be 310,000 people who speak both Gaelic and English, and about 48,800 who speak Gaelic only. [...] Doubtless, it will be a further surprise for many to learn there are nearly three-and-a-half million persons who to-day use one or other of the Celtic dialects, and that of these it is estimated 1,156,730 speak no other than their native tongue. Numerically, it is not Wales that comes first, as commonly supposed, but Brittany, of whose population nearly a million and a-quarter speak the Armorican dialect, while 700,000 of these can speak no other language

He called for the expansion of Gaelic — written and spoken — beyond Ireland, Wales, Brittany, and the western isles of Scotland.

The Fiona letter announced "a new spirit of intellectual and spiritual life is to go forth; not indeed merely to gleam in fantastic beauty, as bewitching but as insubstantial as a rainbow, but to merge into the larger spirit of intense life which makes everywhere for beauty." For that to happen, Highlanders

> must be true to our old love of two of the noblest of human ideals — Beauty and Simplicity. We must not only love but revere Beauty in Nature, in Art, in Life, in the souls of men and women: and we must not only praise

> Simplicity, we must practice it again. It is better to live on porridge and
> have the spiritual birthright of our race, than to be bondagers to the
> palate and the belly, and live less in the spirit and more in the body: and
> it is better to be wrought by what is Beautiful than by social ambitions
> and the chronic pathetic effort to live at a tangent.

Encouraging Macleay in his "timely crusade," Sharp, disguised as
Fiona, thanked him for his "much too generous words" about her
"place and work in this movement." He accepted, on behalf of Fiona,
the leadership role in the Scottish contingent of the Celtic Literary
Revival which Macleay had assigned her in the previous issue of *The
Highland News*. Sharp used the Fiona letter to set forth his expansive
goals for the Celtic Revival and echoed the semi-religious, apocalyptic
rhetoric of several young Irish writers, chief among them W. B. Yeats
and George Russell (AE).

In Macleay, Sharp found the champion he needed for his Celtic
writings. Published in Inverness, *The Highland News* was a perfect
venue. Confident she would be delighted, he sent copies of the paper
to Elizabeth in Italy. He told Murray Gilchrist that "the chief North
of Scotland paper [...] is printing two long articles devoted in a most
eulogistic way to F. M. and her influence 'already so marked and so vital,
so that we accept her as the leader of the Celtic Renaissance in Scotland.'"
Sharp "welcomed the opportunity of appearing in print in two guises for
he believed that would help shield the true identity of Fiona" (*Memoir*,
p. 258). Before long, Macleay began repeating rumors and engaging in
speculation about the identity of Fiona. Forced to write letters of denial,
Sharp became decidedly less enthusiastic about Macleay.

After a hectic month of January — trips to France and Edinburgh;
physical and mental illness; dealing with the affairs of Patrick
Geddes and Colleagues; trying to keep track of the progress of his
publications with Stone and Kimball in Chicago; financial worries; and
the need to keep writing essays, reviews, and stories as two different
people — Sharp went north to the relaxing environment of the Pettycur
Inn on the Firth of Forth for the first two weeks of February. Shortly
after arriving, he wrote a brief note to tell Nellie Allen he was ill the
previous week and sick of London. He canceled his plans to visit Le
Gallienne in Surrey where he would also have called on the Allens.
Instead, he came to "a remote inn on a little rocky promontory on the

Fife coast" where he could hear "the lapping of the tide on the rocks below the windows, and a strange low casual moaning of the sea-wind far out on the water." He would be joined by a friend in a day or so, and he thought Nellie could guess who that friend was. She would guess Fiona Macleod which suggests the guest was Edith Rinder. Several days later, in a letter thanking Macleay for copies of *The Highland News* with his articles on Fiona and the letters from Sharp and Fiona, he assured him "Fiona Macleod is very tangible indeed." She and his sister Mary had been there the day before, and Sharp had to pay for their luncheon. "One doesn't pay for phantoms," he asserted. Macleay had begun to have doubts. Sharp was certain Fiona would not allow her photograph to be published anywhere. She values her privacy, and "it is not too much to say that anyone who once saw her photograph would recognize her in a moment anywhere, for her beauty is of a very striking kind." Once again we can detect that Sharp, in his effort to create Fiona's identity, has conflated her with Edith Rinder.

Elizabeth had written to suggest he focus on his creative work rather than articles, reviews, and essays. He responded positively to her suggestion, promising to concentrate in February on "finishing Wives in Exile and The Washer of the Ford." His diary for the first ten days of the month shows him still balancing both kinds of work. On February 3, he wrote a lengthy *"Prologue"* to *The Washer of the Ford*; while on February 7, he dictated a 1750-word article for the *Glasgow Herald* on "Modern Romantic Art." On February 9, he wrote Fiona's "The Festival of the Birds;" while on February 10, he produced another article for the *Glasgow Herald* on "The Art of the Goldsmith." He also wrote a long Fiona letter to Herbert Stone about publishing and copyright problems. She would be late in completing *The Washer of the Ford* because she had been ill,

> though not so seriously as Mrs. Sharp, who is now in Italy or my dear friend Edith Rinder, whom you know, and from whom at Christmas I received a copy of "The Massacre of the Innocents," so delightfully got up — or as Mr. Sharp himself, who has had influenza, and is still in the doctor's hands, from that cause and a superadded dangerous chill.

All four — Elizabeth, Edith, Fiona, and Sharp — have been ill, and the illnesses, though varying in seriousness, has set them behind in their work.

Still sick and depressed when he returned to London in mid-February, Sharp continued working. On February 21 he told Elizabeth he had finished the introduction and notes to Matthew Arnold's *The Strayed Reveller, Empedocles on Etna, and Other Poems*, which was published by Walter Scott's Canterbury Series in the spring. Also on February 21, Elizabeth's poetry anthology, *Lyra Celtica: An Anthology of Representative Celtic Poetry*, for which Sharp wrote an introduction and extensive biographical and critical notes, was issued in Geddes's "Celtic Library" series. Sharp also finished the remaining tales for Fiona's *Washer of the Ford*, which was published in Edinburgh by the Geddes firm on May 12, and by Stone and Kimball in New York on June 10.

In the *Memoir* (p. 263), Elizabeth included a paragraph about *The Washer of the Ford* from an early April letter she received from her husband. Since it is one of Sharp's most insightful paragraphs about his own work, it is worth reproducing in its entirety:

> I know you will rejoice to hear that there can be no question that F. M.'s deepest and finest work is in this *"Washer of the Ford"* volume. As for the spiritual lesson that nature has taught me, and that has grown within me otherwise, I have given the finest utterance to it that I can. In a sense my inner life of the spirit is concentrated in the three pieces "The Moon-Child," "The Fisher of Men," and "The Last Supper." Than the last I shall never do anything better. Apart from this intense summer flame that has been burning within me so strangely and deeply of late — I think my most imaginative work will be found in the titular piece "The Washer of the Ford," which still, tho' written and revised some time ago, haunts me! and in that and the pagan and animistic "Annir Choille". We shall read those things in a gondola in Venice?

When one lays down *The Sin-Eater* and takes up *The Washer of the Ford*, one moves into a new universe, subjectively and qualitatively. It is the same author writing about similar locales and championing the Celtic cause, but the chief concern is not star-crossed lovers swimming into the ocean never to be seen again and the impossibility of achieving the perfect amorous relationship in this world. For three years, Sharp had been consumed by the barriers preventing his living a full life with the woman he had found too late, and this burden made its way into his writings. Following the psychological maelstrom that beset him in the fall of 1895, described in his letters to Murray Gilchrist, and after Elizabeth left for Italy in January, Sharp, no doubt with the assistance of

Edith and Frank Rinder, began to work his way out of the conundrum, come to terms with the facts of his life, and move on to other concerns and other subjects.

The over-arching aim of *The Washer of the Ford* was to illuminate the transition between the Druidic religion that prevailed in the Western Isles and the new religion St. Columba brought to Iona, and to show how the new religion absorbed many of the beliefs and rituals of the old religion. The title story is Sharp's rendition of the *bean nighe*, or "Washer at the Ford" — a woman who sits beside a stream washing the blood from the linen and grave clothes of those who are about to die. All the stories are infused with the religion of nature or, as Sharp wrote to Elizabeth, the "spiritual lesson" nature had taught him. "Natural religion" was Sharp's recourse from the Darwinian revelations of the mid-century. In stories like "The Fisher of Men" and "The Last Supper", he treats biblical stories as myths with universal applications, and transposes them via dreams or visions into stories set in the Western Isles of Scotland, where they acquire new trappings. In "The Last Supper," for example, Ian Mor of the Hills recounts a dream he had as a young child. Separated from his mother and crying, he was approached by the Prince of Peace, who took him to a hut where a table was set for thirteen men. The Prince told the child he dies daily, and "ever ere I die the Twelve break bread with me." Asked by the child his name, the Prince replied "Iosa mac Dhe," Jesus son of God. The child then saw twelve men sitting at the table with "eyes of love upon Iosa." Each had three shuttles with which they wove phantoms that arose and left the room to enter the lives of men and women. The child liked most to look at the two men sitting on either side of Iosa. One was the Weaver of Joy and the other the Weaver of Love. The remaining men were Weavers of Death, Sleep, Youth, Passion, Laughter, Tears, Prayer, Rainbows, Hope, and, finally, Glory (who turned out to be Judas, and who the Prince named the Weaver of Fear). He left the room and his shadow "entered into the minds and into the hearts of men and betrayed Iosa who was the Prince of Peace." After the child was led by Iosa from the room, he looks back and sees only the Weaver of Hope and the Weaver of Joy "singing amid a mist of rainbows and weaving a radiant glory that was dazzling as the sun." Finally, Ian Mor of the Hills recalls awakening against his mother's heart, with her tears falling on him and her lips moving in prayer. It is a compelling story told with precision, restraint, and compassion.

As Fiona, Sharp dedicated the book to Catherine Ann Janvier who, with her husband Thomas Janvier, was living in Saint-Remy in Provence, where the Sharps often visited them. A lengthy "Prologue" addressed "To Kathia," begins:

> To you in your faraway home in Provence, I send these tales out of the remote North you love so well, and so well understand. The same blood is in our veins, a deep current somewhere beneath the tide that sustains us. [...] You will find much that is familiar to you; for there is a reality, beneath the mere accident of novelty, which may be recognised in a moment as native to the secret life, that lives behind the brain and the wise nerves with their dim ancestral knowledge.

If this sounds like William Sharp writing about a woman fourteen years his senior with whom he had bonded, it is. In what follows, he says things to and about Kathia that would have been difficult had he not attributed them to a woman. In an article titled "Fiona Macleod and Her Creator William Sharp" published in the *North American Review* in 1907, Catherine Janvier recalled receiving a letter from Sharp in April 1896 saying he had dedicated *The Washer of the Ford* to her and commenting "if a book can have a soul that book has one." A copy of the book did not arrive in Provence until mid-May, but on the first of May she received "an especially printed and bound copy of the Prologue, and a letter stating it had been materially improved and strengthened and largely added to." Later, Sharp gave her his original draft of the Prologue. Comparing the draft with the printed version, she noted "the precise choice of word, the careful ordering of phrase and placing of paragraph," and was moved to write "Never was there a more careful writer than Fiona MacLeod, while of her creator this cannot always be said." Catherine Janvier placed a high value on the "Prologue" and her friendship with William Sharp.

Elizabeth included two of the letters Sharp received about *The Washer of the Ford* (*Memoir*, pp. 264–65). One dated June 22, 1896 is from Catherine's husband, Thomas Janvier, who agreed with his wife about the quality of the writing:

> I am sensitive to word arrangement, and some of your work has made me rather disposed to swear at you for carelessness. [...] But these stories are

as nearly perfect in finish, I think, as literary endeavor can make them. [...] Of all in the book, my strongest affection is for "The Last Supper." It seems to me to be the most purely beautiful, and the profoundest thing you have done. [...] I feel some strong new current must have come into your life; or that the normal current has been in some way obstructed or diverted. [...] The Pagan element is entirely subordinated to and controlled by the inner passions of the soul. In a word, you have lifted your work from the flesh-level to the soul-level.

Janvier also thought the stories in *The Washer of the Ford* were quite clearly written by a man. It was not only that the masculine Sharp, though nominally a woman, addressed his wife in the Prologue, but a great part of the book was "essentially masculine."

> If *The Washer of the Ford* were the first of Fiona's books, I am confident the sex of the author would not have passed unchallenged. [...] The "Seanachas," and "The Annir Choille," and the opening of "The Washer": not impossible for a woman to write, but unlikely. [...] The fighting stories seem to me to be pure man — thought I suppose there are Highland women (like Scott's "Highland Widow") capable of their stern savagery. But on these alone, Fiona's sex scarcely could have been accepted unchallenged.

Sharp sometimes said he was more a woman than a man, while Janvier claimed Fiona, in *The Washer of the Ford*, was more a man than a woman. One's head spins at the reversal, but Janvier, like Sharp and many of his close friends, was reaching toward an understanding of human sexuality that became widely accepted in western culture only a century later.

In one story in the volume, "The Annir Choille," Janvier continued, Fiona showed her "double sex" more completely than in any other. The story has "a man's sense of decency and woman's sense of delicacy — and the love of both man and woman is in it to a very extraordinary degree." He concluded by moving beyond the masculine/feminine dichotomy:

> What seems to me plainest, in all the stories together, is not the trifle that they are by a man or by a woman but that they have come out of your spiritual soul. [...] With their freshness they have a curious primordial flavor — that comes, I suppose, from the deep roots and full essences of life which are their substance of soul. Being basic, elementary, they are independent of time; or even race.

Men have feminine traits, and women have masculine traits, and basic human traits are shared by men and women. Though he maintained the distinction between the two sexes, he had come to believe it was not unusual for an author to be both a man and a woman who loved both men and women.

The second letter Elizabeth included is from Frank Rinder:

> My dear Will, From my heart I thank you for the gift of this book. It adds to the sum of the precious, heaven-sent things in life. It will kindle the fire of hope, of aspiration and of high resolve in a thousand hearts. As one of those into whose life you have brought a more poignant craving for what is beautiful in word and action, I thank you for writing it. Your friend, Frank.

The letter is remarkable for the praise it conveys and its expression of gratitude for what Sharp has brought to his life. It also suggests an understanding had been reached between Sharp and the Rinders about the future of their relationship.

If during Elizabeth's absence in the first four months of 1896 Sharp overcame the anxiety and depression that arose from the frustrations of his relationship with Edith Rinder, another problem still plagued him. He was short of money. A letter to Geddes early in March reveals the pressure of his work, and the precariousness of his finances. He had come to rely heavily on an American woman, Lillian Rea, in his work for the Geddes firm. She was based in Edinburgh, but Sharp needed her in London. He was trying to finish Fiona's *Washer of the Ford* and her *Green Fire* for Archibald Constable, and his own *Wives in Exile* for Stone and Kimball. He was also managing the distribution of Elizabeth's *Lyra Celtica*, doing her reviewing work for the *Glasgow Herald*, and corresponding with Stone and Kimball regarding the publication of his books in America. Sharp's doctor ordered him to obtain the help of, or "give up at once" his connection to, Patrick Geddes and Colleagues, and do nothing besides his "own imperative work."

> I am under extreme pressure of work of my own — which has been so terribly interfered with by *Lyra Celtica*, E's work, & my own ill health & absence — and in order to meet E's heavy expenses abroad & my own here I must put my best foot forward. In order to do this work, I must have help for the correspondence etc. involved with printer, binder, & the question of distribution, reviews, etc. etc. of L/C, Rhys, etc. — besides,

Evergreen correspondence, etc. In a word, it is not only W. S.-F. M. who wants an opportunity to get well & to do his own work, but the Manager of P.G. & Co. who wants a clerk or at least an office-boy!

"If I could have Lilian Rea's services clear for about three weeks (or at most a month)," he would be able "to put all straight, for myself and others, at the least possible expenditure of my rather too severely drawn upon reserve."

There was another reason he needed Lillian Rea in London. He had been given "medical injunctions not to be alone," and Geddes, Sharp wrote, didn't realize how "down" he had been: "I don't care to speak about it. I want to forget it. I want to be well. I want to work." Sharp wanted to avoid slipping back into depression, and he informed Geddes he did not feel well if left alone — "particularly in the evenings." There was no one at present who could suitably come to him, except Lillian Rea. Elizabeth was in Italy and Edith Rinder was ill. When alone it was "not only the terrible (& to me novel) depression I then experience, but the paralysis that comes upon my writing energy." The operative word is "depression." It was this condition he described to Murray Gilchrist at the close of 1895. It was this condition he could only hint at in the "chronicle of woe" he sent to Herbert Stone in January. And it was this condition that caused his wife and Edith Rinder to agree that one or the other or a suitable substitute must always be with him. To be sure, he could not work — and sustain necessary income — when alone, but a greater worry was the possibility of his depression leading to suicide.

It becomes ever clearer that Sharp was manic-depressive, a condition augmented and partly caused by the precarious condition of his heart and other physical ailments. In this early March letter to Geddes, he summarized his situation as follows:

> If I find myself unable to do my F. M. work — & it is imperative that for the next six weeks F. M.'s work should prevail — I must sever my connection with the firm. At all hazards, F. M. must not be "killed." *But this is sure*: she cannot live under present conditions. Leaving aside then the Doctor's & E's urgent requests as to my not being alone (partly because of my heart, & partly because of a passing mental strain of suffering and weariness) it comes to this: (1) I have help (& mind you an "outsider" is absolutely worthless to me just now, & probably at any time) & stay here, and do both F. M. & W. S. & P. G. & Co. — each in proportion and harmony: or else I definitely sever my connection — at

any rate pro: tem: — before all correspondence: & go away somewhere where F. M.'s funeral wd. not be so imminent, & W. S.'s nervous health could not be so drained.

My plans all hang upon [...] how much I can get done before the end of March, (2) and at what mental cost. God need not send poets to hell: London is nearer, & worse to endure.

Geddes responded positively to this appeal and sent Lillian Rea to London. Not a frugal person himself, he also responded as far as he could to Sharp's need for money. At the same time, after receiving this letter and considering Sharp's collapse at the Celtic summer session the previous August, Geddes began to realize that, just as working for the firm was not good for Sharp, Sharp was not good for the firm.

By early April, Sharp's need for money reached crisis level. In another letter to Geddes he said Stone and Kimball had not sent the money promised for his books, and what he was writing currently would bear no fruit until summer. It was essential that he receive one-hundred pounds from Geddes before the end of the month. He was due that much for managerial fees and book contracts. Also, he had one-hundred pounds invested in Geddes's Town and Gown Association. Failing money for the work he had done, he would retrieve his investment. With one or the other, he would be able to borrow the rest to cover his expenses in London and those of a trip to Italy he planned for May. It was not only that he wanted to meet his wife and accompany her home, but he had to go abroad because he had come to the end of his tether: it was "no longer a case of an *advisable* complete rest & change — but of that being imperative." Shocked at his "startling loss in vitality," his doctor ordered him not to travel far at a time. Consequently, it would be at least a week or ten days after he left Paris before he met up with Elizabeth. "I am told to go by the Riviera & stay somewhere 3 or 4 days on the way, at least — This for the head." He would spend the next three weeks making "the cauldron boil," but that would produce money only after they return.

Sharp was also trying to understand the lack of communication from Stone and Kimball. On May 4, he vented his frustration in a letter to Herbert Stone;

If, when I wrote to you expostulatingly exactly a month ago today, I was then more than merely surprised and annoyed at the extraordinary delay in hearing from you concerning the matters about which you were to write to me, and in many weeks past-promised receipt of my MS. of "The Gypsy Christ" & Proofs — you may perhaps imagine how I regard the matter now: — now that you have had time to receive and answer that letter sent to you on April 4th.

He was "utterly at a loss to understand this most unbusinesslike and apparently grossly discourteous conduct." He understood Miss Macleod was being treated similarly. For the extraordinary discourtesy, he demanded "an immediate and absolutely explicit explanation." Unless Fiona heard from him before the end of May, she would take legal action in accord with her contract.

With Geddes's aid, he managed to put enough money together to leave for Italy in early May. After stopping briefly in Paris and then in Provence to visit the Janviers, he went on to the Riviera, which turned out to be a profit center. In a May 6 note to Murray Gilchrist he reported that he had made forty pounds on the gaming tables the previous night, half as much as he had asked from Geddes to support his trip. From the Riviera, he went on to Venice, where he joined Elizabeth on May 16. After a few days, they went north to the Italian lakes. On May 28, a card from Bellagio on Lake Como informed Gilchrist they would be in England on June fourth. Elizabeth would go directly to London, but he, having to break up his journey, would spend a few days — as it turned out a week — in Dover. After a week in the remote seaside hotel at St Margaret's Bay, he went on to London for another week, and then north to the Pettycur Inn near Edinburgh, where he stayed until the end of the month.

During his absence, there had been no communications from Herbert Stone. As Fiona, Sharp wrote a letter to Stone dated June 9 in which he said he understood *The Washer of the Ford* had been published in the United States and requested his agreed upon twelve copies and advance of "£25 due on publication." Fiona was "strongly disinclined to publish further" with his firm unless she met with "more prompt courtesy and more satisfactory business relations." The next day — June 10 — Sharp wrote a letter to Hannibal Ingalls Kimball to say he received Kimball's letter dated May 22 which had followed him around Europe. In the letter Kimble said he had bought out Stone's interest in the firm and moved it to New York. He intended to go ahead with the publication of

Sharp's *Wives in Exile* as soon as possible. Sharp replied he was willing to make allowances for the disruption, but he expected to receive 1) the £100 Stone promised on receipt of the manuscript of *Wives in Exile* and 2) proofs of the book to offer Archibald Constable for a possible British edition. As it turned out, within a few months Kimball would run out of money and close the business without publishing *Wives in Exile* or sending Sharp the promised money. Stone and Kimball was an excellent vehicle for introducing Fiona Macleod to the American public. With its dissolution, Sharp was left without an American publisher and a vital source of income.

In early June, Sharp received a letter from W. B. Yeats which must have buoyed his spirits, at least temporarily. In his lengthy introduction to Elizabeth's *Lyra Celtica*, Sharp singled out W. B. Yeats as "pre-eminently representative of the Celtic genius of today," and praised his poetry:

> He has grace of touch and distinction of form beyond any of the younger poets of Great Britain, and there is throughout his work a haunting sense of beauty. He is equally happy whether he deals with antique or with contemporary themes, and in almost every poem he has written there is that exquisite remoteness, that dream-like music, and that transporting charm which Matthew Arnold held to be one of the primary tests of poetry, and in particular, of Celtic poetry.

High praise indeed to assert that Yeats's poems meet the high test of Matthew Arnold, whose poetry Sharp had edited for Walter Scott's Canterbury Poets Series. He went on to quote with praise passages of several Yeats's poems. In the early June letter, Yeats told Sharp he had read *Lyra Celtica* "with greatest delight." No book for a long time had given him so much pleasure. It was certain "to be very influential & to help forward a matter" that meant a good deal to him: "the mutual understanding & sympathy of the Scotch, Welsh, & Irish Celts." Yeats lavishly praised a Fiona Macleod poem in the anthology: "In the Scottish part Fiona Macleod's 'prayer of women' filled me with a new wonder it is more like an ancient than any other modern poem & should be immortal [sic]." These words (as transcribed in *Collected Letters II*) must have given Sharp enormous pleasure and encouraged him to continue putting Fiona forward as the leader of the Scottish contingent of the Celtic Revival. Yeats concluded by accepting Sharp's invitation for dinner as he had some "Celtic matters" to talk over with him, and that meeting may have occurred the following week. When Yeats first met Sharp in the late 1890s, he was not impressed, but *Lyra Celtica* changed his mind. Sharp was a comrade in the Celtic cause. Thus began a close relationship between Sharp and Yeats — a decade his junior — that developed quickly and lasted for several years.

In mid-June, Sharp went north to spend two weeks near Edinburgh in the Pettycur Inn, whereupon Elizabeth wrote a poignant letter to thank Geddes for his friendly welcome home, to tell him she felt stronger and better than she had for years after spending the winter in Italy, and to express her deep concern about the state of her husband's health. When she met him in Venice, he "was so weak and feeble I was very alarmed. He had long fainting fits which at first I thought were heart attacks." Geddes had offered the Sharps his seaside cottage, but Elizabeth could not go north right away because of her work for the *Glasgow Herald*. And Will had to be near the Edinburgh office of Patrick Geddes and Colleagues. She asked Geddes not to allow her husband, when he saw him, "to discuss business matters for any length of time at one sitting. He needs all his time and strength to get well." Each spring, she told Geddes, her husband got worse, and she could see that "if he works at the present speed & with the present complications, he will not see many more springs. The dual work of F. M. and W. S. is a great drain on his strength, at the present moment too great a drain; & his state at present is unsatisfactory." Despite Elizabeth's concern, Sharp, at the Pettycur Inn, continued his work with the Geddes firm. On June 22 and June 30, the day before he left the Pettycur Inn, he wrote long letters to Patrick Geddes about the firm's publications and his work as Literary Director. The positive notices of the Fiona Macleod publications and the praise from Yeats were surely factors in his burst of energy during the last two weeks of June.

Letters: January–June, 1896

To Mrs. William Rossetti, January 6, 1896

...Just back from France where I went so far with my wife on her way to Central Italy. Her health has given way, alas, and she has been sent out from this killing climate for 3 or 4 months at any rate... .

Memoir, pp. 259–60

To Elkin Mathews, January 6, 1896

Monday Night | 6/1/96

Dear Mr. Mathews

On my return from France — where I accompanied my wife so far on her journey South, where she has been abruptly invalided — I send you a hurried line.

Some time ago Mrs. Sharp's health broke down — but we hoped it was not serious. However the doctors said it was imperative she left this country at once, and also give up all work. I have now regretfully to say that she must give up all idea of doing <u>Musa Catholica</u>. Not only has she been unable to do anything material with it (through prolonged ill-health) & has had to desert this fatal climate abruptly — but she will for a long time to come be unable to take up any work of this kind.

In the circumstances, therefore, it would be unfair to you to let any more time lapse without informing you that she is, alas, <u>hors de combat</u>.

At the same time. she fully recognizes the right you have to the title — as you have advertised it: so she waives <u>her</u> right in it freely, as well as her intention to make the anthology — and leaves you free to arrange with Mrs. Meynell, or Mr. Lionel Johnson, or Mrs. Katherine Tynan Hinkson, or any other Catholic poet or critic to compile a <u>Musa Catholica</u>.

It is, let me repeat, with much regret — on every ground — that this decision has been come to: but you will recognize how inevitable it unfortunately is.

With kind regards | Sincerely yours |William Sharp

(Mrs. Sharp wd. send this but she is already in Italy, & in a few days now will be in Central Italy)

ALS University of Delaware Library

To Richard Le Gallienne, [January 6, 1896]

Monday

My dear Le Gallienne

Thanks for your friendly and cordial letter. After all, I could not have joined you yesterday — for I went over to France so as to see my wife so far *en route*. We are both hopeful of her complete recovery in the air of central Italy — but her going was, alas, imperative. It is hard upon us both of course, this 3 or 4 months separation in peculiarly trying circumstances — but it might well be worse, so we look at things hopefully and I may add ungrudgingly, & see what after all is evident — the sunny side.

It will give me very great pleasure indeed to come down to stay with you over a night — sometime after the 20th.

Would Sunday, the 26th suit you?

I am sure you have made a wise move every way –

Affectly yours, | William Sharp

ALS University of Texas, Austin

To Dr. Tebb, [January 6, 1896]¹

Rutland House | Greencroft Gardens | So. Hampstead

My dear Dr. Tebb

I wonder if perchance you have either or both of Matthew Arnold's early vols, "*The Strayed Reveller*" (1849) and "*Empedocles on Etna*" (1852)

If so, could you entrust one or both to me — for a special purpose of collation of the text. All care would be taken & prompt return.

Just came back from France, where I went so far with my wife. I have to go to Edinburgh for a few days shortly — but soon after my return I hope to see you.

With Cordial Regards | Sincerely yours | William Sharp

ALS University of Wisconsin–Milwaukee Library

To Richard Garnett, [January 6, 1896]

Rutland House | Greencroft Gardens | So. Hampstead

My dear Garnett,²

Cordial thanks for "The Age of Dryden" — which I have read with keen appreciation of your sane, sure, & well-balanced judgment & style. It is in every way a serviceable book — as I hope to be able to point out.

Can you do me a great favour, and lend me (if you have the books) either or both the two early vols. of Matthew Arnold: & by "lend" I mean lend me for a few days only — with great care taken & prompt return. I want them for purpose of a rigorous collation of his variant texts. It occurs to me that you are probably owner of *The Strayed Reveller* (1849) and *Empedocles in Exile* (1852).

If you can oblige me, I could call at the B/M on Friday, for the book or books. Just back from Calais, where I went so far with my wife, invalided south for some months I am sorry to say.

In greatest haste | Cordially yours | William Sharp

I am sure no one reading "The Age of Dryden" will fail to realise what range of sympathy & insight you have — a delight in itself.

ALS University of Texas, Austin

To Mrs. Grant Allen, January 10, 1896

Rutland House | Greencroft Gardens | So. Hampstead | 10/1/96

Dear Nellie

(I am sure it sounds ever so much nicer than Mrs. Allen, tho' I shan't feel sure of it till you honour me with "Will") — I find I can manage Sunday of next week (i.e., the 19th) — tho', I fear, only for that day and Monday, & probably with need to return on Monday might. I think, however, I might be able to get to you on Saty by the train due at Haslemere at 5:32 (from Waterloo at 4:10). Will you please send me a line to say if you are to be alone, & if this arrangement will suit you: and please address it to me C/o Miss Lilian H. Rea | Crudelius House | The Lawnmarket | Edinburgh | It was a great pleasure to me to see you and Grant yesterday. If I were Fiona Macleod, as Grant seems to "hanker after believing", I would call you *Deo-Grein'*, for you are of the Sunbeam kind. I go to Edinburgh on Sunday, and hope to return by Thursday.

What a fine woman Mrs. Bird seems to be: I would gladly see more of both, if they care to see more of

Your friend, | Will

ALS Pierpont Morgan Library

To Patrick Geddes, [January 14?, 1896][3]

Patrick Geddes and Colleagues |
Riddles Court Lawnmarket | Edinburgh

My dear Geddes,

It may interest you to see accompanying digest of Press Opinions of Fiona Macleod's book. I am glad that she has had notices so favorable: also, that the book *qua* book, and the new firm have had recognition in many quarters.

Also, herewith I send some typed copies of letters received by Mrs. Wingate Rinder from the eminent Belgian novelists, Georges Eekhoud, Demolder,and Louis Delattre.[4] Please let me have them again. I thought they might interest you. The Belgians are susceptible folk: and now that they believe there is a renascence here as well as with them their interest is extending.

The new "Evergreen" has been much discussed. We must "work them in" some way: and here, socially as well as otherwise, Mrs. E.W.R. might be of real help.[5]

Yours ever | W. S.

"In the incipient Celtic Renascence, Ireland has played a much more conspicuous part than Scotland. But the writings of Miss Fiona Macleod are gradually disclosing to the British public quite another Scotland than that with which lowland writers have familiarised them." (*The Bookman*)

"The Sin-Eater and Other Tales" | (Patrick Geddes & Colleagues.)

Opinions of the Scottish Press: —

The Scotsman: — "The latest of Miss Fiona Macleod's books will infallibly strengthen the spell which she wields over those who have come within the circle of her Celtic incantations, and help to make good her claim to a peculiar place in the literature of her day and race. In all these wild tales from the shore of Iona and the Summer Isles and from the hillsides of Mull — saturated with the sweet and plaintive music, and heavy with the sadness and mystery of the land and people of the Gael — in all these tales, from the beautiful 'Iona' prelude addressed to Mr. George Meredith, the same refrain runs. All are steeped in the gloom and glamour of the gathering mist, the lowering cloud, the breaking wave: in all is the sense of the resistless power of destiny: and in all are manifest Miss Macleod's wonderful ear and delicate touch."

The Glasgow Herald:

— "The new firm of Scottish publishers whose imprint is on the title-page of this daintily-appointed book could scarcely have found a more striking or appropriate work with which to break ground...

If anyone can read them unmoved, or fail alike to shudder, to admire, to marvel at the stories, one does not envy his flat unraised spirit. For such pieces again, as to the beautiful and impassioned 'Harping of Cravetheen', or 'The Anointed Man', with its delicate parable of the poet's soul, hardly any praise can be too high. Indeed, as 'The Mountain Lovers' seemed to us to be an advance on 'Pharais', so this volume of stories seems to us to mark an advance on 'The Mountain Lovers'. It unites beautiful and delicate language to a luxuriant fancy and a knowledge of the Gael that should yet take her very far, indeed, upon that high road of literature with which her individual by-path is now indissolubly connected."

The Aberdeen Free Press: — "It may be said at once that the volume is one of quite unusual literary power.... . All her stories are permeated by a spirit of gloomy fatalism, but while this in less skilful hands would produce an intolerably dreary result, Miss Macleod has handled the theme with great artistic skill, has given a subtle delineation of the mingling in the Celtic mind of this belief in an overpowering destiny and a highly poetic imagination, and has lavished on her sketches a wealth of vivid and picturesque detail."

Opinions of the Irish Press.

The Irish Independent (From a leading Article on Fiona Macleod and the Celtic Renascence.): — "The most remarkable figure in the Scottish Celtic Renascence, Miss Fiona Macleod, has now set three books before the public, and it is time to appraise her seriously. She is a born poet, and the colour and strangeness she gets into her work are as some land east of the Sun and west of the Moon rather than of some earthly island to which one may journey. All she does is namelessly fascinating. She is like her own 'Anointed Man'; she has seen the fairies, and she has also seen the underworld of terror and mystery. Her work is pure romance, and she strikes a strange note in modern literature. The 'Sin-Eater' will assure Miss Macleod's position with literary people; in this book she has 'arrived'. She is a woman of genius, and, like many people gifted so greatly, her message is often gloomy and terrible. But it is the spirit of the Celt, and her work another triumph for the Celtic genius. 'The Englishman can trample down the heather, but he cannot trample down the wind', she says in her dedication to George Meredith, 'Prince of Celtdom', and that wind of romance which breathes among the unpractical and poetical as Celtic peoples stirs in every page of the new writer."

The Northern Whig: — "In 'Pharais' and 'The Mountain Lovers' Miss Fiona Macleod gave abundant evidence of her astonishing range of vocabulary, its richness and its magic. In the present volume, however, it may be said that the gifted writer has surpassed any of her previous efforts. Weird, tragic, and gloomy as are the stories of Neil Ross, the Sin-Eater, Neil MacCodrum, and Gloom Achanna, yet her description of these characters possesses a power of fascination which is absolutely irresistible."

Opinions of the London and English Press (Earliest received)

The Daily News: — "The preface and stories have in their style and treatment that blending of vividness and dreaminess that gives so much distinction to this writer's work. Fiona Macleod is the central figure of the Celtic Renascence curiously going on side by side with the progress of naturalism in fiction. These tales are, we think, the strongest and most characteristic she has yet given us. The charm and interest of the volume lies in the subtle apprehension and imaginative rendering of the ideals of race whose standpoint toward life and the unseen is altogether remote from that of a practical and agnostic generation.

The Morning Leader: — "Miss Macleod has the intellectual and emotional equipment that enables her to appeal effectively to the whole English-speaking race, while she has the intense love — idolatry is perhaps a truer word — for the 'Celtic fringe' that lends to her imagination an unearthly vividness that nothing else could give, and touches her almost with prophetic fire. Her weird story of the wild man of Iona who took upon himself the sins of a dead man whom he hated could hardly be rivalled outside the pages of Maeterlinck. The startling effect made upon the reader's imagination cannot be set down merely to the writer's literary skill, great as that is. Much is due to the racial identification of the writer with the men and women she writes about. Her brain and heart are like unto theirs, and hence the secret of the sympathy and terror she creates."

The National Observer: — "The hand of the authoress of 'Pharais' and 'The Mountain Lovers' has lost none of its cunning. Miss Macleod's new volume is as remarkable as her earlier ones for sombre romance, striking imagery, and poetic expression. She has caught in no small degree the spirit of the Celt with its gloom and superstition, its fixity of purpose, its harshness and nobility. Her tales, full of curious folk-lore, are always powerful and melancholy. The stern, rude nature she describes forms not only a fitting background to her characters, but seems, as it were, a part of them necessary to them — nay they appear to spring from it and be made by it.

The Graphic: — "Critically, it remains to note Miss Macleod's mastery of a not, indeed, untried, but of a hitherto less frequently handled instrument of her art. Her telling of the title story and of certain of the others, notably, the Dan-Nan-Ron, shows that she can command terror as powerfully as pity, which is saying much."

The Western Morning News: — "Written with consummate skill, and is a fine addition to Celtic literature."

Liverpool Mercury: — "The book is full of an art that carries the imagination captive and leads it where it will. Moreover, there is a delicate strength of expression and a power of indicating the finest shades of meaning that is almost, if not absolutely, unique among living writers; at any rate, we know of no one else who possesses it in an equal degree. On nearly every page some phrase strikes home with its freshness and truth. Those who take up 'The Sin-Eater' as a merely entertaining book may be disappointed; but let them read it in the glowing of a winter evening by the 'soft radiance of oil', when the firelight dances on the wall and the imagination has freed itself from the cares that oppress the day, and they will find more than entertainment in the images of beauty, and sadness, and love, with which this most charming abounds.

ALS and typed reviews National Library of Scotland

To Mrs. Grant Allen, [*January 17, 1896*]

Friday

My dear Nellie

After a very fatiguing time in Edinburgh (the night before I came away I had to sit down at 8:30 p.m. and write without a break till 5 a.m.) I got back at midnight last night, but found such a mass of urgent correspondence that I had to write till 3 a.m.; so, this morning, am rather in the condition of the proverbial "boiled owl."

This "cooked" state of mind and body, I hope, will be in the past tense by tomorrow: so that you may have a human creature, & not mere limp material, as your guest — a guest who looks forward very much to seeing you both, tho' it must be a brief visit, as, at the latest, I must leave on Monday morning.

I hope to get away tomorrow by the train due at Haslemere at 5:32.

In great haste, | Cordially Yours, | Will

ALS Pierpont Morgan Library

To Mrs. Grant Allen, [*January 21 or 22, 1896*]

Rutland House | Greencroft Gardens | So. Hampstead

My dear Nellie,

A line of cordial thanks for all the friendly welcome of Grant and yourself. I carry back with me from the sunny uplift of the Hind Head air a delightful memory. The fog & gloom of London make the city seen doubly insupportable. Never let Grant *settle* here, however desirable it may be to be here for 2 or 3 months at a time.

I had good news from Lill, I am glad to say: tho' she is still very far from well.

I think you are an extremely fortunate and happy couple: and if you would both only sleep a little better, and be as brave as your hearts tell you to be, you would know your luck, & feel inclined to throw the cat across your shadow for mere delight! Meanwhile make Grant well content to remain at The Croft. If he came to live in London he would not add a dozen people to his audience — "Milleadh dana, 'bhi 'g a ràdh fer nach tuigear," which being interpreted means ['twould be but a][6] "Waste of Song, reciting where not understood."

Then, too, to fall back upon Gaelic again, "Faodaidh duine sa' bith gàir a dheanamh air enoc" — "any man may laugh on a hill-side" — & Grant I am convinced will come out at the right end of the laugh! Do not trouble to send back the handkerchief you honoured me by appropriating with such unscrupulous selfishness! Let it serve its new owner, with all the joy of a released slave for a gentler master.

But I do deserve a pat on the head, for not being obviously "down" when with you at Hind Head — for I arrived at a moment of great anxiety and profound heart-sinking, & one of the telegrams was not calculated to allay either. It was a relief, however, to throw myself into sympathy with you & Grant. So, after all, I suppose I don't deserve that pat. I hope soon to see the Birds.[7]

Please let you & Grant seek out a convenient rabbit-hole & there bury "Mr. Sharp" — so that when I come again, I may not find that unnecessary acquaintance but only

Your Friend, | Will

ALS Pierpont Morgan Library

To Herbert Stone, January 24, 1896

Rutland House | Greencroft Gardens | South Hampstead |
London | 24th January /96

My dear Herbert

This is merely a hurried line, a chronicle of woe!

(1) When I was in Edinburgh a few days ago, I found Miss Macleod ill, and though now convalescent unable to be at work. She says she cannot now let us have *The Washer of the Ford* till the middle of March, tho' can promise it by then. So that renders publication till beginning of May infeasible: but we hope to issue *then*.

(2) On my return I went to see Mrs. Wingate Rinder, & found *her* ill also, & more seriously: inflammation of the bowels. However, she too is now better, & hopes to be up out of bed in three days or so. <u>But</u> *The Shadow of Arvor*[8] cannot now come to us till about the same date — namely mid-March: and even that can't be taken for granted until next week.

(3) As to W. S. — he admits he is a culprit: & that he is not so far on towards "finis" in *Wives in Exile* as he had hoped. But — apart from the trouble connected with Mrs. Sharp's break-down & going to Italy, & the heavy extra strain thrown on me, & having her work to do for her — I too have been very far from well. Moreover, I have been under a great strain of anxiety & suffering of another kind, as to which I can only hint to you, thus: but, now...[9] anxiety are almost over. Still, with the delay, & with all involved, I must ask you to wait for *Wives in Exile* till well on in February. I am going to do nothing else now till it is finished, & at last can work at it again with verve & pleasure. Believe me, the delay is wise. The book will be all the better for it. There is an interpolated story-episode in the latter portion of it, *"The Man of Two Minds," by The Woman of Two Natures* which, for one thing, I want to rewrite.

I hoped to have had a cable from you about Ernest Rhys's book[10] etc., as I wrote on Jany 4th (abt new books by Rhys, Mrs. Wingate Rinder, & myself — & also abt a proposal by Mrs. Sharp).

In the faint hope that this blood[11] of my crucified patience may better attract your attention, I write to say that I have never yet received the *"Gypsy Christs"* you say in your last were sent a month ago, nor have I seen a copy of that book — though a week or two [ago] I had a very nice letter from Mrs. Moulton[12] about it.

DO SEND SOME COPIES FORTHWITH, OR I SHALL DAMN YOU EVERLASTINGLY.

Affectionately yours | William Sharp

ALS Newberry Library

To John Ross, January 27, 1896

London | Monday: 27: Jan

Dear Mr. Ross

I hope you are now all right again. I, too, have been rather seedy, but am better: & have, I am glad to say, good news of Mrs. Sharp.

I want to send you a *memo* shortly of our Publishing indebtedness — due to White & Co., author's advances — etc. Please meanwhile let me know what the firm's indebtedness is to me — I mean under the arrangement on Agreement as to Salary, & discounting what has already been paid. Am I right in thinking that the sum remaining due to me, to be paid in two more instalments before May (see Agreement as to date of Engagement) is £75.? So far as I recollect, the payments of the firm already made (apart from advance & salary to Miss Rea) are: –

(1) £10 to myself in August (or Sept)

(2) £50 to Miss Macleod Advance on *"Sin-Eater"*

(3) £50 to Mrs. Sharp for *Lyra Celtica*

(4) £30 to myself on a/c Salary as Manager

(5) £20 for purchase of Celtic books etc. required

£160 of which, "W. S." a/c as manager —   (1) £10. 0. 0
                                             (2)   30. 0. 0
                                                  £40. 0. 0
Deducting which from Salary at   £105. 0. 0
Travelling etc. allowance   10. 0. 0 £115. 0. 0
                                                  40. 0. 0
                                                 £75. 0. 0

Is this right?[13]

Yours faithfully | William Sharp

ALS National Library of Scotland

To the Editor, *The Highland News, January 28, 1896*[14]

London, 28th January, 1896

Sir,

In reply to your letter, I would gladly write at some length were it at present practicable for me to do so; for the question is one in which I am profoundly interested.

I have the less reluctance in not writing to you more adequately from the fact that I have recently had an opportunity to say a few words about this Celtic Renascence of which we now hear so often, and shall soon hear much more — remarks that, in a week or so, will appear, forming, as they do, the introduction to *Lyra Celtica*, an anthology of Celtic poetry, to be published by Messrs Patrick Geddes & Colleagues, of Edinburgh, who, as you rightly surmise, have identified themselves with the Celtic movement in literature and art.

But I must take this opportunity to disabuse the minds of some of your readers who may accept the statements so commonly made concerning the extinction of the Celtic speech as a living language — at any rate, of Gaelic.

The assertion so constantly made in England as to the rapid disappearance of the Celtic language and Celtic "nationalism" is based upon surmise rather than upon close observation. It is true that in Eastern Ireland there is almost as little Gaelic to be heard as in Eastern Scotland (though even in Edinburgh, it may be added, the Courts not infrequently need the services of an interpreter); but wherever the native Celtic population is still dominant, the beautiful old tongue survives. The present writer knows a good many places in the Western Isles or Highlands where no English is spoken in ordinary parlance, and some where it is not understood at all; and there are whole districts in Western Ireland, in Wales, and in Brittany of which a corresponding statement could be made. Not only in England, however, but in Edinburgh and Glasgow and Aberdeen, it may be a matter of surprise to learn that the present Gaelic-speaking population of Scotland is larger than that to which Ossian — not the Macphersonian re-creation, but Oisin mac Fhionn himself — sang the Passing of the Fein. For in Scotland at this moment there are estimated to be 310,000 people who speak both Gaelic and English, and about 48,800 who speak Gaelic only — in all, 358,000 Gaelic-speaking folk: while it is almost certain there were not 300,000 Alban Gaels at the time when "Oisin, led by Malvin, wandered blind and desolate in his old age."

Doubtless, it will be a further surprise for many to learn there are nearly three-and-a-half million persons who to-day use one or other of the Celtic dialects, and that of these it is estimated 1,156,730 speak no other than their native tongue. Numerically, it is not Wales that comes first, as commonly supposed, but Brittany, of whose population nearly a million and a-quarter speak the Armorican dialect, while 700,000 of these can speak no other language. Wales comes next, with close upon a million (996,530) inhabitants who use the old Cymric tongue, with the large proportion of over 304,000 who have no English. Then come Ireland and Scotland (the former with 867,570 who speak both English and Irish-Gaelic, and about 103,560 who can understand Erse only), and finally, the Isle of Man, where, it is true, there are very few who know no other language than Manx Gaelic (about 190 is the estimate), but where, it is calculated, at least 12,500 speak Manx as well as English.

There is no longer any Brythonic dialect spoken in Cornwall: indeed, the Celtic tongue practically died out in the Duchy before the Elizabethan era. A solitary native who could speak Brethonec (the Celtic name for the Brythonic dialects) died early in this century, but this old woman was a derelict on a sea that had long been unsailed. On the other hand, the forgoing estimates take no note of the large alien Gaelic-speaking contingent scattered in Australia and New Zealand; considerable in many parts of the United States; and concentrated in large districts of Canada, and particularly in Nova Scotia, where indeed I have come across whole settlements of Gaelic-speaking Highlanders. Moreover, neither Gaelic nor Welsh is, as commonly averred, decreasing. On the contrary, within the last few years there has been a marked arrest of the wane that for adequate reasons had been so long and steadily taking place, and even in some places an unmistakable popular effort to foster and honor the ancestral language. In the West of Scotland many English visitors — and Scots too — infer that Gaelic is no longer spoken because they hear so little of it; but in the first place the Gael has a sense of courtesy that is somewhat foreign to his Southern kinsman, and will seldom indulge in Gaelic conversation before one ignorant of the language: and in the next, English — if often very Highland English — prevails in the summer and autumn seasons almost everywhere from the Firth of Clyde to Macleod's Maids. It is in the winter months that the Gael forgets his English awhile, and returns to his old language. Even in summer, however, and in so frequented a part as the Kyles of Bute or the long reach of Loch Fyne, the fishermen of Tarbert or Strachur habitually use among themselves nothing but Gaelic. In the Inner and Outer Hebrides it is *the* language throughout the dark months. All of us who know this language — in its idioms, I think, the most beautiful of any Aryan speech, and with a flexibility far beyond what is commonly and ignorantly affirmed of it — can be of material help to the Celtic cause in the Highlands in three ways:

1. By speaking Gaelic wherever and whenever it can be used without pedantry or affectation — that is, wherever it can be used naturally.

2. By taking down (with every useful or desirable particular from the mouths of shepherds, fishermen, and others) whatever of local legendary lore or ballad lore they may be willing to impart.

3. For those who can read, but cannot speak Gaelic, there is a wide and fascinating field of research and translation.

Would it not be a good plan to establish in Inverness, with branches in Oban, Glasgow, Edinburgh, and London, a society to be called, say, "The Gaelic Literary Union," with intent to further, in particular, the organization of the second and the initiation of the third of these suggestions?

Yours in strong sympathy, | William Sharp

The Highland News, February 1, 1896

To the Editor, The Highland News, January 28, 1896

Murrayfield, 28th Jan., 1896

Sir:

Your appeal is one that ought to find an echo and a swift response throughout the Highlands. I am convinced that from this our ancient and beloved corner of Gaeldom a new spirit of intellectual and spiritual life is to go forth; not indeed merely to gleam in fantastic beauty, as bewitching but as insubstantial as a rainbow, but to merge into the larger spirit of intense life which makes everywhere for beauty. But we must not expect to work a vital change merely by writing books, however interpretative and freshly stimulating they may be: the change must come from within. Of course, I believe profoundly in the advantages of a Highland league, both as a racial bond and as a system for local union and approach of individual and individual; and am convinced that we can go far towards our goal by lectures, articles, books; still more by fitly directed personal enthusiasm and energy; and by taking the crofter and the shepherd, the labourer and the fisherman, old men and women and the younger generation and even children, into confidence and indeed comradeship. The rebirth must come from within, and be of the people.

So it is now all imperative that we look to the preservation and the realization of the Highland sentiment — of the distinctively Celtic sentiment. But I for one do not believe in this unless we are true to our old love of two of the noblest of human ideals — Beauty and Simplicity. We must not only love but revere Beauty in Nature, in Art, in Life, in the souls of men and women: and we must not only praise Simplicity, we must practice it again. It is better to live on porridge and have the spiritual birthright of our race, than to be bondagers to the palate and the belly, and live less in the spirit and more in the body: and it is better to be wrought by what is Beautiful than by social ambitions and the chronic pathetic effort to live at a tangent.

Here, again, we must not be content with generalities. The Highlander who will deprecate the deep resentment caused by the projected spoliation of national rights in the matter of the Falls of Foyers has no right to claim to be other than a North Briton. It may be a good thing to be a North Briton, possibly much better than to be a Highland Celt: but that is a matter of opinion. Do not let us be ashamed of anything we cherish: but let us be ashamed to seem ashamed. There are some wrongs one should never forget, until they have been undone. One of these wrongs is the Lowland and English tendency to shut us off from our own hills, and locks, and rivers; even, in some instances, from fishing in our sea-lochs; a shutting off that means a narrowing of our national life, a dulling of our ancient pride, and a perversion of our hereditary passion for the beautiful in nature, of our deep intense love for our *Tir nam Beann's nan Gleann's non ghaisgach*, as one of our forgotten old Gaelic poets has it.

Only through this mental atmosphere can we go out, as a regenerating force among ourselves and as a stimulus abroad, our Celtic dream. May it go then, *na's luaithe na earb, na's milse na mill, na's fhearr na an t-or!*

With every cordial wish for your timely crusade, and with thanks for the much too generous words you have for my own place and work in this movement,

Believe me, | Sincerely yours, | Fiona Macleod

The Highland News, February 1, 1896

To Elizabeth A. Sharp, [late January, 1896]

... Only a brief line to thank you for your letter about *me* and *Fiona*. Every word you say is true and urgent, and even if I did not know it to be so I would pay the most searching heed to any advice from you, in whose insight and judgment mentally as well as spiritually I have such deep confidence. Although in the main I had come to exactly the same standpoint I was wavering before certain alluring avenues of thought... . If I live to be an elderly man, time enough for one or more of my big philosophical and critical works. Meanwhile — the flame!

The only thing of the kind I will now do — and that not this year — will be the "Introduction to the Study of Celtic Literature": but for that I have the material to hand, and shall largely use in magazines first... . Well, we shall begin at once. February will be wholly given over to finishing *Wives in Exile* and *The Washer of the Ford*... .

Memoir, p. 260

To Robert Murray Gilchrist, [January 30?, 1896][15]

My dear Gilchrist,

Fiona Macleod has suddenly begun to attract a great deal of attention. There have been leaders as well as long and important reviews: and now the chief North of Scotland paper, *The Highland News*, is printing two long articles devoted in a most eulogistic way to F. M. and her influence "already so marked and so vital, so that we accept her as the leader of the Celtic Renaissance in Scotland." There is, also, I hear, to be a Magazine article on her. This last week there have been long and favourable reviews in the *Academy* and *The New Age*.

I am glad you like my other book, I mean W. S.'s![16] There are things in it which are as absolutely out of my real self as it is possible to be: and I am glad that you recognise this. I have not yet seen my book of short stories published in America under the title *The Gypsy Christ*,[17] though it has been out for some weeks: and I have heard from one or two people about it. America is more indulgent to me just now than I deserve. For a leading American critic writes of *The Gypsy Christ* that, "though it will offend some people and displease others, it is one of the most remarkable volumes I have read for long. The titular story has an extraordinary, even a dreadful impressiveness: 'Madge o' the Pool' is more realistic than 'realism': and alike in the scathing society love-episode, 'The Lady in Rosea,' and in that brilliant Algerian *conte*, 'The Coward' the author suggests the method and power of Guy de Maupassant."

I hope to get the book soon, and to send you a copy. As I think I told you, the setting of the G/C is entirely that which I knew through you. I have made use of one or two features — exaggerated facts and half-facts — which I trust will not displease you. Do you remember my feeling about those gaunt mine-chimneys: I always think of them now when I think of the G/C. Fundamentally, however, the story goes back to my own early experiences — not as to the facts of the story, of course... . Then again, Arthur Sherburne Hardy, who is by many considered the St. Beuve of American criticism — in surety and insight — has given his opinion of a book, i.e., of all he has seen of it (a comedy of the higher kind) for which Stone and Kimball have given me good terms — *Wives in Exile* — that it "is quite unlike anything else — at once the most brilliant, romantic, and witty thing I have read for long — to judge from the opening chapters and the scheme. It will stand by itself, I think."[18]

Personally, I think it shows the best handicraft of anything W. S. has done in fiction. It is, of course, wholly distinct in manner and method from F. M.'s work. It ought to be out by May. Sunshine and blithe laughter guided my pen in this book. Well, I have given you my gossip about myself: and now I would much rather hear about you. I wish you were here to tell me all about what you have been doing, thinking, and dreaming.

Yours, | W. S.

Memoir, pp. 261–62

To Mrs. Grant Allen, [February 2, 1896][19]

[Pettycur Inn] | near Kinghorn, Fife]

My dear Nellie

I did not walk over today from Le Gallienne's to see you & Grant, for the good reason that I was not there, but 500 miles north of you.

I was very far from well last week, and a radical change was imperative: & besides, I was sick of London and longed for the North. So I came to a place I know of — a remote inn on a little rooky promontory on the Fife coast: & here I shall probably remain for a fortnight at any rate. I am alone at present, but tomorrow or next day expect to be joined by a friend. I daresay you can guess who it is![20]

It is as still here tonight (I write on Sunday night) as in Hindhead — though I can hear the lapping of the tide on the rocks below the windows, and a strange low casual moaning of the sea-wind far out on the water.

It is one of the nights in which one both dreams and fears impossible things.

I hope Grant is feeling better. My love to you both,

Ever Cordially your friend, | Will

The news from Elizabeth is good in the main — though she has caught an annoying inflammatory chill in her ear and jaw.

ALS Pierpont Morgan Library

To John Macleay, [February 5?, 1896]

Pettycur Inn | Kinghorn | Fife

Dear Mr. Macleay

Thanks for the H/N[21] copies — in every way very interesting. I shd. like to subscribe to the H/N. Will you send me a form (the first time convenient for you.)

Let me have the *Evergreen* paper[22] at your convenience — the sooner the better, *but no hurry*. After the 13th cancel the above address, for my London one.

Yes, Fiona Macleod is a very tangible reality indeed. She and my sister Mary were here yesterday (She is better, but far from strong), & I had to pay for their luncheon etc. — & one doesn't pay for phantoms. When in the East Country, she stays mostly with my mother & sister (Up. Coltbridge Terrace, Murrayfield) & generally has her letters etc. addressed there when absent. She leads a rather wandering lonely life otherwise: mostly in the West & in the Hebrides, & sometimes in Brittany and the South.

I will send her your message about the photograph, but am certain beforehand she will not consent. A few weeks ago she so far yielded as to send a photograph at the request of the editor of one of the big American monthlies — but a day or two later canceled by telegram the right to reproduce it. Apart from her dislike of publicity, she does not wish to have her freedom of movement affected in any way: and it is not too much to say that anyone who once saw her photograph would recognize her in a moment anywhere, for her beauty is of a very striking kind.[23]

I am very sorry indeed to hear of your ill health. Do you sleep well? Sleep is absolutely the sovereign remedy for all head & nerve troubles. I once cured incipient insomnia by drinking warm milk just before going to bed. If that does not suit you, a tumblerful of water drunk as hot as possible is helpful, both for sleep & overwrought nerves. I trust you will soon be well again, & able to work in the Good cause in which we are all so interested.

Cordially yours | William Sharp

ALS National Library of Scotland

To Mrs. Grant Allen, [February 7, 1896][24]

Pettycur House | Kinghorn, Fife

Just a line to say I am all right again — and the better of this keen salt air, & the isolation, & the beauty of the environment — and circumstances in general!

It is possible now I may visit R. LeG.[25] on Sunday the 23rd. If so, I'll try to get over to see you.

My love to you both. Tell Grant I have sent him a copy of "The Highland News,"[26] with an interesting article (the second, here) on Miss Macleod, with letters from her, Barrie, Crockett, myself, & others, on the new movement in Celtic Scotland. [27]

I send you affectionate Greetings, N. & G.!

Will

ALS Pierpont Morgan Library

To Richard Garnett, [February 7?, 1896]

Pettycur House | Kinghorn | Fife

My dear Garnett

If in your power, will you do my wife & myself a genuine favour by sending to her an Introduction to the head of the National Library in Rome, particularly with a view to the Consultation of Celtic books there, & still more particularly as to traces of the Celtic migration, influence, etc. in Italy.

Excuse a hurried & scrappy note. I expect to be in London again in a week or so: but meanwhile am rejoicing by the sea.

Ever Yours | William Sharp

My wife's address is Mrs. William Sharp / Hotel Hassler / *Rome* but if you will hand the Intro note to my cousin Farquharson Sharp, he will send it on.[28]

ALS University of Texas, Austin

To Herbert Stuart Stone, February 8, 1896

9 Upper Coltbridge Terrace | Murrayfield, Midlothian |
8th. February | 96

Dear Mr. Stone

Your letter of January 28th reached me less than an hour ago, and I now hasten to answer it at once: though I doubt if in time to catch today's mail.

I wish to do nothing unfair, and am distressed that you should think I am acting in any such spirit. You have treated me courteously and fairly in all our intercourse, and I had neither the intention nor any idea of overriding any definite agreement.

As to *"The Washer of the Ford,"* I admit I was somewhat "at sea" as to the terms: and having mislaid your and other publisher's letters (which I have not yet recovered, though I now know where they are) I confused different undertakings and agreements.

I at once accept your assurance that *"The Washer of the Ford"* was to go to you on an arrangement of 25 advance on a 15% royalty (though, I may add, I have two American alternatives for any new book of mine, one of £50 and a royalty of 15%, and one a royalty of 20% and if wished, a small sum in advance thereof.)

From the first I promised to act loyally by your firm, and I have certainly no intention to break my word.

So, as to *"The Washer of this Ford"* let it be as you say: and I hereby formally agree to abide by the above terms, as you say, (and I have no doubt absolutely correctly) they were the terms originally agreed upon.

Pharais

I still do not understand about this matter. Certainly if I had believed I was asked to sign away all American rights, for £10, I should not have agreed.

I see the points you urge, but if matters stand as you say what is to prevent *any* publisher (or, for that matter, myself or any representative) from reprinting *Pharais* in America, if even the slightly amended edition has only a nominal copyright? What I *do* apprehend is, that you wish me to withdraw my stipulation as to your not issuing *Pharais* in other form or in a cheaper edition: and this I now do. In a word, you may cancel my objections, and accept my obligation as indicated in your contract-form. I will say no more than that (1) I have perfect confidence in your good faith; and (2) that it is the last time I shall give my adhesion to a contract that takes away my copyright, or whose terms I do not quite clearly understand.

Date for "The Washer of the Ford".

As I think Mr. Sharp explained to you, I have been unwell (though not so seriously as Mrs. Sharp, who is now in Italy or my dear friend Edith Rinder, whom you know, and from whom at Christmas I received a copy of "The Massacre of the Innocents," so delightfully got up — or as Mr. Sharp himself, who has had influenza, and is still in the doctor's hands, from that cause and a superadded dangerous chill) — and so there has been delay in finishing "The Washer of the Ford," or rather, in rewriting and partially recasting it. I am now under a promise to deliver the book, if possible, by the middle of March, but this means that you cannot have it till about the end of March.

Professor Geddes told me the other day that his firm intended to issue it nominally on May 1st. I need not see proofs of the American edition: but even thus could you manage to issue the book on May 1st? It is about the same length as "The Sin-Eater".

Please let me know by return, if that date, or exactly when will suit, so that I may arrange with Messrs. Patrick Geddes & Colleagues.

In re a New Proposal ("Green Fire")

Messrs. Archibald Constable & Co of London have commissioned a one volume romance by me, of about the same size as *Pharais* or possibly a little longer. They will probably issue it about mid-June. It is, broadly, a love-romance akin to *Pharais* and *The Mountain Lovers*, and will be entitled *"Green Fire."*[29] (The phrase has a particular Celtic significance, meaning at once the intensity and passion of youthful life, and the Rising of the Sap in the green world, in the human heart, and in the brain. Hence, also, the saying: "Green Life to you!")

I had a letter from Messrs. Constable & Co. this morning, in which they said they find they can negotiate satisfactory American terms: and asked for my directions. But I replied that I did not feel myself free to come to any arrangement in America without prior offer of the book to you: though I added: — "It is possible that Messrs. Stone & Kimball may not care to issue another book by me at midsummer, as they are to publish *The Washer of the Ford* early in May: however, as I have explained, I feel bound to give them the offer, and leave them to decide. I shall write to them at once, and as soon as I hear shall communicate with you. In the event of their not caring to issue *"Green Fire"* I shall of course be very glad to accept the generous offer proposed."

Will you please let me know by return about this (1) if you wish *"Green Fire"*, for midsummer (or a week or two earlier) publication — and (2) if you will give me a royalty of 15% plus, on publication, an advance of £50 on said royalty.

Awaiting, then, your reply by the earliest available mail,

Believe me, dear Mr. Stone, with cordial regards, |
Yours very truly, | Fiona Macleod

ALS Huntington Library

To John Macleay, [Feb 18, 1896]³⁰

London | Tuesday |10 p.m.

Dear Mr. Macleay

Your note has just this moment come: & as I have to be out of London tomorrow I answer it at once.

Many thanks about the H/News. Let me have the *Evergreen* article as soon as you conveniently can, please.

Of course you can write to Miss Macleod if you like — though I suppose I ought to say "no," & would if I had the right! For she has been ordered by her doctor to write as little as possible till she is quite right again. She is better — but suffers much from nervous headache & general overstrain. She ought really not to touch a pen for some weeks to come — and it will be a genuine kindness if you & Mr. Macbain refrain from writing to her just now. Altho' I did not know it was noticeable, I am not surprised at Mr. Macbain's noting the Irishicism [sic] of Miss Macleod's Gaelic. As it happens, there is good reason for this, of a private kind! But over & above this, Mr. McB. may not know that the Gaelic spoken in Arran & Iona, two islands where Miss Macleod spent years when a child, before she lived further West, is full of Irish words & idioms. On the whole, Iona Gaelic is probably the least pure in the whole West. There is a marked difference between it & that of Tirie a Coll even. And between an Inverness man & an Iona man there is as marked dialectical divergence as between a Yorkshireman and a Devonian. I daresay Mr. Macbain knows this: but you might draw his attention to it.

I am delighted with the Etymological dictionary. It is a genuine service to the Gaelic cause.³¹

I don't know where Miss M. got the name of "Gloom" from. It is probably her own imagining. Certainly *I* never heard the word as a name. She told me once, though, I remember, that in her list of strange names which she compiled and often draws upon, she has one as strange as "Gloom" — and this within her own knowledge, I am *almost* sure — namely, *Mulad*, meaning, I think, much the same as *Bron* (grief) though possibly rather sadness than grief. This may interest Mr. Macbain.

The name Achanna I think she owes to me. I knew a man of that name: and indeed Miss M's "Gloom Achanna" is one of her most near-to-life characters — for he is founded upon one who is a close relative of Miss M's mother, & a kinsman of my own, & a very undesirable one! The man I knew was called Stephen Achanna, and his son changed the name to its better known form *Hannay*. He is now, I think, settled in Glasgow.

As to what grounds Miss M. had for her "Sin-Eater" I do not know. Certainly the *idea* of it was not recent: for I well recollect her mentioning the superstition, and its fascination for her, some four or five years ago.

I am sorry I cannot give you anything more explicit — but the above may interest you & Mr. Macbain — & save my cousin correspondence. She is a sufferer from the same complaint as your own, I fear. (This, however, between ourselves.)

Sincerely Yours/William Sharp

You are at liberty to show this note to Mr. Macbain (as a private communication of course).

ALS National Library of Scotland

To Hall Caine, February 20, 1896

Rutland House, Greencroft Gardens | South Hampstead, London |
February 20, 1896

Dear Mr. Hall Caine,

To-day Messrs. Patrick Geddes & Colleagues of Edinburgh will post to you a copy of "Lyra Celtica,"[32] which, with all its inevitable shortcomings — and what anthology has not many — will, I hope, meet with your general approval. It is on an ambitious scale, and in its fulfillment several points had to be kept in view, which, taken together militate against perfect proportion in the sections. Still, I think it the first attempt of its kind, and I hope it will tend towards a more general and enthusiastic study of Celtic literature, ancient as well as modern.

Yours sincerely, | William Sharp

Hall Caine, Esq.

P.S. Dear Caine, I hope all goes well with you & yours! My wife is still trying to recover health, in Italy. She has been away since New Year — & dare not come back till end of April at earliest.[33]

TLS Manx Museum, Isle of Man

To Elizabeth A. Sharp, February 21, 1896

London, 21st Feb.

... I am sure *The Highland News*[34] must have delighted you. Let me know what you think of Fiona's and W. S.'s letters... . I am so sorry you are leaving Siena... . I follow every step of your movements with keenest interest. But oh the light and the colour, how I envy you!

I am hoping you are pleased with *Lyra Celtica*. It is published today only — so of course I have heard nothing yet from outsiders. Yesterday I finished my Matthew Arnold essay[35] — and in the evening wrote the first part of my F. M. story, "Morag of the Glen"[36] — a strong piece of work I hope and believe though not finished yet. I hope to finish it by tonight. I am so glad you and Mona[37] liked the first of "The Three Marvels of Hy"[38] (pronounced *Eo* or *Hee*) so well. Pieces like "The Festival of the Birds" seem to be born out of my brain almost in an inspirational way. I hardly understand it. Yes, you were in the right place to read it — St. Francis' country. That beautiful strange Umbria! After all, Iona and Assisi are not nearly so remote from each other as from London or Paris. I send you the second of the series "The Blessing of the Flies." It, too, was written at Pettycur — as was "The Prologue." There is a strange half glad, half morose note in this Prologue which

I myself hardly apprehended in full significance. In it is interpolated one of the loveliest of the "legendary moralities" which I had meant to insert in Section I — that of "The King of the Earth".[39] I will send it to you before long... .

Memoir, p. 262

To the Editor of Blackwood's Magazine, [late February, 1896]

(Letter address.) | 9. Upper Coltbridge Terrace | Murrayfield

Dear Sir

Will the enclosed suit you for Blackwood's? I must add at once (1) that I reserve my copyright, with freedom to reprint in volume form after Xmas 1896: and (2) that the American serial newspaper's rights of this story are already bought beforehand by a New York Syndicate.

The circumstances may make your acceptance of "Morag of the Glen" infeasible — but I hope not, as it would be a great pleasure to me to have one of my Celtic stories in *Blackwood's*.[40]

I am at present in Skye, but I give the address (that of a cousin) where all my letters are sent to.

Believe me | Yours very truly | Fiona Macleod

P.S. May I beg the favour of a reply at your earliest convenience, as I have both Syndicate and Magazine applications for any work of mine I have to dispose of.

ALS National Library of Scotland

To Herbert Stuart Stone, February 28, [1896]

London | Saty 28th Feby

My dear H.

In your letter Feb. 6th (received the 17th) you say 25 copies of the "Gypsy C." go to me on that day. A fortnight has elapsed since receipt of your letter, & still no sign of the books. There seems a fatality abt. this book. (Please see that the address in your books is right: the Chap Book used to be wrongly addressed to "S. Homestead") — as to the earlier package, I have inquired at the G.P.O., & at the Customs at Liverpool & South Hampton, — but without result. Please send me particulars of the dispatch of these books on Nov. 11th: by what line & post etc.

In any case please send me at once 6 copies by post.

How is the book going? I hope to hear any day from you in reply to my note to you with reference to the cancelling of any arrangement with Mr. McClure[41] here. Altogether, this book has "gone wild", so far as I am concerned.

Tho' not quite right yet, I am better. *Wives in Exile* goes well. I hope to dispatch it to you by the mail either of Wednesday 11th or Saty 14th.

Yours Ever, | W. S.

ACS Huntington Library

To Patrick Geddes, [early March, 1896]

My dear Geddes,

I wired to you today, by all means to keep Lillian Rea[42] till Thursday morning if you wish: & so far explained my urgency.

I don't care to go into the matter; but it amounts to this, I neither feel so well, nor *am* so well, if quite alone just now — particularly in the evenings. In fact, I have medical injunctions *not* to be alone. Circumstances have so concurred that there is *no one* at present who can suitably come here just now except L.H.R.

I am under extreme pressure of work of my own — which has been so terribly interfered with by *Lyra Celtica*, E's work,[43] & my own ill health & absence — and in order to meet E's heavy expenses abroad & my own here I must put my best foot forward. In order to do this work I must have help for the correspondence etc. involved with printer, binder, & the question of distribution, reviews, etc. etc. of L/C, Rhys,[44] etc. — besides *Evergreen* correspondence, etc. In a word, it is not only W. S.-F. M. who wants an opportunity to get well & to do his own work, but the Manager of P.G. & Co. who wants a clerk or at least an office-boy!

Primarily, though, it is a matter of health. By the middle of March I hope to be quite right again in every way. The doctor's report is good: only I am to be scrupulously on guard. As for the immediate emergency: I have now arranged to put off my own work, & give up tonight and tomorrow to doing the immediate publishing correspondence etc. I had meant L.H.R. to do for me.

I trust you are not detaining her for the *New Edinburgh* article. That could not be done at once anyhow, but in any case *Harper's* would not want it immediately, as they always arrange these things months in advance. If I can have Lilian Rea's services *clear* for about three weeks (or at most a month) I hope to put all straight, for myself and others, at the least possible expenditure of my rather too severely drawn upon reserve.

My doctor has given me the alternative of having Miss Rea (or Mary[45] or some intimate friend) to be with me, & help me, or else to give up *at once* my connection with P. G. & Co., & do *nothing* except my own *imperative* work? — (& that under new conditions).

My dear boy — you don't realize how "down" I have been. I don't care to speak about it. I want to forget it. I want to be well. I want to work.

To do all this, I must not only have help just now, *but must not be alone*. It is not only the terrible (& to me novel) depression I then experience, but the paralysis that comes upon my writing energy, that distresses me.

January & February *ought* to have been my most remunerative months for some years past. They have been disastrously the reverse: and unavoidably, owing to circumstances. Every day's postponement now means a heavy loss — and yet!

So close have all my arrangements to be knit, that a day's sudden lapse may throw a whole week out of gear e.g. having trusted to L.H.R.'s arriving tonight at latest, I arranged accordingly: but must now sit up all night and work hard tomorrow at detail-work, correspondence, etc. I mention this only to let you understand better. Besides our whole method of work is so different. I could do *nothing* (not even good hackwork) if I worked in your methods — as you would be handicapped and practically paralyzed by mine. My *own* work is primarily the outcome of mental atmosphere — and that *cannot* exist under certain conditions.

I have not made myself or my position clear. I despair doing so. But just as I would absolutely accept any statement of yours, even if I did not understand, so I ask you to accept mine.

And one thing is certain: if I find myself unable to do my F. M. work — & it is imperative that for the next six weeks F. M.'s work should prevail — I must sever my connection with the firm. At all hazards, F. M. must not be "killed". *But this is sure*: she cannot live under present conditions. Leaving aside then the Doctor's & E's urgent requests as to my not being alone (partly because of my heart, & partly because of a passing mental strain of suffering and weariness) it comes to this: (1) I have help (& mind you an "outsider" is absolutely worthless to me just now, & probably at any time) & stay here, and do both F. M. & W. S. & P.G. & Co. — each in proportion and harmony: or else I definitely sever my connection — at any rate pro: tem: — before all correspondence: & go away somewhere where F. M.'s funeral wd. not be so imminent, & W. S.'s nervous health could not be so drained.

My plans all hang upon (1) how much I can get done before the end of March, (2) and at what mental cost.

God need not send poets to hell: London is nearer, & worse to endure.

Wearily yours | Will

To Herbert Stuart Stone, March 4, [1896]

9. Upper Coltbridge Terrace | Murrayfield, Midlothian | 4th March

Dear Mr. Stone,

Just a hurried line, to catch the mail, to thank you for the copies of "Pharais" just received. It makes a very charming book in its "Green Tree" format.

Alas, is Gaelic so terrifying a tongue that there is no hero among the printers of Chicago who is equal to it? I notice several misprints: some from the MS. of the supplementary matter which I sent out, which is not so surprising; and others in the text as printed from the printed copy, which is more a matter for surprise. So far as the Gaelic words go, I do not suppose this very much matters; with the exception of an unfortunate misprint on the last page of the Introduction, where the well-known phrase of Tir-Nan-Og (or, Ogue) — is given as the impossible Tir-Nan-Ogul — a bait for the laughter of all the Celtic gods that are.

You will have received my answer about *Pharais* and *The Washer of the Ford*: and I am now awaiting your expected reply to my query about *Green Fire*. As to *The Washer of the Ford*, I do not expect to be able to post the typewritten copy until the end of March from here. Messrs. Patrick Geddes and Colleagues do not wish to issue it later than about the 10th or 12th of May, if feasible.

With kind regards, | Yours very truly, | Fiona Macleod

P.S. I should be much indebted if you could kindly oblige me with two copies of "The Sin-Eater" in your beautiful little *Carnation Series*, and if you are so good also as to present me with a copy of Mr. Sharp's "Gypsy Christ," which I see you advertise, I shall be still more indebted.

F. M.

ALS Huntington Library

To Herbert Stuart Stone, March 11, 1896

11th March /96

My dear Herbert

That unfortunate "Gypsy Christ" has never turned up yet. I cannot understand it. I wrote to the G.P.O. & Southhampton & Liverpool P.O. — and also to the several Customs — but without result. This as to the packet sent last November. As to that sent on 7th February, it seems to have gone to join the other.

Surely they must have been wrongly addressed.

Meanwhile I am glad to hear from Mr. McClure that he has had a telegram from you confirming me in my wish to try and arrange for the Book here myself — probably under another title, both so as to save copyright — really lost, alas — so far as possible, and because of the name, which seems to be the paramount stumbling block. I doubt if, in the circumstances, it won't be a total loss to me financially; & the utmost I hope for now here is to get the book out here. T'was born under an evil star, I fear.

How has it gone in U.S.A., with reviewers, and as to sales?

I am sorry you have had to cable your rejection of Ernest Rhys's "Fiddler of Carne." Did you not like it. We think highly of it, & advance orders are good.

You will have got the *Lyra Celtica* I sent to you from Mrs. Sharp and myself. How do you like it?

Do post me some of these d____d "G/Cs"! By the way, I paid last year for a "Verlaine's Poems" that never came. It is out, is it not?

"Wives in Exile" should go to you the day after tomorrow — i.e. by the mail of Saty. 14th. It is, I think, a true "Summer Comedy," and, as such will I hope have a wide and cordial reception.

In haste, | Ever yours, and affectionately, | Will

Please send me a line to say if I may write for the *Chap Book* an article on Richard LeGallienne. Have just been reading the MS. of his new book

"The Quest of the Golden Girl" & think it exceedingly fine. I could send a Photo of R. LeG. with the article. Let me know: and also *what length.*

ALS Huntington Library

To Herbert Stuart Stone, March 14, 1896

Rutland House | Greencroft Gardens | So. Hampstead, London | 14:3:'96

My dear Herbert:

By today's post (in postal Tubes) *"Wives in Exile"* goes to you.

I hope you will find it a true Summer Comedy — a true comedy in Romance.

With George Meredith I believe that "comic romance is about us everywhere, alive for the tapping". It has, I think, verve and "go" from first to last, with, as a good friend and critic says, "a note of sunny laughter throughout."

I estimate it to be equivalent to a volume of about 65,000 words. (actual close estimate, *without* same allowances, 63,700)

For sub-title, how do you like

(1) A Summer Comedy

(2) A Comedy in Romance

(3) A Midsummer Month's Dream.

The first, I fancy? I hope, and believe, you will be able to do well with the book. It ought to sell particularly well in June and throughout the summer months — with the "yachting fever" in full swing.

By the next mail (that of Wedny next, 18th) I shall post you the duplicate — *with final revisions in red ink.* These can thus easily be transferred. I have had to send this copy without my final glance through, though gone over carefully by my copyist and revisionist.

So far as America is concerned, *this will obviate you sending proofs.* (Let me, however, have duplicate *page*-proofs, for my own satisfaction — not to send back to you.) I do not know what arrangements you have made, or are going to make in this country. If possible, I had better see proofs *here*, of course.

But the book is now yours to deal with as you see fit — as the young lady said to Don Juan. Its fortune is on the knees of the Gods.

In your agreement-letter of 4th July — and in another note about same date — (from the Portland Hotel) — you undertake that £100 will be paid in receipt of MS.

I am going to ask you my dear Herbert, not to delay an unnecessary mail with this — and for this reason: I have, as soon as it comes, to go & meet *my* Wife in Exile!

The doctor forbids her return meanwhile — and she is fretting at this long separation of ours. I have arranged to go abroad to Venice, & bring her home by sea, towards the end of April. All her & my plans, however, are dependent upon this advance of £100.

So, remember the happiness of a Wife in Exile and a Husband at a Distance — to say nothing of your written vow before God! — !

Ever yours affectly | William Sharp

ALS Huntington Library

To the Editor, Blackwood's Magazine, March 21, 1896[46]

9. Upper Coltbridge Terrace | Murrayfield

Dear Sir

If possible would you let me have an answer soon about my story "Morag of the Glen" — as Mr. Bacheller,[47] whom I have sold the American serial rights, would like to know when the story is to be issued in this country.

Yours faithfully | Fiona Macleod.

To the Editor, Blackwood's Magazine.

ACS National Library of Scotland

To Herbert Stuart Stone, [mid-March, 1896]

My dear Herbert,

Just time for a hurried line by this mail to say that the last "Gypsy Christs" have now come to hand!

The book looks well. I hope it goes well.

I have been so infernally unwell that I have been unable to do any pen work for 3 days — but now I am by the sea (Hastings) and am all right or nearly so. I can't now send out the revised type-pages of *Wives in Exile* till next mail — but from a glance thro' them I see my copyist has not been careful, & that there are many annoying slips and misreadings. These can be put right from my amended copy by next mail. I suppose you are setting up at once.

In great haste | Yours ever | Will

ALS Huntington Library

To Herbert Stuart Stone, [mid-March, 1896]

Rutland House | Greencroft Gardens | So. Hampstead

My dear Herbert,

I write from Hastings — where I still am, recruiting.[48]

Herewith the duplicate of the first 10 Chaps. of *Wives in Exile* overlooked by me.

Still, I do hope I shall have proofs if possible — especially of English issue. (Would you not try A. Constable & Co. first?)

I must send out names for the chaps by next post — with remaining revised chaps.

The long fourth Chap should be divided: I forget if set sent out *is* so divided. I have put it here at bottom p. 66.

My typist has massacred many words. I am correspondingly anxious.

Meanwhile, please see to such alterations as have been made. In extreme haste for the post –

Ever yours | Will

Let me know soon about the Le Gallienne proposal:[49] and *don't forget about my advance cheque like an angel!*

ALS Huntington Library

To Catherine Ann Janvier, April/May, 1896

[Catherine Janvier quoted portions of two Sharp letters to her of April/ May, 1896, in an article about Sharp which appeared in 1907 ("Fiona Macleod and Her Creator William Sharp," *North American Review*, 184/612 (April, 1907), 718–32). Sharp dedicated Fiona Macleod's *Washer of the Ford* to Mrs. Janvier and wrote a Prologue for the volume titled "To Kathia."[50] In April he sent Mrs. Janvier a copy of the book and wrote in an accompanying letter: "If a book can have a soul that book has one." Somewhat later, he sent her a bound copy of the Prologue and told her in an accompanying letter the Prologue had been "materially improved and strengthened and largely added to."[51]]

To Herbert Stuart Stone, April 4, 1896

9 Up. Coltbridge Terrace | Murrayfield, Midlothian, | April 4, 1896.

Dear Mr. Stone,

Herewith I send you the opening pages of "*The Washer of the Ford*" to go on with. The book is the same size as *The Sin-Eater*.

The remainder of the first half of the book will go by next mail, and the rest of the volume complete by the mail thereafter. The Edinburgh printers (Messrs. W. H. White & Co.) are now setting up the book. A duplicate set of revises shall be sent to you when the other is returned to them — so as to save time, and to obviate proofs.

Messrs. Patrick Geddes & Co. have consented to wait if necessary until May 9th for publication. Will this suit you? They are willing to oblige you and me but will not delay publication beyond the 15th of May on any account whatever — and even the 9th (the date fixed for publication) is 9 days later than they wished.[52]

If it is the case that rough sheets of a book — or even part of a book — can be bound in any way, and so nominally be sold and thus entitled to copyright — I wish you would kindly see to this in the case of *"The Washer of the Ford"*. In this case, you might enable Messrs. P.G. & Co. to issue on May 1st. as they urgently wish to do. My illness has prevented my having the book ready earlier. Another time I shall not thus inconvenience you and them.

Herewith I enclose printed list of contents: and some printed press opinions.

In haste,

Yours sincerely, | Fiona Macleod.

Excuse a dictated note. I am on a brief visit to London, and have to save myself from all unnecessary writing at present.

By the way, I suppose I may soon expect a remittance on account of *The Sin-Eater?*

F. M.

TL Huntington Library

To Elizabeth Sharp, [early April, 1896]

... I know you will rejoice to hear that there can be no question that F. M.'s deepest and finest work is in this *"Washer of the Ford"* volume. As for the spiritual lesson that nature has taught me, and that has grown within me otherwise, I have given the finest utterance to it that I can. In a sense my inner life of the spirit is concentrated in the three pieces "The Moon-Child", "The Fisher of Men", and "The Last

Supper". Than the last I shall never do anything better. Apart from this intense summer flame that has been burning within me so strangely and deeply of late — I think my most imaginative work will be found in the titular piece "The Washer of the Ford," which still, tho' written and revised some time ago, haunts me! and in that and the pagan and animistic "Annir Choille". We shall read those things in a gondola in Venice? ...

Memoir, p. 263

To Mrs. James Ashcroft Noble, [April 8?, 1896][53]

6 Patten Road | Wordsworth Common | London SW

My dear Mrs. Noble,

It is with a shock of profound pain and regret that I have just heard of the terrible loss you have sustained. I had no idea that so tragic an ending to a beautiful life was so imminent — and it is piteous that such long and heroic endurance of weakness and pain should not have sustained for a far longer span of life the suffering body that held so fine a spirit.

Mr. Noble must have endeared himself to many whom he did not know personally. For myself I mourn that so true and fine a writer, so generous and sympathetic a critic, has gone into the silence — to use the tender island idiom. But he will live in the minds and hearts of those whom he has helped and encouraged, and be an unknown sweet influence in the lives of hundreds who read his writings signed and unsigned.[54] ~~For you and your daughters, in your great grief, I can find no adequate words. But you have my heartfelt sympathy in your great and terrible loss. Were there time I should send a wreath of laurel and yellow flowers of spring — for him who deserved the one and would understand the exquisite symbolism of the other.~~

To those who like myself do not believe that the soul falls short of its high destiny in the mind and this heart, death is terrible only for the loved ones who have to bear the loss. The others are free of evil things, and move in light

Forgive so slight an expression of what I feel about the true-hearted sweet-souled man who has left us,[55] ~~and left you, and those whom he loved. Once again my deepest sympathy with you and your daughters~~. It is well to remember that he left you on the morning of Good Friday[56] — a day full of the wonder and mystery of earthly death and immortal rebirth.

Believe me, | dear Mrs. Noble, | in the Kinship of sorrow, |
Fiona Macleod

ALS National Library of Scotland

To Patrick Geddes, [*April 9, 1896*]

Thursday Night

My dear old Chap

I do not want to worry you about the enclosed — but alas I have no option.

What I have on hand will just carry me on till the end of the month (or rather till about the 25th or 20th, for some unexpected things always turn up). I had of course calculated on the promise to receive half this managerial £50 in March, & the second half early in April.

Fiona has been giving all her best thought & energies to "The Washer of the Ford" — which is the deepest & best thing she has done — but with disastrous results financially.

To keep to the urgency point. It is absolutely necessary I must have £100 within the next month — and next thing to necessary that I have it by or rather a few days before the end of April.

I must pay the deferred Quarter's Rent before I leave, & must leave a few pounds for the servant & other household expenses: Then I have also to send Elizabeth from £15 to £20 for this month. Finally, I go abroad on the 1st of May if possible — not only to join E., who is forbidden to return till June, but, alas, because I have come to the end of my tether. It is no longer a case of an *advisable* complete rest & change — but of that being *imperative*. In a word, if I don't take from a month to six weeks' cessation from all work & worry, & don't have the change of climate & scene I seem to need (tho' I don't take all the doctor says as quite so urgent as he makes it — though of course he *may* be right) — if I don't have this break, and at the earliest moment practicable, "both head & heart will give way." The doctor was so seriously put out at the startling loss in vitality that he threatened to write to Elizabeth if I did not at once promise on my word of honour that I would check this rapid retrogression in (as he says) the only feasible way. I am forbidden even to travel far at a time, & am to have no night traveling, & none that is continuous beyond a day. It will be at least a week or 10 days after I leave Paris before E. & I meet — as I am told to go by the Riviera, & stay somewhere 3 or 4 days on the way, at least — This for the head. So, after I leave Paris, my pen must rest till mid-June & weary head and "down" body must recuperate *at all hazards*.

It is the *least* menace, that unless I am markedly better by mid-June I shall be ordered away for a long sea-voyage & to do no work for a year!

I trouble you with all this to let you see how urgent the matter is.

First then, à propos of Ross's letter:[57] Can you send me a (managerial) cheque for £50 within the next week — and promise that without fail the "Washer of the Ford" £50 shall be sent to Miss F. M. by May 15th? The book is to be published by the 10th at latest, possibly earlier.

If so, I can manage thus — by getting the consent of the Manager of my Bank to a temporary overdraft at. the beginning of May.

It would be worse than useless for me to go away — to do nothing, & have perforce to incur such heavy & continuous expenses for Elizabeth & myself — unless I can do so with a free mind. I find the strain of anxiety, as it is, telling upon me badly.

With what I have told you you will see that there is not overmuch of even the £100 left for ease of mind & recovery of health — though my anxieties should be at an end by mid-summer if only my American publishers don't prevaricate or in any way play a false game. I know of only one place where I can borrow meanwhile, & that to be avoided if possible: tho' I expect I'll have to do it by June — though perhaps the friends overseas will keep to their undertaking, in which case I'll be able to breathe more freely than I have done for long. I have to keep all these worries from E — who is still so far from being robust again, & who knows (without knowing fully) how absolutely imperative it is that I lay down the reins for awhile.

If I had anything to draw against I would not be so exigent (tho' as you know, in like instances, according to the letter of our Agreements, the payments are, or will shortly be, due) — but all I have in the World is the £100 invested in "The Town & Gown Association"[58] — which reminds me that you have never sent me the promised share Certificates or Warrants — or whatever they are called.

I heard an elderly merchant-friend say the other day that if he only had £2000 it would not only save his credit but prolong his life. I feel inclined to say the same thing, on the more modest scale of £200. *That* would be a very big stitch in time, indeed: but alas, the moon does not come to one because one cries for it.

And now, can you manage that £50 next week, & £50 on May 15th? (The rest I can manage to get some way or other when needed, *if* needed.)

Forgive me that I so press the point. I will say no more if it is to entail actual loss or serious worry upon you and Anna. I love you both too much for that. In that case, I suppose I must simply have my "Town and Gown" £100 back, and have the other sums a little later. What a d——d—d—d —d nuisance these money-difficulties are.

It is now 1.30 a.m. but I found I could not sleep till I had written — for Ross's note came by last post: & as I was writing was not sent to me till midnight.

I hope to return restored in mind & body. There is a kind of grim relief in knowing I cannot go on as I am. Well, a good many things depend on recuperation — & recuperate I *must*. If you shd. happen to be writing do not tell Barclay[59] or anyone that I shall be passing thro' Paris — for I wish to *see no one*.

I do hope you are keeping well — & that things prosper. My love to Anna (to whom I owe a letter, & shall write soon). In the next 3 weeks I have to squeeze enough work in to make a *cauldron* boil: — but that is to live on when we come back.

Ever, Phadrine no Charaid Sileas,

Your friend affectionately, | William Sharp

ALS National Library of Scotland

To Herbert Stuart Stone, April 11, 1896

Rutland House | Greencroft Gardens | So. Hampstead | 11/4/96

My dear Herbert,

You will have received my cablegram which I sent to you yesterday, after receipt of your letter. It was to urge you not to delay longer than inevitable with the first remittance on a/c *Wives in Exile*. Unfortunately I have not been well, & the doctor commands immediate cessation from work, & complete rest & change for at least six weeks. I am to go abroad as soon as possible, & join my wife — who, I regret to say, is still not well enough to be allowed home till mid-June.

I am unable to get away until that money comes, though if I were quite certain of its receipt by the end of April or beginning of May, I would raise a loan meanwhile & so get away. I would not have bothered you, but for the great urgency involved.

I called yesterday on Mr. McClure. I have advised him to submit "Wives in Exile" first to Archibald Constable & Co. when once he has recd. the sheets from you.[60] I shall call on them first myself.

I have discovered that the chief reason (apart from trade reasons as to being late in the season) — for the refusal to have "The Gypsy Christ" was the initial story. Mudie & Co absolutely taboo any story involving possible religious offence — so I am told.

Are you coming over this Summer? I hope soon to be all right again. Possibly this going away may prove the stitch in time to save the fatal number.

Affectionately your friend, | William Sharp

I'll send the Le Gallienne article after June.[61] His "Quest of The Golden Girl"[62] is not to be out now till September. The "Gypsy Christ" original package has been traced at last by the G.P.C. It was wrongly addressed, and has been found unclaimed in Scotland! As I have since received the second set sent, shall I return these earlier copies to you?

ALS Huntington Library

To [John Ross], [April 27, 1896]

... and "Ecce Puella".[63]

II. With regard to our firm's indebtedness for work to be delivered (and apart from bills due for White and Co. and Mr. Wilson), there is not much. There is £50. payable to Miss Macleod on the 15th of May, and either that sum or £25. due to Mr. Stuart-Glennie[64] when he forwards his copy of "Arthurian Scotland" — which he has not done despite his exigency beforehand. As to whether this amount is to be payable directly by the firm, or by Mr. Geddes himself as a personal advance (as I infer from one of Mr. Stuart-Glennie's letters) I leave you to discover from P.G. Then there will be £50 due on my "Ossian",[65] when that is ready, which will be sometime in July. There will be nothing else for Summer payments; and, so far as I am concerned, I have made no binding arrangements with any one, save Mrs. Wingate Rinder, who is to have an advance upon her "Shadow of Arvor," and Miss Macleod for "Ossian Retold." But these are matters for Autumn consideration. By special arrangement Mrs. Rinder is to have two guineas (£2-2-0) for Evergreen contribution, Miss Nora Hopper (£1-1-0).[66]

I hope the Company matters prosper. Perhaps you will kindly drop me a line as to how things go. Naturally, I am much handicapped at present — discussing literary prospects for the firm when I am in the dark as to what means may be at my disposal.

Some time ago, when you sent Miss Rea a cheque for £8:6:8, she drew your attention to the fact that £3:6:8 of this was not due to her while she was my guest. She consulted me on the matter, and I advised her to pass the said sum £3:6:8 over to current office expenses, postages etc., which she has done, and of which she has kept an account. As her next salary is not due until the 17th of May, and she leaves London to return to Edinburgh on or about the 5th of May, will you kindly remit to her a cheque for her traveling expenses: say £2?

I am returning Mr. Eyre-Todd's[67] MSS, as we are at present quite unable to undertake any work, however good of its kind, that does not open up a prospect of repaying us with some surety for outlay, and even if his book were well received, it is in the least degree unlikely that it would pay expenses. To save you the trouble, I shall have these

MSS. returned with a suitable letter direct to Mr. Eyre-Todd, as from the firm.

Yours very truly, | William Sharp

P.S. In case I forget, please note that when due Miss Fiona Macleod's cheque is to be crossed "National and Provincial Bank, Piccadilly Branch," and is to be sent to her C/o Frank Rinder Esq | 7 Kensington Court Gardens | *London* W.

ALS National Library of Scotland

To Herbert Stuart Stone, May 4, 1896

Rutland House, | Greencroft Gardens, | South Hampstead. | London | Saturday 4th May

My dear Sir,

If, when I wrote to you expostulatingly exactly a month ago today, I was then more than merely surprised and annoyed at the extraordinary delay in hearing from you concerning the matters about which you were to write to me, and in many weeks past-promised receipt of my MS. of "The Gypsy Christ" & Proofs — you may perhaps imagine how I regard the matter now: — now that you have had time to receive and answer that letter sent to you on April 4th.

I am utterly at a loss to understand this most unbusinesslike and apparently grossly discourteous conduct.

I understand that the same inexplicable attitude has been taken by you towards Miss Macleod. You seem anxious to alienate not only Miss Macleod & myself but others here.

When I wrote this day last month I felt certain a letter from you would cross my letter. Surely, the most ordinary courtesy will bring me an apology and explanation before this reaches you by mid-May: but, if you have not written, I must formally request *an immediate and absolutely explicit explanation and statement* from you.

For a time I thought illness might be the cause: but that would not excuse such prolonged silence, for you have a partner.

Hurt as I am, I am doubly annoyed by your conduct to Miss Macleod, as I am responsible for having urged her to write to you. She has lost time & money through your inexplicable negligence, and, I understand, will send you a formal legal communication as to the breaking of her contract with you, & possibly on another matter if she does not hear from you satisfactorily by the end of May.

Yours truly, | William Sharp

ALS New York Public Library, Berg Collection

To Robert Murray Gilchrist, [May 6, 1896][68]

Monte Carlo

Just a line to say that the friends about whom I wrote to you are here, & that *possibly* all may yet go well, at any rate for a time. Indeed, one of them told me nothing wd. happen now till September at any rate.

It is most glorious weather here, though so hot. I went to the Gaming Tables last night, & in half an hour made £40. Shall write some days or a week later.

W. S.

ACS Sheffield City Archives

To William Butler Yeats, [May10?, 1896][69]

9. Upper Coltbridge Terrace | Murrayfield | Midlothian

Dear Sir,

Please accept from me, in return for so much pleasure, the new book of mine I have directed to be sent to you.

I hope you will find something both in the prose and verse of this volume to appeal to you.

Yours very sincerely | Fiona Macleod.

ALS Private

To William Meredith, [May 15?, 1896]

Dear Mr. Meredith[70]

Just a brief line, as I am not supposed to be writing just now. I am distinctly better, and enjoying the heat and colour immensely.

I traveled with Mr. Sharp as far as Avignon, and have now met Mrs. Sharp in Italy, where her husband will join us shortly.

My addresses are very uncertain, so I do not like to give even Venice. With this (or perhaps before it) you will receive *Green Fire*, which I hope you will like.

It will, after all, be best for me to see a final revision of the book. If there is time for me to see a final revise in page form, please send in duplicate to Miss Lillian Rea who will forward to me wherever I am, for my immediate return — if not, then please let me have (through her) duplicate first-proofs, which I shall return through her. I want, if possible, to avoid more textual revision than is necessary, because of my eyes.

Sincerely yours | Fiona Macleod

ALS University of Wisconsin–Milwaukee Library

To Robert Murray Gilchrist, [May 28, 1896][71]

Bellagio | Lake of Como

Just a line to say that I am better — & that meanwhile all goes well. I met my wife in Venice — & we came here. We shall be in England again on the 4th — tho' I shall not go to London for a few days thereafter.

Send me a line by return to Poste Restante, Bâle, Switzerland. I hope you have recd. "The W. of the Ford" & that you & Mrs. Gilchrist[72] both find in it something to care for.

My love to you.

Wearily | W.

ACS Sheffield City Archives

To _____, [late May, 1896][73]

... They are studies in old Religious Celtic sentiment so far as that can be recreated in a modern heart that feels the same beauty and simplicity of the Early Christian faith.

[William Sharp]

Memoir, p. 263

To Herbert Stuart Stone June 9, 1896

9. Upper Coltbridge Terrace | Murrayfield. | Midlothian | 9th June

Dear Sir

I cannot understand your silence. I have had no answer to my last letters (tho' long overdue) about *The Washer of the Ford*.[74] I understand, now, that the book is to be published by you today, the 10th.

Please remit me by return, if you have not already done so, the advance of £25 due on publication: and also, please, the stipulated twelve copies.

I have been in constant expectation of a remittance for the sum due on royalties on *The Sin Eater*, published last autumn.

I have so many requests for work, from America as well as from England, that I am strongly disinclined to publish further with your firm, unless I meet with more prompt courtesy and more satisfactory business relations.

Yours faithfully, | Fiona Macleod

ALS Huntington Library

To Hannibal Ingalls Kimball June 10, 1896

Rutland House | Greencroft Gardens | South Hampstead | London

My Dear Sir,

Your letter of May 22nd followed me abroad and has just been reforwarded. I have barely time to catch this mail — so must send a hurried line.

I am willing to make all allowances for confusion & delay arising through the dissolution of partnership[75] — but what I do not excuse is Mr. Stone's having apparently left you so partially informed. Besides, in *March* (30th I think) he writes that *Wives in Exile* has gone to the printers, & that duplicate proofs will be with me shortly. On the head of that I at once went to consult Mr. R. McClure, with an urgent suggestion that the first offer should be made to Messrs. Archibald Constable and Co. of 2 Whitehall Gardens.

Not a proof has ever come, & now on May 22nd you write that you are proceeding with the book as rapidly as possible.

If the proofs come I can submit them to Constable and Co. But you give no particulars of any kind, as to terms, conditions, etc.

As to my own delay, Mr. Stone was duly warned that this might be — & there was indeed an express understanding. But I must again beg you to observe the signed stipulation and agreement, that this initial payment of £100 *has nothing to do with the date of publication*, but was payable on receipt of MS. Mr. Stone guaranteed this *officially*, by a personal note, and by his word of honour.[76]

I have been very seriously inconvenienced in consequence — on account of my wife's illness abroad — and I must again ask you, as I am sure you will now readily do, honourably to fulfill your pledged undertaking.

I hope the book will be a success everyway: and that we may have many pleasant relations in the future.

Yours faithfully, | William Sharp

ALS New York Public Library, Berg Collection

To Richard Garnett, [June 14, 1896][77]

Sunday

My dear Garnett,

I was a week later than my wife in reaching home, as I stopped for a few days at Dover: hence I received your book,[78] for which I thank you most cordially, only yesterday.

It has been my companion all forenoon today, & indeed most of the afternoon as well, and has given me keen pleasure because of its beauty and poetic distinction. You seem to have a very remarkable faculty for entering not only into the heart but into the style of each author — to feel with his nerves, to see with his eyes, to imagine with his brain, and to speak with his own elect words. There is, therefore, a double pleasure in reading your book — not only to find the fine work of an English poet but that of a born interpreter — & to interpret worthily is a second creation.

If, on the whole, I have derived most pleasure from those of Camoenshat is doubtless in part because they are newer to me — & because I now feel as though I had at last read the Portuguese poet. One or two of these I find very haunting — e.g. the 28th, beginning "Sky, earth, and air are sleeping silently".[79] I wonder, by the way, if I have ever told you that my favorite verse by any modern poet is the lovely quatrain by yourself

> Seclusion, quiet, silence, slumber, dreams,
>
> No murmur of a breath;
>
> The same still image on the same still streams
>
> of Love caressing Death.

Forgive me if these lines are not quite correct, as I quote from memory.

I am afraid it may now be too late for me to get the book for the *Academy*, but if I can I will.

> With cordial regards | Sincerely Yours | William Sharp

ALS University of Texas, Austin

To Patrick Geddes, [June 20?, 1896][80]

> Rutland House | *Saturday.*

Dear Patrick

How nice of you to send me so friendly a welcome home! I have come back refreshed indeed — stronger & better than I have been for years. It is a new & delightful sensation. I look forward to the strong Scottish air to put the finishing touches, this autumn. I wish my Poet were half as well. He met me at Venice, so weak & feeble I was very alarmed. He had long fainting fits which at first I thought were heart attacks. As soon as I got home I summoned the doctor. He told me that Will has so greatly overworked that he had reduced himself to a dangerous point of weakness; that the danger to be avoided is heart failure. He is a little better again, but not strong enough to take the journey from London to Edinburgh without a break. Had I known he was in this state I would never have consented to his going to Venice. We had to take the journey home in short breaks & even then, his fatigue was distressing to see.

It is very good of you to ask us both to your seaside Cottage, but I cannot come north just now; & it is better Will should add nothing to his journey to and fro — besides he requires to be near Edinburgh — And now I am going to ask you a favour; and that is not to allow him — when you see him — to discuss business matters for any length of time at one sitting. He needs all his time and strength to get well –

Each Spring he grows worse — & I can see that if he works at the present speed, & with the present complications, he will not see many more Springs. The dual work of F. M. and W. S. is a great drain on his strength, at the present moment too great a drain; & his state at present is unsatisfactory.

With regard to your second kind proposal which is very seductive (only *I* should bid for the post of under-gardener!) it, too, alack! must regretfully be refused. For, I cannot get away till about the end of July. I have taken up my *Herald* work again & must stick to it till the end of the summer.[81]

I look forward with so much pleasure to seeing Anna and you in August — for we shall be at Petticur for part of that month in any case, I think. And then I shall run in and out of Edinburgh to see & hear what is going on.

I do hope you, too, are resting a little! I know you usually consider the Dundee term a time of partial rest and recuperation and I feel sure you need it greatly before the arduous work of the Summer Meeting begins. Please give my love to Anna and the Godson[82] & to his father.

Cordially yours | Elizabeth A. Sharp

I have forwarded your note to Fiona to Petticur.[83]

ALS National Library of Scotland

To Patrick Geddes June 22, 1896[84]

Patrick Geddes and Colleagues | Lawnmarket | Edinburgh |
June 22, 1896

In re Dr. Croll.

My dear Geddes,

I am at a loss what to write to Mr. Campbell Irons: and for the following reasons:

I. Are we to publish the book on our own account, or simply as agents for Mr. Irons?[85] It is being set up, I see, by Morrison & Gibb, and I presume, from what you told me before, at Mr. Irons' expense.

II. If we are to be the publishers, why is there any need to bring Fisher Unwin's name into the matter? It is not customary to have two British publishers' names on a book.

III. Would it not be a better plan for our firm to publish the book for Mr. Campbell Irons in Scotland, for Mr. Unwin to act as English distributor, and, if possible, to arrange with Stone & Kimball or elsewhere in America? At present I am quite in the dark as to what actual negotiations have taken place.

By no possibility can this book of 400 pages pay expenses — since it is not to be brought out by private subscription: really the only suitable way for a book of this kind. Even if Croll were far more commanding a personality, any book about him written as Mr. Irons' is, would be heavily handicapped. You will gather my opinion of the book when I say that it is with extreme regret that I think our firm should issue anything so incapable and amateurish. Almost every sin possible to the Biographer is committed, with a promiscuity which is literally offensive! Excuse such plain speaking of one who is, I understand, a friend of yours; but here, of course, I am writing simply as a critic. If you have a copy of the proofs, read the first five or six pages of Mr. Irons' biographical introduction, and I am sure you will realise the hopeless ineptitude of his matter.

However, if a definite pledge has been given to Mr. Campbell Irons I presume there is nothing for it but for P.G. & Coll. to issue this ugly duckling. It may well be that you are a better judge of the likelihood of the success of such a book as this, at any rate with the scientific world; but the question is, is it meant for the scientific world, or for the general reader? If for the latter, it is foredoomed.

But now about what I am to write to Mr. Irons. He says that he understands that you propose to publish in England through Mr. Fisher Unwin. Kindly advise me as to what definite proposal of the kind you *have* made. As to America, there is now no possibility of issue this summer — even if, as seems to me incredible, any firm would take up the book for separate issue there. The very most we could expect is that some firm would take a certain number of copies on sale. It would, I know, be useless to apply to Mr. Kimball (Stone & Kimball dissolved), as his firm publishes no books of this nature. Probably the best publishers to apply to, owing to their scientific connection, would be Messrs. Appleton. We can, of course, write there, but before doing so I must know on what terms we are publishing the book, and what conditions and terms we can grant to our American agents, whoever they may be.

Again, are we to bind the book, or is it to be bound by Mr. Irons himself? and what about expense of distribution and advertisement? Are we to undertake these on commission, or are they his affair? His letter and yours alike leave me quite in the dark on these important details. Meanwhile, I refrain from sending him more than a mere acknowledgement. Please let me hear from you at your earliest convenience.

Yours faithfully, | William Sharp | per L.H.R.

Pettycur House, | Kinghorn, Fife.

TL National Library of Scotland

To Herbert Stuart Stone, June 24, 1896

9 Upper Coltbridge Terrace, | Murrayfield, Midlothian, |
June 24, 1896.

Dear Sir,

I have received your statement as to additional sales of "The Sin-Eater",
and note that you have credited the small amount in question to me. You
will, however, have by this time received my letter asking you to remit
me by return the amount already due to me upon that book, as also the
sum due on "The Washer of the Ford" on the day of publication.

I am hoping the last-named is in the same bind etc. as its predecessor,
for I like the Carnation Series format much better than that of the Green
Tree. In my note I asked you kindly to let me have the promised copies
as soon as ready.

In haste for this mail,

Yours very truly, | FIONA MACLEOD.

TL Huntington Library

To Patrick Geddes, June 30, 1896[86]

Patrick Geddes & Colleagues | Lawnmarket, Edinburgh |
June 30, 1896

My dear Geddes,

As I shall be leaving Pettycur immediately in any case, and probably going
south on Thursday or Friday at latest, you need not reply to this here.

Herewith I send you a letter which Mdme. Janvier asks me to read
and forward to you. After you have read it, consider the advantage of
a paper from her for the *Evergreen* — say Provençal and other southern
Celtic points of affinity with North Celtic folklore and customs.[87]

By the way excuse that the last page of her letter is copied — but the remaining page and a half belong to a letter intended for myself Perhaps when you have read it, you will let me peruse it, as I have not had time to do so — or let Miss Rea make a copy of it.

In accordance with your wish — and with my own concurrence—"Lyric Runes" will not now be published until the Autumn. So that the only two books we shall be issuing this next quarter will be the Ossian in July, and "The Shadow of Arvor" in September.

A propos, it will, of course, be absolutely necessary to spend a certain sum in advertisement. The best way will be to do so on a limited scale sufficient to give the books that preliminary start-off which is absolutely essential. The main question of advertisement we shall leave over, as agreed, for final settlement next year. Meanwhile I shall endeavour to make peace with our sole three authors, Mrs. William Sharp, Miss Fiona Macleod, and Mr. Ernest Rhys, each of whom will naturally regard the suspension of all advertisement pro tem with dismay.

However, that is a matter into which we need not enter again just now.

With regard to the "Ossian" I find that a contract concerning this book was drawn up between us at the time of arrangement. I find also that the "Lyre Celtica" duplicate agreement has not been signed — that is the duplicate on the part of the firm.

As I shall not now have time to call on Arthur Thomson this visit, will you kindly see him at your convenience, after your return, and discuss with him (1) The Natural History of Woman project; (2) If he can be preparing for issue next year the "Three Fates" volume — or, if preferred, the more popular and remunerative "Romance of Ornithology" the title and, so to say, good will of which I will so gladly hand over to him.[88] Also, what about Miss Marion Newbiggin?[89] (3) You spoke to me about my own "Critical Essays." I can say nothing about these meanwhile. My idea is not to reprint any of these past essays of mine intact, even the best of them (Concentrations of books on Heine, Browning etc.[90]); but rather in three long essays or addresses to give the gist of my best writing and later thought, and this throughout the three following essays, which would really sum up the essential part of what I have to say:

THE LITERARY IDEAL

LIFE AND LITERATURE

INTRODUCTION TO THE STUDY OF CELTIC LITERATURE[91]

These three being each of considerable length, would make a good volume, to be published under the title "The Literary Idea."

This, however, is merely a statement as to what I think will be best to do: and, if you wish to have them next year, as you suggest, let me know in due time.

There is only one other point which needs to he alluded to just now: and that is one of necessary administration. Do you remember our contracts, or rather the clause in these contracts dealing with the matter of rendered statements? By this clause, the authors were promised a definite statement of sales and royalties to account every six months. Of course, the only omission as yet is in the instance of "The Sin-Eater" no statement of account, etc. having been sent to Miss Macleod at the expiry, in April, of the six months from date of publication, as per contract. But, of course, this should be done, and in each case, as occasion demands. I have, therefore, instructed Miss Rea to attend to this matter — another publishing item which will take up some of her time, involving as it does the gathering of complex details from White and the other distributors, as well as from Wilson, etc.

Thus, on the 15th of September, we shall have to render to Mr. Rhys an exact statement as to number of copies sold of his book. This, of course, is an instance where Miss Rea can take over from me detail work of a kind that I could not myself adequately fulfill from London.

I have written to Mr. Yeats to tell him that while we are in complete sympathy with him in his project, we cannot take up the book. Of course, I have not been so curt as this — as you can see any time you glance over the firm letters kept by Miss Rea.

The Standish O'Grady idea must also lapse on account of expenses involved. The same reason, I think, should at present militate strongly against your idea of the Universities of Scotland volume.

There is decidedly comfort in the maxims from Montrose, Solomon, P.G., and other prophets. They were and are a bad lot, but I suppose one must still believe in them.

Yours ever, | WILLIAM SHARP | L.H.R.

TL National Library of Scotland

Chapter Fifteen

Life: July–December, 1896

Less than three weeks after Sharp returned to London from Edinburgh in early July, he and Elizabeth left for a long summer holiday in the north. Before leaving, Sharp asked his friend Murray Gilchrist to join them for a few days on the Northumberland coast. In mid-letter, he changed course and asked Gilchrist if it would be convenient for him and Elizabeth to spend a few days with Gilchrist's mother at Cartledge, her home in Derbyshire. Neither alternative materialized. They spent the night of July 20 at the Station Hotel in York and went on to Bamborough, a coastal village in Northumberland. After a week of "sea bathing," as Elizabeth described it, they crossed to "the little Holy Isle of the Eastern Shores, Lindisfarne, Iona's sister." During the years he was writing as Fiona Macleod, Elizabeth noted, her husband "was usually in a highly wrought condition of restlessness, so that he could not long remain contentedly anywhere" (*Memoir*, p. 266). After two weeks on Lindisfarne, they went to Edinburgh, and, after a few days there, left for Dunoon, a seaside resort town on the Firth of Clyde west of Glasgow, to be near Sharp's mother and sisters who were there on holiday.

In Bamborough, in late July, Sharp wrote a long letter to John Macleay of *The Highland News* in which he tried to dispel rumors he was Fiona.

> I confess I share to some degree in Miss Macleod's annoyance in this persistent disbelief in her personality to which you allude — as, indeed, to some extent in her resentment against the impertinence of those persons who try to intrude upon her privacy or seek to ascertain what for good reasons of her own she does not wish made public. [...] Did you not see the explicit statement I caused to be inserted in the "Glasgow Evening News," & elsewhere (because of one of these perverse misstatements) to the effect that "Miss Fiona Macleod is not Mr. William Sharp; Miss

    https://doi.org/10.11647/OBP.0196.04

Fiona Macleod is not Mrs. William Sharp; and that Miss Fiona Macleod is — Miss Fiona Macleod." Surely that ought to have settled the matter: for it is scarcely likely, I imagine, that I should put forth so explicit a statement were it not literally true. I trust, therefore, that you will do your best at any time to counteract all other misstatements.

Near the close of this letter, Sharp mentioned that he might be able to go north to Inverness in early October and, if so, he "might perhaps say something on, say, 'The Celtic Spirit.'" Macleay took that possibility seriously and informed Sharp he was working with others to find a venue for Sharp's lecture, which would be welcomed by many in Inverness. In Edinburgh, on his way to Dunoon, Sharp quashed the idea in a letter to Macleay. He said he had received a letter from his doctor forbidding him from lecturing "on any condition whatever, this year at any rate." Sharp thanked Macleay and others who would have given him a friendly welcome, and asked to defer his address till the spring, or even the autumn, when Inverness would host the Mod, a large annual gathering of Celtic enthusiasts which still moves from city to city in Scotland.

When Sharp arrived in Dunoon on August 15, he saw the August 14 issue of *The Highland News*, which contained a lead article by John Macleay titled "Mystery! Mystery! All in a Celtic Haze." Hoping to attract attention and increase readership and disregarding Sharp's assertions, Macleay described an article in *The Glasgow Evening News* that asserted Fiona Macleod was William Sharp. This unexpected development produced a flurry of letters from Sharp to Macleay during the next week — nearly one per day — in which he indignantly denied he was Fiona and tried, with expressions of camaraderie and implied threats of legal action, to dissuade Macleay from pursuing the issue further. Intended as an interlude of rest and relaxation, the visit with his family in Dunoon turned stressful as Sharp worried Macleay was intent on discovering and broadcasting the truth. He summoned all his verbal skills in a hasty effort to preserve the fiction and thus prevent both embarrassment and erosion of his income. He had received a letter from Fiona which expressed "deep resentment" against the writers of *The Glasgow Evening News*. She was especially insulted by the cruel & inexcusable phrase: "I hear again & again that she is a greater fraud than Macpherson of Ossianic fame." She would "ignore all unwarrantable interference, conjecture, & paragraphic impertinence." Macleay's initial praise of the Fiona writings and support for the cause of Scottish Celticism was a welcome stimulus for the sale of the Fiona books in Scotland. Now Macleay's pursuit of Fiona's identity, unless handled properly, threatened a public debacle. By the end of the week, Sharp had derailed Macleay's probes and decided that even this conflict had the beneficial effect of focusing more attention on Fiona and her writings.

On Saturday, August 22, the Sharps took his mother to Edinburgh, stayed for only two days, and left again on Monday with Sharp's sister Mary for Tigh-Na-Bruaich, a small village west of Glasgow on the Kyles of Bute. From there, in early September, William and Elizabeth paid a brief visit to Inverness, where they met Macleay, and went on to see the Falls of Lora. In mid-September, Elizabeth returned to London and her work as art reviewer for the *Glasgow Herald*. William and his sister took the ferry across Loch Fyne to Tarbert where Edith and Frank Rinder were vacationing. Elizabeth reproduced (*Memoir*, pp. 166–67) a section of a letter Sharp wrote to her from Tigh-Na-Bruaich, and sections of two letters he wrote from Tarbert, one on September 23 and one on September 26. His writing was going well, but he was not well enough to carry out his plan to go off by himself in the Hebrides.

Sharp found it easier to write as Fiona Macleod when Edith Rinder was nearby, and a burst of creativity in Tarbert produced many pseudonymous stories, poems, and letters. On September 23 he told Elizabeth in a letter he had written "the long-awaited 'Rune of the Passion of Women' the companion piece in a sense to the 'Chant of Women' in *Pharais*." On September 26 he said he had finished what had stirred him "so unspeakably, namely the third and concluding 'Rune of the Sorrow of Women.'" That rune, he said, had tired him "in the preliminary excitement and in the strange semi-conscious fever of composition." All three runes appeared in *From the Hills of Dream* where he said he did not use the word "Rune" in "its ancient or exact significance, but rather as a suitable analogue for "Chant." Occasionally, he wrote, they have "something of the significance of the old Ru'n, meaning a mystery, or the more or less occult expression of mystery." The three runes express in detail the travails of women who suffer at the hands of men. Recalling Sharp's early poem called "Motherhood," they focus particularly on the burden of bearing children and then being cast aside for younger women. The runes deserve attention for the varied nuances of Sharp's critique of the repression of women. Equally interesting is his description of the composition process in his letter to Elizabeth:

> In a vague way not only you, Mona, Edith and others swam into my brain, but I have never so absolutely felt the woman-soul within me: it was as though in some subtle way the soul of Woman breathed into my brain — and I feel vaguely as if I had given partial expression at least to the inarticulate voice of a myriad women who suffer in one or other of the triple ways of sorrow.

Images of breath entering the brain aside, Sharp felt like he was a woman when he wrote as Fiona Macleod, but his propensity to identify with women began long before he began to write and publish as a woman. Like Mona Caird, Sharp was a strong advocate for the rights of women. He projected himself into the minds of three women he knew well (Elizabeth, Mona, and especially Edith), identified qualities he shared with them, and coalesced those qualities into a fourth woman he introduced to the world as Fiona Macleod who was, herself, an advocate of women's rights.

A letter he wrote to W. B. Yeats from Tarbert exemplified his effort to project that woman, and it also opened a lengthy and complicated relationship between the Irish poet and Sharp, as himself and as Fiona. In an August 25 letter to Sharp from Tillyra Castle, Edward Martin's home in western Ireland, Yeats described a recent vision:

> I invoked one night the spirits of the moon & and saw between sleep & waking a beautiful woman firing an arrow among the stars. That night she appeared to [Arthur] Symons who is staying here, & so impressed him that he wrote a poem to her, the only one he ever wrote to a dream, calling her the fountain of all song or some such phrase. She was the symbolic Diana (*Collected Letters II*, pp. 47–49).

A letter Yeats wrote to Fiona the previous day has not surfaced, but it also described his archer vision. At Tarbert in mid-September Sharp composed Fiona's response, which began with an apology for "unforeseen circumstances" that prevented her from writing sooner. She began a letter earlier, before receiving Yeats's August letter, which described her archer vision, but

> Alas, a long pencilled note (partly apropos of your vision of the woman shooting arrows, and of the strange coincidence of something of the same kind on my own part) has long since been devoured by a too voracious or too trustful gull — for a sudden gust of wind blew the quarto-sheet from off the deck of the small yacht wherein I and my dear friend and confrère of whom you know were sailing, off Skye.

Sharp's goal was to convince Yeats of Fiona's visionary compacity, and he made further use of the archer vision by tacking it to the end of a Fiona story he had finished earlier called "The Last Fantasy of James Achanna."

Fig. 8. William Butler Yeats (1865–1939). Photograph by Alice Boughton (1903), Wikimedia, Public Domain, https://commons.wikimedia.org/wiki/File: Yeats_Boughton.jpg#/media/File:Yeats_Boughton.jpg

The story begins in the authorial voice of Fiona, who says she will tell a story she heard from a fisherman named Coll McColl. In the story, a woman who is married falls in love with another man but finally chooses to remain with her husband. It would kill him to choose otherwise, and, not surprisingly, the body of the spurned lover is found several days later. To this depressing story he attached two archer visions, and changed the name of the story to "The Archer." On the night the dead body was found, Coll McColl saw "a tall shadowy woman" draw "a great bow" and shoot an arrow through the air, which pierced the heart of a fawn. He believes "the fawn was the poor suffering heart of Love" (or the spurned lover) and the "Archer was the great Shadowy Archer that hunts among the stars." The next night, Coll saw a woman "shooting arrow after arrow against the stars." Encouraged by Yeats, Arthur Symons, editor of *The Savoy*, had asked Fiona to submit a story for publication. Sharp told Elizabeth in a letter of September 23 that he had "done the *Savoy* story 'The Archer' (about 4,500 words)," and shortly thereafter he sent it to *The Savoy*. Symons was staying with Yeats at Edward Martin's Tillyra Castle in late August and September, and he too had a dream about an archer shooting arrows at the sun. It was so vivid he composed a poem about it. Sharp assumed correctly Symons would mention Fiona's archer story to Yeats when they returned to London in early October. Yeats decided Fiona could not have heard about his vision before she wrote "The Archer," and that was enough to convince him that Fiona had visionary powers.

In the last paragraph of the Fiona letter to Yeats, Sharp further burnished her visionary powers by recounting yet another vision:

> I had a strange vision the other day, wherein I saw the figure of a gigantic woman sleeping on the green hills of Ireland. As I watched, the sun waned, and the dark came, and the stars began to fall. They fell one by one, and each fell into the woman — and lo, of a sudden, all was wan running water, and the drowned stars and the transmuted woman passed from my seeing. This was a waking dream, an open vision.

Fiona first claims not to know what it means and then suggests a meaning:

> I realise that something of tremendous moment is being matured just now. We are on the verge of vitally important developments. And all the heart, all the brain, of the Celtic races shall be stirred. There is a shadow of mighty changes. Myself I believe that new spirits have been embodied among us. And some of the old have come back. We shall perish, you and I and all who fight under the "Lifting of the Sunbeam" — but we shall pioneer a wonderful marvelous new life for humanity.

Sharp was not only pressing Fiona's supposed visionary powers. He knew this forecast of a new life for humanity arising from the spiritualist heart of the Celtic revival in Ireland and Scotland would bring Fiona perfectly in line with Yeats's aspirations.

Sharp incorporated another stratagem in the Fiona letter. She was sailing off Skye with "my dear friend and confrère of whom you know." That good friend, clearly William Sharp, has been with her during "much sailing about and faring in remote places," and he has participated in the "work we are doing, and putting together the volume of verse." The volume of verse is *From the Hills of Dream: Mountain Songs and Island Runes* which was published in Edinburgh by Patrick Geddes and Colleagues in November 1896. When he composed the Fiona letter, Sharp and his sister Mary were in Tarbert. It is unique in that two manuscripts survive: Sharp's draft is in the National Library of Scotland, and Mary's copy (in the Fiona Macleod handwriting) is in the Beinecke Library at Yale University. In Sharp's draft, he first wrote "our" when referring to the volume of poetry, but crossed this out and replaced it with "my own book of verse." Mary copied "my own book of verse," but in the letter Yeats received, there is a caret after "my," and "(our)" is written above the line in Sharp's hand and then lightly crossed through. He was signaling his ambivalence about how much responsibility to claim for the poems themselves as well as the "putting together."

Yeats had become a friend of Sharp, but he was interested in the writings of Fiona Macleod, not those signed William Sharp. Sharp's desire for acceptance as a colleague in the Celtic Revival was frustrated since he could not claim credit for the poetry and prose fiction he was contributing to the movement. The Fiona letter was brilliantly contrived to convince Yeats he had found in Fiona a fitting companion in the Celtic cause. It also featured Sharp as an enabler of the Fiona writings, and introduced the possibility of some collaboration. Yeats accepted Fiona as a real person in his review of *From the Hills of Dream* in *The Bookman* of December 1896, and his reply in January 1897 to the September Fiona letter. Through 1896, and well into 1897, Yeats accepted the fiction Sharp had constructed. Eventually, he would tell Yeats she was not a separate person, but a secondary personality of William Sharp, who was the author of the Fiona writings.

Sharp left Tarbert on October 2, spent that night at the Caledonian Station Hotel in Glasgow, continued to Edinburgh and then to London. Before leaving Tarbert, he decided his difficulties with Stone and Kimball were such that he should go to New York to try to recover the money promised for works the firm had published or promised to publish.

He asked Murray Gilchrist to accompany him to America, both for the sake of Gilchrist's health, and for "friendship's sake." Gilchrist declined this unexpected invitation, and Sharp wrote from London on October 18 to say he wanted to see Gilchrist soon after he returned from New York in December. Also, before leaving Tarbert, Sharp wrote one of his exuberant birthday letters to E. C. Stedman, in which he announced his intention to come to New York in early November. After three weeks in London, Sharp went to Southampton on October 22 and sailed from there to New York the next day.

He arrived in New York aboard the "Augusta Victoria" of the Hamburg American line on Saturday, October 31, where he saw "the streets thronged with over two million people" in the weekend before the fiercely contested Presidential election in which the Republican Party candidate William McKinley defeated the Democratic Party candidate William Jennings Bryan. Since no business could be done until the following Wednesday, he crossed the Hudson River to spend a few days with his friend Henry Mills Alden, editor of *Harper's Magazine*. On Sunday, he described the pre-election scene to his wife:

> New York itself is at fever heat. I have never seen such a sight as yesterday. The whole enormous city was a mass of flags and innumerable Republican and Democratic insignia. The whole business quarter made a gigantic parade that took 7 hours in its passage — and the businessmen alone amounted to over 100,000. Everyone — as indeed not only America but Great Britain and all Europe — is now looking eagerly for the final word on Tuesday night (*Memoir*, pp. 174–75).

Following McKinley's defeat of Bryan, business resumed, and Sharp returned to the city where E. C. Stedman's son Arthur had arranged for him to stay as a temporary member at the Century Club.

Before leaving London, Sharp threatened lawsuits against Stone and Kimball and armed himself with power of attorney from Fiona Macleod so he could act on her behalf as well as his own. One wonders who drew up a document that authorized one aspect of Sharp's personality to act for the other. During his week in the city, however, Kimball succeeded in charming Sharp into submission. He described Herbert Stone's loss of interest in the firm, the withdrawal of financial support by Stone's father, Kimball's acquisition of the firm's stock of bound volumes, sheets, and plates, and his move of the enterprise to New York, where he was determined to make a success of it. The firm remained in perilous condition, but Kimball managed a small check for Sharp to take back to Fiona Macleod. On Friday November 13 Sharp thanked Kimball for his hospitality and expressed his hope that Kimball would soon visit London, where his kindnesses would be repaid. His faith in Kimball had been rekindled to the extent that, ever optimistic, he proposed a book for him to publish the following year. When Sharp boarded the Fürst Bismarck on Saturday November 14 for his return to London, he was satisfied with the results of his American trip.

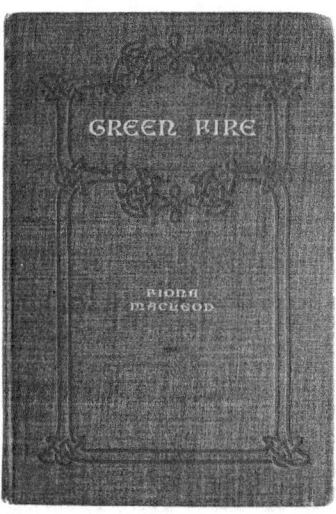

Fig. 9. The first American edition of Fiona MacLeod's *Green Fire. A Romance* (New York: Harper & Brothers, 1896). Photograph by William F. Halloran (2019).

During his absence, Archibald Constable and Co. in London, and Harpers and Brothers in New York published Fiona Macleod's *Green Fire: A Romance.* The first half of the novel takes place in Celtic Brittany, and the second on a remote island near Skye in the Hebrides. The two parts are held together by the love of Alan de Kerival for his beautiful cousin Ynys de Kerival. When Ynys' father kills Alan's father in a duel, the two realize they cannot remain together in Brittany and escape to the Hebridean island where they both have family roots and where the second half of the romance, "The Herdsman," takes place. Years later, Sharp rewrote the Hebridean section and published it separately in Fiona Macleod's *The Dominion of Dreams*. Before he died in 1905, he asked Elizabeth to promise she would never reissue *Green Fire* in its entirety. In fulfilling that promise, she said Sharp thought only the second "Herdsman" section was produced by the Fiona impetus, while the first — "The Birds of Angus Ogue" — was the work of William Sharp.

While it is true that the first half of the romance sounds more like Sharp and the second, set in the Hebrides and focusing on a deeply held folk belief of the native Gaels, sounds more like Fiona, a closer look at the two sections reveals a deeper reason for suppressing the Brittany section of the romance. While studying in Paris, Alan dreamed of Ynys with "ever deepening joy and wonder." She was his "real life; he lived in her, for her, because of her [...] she was his strength, his inspiration." When Alan returned to Brittany, Ynys saw him as "the fairest and comeliest of men," and when Alan turned

> the longing of his eyes upon Ynys he wondered if anywhere upon the green earth moved aught so sweet and winsome, if anywhere in the green world was another woman so beautiful in body, mind, and spirit as Ynys — Ynys the Dark, as the peasants call her, though Ynys of the dusky hair and hazel-green eyes would have been truer of her whom Alan de Kerival loved. [...] there was but one woman in the world, but one Dream, and her name was Ynys.

Alan was a poet, and Ynys "was the living poem who inspired all that was best in life, all that was fervent in his brain." Beyond that, recalling Sharp's fascination with women, it was Ynys who gave Alan his "sense of womanhood, [...] In her, he recognized the symbol as well as the individual." She was "his magic; the light of their love was upon everything: everywhere he found synonyms and analogues of Ynys. Deeply as he loved beauty, he had learned to love it far more keenly and understandingly, because of her." Recalling Sharp's early poem "Motherhood," Alan, through his love for her, "had come to understand the supreme hope of our human life in the mystery of motherhood." Ynys "was at once a child of nature, a beautiful pagan, a daughter of the sun; was at once this and a soul alive with the spiritual life. [...] Indeed, the mysticism which was part of the spiritual inheritance came with her northern strain that was one of the deep bonds which united them."

In Alan, Ynys "had found all that her heart craved," but she had found that "nearly too late." While Alan was in Paris, Ynys was "formally betrothed" to Andrik, a friend of her childhood, and in Brittany a betrothal was "almost as binding as marriage." Ynys asserted that "betrothal or no betrothal" she belonged only to Alan: "How could she help the accident by which she had cared for Andrik before she loved Alan." She still cared for Andrik, but what she felt for him paled in comparison to her love of Alan. She was the flame that lit his torch. Even if forced to marry Andrik, she would still love only Alan. "Affection, the deepest affection, is one thing; the love of man and woman" as they knew it was "a thing apart."

The only way they could escape the betrothal and build a life together was to board a ship and sail to the Hebrides, where their love prevailed, despite further complications arising from the case of mistaken identity that became the story of the Herdsman. Those complications caused Alan to slip in and out of depression, "a melancholy from which not even the love of Ynys would arouse him." To ward off that depression, he dwelt upon the "depth and passion" of his love for Ynys,

> upon the mystery and wonder of that coming life which was theirs and yet was not of them, itself already no more than an unrisen wave or an unbloomed flower, but yet as inevitable as they, but dowered with the light which is beyond where the mortal shadows end. Strange, this passion of love for what is not; strange this deep longing of the woman — the longing of the womb, the longing of the heart, the longing of the brain, the longing of the soul — for perpetuation of the life she shares in common with one whom she loves; strange this longing of the man, a longing deep-based in his nature as the love of life or the fear of death, for the gaining from the woman he loves this personal hostage against oblivion. For indeed something of this so commonplace, and yet so divine and mysterious tide of birth, which is forever at the flow upon this green world, is due to an instinctive fear of cessation. The perpetuation of life is the unconscious protest of humanity against the destiny of mortality.

When this abundance of overwrought prose is disentangled, we identify the belief often expressed by Sharp — that the love between a man and a woman reaches its zenith only in the production of children as "hostages against oblivion". When the complexities of the Herdsman section were cleared away, Alan and Ynys boarded a ship and returned to Brittany, where Alan assumed his rightful position as Lord of the Manor, and the two lovers would produce a child. Unlike the lovers in earlier Fiona Macleod productions, Alan and Ynys find a way to consummate their love and live happily ever after.

The love story of Alan and Ynys is the central theme of both sections of *Green Fire*. As is likely obvious by now, Sharp, disguised as Fiona, was both describing and attempting to reconcile the affectionate love he felt for his wife, and his intense, passionate love for Edith Rinder. In a letter to John Macleay dated late July 1896, Sharp said the book was written "a year or so ago," which would be the late summer and fall of 1895, a period in which he was in agony over the conundrum. The title page carries the following lines below the author's name: "While still I may, I write for you | The love I lived, the dream I knew." The book is dedicated "To Esclarmoundo" followed by the Latin phrase from Ovid, "Nec since te nec tecum vivere possum," which translates: "Neither without nor with you is it possible to live." The book was written for and about Edith Rinder.

Esclarmonde of Foix was a prominent figure associated with Catharism in thirteenth-century southern France. She figured prominently as a heroine in several medieval epic poems, including one titled "Esclarmonde" by Bertran de Born. Esclarmonde was also the heroine of an opera by that name composed by Jules Massenet and first performed in Paris in 1889. Sharp's more immediate source for the name was a Provençal poem, *La Glorie d'Esclarmonde*, edited in both Italian and French by Marius Andre, and published by J. Roumanille in Avignon in 1893. Characteristic of the Provençal tradition, a beautiful woman inspired the poem. Sharp dedicated his novel, which recounts his own love of a beautiful woman, to Edith Rinder — the object of his love, disguised as the heroine of a Provençal love poem, and further protected from discovery by his female pseudonym (Fiona).

Indeed, this interpretation of "Esclarmoundo" finds further support elsewhere. While Sharp was in America, Fiona Macleod's *From the Hills of Dream: Threnodies, Songs and Other Poems* was published. Sharp dedicated it to Arthur Allhallows Geddes, the newborn son of Patrick and Ann Geddes, and Sharp's godson. Arthur was born on Halloween, the day Sharp arrived in New York, and the anniversary of William and Elizabeth Sharp's marriage. The last section of the volume, a

Fig. 10. Poster advertising the premiere of *Esclarmonde*, libretto by Alfred Blau and Louis de Gramodt, music by Jules Massenet's, Paris, May 1889. August François-Marie Gorguet, *Esclarmonde* (1889), chromolithograph. Wikimedia, Public Domain, https://commons.wikimedia.org/wiki/File:Esclarmonde.jpg#/media/File:Esclarmonde.jpg

series of "prose rhythms" called "The Silence of Amor," is dedicated "To Esclarmoundo." Cast in the usual heightened Fiona prose, the dedication exposes the intensity of Sharp's love for Edith and his manic state of mind:

There is one word never spoken in these estrays of passion and longing. But you, White Flower of these fugitive blossoms, know it: for the rustle of the wings of Amor awakens you at dawn, and in the last quietudes of the dark your heart is his dear haven of dreams.

For, truly, that wandering voice, that twilight-whisper, that breath so dewy-sweet, that flame-wing'd lute player whom none sees but for a moment, in a rainbow-shimmer of joy, or a sudden lightening-flare of passion, this exquisite mystery we call Amor comes, to some rapt visionaries at least, not with a song upon the lips that all may hear, or with blithe viol of a public music, but as one wrought by ecstasy, dumbly eloquent with desire, ineffable, silent.

For Amor is ofttimes a dreamer, and when he dreams it is through lovely analogies. He speaks not, he whispers not, who in the flight of the wild swan against the frosty stars, or the interlaceries of black branches against the moonlight, or the abrupt song of a bird in the green-gloom of the forest, hears the voice that is all Music for him, sees the face of his unattainable Desire. These things [the poems that follow in this section] are his silences, wherein his heart and his passion commune. And being his [Amor's], they are mine: to lay before you, Dear; as a worshipper, wrought to incommunicable pain, lays white flowers before the altar, which is his Sanctuary and the Ivory Gate of his Joy.

The author of this dedication, presumably Fiona, identifies with Amor or Cupid, the male personification of love. Since he cannot express his love openly, the poems that follow are silences, but in them his heart and passion "commune." He lays them before the object of his desire just as a worshipper, hoping for salvation, lays flowers before an altar. He is "dumbly eloquent with desire" and "wrought by ecstasy," but also wrought to "incommunicable pain" by the need to be silent about the love and passion he shares with his beloved.

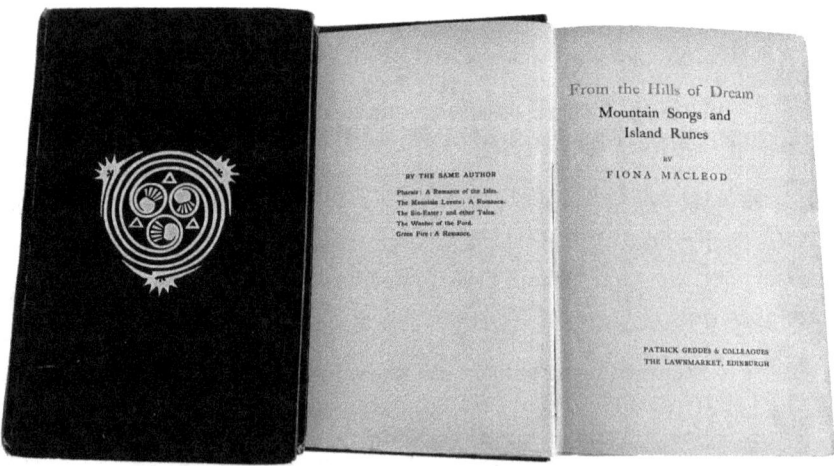

Fig. 11.   Cover and title page of the first edition of Fiona Macleod's *From the Hills of Dream* (Edinburgh: Patrick Geddes & Colleagues, 1896). Photograph by William F. Halloran (2019).

Was anyone paying close attention to what Fiona was saying in this dedication? Surely Elizabeth Sharp, a bright and well-educated woman fluent in French, knew what her husband was saying under the cover of Fiona. Edith and Frank Rinder surely knew. One can only conclude that by the fall of 1896, when *Green Fire* and *From the Hills of Dream* were published, the two couples had reached an understanding that Sharp and Edith would continue their intimate relationship discretely, but neither would leave the spouse they also loved and cared for. Sharp may have assumed Fiona's readers would think she was inventing a male persona, an interesting reversal to be sure. More likely, neither Sharp nor his readers gave the matter much thought. He was able to disguise the identity of Fiona Macleod for a decade because a part of the reading public needed her. Sharp recognized the need and set about fulfilling it. Descent into the Celtic past was an escape from the negative effects of rapid industrialization and the scientific discoveries challenging the tenets of Christianity. Yet more important — considering the content of Fiona's writing — was her sentimentalizing of love and passion, which offered a convenient escape for women, and also for some men, a few of whom fell in love with Fiona.

In his October 18 letter to Murray Gilchrist, who knew its true authorship and would read it as disguised account of Sharp's love of a beautiful woman, Sharp called *Green Fire* "a strange book — some will say a mad book." By 1899, when the flame of his passion had dissipated, Sharp decided to repress the book's astonishing revelations. He dropped the first half of the book and erased from the second half any mention of the love affair between Ynys and Alan. There is no Ynys, and there is no dedication to Esclarmoundo. When Alan Carmichael leaves Brittany and lands on a small island near Skye at the start of the revised "Herdsman," he has "wed and lost" the unnamed daughter of the man who killed his father. His only companion is his "servant and old friend Ian M'Ian," who becomes his interlocutor. Sharp also eliminated "The Silence of Amor" section and its dedication to Esclarmoundo from editions of *From the Hills of Dream* published after 1900. In 1902, Thomas Mosher of Portland Maine printed *The Silence of Amor | Prose Rhythms by Fiona Macleod* in a beautifully designed book on Van Gelder paper limited to 400 copies. For that edition, Sharp wrote a "Foreword" asserting the content of the volume should not be called "prose poems," but "prose rhythms." He also dropped the dedication to Esclarmoundo and revised both the dedicatory statement he had addressed to the dedicatee and many of the prose pieces that follow. He prefaced the revised dedicatory statement with the following quotation from Fiona Macleod's *The Distant Country*: "Love is more great than we conceive, and Death is the keeper of unknown redemptions." In this edition the intense passion of the first is absent. It is still Sharp disguised as Fiona Macleod laying before his "Dear" the prose rhythms, but he does so calmly "as a wind, that has lifted the blossoms of a secret orchard stoops, and lays milk-white drift and honeyed odors at the open window of one who within sleeps and dreams."

Despite the perceived success of Sharp's New York trip and the publication of two Fiona Macleod books in his absence, matters soon took a turn for the worse. He fell ill again, this time with influenza, and needed money to recuperate in a warmer climate. Herbert Stone, acting for the firm, had promised Sharp £300 (£100 on the submission of the manuscript and £200 upon publication) for a yachting romance called *Wives in Exile*. Claiming ignorance of this commitment, Kimball could not, in any case, afford to honor it. The book was submitted for copyright under the Stone and Kimball imprint in September 1896, but not issued. When they met in New York, Kimball agreed to relinquish all rights to the book, whereupon Sharp arranged for a young Boston publishing firm, Lamson, Wolffe & Company, to buy the loose sheets and the plates, and they published the book in January 1897 with a new title page. The Boston firm gave Sharp a promissory note due in January for £150, which he carried home only to discover it was not negotiable in Britain. He had hoped to borrow against it but was forced to send it to Stedman and ask him to advance the money until the note could be redeemed in January. While in New York, Sharp also met with Melville Stone, Herbert's father, to recover the remaining £150 due for *Wives in Exile*. The elder Stone agreed his son was morally, if not legally, obliged to pay Sharp some of the missing £150. He suggested E. C. Stedman arbitrate the matter, and Sharp accepted his suggestion. In his December 5 letter to Stedman, Sharp presented the history of the affair in a manner that might move Stedman to award him at least some of the compensation he thought due from the Stone family.

After recovering from influenza, Sharp began to exhibit in early December "disquieting symptoms of nervous collapse" which were brought on, Elizabeth said, by "the prolonged strain of the heavy dual work added to by an eager experimentation with certain psychic phenomena with which he had long been familiar but wished further to investigate, efforts in which at times he and Mr. W. B. Yeats collaborated" (*Memoir*, p. 282). Sharp had engaged in various attempts to communicate with the spirit world, augmented by drugs, while living at Phenice

Croft in 1891–1892. That was one reason Elizabeth disliked the place and insisted they give it up and return to the city. He resumed those investigations in late November and early December after returning from America. Suffering both physically and mentally, he needed a respite from damp and depressing London.

Although Stedman's efforts to recover money from the Stone family had not produced results, Stedman loaned Sharp — against Lamson's promissory note — enough money to leave England. In a letter of December 16, Sharp thanked him profusely for his generosity, and said that he was leaving the next day for the South of France. He would spend a few days in Tarascon with the Janviers before going on to Tamaris and St. Maxime on the Riviera. From Tarascon, he told Elizabeth he hoped to recover his "old buoyancy and nervous strength" through prolonged rest in the open air. In her article on "Fiona Macleod and her Creator William Sharp" (*North American Review*, 184/612, April 5, 1907, pp. 718–32), Catherine Janvier described Sharp's visit (p. 722):

> In December of 1896 — preceded by the announcement that he was old and gray-haired — William Sharp superb as a young Viking, burst in on us in quiet Saint-Remy. After the excitement of the first joyous meeting was over, it was plain to see that this magnificent presence gave false promise. He was exhausted by the long strain of double work and had been ordered away from the smoke and fog of London to the sunshine of the Riviera, there to seek the rest he nowhere had found. While with us strange moods possessed him; and, perhaps, because of these strange things happened. At times it was as though he struggled against an evil influence; was forcing back a dark tide ever threatening to overwhelm his soul. Warring presences were about him, he thought; and he believed that these must be conquered, even at the risk of life. The culminating struggle came, and through one winter night my husband watched over him as he battled against unseen but not unfelt influence. The fight was won, the dark tide stemmed, but at great cost of vitality, his victory leaving him faint and exhausted. "Nevermore," he told us, "would he tamper with certain forces, for such tampering might mean destruction."

Having passed through the dark night, according to Mrs. Janvier, Sharp recovered from his severe psychic episode and enjoyed the Christmas celebrations in the village. After Christmas he left for the warmer Riviera where, according to Mrs. Janvier, "he wandered restlessly from place to place" before returning to the Janviers in St. Remy shortly after the start of 1897. As it turned out, the New Year brought another adventure that, despite his "Nevermore," involved his return to spiritualist experiments.

Letters: July–December, 1896

To Catherine Ann Janvier, July, 1896

... I resent too close identification with the so-called Celtic renaissance. If my work is to depend solely on its Gaelic connection, then let it go, as go it must. My work must be beautiful in itself — Beauty is a Queen and must be served as a Queen.

... You have asked me once or twice about F. M., why I took her name: and how and when she came to write *Pharais*.[1] It is too complex to tell you just now. The name was born naturally: (of course I had associations with the name Macleod.) It, Fiona, is very rare now. Most Highlanders would tell you it was extinct — even as the diminutive of Fionnaghal (Flora). But it is not. It is an old Celtic name (meaning "a fair maid") still occasionally to be found. I know a little girl, the daughter of a Highland clergyman, who is called Fiona. All my work is so intimately wrought with my own experiences that I cannot tell you about Pharais, etc., without telling you my whole life.

William Sharp

Memoir, p. 227

To Louise Chandler Moulton, July 17, 1896[2]

My dear Friend

It is with singular pleasure I introduce to you my friend, Mr. Eugene Lee Hamiltonwhose name will be so familiar to you who love what is best in contemporary English poetry.[3] You will remember, too, how much our dear Philip loved & admired Mr. Lee Hamilton's Sonnets.

You will be glad to meet him for these reasons, for himself, & because he is an old friend of

Your ever affectionate | William Sharp

ALS Library of Congress, Louise Chandler Moulton Collection

To Robert Murray Gilchrist, [July 19, 1896]

My dear Friend,

Could you not join us for a few days — I mean my wife & myself — on the Northumberland coast: say at Alnmouth? say on Saty the 25th, i.e. Saty of this week? It would be so pleasant, & I want much to see you.

Again, from 1st August for a fortnight or so we shall be at Sea View | Holy Island off the North Northumberland coast. Perhaps you wd. rather go there!

But could you not manage to get away for a few days on the 25th or 27th?

Your mother once asked me to bring my wife with me, & to stay at Cartledge. Supposing that this were feasible for Mrs. Sharp & myself — & I have said nothing of it to her — & supposing that you cannot get away — would it be convenient & agreeable to your mother that Elizabeth & I came to you on the evening of the 24th (Friday) till Monday? This is a mere idea, though.

If this reach you any time on Monday (tomorrow)⁴ or Monday evening — please telegraph to me at Station Hotel | York. I reach there in the evening, & leave it again for the North about 9.30 on Tuesday morning. If you do not get it, then hold over telegram till you receive mine from wherever I may go to on Tuesday — probably Belford.

In great haste | Yrs Ever | W. S.

P.S. I have just spoken of the idea to my wife — of Friday evening till Monday: & she would like it very much. Is it feasible or not? Say frankly, in every way.

I enclose telegraph form for me to save you trouble. (The house in London is closed pro-tem as my [wife] will be at her mother's.)

My cordial regards to your mother.

If we can come, it will be a great pleasure to see her again. Also, *if* so — may we come as simply in all respects as "wayfarers." W.

ALS Sheffield City Archives

To John Macleay [July 28?, 1896][5]

4 Victoria Terrace | Bamborough | Northumberland

Dear Mr. Macleay

Thanks for your note. As regards the "Evergreen" winter number, you are mistaken in thinking "the time for such considerations," as Falstaff or someone says, remote. I understand that August 1st is the nominal, & August 15th the latest date for matter to be sent in.

I confess I share to some degree in Miss Macleod's annoyance in this persistent disbelief in her personality to which you allude — as, indeed, to some extent in her resentment against the impertinence of those persons who try to intrude upon her privacy or seek to ascertain what for good reasons of her own she does not wish made public. She has ever been willing to meet the few persons who have any right to expect an interview — and the other day, I hear, met by appointment, in Edinburgh, one of the firm of Messrs. A Constable & Co. Formerly, I used to transact much of her business for her: now, I am glad to say, she attends to her literary negotiations etc. herself — & so has perforce to break her determination so far, i.e. her determination not to be "interviewed" in any sense, or in any way have her privacy pried into.

The other day in London I met one of the Constables, & heard that Miss Macleod had written to them for advice as to certain statements etc. — & I am pleased to say they gave her the same advice as I did & that was to hold herself as absolutely aloof as she liked from all busy bodies & everyone who had no concern in her private affairs.

Did you not see the explicit statement I caused to be inserted in the "Glasgow Evening News," & elsewhere (because of one of these perverse misstatements) to the effect that "Miss Fiona Macleod is <u>not</u> Mr. William Sharp; Miss Fiona Macleod is <u>not</u> Mrs. William Sharp; and that Miss Fiona Macleod is — Miss Fiona Macleod."

Surely <u>that</u> ought to have settled the matter: for it is scarcely likely, I imagine, that I should put forth so explicit a statement were it not literally true.

I trust, therefore, that you will do your best at any time to counteract all other misstatements. These, I fancy, originate chiefly from Dr. Robertson Nieal or his Edinburgh agent, & from Mr. Neil Munro: i.e. so far as I have reason to say so.[6]

By the way, there were some recent misstatements both in the "Evening News" & the "Highland News." (e.g. Prof Geddes has not withdrawn from the firm of P. G. & Co — of which he is the head: nor has he any intention of doing so).

Miss Macleod's poems will not be issued till mid-September at the earliest.

About the same date (I understand) Messrs. A. Constable & Co. are to issue her new one-vol romance "Green Fire," written a year or so ago I believe.[7] From what she wrote to me recently, I understand there will be no other book by her published this year, unless it be a short story (in Messrs Constable's new 2'/6 series) called "The Lily Leven." This will be a new departure for her, as it does not deal with the gloom, but rather with the gaiety or abandon of the Celtic character at certain times and seasons.

Her work is now much sought for by the leading American & English magazines, though she will accept very few commissions & these only conditionally: so this, and the press opinions etc. show that she has really struck a deep note, and that there is a public for a Celtic writer.

The chief obstacle for writers like Miss Macleod is in jealous or parochial criticism among those where it should be least likely to be seen. Surely the spirit is all important — but, to judge from some comments, there is in Inverness & perhaps elsewhere a tendency to thwart a new influence by an ignoring of the "spirit" for the sake of some pedantic or unimaginative insistence on the barren side of the "letter."

With regard to the suggestions in your note: I think they are excellent, and may well be fruitful. Later, if I think of any suggestions I will send them. As to my coming north to Inverness, I fear the only chance this year (& that uncertain) would be about the beginning of October: & that would be too early for you I suppose. If I <u>were</u> in Inverness then I might perhaps say something on, say, "The Celtic Spirit." But this is <u>in nubibus</u> meanwhile.

Hoping you are in better health | Sincerely Yours | William Sharp

Miss Macleod's latest address was the isle of Colonsay — but she may be gone from there now as she is yachting. I'll send on your letter, as soon as I know definitely where to write to. She is due in the Clyde region soon.

P.S. If you think advisable you could reprint in the *H/News* that explicit statement about Miss F. M.

ALS National Library of Scotland

To the Editor of Blackwood's Magazine, August 6, 1896

(Temporary) | Viewpark | Clynder | Garelock | 6th August

Dear Sir,

I trust that the receipt of "The Washer of the Ford" showed you that I appreciated your courteous letter à propos of the rejection of a story, the English serial right of which I had offered you.[8] I meant to write at the time, but I fear I omitted to do so, as I was then on the point of departure for Italy. "The Washer of the Ford" into which I have put the best I have been able to do, as I think, has, I hope, not disappointed you as my unfortunate MS. story did. You were, I am more than ready to believe, so right in that instance that I should be gratified if you found in this book the genuine effort of one who is slowly learning how easy it is to write "something," how supremely difficult it is to write well.

Believe me | Yours very truly | Fiona Macleod

ALS National Library of Scotland

To Coulson Kernahan, August 15, 1896[9]

Myrtle Grove | 4, Auchamor Road | Dunoon | Argyll | 15/Aug/96

Just a line, cher ami, to acknowledge your thrice-forwarded letter — & to say that I shall write to you Tuesday or Wedny next, as soon as I can hear from Scotts'.[10]

Yours ever, | William Sharp

ACS Princeton University

To John Macleay, [August 10, 1896][11]

till 21st Aug: after that c/o Messrs. P. G. & Co.

Myrtle Grove | Auchamore Road | Dunoon

Dear Mr. Macleay

Many thanks for your letter — & all the trouble you have taken.

It is with very great regret that I have to tell you I have just received from my doctor an imperative letter forbidding me to lecture in Inverness, Edinburgh, or Dublin this year: even to such a semi-private audience as at the Celtic Union in Edinburgh.

This is a great disappointment to me — & in a double way: for I had believed I was much stronger, & could quite well risk at any rate the Inverness lecture. But the truth is: I have an inherited heart-trouble complicated by harm done to me by a very serious (second) & prolonged attack of rheumatic fever. I have, however, been so much better of late, & felt so sure of my restored vigour, that I thought I could safely undertake the Inverness address at any rate. However, it is not to be: "not on any condition whatever, this year at any rate: whether you may undertake anything of the kind for next year or not" — so writes my doctor.

You will understand my chagrin as well as my disappointment — & I can only thank you & others who would have given me a friendly welcome, & ask you to permit me to defer my address till next Spring (or possibly till the Mod at Inverness!)

Sincerely Yours | William Sharp

P.S. It is quite likely my wife & I may now be in Inverness for a night at any rate on or about the 3rd of September. Will there be any chance of my having a glimpse of you?

ALS National Library of Scotland

To John Macleay, [August 17, 1896][12]

Dear Mr. Macleay

In reply to what you tell me in your letter, & to the article in the current H/News headed "Mystery! Mystery!" I can only say that I regret the ill-bred impertinence of the Glasgow busybodies in question, and the personalities & tone of the said article. They seem to me in very bad taste. I think a paper that respects public & private right should not lend itself to unwarrantable personalities — favourable or unfavourable: but perhaps I am too old-fashioned in my views on this matter.

The thing lies in a nutshell. For good reasons of her own, a lady wishes to preserve absolutely her privacy. As a friend & relative I happen to be in her confidence (though of course, both as individual & writer, she is known intimately to a few others as well) — & I have, on her behalf, done what I could, by that explicit statement requoted in the H/N.[13] By common courtesy, this matter should stop there.

If the Glasgow busybodies are ludicrously wrong in their conjectures (& maliciously wrong, as in that absolutely unfounded rumour (to which you allude) about Constable & Co., America, etc. — for, as I happen to know, this contract with her about "Green Fire" was signed several months ago. They have, too, behaved with eager courtesy throughout: as indeed have not only Messrs. Constable & Messrs. P. Geddes & Co., but also the Harpers & Stone & Kimball in America) — if, as I say, they are wrong, so also is "Mac" — for I am not, and I have never said or implied that I was, Miss Macleod's "uncle." I am a relation & a friend: *c'est tout*. Nor has Miss Macleod any residence in Edinburgh at which to call upon her. When in Ed. she stays sometimes with my relatives in Murrayfield, sometimes with other friends & Prof Geddes or others. Fortunately, all this rather vulgar prying cannot have any result: for, as a matter of fact, Miss Macleod's privacy is now so-well safeguarded by her & her friends that she is as "safe" either in Edinburgh or Glasgow as Prince Charlie in "the heather." It is amusing — when a thing is very simple — how it can be made into a mystery.

For the rest — I am certain Miss Macleod needs no urging from me: — but I am writing saying that I hope she will absolutely ignore all personal remarks of any kind, & indeed any controversy about her writings.

There are other ideals of conduct than those which prevail with the writer or writers in the "Glasgow Evening News" — & from what I know of Miss Macleod I do not think it is likely she will stoop to any undignified "disclaimer" in "explanation," or "reply," of any kind. She writes, as best she can: for the rest she is a woman in private life: that, she holds (and I & those who know her hold also), is her ground, and from that she will not budge an inch.

I would like to be able to tell her that she can count upon you (as one of her unknown friends) to help in this safe-guarding of her privacy, which, rightly or wrongly, she considers essential to her happiness & literary welfare.

Yours very truly | William Sharp

ALS National Library of Scotland

To John Macleay, [August 18, 1896]

Myrtle Grove | Auchmore Road | Dunoon | Tuesday night

Dear Mr. Macleay,

The last post has brought me a line from Miss Macleod apropos of the article "Mystery." She writes in deep resentment against what she considers its altogether unwarrantable personalities, and against "the insulting opening, the note of which is more fully emphasized in the cruel & inexcusable phrase: 'I hear again & again that she is a greater fraud than Macpherson of Ossianic fame.'"

She adds that any temptation she had to forego her rule — & write to the H/News on any controversial point — no longer exists: and that more than ever she is determined to safeguard her privacy — as I wrote to you yesterday — and absolutely to ignore all unwarrantable interference, conjecture, & paragraphic impertinence.

I admit I am glad she writes as she does: for I should deeply regret to see her yield to the vulgar temptation to a public controversy concerning herself — whether "a rather peculiar" one or any other.

I have already written you about the misstatements as to my being her uncle (I am a second cousin) and as to Miss M. having a residence in Edinburgh where "literary detectives" could call. As I said, she stays, when east, sometimes with my people in Murrayfield: sometimes with other friends, generally with her friend Miss Rea.

She, and I, resent the cool impertinence of the words: "No one seems to have seen her." Who is "no one"? The "Evening News" man — or the "British Weekly" man — & the like? If it were not so grotesque, one might well be angry at the blank insolence of such a statement.

Let me add, apropos of a remark in this article: that nothing of Miss Macleod's ever appeared in any American paper or magazine, or in any like form, till the Christmas number of Harper's, last Xmas — when the gist of what is now "The Shadowy Seers" in her last book appeared. I believe that this Spring she has serialized one short story there: but am not sure as to where, or if it has appeared. For the rest, Messrs. Stone & Kimball published, in a most dainty & charming format, her "Pharais": later, in the charming "Carnation" series, her "Sin-Eater": and, recently, her "Washer of the Ford," one of the prettiest books in get-up I have seen. Messrs. Roberts Bros. published her "Mountain Lovers" in the American "Keynotes" series. Messrs. Harpers are to issue her "Green Fire" simultaneously with Messrs. Constables' edn.

In each instance (save with Messrs. Roberts Bros, with whom the English publisher arranged) Miss M. has dealt direct, & with most satisfactory results.

There — you have, in this letter & my last — all necessary data at next to first hand. You will excuse me henceforth, I am sure, from further details on a subject which concerns another & another who wishes "to steer clear of the personal paragraphist."

Miss M. adds that she has sent a little note to Mr. W. C. Mackenzie. She is in Edinburgh for a day or two, but leaves tomorrow morning for a yachting cruise among the Isles. She was lately in Skye & the adjacent isles — & to be off again has luck indeed.

Yours very truly | William Sharp

ALS National Library of Scotland

To John Macleay, [*August 19, 1896*]

Myrtle Grove | Wednesday forenoon

Dear Mr. Macleay,

In reply to your letter received this morning, I need not again go into a matter explained in extenso in enclosed note which I wrote to you last night.[14]

Even if Miss Macleod — as mentioned there — were not leaving tomorrow for a yachting cruise in the West — there could now be no question of an interview.

I knew this, of course, but as this was a matter in which it was not right for me to decide without consultation I telegraphed to her. I have just had her answer & give it you as I received it. "I absolutely refuse now or at any time. If not all gratuitous impertinence it is quite unwarrantable as explained in my letter yesterday. Am writing. F.

As for myself — I leave here (Dunoon) on Saty.[15] I could see you at No. 9 Upper Coltbridge Terrace, Murrayfield, (Edinburgh) — on either Saturday evening or Sunday evening — or on Monday morning (not later than 11) — but it is probable I leave Edinburgh for the Clyde again on Monday.

As I wrote to you yesterday we expect to be in Inverness for a night on or about the 4th or 5th Sept.

Please send me a wire by return if you wish to see me on Saturday night or Sunday night, as I have other arrangements to consider.

Yrs Trly, | W. S.

To John Macleay, [August 21, 1896][16]

Murrayfield, Midlothian | (Dunoon)

My dear Mr. Macleay

I quite understand: & I thank you for your letter. Pray overlook any resentment that seemed of a personal kind against you: that certainly was not meant by me, & equally certainly would never be intended by Miss Macleod. I may perhaps be able to give you a hint as to an apparent mystery when we meet in Inverness.[17]

Meanwhile, immediately on receipt of your letter this morning I sent it on to Miss Macleod. She will doubtless write to you tonight or tomorrow.

My wife & I go to Edinburgh tomorrow — & I shall then see Miss M. & talk over certain points — as she has wired saying she will postpone going west till Monday or Tuesday.

Thanking you for what I assure you is a wholly satisfactory explanation, & for your friendly words.

Believe me | Yours sincerely | William Sharp

To John Macleay, [August 22, 1896][18]

c/o Miss Lilian Rea | Crudelius Hall | 457 Lawnmarket | Edinburgh

My dear Sir

Mr. Sharp has forwarded me your letter to him. I quite understand, and thank you cordially not only for all your generous friendliness in the past, and for all you say, but for your courteous and forbearing letter.

It is possible — I cannot say yet — that I may write something in the lines you suggest.

May I ask your acceptance from me of a copy of the American issue of "The Washer of the Ford?" A few copies were kindly sent to me by the publisher. I send it by this post.

I had intended to leave Edinburgh today, but shall now wait till Monday or Tuesday, as Mr. and Mrs. Sharp are coming here for a day or two.

Yours very truly / Fiona Macleod

If perchance you should be writing to me on Sunday or Monday, please address to me at No. 9 Upper Coltbridge Terrace | Murrayfield | Midlothian as though not staying there I expect to be there most of the next day or two.

ALS National Library of Scotland

To Patrick Geddes [August 23, 1896][19]

Sunday

I forget if I gave you my address, where we are to go tomorrow morning: — Woodside | Tigh-Na-Bruaich | The Kyles of Bute | Will you kindly direct that an (editorial) copy of No I of *The Evergreen* be sent to me there.

Advise me, if possible, a day or two beforehand as to when Proofs of the new number are likely to reach me: also if you will be at your present address throughout September, or for how long.

William Sharp

ACS National Library of Scotland

To John Macleay, [August 24, 1896]

Dear Mr. Macleay,

Thanks for your letter. I have had a long talk with Miss Macleod, who has delayed her return to the West on account of my wife & myself being here for a day or two: and I think that while she is steadfast in her main contention and position she is alive to the point of view you brought forward.

I have not said anything to her about your hint about someone "thinking he might add zest to the Mod by attacking Miss M's writings." Personally, I think this would be a mistake (apart from the obvious discourtesy of attacking one where there could be no means of immediate reply) — and while it would do little harm to Miss Macleod [it] would certainly hurt the Celtic cause in the Highlands, for if the average Anglo-Saxon reader (& as much in Edinburgh & Glasgow as in England) sees division and scornful raillery in the Camp itself, he will simply say "it's the same all over: there is no Irish union possible, & now there's the same mutual bickering in Gaelic Scotland."

I am very disappointed not to give my address — but look upon it as a postponement rather: for I was going to lay utmost stress on this very point of loyal cooperation &, in treating of the Celtic Spirit, try to keep clear of the Parochial in every form. However, in good time.

Yrs sincerely / William Sharp

P.S. Will you kindly have the H/News of this week sent to me at Post Office, Tighnabruaich, Kyles of Bute, as I shall call there on Friday or Saty.

ALS National Library of Scotland

To Katharine Tynan Hinkson, August 25, 1896

c/o Miss Lilian Rea, | The Outlook Tower, | The Lawn Market, | Edinburgh, 25.8.96.

My dear Mrs. Hinkson,

My cordial thanks for your most generous and friendly words about my last book — in the "National Observer" and now again in "The Sketch." Your words, indeed, give me singular pleasure. For one thing, I am always much more susceptible to praise or blame, when the critic is one whose own writings I hold in especial regard — and, as I think I have told you, I delight in your beautiful poetry, and find too in your imaginative prose the same corresponding charm and delicacy of emotion and execution. Let me add here a sentence from a letter from my intimate friend, Mrs. Edith Wingate Rinder, whose forthcoming "The Shadow of Arvor" (a vol. of Breton legendary romances) will, I am sure, delight you: — "I am delighted with Katharine Tynan's review of "The Washer of the Ford" in the Sketch. It is so very sympathetic, and intimately appreciative. Her phrase "The warp and woof of the book are gold and shadow" is peculiarly happy: and the whole article is so free from the commonplaceness of the ordinary review that in itself it is a delight."

Though not to be there again till late autumn, Mrs. Wingate Rinder lives in London, and I would like you and her to meet some day. When (in October, I expect) my little first volume of verse is published, I shall so gladly send you — as the comrade, not as the critic! — a copy.[20]

Meanwhile, dear Mrs. Hinkson, | Believe me, | Cordially yours, |
Fiona Macleod

ALS Private and Middle Years, pp. 129–30

To Henry Chandler Bowen, August 26, 1896[21]

c/o Miss Lillian Rea | The Outlook Tower | The Lawnmarket |
Edinburgh | 26: 8: 95

Dear Sir,

I do not know, of course, if you are acquainted with my name — though my first four books have all been republished (simultaneously published, I should say) in the United States: and Messr^s Harpers are to publish on about Sept 15th my new Celtic romance *"Green Fire"*: but in any case you may care to consider for publication in the *Independent* (if before Nov. 15th, when it may appear in book form) the enclosed story, if that may be called a story which is rather "a spiritual episode," as someone describes the "legendary moralities" in my recent book, *"The Washer of the Ford."* I hope it may please you, and be acceptable to your readers.

Believe me | Yours very truly | Fiona Macleod

ALS Princeton University

To Elizabeth Sharp, [mid-September, 1896][22]

[Tighnabruaich Hotel | Kyles of Bute]

... I am glad to be here, for though the weather has changed for the worse I am so fond of the place and neighbourhood. But what I care for most is I am in a strong Fiona mood, though more of dream and reverie — creatively — than of actual writing: indeed it is likely all my work here, or nearly all shall be done through dream and mental-cartooning. I have written "The Snow Sleep of Angus Ogue" for the winter *Evergreen*,[23] and am glad to know it is one of F. M.'s deepest and best utterances...

Memoir, pp. 267–68

To Elizabeth A. Sharp, September 23, 1896

September 23rd

... I am now well in writing trim I am glad to say. Two days ago I wrote the long-awaited "Rune of the Passion of Women" the companion piece in a sense to the "Chant of Women" in Pharais — and have also done *The Savoy* story "The Archer" (about 4,500 words) and all but done "Ahez the Pale". Today I hope to get on with the "Lily Leven"... .[24]

I must make the most of this day of storm for writing. I had a splendid long sleep last night, and feel "spiff"... . I am not built for mixed companies, and like them less and less in proportion as the imperative need of F. M. and W. S. for greater isolation grows. I realise more and more the literal truth of what George Meredith told me — that renunciation of ordinary social pleasures (namely of the ordinary kind in the ordinary way) is a necessity to any worker on the high levels: and unless I work that way I shall not work at all.

Memoir, pp. 266–67

To Elizabeth A. Sharp, September 26th, 1896

September 26th

... Yesterday turned out a splendid breezy day, despite its bad opening: one of the most beautiful we have had, altho' too cold for bathing, and too rough for boating. I went off by myself for a long sail — and got back about 4. Later I went alone for an hour or so to revise what had stirred me so unspeakably, namely the third and concluding "Rune of the Sorrow of Women." This last Rune tired me in preliminary excitement and in the strange semi-conscious fever of composition more than anything of the kind since I wrote the first of the three in Pharais one night of storm when I was alone in Phenice Croft.

I have given it to Mary to copy, so that I can send it to you at once. Tell me what you think and feel about it. In a vague way not only you, Mona, Edith[25] and others swam into my brain, but I have never so absolutely felt the woman-soul within me: it was as though in some subtle way the soul of Woman breathed into my brain — and I feel vaguely as if I had given partial expression at least to the inarticulate voice of a myriad women who suffer in one or other of the triple ways of sorrow. For work, and rebuilding energy, I am thankful I came here. You were right: I was not really fit to go off to the Hebrides alone, at the present juncture, and might well have defeated my own end. Tomorrow morning I shall be writing — probably at From the Hills of Dream.

Memoir, p. 267

To William Butler Yeats, [late September, 1896][26]

Strath-Na-Mara | Tarbert of Loch Fyne | Argyll

Dear Mr. Yeats

Unforeseen circumstances have prevented my writing to you before this, and even now I must perforce be more brief than I would fain be in response to your long and deeply interesting as well as generous letter. Alas, a long pencilled note (partly apropos of your vision of the woman shooting arrows, and of the strange coincidence of something of the same kind on my own part) has long since been devoured by a too voracious or too trustful gull — for a sudden gust of wind blew the quarto-sheet from off the deck of the small yacht wherein I and my dear friend and confrère of whom you know were sailing, off Skye.[27]

Private matters have combined to distract me very much just now — and this, and much sailing about and faring in remote places — and the work we are doing, and putting together the volume of verse[28] — have together frayed the edges of my small fragment of actual leisure for writing.

How good of you to write to me as you did. Believe me, I am grateful. There is no other writer whose good opinion could please me more — for

I love your work, and take an endless delight in your poetry, and look to you as not only one of the rare few on whose lips is the honey of Magh Mell but as one the dark zone of whose mind is lit with the strange stars and constellations of the spiritual life.

Most cordially I thank you for your critical remarks.[29] Even where I do not unreservedly agree, or where I venture to differ (as for example, in the matter of the repetition of the titular words in "The Washer of the Ford" poem) I have carefully pondered all you say.

I am particularly glad you feel about the "Annir Choille" as you do. Some people whom I would like to please do not care for it: yet I am sure you are right in considering it one of the most vital things I have been able to do.

With what delight I have read your lovely poem "O'Sullivan Rua to the Secret Rose."[30] I have read it over and over with ever deepening delight. It is one of your finest poems, I think: though perhaps it can only be truly appreciated by those who are familiar with legendary Celtic history. We read it to each other, my friend and I, on a wonderful sundown "when evening fed the wave with quiet light," off one of the Inner Hebrides (Colonsay, to the south of Oban). The only thing we both note is the use of "heavy" in the 7th as well as in the sixth line. Is not the effect of that in the 7th consequently lost? And would not "slumberous" or some other apt epithet be better? It is but a suggestion — and it is only because you love so truly what is beautiful and so are heedful to any suggestion, right or wrong, that I venture to make it. I cannot quite make up my mind, as you ask, about your two styles. Personally, I incline not exactly to a return to the earlier but to a marriage of the two: that is, a little less of the remoteness, or subtlety, with a little more of the earlier rippling clarity.

After reading your Blake paper[31] (and with vivid interest and delight) I turned to an early work of yours which I value highly, *Dhoya*: and I admit that my heart moved to it.[32] Between them lies, I think, your surest and finest line of work — with the light deft craft of *The Celtic Twilight*.[33]

I hope you are soon going to issue the promised volume of poems.[34] When my (our) own book of verse is ready — it is to be called *From the Hills of Dream* — it will give me such sincere pleasure to send you a copy. By the by, I must not forget to thank you for introducing my work to Arthur Symons. He wrote to me a pleasant letter, and asked me to contribute to the Savoy, which I have done.[35]

I daresay my friend (who sends you comradely greetings, and says he will write in a day or two) will tell you more from me when he and you meet. I had a strange vision the other day, wherein I saw the figure of a gigantic woman sleeping on the green hills of Ireland. As I watched, the sun waned and the dark came and the stars began to fall. They fell one by one, and each fell into the woman — and lo, of a sudden, all was wan[36] running water, and the drowned stars and the transmuted woman passed from my seeing. This was a waking dream, an open vision: but I do not know what it means, though it was so wonderfully vivid. In a vague way I realise that something of tremendous moment is being matured just now. We are on the verge of vitally important developments. And all the heart, all the brain, of the Celtic races shall be stirred. There is a shadow of mighty changes. Myself I believe that new spirits have been embodied among us. And some of the old have come back. We shall perish, you and I and all who fight under the "Lifting of the Sunbeam" — but we shall pioneer a wonderful marvellous new life for humanity. The other day I asked an old isles woman where her son was buried: he was not buried" she said, "for all they buried his body. For, a week ago, I saw him lying on the heather, and talking swift an' wild with a Shadow." The Shadows are here.

I must not write more just now.

My cordial greetings to you — | Sincerely | Fiona Macleod

My best letter-address (for you) is | 9. Upper Coltbridge Terrace | Murrayfield | Midlothian.

ALS Yale, Sharp's draft in National Library of Scotland,
and excerpted in Memoir, pp. 270–72

To Robert Murray Gilchrist, [September 28?, 1896]

Strathnamara | Tarbert | Loch Fyne

My dear Boy

I have to go to America on or about the 14th of Oct. — only there & back & about 10 days there: having urgent literary business to see to. Have been rendered next to bankrupt by disaster & fraud — but hope to "work thro."

I write now to ask you if for your own health's sake — the stimulus & general good — for what you might arrange in U.S.A. — & for friendship sake — you will come too? This is sudden — but, well, come!

Your Friend | Wilfion

I shall be here till Thursday inclusive — on Friday night or Saty morning, the Caledonian Station Hotel, Glasgow — on Saty night or Monday morning Murrayfield.[37] If you can come telegraph "yes." Again, for your own sake & mine come!

ALS Sheffield City Archives

To Edmund Clarence Stedman, [September 30?, 1896]

Strath-Na-Mara | Tarbert of Loch Fyne, Argyll

Dear Poet, Friend, Comrade | & Edmund-mo-ghraidh | & Stedman-mo-caraid[38] —

Slainte, 's Mile Faillé! which, being interpreted, means "Hail, and a Thousand Greetings!"

I hope this will reach you on your birthday, and that it will carry to you my loving good wishes. May your new year bring you health, weal, peace, joy, and happiness of all kinds. Only, don't be too good. The gods only bless with the left hand when one is too good. A right hand blessing, even with the occasional severe spank that goes therewith, is much better. Seek it, my dear silver-haired Youth. What a good thing it is to be alive — and to be, like you, a poet. That is, to love. We are the crowned lovers of the world, we, and our lovely embodied Dreams — the gods bless their leaping pulses, their red lips, their white breasts, their brave laughing souls, beautiful Sunbeams of life that they are![39]

Do not think because I have not written but once this year that I am forgetful. For one thing, I've had a decade boiled down into this year! Then, too, I have been away so much in France, Italy, and Scotland. Then, I have suffered — but of this, nothing in a birthday letter. And — well, I've been a "Poet"!

In a day or two now I leave the West Highlands. Then I go to London. Somewhere about mid-October (14th or 17th) I leave for a brief visit to New York, primarily to recover heavy indebtedness & to safeguard literary property, due to me by Mr. Kimball (Stone & Kimball). Alas, I am rendered bankrupt by their broken pledges. My affairs have all gone to smash. However, I'm taking it philosophically and hope to put things straight within some months. (But this perhaps had best be strictly entre nous. It would not do to get about.) I know you are off somewhere — but if near New York may I pay you a flying visit?

I expect to leave on either the 14th or 17th via Southampton, either by the Hamburg American or the North German Lloyd, but the former if it calls in Southampton, I expect.

I have a great deal to tell you, and to talk about — but meanwhile can only send you my love and loyal homage and greetings. (You have no loyaler friend or advocate here, dear E. C. S., I'm sure I can say.)

> Till we meet, then — and with my love and "obeisance" to Mrs. Stedman, and love to Arthur. Ever affectionately yours, |
> William Sharp

I shall write later as soon as I know exactly when and by what boat I sail.

ALS Columbia University Library

To John Ross, October 9, 1896

Thursday 9th Oct

Dear Mr. Ross,

I suppose in Miss Rea's absence I had better address to you, tho' neither she nor I wish to add unnecessarily to your business distractions.

I had a wire today from Mrs. Wingate Rinder saying that the promised remittance of £50 had not reached her up to this afternoon. I wired back to her to telegraph to you if on her return (to Kensington Court Gardens) she did not find it there. I told her it was quite right — merely a slip somewhere — as you had promised to send it.

Please see that among the earliest copies of *Arvor*[40] to be sent out for review are those for *The Bookman* and *The Highland News,* and note that the copy for the latter (marked "for review") had better be sent direct to John Macleay Esq | Rosehall | Fairfield Road | Inverness.

Please send 6 copies (Author's Copies) to Mrs. Wingate Rinder at her London address.

If procurable at once please send me the Review-Copies list as used for "The Washer of the Ford", which I shall return revised for "Arvor". Also the advt. List.

In haste | Cordially yours | William Sharp

Also addresses please (see Evergreen contributors list) of a Mrs. Clothilde Balfour,[41] and of J. H. Pearce:[42] & if you have it name etc. of editor of the Birmingham paper that reviews our books so well.

NOTE: Miss Macleod's Two Books

Please consult with Mr. Cuthbertson[43] as to the following proposal, to which I have Miss Macleod's consent and approval.

How would it do, early in the Spring of 1897 — both for Miss F. M.'s sake, and markedly for the firm's, I think — to reissue, in the form proposed by Miss Macleod, her Tales — in 3 vols, and each to be bound simply in paper, with artistic design (like that of "Vamireh" etc. you had done for Prof. Geddes & myself.)

I do not think this wd. hurt the Sale of Stock, if, as Mr. W. C. says, they are too artistically (or remotely) got up to fetch the buying public. There will always be buyers who want these, both for themselves, and as original issues, etc. Moreover, a reissue might give even them a lift.

I believe that these books, issued with paper covers, at say 2/6 nett, would have a good sale, | Vol. I. Spiritual Tales | Vol. II. Barbaric Tales | Vol. III. Tragic Romances | to be sold separately, or in sets for those who prefer. Of course (particularly as they wd. be thoroughly revised by Miss Macleod, & have notes where called for — & also as some new matter (as you will see) is to be added — the vols would have to be reprinted.

But a less expensive paper cd. be used.

I am convinced that, Miss M. working with us, we may yet redeem our fortune successfully.

Herewith the Dft of Rearrangement.

Yours ev. | W. S.

ALS National Library of Scotland

To John Macleay, October 13, 1896

Please acknowledge receipt of MS.

Rutland House | 15, Greencroft Gardens, | South Hampstead | 13/Oct/96

Dear Mr. Macleay,

I like the enclosed the best thing of yours that I have seen. It is full of the Celtic atmosphere — and is told with genuine skill & insight.

But I see two objections: viz, that it is too long for a short story, and too short for book-issue. My advice to you is — shorten it by a scrupulous deletion: bring it to say 3,000 words: & then send it to *Blackwood's*. Or, if you prefer it, work it up into more of a story — make this its central plot — & then try it with one or other of the firms who are bringing out short romances of say 25,000 or 30,000 words. Otherwise I am afraid you will find it difficult to get quit of this as it stands — for all that it is so admirable in itself.

By the way, I notice the influence of your friend Miss Macleod. In the circumstances, therefore, I think it unwise of you to challenge comment by the use of Eilidh as the name of your heroine — as that is the name most used by Miss M. both in her prose writings & poems. It is not as if it were as relatively common a Gaelic name as Silis or Girasol. However, this is only a suggestion for your consideration.

I directed a copy of Mrs. Wingate Rinder's *Shadow of Arvor* to be sent to you at the H/N. I hope it reached you, & that you may be able to notice it. I like the book exceedingly every way, tho' I differ in certain minor respects from Miss Macleod's article on it in the current *Bookman*.

By the way, Miss Macleod's book of poems is all but printed, & ought to be out by mid-November at latest. It is now definitely entitled "From the Hills of Dreams | Mountain Runes & Island Melodies" I am very glad she discarded "Gold and Shadow," not nearly so indicative or good a title in my opinion.

I am not certain, but fancy that about half the book is new in print: as is, certainly, the final section, a series of rhythmic prose studies, or poems in prose rather, connected by a simple dominant emotion.

Alas, I have had little time for reading Miss M's or any other books — for I am under extreme pressure at present, as I have a great deal to see to before I leave (latter-end next week) for New York, where I go on literary business of my own. I hope, however, to be back by the end of Nov[r].

In great haste | Sincerely yours | William Sharp

If you decide to expand the story for book publication, let me hear from you when I return, & I may be able to give you some useful advice.

ALS National Library of Scotland

To Arthur Stedman, October 14, 1896

London | 14 Oct /96

My dear Arthur,

As you will have heard from E. C. S. I have shortly to be in N.Y. on literary business. Of course I hope to see you, cher ami.

If you can do so, and easily, will you again do me the service & pleasure of making me a Pro-tem member of the Century (for say the first half of Nov.)?

I sail from Southampton on the 23rd, by the "Augusta Victoria" of the Hamburg American line, due at New York early on Friday 30th — where my letter-address will be c/o The H. A. Line Agents, 37 Broadway. (I shall probably be with Alden till Monday.) Please tell E. C. S. whose new address I do not know (I wrote to him for his birthday). Excuse a P/C in great pressure.

Ever cordially yours, | William Sharp

ACS Columbia University Library

To Stone and Kimball, October 16, 1896

Rutland House, Greencroft Gardens, | South Hampstead, London. | 16th October, 1896.

Messrs. Stone & Kimball, New York.

Dear Sirs,[44]

I shall not now enter into the question of "Wives in Exile".

I send you this formally to notify to you that I shall arrive in New York at the end of the month, and immediately after the elections, shall call upon you, preliminary, if necessary, to my taking steps to enforce my legal claims against you.

I may add that I shall have a power of attorney from Miss Fiona Macleod to enable me to act for her. She has placed her letters with me, including that wherein you acknowledge your indebtedness for the advance of £25 on "The Washer of the Ford"; but which you have never yet paid, despite your promises to the contrary.

I make no comment upon your procedure in these matters of Miss Macleod or of my own.

I am, Sirs, | Yours truly, | William Sharp

P.S. I expect to be staying first with Mr. Alden of Harper's, but my letter-address will be: 37 Broadway | (c/o The H. A. Line Agents)

ALS Huntington Library

To William Meredith,[45] October 17, 1896

C/o Miss Lilian Rea. | The Outlook Tower. | Lawnmarket | Edinburgh. | 17th Oct.

Dear Mr. Meredith

I have only today, on my happening to be in Edinburgh (I am at present visiting in Roseburghshire) received the copies of "Green Fire" — the delay in my hearing of their arrival being due to the temporary absence of Miss Rea, but chiefly to the fact that she has now left Crudelius House. Please cancel that address. (Henceforth all communications should be addressed to me as above.) (I expect to be very rarely in Murrayfield now, as, when I am on the East Coast, I shall probably be with a relative who lives near Hawthornden, a more sheltered locality. I never feel well, however, in the east, and wish to live more and more in the west, though private domestic affairs involve my being here frequently for a day or so at a time.)

And now my thanks for the copies of "Green Fire." The book is beautifully bound (and the printing and paper are delightful), and I am very pleased indeed with the design. Strangely, it is very like the island where I lived a long time as a girl — and which appears as Ithona in "Pharais." I thank you, and your firm, for the care and taste shown. And now, I can only hope that the book will go well, notwithstanding that it is not of a nature to appeal to the general public. I doubt if anything of mine ever will really reach the general public till "In the Old Magnific Way," of which I have great hopes. For the rest, I can write only as "Orchel has woven me."

I regret to say that the imperative need of nervous rest involves some delay with "The Lily Leven".[46] I made a fatal mistake when, wishing to save my eyes and nervous headaches, I dictated a great portion of this book. It is not my way of work, and I ought to have known better. The result is complete dissatisfaction. So, I have destroyed what I had done (save for some pages here and there, and a single chapter), and am now rewriting it — to my genuine satisfaction, I am glad to say. But, as things are, I cannot hope to send it to my cousin at Murrayfield or to Miss Rea, or to be copied, for a month or more to come. I am not at present allowing myself to write more than two hours a day — and I have besides had much moving about of late. Then, too, I have had all the putting together, and the revision, of my volume of poems. (It is called "From the Hills of Dream", and I shall have pleasure in sending you one of the earliest copies.) However, as I know you are not in any way inclined to be exigent in the matter, I shall be under no sense of strain, and be content to work to my own satisfaction and thereafter to send MS. to you at the earliest practicable moment. At the very latest, you may depend on receiving it, I feel confident, by mid-December. In any case, now, I suppose you would not issue it till well after the turn of the year?

Let me know if this is agreeable to you. Also, please, when writing, let me know when I may expect to receive the cheque from Messrs. Harpers, and if through you or their London agents.

I am looking forward to a fine St. Martin's Summer among the Isles, for a fine November generally follows a stormy October.

Yours very Sincerely | Fiona Macleod

P.S. You need not send a copy of "Green Fire" to Mr. Sharp, as I am sending him one of the six you sent to me. (By the way, do you know of his sudden departure for America — though only for two or three weeks I understand.) But will you please at once send a review-copy of "Green Fire" to | John Macleay. Esq. | The Highland News. | Inverness.

ALS Private

To Robert Murray Gilchrist, October 18, 1896

London | 18. Oct. 96

My dear Robert

Adieu for the present. But I want to see you soon after I return, sometime in December.

My love to you, & comradely greetings.

I leave London on Thursday morning, & on Friday (sailing from Southampton) shall be on the ocean, on board the "Augusta Victoria" of the Hamburg American line due at New York (where my letter address is 37 Broadway) on Friday 30th.[47] I shall not leave N.Y. till mid-November, whatever else I do, I expect.

"Green Fire" is just published. I have no copies to send, alas, or would send one to you. Constables sent only one or two. It is a strange book — some will say a mad book.

About first November your mother will receive from me a copy of "From the Hills of Dream" (F. M.'s first book of verse) — with my affectionate regard. She and you must look to what I have tried to say, in a new way, in the last section ("The Silence of Amor").

To both of you, Comrades, the greeting of | Your friend |
William Sharp | (& to you, | Will)

I had an unexpected (& unwished for) call the other night from Mr. Platt.[48] He does not in any way appeal to me, & he had underbred familiarities.

ALS Sheffield City Archives

To Stone and Kimball, October 21, 1896

9. Upper Coltbribge Terrace | Murrayfield, Midlothian | Oct. 21st. 1896.

Dear Sir,

I was more than astonished in reply to my cablegram to receive your extraordinary statement of accounts of a dollar or two as all due to me. This has the unpleasant appearance of adding insult to injury. I will not go into a matter which will have to be legally seen to, beyond stating that I have your firm's written agreement (1), about the royalties on *The Sin-Eater*, and the number of copies sold from the 1st. (2) Your firm's agreement as to the royalty of £25. to be advanced on the day of publication of *The Washer of the Ford*; and (3) Your own personal letter admitting this responsibility with a definite promise that it would be sent immediately.

I demand immediate fulfillment of these just claims. Meanwhile I have granted a Power of Attorney and full letter of authorisation to my friend, Mr. William Sharp, to act for me, as he is going out himself to take action against you, if necessary, on account of your extraordinary procedure in the matter of your business negotiations with him.

I am, etc., | Yours truly, | Fiona Macleod

To, Messrs. Stone and Kimball.

ALS Huntington Library

To Edmund Clarence Stedman, [October 21, 1896]

London

I cannot remember if I gave you my address in U.S.A. for my flying visit. I arrive (by the "Augusta Victoria" of the Hamburg American line) on Friday October 3rd[49] — and go to Alden's[50] at Metuchen till Monday. My letter address (before that and after) is | c/o The H. A. Line Agents | 37 Broadway | It will be a great happiness to see you and yours again — tho' alas the glimpse must be literally a glimpse, I fear.

W. S.

ACS Columbia University Library

To Elizabeth A. Sharp, October [21?], 1896

... to her [E. W. R.][51] I owe my development as "Fiona Macleod" though, in a sense of course, that began long before I knew her, and indeed while I was still a child.... without her there would have been no "Fiona Macleod."

Memoir, p. 222

To Coulson Kernahan, [October 22, 1896][52]

London

Many thanks for the card. I hoped I might sail with L.C.M.[53] — but now impossible. I leave tomorrow (on a flying visit on lity business of my own) for New York by the "Augusta Victoria" of the Hamburg American line, due New York on Friday 30th. (Address, c/o The H. A. Line Agents,

37 Broadway, New York). I hope to be in Boston for 2 days somewhere about 12th, I expect, and shall see L.C.M.

W. S.

As this now too late to catch L.C.M. at Paris, please forward to her. Au revoir cher ami, and heartiest congratulations on your vivid story. W. S.

ACS Princeton University

To Elizabeth A. Sharp, November 1, 1896

Metuchen, N.J. | 1st Nov., 1896

... Of course nothing can be done till Wednesday. All America is aflame with excitement — and New York itself is at fever-heat. I have never seen such a sight as yesterday. The whole enormous city was a mass of flags and innumerable Republican and Democratic insignia — with the streets thronged with over two million people. The whole business quarter made a gigantic parade that took 7 hours in its passage — and the business men alone amounted to over 100,000. Everyone — as indeed not only America, but Great Britain and all Europe — is now looking eagerly for the final word on Tuesday night.[54] The larger issues are now clearer: not merely that the Bryanite 50-cent dollar (instead of the standard 100 cent) would have far reaching disastrous effects, but that the whole struggle is one of the anarchic and destructive against the organic and constructive forces. However, this tremendous crisis will come to an end — pro tem. at any rate — on Tuesday night...

Memoir, pp. 274–75

To Elizabeth A. Sharp, [early November, 1896]

... I am indeed glad you like *Green Fire* so well.[55] And you are right in your insight: Annaik is the real human magnet. Ynys is an idealised type, what I mean by Ideala or Esclarmoundo, but she did not take hold of me like Annaik. Allan, too, is a variation of the Ian type. But Annaik has for me a strange and deep attraction and I am sure the abiding personal interest must be in her. You are the only one who seems to have understood and perceived this — certainly the only one who has noticed it. Some day I want to tell Annaik's story in full... .

Memoir, p. 275

To George Cotterell, [November 6, 1896][56]

9. Upper Coltbridge Terrace | Murrayfield | Midlothian

Dear Mr. Cotterell

Please accept from me the accompanying volume of "From the Hills of Dream," in which I hope you my find, here or there, something arresting.

It is but a small acknowledgement of the keen pleasure your own beautiful work in verse has given me.

Believe me | Yours most faithfully | Fiona Macleod

ALS Private

To Bliss Carman, [November 9, 1896]

The Century Association | 7 West Forty-Third Street

My dear Bliss,

If possible — or if you have not already written — please let me hear from you tomorrow (i.e. for my receipt on Wednesday) — about "From the Hills of Dream."[57]

Will you kindly do something for me?

Please call at the book store in Washington St. (or at H-M. & Co if they sell at discount) & get another copy of | Clement & [others?] "Artists of the 19th Century" | the 1896 One-Vol edition. | I forget the amount, but when you write on Tuesday let me know, & I will remit. | Please direct it to be done up and posted to | Mrs. William Sharp| Rutland House | 15 Greencroft Gardens | South Hampstead | London | England

Again, when you are at Copeland & Day's, will you ask them to send me, if they care to do so, review copies of any recent vols of verse — i.e. from say midsummer 1895.

(I have to write a "Fortnightly" article on recent American poetry)

If so, let them post to me at my London address as above.

In haste, Ever Yours, Dear Old Chap, | Will

ALS Pierpont Morgan Library

To [E. C. Stedman], [November 12, 1896]

The Century Association | 7 West Forty-Third Street

Dear Poet-Comrade

As the copy[58] I sent you has apparently gone astray for good (perhaps thro' being put in an open envelope, as the custom in England) I send you herewith my own, & the only one I have.

With love | Yours ever | Will

Steamer now goes Friday night or Saty morning.

ALS University of Washington Libraries, Walter Beals Autograph Collection

To Hannibal Ingalls Kimball, [November 13, 1896][59]

Century Club

My dear Mr. Kimball

Herewith receipt as from Miss Macleod. I will send her a cheque immediately on my return for exact English equivalent.

So very sorry I fear I can't see you again — but hope we may meet before very long in London, where you will be welcome, & where I hope to repay your friendly courtesies.

I am indebted to Mr. Barrie[60] — & indirectly to you of course — for the generously friendly & appreciative notice of W. S. in *The Tatler*. May its shadow grow longer & broader! — and by "it" I mean the daily one!

If this reach you in time to send me a line — either, if posted today, to the Century Club, where I'll call tomorrow forenoon — or, if sent tomorrow, to 37 Broadway, before 12 (my steamer, the Fürst Bismarck, goes from Hoboken at 1:30 or 2 p.m.) — you might let me know how you take to the idea of a small book next year to be called "A Northern Night and other Tragic Romances."[61] Nothing that I have done has made as much impression here as "A Northern Night" in *Vistas*. It is the only one of the "Vistas" I shd. reprint in the proposed book: which would consist of four or five other short pieces, including the strongest thing I have ever done, unpublished in any form, called "The Father's Tragedy."[62]

Let me know what you think.

In great haste, | [William Sharp][63]

P.S. I was delighted to make the acquaintance of your wife. I hope we may see her too in England.

ALS Huntington Library

To Ernest Rhys, November 23, 1896

23:11:96.

Dear Mr Rhys

On my coming from the West to Edinburgh, for a few days, I found your very welcome and charming letter, among others forwarded to me from the Outlook Tower.

It gratifies me very much that you, whose work I so much admire and with whose aims and spirit I am in so keen sympathy, care so well for the "Hills of Dream." These are hills where few inhabit, but comrade always knows comrade there — and so we are sure to meet one another, whether one carry a "London Rose" or a sheaf of half-barbaric Hill-Runes. I may say, however, that my life is mainly spent in the Western Highlands, and Isles, and that save for a week or so now and again in Edinburgh, I am never in towns, which depress me beyond words, and which I care (aside from friends) only for the music that I can hear there.[64] It may interest you to know that the name which seems to puzzle so many people is (though it does exist as the name "Fiona," not only in Ossian but at the present day, though rarely) the Gaelic diminutive of "Fionaghal" (i.e. Flora). "Fiona," however, and not "Fionaghal," is my name. For the rest — I was born more than a thousand years ago, in the remote region of Gaeldom known as the Hills of Dream. There I have lived the better part of my life, my father's name was Romance, and that of my mother was Dream. I have no photograph of their abode, which is just under the quicken-arch immediately west of the sunset-rainbow. You will easily find it. Nor can I send you a photograph of myself. My last fell among the dew-wet heather, and is now doubtless lining the cells of the wild bees.

All this authentic information I gladly send you!

Sincerely yours, | Fiona Macleod

Memoir, pp. 279–80

To Edmund Clarence Stedman, November 25, 1896

Rutland House | 15 Greencroft Gardens | South Hampstead |
London | 25/Nov/96

My dear Stedman,

You told me I was to come to you in any difficulty — and I take you at your word: always with the proviso that if you are too busy or are unwell you will be equally frank.

Well, what I write about now is the enclosed IOU from Lamson Wolffe & Co.[65] It is in the form, as you will see, of a Promissory Note, due on 6th (i.e. 9th) Jany/97. I did not realise in accepting it that the document would be useless here.

If at all possible, & if not at a heavier discount than say, in all, £5 (Five Pounds), I would thankfully have this money at once, <u>of which I am imperatively in need</u>. Can you manage this for me? I mean — if impracticable for yourself to advance the amount, less discount — then as a broker, on the spot?

If you think this cannot be done, & that it is best to await due date, will you like a good fellow put the document in your safe — have it presented when due, and then remit me the amount in a draft payable in London?

In this latter case I must just manage meanwhile as best I can, heavily handicapped as I am.

It will be a very great relief to my wife & myself if the first suggestion can be fulfilled: but you, I know, will do what is practicable, & know what is best. And so I leave it.

(My next year or two really hinge on this single joint.)

There is no need to waste words: I know you will do what you can to help me, and <u>you</u> know how grateful I am for "all and every" of your loving service & friendship.

Ever yours affectly, | William Sharp

ALS Columbia University Library

To Edmund Clarence Stedman, November 28, 1896

London | 28th Nov./96

My dear Stedman,

You will think me an infernal nuisance to trouble you again (after that last letter of mine with the Bill for $719, and my stupid oversight or rather ignorance about the $10 cheque) — but it will be a great obligation if at your convenience you will instruct your Clerk (or anyone else, at my expense) to go to Customs, & claim the enclosed.[66] (They should not be dutiable, as they are not for sale: but were sent to me, from Miss Macleod, as Presentation copies. However, if necessary, please pay the 60 cents, & let me know total amount expended, including postage of them. Miss M. wanted one to go to

1. E. C. Stedman, Lawrence Park, Bronxville, N. Y.

2. H. M. Alden, Metuchen, New Jersey

3. Bliss Carman, c/o Copeland and Day, 69 Cornhill

4. William Sharp, Rutland House, Greencroft Gardens, South Hampstead, London.

In the first 3 instances a written line was to go | To so and so, from Fiona Macleod | (C/o Miss Rea | The Outlook Tower | Castle Hill | Edinburgh).

Just in time for the mail, & no more. You and Mrs. Stedman and Miss McKinney will have had my other letters.

With love to you & yours, | Ever affectionately, | William Sharp

ALS Columbia University Library

To Robert Murray Gilchrist, [*Early December, 1896*]

15 Greencroft Gardens | So. Hampstead

My dear Robert,

As you will see, I am back again.

Health and divers circumstances rather frown upon me for the moment. It is possible I may have to knock off all work for two or three weeks or so: only, alas, if so, I am not to go north but south. That being so, Paris draws me more than anywhere else. But I might go afoot. How are you? Are you to be seduced?

Ever affectionately | Your friend | Will

I hope Mrs. Gilchrist duly received the copy of "From the Hills of Dream" I directed to be sent to her — and that both you and she have found in it something arresting.

ALS Sheffield City Archives

To Edmund Clarence Stedman, December 5, 1896

London | 5th Decr 1896

My dear Stedman,

Your welcome and unexpected letter has come just in time for me to catch the mail, having gone astray for 2 or 3 days chasing me!

I have time then only to say that I thought I had told you all about the Stone & Kimball matter, & left Stone's letter etc. —

To recapitulate, however, as briefly as possible:

(1) Stone persuaded me to promise to give him for S&K. "Wives in Exile," and not (as was my intention, after "A Fellowe and His Wife") to send it to Houghton Mifflin & Co.

(2) He gave me his own, & firm's undertaking to pay me £300 advance against royalties — £100 on receipt of MS. and £200 on publication.

No stipulation as to time when sent in, tho' we both hoped for late autumn issue, 1895. Illness delayed this. MS. was not sent complete till early in 1896. It was to come out in Spring.

(3) No option was given me, when S. & K. separated — and I knew nothing of it till a cool renunciatory note from S. & later a formal communication from K.

(4) S. wrote saying all would certainly be well, & contract honourably fulfilled.

(4)[67] After cabling as well as writing again & again, still failed to obtain the £100 due on the <u>receipt</u> of MS.

(5) Delays after delays, involving loss of Spring, Summer, & Autumn sales.

(6) Letter from K. saying S. had never told him how much he was in for: that he simply couldn't pay: etc., etc., etc.

(7) Letter from me to S. holding him to his personal pledge — & explaining how nothing but this debt of his, or his & K.'s, to me stood between me and bankruptcy.

(8) Clear evasion on part of S. & K.

(9) Decide to go to New York.

(10) In place of the <u>first</u> stipulation, K. ultimately relinquishes to me his rights in the book, & agrees to give over to any publisher I name, the printed sheets & plates.[68]

This gives me no money, of course, but only makes a fresh arrangement possible at once.

(11) Find that state of literary market makes any good bargain at moment impossible.

(12) Lamson said £300 utterly beyond him. When at last I suggested £150, he said that too was more than he could afford to give. Ultimately, when I explained that K. relinquished the sheets etc., he agreed to give me £150, on a bill at 2 months.

(13) I wrote to Stone, telling him of my loss of £150 (besides over £60 in coming to America etc. & returning & incidental expenses, apart from loss involved in leaving England and work) — due entirely to his broken pledges.

(14) Saw Mr. Melville Stone. He admitted H. S.'s moral obligation.

(15) I agreed to let the matter go to you for arbitration.

(16) My talk with you.

(17) Stone's letter to you.

(18) Final issue unknown.

In haste at the very last moment | Yours ever affectly |
William Sharp

ALS Columbia University Library

To John Ross, December 6, 1896[69]

Rutland House | 15 Greencroft Gardens | N.W. | 6/12/6

Dear Ross

Herewith I am sending my certificate for 100 shares in Town & Gown Association to Messrs. Whitson & Methuen to be transferred at their earliest convenience, the amount to be paid to you on behalf of Patrick Geddes & Colleagues, to whom you will advise the same.

Yours faithfully, | William Sharp

John Ross Esq.

ALS National Library of Scotland

To John Ross, December 9, 1896

Rutland House | Greencroft G'dns | So. Hampstead | 9/Dec/96

This note had better be filed with the other Papers & Receipts on this matter.

Dear Mr. Ross

Today I recd. back the Certificate, from Messrs. Whitsun & Methuen — who say "We regret we cannot undertake at present to find a purchaser of your shares — but should you do so, and let us have the particulars of transfer, we shall be glad to lay them before our Directors. We return Certificate herewith."

I have sent their letter to Prof. Geddes, as it is in direct contradiction of his assurances to me: and added, "I have sent the Certificate today to Mr. Ross, requesting him to hold it over for you, till he receives your instructions."

Please send me formal notification of Receipt of Certificate.

In gt. haste, | Yrs sincerely, | William Sharp

ALS National Library of Scotland

To [John Ross], December 16, 1896

London: 16th Dec '96

Dear Sir

I have no papers I can send you relative to Messr. White or to Mr. Wilson.[70] All the latter's business arrangements were with Mr. Geddes, and all Mr. White's with me were oral, save for a memorandum or two which I cannot now get till my return about middle or end of January; when also I will return any contracts etc. with authors now in safekeeping. These cannot be got without my personal application at my bank — and as I say I must now wait with this till after my return. I have, however, nothing of any kind that could bear upon the business footing of transactions with Mr. White.

Yours truly | William Sharp

ALS National Library of Scotland

To [John Ross], December 16, 1896

London: 16th. Decr.

Dear Sir,

Herewith a letter from an Armenian gentleman, Mons. A. Tchobanian[71], recommended by Prof. Geddes. Prof. G. also expresses his hope that P.G. & Co. may be able to bring out this book if it can be arranged.

All I can say is that I approve the idea in the abstract — but as for a success here all wd. depend (1) on the interest of the subject-matter and (2) on the translation. If gone on with, the translation could safely be left in the hands of Miss Lilian Rea, who has had ample experience. It is difficult to judge without seeing something to go by, or at least without knowing the kind of material.

Yours faithfully, | William Sharp

ALS National Library of Scotland

To John Ross, December 16, 1896

To The Manager "Patrick Geddes &Colleagues"

London | 16th Decr./96

Dear Sir

Reissue of Miss Macleod's Tales

As I have to see Miss Macleod shortly — where she is visiting friends in the South of France — I can discuss this matter further.

Meanwhile, as she has deputed to me the management pro.tem. of all her literary affairs I may say that

(1)   if you mean P.G. & Co. should reissue *The Sin Eater* and *The Washer of the Ford* intact, save for paper covers, the idea must be given up at once as quite untenable.

(2)   if, on the other hand, you mean that P.G. & Co. could reissue the tales in the new order suggested by Miss Macleod avoiding resetting up of type, but simply altering the moulds in so far as pagination is concerned (& correcting a few misprints) — then she might consent.

I am strongly of opinion that it would be worthwhile to reissue these tales, in the manner and sequence suggested by Miss Macleod, — keeping to the moulds save for the pagination & a few corrections: equally of opinion that her own division into 3 vols. is best ("*Spiritual Tales*," "*Barbaric Tales*," and "*Tragic Romances*"): and, from every point of view, would urge the advisability (save indeed for Miss M's own sake, for she proposes to give up to this end what she could easily print in book form elsewhere) that the one long important new tale, "Morag of the Glen" should be printed for the 3rd vol.

The amended list would be

Vol. I. *Spiritual Tales*

  1. The Washer of the Ford

2. St. Bride of the Isles

3. The Three Marvels of Iona

4. The Fisher of Men

5. The Last Supper

6. The Anointed Man

7. The Dark Nameless One

(All from *The Washer of the Ford* except no. 6)

Vol. II. *Barbaric Tales*

   The Harping of Cravetheen from "The Sin-Eater"

   The Song of the Sword from "Washer of the Ford"

   The Flight of the Culdees from "Washer of the Ford"

   Mircath from "Washer of the Ford"

   The Laughter of Scathach the Queen from "Washer of the Ford"

   Silk o' the Kine from "Sin-Eater"

   Ula and Urla from "Washer"

   The Annis Choille from "Washer of Ford"

(N.B. Miss Macleod offers her unpublished barbaric tale "Ahez the Pale" to add to this vol.)

Vol. III. *Tragic Romances*

   Morag of the Glen Proposed to be added to this vol., by Miss Macleod

   The Dan-nan-Ron

   The Sin-Eater

   The Ninth Wave from *The Sin-Eater*

   The Judgment o' God from *The Sin-Eater*

   Green Branches from *The Sin-Eater*

The Archer Proposed to be added

These additions would of course materially help the sale.

If, however, all this is considered inadvisable, it is possible Miss Macleod might agree to *The Sin-Eater* and *The Washer of the Ford* being reissued in paper-covers <u>thus</u>, in 2 Vols,

I. *Spiritual Tales*

The Washer of the Ford

St. Bride of the Isles all below from "The Washer of the Ford" & in order as they are in that book

The Fisher of Men

The Last Supper &

The Dark Nameless One in order as they are in that book

The Three Marvels of Iona

The Annir Choille

The Anointed Man .... from "The Sin-Eater"

II. *Barbaric Tales and Tragic Romances*

I.

The Harping of Cravetheen from "Sin-Eater"

The Song of the Sword from "Washer of Ford"

The Flight of the Culdees from "Washer of the Ford"

Mircath from "Washer of the Ford"

The Laughter of Scathach the Queen from "Washer of the Ford"

II.

The Dan-nan-Ron from "Sin-Eater"

The Sin-Eater from "Sin-Eater"

The Ninth Wave " from "Sin-Eater"

The Judgment o' God from "Sin-Eater"

Green Branches from "Sin-Eater"

Isla and Eilidh from both books

This would, also, leave the present vols with some unreissued matter (Prologue and Sections III & V in "The Sin-Eater", and Prologue and "The Shadow Seers" in The W. of the Ford).

I agree with her in thinking the 3-vol, with additions, much the best and most advantageous plan.[72]

The second, however, is worth consideration also.

Please let me hear by return about this, as I shall then be able to discuss the matter with Miss Macleod, addressing me at | Poste Restante | Tarascon | Bouches du Rhone | France | (I understand that Miss M. is willing to accept an arrangement whereby she is paid by royalty on sales.)

Yours faithfully, | William Sharp

P.S. I cannot return the dummy copies of the paper-covered specimens sent by Miss Rea, who, however, can surely get others at once from Miss Hay, as I do not think the designs were done by hand. Prof. Geddes may have taken them, along with the other papers he took away.

P.S. II As I find I cannot leave London tomorrow in the morning after all, & do not now leave my house till 4 p. m. — please telegraph to me about above proposals of Miss M. — so that if possible I may decide for her before I leave.

ALS National Library of Scotland

To Edmund Clarence Stedman, December 16, [1896]

Wedny Night 16th Decr

(Latter part private)

My dear Stedman,

Just 3 hours after the American mail has gone your two letters have come to hand. No mail goes out again till Friday night (for Saty, 19th).

Let me first thank you from my heart for all the worrying trouble you have so generously taken — & to ask you to believe me when I tell you that I am deeply distressed that in my hurry and influenzic perturbation I sent off the bill without endorsement, and so added greatly to your trouble & just annoyance. What a good & generous fellow you are: I can think of few men who would have taken so much trouble over this matter, as you have done. Again, dear friend, I thank you.

Tomorrow I will telegraph "Sincerest thanks, Returning note tomorrow," both to let you see I have duly recd. your regd. letter & enclosure and that I am at once returning it. (I daresay "Stedman, Bronxville, N.Y." will be enough to find you).

As things are, I am just as glad Lamson didn't discount the Bill, for I have had a loan & am for the moment out of the wood, & can't afford to realise at a heavy discount.

Herewith I return this note, duly endorsed: & again accept frankly your generous aid, & will leave it with you to realise for me at due date (January 6th-9th). I am sorry Lamson added to your worry by his prolonged silences. (He seems to be quite "square" from all I hear.)

As to the Stone & Kimball matter, you will before this have received my letter on this matter. (No, Mr. Stone & I settled nothing on the way home. He seemed to think his son would at once pay up whatever you adjudged, if at all, & there each of us left it.)

A few days ago I sent to you & Mrs. Stedman, as a Xmas Greeting, the new "Evergreen": & today I posted a copy of my edn. of M. Arnold to Miss McKinney. I also asked Lamson to send you for Xmas one early copy of "Wives in Exile."

If you have not done anything with the spare 4th vol. of "The Hills of Dream," kindly direct it to be sent to C. G. D. Roberts (Kingcroft, Fredericton, New Brunswick).

By the way, please do not omit to instruct Miss McKinney kindly to inform me of all outlays on my behalf, over & above what I remitted to her — including those "Hills of Dream" copies, the telegram & other Lamson matters, etc.

I beg you will not refuse this. I do not think anyone has a right to inflict these small expenses on friends — and it will really make me uncomfortable. As it is, I presume greatly on your loyal & affectionate good will.

Private

Alas, I found F. M. far from well. However, things go better. But as for myself worry & God knows what all have thrown me back a good deal — with the result that I am to knock off all work for 4 or 6 weeks, & go away at once from these killing fogs & damps.

So, tomorrow night or Friday morning, I leave London. I go first straight to Tarascon in Provence, to spend a few days with the Janviers — & then on to Tamaris & St. Maxime on the Riviera. I'll be back in London (to new & happier circumstances in every respect) before the end of January, thoroughly set-up again,

Love to you and Mrs. Stedman, in which my wife (who says you must be an angel) joins.

Ever gratefully yours | William Sharp

F., who has a weakness for poets & disreputable sinners generally, has taken an unnecessarily strong fancy to your photograph & to yourself as realized thro' me.

ALS Columbia University Library

To Patrick Geddes, [late December, 1896]

Please note (canceling any earlier direction) that, till further notice, my address will be | c/o Mons. Thos. A. Janvier | St. Remy-de-Provence | (Bouches du Rhone) | France | telegraphic | Sharp c/o Janvier | St. Remy-de-Provence (one word)

If I telegraph any arrival, change of plans, or change of address, please at once advise Elizabeth and Mary.

ALS National Library of Scotland

To Elizabeth A. Sharp, [late December, 1896]

St. Remy, France

... I am not going to lament that even the desire to think-out anything has left me — much less the wish to write — for I am sure that is all in the order of the day towards betterness. But I do now fully realise that I must give up everything to getting back my old buoyancy and nervous strength — and that prolonged rest and open air are the paramount needs... .

However, enough of this, henceforth I hope to have to think of and report on the up-wave only.

I am seated in a little room close to the window — and as I look out I first see the boughs of a gigantic sycamore through which the mistral is roaring with a noise like a gale at sea. Beyond this is a line of cypresses, and apparently within a stone's throw are the extraordinary wildly fantastic mountain-peaks of St. Remy. I have never seen anything like them. No wonder they are called the Dolomites of France. They are, too, in aspect unspeakably ancient and remote.

We are practically in the country, and in every way, with its hill-air and beauty, the change from Tarascon is most welcome... . There is a strange but singularly fascinating blend of north and south here just now. The roar of the mistral has a wild wintry sound, and the hissing of the wood fire is also suggestive of the north: and then outside there are the unmistakable signs of the south and those fantastic unreal like hills. I never so fully recognise how intensely northern I am than when I am in the south... .

Memoir, pp. 282–83

Chapter Sixteen

Life: 1897

After visiting the Janviers in St. Remy in late December, Sharp went on to the Riviera where, according to Catherine Janvier in her article on "Fiona Macleod and Her Creator William Sharp" (*North American Review*, 184/612, April 5, 1907, pp. 718–32), he "wandered restlessly from place to place" (p. 722). On New Year's Day, he wrote to the Janviers from Saint-Maxime to say he felt lonely and "craved help and companionship in a way foreign to his self-sufficing nature" (p. 722). After sending the Janviers several telegrams, he reappeared in St. Remy "with the statement that he wished to be looked after and to be made much of" (pp. 722–23).

> During this second stay with us, he was utterly unlike the mystery-surrounded, dual-natured dreamer of his previous visit: he was William Sharp, and William Sharp in his blithest mood. Though Fiona might smile, it is impossible to imagine her as bursting into a hearty laugh; while her creator could be the gayest of companions, full of fun and frolic, displaying at times a Pucklike impishness worthy of a twelve-year-old boy. He left our town in this joyous trim, waving his blue beret from the carriage window until the train was out of sight (p. 723).

Sharp intended to spend the entire month in the south of France, but his health had improved, finances were a continuing problem, and, most importantly, W. B. Yeats, who was scheduled to return to London in mid-January, asked Sharp to meet him in Paris. The carriage in which he left, according to Janvier, in "joyous trim" headed for Paris on January 4 or 5. In late December, Yeats had written a lengthy letter to Fiona Macleod in which he suggested she write a short play in the Celtic vein for performances sponsored by one of the various Irish literary and political

 https://doi.org/10.11647/OBP.0196.05

organizations he was promoting. He described his interest in the occult
and his intent to incorporate occult materials in his writings, and he
hinted at plans to create a Celtic Mystical Order. He also expressed
his hope that William Sharp would "come to Paris on his way back to
England" for "I have much to talk over with him." Mary Sharp received
the letter in Edinburgh and sent it on to Sharp in St. Remy.

Although Yeats and Sharp had moved in some of the same London
circles since the late 1880s and experimented together in drug-induced
(hashish and mescal) spiritualist experiments, they were not close
friends. Ten years younger than Sharp, Yeats had begun to attract a great
deal of critical notice for his poetry, and Sharp wanted to get to know
him better. Having invented Fiona Macleod and positioned himself as
either her friend or her relative, Sharp hoped to be drawn more closely
into the Celtic Revival where Yeats figured prominently. Yeats's January
letter to Fiona was precisely the entrée Sharp sought, just as Sharp
was Yeats's entrée to the mysterious highland lady whose writings he
admired. Yeats hoped Sharp would encourage Fiona to contribute to
the Celtic Revival by writing plays to be performed in Ireland. It is no
wonder Sharp shifted his plans and went to Paris.

Far more significantly, given later developments, Yeats wanted to test
Sharp's powers of clairvoyance. The ruse Sharp perpetrated the previous
August involving the Archer vision assured Yeats of Fiona's visionary
powers. Now, Yeats wanted to know if Sharp was able to communicate
with spirits. Years later, Yeats recalled Sharp visiting him in his hotel in
the Boulevard Raspail:

> When he stood up to go, he said, "What is that?" pointing to a
> geometrical form painted upon a little piece of cardboard that lay upon
> my windowsill. And the before I could answer, he looked out of the
> window, saying, "There is a funeral passing." I said, "That is curious, as
> the Death symbol is painted on the card." I did not look, but I am sure
> there was no funeral. A few days later he came back and said, "I have
> been very ill; you must never allow me to see that symbol again" (W. B.
> Yeats, *Autobiographies* (London: Macmillan, 1955), pp. 339–40).

Sharp may have known the geometrical form was a death symbol, but
Yeats assumed he did not and that reassured him of Sharp's visionary
powers. Yeats proceeded to recount a more interesting demonstration
of Sharp's psychic abilities. A phantom woman appeared in Sharp's

Paris hotel suite. After appearing and disappearing, she escaped down a flight of stairs into the street. Sharp followed her around many corners constantly seeing and losing her, until he came to the Seine. She was standing at an opening in the wall looking down into the river.

> Then she vanished, and I [Yeats speaking as Sharp] cannot tell why, but I went to the opening in the wall and stood there, just as she had stood, taking just the same attitude. Then I thought I was in Scotland, and that I heard a sheep-bell. After that I must have lost consciousness, for I knew nothing till I found myself lying on my back, dripping wet, and people standing all around. I had thrown myself into the Seine (*Autobiographies*, p. 340).

Yeats continued: "I did not believe him, and not because I thought the story impossible, for I knew he had a susceptibility beyond any one I had ever known to symbolic or telepathic influence, but because he never told anything that was true; the facts of life disturbed him and were forgotten." Yeats recalled this amazing story many years after discovering Fiona was Sharp. By then he had decided Sharp was an unwitting prevaricator and succumbed to the general opinion he was to be dismissed as an oddity because he pretended for so long to be a woman. Yeats's opinion of Sharp was quite different when he heard the story in 1897.

In Paris, Sharp was elated to receive Yeats's invitation to join him and Maud Gonne, who was with him in Paris, in evoking visions to obtain the talismans and rituals of a Celtic Mystical Order which would be centered in the Castle of the Rock in Loch Key in the West of Ireland. The Order would "unite the radical truths of Christianity to those of a more ancient world." Young men and women would be invited to the castle to learn the Order's rites and then go out into the world to spread the word and recruit others using the Castle as an "occasional retirement from the world." To begin this difficult, but necessary project, Yeats needed "mystical rites — a ritual system of evocation and meditation — to reunite the perceptions of the spirit of the divine, with natural beauty." He was deeply in love with Maud Gonne, and he thought she exceeded him in "seership." She shared his ideas, and he hoped he would "entirely win her" for himself as they engaged in the evocations together. That hope led him to an elaborate theory of partnership between a man and woman who loved each other.

I could therefore use her clairvoyance to produce forms that would arise from both minds, though mainly seen by one, and escape therefore from what is merely personal. There would be, as it were, a spiritual birth from the soul of a man and a woman. I knew the incomprehensible life could select from our memories and, I believed, from the memory of the race itself; could realize of ourselves, beyond personal predilection, all it required of symbol and of myth. I believed we were about to attain a revelation. [This quotation and those preceding in the paragraph are taken from the first draft of Yeats's autobiography in W. B. Yeats, *Memoirs*, transcribed and edited by Denis Donoghue (London: Macmillan, 1972), pp. 123–25]

Sharp was not to engage in evoking visions alone, but in the company of and in partnership with Fiona Macleod. Since Sharp and Fiona had clairvoyant powers and were in love, Yeats thought their relationship paralleled his with Maud Gonne. The two couples would augment each other's visionary capacities in the secret and laborious work of finding the symbols and rituals of the Celtic Mystical Order.

During the ten days he spent in Paris with Yeats and his friends — Maud Gonne, and Moina and Macgregor Mathers who were busy setting up a Paris branch of the Golden Dawn — Sharp was in a heightened state of mind. The invitation to join the inner sanctum of a revolutionary movement whose ultimate purpose was to prepare the world for the apocalypse produced a state of euphoria. There was one missing part; he had to enlist Fiona Macleod in the undertaking. He left Paris on or about January 15 and, stopping only briefly in London, went straight to Edinburgh where he crossed the Forth to the Pettycur Inn. He told Stedman in a January 25 letter he was "staying with a friend, F. M." at a "remote place among the hills." He had led Stedman to believe he was having an affair with Fiona, but it was Edith Rinder who was with him at the Pettycur Inn. It was she he had to convince to play the role of Fiona in the spiritualist work. It was she who must play Maud Gonne to his W. B. Yeats. One imagines Edith was both astonished by and skeptical of the proposal Sharp brought from Paris, but Sharp succeeded in convincing her to play at least a passive role in the enterprise. By 1897, their original passionate commitment had begun to fade. The search for talismans and rituals gave their relationship a new and serious purpose. Sharp continued to write as Fiona for the rest of his life, but his experience in Paris in

January 1897 was a critical turning point. The occult and its psychic experiments influenced the prose he wrote as Fiona during the last three years of the century and published in *The Dominion of Dreams* (1899) and *The Divine Adventure* (1900). From writing stories about the simple people who lived amid tragedies and in close touch with ancient myths and the spirits in the West of Scotland, Sharp turned to symbolic and ritualistic stories and essays. Though Edith Rinder was not, I believe, an enthusiastic participant in the psychic investigations, she was a significant enabler of the Fiona development.

Sharp's long January 25 letter to Stedman was dictated to and typed by Lillian Rea, an American girl employed by the Geddes firm who helped Sharp secretarially. He thanked Stedman for a check which was about half what he was due from Lamson for *Wives in Exile*. He deposited it right away, to the relief of his wife and his bank manager, since his "worldly fortune" had sunk to "about £3." After signing the typed letter, Sharp added a handwritten note:

> The time on the Riviera did me a lot of good and still more this unexpected and wild flight straight from France to the Scottish hills. And now I am going back to settle down to hard work till the end of July — and at the same time manage to give both my wife and myself a good time — and be a good boy — and always endorse my cheques — and love you and Mrs. Stedman and Miss McKinney — and "Generally" be your loving and grateful W. S.

It may have been Miss McKinney, Stedman's secretary, who sent Sharp a check he forgot to endorse, but Sharp's less than subtle message was he was ensconced with Fiona in "a remote place among the Scottish hills" where he was being less than a "good boy."

Financial problems continued to plague Sharp through the winter and spring, aggravating his physical and mental illnesses. He was so short of funds he asked the Geddes firm as Fiona Macleod for an advance of twenty-five pounds against the royalties of a three-volume edition of her short stories that would be published in March. If twenty-five pounds was too much, she hoped for at least ten pounds. Another Fiona letter went to Hannibal Kimball in New York asking if he would like to undertake the American publication of the three-volume edition or, if not, a single volume edition of her stories. In mid-February, he asked Murray Gilchrist whether he would like to contribute a serial romance to *My Social World*, a periodical Frank Rinder, his "intimate friend," was editing. He also offered Gilchrist a glimpse of his current state of mind:

> Alas, my dear boy, I can tell you neither that I am well nor happy. I am content, at present, to tell you that I am not actively unhappy, and that I am, I hope, slowly gaining ground physically. I have not done a stroke of original work for weeks past but am eagerly hoping to be able to begin again soon.

In late February letter, he invited Richard Le Gallienne to be his guest at an Omar Khayyam Banquet at Frascati's, an elegant and expensive restaurant on Oxford Street. Shortage of money seemed not to limit his expenditures. Another Fiona letter went to Kimball, who was planning a trip and hoped to meet Fiona. She informed him it would be "unpractical" for her to see him because she was "going to Italy immediately, and when I return in the late spring or early summer it will be direct to Glasgow or rather Greenock, to sail thence to my relatives in the Hebrides."

Though Sharp told Stedman in his January 25 letter he was going to work hard until July, give his wife a good time, and be a "good boy," he wrote again in early March to thank him for a twenty-pound advance from Lamson. He added a personal note:

> Pour moi, my brief spell of reform (three weeks and three days) convinced me that systematic reform would never suit me in mind or body. I have very happily relapsed into my Pagan ship, and the Sunbeam flies again at the Peak. My mate in this delectable craft smiled at my attempt, and now laughs joyously that I am myself once again.

A postscript which he asked Stedman to destroy clarified the identity of the mate: "Two days ago I was by the sea, with F. M. In mind and body, I am ten years younger, with that joy and delight." The improvement in his mental and physical state did not last long. On March 10, he told Catherine Janvier he had "an unpleasant mental and physical set-back the last three days." He had not been able to regain the "health and spirits" he was in during his visit to St. Remy though even then he was "far more worn in mind and body" than even she had guessed.

When the three volumes of tales were published in mid-March, Sharp asked his friend and fellow writer Coulson Kernahan to do what he could for them. Elizabeth had been in bed several days with an attack

Fig. 12. Fiona Macleod stories reissued in paperbacks by Patrick Geddes and Colleagues in 1896. Photograph by William F. Halloran (2019).

of rheumatism. Gilchrist had made it to London, and when he left — the "other night" — Sharp's study caught fire, probably from a misplaced cigarette. There was no harm to books or pictures, but between the fire and Elizabeth's illness, Sharp was "distracted." Though he was not producing much writing, he was quick to escape into Yeats-inspired millennialism. Energized by the beginning of Spring, he proclaimed to Catherine Janvier on March 23:

> It is the season of sap, of the young life, of green fire. Heart-pulses are throbbing to the full: brains are effervescing under the strong ferment of the wine of life: the spiral flames of the spirit and the red flower of the flesh are fanned and consumed and re-created and fanned anew every hour of every day... .
>
> This is going to be a strange year in many ways: a year of spiritual flames moving to and fro, of wild vicissitudes for many souls and for the forces that move through the minds of men. The West will redden in a new light — the "west" of the forlorn peoples who congregate among our isles in Ireland — "the West" of the dispeopled mind. The common Soul is open — one can see certain shadows and lights as though in a mirror.

Printing this passage in the *Memoir* (p. 284), Elizabeth simply noted "The letter ends abruptly." We recall her writing: "During the most active years of the Fiona Macleod writings, the author was usually in a highly wrought condition of mental and emotional tension," and, later: "The prolonged strain of the heavy dual work added to by eager experimentation with certain psychic phenomena with which he had long been familiar but wished further to investigate, efforts in which at times he and Mr. W. B. Yeats collaborated — began to tell heavily on him and to produce very disquieting symptoms of nervous collapse" (*Memoir*, pp. 266, 282). The periodic escapes with Edith Rinder provided passing relief from depression and enabled him to think and write as Fiona. They also enabled him in Edith's presence to engage in psychic experiments, but those evoked manic episodes that collapsed into deeper depressions upon his return to London. Both Elizabeth and Edith were clearly worried about Sharp's state of mind.

The Irish writer Katherine Tynan Hinkson, after favorably noticing Fiona's *From the Hills of Dream* in *The Speaker,* wrote to ask for more information about her personal life for an article she proposed to write for *The English Illustrated Magazine*. Sharp was moved to compose a long reply, dated March 24, designed to project Fiona as the preeminent Scottish female contributor to the Celtic revival, just as Hinkson assumed that role in Ireland. He responded first to Hinkson's mention of the questions about Fiona's identity.

> Oh yes, dear Mrs. Hinkson, I am now well aware of much of the mystery that has grown up about my unfortunate self. I have even heard that Fleet Street journalist rumour to which you allude — with the addition that the said unhappy scribe was bald and old and addicted to drink. Heaven knows who and what I am according to some wiseacres! A recent cutting said I was Irish, a Mr. Chas. O'Connor, whom I know not. A friend of a friend told that friend that I was Miss Nora Hopper and Mr. Yeats in union — at which I felt flattered but amused. For some time, a year or so ago, there was a rumour that "Fiona Macleod" was my good friend and relative, William Sharp. Then, when this was disproved, I was said to be Mrs. Sharp. Latterly I became the daughter of the late Dr. Norman Macleod [a distinguished minister of the Scottish Church]. The latest is that I am Miss Maud Gonne — which the paragraphist "knows as a fact." Do you know her? She is Irish, and lives in Paris, and is, I hear, very beautiful — so I prefer to be Miss Gonne rather than the Fleet Street journalist!

Sharp tried to project the consummate feminine voice writing to another woman, placing himself in the middle of other "wiseacre" speculations to deemphasize the wisest. He went on to stress Fiona's need for privacy: "I do most urgently wish not to have my privacy made public, partly because I am so "built" and partly for other reasons: but I would not perhaps let this stand in the way of the urgent wishes of friends, were it not that there are other reasons also." Next, Sharp revealed just a bit:

> But this much I will confide to you, and gladly: I am *not* an unmarried girl, as commonly supposed, but am married. The name I write under is my maiden name. Perhaps I have suffered, as well as known much joy, in my brief mature life: but what then — all women whose heart is in their brain must inevitably suffer. And so, you will, I know, at once excuse me and forgive my inability to give you any material particulars. This past week I have had no fewer than four editorial applications for my photograph for reproduction — but now, as ever, I have had to decline. Two friends in London have my photograph, and perhaps you may see it someday: but now I do not even let friends have a photograph, since one allowed someone to take a sketch of it for an American paper. I can't well explain why I am so exigent. I must leave you to divine from what I have told you.

And a bit more: "I don't object to its being known that I come of an old Catholic family, that I am a Macleod, that I was born in the southern Hebrides, and that my heart still lies where the cradle rocked." Mixing his own plans with those of Fiona, he continued: "If, perchance, I should be in London this autumn or early winter — on my way to the Riviera (for I am not strong) — I hope to be able to make your acquaintance in person." Fiona had heard about Mrs. Hinkson from several friends, whereupon Sharp inserted himself as one such friend: Mr. William Sharp "is a great admirer of your writings, both in prose and verse." The letter is a carefully wrought work of art and one of Sharp's most revealing and extensive efforts to construct the personality of his invention.

Since Fiona suggests she and Hinkson should meet in London should they happen to be there at the same time, Sharp was toying with the idea of inducing Edith to impersonate Fiona. Two days later he broached the idea in a Fiona letter to George Meredith: "There is a chance I may be south this Spring or early Summer. If so, I look with keen pleasure to the often-anticipated visit to you." Sharp succeeded in convincing Edith to play the role, for he took her to meet Meredith at Box Hill on June 10, 1897. In a letter to Alice Meynell dated June 13, Meredith described her as "a handsome woman, who would not give me her eyes for awhile." In a letter to Maud Gonne dated January 14, 1907, Yeats recalled Meredith saying, "she was the most beautiful woman he ever saw." It is no wonder Edith appeared shy and nearly voiceless, and this is the only time, to my knowledge, she agreed to meet one of Sharp's friends as Fiona. The ruse was successful because Meredith lived in relative isolation in Surrey and never engaged in London society where he might have come upon Edith.

Fig. 13. William Sharp (1855–1905). William Strang, *William Sharp* (c. 1897), etching, printed by David Strang. Photograph by William F. Halloran of author's copy (2019).

In late March, he sent his latest "phiz," or photograph, to Louise Chandler Moulton for her birthday and told her he was leaving England for three weeks or so and hoped to find her in London when he returned. He sent the same message to Stanley Little. If he planned to go abroad, he changed plans and opted for a hotel in St. Margaret's Bay, near Dover. There, apart from the pressures of life in London and, for part of the time at least, with Edith Rinder he hoped to regenerate his writing as Fiona and renew efforts to find talismans and rituals for Yeats. In the *Memoir*, Elizabeth recalled: "Towards the end of April I went to Paris to write upon the two 'Salons,' and my husband, still very unwell, went to St. Margaret's Bay" (*Memoir*, p. 285). Since the "Old Salon" opened on April 14 and the "New Salon" on April 20, Elizabeth must have been in Paris for the "Press Preview" of the "Old Salon" on April 13.

On a Sunday that must have been April 18, Sharp wrote to Elizabeth from St. Margaret's Bay where he was "on the shore by the sea and in the sunshine" and felt very near her in spirit, as he always did when he was "reading, hearing, seeing any beautiful thing." Filled with "a passion of dream and work," he felt he would soon be able to write again. "More and more absolutely," he wrote, W. S. and F. M. were "becoming two persons — often married in mind and one nature, but often absolutely distinct." Omitting passages of the letter, Elizabeth added a final sentence: "Friendship, deepening into serene and beautiful flame, is one of the most ennobling and lovely influences the world has." She may have wanted to imply the sentence referred to her or Fiona, but Sharp habitually used the flame metaphor to describe his relationship with Edith. Used here, it increases the likelihood that she was with him at least part of the time in St. Margaret's Bay. How neatly it coalesces with the splitting of selves, since she was the physical embodiment of the second person he felt within.

The letter is signed "Wilfion," a name Elizabeth described in the *Memoir* as follows:

> In surveying the dual life as a whole I have seen how, from the early partially realised twin-ship, "W. S." was the first to go adventuring and find himself, while his twin, "F. M.," remained passive, or a separate self. When "she" awoke to active consciousness "she" became the deeper, the more impelling, the more essential factor. By reason of this severance, and of the acute conflict that at times resulted therefrom, the flaming of the dual life became so fierce that "Wilfion" — as I named the inner and third Self that lay behind that dual expression — realised the imperativeness of gaining control over his two separated selves and of bringing them into some kind of conscious harmony (*Memoir*, p. 423).

Having postulated yet a third self which tried to gain control over her husband's two separated selves, Elizabeth went on to ascribe at least one characteristic of the unifying self. "The psychic quality of seership," she thought, "linked the dual nature together" for both as F. M. and W. S., Sharp "dreamed dreams" and "saw visions." Elizabeth said little about her husband's psychic experiments because she was concerned about their effects, but a few friends, she wrote, knew him only as a "psychic and mystic." From time to time, "he interested himself in definite psychic experimentation, occasionally in collaboration with Mr. W. B. Yeats; experimentation that sometimes resulted in such serious physical disturbance that he desisted from it in later years" (*Memoir*, p. 424). That brings us back to William and Edith together in St. Margaret's Bay and the likelihood — recalling Yeats's opinion that visions come more readily when a man and woman who love each other evoke such visions together — that they were engaged in the work Yeats set for them.

Before Sharp left for St. Margaret's Bay, he dictated a Fiona letter which Mary dated April 9, to Benjamin Burgess Moore, an undergraduate at Yale University who had authored an article about Fiona in the *Yale Literary Magazine*. She thanked him for his "profoundly sympathetic" and "most welcome appreciation" of her work. She had seen nothing in any American paper or magazine which "can be compared with it — either in knowledge of the writings, sympathetic understanding, and general insight — and this, I may add, not merely because you honour me with such cordial praise." She then went on as in the letter to Katherine Hinkson to flesh out the Fiona character. Adopting what he considered a feminine voice, Sharp revealed a good deal of his own approach to human life:

> I believe in one intensity of emotion above all others, namely the intensity of this brief flame of life in the heart and the brain, an intensity no one can have who does not account the hours of every day as the vanishing pawns in that tragic game of chess for ever being played between Time and Eternity. [...] I live truly only when I am in the remote Isles or among the mountains of Argyll — a solace and inspiration which come to me much attenuated through the human medium. [...] though young in years, I have a capacity for sorrow and regret which has come to me through my Celtic ancestry out of a remote lost world.

Nonetheless, Sharp states that Fiona was not a melancholy person, "I am young, and life has given me some of her rarest gifts, and I am grateful." When her hour comes, she will be ready, having lived. At the same time, she is "ever aware of the menace of the perpetual fugitive shadow of Destiny." Lying among the dunes in Iona, writes Sharp, Fiona once had a dream which summed up her approach to life. She "heard a voice saying in Gaelic that the three Dominions or Powers were 'The Living God, the Dying World, and the mysterious Race of Man,' and that behind each gleamed the shadowy eyes of Destiny." Hoping Burgess will shore up Fiona's reputation in the United States, Sharp sent him a copy of *The Washer of the Ford*, *From the Hills of Dream*, and a sympathetic review of the latter. Later, when Burgess decided to seek out Fiona in Scotland in the hope of a Celtic romance, Sharp had cause to regret Fiona's openness in this letter.

Fig. 14. Cartledge Hall, Holmesfield, Derbyshire. Home of R. Murray Gilchrist and family. Photograph by Dave Hobson (2014). Courtesy of Vale of Belvoir Ramblers, https://vbramblers.blogspot.com/2014_04_01_archive.html

In early May, Sharp was back in London, and Elizabeth, whose health was not good, had gone south from Paris to stay in St. Remy where their friends the Janviers lived in the winter months. On May 3 Elizabeth wrote to thank Murray Gilchrist for his photograph which she had requested to become better acquainted with "Will's firm friend." She writes that she was gathering strength, resting and enjoying herself in a lovely sunny spot where she found it extremely interesting to be taken to the heart of a "wonderful literary movement" — the Provençal poets, led by Frederick Mistral, who she hoped to meet soon. Sharp went north to spend the night with Murray Gilchrist on Saturday, May 8, and returned to London the next afternoon. In a letter of thanks, he reminded Gilchrist to include his photograph when he wrote to Mrs. Wingate Rinder, whose address was 11 Woronsow Road, in St John's Wood, a fashionable area of northwest London. Despite his worries about finances, Sharp, restless as ever, decided to surprise his wife in St. Remy on her birthday. He left London on Friday, May 14, arrived in

St. Remy Sunday morning, celebrated Elizabeth's birthday on Monday, left that evening, and was back in London late on Wednesday. Elizabeth described the occasion as follows:

> On the early morning of the 17th of May the waiter brought me my coffee and my letters to my room as usual and told me gravely that a large packet had arrived for me, during the night, with orders that it should not be delivered to me till the morning. Should it be brought upstairs? The next moment the door was pushed open and in came the radiant smiling unexpected apparition of my Poet!" (*Memoir*, p. 286).

The "interlude" seemed "strange and dreamlike," he wrote to Elizabeth, the "hurried journey, the long afternoon and night journey from Paris, the long afternoon and night to Tarascon — the drive at dawn and sunrise through beautiful Provence — the meeting you — the seeing our dear friends there again. And then that restful Sunday, that lovely birthday!" After returning to London Wednesday night, he left again to spend the weekend with his mother and sister in Edinburgh. When he returned the following Monday, May 24, he told Little he could not go down to Sussex to visit him and his wife until Elizabeth returned from St. Remy on the June 14 or 15. He was busy all week and planned to leave again on the weekend. He went on to say:

> What with the autumn in Scotland, the early winter in America, Jany in the Riviera, Provence, Scotland, & France three times, I've not been much here since last summer! I'm as nearly bankrupt as I've ever been in my life — but I've lived up to the hilt, and it's Spring, and Summer's still to come, and heads or tails it's still good to be alive, and may the Dispenser of Laughter & Tears smile benignly on both of us, cher ami!

In that spirit he left at the end of May to spend the first week of June with Murray Gilchrist and his family at Cartledge Hall in Derbyshire. Following his stay in St. Margaret's Bay, his trip to St. Remy, his visits to Gilchrist, and the advent of Spring, his spirits were high, but the constant movement — reflecting his efforts to stave off loneliness and depression — prevented him from writing much as W. S. or F. M.

For most of June, Sharp was in London. As the summer progressed, he worked on several Fiona tales which would appear in 1899 in *The Dominion of Dreams*. He also wrote, as Fiona, *The Laughter of Peterkin* — a collection of Celtic stories for children, which Archibald Constable and Co. published in November. In mid-August, he and Elizabeth spent two weeks in Southwold, Sussex with the Janviers, who were visiting England. They returned to London for two days on August 28 and then left for Parkstone in Dorset, where they stayed until September 12, Sharp's forty-second birthday.

While in Dorset, Sharp constructed a birthday letter from Fiona to Will which is in Sharp's hand, not Mary's Fiona hand. It reflects the splitting defined by Elizabeth and his belief Fiona was becoming a separate personality distinct from that of W. S. In it we glimpse how Sharp viewed his life in the fall of 1897:

> Now, dear Billy, forgive me if I say that I am very much disappointed with you this past year. You have not been well, it is true: but you have also been idle to a painful degree, and your lack of method makes me seriously anxious. I will not dwell upon your minor and to me irritating faults: you know well to what I allude, and I think too you are often greedy, for it is not necessary always to have both marmalade and butter at breakfast. That is a small thing, but it is significant: I can only hope that you will control your appetites better in 1897–8.
>
> But do for heaven's sake put your shoulder to the wheel and get soon in good working trim at something worth doing. You ever put pleasure first and think so much of youth that you don't like billiards merely because the balls are bald. This is sad, Billy.
>
> I shall keep all the rest till we meet. What an uncomfortable half hour you will have!
>
> Still, you're a dear, and I like you with all your faults. Be a good boy and I'll love you.
>
> Your loving twin, | Fiona

It is Sharp's view of himself, but it also that of a sister, even a mother figure, who expresses her displeasure about Sharp's putting pleasure first and his failure to control his appetites. One can imagine Elizabeth so expressing herself to her "poet." It might also reflect Sharp's sense of the views of other women who loved him — Edith Rinder, Mona Caird, and Catherine Janvier — to name but three.

Back in London on September 14, Sharp sent the typed manuscript of Mona Caird's "The Pathway of the Gods," to William Meredith with the recommendation that it be published by Archibald Constable and Co., which was about to publish Fiona Macleod's *Laughter of Peterkin*. He was in London but would be leaving the next day. If he did indeed leave London then, we do not know his destination. Sharp was back in London when he wrote to Edward Martyn on September 22. Yeats had encouraged Martyn, a well-off member of the Irish landed gentry, an Irish nationalist, and an aspiring playwright, to invite Sharp and others to his home, Tillyra Castle in County Galway, to discuss the kind of plays Yeats wanted for his projected Irish Theater. With the dates for the theater discussion set for early October, Sharp told Martyn he was leaving the next day (Thursday 23) for Dublin, where he would see George Russell (AE) on Friday and, on Saturday morning, go on to the Royal Hotel in Greenore, a port village on the East coast north of Dublin. Here, he could be contacted on Sunday and Monday morning (September 26 and 27). His plans after that, he told Martyn, would be "guided by weather and other circumstances," but he implied he would be travelling in Ireland until Saturday October 2, when he would take the train Martyn had suggested to Ardrahan in Galway. Letters that follow show, however, that he made his way on September 27 back across the Irish Channel to the Isle of Arran off the west coast of Scotland, where he stayed four nights, before returning to Ireland and boarding the train to visit Martyn.

Sharp's annual birthday letter to E. C. Stedman, dated September 28 from The Corrie, Isle of Arran, began: "I send you a line from this beautiful island (more beautiful than ever to me because of a beautiful friend and comrade who is here too)." He went on to name that comrade as F. M. The brief Arran interlude seems to have been preplanned to enable him to be alone for a few days with Edith Rinder, who was spending September, as usual, on the mainland near Tarbert just north of Arran. After leaving Arran, he told Stedman, he would be going "to the West of Ireland (Connemara) to stay at an old castle with a strange and delightful host — with a fellow guest, my friend W. B. Yeats." In a September 29 letter from Arran, he asked John Macleay to see that *The Highland News* "for this and the next two weeks" be sent to him at Tillyra Castle.

After arriving at Tillyra on Saturday October 2, he wrote a long letter to Elizabeth on October 4 which described his hazardous arrival two days earlier and Martyn's plans to take him to see the Cliffs of Moher and other West Country sights before Yeats arrived on Thursday. He was delighted to have finally made it into the heart of the Irish literary revival, a distinguished group that included, besides Martyn and Yeats,

Fig. 15. This photograph of William Sharp was taken in Dublin in late September, 1897, and sent to Henry Mills Alden, editor of *Harper's Magazine* and Sharp's friend, at Christmas, 1897. Courtesy of the University of Delaware Library (The Henry Mills Alden Papers), Public Domain.

Lady Gregory (whose Coole Park was nearby), Douglas Hyde, and Martin Morris, a neighbor who would become, in 1901, Baron Morris of Killanin. As the days went by, he was less than well-received by the group. Lady Gregory memorably described him (*Diaries*, 153–54) as "an absurd object, in velvet coat, curled hair, wonderful ties — a good natured creature — a sort of professional patron of poets — but making himself ridiculous by stories to the men of his love affairs & entanglements, & seeing visions (instigated by Yeats) — one apparition clasped him to an elm tree from which he had to be released." I have described Sharp's strange and amusing visit to Tillyra for what Lady Gregory called a "Celtic party" at some length in a section called "The Soul of the Tree and the Hermaphrodite" in *Yeats Annual, No. 14*, pp. 184–99 (see Endnote 1). Lady Gregory recalled having suspected Sharp was Fiona Macleod. That may have been only hindsight, but Yeats knew Sharp was the key to Fiona Macleod, and he wanted Fiona, not Sharp, to contribute plays for the theater. Throughout the visit Sharp played a double role, and portraits taken in a Dublin studio on his to or from Tillyra confirm Lady Gregory's description. With two enormous blond curls on his forehead, he seems to have decided — for a brief period at this time — that his appearance should offer at least a hint of his feminine self.

Writing to the Grant Allens from London on November 5, Sharp reported that he had returned a few days earlier from the west of Ireland, where he had had a delightful time. Having left Tillyra in mid-October, he spent some time in Dublin and Scotland. But he was not long in London. "Owing to the excitable condition of his brain," according to Elizabeth (*Memoir*, p. 290), "London proved impossible, and "he took rooms in Hastings." That decision recalls his residence in Phenice Croft in 1893, when he was alone and experimenting with drugs to evoke visions. One reason for the "excitable condition of his brain" which Elizabeth did not mention was the need for a place where he could be alone — and at times with Edith Rinder — to conduct psychic experiments for Yeats. The fragment of a letter he sent Elizabeth from Hastings which she included in the *Memoir* reflects the state of his mind as 1897 drew to a close:

> I am so glad to be here, in this sunlight by the sea. Light and motion — what a joy these are. The eyes become devitalized in the pall of London gloom.... There is a glorious amplitude of light. The mind bathes in these illimitable vistas. Wind and Wave and Sun: how regenerative these elder brothers are. Solomon says there is no delight like wisdom, and that wisdom is the heritage of age: but there is a divine unwisdom which is the heritage of youth — and I would rather be young for a year than wise for a cycle. There are some who live without the pulse of youth in the mind: on the day, in the hour, I no longer feel that quick pulse, I will go out like a blown flame. To be young; to keep young: that is the story and despair of life.

Sharp fixated on the image of the as a representation of the youth and desire which he felt slipping away from him, but which he desperately wanted to preserve. The desire to "keep young" is central to the story of Sharp's life. The increased difficulty of sustaining his youth, and the inevitability of losing it, was a cause for the despair he was desperately trying to avoid in 1897, and indeed for the rest of his life.

On December 4 he was back in London briefly to attend a meeting of The Irish Literary Society, where Yeats read an important lecture on "The Celtic Movement." Without Yeats's approval, the Society officials had asked Sharp to chair the meeting. Influenced no doubt by Sharp's behavior at Tillyra Castle, but also because it was an Irish society, Yeats asked him to withdraw. He refused, whereupon Lady Gregory, ever ready to come to the aid of Yeats, intervened and charmed Sharp into acceding to Yeats's request. She arranged what she called "a little festa" after the lecture at the Metropole restaurant for a group that included the Sharps, Yeats, Yeats's father and sisters, and Arthur Symons. She said: "It went off very pleasantly." The rest of December seems to have passed uneventfully, though at the end of the month, Elizabeth, who Lady Gregory came to like very much, contacted the flu, whereupon her husband took her to his flat in Hastings to recuperate. 1897 was a full year for the Sharps, with many highs and many lows.

Letters: 1897

To Patrick Geddes and Colleagues, [early January, 1897][1]

Hotel St Romain | 5 Rue St Roch | 5 Rue St Roch | Paris

I have tonight telegraphed to you to send me | The Sin Eater | The Washer of the Ford (2) | Hills of Dream | Lyra Celtica | and Papers of the Franco-Scottish Socy. Put all down to Firm, as they are for an important writer here who has promised to do best for us.

W. S.

Have also interviewed Flory the bookseller who is much interested.

ACS National Library of Scotland

To Robert Murray Gilchrist, [January 15?, 1897][2]

The most hurried line, dear friend, to say that I am leaving London in an hour — My address for the rest of this month (at any rate) is Pettycur House | Kinghorn | (Fife)

Your friend | William Sharp

ALS Sheffield City Archives

To Edmund Clarence Stedman, January 25, 1897

Rutland House, Greencroft Gardens | South Hampstead, London |
25. January, 1897.

Excuse a type-written letter (done, to save time and for my eyes which have neuralgia today, at my sister's in Edinburgh — where I have come in for an hour from the remote place among the hills where I am staying with a friend, FM.[3]

My dear Stedman,

Let me at once hasten to thank you for the generous and loyal way in which you have taken my interests under your care. Not only am I grateful to you for all your many kindnesses, and for the unselfish trouble and responsibility you have taken on my behalf, but also I realize how much more efficaciously you have carried through all this business with Lamson than I could possibly have done, partly from being at such a distance, and largely, I admit, from business incapacity, or rather lack of experience and knowledge of how such financial negotiations are best conducted. Everything that you have done in this matter seems to me wise and discreet. I have received the draft for £ 64.5.6 (that is, the $319.00 less the small item due Miss McKinney), and duly passed it into my bank, to my own and my wife's great relief, seeing that our worldly fortunes had sunk to about £3, and also, no doubt, to the re-establishment of my waning financial repute with my much tried bank Manager. In the circumstances, I think you were certainly wise, as well as alert in getting hold of those $319.00, though from all you say, and the collateral security of Merriam & Cop's notes, I have no doubt the whole matter will be settled satisfactorily. I have also by this post written to Mr. Lamson. In that letter I have, of course, dissipated any possible misunderstandings about the English rights of Wives in Exile having surreptitiously been disposed of. Lamson ought to have known that any such action on my part was impossible for me, but over and above any sense of honour and squareness on my part, he should also have remembered that in our signed contract he is absolutely protected on this point. Of course, nothing of the kind has happened, or anything that could possibly give colour to such an idea: as a matter of fact, not even a single word has been said about the book in question to anybody, for the good reason that I have all along been awaiting Lamson's own action in England as agreed upon between us. However, I fancy that possibly he merely mentioned to you some statement made by Kimball, Kimball speaking or writing inadvisedly or misapprehendingly.

I have already written to you about the Stone arbitration matter, and explained that so far as I am aware, nothing whatever was kept back from you. There was no gain to me either from Kimball or from Lamson in the fact of the sheets being got from Kimball. I insisted upon this seeing that Kimball could not pay up anything at all, and as I had lost heavily through the year's loss of this book through non-publication and it was simply in order to strengthen my hands by coming to an immediate arrangement with some other publisher that I got Kimball to yield this point in lieu of what he felt I might otherwise claim as damages. And, as a matter of fact, as I think I told you, Lamson would not have taken the book, even at the half of the original sum (that is £150. instead of £300.), if it had not been for this that he got the printed sheets thrown in. He, therefore, was the gainer by my insistence on this point with Kimball, but it put nothing in my pocket — so that the upshot was my having £150 on a bill of exchange instead of £300, the loss of a year's usufruct of the book in Great Britain and America, and other incidental losses — to say nothing of my voluntary but still necessitated action in coming out to America — all brought about through Herbert Stone's shiftiness in fulfilling his obligations firstly to me, and secondly to Mr. Kimball in connection with me.

I do hope your own affairs will already have taken, or will promptly take, a convincing upward turn and that in means and in health you will soon have that leisure which you so much need for the beautiful work all of us who know you are looking for you still to do, and add to that so fine achievement in prose and verse which is already associated with your name. We talked often of you and your work and common friends — and by "we" I mean the Janviers and myself — when I was with them recently in Provence. My stay on the Riviera did me good, and after I left the Janviers, I went to Paris for a week or so, and thence abruptly came to Scotland, *for a special reason* — where after a week or two I am now on the point of returning to London to settle down and be the good boy you have so often foolishly exhorted me to be — foolishly, because a preacher should always be able to exhort out of example as well as from precept![4]

Finally, do not forget my glad willingness at all times to do anything I can for you over here. And, by the way, let me take this opportunity to tell you about a friend of mine, about whom in any case I will write you later, who is starting literary and agency work in London, chiefly of the Literary Agency nature. This is Miss Lilian Rea (who for some time hence can best be addressed through me) an American girl who after much residence abroad and fairly wide experience came to

London first to assist me secretarially, and afterwards succeeded to a responsible position in the firm of Patrick Geddes & Colleagues. She is now settled in London, and going to do all kinds of miscellaneous literary work at first and second hand: typing, copying, researching at the British Museum, translating, obtaining books, in fact everything that comes under the heading of Literary Bureau and Agency. As she is just about to take a new office and rooms, there is no use in giving present address, so if you or any of your friends want to employ her on any matter, from procuring English books up to researching or any literary undertaking, she can be addressed, meanwhile, through me. Later you will have a circular prospectus from herself, but it will be a month or so yet before she is definitely settled in her new quarters and with her new partner. I may add, of course (otherwise I would not venture to recommend her), that she is absolutely trustworthy, thoroughly business like, and will be found to fulfill every kind of transaction on the most moderate scale practicable. I cannot but think that you and others might find her services of great use even in the minor matter of the swift and economical procuring of English books old and new and second hand. She is also, I understand, prepared to act as literary agent for any American authors — that is, as to the piloting of their MSS., or arranging for the English issue of their books with English publishers — and once more, to do what is really necessary for the successful appearance of the works of any American author here, to go through typewritten or printed copies of books and see that all American spellings are made conformable with English usage.[5]

Ever affectionately, | William Sharp

I expect to be in London this day week. The time on the Riviera did me a lot of good and still more this unexpected and wild flight straight from France to the Scottish hills. And now I am going back to settle down to hard work till the end of July — and at the same time manage to give both my wife and myself a good time — and be a good boy — and always endorse my cheques — and love you and Mrs. Stedman and Miss McKinney — and "Generally" be your loving and grateful W. S.

Miss M. greatly pleased by your message, and encouraged too. (The tales of *The Sin-Eater* and *The Washer of the Ford*, rearranged and sectioned, and with a few others added, are about to be reissued in three vols. in a cheaper but artistic paper-cover edn. I. Spiritual Tales; II. Barbaric Tales; III. Tragic Romances.)[6]

TLS Columbia University Library

To P. G. Geddes and Colleagues, January 28, 1897

28:1:97.

Dear Sirs

Will it be practicable for you to let me have at once — in whole or in part — the £25 agreed upon as an advance against royalties on the new cheap 3. vol edition of my *Sin-Eater* and *Washer of the Ford* (augmented).

I believe the stipulated date was the day of publication, and so I ask for this favour only as one of convenience. If it is not convenient for you to pay me that sum at present, could you let me have £10 to account.

Apologizing for troubling you with my personal needs in this way —

Believe me, | Yours sincerely, | Fiona Macleod

P.S. I send you this through my cousin, Miss Mary Sharp, 9. Upper Coltbridge Terrace, etc. to which please post your reply.

ALS National Library of Scotland

To Hannibal Ingalls Kimball, January 28, 1897

9. Upper Coltbridge Terrace | Murrayfield, Midlothian | 28:1:97.

Dear Mr. Kimball

Do you care to come to any arrangement with me as to an American reissue of my shorter tales, such as indicated in the enclosed prospectus.

Or would you care for a new short volume, to consist of the new tales only — Morag of the Glen | The Melancholy of Ulad | Ahez the Pale | The Hills of Ruel | The Archer | The Awakening of Angus Ogue — to be called either (after much the longest and most dramatic) Morag of the Glen | And other Tragic Romances | or simply Tragic Romances[7]

As, apart from Messrs. Harpers who published "Green Fire" (after I had duly submitted the offer to you first), there are one or two other firms in the U.S.A. who want my work, may I ask you for a reply at your very earliest convenience.

(Of course, in referring to other firms, it is only in the instance of this new vol. of the new matter.)

To you, my terms would be £25 paid to me on receipt of copy, and 15% royalty thereafter

In haste | Sincerely Yours, | Fiona Macleod

P.S. If you care to present me with a copy of my "Stone & Kimball" *Pharais, Sin-Eater* and *Washer of' the Ford*, I should be very grateful. I have none left, for these American editions were much admired, and I was weak against the solicitations of friends. I wrote on this matter to Mr. Sharp when he was in New York but my letter failed to reach him in time before he left.

ALS Huntington Library

To Edmund Clarence Stedman, January 30, 1897

York (en route, returning | to London, staying | with Geo. Cotterell[8]) |
Saty, 30th

My dear Stedman

I wrote you the other day a long letter of grateful thanks about all your care for my interests in re. Lamson etc.

And now I have just recd. your arbitration-letter. I thought I had made all clear: But in any case my preceding letter should do so. The mail goes out in less than an hour, and as there is no other till Wedny., I must be very brief.

The primary claim is that admitted by Mr. Stone (Senior) — the document signed by H. S. Stone. But that, I fancy, is no longer worth anything legally. But in any case — as I thought I had explained — he having persuaded me to give him the book, & given his personal pledges that all wd. be fulfilled — & that it is thro' these broken pledges, & particularly when he transferred (without explanation) to Kimball. It is to this shiftiness that I owe so much loss of time, health, & money. Cotterell (who sends you greeting) says I haven't another moment — I must regretfully close.

My love to you, dear friend & Poet — Your bad (trying to be good) |
Will

ALS Columbia University Library

To Robert Murray Gilchrist, [*mid-February, 1897*]

My dear friend

If you can put the spur to the Inventive Steed which you ride so well, when opportunity permits, do you think that you can do so now?

Mr. Frank Rinder will write to you on the part of *The Social World* to ask you if you will write a serial romance for them at once. The advantages are your preservation of copyright, freedom to arrange for book publication immediately on cessation of serial publication and a certain sum down: small, perhaps, but sure.

Mr. Rinder (who is my intimate friend) will write more fully with this.

In haste | Ever Yours Affectly | William Sharp

ALS Sheffield City Archives

To Robert Murray Gilchrist, [mid-February, 1897]

Century Club | New York[9]

My dear Robert

Thanks for your note. I think that either I or Mr. Rinder must have inadvertently misled you — for there was no intention on his part to ask for you to undertake anything to do with politics — only an ordinary "fantastic thriller."

However, he has doubtless understood, and written to you himself. It is just possible I may be seeing him tonight.

So glad to hear you are to be in London soon. Do please let me know well in advance before you come: partly because many engagements are made long in advance, & partly because I might be away from town just when you come. Is it likely to be early in March?[10] (I shall be away the middle of April.)

Alas, my dear boy, I can tell you neither that I am well nor happy. I am content, at present, to tell you that I am not actively unhappy, and that I am, I hope, slowly gaining ground physically. I have not done a stroke of original work for weeks past but am eagerly hoping to be able to begin again soon.

My love to you and cordial remembrances to your mother & sister.

Yours affectionately | Will

Please send me a line by return to say if your coming is not immediate — i.e. if you will not be leaving home for a week or two. I have a special reason for asking.

ALS Sheffield City Archives

To [Richard Le Gallienne?], February 19, 1897

19:2:97

Cher Confrere

If you are disengaged, and otherwise able to come, will you be my guest at the Omar Khayyam Banquet to be held on March 25th. I do not think you are a member: if you are, forgive my not knowing it. I am a recent member of the 49 myself, for last year or rather the Autumn of '95, when the last vacancies occurred, the council elected Andrew Lang, George Gissing, and myself. This year Austin Dobson and someone else have been elected — so they will be there and have to speak: also the guest of the evening, Lord Wolseley.[11]

The "banquet" is at 7: at Frascati's — morning dress. Each guest must "sport" a white rose, as each member a red one — and all must drink of "the red, red wine."

Let me know if you can come — as I must notify.

Looking forward to Saty. of next week.

Ever Yours, | William Sharp

ALS Pierpont Morgan Library

To Hannibal Ingalls Kimball, February 20, 1897

9. Upper Coltbridge Terrace | Murrayfield, Midlothian | 20:2:97.

My dear Sir

Thanks for your letter. But please send me a specific answer to my proposal, so that I may arrange accordingly: the more so as it will, unfortunately, be impractical for me to see you when you are in Great Britain, as you suggest — for I am going to Italy immediately, and when I return in the late Spring or early Summer it will be direct to Glasgow or rather Greenock, to sail thence to my relatives in the Hebrides.

I am hardly ever in London, and indeed rarely even in Edinburgh, though it has been convenient for me to have my letters addressed there.

My friend Miss Rea, who attends to my typing and correspondence, is, however, shortly going to London to settle there as a literary agent: and thenceforth all my correspondence will be addressed to her there.

When she has a definite official address (about the beginning of March) she will send it to you. Or if you come sooner, you can learn it from Mr. William Sharp, or if he is out of town, by card to Messrs. Patrick Geddes & Colleagues, Edinburgh.

If necessary, you can talk over any literary matters with Miss Rea, who will have all my instructions. But please write at once in reply to my letter.

Personally, I think the best plan would be for you to issue a small volume containing the new tales: viz "Morag of the Glen" (10,000 to 12,000 words), "The Melancholy of Ulad", "The Hills of Ruel", "Ahez the Pale", (8000) and "The Archer" (to be renamed) — in all, about 25,000 words — the whole to be called "Morag of the Glen".

In haste, | Yours very truly, | Fiona Macleod

P. S. Very many thanks for the books, which will doubtless come by next post.

ALS Huntington Library

To Bliss Carman, February 24, 1897

15 Greencroft Gardens | South Hampstead | London N.W. | 24/Feb/97

Dear Bliss

Will you please propose to Copeland & Day, from me, the following — An anthology of the rarest and finest poems & lyrics by modern French poets, chosen solely by personal taste — just the few lovely things by a score or so of poets, known and little known — The small vol. to be called, say, "*Le Petit Parnasse Contemporaire*" or, if preferred, "*A Little Treasury of Contemporary French Poetry*" with an introductory note on the Symbolists and the Evolution of Symbolism. I would do this *con amore* (have already many lovely little poems previewed to this end — and though I would prefer to dispose of American rights only, so as to issue here myself, would be willing to dispose of both British & American selling rights if Copeland & Day prefer, & wd. issue in both countries. My terms are £50 on receipt, as an advance against a royalty of 15% — if for both rights: & half, if for the American book only: & six free copies.

A small anthology of the *fine-fleur* of Celtic poetry to be called "*The Golden Treasury of Celtic Poetry*" or "A Little Treasury of Celtic Poetry" — It would be in two parts: ancient and modern. Or if preferred, wholly ancient. It would be about the usual "Golden Treasury" vols size. Here would be nothing but what is absolutely & authentically Celtic — & would, as I say, consist of the very *fine-fleur* of the Celtic genius.

Here again, same terms as above, & same conditions: though I would not agree to give up English issue, so that the book would have to be issued in both countries.

Let me know from them, please, at their very earliest convenience, as I wish to arrange abt both, but particularly the Celtic vol., immediately.

In both instances, as I say, I am willing to arrange outright if Messrs. C. & D. prefer, but only on an undertaking that the book be published simultaneously in this country. Or, only for American issue.

Meanwhile, I shall make no arrangements but expect early reply.

Yours Ever | William Sharp

P.S. I am still awaiting to hear from you, for Miss Macleod, about her "Hills of Dream," left with you in Oct-Nov.

ALS New York University, Fales Library

To Edmund Clarence Stedman, March 3, 1897

London | 3 March

Just returned from a short visit to a friend, and find I have barely time to catch today's mail — so must send only a hurried P/C. I'll write by next mail, when also I'll send the letter to be read at the Stoddard dinner,[12] of which event I am very glad to hear. Meanwhile, my grateful thanks not only for the Dft for £20 safely to hand (& most welcome) advance from Lamson on a/c but also for all your trouble & forethought.

In extreme haste for the mail, W. S.

ACS Columbia University Library

To Mr. Cuthbertson, March 5, 1897

London | 5th March/97

Dear Mr. Cuthbertson

I do not quite understand why Prof. Geddes writes a joint letter to you and me, particularly as he knows that I have no longer any connection with the firm. At the same time I am very willing to advise on this point.

I think that Tchobanian's book might very well be published by P.G. & Co., since in the first place Prof. Geddes is himself so anxious for it, and, in the next, it is to be brought out in a cheap form.[13]

If it were to be brought out like the "Celtic Library" that would mean a direct appeal to the literary world — or rather to a small section of it: and the result would be unsatisfactory to say the least of it, as the book would then *primarily* be judged on its artistic merits. As a cheap edition, however, and above all with a preliminary note on the lines indicated in Prof. G's letter, I think there would certainly be a large sale for the book — particularly if a shilling volume.

Were I advising another firm I should say "yes, certainly" (in the circumstances) — and my only hesitation is on the question of distribution. Advt. is of little use in a book of this kind, and P.G. & Co's means of distribution (except thro' Simpkin Marshall) are neither extensive nor effective. I think some such title as "Armenian Sorrow" would be better for a book of this kind than Lyra etc.

Yours sincerely | William Sharp

ALS National Library of Scotland

To Edmund Clarence Stedman, March 5, 1897

London | 5th March/97

The P.S. is private (Destroy)

My dear Stedman,

As my card will have informed you, I received your last letter all right — also its enclosed dft for £20, (which came as a most welcome lift at an awkward juncture) — Lamson's advance against his Bill for $250.

I am indeed most indebted to you for all the trouble you have taken and are taking on my behalf. "A friend in need is a friend indeed," as I have found again and again with you.

I entirely approve of all you have done. As for Lamson, I think he ought not to have assured me so emphatically that all was well with the Lamsonian state of Denmark, when he knew its present instability. However, I daresay he will loyally fulfil his engagements: & certainly I hope so — for what with ill health etc. this year has been a disastrous one for me financially. I begin to see daylight all the same.

Among the good news I am waiting for is that of your own well-being in fortune and personal estate. I do hope your worries will disappear, and that all will go well with you in every possible way.

Pour moi, my brief spell of reform (three weeks and three days) convinced me that systematic reform would never suit me in mind or body. I have very happily relapsed into my Pagan ship, and the Sunbeam flies again at the Peak. My mate in this delectable craft smiled at my attempt, and now laughs joyously that I am myself once again.[14]

I am gratified at the invitation to the Stoddard dinner, but find it impossible to be present. I have sent a letter to the Committee (c/o R. Hitchcock) — but in case of miscarriage send a duplicate to you. If there is anything in it you judge ill-timed or inapposite I leave you a free hand.

Sorry you have lost Miss McKinney, but trust her successor consoles you for that bright and cheery presence.

With grateful affection, dear Poet, and my affectionate greetings to Mrs. Stedman,

Ever Yours, | William Sharp

Cotterell much gratified with your cordial message.

(P.S.) Two days ago I was by the sea, with F. M. In mind and body I am ten years younger, with that joy and delight.

ALS Columbia University Library

To Edmund Clarence Stedman, March 9, 1897

London | 9th March/97

My dear Stedman

I have got back from a flying visit to a relative in Tunbridge Wells just in time to write to you by this mail.

First, let me thank you again for all your kindness in this troublesome Lamson matter — and also with thanks acknowledge the safe receipt of the £10 dft. which you sent to me. I note also that you have given Lamson the extension he wants for his own small note for $150, nominally due March 1st, to May 8th — and also his intention, if practicable, to advance upon or pay off these notes by installments. Since you are satisfied with the genuineness of F. R., I am.[15]

I understand also that the case as you put it, now stands thus: $250 still due: — against which you hold L.W. & Co's new note for $101.37 payable April 11 and note for $150 payable May 8th. I have by today's mail sent to Lamson the proofs of a serial romance (of the Garibaldian campaign) the copyright of which has just lapsed to me.[16] It was a "pot boiler," but I think good at that, and was serially a marked success — so that now in book form it may well serve Lamson's purposes better than a more ambitious literary work. I find myself, both as to health and means, wholly unable to devote myself to the book ("Sister Eunice")[17] he wants — apart from the extreme uncertainty of getting the £100 advance promised by him.

But now to leave business, and say how profoundly vext I am to hear of your having had a bout of rheumatic fever. If superb vitality can carry any man through, I [know] you are "through" — but all the same I am anxious. How I wish you were free from all business worries (this sounds ironical from me who cause you so much "botheration" just now) and able to devote yourself wholly to the pen. That would indeed be good news.

Hoping soon to hear you are feeling better

Gratefully and affectionately yours | William Sharp

By last mail I posted the Stoddard letter.

ALS Columbia University Library

To Catherine Ann Janvier, March 10, 1897

Grosvenor Club, | March 10, 1897.

... Although I have had an unpleasant mental and physical set-back the last three days,[18] I am steadily (at least I hope so) gaining ground — but I have never yet regained the health or spirits I was in at St. Remy, tho' even there far more worn in mind and body than even you guessed. But with the spring I shall get well.

I am heart and soul with Greece in this war of race and freedom[19] — and consider the so-called "Concert"[20] a mockery and a sham. It is a huge Capitalist and Reactionary Bogus Company. Fortunately the tide of indignation is daily rising here — and even the Conservative papers are at one with the Liberal on the central points. Were I a younger man — or rather were I free — I would now be in Greece or on my way to join the Hellenes. As you will see by the enclosed, I am one of the authors who have sent a special message to the Athenian President of the Chamber. It is a stirring time, and in many ways... .

Memoir, pp. 283–84

To Coulson Kernahan[21] [*mid-March, 1897*]

15 Greencroft Gardens | South Hampstead

My dear Kernahan,

As you generously promised to do what you could for the Reissue of Miss Macleod's shorter tales, with others added — and, as I told you, I shall personally be indebted to you for any helpful word you may say, for the reasons I hinted to you — I have asked the publishers to send you today, the day of issue I believe, a set of the 3 vols. complete.

Sorry to hear the other day that Harvey Moore was ill[22] — He alluded to your kindness in going over to sit with him. However, I saw him on Saturday at the Royal Academy, and looking all right again — perhaps in part because of a young and pleasing lady companion!

Please thank your wife for her kind letter. I am glad she was pleased to have *Vistas*,[23] and so well liked the added matter. You, I hope, duly received "Flower 'o the Vine."[24]

I hope all goes well with you and your projects.

Elizabeth, alas, is hors-de-combat: for she has been some days in bed, and will likely be a day or two there still, with an attack of rheumatism.

Then, the other night, just after Murray Gilchrist left me, my study caught fire — and it was with difficulty that the conflagration was extinguished. Fortunately no harm was done to books or pictures, and the insurance covers the rest.

Have just seen one or two new American reviews of your last book. There as here "The Child etc."[25] seems to be a great and deserved success —

Ever, my dear fellow, | Affectionately Yours, |
William Sharp

ALS Princeton University

To Hamilton W. Mabie [mid-March, 1897][26]

15 Greencroft Gardens | South Hampstead | London

My dear Friend,

I have been in France again or would have answered your letter before this — a letter I was very glad to receive. I have been reading certain chapters from your two last books[27] to my wife, who has had a bout of rheumatism which has kept her in bed for a week: and she appreciates as deeply as I do their beauty of thought, sentiment, and structure. Your work has great winsomeness as well as distinction. As Miss Macleod (who has read them) says: "Mr. Mabie appeals to me all the more in that he is so fine an idealist, and yet does not disdain the actualities. He has tempered himself to fine thought and fine speech. That he has distinction is good: that he frequents the attitudes of thought and art is perhaps better still: and that his quest and his work are together the expression of himself, is best of all. Or you can reverse these if you like, — for extremes meet: and his formative impulse and his ultimate distinction are really one and the same."

I have the more pleasure in quoting this, as it is about Miss Macleod's Reissued Tales I am writing, for I have no time at the moment to write to you a proper letter.

I have asked the publishers to send you by this mail a set of the 3 vols. of the Reissued Shorter Tales, with others added, in the hope that you may be able to help her & them in America. If you can do so, I am sure you will. I am glad to hear that my Comedy in romance, "Wives in Exile" recently pub.d in U.S.A. by Lamson Wolffe & Co. has had so favorable a reception. It is not out here yet.

I had to be photographed recently for some public reason & when I get copies I'll send one to you as a remembrancer of

Your friend | William Sharp

ALS Library of Congress, Louise Chandler Moulton Collection

To J. Stanley Little, [March 15?, 1897]

Monday Night

My dear Stanley

I have time only for a brief note in reply to your letter — but hope to see you some day soon.

Elizabeth and I learned with genuine regret that Maud is not "up to the mark" at present, & we both hope she is by this time quite right or well on the mend: also that your Abigail no longer puts her trust in the Lord, but is up & about again, spotless (in appearance at least) as Abigails should be.

I am distressed at your S/A Rev. & other embarrassments, and hope you will soon be able to note the inflow of a new & more prosperous tide. I would try short fiction if I were you (i.e. stories not exceeding 50,000 words) also short tales for magazines. Is not the Drama as remote & indifferent a Deity as the aforesaid Lord? However, there is no reason why you should not sacrifice at both altars. (I have "The Doctor" in safe keeping: when you want it, say so.)

I am glad you like "Madge o' the Pool" & thank you for reviewing it. I am, I may add, agreeably surprised at the way it has been reviewed as yet. Some papers are generously eulogistic, & even my usually hostile critics give genuine if qualified praise.[28]

In haste

Ever affectionately yours, dear Stanley | William Sharp

Love from us both to you and Maud.

ALS University of British Columbia Library

To John Macleay, March 16, 1997

London

Dear Mr. Macleay

I have to thank you for your most appreciative & kind notice of "Madge of the Pool." It is pleasant to me to know that you like it so well.

The book had had quite a remarkable success, I am glad to say: the reviews having been practically unanimous in their cordial recognition.

And so — to other matters!

If Miss Macleod has not done so herself, Messrs. P/ G. & Co. will send you a set of the Reissue in 3 vols of her Shorter Tales, (from her two P. G. books) with others added. There are some satisfactory corrections in the reprinted matter I am glad to know — and what I consider a wise note prefatory to the actual basis of "The Sin-Eater" story — and to "The Anointed Man" (or if not that, then one of the kindred stories) apropos of the use of the name "Gloom."

Personally, I think that two of the new tales — the long "Morag of the Glen" and the short Highland fisherman story "The Archer" (both in *Tragic Romances*) are among Miss M's best work. She concurs as to the "Archer," I fancy, though not emphatic about "Morag" — possibly, as I urge, because it is so "near" her, so to say.

Hoping you are well & at work

Sincerely Yours | William Sharp

ALS National Library of Scotland

To Richard LeGallienne, March 16, 1897

C/o. Miss Rea | The Outlook Tower | Castlehill | Edinburgh | 16:3:97

Dear Mr. LeGallienne,

Herewith goes (or should go) to you the reissue of my shorter stories — with others added — rearranged into their proper interrelation. I heard a few days ago (on one of those rare occasions when I was south for a flying visit) of your marriage, and I beg that you and your wife will accept this "set" from me with my cordial good wishes, both for Mr. and Mrs. LeGallienne and for the author of "The Quest of the Golden Girl", with which I have been greatly charmed.

Believe me, | Sincerely yours, | Fiona Macleod

ALS Stanford University

To Catherine Ann Janvier, March 22, 1897

March 22nd

... What a whirl of excitement life is, just now. I am all on fire — about the iniquities of this Turkish-Finance triumph[29] over honour, chivalry, and the old-time sense that the world can be well lost. There are many other matters, too, for deep excitement — international, national, literary, artistic, personal. It is the season of sap, of the young life, of green fire. Heart-pulses are throbbing to the full: brains are effervescing under the strong ferment of the wine of life: the spiral flames of the spirit and the red flower of the flash are fanned and consumed and re-created and fanned anew every hour of every day... .

This is going to be a strange year in many ways: a year of spiritual flames moving to and fro, of wild vicissitudes for many souls and for the forces that move through the minds of men. The West will redden in a new light — the "west" of the forlorn peoples who congregate among our isles in Ireland — "the West" of the dispeopled mind.

The common Soul is open — one can see certain shadows and lights as though in a mirror.[30]

Memoir, p. 284

To Katherine Tynan Hinkson, March 24, 1897[31]

C/o Miss Rea | The Outlook Tower | Castlehill | Edinburgh | 24:3:97.

Dear Mrs. Hinkson,

The Re-issue of my shorter tales has brought me so many letters: then my present visit to Edinburgh is a brief one: and, once more, very uncertain health has been like a foe knocking at my gates: for all which triple reasons I beg you to forgive me for not having sooner acknowledged your kind little note.

Yes, I *did* see, and much appreciate the *Speaker* notice[32] of "From the Hills of Dream" — tho' I did not have the added pleasure of knowing it was by yourself. I thank you for it, and all the generous interest you have shown in my work.

I did not wish to trouble you with all the 3. vols of the Reissue set — and moreover wished to make it clear that I was sending you one of a set to mark it as a personal offering to a writer whose work has always singular charm for me, and whose generous recognition of my own work has been one of my abiding pleasures. But as you say you intend a little article about me and my work, in the *English Illustrated Magazine*,[33] I have directed the publishers to send to you the two companion vols.

The third, "Tragic Romances", contains my strongest contemporary short story, by common consent (viz., "Morag of the Glen") — and what I myself think to be my best, the shorter story called "The Archer".

Oh yes, dear Mrs. Hinkson, I am now well aware of much of the mystery that has grown up about my unfortunate self. I have even heard that Fleet Street journalist rumour to which you allude — with the addition that the said unhappy scribe was bald and old and addicted to drink.

Heaven knows who and what I am according to some wiseacres! A recent cutting said I was Irish, a Mr. Chas. O'Conor,[34] whom I know not.

A friend of a friend told that friend that I was Miss Nora Hopper and Mr. Yeats in union — at which I felt flattered but amused. For some time, a year or so ago, there was a rumour that "Fiona Macleod" was my good friend and relative, William Sharp. Then, when this was disproved, I was said to be Mrs. Sharp. Latterly I became the daughter of the late Dr. Norman Macleod.[35] The latest is that I am Miss Maud Gonne[36] — which the paragraphist "knows as a fact". Do you know her? She is Irish, and lives in Paris, and is, I hear, very beautiful — so I prefer to be Miss Gonne rather than the Fleet Street journalist!

Seriously I am often annoyed by these rumours. But what can I do? There are private reasons, as well as my own particular wishes, why I must preserve my privacy.

I do most urgently wish not to have my privacy made public, partly because I am so "built" and partly for other reasons: but I would not perhaps let this stand in the way of the urgent wishes of friends, were it not that there are other reasons also. But this much I will confide to you, and gladly: I am *not* an unmarried girl, as commonly supposed, but am married.

The name I write under is my maiden name. Perhaps I have suffered, as well as known much joy, in my brief mature life: but what then — all women whose heart is in their brain must inevitably suffer. And so, you will, I know, at once excuse me and forgive my inability to give you any material particulars. This past week I have had no fewer than four editorial applications for my photograph for reproduction — but now, as ever, I have had to decline. Two friends in London have my photograph, and perhaps you may see it someday: but now I do not even let friends have a photograph, since one allowed someone to take a sketch of it for an American paper. I can't well explain why I am so exigent. I must leave you to divine from what I have told you.

I have looked among my newspaper excerpts for some cuttings of a personal kind, and particularly for a longish account in "The Highland News" — but they are mislaid. I can find only two, which appeared about the time of the publication of "The Mountain Lovers" a couple of years ago. Perhaps you will kindly let me have them again. There was also a (slightly) personal article on me as a "new writer" in *The Bookman*[37] for some autumn month in 1895.

But, of course, if wished, I could give you any information about my books, my work, and "what I feel about things in general", as one (would-be) American interviewer puts it: (of course I don't object to its being known that I come of an old Catholic family, that I am a Macleod, that I was born in the Southern Hebrides, and that my heart still lies where the cradle rocked.)

If, perchance, I should be in London this autumn or early winter — on my way to the Riviera (for I am not strong) — I hope to be able to make your acquaintance in person. I have heard of you from several friends, and particularly from Mr. William Sharp, who is a great admirer of your writings, both in prose and verse.

But now I have taken up too much of your time.

Believe me, dear Mrs. Hinkson, | Cordially yours, | Fiona Macleod[38]

ALS University of Toronto Library

To J. Stanley Little, [March 24?, 1897]

Wedny

My dear Stanley

Ever so many thanks, my dear fellow, for your most generously worded review of "Madge".[39] I wish the book really deserved half you say of it — which is a genuine and not an "epidermic" wish! It has had quite a remarkable reception all round. But apart from any public criticism, I am gratified it appeals so much to so good a judge as yourself.

Sorry I can't give you exact particulars about the Salons[40] — as I don't know them myself. I understand, however, that the dates are as follows: (you know that both Salons are opening a fortnight earlier than usual?)

The "New Salon" (Champ de Mars) is said to open on Apr. 14th — and the Champs-Elysées or Old Salon on the 20th.

Probably these dates mean the "Tour du Vermissage" — our "Private-View". If so, it will mean that the N.S. press day is the 12th or 13th — and that of the O.S. the 19th or even the 17th.

There is no way to get tickets save by application to the Directeur, & *on the part of the paper* (not the critic himself). *Personal* application *might* do as an emergency, but cannot be trusted. After talking fluently & arguing in rapid French for an hour, one might succeed — but probably not.

Separate tickets are needed for the Tour du Vermissage. Tickets *only* for the O.S. — for the new, there is public admission also, price 10 fcs. I fancy the New keeps to a uniform 1 fc rate for other days: the O. S. has a 5 franc day, & a 2 fc. day. On Sundays, 1 fc till 12, & free after. When I know anything more definite I'll let you hear.

Frantically busy just now & in deep arrears — the more so as from the 4th I expect to be away (abroad) for 3 or 4 weeks. Hope Maud is all right now. E. has been very seedy, but is better.

Ever affectly Yours, | Will

Are you ever Bond St. way in the afternoon? Someday I wish we could meet at the Grosvenor Club & have a chat over a cup of coffee.

ALS University of British Columbia Library

To George Meredith, March 26, 1897

c/o Miss Lilian Rea / The Outlook Tower / Castlehill / Edinburgh |
26:3:97

Dear Mr. Meredith

Herewith I send to you, begging you to give me the pleasure of its acceptance by you, a copy of one of the three vols. of the just published Reissue of my shorter tales. These have been rearranged, and organically grouped, and (with others added) have just appeared as a new and cheaper edition in three volumes. I was tempted to burden you also with "Spiritual Tales" and "Barbaric Tales" — but have refrained. I wonder if you will be cynical, and say "Ah, why has she not been equally reticent with "Tragic Romances"! But I hope not: for it is a pleasure to me to bring any small flower o' the mind to you, if you will accept both the homage of the gift and the shy pleasure with which it is given.

I chose "Tragic Romances" because it contains my longest modern short story, "Morag of the Glen," and the story which I myself think the nearest to what I want to do in this particular *genre* — "The Archer."

The other stories are from either *The Sin Eater* or *The Washer of the Ford*. I saw a paragraph in "The Highland News" that you had been ill, but are now quite well again. I hope the latter is true.

There is a chance I may be south this Spring or early Summer. If so, I look with keen pleasure to the often anticipated visit to you.[41]

I am deep in a big historical romance: and having sloughed the immature manner of "Pharais" and "Green Fire," I venture to hope I may not displease those who are kind enough to hope good things of me.

Ever Sincerely yours / Fiona Macleod

ALS Private

To Louise Chandler Moulton, March 31, 1897

15 Greencroft Gardens | South Hampstead | London | 31/Mch/97

Dear Louise,

The mail day finds me so close run for time that I can do no more than send you my affectionate greetings for your birthday — & therewith my latest "phiz."[42] I leave England next week for 3 weeks or so — & perhaps when I return it may be to find you here. I hope so.

Ever dear friend, | affectionately yours, | Will

Did you receive the copy of "Wives in Exile" I asked to be sent to you?

ACS Princeton University

To W. E. Henley, April 1, 1897[43]

To W. E. Henley Esq. | Stanley Lodge | Muswell Hill |
London, N. | 1:4:97

Dear Mr. Henley

I thank you for your kind letter. Any word of recognition from you means much to me. Your advice is wise and sane, I am sure — and you may be certain that I shall bear it in mind. It will be difficult to follow — for absolute simplicity is the most difficult of all styles, being, as it must be, the expression of a mind at once so imaginative in itself, so lucid in its outlook, and so controlled in its expression, that only a very few rarely gifted individuals can hope to achieve the isolating ideal you indicate.

I sent you only the second volume of the Reissue of my shorter tales — but I would now like you to see what I have written last (with no implied compulsion on you to express your opinion, however!).

The three latest things I have written are the long short-story "Morag of the Glen", "The Melancholy of Ulad", and "The Archer". The second appears in the first volume, "Spiritual Tales" — but the two others in the third, "Tragic Romances": so I will direct the publishers to send you a copy. I would (if you <u>do</u> write — but, let me repeat, I do not ask or in a sense expect this, knowing how preoccupied you must ever be) particularly like to know what you think of the style & method of "The Archer" (I mean, apart from the arbitrary fantasy of the short supplementary part — which affords the clue to the title) — as there I have written, or tried to write, with the accent of that life as I know it.

I was visiting friends in an old house among the Pentlands when your kind letter was posted, and by mischance I did not receive it till last night. I expect to be in (or near) Edinburgh for a week yet, when I return to Assynt[44] for a season.

Do not for a moment think that I take your "imposing yourself editorially" upon me as "an offense" — or anything but a welcome and honourable tribute of interest.

Believe me, | Sincerely yours, | F. M.

ALS National Library of Scotland

To Katherine Tynan Hinkson, April 3, 1897

C/o Miss Rea, | The Outlook Tower, | Castlehill, | Edinburgh | 3.4.97.

Dear Mrs. Hinkson,

I have asked my friend Miss Rea, who has now gone to London (and will still, as before, look after my correspondence), to send you some notes "she took of me" for an American article she has been commissioned to write.[45] These, if I remember aright, will give you the main drift of my possible publicities. For the rest, let me answer briefly that my first encouragers were (first and foremost) Mr. George Meredith — then Mr. Grant Allen, Mr. Traill, and very soon Mr. Yeats and fellow-Celtic writers, including Katharine Tynan Hinkson.

   In great haste,

Most cordially yours, | Fiona Macleod

Middle Years, p. 130

To Benjamin Burgess Moore,[46] April 9, 1897

The Outlook Tower | Castle Hill | Edinburgh | 9:4:97

Dear Mr. Moore,

— For "Sir" and "Madam" seem incongruous with the expression of a friendly sympathy such as yours and of a gratified acceptance such as mine.

   I write at the earliest date practicable since I heard from you, to thank you most cordially for your friendly letter, and for the accompanying copy of the Yale Literary Magazine, with its profoundly sympathetic and therefore to me most welcome "appreciation" of my work. It is a keen pleasure to me that I have won many friends in the United States — as I discover, apart from my publishers, from reviews and from unknown correspondents. And now I have to add a new friend to my unknown friends oversea — and believe me it is a true encouragement as well as a pleasure to win the deep and keen sympathy of one like yourself. As to the article itself, I have seen nothing in any American paper or magazine which can be compared with it — either in knowledge of the writings, sympathetic understanding, and general insight — and this, I may add, not merely because you honour me with such cordial praise.

There are some writers who dwell apart, in every sense of the word: and I am one of these. My wishes and my tastes, as well as certain exigencies in my private circumstances, incline me towards a greater privacy or isolation than suits that ethic of publicity which prevails and is to me so undignified and even distressing: and hence have arisen many strange rumours about me and as to "who I am" etc. And in like manner, even those who know me say that I am a survival from a remote past, and not a proper modern at all. This is not quite true, for I believe in one intensity of emotion above all others, namely the intensity of this brief flame of life in the heart and the brain, an intensity no one can have who does not account the hours of every day as the vanishing pawns in that tragic game of chess for ever being played between Time and Eternity. All the same, I have ever mentally been impassioned for the past and so it is that I find myself, both in the inner and outer life, much aloof from my fellows. I find in the close and intimate communion with nature, which is so much more possible away from towns — and I live truly only when I am in the remote Isles or among the mountains of Argyll — a solace and inspiration which come to me much attenuated through the human medium. Perhaps this is because, though young in years, I have a capacity for sorrow and regret which has come to me through my Celtic ancestry out of a remote lost world: because, indeed, I have myself walked the blind way between Joy and Sorrow and been led now by the one now by the other. But do not think I am a melancholy person. I am not, in the ordinary sense. I am young, and life has given me some of her rarest gifts, and I am grateful: and, when my hour comes, shall be ready, having lived. Not even in my vision of life am I melancholy. All the same, I am, as you discern, I am young, and life has given me some of her rarest gifts, and I am grateful from one vital point of view: and am ever aware of the menace of the perpetual fugitive shadow of Destiny. It is summed up in a dream I had once, lying among the grassy dunes in Iona: a dream wherein I heard a voice saying in gaelic that the three Dominions or Powers were "The Living God, the Dying World, and the mysterious Race of Man", and that behind each gleamed the shadowy eyes of Destiny.

I write to you thus, and of course in all privacy, because you will understand, and care that I should do so. I am glad my books appeal to you so. As you do not seem to know my most mature and most characteristic book, "The Washer of the Ford", I send you a copy. If I am mistaken, and you already have one, this or the other can be given to some friend who will care to hear what a far away and rather weary dreamer of a beautiful if perhaps vain Dream has to say out of her vision of life temporal and spiritual. As, also, I gather from a phrase in your article that you have not seen my most intimate book of all, the poems collectively entitled "From the Hills of Dream"; I send you also a copy of that book. It is almost certain I shall never publish another volume of poems. It is giving up too much of oneself, exposing to curious or indifferent eyes the emotions which, as Plato says, colour that strange flame, the soul.

Please let know if you received this too-long note and the accompanying books — and believe me

Most Sincerely Yours | Fiona Macleod

P. S. I enclose a review of "From the Hills of Dream" by an unknown but as sympathetic a critic as yourself.

ALS Huntington Library

To Elizabeth Sharp [April 18, 1897][47]

St. Margaret's Bay

Sunday (on the shore by the sea, and in the sunshine). I wonder what you are doing today? I feel very near you in spirit as I always do when I have been reading, hearing, or seeing any beautiful thing — and this forenoon I have done all three, for I am looking upon the beauty of sunlit windswept sea, all pale green and white, and upon the deep blue sky above the white cliffs, upon the Jackdaws and gulls dense black or snowy against the azure, upon the green life along and up the cliff-face, upon the yellow-green cystus bushes below — and am listening to the sough of the wind, soft and balmy, and the rush and break of the sunlit waves among the pebbly reaches just beyond me — and have been reading Maeterlinck's two essays, "The Deeper Life" and "The Inner Beauty."[48]

I am longing to be regularly at work again — and now feel as if at last I can do so... .

More and more absolutely, in one sense, are W. S. and F. M. becoming two persons — often married in mind and one nature, but often absolutely distinct. I am filled with a passion of dream and work... .

Friendship, deepening into serene and beautiful flame, is one of the most ennobling and lovely influences the world has... .

Wilfion[49]

P.S. Again some more good tidings. Constables have accepted my giving up *The Lily Leven* indefinitely — and instead have agreed to my proposal to write a child's book (dealing with the Celtic Wonderworld) to be called *The Laughter of Peterkin*.[50]

Memoir, p. 285

To Robert Murray Gilchrist, [May 3, 1897]

Hotel Teston | St. Rémy de Provence | Bouches du Rhone | Monday

Dear Mr. Gilchrist

Do not, please, measure my pleasure at receiving your photograph by my apparent forgetfulness in writing more fully than the post card permitted me to thank you for your kind remembrance of my wishes. I am very glad to have your photograph, and I am daily becoming better acquainted by means of it with Will's firm friend.

I hope you will find some opportunities of seeing you. A chat of half an hour is too little in which to become really friends, and that is what I wish.

Will was very disappointed at the failure of the Ronen plan, and I hope he will carry out his present idea of going to see you within the next few days.

Here in this lovely, sunny spot I am gathering strength, and resting, and enjoying myself. The charm is as appealing as that of Italy; but it is different — a little more direct — I find. And I am much interested in meeting some of the members of the Felibre: Felix Gras,[51] and the lovely Queen of the Felibres Mme Gasquet.[52] Mistral[53] I hope to meet next week. It is extremely interesting to be taken into the heart of this wonderful vital literary movement[54]

[Elizabeth A. Sharp]

ALS Frag. Sheffield City Archives

To Robert Murray Gilchrist, [May 4, 1897]

15 Greencroft Gardens | So. Hampstead | NW

My dear Robert

Will you be at home, & free this week-end?

There is *just a chance* I could come to you on Saty, for a couple of days.

If so, I would come via Chesterfield. Is it an easy drive from there to you?

Affectionate greetings to you & yours. W. S.

Do send me the promised photograph.

ACS Sheffield City Archives

To Robert Murray Gilchrist, [May 6, 1897][55]

It is possible I may not be able to get away on Saturday till the train which leaves at 3 (due Chesterfield 6.14) — in fact it had better be arranged so: so (if convenient for you) I shall hope to see you at Chesterfield Station at 6.14.

W.

If, on Saty. Morning early, I see that I can get to the train due at C at 3.40, I'll wire.

ACS Sheffield City Archives

To Robert Murray Gilchrist, [May 10, 1897]

Monday Night

My dear Robert

I reached Chesterfield, I reached Stretton, I reached Ashover by bus, and I reached Liedernot. There I learned that Mr. & Mrs. Murray had left home for a fortnight. This was 11.30, & there was no bus till the evg, no train till the afternoon!

So I got a dog-cart, & drove the 3 or 4 miles to Stretton for my bag, & then the 6 or so to

Chesterfield, where I had an hour & a half to wait. Well, I console myself by saying that I reached home 2 or 3 hours earlier than I expected to do — so all's well that ends well.

I enjoyed greatly my brief visit to you. It is true I am suffering from the effects of that long detour you involved me in on Sunday, & deeply resent that dream about the pig — but by the time I have written to my wife about your unfortunate dropsical mania, & general anaemic decay; & to Mrs. W. R. about your loving intimacy with Death; & to Madame Janvier about your most unwarrantable and lewd dream; & to Grant R. about what you told me about his horrid Complaint; by *then*, I shall have no other than happy thoughts of you, you deeply ungrateful & foolish youth.[56]

I think it is not improbable I shall get south, on Friday or Saty: but cannot tell for certain till Friday comes.[57] So if you write them you had better not say that you know I am to be there, in case I cannot manage it. I am very anxious to do so, however, if I can — though four days incessant travelling (i.e. there & back) & over 1000 miles, is a good deal to do for one day — at most for two: for I wd. need to leave again on the 18th or at latest the 19th.

However, I'll try & let you know in advance. At the present moment my getting away *seems* impossible — and indeed with the best will in the world it may well prove to be so.

Do not forget to put your shorter stories together, and as soon as possible. I do hope you will do this — & also that you will soon work at "The Labyrinthe".

When you write to Mrs. Wingate Rinder do not forget your photograph. Her address is 11Woronzow Road | St. John's Wood. If you are getting any more, get an *unmounted one* for her, so that she could put it into "The Stone Dragon".[58]

How strange life is, indeed. Today we laughed and chatted, and everything was as usual — & yet I received at Cartledge[59] today a letter of the most vital & far-reaching importance in my life! But so it is, often & oftener with all of us, or many of us.

My loving greeting, Camerado mio | Your friend | Will

I have written to your mother also, so send no messages with this.

ALS Sheffield City Archives

To Edmund Clarence Stedman, May 12, 1897

12/May/97

P.S.[60] After all, I am just going abroad again on important work — and shall not be back for a week or 10 days, so cannot write at the moment. I wrote by preceding mail to thank you most cordially for your ever watchful and helpful care of my interests. You were, of course, quite right abt. this last postponement, though I do trust I.[61] will pay up

Thursday as I urgently need it. Meanwhile my most grateful thanks to you, ever kind friend, W. S.

ACS Columbia University Library

To Elizabeth A. Sharp [May 21, 1897][62]

London

It seems very strange to be here and at work again — or rather it is the interlude that seems so strange and dreamlike. This time last week it was not quite certain if I could get away, as it depended partly upon finishing the Maeterlinck Essay and partly upon the postponement of due date for the monograph on Orchardson.[63] Then Richard Whiteing came in. Then at last I said that since fortune wouldn't hurry up it could go to the devil — and I would just go to my dear wife: and so I went. And all is well. Only a week ago today since I left! How dramatic it all is — that hurried journey, the long afternoon and night journey from Paris, the long afternoon and night to Tarascon — the drive at dawn and sunrise through beautiful Provence — the meeting you — the seeing our dear friends there again. And then that restful Sunday, that lovely birthday!

Memoir, p. 286

To Thomas Wentworth Higginson, [May 22?, 1897]

Murrayfield | Midlothian

Dear Mr. Higginson,[64]

In passing thro' London from abroad on Saty I found your card among many other letters etc. awaiting me. I am very glad indeed to hear that you and Mrs. Higginson are here, and shall hope to see something of you, after my return South — which will be when my wife comes back from the South of France — probably about the 16th. Meanwhile, cordial greetings.

Yours very truly, | William Sharp

ALS Harvard University, Houghton Library

To J. Stanley Little, [May 24, 1897][65]

Monday

My dear old man,

On returning to London this evening I found your note awaiting me.

Elizabeth is still in the South of France, & will not be back till either the 14th or the 15th of June. Much as I want to see you again, I fear it will be impracticable until E. returns — & then we shall both gladly come — for tho' I am to be here till this week-end I go away again then for a week, and meanwhile am engaged every day and night. What with the autumn in Scotland, the early winter in America, Jany in the Riviera, Provence, Scotland, & France three times, I've not been much here since last summer! I'm as nearly bankrupt as I've ever been in my life — but I've lived up to the hilt, and it's Spring, and Summer's still to come, and heads or tails it's still good to be alive, and may the Dispenser of Laughter & Tears smile benignly on both of us, cher ami!

Ever yrs affectly, | Will

If I can't get away this week-end, i.e. if free this Saty or some day next week I'll send you a preliminary wire, and try to get to see you — but it is unlikely.

ALS Princeton University

To Patrick Geddes, [May 24, 1897][66]

Monday

My dear Geddes,

Excuse a pencilled line in great haste. I have just returned home, & find many things awaiting immediate attention.

Yes — I had already thought and certainly do think it wd. be a mistake for P. G. & Co. & for you not to take advantage of the Iona pilgrimage-celebrations. Among other things I thought it wd. be a paying thing to ask Miss Muir (if she is still there — or other representative of the small Iona Press — a little, primitive, right, Iona printing company of two or three persons) or some one to sell the paper and indeed other copies of F. M. The best place would be a little stall near the Ferry landingstage — or at the north entrance to the "Cathedral" —

Much the most suitable thing of Miss F. M. would be what she suggested last year as a cheap Xmas reprint in pamphlet — or paper-cover booklet form, of "The Three Marvels of Iona." (As thus reprinted in the Reissue — Vol. I, abt 30 pp in all.) In some respects, "St. Bride of the Isles" ("Muime Chriosd") is considered her most typical Iona tale — but I imagine that some of the good folk of the Kirks would not like the Bethlehem and Biblical parts. What do you think about this? For that matter, both "St. Bride of the Isles" (which might be rechristened "St. Bride of Iona") and "The Three Marvels of Iona" might each be done in booklet form.

Miss M. says she is quite willing, and indeed glad: but at the same time wishes me to see for her that she obtains her just share in the returns of any such sales: i.e. a direct proportion, to be agreed on, on all copies in this proposed reprint, to be duly accounted for and duly paid in ordinary course. On these conditions, I agree for her.

It is impossible to say right away if she can send a poem. Send me a P/C to say the latest date it wd. need to be recd. — and I'll let her know.

It must be strange for you both to be in Dundee after the East. Well, Life has been kaleidoscopic enough for you of late?

Love to you both —

In haste, | Yrs Ever, | W. S.

ALS National Library of Scotland

To Robert Murray Gilchrist, May 24, [1897]

St. Rémy de Provence | May 24

Dear Mr. Gilchrist,

Your letter on my birthday gave me great pleasure, bringing as it did not only kindly wishes but the pretty message from the wood sorrel.

You knew of the delightful surprise that was in store for me & you will therefore readily believe this birthday of mine is very memorable. The whole establishment was in a ferment; for the landlord & landlady had kept the secret since the previous day. They decked our dinner table with masses of lovely roses of all sizes and colors: a central pyramid & star-like rays to the edge of the table — very lovely.

Will is back again in London, & his coming now seems like a beautiful dream. He told me how much he enjoyed his visit to Cartledge Hall.

Someday I hope to avail myself of Mrs. Gilchrist's kind proposal that I should accompany him when he goes to see you. He has spoken so much to me of your mother that I am doubly wishful to have the privilege of meeting her.

I have your message to Mr. Janvier who is greatly gratified thereby.

I am charmed with the sound of the Provencal language. It is so much more sonorous and liquid than the concise clear cut French. It is eminently suited to the lips of poets. Hearing it, and seeing the beauty and richness of this southern land, one understands why this was & still is the land of Troubadours, Sunshine, and sweet sounds — the heart must needs sing it seems to me.

I hope you are writing. I like your work — and look forward expectantly to what you will give us to read & ponder over.

Sincerely yours | Elizabeth A. Sharp

Hotel Teston

ALS Sheffield City Archives

To Elizabeth A. Sharp, [late May, 1897]

Herewith my typed copy of your Wilfion's last writing. Called "The Wayfarer"[67] though possibly, afterwards, "Where God is, there is light," it is one of the three Spiritual Moralities of which you know two already, "The Fisher of Man" and "The Last Supper."[68] In another way, the same profound truth is emphasized as in the other two — that Love is the basic law of spiritual life. "The Redeemer liveth" in these three: Compassion, Beauty, Love — the three chords on which these three harmonies of Fiona's inner life have been born... .

Memoir, pp. 286–87

To R. A. Streatfeild, [June 4?, 1897]

Cartledge Hall | Holmesfield | Derbyshire

Dear Mr. Streatfeild,[69]

Your note and "Nepenthe" have been forwarded to me here — where I came for a few days after my return from France, where my wife is still, in the extreme south.

Today I can do no more than thank you for your friendly gift. I am much interested in Darley[70] — and am very glad indeed to have this pleasant little edition of the mysterious "Nepenthe." I hope to be able to say something about it somewhere.

I had no idea that Lawrence Binyon[71] was "a new Blake"! His design is .... well, I've lost my vocabulary pre-tem, so I'll leave the right epithet in peace!

In haste | Yours sincerely | William Sharp

I look forward very much to re-perusal of the poem & to your Introductory Note.

ALS New York Public Library, Berg Collection

To Robert Murray Gilchrist, June 14, 1897

14th June/97

My dear Robert,

I must tell you at once that I am delighted more than I can say with your new book. Frankly, I had not expected this. I knew I should be interested: I knew there would be good & fine work: but I had imagined the contents to be, however good, still of the pot-boiler nature. Instead, I find them the best you have done as yet. I mean what I say when I add that I can compare them only with Guy de Maupassant, different as they are in atmosphere. You have observed so truly, depicted so masterly, and with so true a sense of proportion, and with, too, so much of poignant if always controlled pathos, and humour of a rare kind, that I almost dare to hope "A Peakland Faggot" will go straight to the mark. I do not think the title will take the public, & it is a bad time for books just now — yet surely such altogether exceptional work must find a public.[72]

The first six tales seem to me absolutely perfect in their kind. (The first I remembered in a moment, and found it as impressive & reaching as ever). The seventh I did not find convincing. It put me too in mind of a tale of Hardy's — I don't mean in facts, but in atmosphere & treatment. It is followed by five charming studies. "The End of the World" is the best thing of its kind I have read for very long. The dialogue throughout is admirable, colloquially consistent, & convincing.

Altogether I do most heartily congratulate you on such notably fine work. Work now on a bigger scale, on a broader canvas, with a still freer touch, and you will be in the front rank of our creative writers.

My love to you & yours, & all cordial greetings. I am just off to meet my wife, who arrives tonight. If I cannot do anything at first hand I'll do what I can at second hand to help the book.

Ever affectionately | Your gratified friend | Will

ALS Sheffield City Archives

To Mrs. Coulson Kernahan [*August 4, 1897*]

I — we — had meant to write before this — but as Mrs. Malaprop says "suckingstantial suckcumstances have been agin us", up till tonight.

But I'll write soon, tomorrow I hope, with the cook etc. Love to you both —

W. S.

ACS Princeton University

To Robert Murray Gilchrist, [*mid-August, 1897*]

18 Park Lane | *Southwold* | Suffolk

My dear Robert

I was glad to see your fist[73] again — though sorry to learn that your old enemy neuralgia (or is it cancer-cum-dropsy, as you vowed of old) has been visiting you.

I have had a troubled & wearing time since I saw you — save for a brief happy spell in the early part of July. But, where there is nothing to be said, words are idle.

I have liked being here, where Elizabeth & I came with our friends the Janviers from Provence at the end of July. It is one of the pleasantest English coast places I know. We leave again on Saty the 28th, & return to London for two days, when we go to the Dorset coast till the 12th Sept (my birthday, by the way, so send me a line, mind!) to stay with friends — | Good Rest | *Parkstone* | Dorset | Then I go north (by sea to Ireland, & thence to the Inner Hebrides) for 2 or 3 weeks.

I have heard many (literally) good reports of the "Faggot", tho' I fear it has not gone very well, owing to Jubilee etc.[74]

What are you doing now? You are I hope engaging in some big thing?

W. S. is busy with the architectonic & other preliminaries of two books, very different in kind, though both imaginative fiction: and, later, will be busy on a play. F. M. has recently finished "a retelling of old tales" volume, partly what is called a child's book[75] — & is now planning out preliminaries of a long historical romance, & also of a short imaginative dramatic poetic play called "The Hour of Beauty."

Elizabeth is much better & well & happy, tho' enviably idle. Mrs. Wingate Rinder is at present in Cornwall — but I shall see her before long.

Of my love take what you will for yourself, & give also to your mother & sisters. In the pipe put no hashish (which I refuse to send to you) but put in it an Imperishable Dream, and smoke it whenever Silence, Solitude, & Reverie concur.[76]

Your friend | Will

ALS Sheffield City Archives

To William Sharp [September 12, 1897][77]

My dear Will,

I would like to write you a longer note, but I find it impracticable today. However, you know how sincere my good wishes are: and I trust from my heart that you may have a happy and prosperous new year.

Now, dear Billy, forgive me if I say that I am very much disappointed with you this past year. You have not been well, it is true: but you have also been idle to a painful degree, and your lack of method makes me seriously anxious. I will not dwell upon your minor and to me irritating faults: you know well to what I allude, and I think too you are often greedy, for it is not necessary always to have both marmalade and butter at breakfast. That is a small thing but it is significant: I can only hope that you will control your appetites better in 1897–8.

But do for heaven's sake put your shoulder to the wheel, and get soon in good working trim at something worth doing. You ever put pleasure first, and think so much of youth that you don't like billiards merely because the balls are bald. This is sad, Billy.

I shall keep all the rest till we meet. What an uncomfortable half hour you will have!

Still, you're a dear, and I like you with all your faults. Be a good boy and I'll love you.

Your loving twin, | Fiona

I have a lovely present for you. I'll tell it when we meet. I shall also, later, send you "The Laughter of Peterkin."

ALS Private

To William Meredith, September 14, 1897

15 Greencroft Gardens | South Hampstead | 14/Sept/97

Dear Mr. Meredith,

My friend, Mrs. Mona Caird, with whose name you are of course familiar, & some of whose books you may have seen, sent me a short time ago the (typed) MS. of her new novel, "The Pathway of the Gods," with the request that I should advise her where to send the book. (She did not wish it to go to the publishers to whom, at their request, she gave her last book, "The Daughters of Danaus").[78]

I have read "The Pathway of the Gods" with deep appreciation & sustained interest — and I think your firm may be glad of the opportunity to consider it — so I send it to you herewith.

Whatever your decision it will be simplest if you will communicate with Mrs. Caird directly (I understand that her foremost wish is not so much as to terms as to early publication). Mrs. Mona Caird's private address is Mrs. Henryson Caird | Cassencary | *Creetown* | N.B.

I hope you are well, & having a pleasant summer. I have just returned from some delightful cycling in Dorset: but have not been able to get to Scotland yet, where however I hope to go for October.

I am here only for today & till tomorrow — so please send me here by return a line of acknowledgment of Mrs. Caird's book.

I trust you have good news of your father[79] — & that you and yours are well.

Sincerely Yours | William Sharp

ALS University of California, Berkeley

To Edward Martyn, [September 22?, 1897][80]

Rutland House | Greencroft Gardens | South Hampstead | London

My dearest Martyn,[81]

Many thanks for your letter and the response to my telegram. It would have been a great disappointment if I had been unable (or you) to make this much looked forward to visit a reality. I am anticipating with exceptional pleasure my visit to the west of Ireland, and to long talks with you and Yeats on the Celtic and other subjects so dear to us all.

I go to Dublin tomorrow — till Saty morning (Poste restante G.P.O.) where I shall see George Russell[82] but have no other address meanwhile, as my movements in north or n. Western Ireland will be guided by weather and other circumstances. I expect to be at the Ry. Hotel at Greenore on Sunday and Monday morning — and after that at present know nothing more. But when I know an address later — and in any case nearer the time — I shall communicate with you in case for any reason you wish to postpone my visit.

Otherwise with keen pleasure I shall arrive at Ardrahan by the train you mention on Saty the 2nd of October. I hope the poetic drama of the Return of the Gods is finished. I am eager to hear that and other achievements of you and our brilliant comrade.

Sincerely yours, | William Sharp

ALS National Library of Ireland, text from transcript made by Library staff

To William Meredith, September 24, [*1897*]

Isle of Arran | Friday. 24th Sept. | En passant.

Dear Mr. Meredith

I had not time to do more than send a formal acknowledgment of the cheque for £50 advance against royalties on "Peterkin"[83] — which at my request you kindly forwarded to me, and for which I now send you and "A. Constable & Co" my cordial thanks.

I do hope the book will be a success, and reward you for all the trouble and outlay, as well as the friendly interest shown by you.

I asked Miss Rea some time ago to request a finished proof-copy for me (not for revision) and, if ready, for proof illustrations with it.

If this gale abates we sail from here tomorrow. For several weeks to come I shall be among the inner and outer Hebrides, and am never happier than when thus addressless. However, as you know, I can always be communicated with through Miss Rea, with whom whenever practicable I keep myself in telegraphic communication.

I hope, soon, to work uninterruptedly on "In the Old Magnific Way",[84] and *possibly* finish it by the turn of the year or early in 1898, but I can say nothing definite yet.

I hope soon to see Mr. Sharp who is at present in Ireland, and after seeing him to write to you a suggestion about my first book *Pharais*, which he negotiated for me.

With kind regards | Believe me, | Yours very sincerely, | Fiona Macleod

ALS University of California, Berkeley

To Edmund Clarence Stedman, September 28, [1897]

Temporary | The Corrie | Isle of Arran | Western Isles | 28:Sept

My dear friend, Comrade, and Poet

I send you a line from this beautiful island (more beautiful than ever to me because of a beautiful friend and comrade[85] who is here too) to wish you all of good luck, of good weal, of good fortune in the deepest sense, that loving friendship can wish for you. And not least do I hope that in this coming year you will find more leisure for your literary work, and for a fuller and richer expression still of your lovely lyric gift. If love, dear Stedman, can bring you your heart's-desire in all things, you shall be well served by "the silent ministers." I am eager to hear where you are, how you are, what you are doing, and how things are going with you. I forget when I last wrote to you — it was from Paris I think, or en route, and just after I had received the final settlement of that Lamson matter. Let me once more thank you lovingly for all the trouble, scrupulous heed, and wise discretion you showed throughout — and once more to tell you how grateful I am. You are of those who are indeed loyal in friendship.

I hope the delightful household at Bronxville flourishes — tho' your good friend (and mine I hope in a less ambitious way) Miss "Mary Stuart"[86] is gone. When is she to be married? and your dear wife — she is well I hope? You have been away of course: I wonder where.   A n d that other friend? Does all go well, there? I have often thought of this.

Tomorrow F. M. and I leave Arran. Then I go to the West of Ireland (Connemara) to stay at an old castle with a strange and delightful host — with a fellow guest, my friend W. B. Yeats. If you have time to send me a line after receipt of this, let it be to c/o Edward Martyn Esq, Tillyra Castle, Ardrahan, Co. Galway, Ireland. About the end of the month I shall be in Ireland again. (F. M. says you are to have from her her new book — but as it will not be out till end November it must be combined birthday and Xmas present — and be from us both!)

Ever, dear friend, Admiringly & Affectionately, |
Your Comrade | William Sharp

ALS Huntington Library

To John Macleay, [September 29, 1897]

Isle of Arran | 29th Sept.

My dear Mr. Macleay,

Pray excuse a penciled note. I have been yachting with some friends, & have put in at Arran, where I have found a budget of letters. I am now about to go to the West of Ireland, and shall stay at an old castle in Iar-Connacht (the coast-end of County Galway) with, for fellow-guest, W. B. Yeats.

I can give you little information about Miss Macleod's new work that, I fancy, you do not know already. There is this, however: Messrs. Geddes & Co have found that the cheap 3. Vol reissue (in sets & separable) much appreciated — & there has been a great advance of late in the sales of Miss M's works — & in America as well as here. Then again: Messrs A. Constable & Co. will issue, a month or so hence (Sooner or later, but that's what I heard from Miss F. M. a day or two ago) a new volume by her, mainly for young readers — tho' not what is called a child's book — called "The Laughter of Peterkin." It consists *mainly* of a retelling of the three beautiful old Irish-Gaelic & Alban-Gaelic tales known as "The Three Sorrows of Story Telling" — i.e. "The Four White Swans" ("The Children of Lir"), "Deirdre and the Sons of Usna," and "The Fate of the Sons of Tureen." I have seen these in proof, but not the original preliminary or appendical matter. The book is to be illustrated, but, if I ever heard, I forget by whom.

Finally, as to Miss M.., she is devoting her time wholly to her historic romance — the first draft of a trilogy dealing with "the epic" of the fall of the Stuart dynasty. All that she has already done has been mere scaffolding towards this ambitious structure — and has been destroyed now that the plan is clear: but, I understand, it will be the Spring before she finishes the writing of the initial volume (Each will be a distinct romance, i.e., independent of each other: but, all the same, the trilogy will be a complete sequence.) It has been commissioned to appear serially first — but I am not at liberty at present to say where or under what title.

As for myself, I am now within 2 or 3 months from the end of a romance I began last Spring, and hope to see it published about the middle of next Spring, I am also at work on a new play (for appearance in America first). For the rest, I am (or should be!) busy with commissioned articles for Harper's, the Atlantic Monthly, Nineteenth C., & Fortnightly.

I don't think I have any other news that wd. Interest you — unless it be that Mrs. Wingate Rinder (whose "Shadow of Arvor" you liked so much, & which by the way an eminent French critic has just praised for its high quality as at once faithful to the originals and yet individual in the retelling) is shortly to bring out a little volume through Messrs. Constable, a translation, under the title "The Dark Way of Love," of the chief work of the Breton romanticist Charles Le Goffie, "Le Crucific de Keralies."

I hope things are going well with you as to private pen-work. If possible, get out some romance or something of the kind. That, if at all successful, would help you better than anything else. I trust, too, you are in better health.

Perhaps you will kindly see that the H. N. for this & the next two weeks be sent to me at Tillyra Castle/ Ardrahan/Co. Galway/Ireland.

> With cordial regards & good wishes |
> Yours very truly | William Sharp

P.S. I expect to be in Edinburgh from about the 15th to 20th Oct. (Address Murrayfield) Is there any chance of your being South then. If so let us meet.

ALS National Library of Scotland

To Catherine Ann Janvier, October, 1897

Ireland

I hope to be dreaming in that old castle in what the Gaels called Far Connaught. Think of me there at the extreme verge of the passing Celtic world. There I know that some spiritual tidings or summons await me.

William Sharp

North American Review, April 5, 1907

To Elizabeth A. Sharp, [October 4, 1897][87]

Tillyra Castle | Galway, Ireland

... I find it almost impossible to attempt to tell you the varied and beautiful delights of this lovely place... . The country is strange and fascinating — at once so austere, so remote, so unusual, and so characteristic... .

Lord Morris,[88] and Martyn and I go off today "to show me the beauties of the wild coast of Clare." It is glorious autumnal weather, with unclouded sky, and I am looking forward to the trip immensely. We leave at 11, and drive to Ardrahan, and there get a train southward into County Clare, and at Ennis catch a little loopline to the coast. Then for two hours we drive to the famous Cliffs of Moher, gigantic precipices facing the Atlantic — and then for two hours move round toe wild headlands of Blackhead — and so, in the afternoon, to the beautiful Clare "spa" of Lisdoonvarna, where we dine late and sleep. Next day we return by some famous Round Tower of antiquity, whose name I have forgotten. Another day soon we are to go into Galway, and to the Arran Isles.

On Thursday Yeats arrives, also Dr. Douglas Hyde, and possibly Standish O'Grady — and Lady Gregory,[89] one of the moving spirits in this projected new Celtic Drama. She is my host's nearest neighbour, and has a lovely place (Coole Park) about five miles southwest from here, near Gort. I drove there, with Sir N.G.[90] yesterday, in a car, through a strange fascinating austere country.

The people here are distinct from any I have seen — and the women in particular are very striking with their great dark eyes, and lovely complexions and their picturesque "snoods."

The accent is not very marked, and the voices are low and pleasant, and the people courteous to a high degree.

In the evening we had music — and so ended delightfully my first delightful day in the west...

I forgot to tell you that I arrived late — and of course at Athenry only — some 14 miles from here. I had to wait some time till a car could be got — and what a drive I had! The man said that "Plaze God, he would have me at Tull-lyra before the gintry had given me up entoirely" — and he was as good as his word! The night was dark, and the roads near Athenry awful after the recent gale and rains — and it was no joke to hold on to the car. Whenever we came to a particularly bad bit (and I declared afterwards that he took some of the stone dykes at a leap) he cried — "Now thin yer honour, whin I cry *Whiroo!* you hould on an' trust to God" — and then came his wild *Whiroo!* and the horse seemed to spring from the car, and the jarvey and I to be flying alongside, and my rope-bound luggage to be kicking against the stars — and then we came down with a thud, and when I had a grasp of refound breath I asked if the road was as smooth and easy all the way, whereat my friend laughed genially and said "Be aisy at that now — shure we're coming to the bad bit soon!"

Not far from here is a fairy-doctor, I am going to see him some day. It is strange that when one day Lady Gregory took one of Russell's mystical drawings (I think of the Mor Reega) and showed it to an old woman, she at once exclaimed that that was the "photograph" of the fairy queen she had often seen, only that the strange girdle of fan-flame was round her waist and not on her head as in the drawing. An old man here also has often met "the secret people," and when asked to describe one strange "fairy lord" he has encountered more than once, it was so like G. R.'s drawing that that was shown him among several others, and he at once picked it out!

It is a haunted land.

In haste (and hunger), | Wilf.

P.S. I have been thinking much over my long-projected consecutive work (i.e. as W. S.) — in five sequel books — on the drama of life as seen in the evolution of the dreams of youth — begun, indeed, over ten years ago in Paris — but presciently foregone till ten maturing years should pass.

But now the time has came when I may, and should, and indeed, now, *must*, write this Epic of Youth that will be its general collective name — and it will interest you to know the now definitely fixt names of these five (and all very long) books; each to be distinct and complete in itself, yet all sequently connected: and organic and in the true sense dramatic evolution of some seven central types of men and women from youth to maturity and climax, along the high and low, levels.

Name: The Epic of Youth.

I.   The Hunters of Wisdom.

II. The Tyranny of Dreams.

III. The Star of Fortune.

IV. The Daughters of Vengeance.

V.   The Iron Gates.

This will take five years to do — so it is a big task to set, before the end of 1902! — especially as I have other work to do, and F.M's herself as ambitious. But method, and maturer power and thought, can accomplish with far less nervous output, what otherwise was impossible, and only at a killing or at least perilous strain.

So wish me well![91]

Memoir, pp. 287–90

To Mr. and Mrs. Grant Allen, November 5, 1897

15 Greencroft Gardens | South Hampstead | 5th Nov /97

My dear Grant and Nellie,

The appearance of "God" in the hearts of man seems a just cause for congratulation — so I write to wish you (G.A.) heartiest good-fortune with it.[92] I hope your other undertakings, also the plans of both, go well.

We returned a few days ago — or rather Elizabeth did some short time ago, and I dropped casually from an unexpected place I found myself in — the West of Ireland. I had a very delightful time there, as also in the Highlands.

We hope you are to be in town this winter, or a part of it — selfishly that is, for I don't doubt but that you are infinitely better at Hindhead — or, failing that, abroad.

I saw Dick Le Gallienne last night. He has just published a weak and malapropriately named little booklet[93] — but, I am glad to say, is at the moment writing the best and in every way finest thing he has yet done. You know, I daresay, that he and Julie have temporarily (amicably, of course), separated, on account of his inability to live at Waggoners Wells, because of his asthma, and also for financial reasons. She is now in Copenhagen, but is to join him again at the end of December, and both go then to America for a long time. In every way, Dick is pulling himself together.[94]

To show you that I am more faithful to my promises than either of you are, I enclose my promised photograph. This particular "phiz" was taken a week or two ago in Dublin. (If E. were in, she would doubtless send a new one of herself too: but she isn't, and won't be here till Monday. Won't you fulfil your solemn promises, you unfaithful twain?

Ever Yours, | William Sharp

ALS Pierpont Morgan Library

To Elizabeth A. Sharp, November 21, 1897

I am so glad to be here,[95] in this sunlight by the sea. Light and motion — what a joy these are. The eyes become devitalised in the pall of London gloom... .

There is a glorious amplitude of light. The mind bathes in these illimitable vistas. Wind and Wave and Sun: how regenerative these elder brothers are.

Solomon says there is no delight like wisdom, and that wisdom is the heritage of age: but there is a divine unwisdom which is the heritage of youth — and I would rather be young for a year than wise for a cycle. There are some who live without the pulse of youth in the mind: on the day, in the hour, I no longer feel that quick pulse, I will go out like a blown flame. To be young; to keep young: that is the story and despair of life... .

Memoir, p. 290

To Lady Augusta Gregory, [November 27?, 1997]

Rutland House | Greencroft Gardens | South Hampstead

Dear Lady Gregory,

I have written definitely withdrawing, both to Yeats & the Committee.

Cordially Yours | William Sharp[96]

ALS New York Public Library, Berg Collection

To Edmund Clarence Stedman, December 3, 1897

30 Greencroft Gardens | South Hampstead | London NW | 3/Dec/97

My dear Stedman

Let me send you not only my cordial thanks for the welcome copy of your Poems, but also my congratulations on the beauty and variety of the poems themselves.[97] I have read the book with delighted interest from first to last — & much of it over and over (some of course I knew well — some I had read before in some magazine or other — & some was new to me). What a wonderful fellow you are! Here is a volume coming out late in life (you, you Viking-bard, will be young till your last breath) — and it is enough to set up any new poet with a very high reputation indeed. After fresh joy in old favourites such as the exquisite "Ancassin," I turned with keen pleasure to the Caribbean section. What glow and colour and life! And what a splendid ballad is the one (new to me) entitled "Captain Francisca." It is bound to pass into the permanent ballad literature of our language. "Christophe," too, how noble & stirring it is. I am glad, also, that you ended the volume with the stately & beautiful "Ariel" — with which I am more impressed than ever.

My wife was deeply gratified to receive a copy from you, & is charmed (in the best sense of a much abused word) by it. She — like myself — has been home only a few days — & so cannot write to you by this mail: but will do so two or three days hence she says. I was going to get and send a copy to Miss Macleod — but this morning heard that she had just received one that had been forwarded from Edinburgh, & from you yourself. She says she is writing, but cannot post till she returns to Edinburgh at the week-end, as she is off to a remote Highland spot. She seems deeply touched by your courtesy, & kindness in sending her the book — which, she adds, more Celtico, "I have taken into my heart."

I will write again later. (Have applied two places to review the book.) Meanwhile my renewed thanks & loving congratulations.

Love to you & yours, dear Poet and Friend, | William Sharp

P.S. I hope you got my note on your birthday.

ALS Huntington Library

To John Macleay, [*mid-December?, 1897*]

30 Greencroft Gardens | South Hampstead

My dear Mr. Macleay,

I have read your book of stories with very great interest. They are full of "good stuff" — and it is quite clear that you have a real & fine faculty. But having said this much I am puzzled as to how best to advise you. It seems disheartening (after you have already worked at them so much) to say that they lack finality — but so, frankly, it seems to me they do. It is just because they are potentially so good, that I say so: otherwise it would be useless. I have not come to this conclusion through perusal in adverse circumstances or when not of the mood — and have, for greater surety, reread. I think a fine, strong, & interesting book lies here — but it wants re-writing in parts, reshaping in phrase and section every here & there, & <u>throughout</u>, lowering in key and a definite, a scrupulous almost austere <u>finishing up</u> "line by line." Frankly, too, there are too many pages which (rightly or wrongly seem to me to) reflect the influence now of Neil Munro, now of Miss Macleod. Both these writers can influence to strength & beauty, but, also, both can influence to self-conscious mannerism of strength & to a mannerism of sentiment that easily outruns itself. I think your work is too good to be other than <u>your</u> <u>own</u>.

<u>Critically</u>, I should advise you to make the book <u>wholly</u> of fiction (tale or episode) — & to keep out "An Old Capital" etc. for a book to be called, say, "Highland Essays." If I were asked by a firm as a "reader" I should indicate the inclusion of a long piece of discursive non-narrative prose such as this as out of place & likely to interfere with the particular reception wanted. A volume of stories & imaginative life-renderings called "From the Upper Glens" (an admirable title) should go well.

I think I like best "Neil the Harper," "Uistean the Seer," and "John Pane." But I would make the book as uniform in <u>general</u> sentiments as possible. Personally, I don't believe in "mixtures." In any case, before you submit it anywhere (I wd. try *Blackwoods* first) you should revise the typed copy. It is full of mis-typing — & experience teaches me how important it is not to prejudice a publisher or his reader by seeming carelessness or indifference. If your book had come to me as a reader, I shd. have added a rider to the effect that if a contract were made, the author shd. be responsible for extra corrections in proof — as his "MS" was so careless!! (E.g., just take the first I light on, the first & last pp. of the "Servant Girl" — where "glow the *rich* plain furnishings," and where a "<u>striven</u> heart" is left for presumably "a stricken heart."

It is only my genuine interest in you & your work that makes me write as I have done — & at a time & on a day when I am overwrought with unavoidable continuous pressure. It would be no true friendly service to have sent you compliments just on what was good, & to have been silent on essential things. You will understand, I am sure. I may well, of course, be wrong in my opinions — but they are at least the sincere expression of what your very promising & interesting work leaves in the mind of

Your friend | William Sharp

ALS National Library of Scotland

To Coulson Kernahan, [December 28, 1897][98]

3 Pelham Crescent | Hastings

So very sorry that, by doctor's orders, Elizabeth (who has had influenza) is forbidden to go to Scotland — and by the doctor's advice I brought her here today, at a few hour's notice. She will be here for a week or so — and I when I can. But sometime later I hope our Scotland visit may come off.

Cordial and affectionate regards to you both. W. S.

ACS Princeton University

Chapter Seventeen

Life: 1898

Early in 1898, Sharp suffered a "severe nervous collapse" which caused "an acute depression and restlessness that necessitated a continual change of environment." Elizabeth attributed it to the strain of maintaining a double identity:

> The production of the Fiona Macleod work was accomplished at a heavy cost to the author as that side of his nature deepened and became dominant. The strain upon his energies was excessive: not only from the necessity of giving expression to the two sides of his nature; but because his desire that, while under the cloak of secrecy F. M. should develop and grow, the reputation of William Sharp should at the same time be maintained. Moreover, each of the two natures had its own needs and desires, interests, and friends. The needs of each were not always harmonious one with the other, but created a complex condition that led to a severe nervous collapse (*Memoir*, p. 292).

As he moved from place to place on the south coast of England — Bournemouth, Brighton, and St. Margaret's Bay near Dover — he "was much alone, except for the occasional visit of an intimate friend." The sea, and solitude "proved his best allies." Elizabeth and Edith Rinder, the "intimate friend," were co-operating to provide whatever companionship and affection was needed. Elizabeth recognized the extent of Edith's "intimacy" with her husband, but she expressed no concerns about their relationship here or elsewhere in the *Memoir*. She focused on her work in London as an art critic, and on supporting her husband's physical and mental health.

In a letter describing his illness to Catherine Janvier, Sharp implied he was trying, aided by drugs, to communicate with spirits. He was "skirting the wood of shadows," "filled with vague fears," in "a duel

  https://doi.org/10.11647/OBP.0196.06

with other forces than those of human wills." Periodically he recovered his "psychic control over certain media," but the control was only temporary, a few days or weeks, but in that time he was himself. He wished for her peace of heart and "no gloom, but light, energy, full life" and in her "whole being, the pulse of youth, the flame of green fire." In the months ahead he returned often to the flame imagery, sometimes green and sometimes red, to signify the youthful vitality he felt slipping away.

Elizabeth thought her husband's efforts to obtain rituals for Yeats's Celtic Mystical Order undermined his health. She attributed his illness in December 1896 to both the "heavy dual work" and "experimentation with certain psychic phenomena [...] efforts in which at times he and Mr. W. B. Yeats collaborated" (*Memoir*, p. 282). Though she did not mention those efforts as a cause of Sharp's illness in early 1898, they must have worried her. Her reticence here and elsewhere in the *Memoir* may have been due to her desire to protect Yeats and other living participants. There was also the fact that Edith Rinder was Sharp's confederate in the psychic experiments. She valued her friendship and wanted to protect her as well. Though Sharp and Yeats may have engaged in psychic experiments together earlier, their collaboration began in earnest in January 1897 when Sharp joined the search for rituals for the Celtic Mystical Order. Yeats convinced Sharp, referencing his own relationship with Maud Gonne, that visions came more easily when jointly evoked by a man and a woman who were in love. He urged Sharp to partner with Fiona in the project, whereupon Sharp convinced Edith Rinder to join him, and the experiments continued for several years.

Although Elizabeth attributed her husband's movement from place to place along England's southern coast to his poor health and mental instability, he was also trying to create conditions that induced dreams and visions he could share with Yeats. He had convinced Elizabeth he needed to be alone with Edith to summon the female persona that enabled him to write as Fiona. Following Yeats's advice, he needed to be alone with Edith to evoke necessary dreams and visions. Whether or not Edith shared his faith in the supernatural, her participation in the spiritualist activities reflected her love for Sharp and her desire that he remain healthy and productive. In this regard, it is interesting to note that a diary, now in the British Library, which Elizabeth kept for some years after her husband died in 1905, records in considerable detail her contacts through a medium with the spirit of her dead husband. Such spiritualist sessions were in vogue, and Edith must have had at least an open mind about Sharp's communications with spirits.

In mid-February, he wrote a letter to his wife from the St. Margaret's Bay Hotel shortly after arriving there from Dover. He expressed the sense of peace and happiness that came to him that afternoon after leaving the station, walking through the village, and finding himself "alone, alone 'in the open.'" It was not "merely healing to me but an imperative necessity of my life." He was weary of "the endless recurrence of the ordinary in the lives of most people." To his own "wild heart [...] life must come otherwise or not at all." He wished he was "a youth once more" so he could "lie down at night smelling the earth and rise at dawn, smelling the new air out of the East, and know enough of men and cities to avoid both, and to consider little any gods ancient or modern, knowing well that there is only 'The Red God' to think of, he who lives and laughs in the red blood." He described the tension between the need to produce articles and reviews that generated income and his desire to live freely in nature, "a wild instinct to go to my own." In a letter about this time to "a friend," who may well have been Edith Rinder, he was even more specific about his desire to shed his human qualities and become a creature of nature:

> I wish I could live all my hours out of doors: I envy no one in the world so much as the red deer, the eagle, the sea-mew. I am sure no kings have so royal a life as the plovers and curlews have. All these have freedom, rejoice continually on the wind's wing, exalt alike in sun and shade: to them day is day, and night is night, and there is nothing else (*Memoir*, p. 298).

Elizabeth said the February letter to her provides "an insight into the primitive elemental soul that so often swayed him and his work." Taken together, the two letters — that to Elizabeth and that to a friend — express an intense desire to escape the bonds of rational life, to live an "elemental life" in the natural world, to recover the freedom he experienced as a youth when he joined the band of gypsies.

Before leaving St. Margaret's Bay, he explained his illness to Murray Gilchrist and said his two weeks there had been restorative:

I know you will have been sorry to hear that I have been ill — and had to leave work, and home. The immediate cause was a severe and sudden attack of influenza which went to membranes of the head and brain, and all but resulted in brain fever. This evil was averted — but it and the possible collapse of your friend Will were at one time, and for some days, an imminent probability. I have now been a fortnight in this quiet sea-haven and am practically myself again.

At the letter's close, he added: "I have suffered much, but am now again fronting life gravely and with laughing eyes." After returning to London, he wrote to Stedman on March 1. He had been seriously ill, had just returned from two-months convalescence, and was well again partly due to what he called "alleviations" or "to be more exact, it should be in the singular! You can guess the name, & perhaps remember something of a rare beauty, of life-lifting eyes." He must have shown Stedman a photograph of Edith Rinder during his trip to New York in November 1896. Later in the letter he was more specific about his illness and Edith's role in his recovery:

Although I have had so bad a time with a dangerous collapse (culminating in severe meningitis) I am now feeling better than I have done for at least two years past — and am quite determined not only to work hard but to get as much of the sunshine & joy & romance and dear delight of life as may be! And what's more, I've had it! And what's more, I have laid in a treasure of it quite recently! And what's more — by my Queen's full consent and approval — I've been a very bad boy with a very dear & delightful "friend," now alas returned to her home in Brussels — & generally I've been "spoilt" & made much of, & have enjoyed it, and am thinking of reforming 20 years hence, but meanwhile cling to my Sunshine Creed — to live sunnily, to think blithely, to act on the square even in my "sinning," & to try to give sunshine to others. After all, it's not such a bad creed — indeed, it's a very good one, and it has my dear poet E. C. S. as Prophet!

In the *Memoir*, Elizabeth said she welcomed Edith's cooperation in the efforts to maintain her husband's health, but this paragraph is perhaps the only instance of Sharp's stating explicitly that Elizabeth (his Queen) consented in and approved of his relationship with Edith. It also suggests Edith may have been living temporarily in Brussels to learn more about the Belgian writers whose stories she had translated and published in *The Massacre of the Innocents*.

Toward the end of the letter, in a burst of enthusiasm reflecting his restored health and enhanced devotion to the creed of which Stedman was the prophet, Sharp revealed his plan to meet Edith again in France in mid-April:

> If all goes well, you can think of me (and my friend) in a lovely green retreat, on the Marne, near Paris, during the last fortnight of April. If you were there too I would drink to you in white wine, and she would give you a kiss — which, with the glory in her beautiful eyes, would make you "wild with the waste of all unnumbered Springs". You will be with us in Spirit, dear poet of youth & romance — and *I* will kiss her for you, & likewise drink the sweet wine of France!!

Following this passage several lines are blacked out and are not decipherable. They precede the following lines which are also crossed through but can be read: "... hope, and I trust that her sunny smile and youthful heart often rejoice you. You will be a dear youth till the end, E. C. S., — & may the Gods reward you!" Apparently, Stedman's life was also enriched by a beautiful young woman as he tried to live the creed of which he was the prophet. Sharp concluded by saying his letter had better be entrusted to "the oblivious flame." Stedman did not so entrust it, but he, or someone else, expunged the name of the young woman who brought joy to his life.

In his St. Margaret's Bay letter to Gilchrist, Sharp said that Fiona, "before she got ill," had nearly finished a group of stories that might appear in the spring under the title *There is But One Love*, a volume Elizabeth identified as Fiona's *The Dominion of Dreams*, which was not published until the spring of 1899. Four of those stories were published in 1898: "Children of the Dark Star" (*The Dome*, May); "Enya of the Dark Eyes" (*Literature*, September); "The Wells of Peace" (*Good Words*, September); and "The White Heron" (*Harper's*, December). Two more that did not make their way into *The Dominion of Dreams* appeared in periodicals in 1898: "The Four Winds of Desire" (*Good Words*, 245) and "The Wayfarer" (*Cosmopolis*, June). Despite his illnesses during the first several months of 1898, Sharp produced by mid-year a considerable volume of writing.

Yet another spiritualist entered Sharp's life in late March when he wrote the first of several Fiona letters to Dr. John A. Goodchild, whom he met through their mutual friend Grant Allen. As Fiona, he thanked

Goodchild for a copy of a book of his poems and for a proof copy of his *Light of the West*, which would be published in April by Allen's nephew, Grant Richards. Goodchild was a highly regarded medical doctor who cared for his British patients both in England and in Italy where many spent the darker months. He was also a serious student of the early civilizations of Ireland, England, and Scotland and had a special affection for the Celts and the early converts to Christianity. More significantly, he was a spiritualist to whom important messages were delivered during sleep and reveries. He had bought from a tailor in Italy a beautiful glass bowl he thought might be the Holy Grail, the cup Jesus used at the last super. After keeping it on display in his library for several years, a master spirit directed him to bury it in a stream near Glastonbury in the West of England, the reputed domain of King Arthur and his grail-seeking knights. The purpose of the burial is not clear, but it had some interesting results. Given Sharp's involvement with Yeats's Celtic Mystical Order, it is not surprising that he was drawn to Goodchild who, in turn, was drawn to the Celtic stories of Fiona Macleod.

Since Elizabeth included in the *Memoir* (pp. 294–96) part of a letter her husband wrote to her dated March 29, he must have been away again. Many have wondered why Elizabeth was so accepting of her husband's relationship with Edith Rinder. Her inclusion of this letter in the *Memoir* addresses that concern as it is a carefully crafted argument not for free love, but for loving more than one person at a time. Elizabeth introduced the letter by saying it expressed views she and her husband held in common, and that echoes Sharp's opening assertion:

> Yes, in essentials, we are all at one. We have both learned and unlearned so much, and we have come to see that we are wrought mysteriously by forces beyond ourselves, but in so seeing we know that there is a great and deep love that conquers even disillusion and disappointment.

Having assured Elizabeth of his continuing love for her, he portrays his love for Edith as a powerful force impossible to control:

> Not all the wishing, not all the dreaming, not all the will and hope and prayer we summon can alter that within us which is stronger than ourselves. This is a hard lesson to learn for all of us, and most for a woman. We are brought up within such an atmosphere of conventional untruth to life that most people never even perceive the hopeless futility in the arbitrary ideals which are imposed upon us — and the result for

the deeper natures, endless tragic miscarriage of love, peace, and hope. But, fortunately, those of us who to our own suffering *do* see only too clearly, can still strike out a nobler ideal — one that does not shrink from the deepest responsibilities and yet can so widen and deepen the heart and spirit with love that what else would be irremediable pain can be transmuted into hope, into peace, and even into joy.

For those of us who recognize that loving more than one person can "widen and deepen the heart and spirit," he asserted, what otherwise would cause deep pain can become a source of hope, peace, and even joy.

It strains credulity to believe Sharp's relationship with Edith Rinder brought "hope, peace, and even joy" to Elizabeth, but her inclusion of the letter is a clear sign she shared its basic opinions. For most people, Sharp wrote, "the supreme disintegrate" of happiness is

the Tyranny of Love — the love which is forever demanding *as its due* that which is wholly independent of bonds, which is as the wind which bloweth where it listeth or where it is impelled, by the Spirit. [...] That ought not be — but it must be as long as young men and women are fed mentally and spiritually upon the foolish and cowardly lies of a false and corrupt conventionalism.

Mona Caird, Elizabeth's best friend and Edith's cousin by marriage, was arguing forcefully in widely read periodicals and in novels against the conventional constraints of marriage. Elizabeth asserted several times in the *Memoir* that she and her husband shared her views. Mona's main goal was to free women from the legal and conventional constraints of marriage and recognize them as equal partners. Sharp, however, in this letter goes much further to argue that both men and women ought to be freed from the convention that marriage required them to love and have intimate relations with only their marital partner.

An admission in the last two paragraphs of the letter casts an important light on the psychological make-up of William Sharp. "False and corrupt conventionalism," he wrote, subjects "many fine natures, men and women," to "lifelong suffering." Some never learn their unhappiness is the result of impossible ideals, while others "learn first strength to endure the transmutations and then power to weld these to far nobler and finer uses and ends." Both suffer, and Sharp places himself among the second class of sufferers. Everyone, he says, tends to nurse grief. "The brooding spirit craves for the sunlight, but it will not leave the shadows. Often, *Sorrow* is our best ally." Sharp's frequent bouts of depression which he described to his intimate friends, principally to Murray Gilchrist, were rooted in the impossible ideals installed in his youth.

> I dreamed that a beautiful spirit was standing beside me. He said, "My Brother, I have come to give you the supreme gift that will heal you and save you." I answered eagerly: "Give it me — what is it?" And the fair radiant spirit smiled with beautiful solemn eyes and blew a breath into the tangled garden of my heart — and when I looked there, I saw the tall white Flower of Sorrow growing in the Sunlight.

Whether or not such a dream occurred, Sharp's rendition of it reveals a great deal. When he was twenty-one, his father, with whom he had a strained relationship, died. From that point onward, he had an overpowering need for intimate relationships with both men and women to whom he revealed his deepest thoughts and feelings. Elizabeth and Edith fulfilled his need for a female confessor, and a succession of men — Hall Caine, J. Stanley Little, R. Murray Gilchrist, and starting in 1900 Alexander Nelson Hood, the Duke of Bronte — fulfilled his need for a male confessor, a brother who would blow a breath into the tangled garden of his heart, that would allow his sorrow to grow into a beautiful white flower in the bright sunlight. Among his surviving letters, those to Murray Gilchrist express that need most vividly. There is no evidence that any of these relationships — with women or with men — involved sexual intimacy just as there is no evidence they did not. But there is abundant evidence that these individuals and others fulfilled a deep psychological need that reasserted itself throughout his troubled life.

Sharp's trip to France was delayed. On April 22, he told Gilchrist he was leaving for Paris "next Friday," April 29. The main purpose of the trip to Paris was to introduce Fiona Macleod to Yeats and Maud Gonne, and to Macgregor Mathers and his wife Moina who were helping him with the Celtic Mystical Order. The six would engage in psychic experiments, and Yeats would discuss with Fiona the plays he wanted her to write for the Celtic Theatre he was creating in Dublin. Sharp left for Paris on April 29, but he made it only as far as Dover where he again checked into the St. Margaret's Bay Hotel. He wrote to Yeats the next day: "A sudden and serious collapse in health will prevent Miss M. from coming to Paris" and will "probably end in her having to go to some remote Baths for 2 months." He added, "As for myself, partly for this and partly because being myself (as you will understand) seriously indisposed in the same way, I am unable to go to Paris either." This sentence indicates that Sharp had told Yeats confidentially that Fiona was a woman who had emerged in his body. When she was sick, he was sick. She generated the Fiona writings, and Sharp was the vehicle for bringing them to the world. However improbable that construction may be, Yeats at the time accepted it, along with Sharp's claim that there was a real woman who facilitated the emergence of Fiona. She was the woman Sharp loved and the woman who was working with him psychically on the Celtic Mystical Order. Since neither Maud Gonne nor the Mathers knew the truth, the woman he was taking to Paris would have to pretend to be Fiona.

Sharp thought he could take Edith to Paris, where they would engage briefly with Yeats and company, and then go to "the lovely green retreat on the Marne, near Paris," he had described to Stedman on March first. If Edith knew Sharp expected her to play the role of Fiona in Paris as she had done for an hour or two with George Meredith the previous June, she would have been at least apprehensive. Though sympathetic to the Celtic Revival, she was neither a Scot nor immersed in the myths and legends of the Hebrides. She must have considered the Paris plan as one of Sharp's romantic fantasies that would evaporate as so many did. When she realized he was about to implement the plan, she put her foot down and refused to go to Paris. Her refusal presented a problem for Sharp who seems to have been blissfully unaware of the inherent difficulties. Having refused to go to Paris as Fiona, Edith worried about leaving Sharp alone and either accompanied him to St. Margaret's Bay or joined him there, where ensuing events bordered on the fantastic.

Yeats described the planned visit in a letter to Lady Gregory on April 25:

> I have been here in Paris for a couple of days. [...] I am buried in Celtic mythology and shall be for a couple of weeks or so. Miss Gonne has been ill with bronchitis. [...] She comes here to-morrow to see visions. Fiona Macleod (this is private as she is curiously secret about her movements) talks of coming here too, so we will have a great Celtic gathering (*Collected Letters II*, pp. 214–15).

Fig. 16. Maud Gonne McBride (1866–1953), Wikimedia, Public Domain, https://
commons.wikimedia.org/wiki/File:Maude_Gonne_McBride_nd.jpg#/
media/File:Maude_Gonne_McBride_nd.jpg

In a postscript, he told Lady Gregory he was staying with Macgregor
Mathers, who was "a Celtic enthusiast who spends most of his day in
highland costume to the wonder of the neighbors." When he learned
Sharp and Fiona were not be coming to Paris, Yeats sent Sharp a letter
on May 3, in which he asked about Sharp's family tartan and wanted to
know what sort of person Fiona Macleod's father was, what he looked
like, and what *his* tartan was (*Collected Letters II*, pp. 219–20). He then
asked Sharp if he had been "conscious of being in any unusual state on
either May 1 or May 2." He would explain later why he was asking these
questions. For now, he could only say he has "had an astral experience of
the most intense kind" and that Sharp's "answers are necessary before
certain things, which I was asked to do can be done." With his letter to
Sharp, Yeats enclosed a sealed letter to Fiona which clarified the matter.
On the night of May 2, he was "suddenly visited by the intellectual body
of someone who was passing through an intense emotional crisis." He
was "inclined to believe" the visitor was Fiona, and he needed to know if
she, "either last night [May 2] or Sunday night [May 1] (the intellectual
body sometimes appears a little after the emotional crisis that causes
its appearance)" passed through "some state of tragic feeling?" Since

Yeats knew Sharp was producing the Fiona writings, the enclosed letter must have been intended either for that separate person within the body of Sharp or for the woman who inspired the Fiona writings and was helping Sharp obtain rituals for his Order.

Yeats told Fiona he needed to know if she passed through some state of tragic feeling because someone "asked last night" for his help and the help of the "far more powerful occultist," with whom he was working. Though not named in the letter, the more powerful occultist was probably Maud Gonne, and the person who asked for help was probably Macgregor Mathers. A professional Scott, Mathers wore a Macgregor tartan in Paris where, with help from his wife Moina, he was trying to set up a Paris branch of the Order of the Golden Dawn. He must have had some doubts about the Sharp/Fiona duo. Their tartans, if they had them, would prove they were legitimate Scotts. In a postscript to the Fiona letter, Yeats said he had hoped to see her in Paris and informed her that "the opening ceremonial of the Celtic mysteries, of which he [Sharp] will have told you, is now ready to be considered."

Fig. 17. Moina Mathers (1865–1928), the wife of Macgregor Mathers and sister of Henri Bergson, was an artist, occultist, and founder of the Alpha et Omega Lodge of the Golden Dawn. Left: Moina Mathers from her performance in the Rites of Isis in Paris (1899), Wikimedia, Public Domain, https://commons.wikimedia.org/wiki/File:Picture_of_Moina_Mathers_from_her_performance_in_the_Rites_of_Isis_in_Paris.jpg. Right: Moina Mathers (c. 1887), Wikimedia, Public Domain, https://commons.wikimedia.org/wiki/File:Moina_Mathers.jpg

Sharp's response to Yeats's letter posted two days later (Thursday, May 5) is a remarkable and amusing reflection of the predicament in which he found himself. No, he had not experienced anything but "a singular depression, and a curious sense of unreality for a time" on Sunday, but on Monday, May 2, he "suffered in a way I can't explain, owing to what seemed to me an unaccountable preoccupation of Miss M." That is vague enough. Ignoring Yeats's tartan questions, Sharp described Fiona's father as a "tall, fine looking man," and then, surprisingly, "Fiona sees at times a startling likeness between me & her father, though I am taller & bigger & fairer than he was." Among the similarities between them, he continued, was their first name: William. One need not look far for the origin of that detail; Edith Rinder's father was *William* Wingate (1828–1884) of Ludford, Leicestershire.

In a hurried postscript, Sharp informed Yeats that Fiona had awakened and read his letter to her. In response, she said she had experienced a series of emotions like those of Sharp. She told Sharp to tell Yeats she was "going through an intense emotional crisis." There was one "poignant period" on the Sunday night, she said but a far more poignant period on Monday:

> But of this, being private, I cannot speak further. I was, on both occasions (though differently & for different reasons) undergoing tragic feeling. I am at present at a perilous physical & spiritual crisis. I can say no more. The one who shares my life & self is here. It is as crucial for him. I will talk over your letter to us — for to us it is, though you send it to me.

Sharp then added a question from Fiona: "Are you sure it was not Will whom you felt or saw?" He wondered why Yeats was asking about Fiona's father rather than his father. He was unaware of Mather's role in the matter. It was Mathers who had some suspicions about Fiona and wanted to know more about her Macleod ancestry. Sharp saw no need to shift the spotlight by introducing another male into the picture, and he certainly didn't want to be drawn into speculations about Fiona's ancestry.

In a second postscript, Sharp added for Yeats's benefit a more immediate and serious element of stress:

> Hurriedly adding this at the PO to say that my friend's neuralgia was too severe to talk any more. The subject too was exciting her. She will show me your letter when I get back. Note *this* time today. About 3 p.m.

today Thursday she went through (& I too) a wave of intense tragic emotion — and last night, between 10 and 12 or later, we nearly lost each other in a very strange way. Something I did by the will was too potent, & for a time severed some unconscious links (we were apart at the time: I thought she was sleeping) — & we both suffered in consequence. But I think the extreme crisis of tragic psychic emotion is over.

Most of this frenetic activity was invented for the consumption of Yeats in order to sustain his belief in Sharp's psychic abilities, but it also reflects the pattern of emotions Sharp and Edith were experiencing as they attempted to establish contact with spirits in another realm. It is always difficult to distinguish between what Sharp was fabricating in a calibrated effort to mislead people, and what arose from genuine experiences. Although the mix differed from time to time, it was always a combination of the two. That said, the letter exemplifies the mental instability that resulted from having joined Yeats's spiritualist quest.

Yeats's response on May 7 was even stranger than Sharp's May 5 letter (*Collected Letters of W. B. Yeats, II*, pp. 222–23). He described in detail the dreams and visions he and the Mathers were having about Sharp/Fiona. The letter illustrates the depth of Yeats's interest in and psychic involvement with his mysteries and with Sharp. Fiona's father had appeared in a Macleod tartan to Mathers in a dream on Sunday. On Monday, Yeats said, he "fell into a strange kind of shivering & convulsive trembling" whereupon he felt the astral presence of first Fiona and then Sharp. Moina Mathers then saw a face which she drew, and it seemed to Yeats to be the face of William Sharp's daemon which George Russell (AE) had seen in the spring of 1897. Next, Moina saw someone who must have been Fiona and then a man with a tartan who, Yeats wrote, "was probably the astral of some dead person." After all these sightings, Yeats, Moina, and Macgregor retired "into a room used for magical purposes" and there made themselves "magical principals rather than persons." Fiona appeared, Yeats continued, and told them "certain things about her spiritual & mental state & asked for Occult help, of which I prefer to talk rather than to write." Fiona, he affirmed, "is suffering physically," as Sharp had just told him, "but the cause of this suffering is not physical & can be remedied." It would be best if Sharp and Fiona "could come to Paris for a couple days on (say) Monday [May 9]." Otherwise, Yeats might see Sharp in London at the end of the next week.

Yeats was left shaken for a time by this very intense experience. He had spoken in a dream to Sharp's daemon during the past night. If Sharp can come to Paris, his friends in "the order of the Rosy Cross," really the Order of the Golden Dawn, and specifically the Mathers, will give any help they can. These friends "have a boundless admiration for the books of Fiona Macleod." As if all this was not enough to set Sharp's teeth on edge and feed his manic fantasies, Yeats added a postscript, which reads as follows:

> I think you should do no magical work with Miss Macleod until we meet. I mean that you should not attempt to use the will magically. The danger of doing so just now is considerable. You are both the channels of very powerful beings & some mistake has been made. I tried to send a magical message, as I have said, last night. It was something which you were to say to Miss Macleod. I can but remember that it was a message of peace. I did not try to appear or make you aware of my presence. I was in a dream for a [...] time too, far off from my surroundings, & believe that our daemons met in someplace of which my bodily self has no memory & that the message which I spoke with my bodily lips was carried thither.

Yeats was an active member of the London chapter of the Order of the Golden Dawn where his motto was *Daemon est Deus*. His encounter with Sharp's daemon was rooted in the secret rituals of the order, and Sharp, as a less active member of the London chapter, knew something of its rituals.

Many years later, Yeats wrote of the St. Margaret's Bay exchange of letters:

> I was fool enough to write to Sharp and [received] an unbelievable letter from a seaside hotel about the beautiful Fiona and himself. He had been very ill, terrible mental suffering and suddenly my soul had come to heal him, and he had found Fiona to tell her he was healed — I think that I had come as a great white bird. I learnt, however, from Mrs. Sharp years afterward that at the time he was certainly alone but mad. He had gone away to struggle on with madness (W. B. Yeats, *Memoirs*, transcribed and edited by Denis Donoghue (London: Macmillan, 1972), p. 105).

In response to Yeats's May 7 letter, Sharp may have written another to Yeats that contained the "great white bird." If he was referring to Sharp's May 5 letter, his recollection was inaccurate. Not only is there no bird, but the assertion — attributed correctly or falsely to E. A. S — that

Sharp was surely alone and struggling with madness was wrong. Since the descriptions of Fiona's actions were, I believe, beyond even Sharp's ability to create out of thin air, Edith must have been with him in St. Margaret's Bay. Moreover, many of the letters he wrote to others during the two weeks were perfectly sane and rational. He was experiencing depression, a condition worsened by the psychic experiments, but he was not insane. The description in his May letter to Yeats of his depression and "tragic emotion" and Fiona's "perilous physical & spiritual crisis" had some basis in fact, but the letter's main purpose was to sustain Yeats's confidence in his psychic abilities.

Yeats's three May letters from Paris — one to Fiona and two to Sharp — also exhibit his genuine attraction to the idea of Fiona in 1898 and the closeness of his relationship with Sharp. They were joined in a secret project known to only a few of Yeats's close friends. His later disparaging remarks arose, in part I believe, from his effort to obscure the extent of his own psychic activities in the 1890s. Sharp was trying his best to follow Yeats's directions and contribute to his project. In the first draft of his "Autobiography," Yeats wrote of Sharp,

> I feel I never properly used or valued this man, through whom the fluidic world seemed to flow, disturbing all; I allowed the sense of comedy, taken by contagion from others, to hide from me my own knowledge. To look at his big body, his high colour, his handsome head with the great crop of bristly hair, no one could have divined the ceaseless presence of that fluidic life (*Memoirs*, pp. 128–29).

On the other hand, we recall Yeats's remark many years later that Sharp "never told one anything that was true" (*Autobiographies*). Taken together, the two comments show Yeats continued for years the effort to unravel the mysteries and grasp the truth about Sharp/Fiona. His failure reflects the complexity of Sharp's personality and exemplifies the difficulty his friends faced understanding him while he lived, and everyone has faced since he died.

The astonishing letters Sharp wrote to Yeats from St Margaret's Bay contrast starkly with the perfectly sane business letters he wrote to his publisher Grant Richards, to his friend John Macleay, and to Fiona's suitor Benjamin Burgess Moore. It is no wonder Sharp's state of mind was fragile, that he was often depressed and on the edge of mental collapse. His life was defined by dichotomies and contradictions — all of his own making — as he tried to comply with Yeats's spiritualist expectations, write poems and stories as though by two different writers, get them published to produce income, and deal with the tensions that inevitably arose from his love for two remarkable women, both of whom loved him and worried about his mental and physical health. Yeats's warning that Sharp not engage with Miss Macleod in any "magical work' until they could meet freed Edith to leave St. Margaret's Bay after a week, so I believe, and provided Sharp some respite for serious writing during his second week at the St. Margaret's Bay Hotel.

After returning to London on May 13, Sharp described his condition to Gilchrist: "After months of sickness, at one time at the gates of death, I am whirled back from the Iron Gates and am in the maelstrom again — fighting with mind and soul and body for that inevitable losing game which we call victory." After mentioning what he was writing as Fiona and as himself, he asked Gilchrist to write to him soon, "by return best of all. You can help me — as I, I hope, can help *you*." Despite his return with renewed health to the "maelstrom," his condition remained fragile, since he needed Gilchrist's help, if only through a letter. "It is only the fullest and richest lives," he wrote, "that know what the *heart* of loneliness is." He placed Gilchrist and himself among those who live full and rich lives. Sharing confidences about their deepest feelings and desires would, he thought, alleviate their loneliness. He concluded by calling Gilchrist his "comrade" and assuring him he had his love. More openly here, but throughout his correspondence with Gilchrist, there is the suggestion that Sharp had shared with Gilchrist, whose desires were directed entirely toward men and who lived with a male lover, his need for an intimate relationship with another man and the duality of his sexual orientation.

After his return from St. Margaret's Bay, Sharp stayed in London only long enough to celebrate Elizabeth's birthday on May 17, before leaving again on May 18 for what she called "a delightful little wander in Holland" with Thomas Janvier, "a jovial, breezy companion." She hoped a walking trip with a sane friend would be restorative, and it had that effect for a time. On May 20, Sharp wrote to Elizabeth from the south Zuyder Zee about the "marvellous sky effects" and the island of Marken where "the women are grotesque, the men grotesquer, and the children grotesquest" and where the babies are "gorgeous-garbed, blue-eyed, yellow haired, imperturbable." They alone, Sharp wrote, were worth coming to see.

Only a few Sharp/Macleod letters survive from the summer of 1898, and surprisingly few from the last half of the year. Elizabeth glossed over this seven-month period by commenting only that her husband had to sustain the reputation of William Sharp despite his need to write as Fiona Macleod.

> There was a great difference in the method of production of the two kinds of work. The F. M. writing was the result of an inner impulsion, he wrote because he had to give expression to himself whether the impulse grew out of pain or out of pleasure. But W. S., divorced as much as could be from his twin self, wrote not because he cared to, because the necessities of life demanded it (*Memoir*, p. 301).

In this context, Elizabeth referred to two William Sharp novels: *Wives in Exile, A Comedy in Romance* which he wrote in 1895 for the Stone and Kimble firm in Chicago; and *Silence Farm*, the novel he was writing in 1898.

When Grant Richards started his publishing firm in 1897, Sharp moved in on the ground floor. He convinced Richards to publish a British edition of *Wives in Exile*, which, Stone and Kimball having dissolved, was published by Lamson, Wolffe and Co. in Boston in 1897. He made some revisions in the spring of 1898, and the book appeared in the summer. It is a light romance in which the men go off sailing, leaving their wives behind to make do. He also started a new novel, *Silence Farm*, which Richards would publish in 1899. According to Elizabeth, he felt he had to publish works by William Sharp and "show some result of the seclusion he was known to seek for purposes of work" in order support the fictional existence of Fiona. In writing *Silence Farm*, "a tragic tale of the Lowlands, founded on a true incident," Sharp

> never forgot that the book should not have obvious kinship to the work of F. M., that he should keep a considerable amount of himself in check. For there was a midway method, that was a blending of the two, a swaying from the one to the other, which he desired to avoid, since he knew that many of the critics were on the watch. Therefore, he strained the realistic treatment beyond what he otherwise would have done. [...] Nevertheless, that book was the one he liked best of all the W. S. efforts, and he considered that it contained some of his most satisfactory work (*Memoir*, p. 301).

Despite his fondness for *Silence Farm*, neither it nor *Wives in Exile* were successful. Elizabeth's comments about the two writing methods and styles, and a third "midway method," are interesting. Beginning in 1897, the Fiona writings begin moving away from the retelling of Celtic myths and stories about people of the Western Isles into mystical allegories and ruminations on the beauties of the natural world and the presence of spiritual forces within it. After the failure of *Silence Farm* to attract a sizable readership, Sharp turned increasingly to travel writing, art history and criticism for publications signed William Sharp. "Middle method" or not, the distinction between publications signed F. M. and those signed W. S. began to fade despite, Sharp's continuing efforts to sustain it.

In June 1898, however, the origin of the "two writing methods" and the relationship between them, were on Sharp's mind. On June 28, Fiona Macleod responded to a Yeats letter which has not yet surfaced. In that letter, Yeats praised two Fiona stories and asked for a further explanation of the relationships between the man the world knew as William Sharp, the real woman who inspired Sharp to write as F. M., and the female personality within Sharp responsible for the Fiona writings. It is not surprising that Yeats, who at this time accepted the possibility of more than one person inhabiting a single body, remained curious about Sharp/Fiona. In Fiona's response, Sharp invoked the metaphor of a torch, a match, and a flame to explain his relationship with Edith Rinder and her role in the creative process. Portions of the letter have been crossed out or erased, but it is possible to read some lines through the markings and infer some of the erased words. In a postscript that is not decipherable, he asked Yeats to destroy the letter, and when he had not received word that Yeats had done so, Sharp wrote again as Fiona on July 6 to tell Yeats he was anxious about the letter. In a July 4 letter to Sharp, Yeats said he had heard from Fiona and "done as she wished about the letter" (*Collected Letters II*, p. 250). Fortunately, he had not done as she wished, and the letter survives.

The relevant section reads as follows:

> I have been told that long ago one of the subtlest and strangest minds of his time — a man of Celtic ancestry on one side and of Norse on the other — was so profoundly influenced by the kindred nature and spirit of a woman whom he loved, a Celt of the Celts, that, having in a sense

accidentally discovered the mystery of absolute mental and spiritual union of two impassioned and kindred natures the flame of [?vision] that had been his in a far back day was in him, so that besides a strange and far [?reaching] ancestral memory, he remembered anew and acutely every last clue and significance of his boyhood and early life, spent mostly among the shepherds and fishers of the Hebrides and Gaelic Highlands. His was the genius, the ancestral memory, the creative power — she was the flame — she, too, being also a visionary, and with unusual and all but lost old wisdom of the Gael. Without her, he would have been lost to the Beauty which was his impassioned quest: with her, as a flame to his slumbering flame, he became what he was. The outer life of each was singular, beyond that of any man or woman I have heard of: how much stranger that of their spiritual union. A profound and resolute silence lay upon the man, save when he knew the flame of the woman "through whom he saw Beauty," and his soul quickened. She gave him all she could, and without her he could not be what he was, and he needed her vision to help his own, and her dream, and her thought, and her life, till hers and his ceased to be hers and his and merged into one, and became ...... a spirit of shaping power born of them both.

Although he cast the vignette in the ancient past, he was talking about himself (half Celt and half Norse) and describing how his relationship with Edith Rinder enabled him to write as Fiona Macleod. She was the match that brought flame to the otherwise dark and silent torch. They became one in the resultant fire, which was the fire of passion, the fire of creativity. The torch (Sharp) was the vehicle that carried that fire while the match survived within the fire and sustained it. This metaphor of creativity came to dominate Sharp's imagination. After describing it, Fiona asked Yeats: "How does that strike you as a subject for a tale, a book? It would be a strange one. Does it seem to you impossible? It does not seem so to me." Indeed, it did not, for Sharp as Fiona incorporated the match, the torch, and the flame into "The Distant Country," a story he began writing in the summer of 1898 and included in Fiona's *The Dominion of Dreams* which Archibald Constable and Co. published in May 1899. The story will be discussed in some detail in the next chapter.

Sharp was in London for most of July writing and dealing with the publication details of *Wives in Exile*. In mid-July, he received a letter from Yeats addressed to Fiona informing him that a certain legal obstacle to the establishment of a Celtic Theater in Dublin had been resolved, and asking which plays Fiona would have for production by the fall. In her reply, Fiona said that three plays ("Fand and Cuchulain," "The King of Ys," and "Dahut the Red') would be ready for consideration. And there might be a fourth, "The Hour of Beauty." The first three were never finished, but "The Hour of Beauty," having become "The Immortal Hour," was published in *The Fortnightly Review* in 1900. The play was not performed in Dublin, but it became the libretto for Rutland Boughton's opera, which was an enormous success on the London stage in the 1920s and is still performed. Though Sharp was working on plays during the summer of 1898, he managed to complete only two ("The Immortal Hour" and "The House of Usna"). His plan to write a series of short dramas under the general title *The Theatre of the Soul* came to naught, but "The House of Usna" was also published in *The Fortnightly Review* in 1900 and, on April 29 that year, it was performed at the Globe Theatre in London under the auspices of the Stage Society of which William Sharp was President. Only a few of those who joined Sharp in the audience knew he was the author of the play.

On the July 19, 1898, William and Elizabeth went to Holmesfield in Derbyshire to visit Murray Gilchrist at Cartledge Hall, where he lived with his mother, his two sisters, and his companion George Garfitt. They returned to London on July 26, and Sharp left for the West of Scotland on July 31. A letter carrying that date from Fiona to Benjamin Burgess Moore, the American fan she had enlisted in approaching publishers, informed him that "it is not quite true that Mr. Yeats and I are collaborating on a drama: but we are each writing a drama, which we hope to see brought out in the new Celtic Theatre in Dublin next year." She concluded by telling him that as soon as she finished her new book (*The Dominion of Dreams*) she would "get on with two short plays, 'The Hour of Beauty' and 'The King of Ys and Dahut the Red.'" Yeats's efforts to encourage Sharp/Fiona to write plays for his projected theatre in Dublin soon came to an abrupt end when he was forced, under the pressure of Irish Nationalists, to change its name to the "Irish Theatre," and to exclude all but Irish authors.

In a July 4 letter from Coole Park, Yeats told Sharp that Edward Martyn was too upset by his mother's death (on May 12) to invite anyone to Tillyra Castle, his home in County Galway where Sharp was a guest the previous October. If he changed his mind, Yeats would speak to him about inviting Sharp. Apparently, Martyn did invite Sharp, but the formality of Sharp's early August letter to Martyn suggests the invitation was less cordial and welcoming than that of the previous year which led to Sharp's spending nearly three weeks at Tillyra, proving an embarrassment to Martyn and some of his friends. Sharp stayed in and around Kilcreggan in Scotland, near where Edith Rinder was vacationing, until August 24, when he returned to London and went on to Holland to gather material for an article on Rembrandt which *Cosmopolis* had commissioned and which appeared in its November issue. He was back in London by September 17, the date of a Fiona Macleod letter to Benjamin Moore which mentioned "prolonged absence" as reason for his delay in writing. Sharp's annual birthday letter to E. C. Stedman on September 28 mentioned "illness — followed by heavy work & latterly a big exigent writing commission in Holland for *Cosmopolis*" (the Rembrandt article) as excuses for the relative brevity of the letter. Still, he managed to inform Stedman that he "had a very wonderful & happy time this summer with the dear friend of whom you know, & whose writings you admire so much — & I look to another week at least about mid-October." The dear friend was Edith Rinder, who Stedman thought was Fiona Macleod, and who was with Sharp often during the three weeks he spent in the West of Scotland. He concluded the Stedman letter by highlighting his recent successes: "In another letter I must tell you of my many literary doings — more ambitious now. (In a magazine way, see *Fortnightly* for August, etc. etc. Also *Cosmopolis* in Nov. — am now writing for *all* the big mags here and U.S.A.)." *The Fortnightly* printed his tribute to Edward Burne Jones, the Pre-Raphaelite painter who had recently died.

It is difficult to chronicle Sharp's activities in the fall of 1898 because very few letters survive from those months. He may have had another holiday with Edith Rinder in October, as he told Stedman he was planning, and he was continuing the mystical efforts to obtain talismans and rituals for Yeats. In that connection, it is interesting to note that Sharp proposed Grant Richards ask Edith Rinder to translate Jules Bossière's *Fumeurs d'Opium*, a collection of stories first published in 1896 examining the effects of opium on mind and body.

Near the end of December, just before Christmas, he was at the Pettycur Inn across the Forth from Edinburgh. From there he wrote to Catherine Ann Janvier with enthusiasm and optimism. His time there had been "memorable,'" and he had written three stories for *The Dominion of Dreams* that he thought some of his best work.

> What a glorious day it has been. The most beautiful I have ever seen at Pettycur I think. Cloudless blue sky, clear exquisite air tho' cold, with a marvellous golden light in the afternoon. Arthur's Seat, the Crags, and the Castle and the 14 ranges of the Pentlands all clear-cut as steel, and the city itself visible in fluent golden light.

Then, as 1898 came to a close, he was moved to reflect on what he had accomplished and to welcome "a new birth," without specifying whether it would occur in this world or the next:

> And now I listen to the gathering of the tidal waters under the stars. There is an infinite solemnity — a hush, something sacred and wonderful. A benediction lies upon the world. Far off I hear the roaming wind. Thoughts and memories crowd in on me. Here I have lived and suffered — here I have touched the heights — here I have done my best. And now, here, I am going through a new birth. "Sic itur ad astra!" [Thus onward to the stars]

It is fitting that the first and last surviving letters of 1898 were addressed to Catherine Ann Janvier, an American artist and writer who was fourteen years older than Sharp, and with whom he shared his deepest thoughts and dreams.

Letters: 1898

To Catherine Ann Janvier, [January/February, 1898]

... I am skirting the wood of shadows. I am filled with vague fears — and yet a clear triumphant laughter goes through it, whether of life or death no one knows. I am also in a duel with other forces than those of human wills — and I need all my courage and strength. At the moment I have recovered my physic control over certain media. It cannot last more than a few days at most a few weeks at a time: but in that time *I am myself*...

Let there be peace in your heart: peace and hope transmuted into joy: in your mind, the dusking of no shadow, the menace of no gloom, but light, energy, full life: and to you in your whole being, the pulse of youth, the flame of green fire... .

Memoir, pp. 292–93

To Elizabeth A. Sharp, [mid-February, 1898][1]

St. Margaret's Bay

I have had a very happy and peaceful afternoon. The isolation, with sun and wind, were together like soft cream upon my nerves: and I suppose that within twenty minutes after I left the station I was not only serenely at peace with the world in general, but had not a perturbing thought. To be alone, alone "in the open" above all, is not merely healing to me but an imperative necessity of my life — and the chief counter agent to the sap that almost every person exercises on me, unless obviated by frequent and radical interruption.

By the time I had passed through the village I was already "remote" in dreams and thoughts and poignant outer enjoyment of the lovely actualities of sun and wind and the green life: and when I came to my favourite coign where, sheltered from the bite of the wind, I could overlook the sea (a mass of lovely, radiant, amethyst-shadowed, foam-swept water), I lay down for two restful happy hours *in which not once a thought of London or of any one in it, or of any one living*, came to me. This power of living absolutely in the moment is worth not only a crown and all that a crown could give, but is the secret of youth, the secret of life.

O how weary I am of the endless recurrence of the ordinary in the lives of most people — the beloved routine, the cherished monotonies, the treasured certainties. I grudge them to none: They seem incidental to the common weal: indeed they seem even made for happiness. But I know one wild heart at least to whom life must come otherwise, or not at all.

Today I took a little green leaf o' thorn. I looked at the sun through it, and a dazzle came into my brain — and I wished, ah I wished I were a youth once more, and was "sun-brother" and "star-brother" again — to lie down at night, smelling the earth, and rise at dawn, smelling the new air out of the East, and know enough of men and cities to avoid both, and to consider little any gods ancient or modern, knowing well that there is only "The Red God" to think of, he who lives and laughs in the red blood... .

There is a fever of the "green life" in my veins — below all the ordinary littleness of conventional life and all the common place of exterior: a fever that makes me ill at ease with people, even those I care for, that fills me with a weariness beyond words and a nostalgia for sweet impossible things.

This can be met in several ways — chiefly and best by the practical yoking of the imagination to the active mind — in a word, to work. If I can do this, well and good, either by forced absorption in contrary work (e.g. Caesar of France),[2] or by letting that go for the time and let the more creative instinct have free play: or by some radical change of environment: or again by some irresponsible and incalculable variation of work and brief day-absences.

At the moment, I am like a man of the hills held in fee: I am willing to keep my bond, to earn my wage, to hold to the foreseen: and yet any moment a kestrel may fly overhead, mocking me with a rock-echo, where only sun and wind and bracken live — or an eddy of wind may have the sough of a pine in it — and then, in a flash — there's my swift brain-dazzle in answer, and all the rapid falling away of these stupid half-realities, and only a wild instinct to go to my own.

Memoir, pp. 296–98

To a friend, [mid-February, 1898][3]

... but then, life is just like that. It is glad only "in the open" and beautiful only because of its dreams. I wish I could live all my hours out of doors: I envy no one in the world so much as the red deer, the eagle, the sea-mew. I am sure no kings have so royal a life as the plovers and curlews have. All these have freedom, rejoice continually on the wind's wing, exalt alike in sun and shade: to them day is day, and night is night, and there is nothing else... .

Memoir, p. 298

To Robert M. Gilchrist, [mid-February, 1898][4]

My Dear Friend:

I know you will have been sorry to hear that I have been ill — and had to leave work, and home. The immediate cause was a severe and sudden attack of influenza which went to membranes of the head and brain, and all but resulted in brain fever. This evil was averted — but it and the possible collapse of your friend Will were at one time, and or some days, an imminent probability. I have now been a fortnight in this quiet sea-haven, and am practically myself again. Part of my work is now too hopelessly in arrears ever to catch up. Fortunately, our friend Miss F. M. practically finished her book just before *she* got ill too — and there is a likelihood that *There is But One Love*[5] will come out this Spring. A few days will decide... .

Your friend and Sunlover, (in the deep sense you know I mean — for I have suffered much but am now again fronting life gravely and with laughing eyes),

Will

Memoir, p. 293

To Benjamin Burgess Moore, February 25, 1898

c/o Miss Rea. | The Columbia City Agency | 9. Mill Street. | Conduit
Street. | London. | 25:2:98 Dear Mr. Moore

I was very pleased to get your letter, which ill health prevented my
answering before this; and to learn that you like "The Laughter of
Peterkin" so well. Its reception altogether has been a pleasant surprise to
me — for though but a volume of old tales of beauty re-seen and re-told
across an individual temperament, it has had many long articles and
important reviews as well as the ordinary run of notices. In America,
however, I understand there was little or no demand for it — partly due
to the fact that the book was not published there.

My English publishers did what they could — but the invariable
reply was "there is no market here for such books."

I am sorry.

I had intended to publish this Spring a volume of tales — but on
account of an important historical romance on hand have postponed
publication of the vol. in question indefinitely — certainly for a year
hence at least. Till the publication of this historical romance (sometime
in 1899) I intend to issue no volume, with the possible exception of a
volume of poems and short old-world dramas, but even that not till
next Spring, or, at earliest, the late Autumn of this year. On the other
hand stories etc. by myself are to appear in serial magazines, British and
American, throughout this year. In particular, I would care for you to
look at (when they *do* appear) "The Wayfarer" in *Cosmopolis*[6] and "The
Wells of Peace" in *Good Words*.[7] I have no other personal news to give
you save that some of my tales are being translated into French.

Hoping that the exigent life oversea leaves you time sometimes to
stroll quietly off through the Gates of Dream —

With kind regards, | Yours very truly, | Fiona Macleod

ALS Huntington Library

To Mary Stuart, March 1, 1898

30 Greencroft Gardens | South Hampstead, London | 1st March/98

My dear Miss Stuart,

It was a great pleasure to me on returning to London today (after a two months absence, recruiting from serious illness) to find that the American mail just in had brought me a letter from you. I said to myself "what a dear she is" — and envied Mr. Mielatz,[8] for I can only hug you in imagination and with the Atlantic between us!

I thank you very much for your kind letter. But I am indeed distressed to hear how ill E. C. S. has been and I fear still is, tho' I hope now along the upgrade. I am thankful you have returned to his aid — and glad that you are working with him in the Amer. Anthology.[9] If I can possibly manage it I'll send him a cheery letter by this mail. I am certain he needs to take very great care of himself — and above all to be on guard against nervous weariness. His real illness, alas, is a nostalgia for impossible things. We all (soon or late) suffer from it in some degree. I do not know any friend who can do more for him than you can — and again I say I am thankful you are with him. He is so naturally sweet and sunny, but his nervous life is forever on the rack — much of it unavoidably alas, but some of it amenable by sympathy, loving camaraderie, and alert cooperation.

I am interested in what you say about Mr. Mielatz's recent work. Well (except for E. C. S.) I hope you *will* get married soon — & have a happy time, as you deserve — and that you will both come over to London, for Mr. Mielatz not only to win wider repute & ampler cash but also to be introduced to one of the staunchest of your admirers and your sincere friend

William Sharp

My other news in my note to E. C. S.

ALS Columbia University Library

To Edmund Clarence Stedman, March 1, 1898

30 Greencroft Gardens | South Hampstead | London NW | 1st March/98

Dear & well-loved Poet & Friend,

Today is the first day of Spring — and what better could I do than send a line to a friend whom I love right well, and who happens also to be a poet of Springtide and of romance and love & youth?

But first, Edmund of the Gypsy Eyes, bear in mind that you are just to read, & have a handshake across the Atlantic, & then *not to dream* of answering. Half the pleasure of hearing from a friend is gone — for one so wrought as yourself by many things, & so waylaid by Protean circumstance — if a letter has the ill-manners to kick at the conscience while smiling in the eyes! So know that I am simply writing you a brief greeting out of loving camaraderie. You have many friends over here, & doubtless some whose friendship you value more than mine — but there is none more loyal to you, in every way, and none who loves you more truly.

I know you will be sorry to hear that I have been seriously ill, & am just back from 2 months convalescence — but, then, I am better now, & so there is no more to be said about it. Then, too, latterly I had ...... alleviations. To be more exact, it shd be in the singular! You can guess the name, & perhaps remember something of a rare beauty, of life-lifting eyes.[10] Anyway, I am well again: & youth, romance, beauty, the passion of keen life, hope, eager outlook, eager work, are all realities once again.

My latest news of you was that you were very "fagged" — nervously overwrought. I do hope you are now more rested, and better able to get to your work — I mean *the* work for which God & nature meant you. Your book of poetry — for it is not "a book of verse" — has made a very distinct impression here.[11] I have not seen many notices, but what I saw were respectful & appreciative — & from individuals & from letters I hear of nothing but high praise.

Did Miss F. M. ever write to you? I know she intended to — & indeed I remember seeing the first page or two of a letter (for she wrote when we were together somewhere) — for she very sincerely admired your poems and was touched and gratified by your sending her a copy. A photograph of your handsome "phiz" ornaments said copy of the Poems — not given, I must add, but forcibly & insistently stolen from me!

Although I have had so bad a time with a dangerous collapse (culminating in severe meningitis) I am now feeling better than I have done for at least two years past — and am quite determined not only to work hard but to get as much of the sunshine & joy & romance and dear delight of life as may be! And what's more, I've had it! And what's more, I have laid in a treasure of it quite recently! And what's more — by my Queen's full consent and approval — I've been a very bad boy with a very dear & delightful "friend", now alas returned to her home in Brussels — & generally I've been "spoilt" & made much of, & have enjoyed it, and am thinking of reforming 20 years hence, but meanwhile cling to my Sunshine Creed — to live sunnily, to think blithely, to act on the square even in my "sinning", & to try to give sunshine to others.[12] After all, it's not such a bad creed — indeed, it's a very good one, and it has my dear poet E. C. S. as Prophet!

As for work — a great change has taken place in me. Hence forth you will see work at once more controlled, more thorough, stronger, and with more of controlled imagination, of more scrupulous art — & this both in prose & verse, tho' indeed of the latter I am writing little. My *immediate* long undertakings (& I have also many important magazine commissions to fulfill) are "a romance of the destinies of France," and an ambitious play.

For ten years, too, I have been slowly preparing for a big series depictive of Contemporary Life — and the first (to be called either *Camaraderie* or *The Hunters of Wisdom*, may be out in book form next Spring).[13]

If all goes well, you can think of me (and my friend) in a lovely green retreat, on the Marne, near Paris, during the last fortnight of April. If you were there too I would drink to you in white wine, and she would give you a kiss — which, with the glory in her beautiful eyes, would make you "wild with the waste of all unnumbered Springs". You will be with us in Spirit, dear poet of youth & romance — and *I* will kiss her for you, & likewise drink the sweet wine of France!!

... hope, and I trust that her sunny smile and youthful heart often rejoice you. You will be a dear youth till the end, E. C. S., — & may the Gods reward you![14]

If you, or Miss Mary Stuart (God bless her!) will (*not* write, but) send me a P/C to say that this has safely reached you — and it had better be entrusted to what old Sir T. Browne calls "the oblivious flame" — I will be glad.[15]

My dear wife sends you cordial greeting — & and tells me to say to you that she insists on your keeping well & young till she comes out to Bronxville to see for herself! Possibly she may take a run over sea next Spring! So she says, & I believe intends. (I hope *she'll* find the funds!)

My love to dear Mrs. Stedman — & if Miss Mary Stuart will accept it, it is hers too. As for you, dear friend, you know you have it.

Ever loyally & lovingly yours, | William Sharp

ALS Columbia University Library

To John Macleay, [mid-March?, 1898]

Greencroft Gardens/So. Hampstead

My dear Mr. Macleay

I congratulate you on your appointment — and trust it may be a stepping stone to good fortune.[16] I am sorry, otherwise, that you are leaving the Highland — & that the H/News loses one of its best contributors. There is sore need of more men like yourself, in the newspaper offices of the north. But probably you will continue to write occasionally for the H/N — and give a good but difficult, tho' I hope in the end triumphant cause, what lift you can.

If ever I can be of any help to you, let me know: & if I can I will.

You go to a good paper — & Liverpool is one of the lucky schools of journalism.

May you reach your heart's desire!

Yrs very sincerely/William Sharp

ALS National Library of Scotland

To Elizabeth A. Sharp, March 29, 1898[17]

... Yes, in essentials, we are all at one. We have both learned and unlearned so much, and we have come to see that we are wrought mysteriously by forces beyond ourselves, but in so seeing we know that there is a great and deep love that conquers even disillusion and disappointment... .

Not all the wishing, not all the dreaming, not all the will and hope and prayer we summon can alter that within us which is stronger than ourselves. This is a hard lesson to learn for all of us, and most for a woman. We are brought up within such an atmosphere of conventional untruth to life that most people never even perceive the hopeless futility in the arbitrary ideals which are imposed upon us — and the result for the deeper natures, endless tragic miscarriage of love, peace, and hope. But, fortunately, those of us who to our own suffering *do* see only too clearly, can still strike out a nobler ideal — one that does not shrink from the deepest responsibilities and yet can so widen and deepen heart and spirit with love that what else would be irremediable pain can be transmuted into hope, into peace, and even into joy.

People talk much of this and that frailty or this or that circumstance as being among the commonest disintegrants of happiness. But far more fatal for many of us is that supreme disintegrant, the Tyranny of Love — the love which is forever demanding *as its due* that which is wholly independent of bonds, which is as the wind which bloweth where it listeth or where it is impelled, by the Spirit. We are taught such hopeless lies. And so men and women start life with ideals which seem fair, but are radically consumptive: ideals that are not only bound to perish, but that could not survive. The man of fifty who could be the same as he was at twenty is simply a man whose mental and spiritual life stopped short while he was yet a youth. The woman of forty who could have the same outlook on life as the girl of 19 or 20 would never have been other than one ignominiously deceived or hopelessly self-sophisticated. This ought not to be — but it must be as long as young men and women are fed mentally and spiritually upon the foolish and cowardly lies of a false and corrupt conventionalism.

No wonder that so many fine natures, men and women, are wrought to lifelong suffering. They are started with impossible ideals: and while some can never learn that their unhappiness is the result, not of the falling short of others, but of the falsity of those ideals which they had so cherished — and while others learn first strength to endure the transmutations and then power to weld these to far nobler and finer uses and ends — for both there is suffering. Yet, even of that we make too much. We have all a tendency to nurse grief. The brooding spirit craves for the sunlight, but it will not leave the shadows. Often, *Sorrow* is our best ally.

The other night, tired, I fell asleep on my sofa. I dreamed that a beautiful spirit was standing beside me. He said: "My Brother, I have come to give you the supreme gift that will heal you and save you." I answered eagerly: "Give it me — what is it?" And the fair radiant spirit smiled with beautiful solemn eyes, and blew a breath into the tangled garden of my heart — and when I looked there I saw the tall white Flower of Sorrow growing in the Sunlight.

Memoir, pp. 294–96

To Robert Murray Gilchrist, [April 22, 1898]

I forgot to answer your question: Forgive me. E's birthday is the 17 of May — & she will be at home.

I am hard pressed with work just now, as this is my busiest time. Next Friday[18] I go to Paris for a week or 10 days.

I hope all goes well with you and yours.

W. S.

ACS Sheffield City Archives

To Grant Richards, April 26, 1898

30 Greencroft Gardens | South Hampstead | 26/Apr/98

My dear Richards,

Thanks for your note. Glad you like the exiled ladies so well.[19] I daresay I might improve the opening a bit. I can see about this.

My terms, as I stated, are £25 (not £20) down on day of publication on a/c of a 15% royalty: & to this I agree. (It is the miscarriage I explained to you that induces me to mention so modest a sum — but that is absolutely my minimum.)

When will you begin printing? I should strongly advise publication before the end of May *if possible* — so as to catch that large public which begins to move off towards mid-June — a public interested in such a yachting romance as this.

The copy I sent you was an unrevised one. I have a partially revised one somewhere — & this I could take with me to Paris & send to you for printing from, with revisions, & perhaps some improvement in first chap. Please let me have the other some time.

It is fairly possible I may be able to snatch a half hour tomorrow (Press day Royal Academy) & look in on you abt this & these d–d "Love Letters"[20] but I can't tell yet.

Excuse a scribbled line in extreme haste, with a telegram from one big daily & a printer's devil from *Literature* both "pawing the air" for me.

Yours sincerely | William Sharp

ALS Stanford University

To William Butler Yeats, April 30, 1898[21]

St. Margaret's Bay Hotel | Dover

My dear Yeats

I was just about to write to you when your note came, to tell you that a sudden & serious collapse in health not only will prevent Miss M. from coming to Paris, but will probably end in her having to go to some remote Baths for 2 months for special treatment. This may prove unnecessary: I trust so. Meanwhile it has materially affected immediate plans. As for myself, partly for this and partly because of being myself (as you will understand) seriously indisposed in the same way, I am unable to go to Paris either, & have had to cancel my art-work etc.[22] I shall now be at above address for a week or more to come.

No I do not recall the new Revue Celtique address — but think it is in the Rue Bonaparte. Parts cannot be had separately — as it is by yearly subsc. Your easiest plan wd. be to borrow the Moytura[23] part either from Jubainville[24] or from Douglas Hyde[25] who, I know, takes the R.C. or you could easily copy what you want at the Bibliotheque Nationale. Send me a p/c to say you have recd this.

ACS Yale, printed in Letters to Yeats, I, pp. 35-36

To Grant Richards, May 2, 1898

St. Margaret's Bay Hotel | Lanzardle | near Dover | 2/May/98

My dear Richards

Herewith the contracts. I return mine to be initialled or cross-signed by you opposite Clause I.

(1) As I explained to you at the time I called on you about *Wives in Exile,* the American sale covers the U.S.A. *and* Canada, and the condition on which publication is now feasible in this country is that of non-interference with the Transatlantic sale.

(2) I make it an invariable rule (a wise condition voluntarily adopted also with all their books, by John Lane and at least 3 other Publishers) to sign away no copyright for more than seven years. It goes without saying that self-interest as well as courtesy & square dealing make this stipulation a merely precautionary one.

In this instance I need make no objection to Clause 7 — as the printing will be from revised printed pages, and so there will naturally be very few Author's corrections: but as a rule I refuse to sign any such stipulation, unless indeed in some special instance where expense would run high.

Again, in Clause XI, I prefer the more expeditious & more business-like procedure of Constable & Co., Lane, etc. who remit within a calendar month after June 30th & Dec. 31.

Love Letters[26]

I regret that continuous pressure of work since I came here has prevented my reading through the long installment of these letters. From the hurried glimpse I have been able to take of them, I feel as I already told you that the vocative-beginnings should be omitted, or used very rarely, as they are monotonous and (except doubtless to the two concerned!) ultimately wearisome. My own (perhaps far too swiftly and inadequately gained) impression is, that the man is sexually distraught and that the woman is neither his holy saint nor even a *virgo intacta*! However, I send on the signed copy for you to judge: it is quite possible that there might be a big sale for a book of this kind. Pour moi, le dis que le propre titre, c'est "Le monde ou l'on s'ennuie".

Tomorrow I hope to be able to go through *Wives in Exile*. So I can see my way to improving the opening by making clearer the point to which you allude I will do so. In any case I will revise for press as soon as I can — for certainly I think it important that this book should come out as early as practicable.

In haste | Yours sincerely | William Sharp

ALS State University of New York at Buffalo

To John Macleay, [May 3?, 1898]

Lanzardle | near Dover

Dear Mr. Macleay,

Your note has reached me at a little seaside place near Dover where I came a few days ago after a specially hard spell of literary and art-journalistic work: tho,' now, I may leave tomorrow.[27]

I am glad to hear from you, and that things go fairly well with you: and glad also that you are finding leisure for that literary pen-work for which you care so much and in which you have shown so much genuine promise. It is of the very greatest advantage that Liverpool suits you, and that you have so fortunate a domestic environment. You ought now to set yourself (always keeping a scrupulous hold over your nervous health) to write imaginatively, that is to re-create observation and impression and give forth in a new because individual way. I shall look for any Highland work from your pen with genuine interest. Almost certainly, I should fancy, you will do better away from Inverness than in it — I mean about Inverness & Highland life.

I have never seen *The Highland News* since you left, so don't know if you are still (as I hope) contributing to it. I believe Miss Macleod had a long letter in it, in response to a request from the Editor, but I have not seen it.

She is in better health now, you will be interested to hear: but I'm not sure what she is doing just now — probably working slowly at her historical Jacobite romance. There is a long short-story of hers in the just pubd. new number of that marvelous shillings worth, the little quarterly *The Dome*: and, I hear, one of the Summer issues of *Cosmopolis* is to have one of her most ambitious short stories. As to Mrs. Wingate Rinder's new Breton translation — yes, it has been well received already, tho' just published, *The Scotsman* of May 2nd which I have just found here, on file, has a very good notice. I have read the book with much interest, though I do not hold the high opinion of Le Goffic that many French critics have.[28] I think Mrs. W. R.'s translation excellent *as* a translation, and wonderfully literal while deft and idiomatic — but I wd. far rather see her translating and better still paraphrasing the Breton legendary tales of which she gave so fine an installment in "The Shadow of Arvor." However, when last I heard from her, she alluded to her intention to do another such volume — & would have the advice & help of the great Breton Specialist, Anatole Le Braz.

As for myself I have been very busy, but largely with writing for the weeklies, and upon a new book, and upon as yet unpublished magazine articles. At the end of this month, or beginning of June, Grant Richards will publish a story, a "Comedy in Romance" of mine, entitled *Wives in Exile*.

I'll postpone Neil Munro's story till it appears in book-form. It seems to me very good indeed, but its Gaelicism to be far too self-conscious and in any case overdone. Another Glasgow man (Benjamin Swift) has, in my judgment, produced a very disappointing book in *The Tormentor*, tho' I had hoped big things from him. He may do well yet. The book, all the same, is very clever, very able. *Spanish John* I liked, and was the more interested in as I know the author, a Scoto-Canadian who lives in Montreal. But he does not know the real Gaelic nature, I fancy. I have read nothing so imaginatively good for a long time as F. Mathews *The Spanish Wine*. That is romance.

With cordial regards and good wishes, / Yours sincerely / William Sharp

ALS National Library of Scotland

To Benjamin Burgess Moore, May 3, 1898

Letter-address | c/o Miss Rea | The Columbia City Agency | 9 Mill Street | Conduit St. |

London | 3rd May 98

Dear Mr. Moore

Very many thanks for your friendly letter and its accompanying most sympathetic and appreciative review of "Peterkin".

I wish there could be an American edition of that book, for I find now I have a greater number of readers than I knew. If chance should take you to Boston I wish you would ask Mr. Lamson (Lamson, Wolffe & Co.) or Copeland & Day or Houghton Mifflin & Co. if they would care to issue an American edition of it[29] — either as it stands or without the Peterkin prologue and interludes — and in the latter case (which for some reasons I should prefer) under the title "The Three Sorrows of Old", or "Heroic Tales of the Celt", or "The Story of Deirdre the Beautiful". In the circumstances I should expect no payment beyond a

15% royalty, and say 25 copies free. Would it be possible for you to see to this for me? You could add that the *Spectator*,[30] *Literature*, and indeed all the important English literary papers have spoken most highly of the book, — and perhaps you could emphasise this point by sending your own admirable "Yale Review" notice.

On the other hand do not hesitate to let me know if this is inconvenient for you. (If it had not been for the failure of Stone & Kimball of New York, who published my two previous books *"The Sin Eater"* and *"The Washer of the Ford," Peterkin* would probably have been out in U .S. A. before this.)

I have directed the publisher to send you a copy of that delightful quarterly magazine, *The Dome*,[31] which is published today I believe. It contains a story of mine which you may care for (*Good Words* for April had a brief episodic narrative, "The Four Winds of Desire".[32] One of the Summer issues of *Cosmopolis* will contain "The Wayfarer"[33] of which I wrote to you, and *Good Words* "The Wells of Peace".)[34]

I am writing this to send it with other notes to be posted in Edinburgh, (as am postless here in a remote little haven by the sea.)[35] What peace and wonder and mystery lie in the ceaseless noise of a lonely sea. I send you a sea-breath of this old-world you love so well.

Sincerely Yours, | Fiona Macleod

ALS Huntington Library

To William Butler Yeats, May 5, 1998

St. Margaret's Bay Hotel | Nr. Dover | 5th May 1898

My dear Yeats

In strict privacy, my friend Miss Macleod is here just now. She was on her way to Paris, but as I told you she was suddenly taken too unwell. She was sleeping when your letter came, but I left the enclosure for her at her bedside — & if she wakes before the post goes she will doubtless give you a message through me, unless she feels up to writing herself. If well enough, she leaves here on Saturday morning — but to go north again.[36]

You ask me if I were in any unusual state on either May 1st or 2nd. I do not remember anything on Sunday 1st beyond a singular depression, and a curious sense of unreality for a time, as though I were really elsewhere. But on Monday 2nd, late, I suffered in a way I can't explain, owing to what seemed to me an unaccountable preoccupation of Miss M.

All this is very private — but I trust you.

Her father was tall, fine-looking, with a rather singular concentrated expression. The Macleod tartan is dark (dark green & dark blue almost black). I don't quite understand why you ask. I forgot to add that F. M. herself at times sees a startling likeness between me & her father, though I am taller & bigger & fairer than he was. There are, however, many similarities in nature, etc., and also in the accident of baptismal name.

In case you do not get it, I ordered to be sent to you in Paris (at her & my simultaneous suggestion) a copy of *The Dome*.[37] Perhaps you will care for the story there. Your own poems there are very lovely.

I am afraid I must now go and post this: but

P.S. Have just time to say that Miss M has awaked, & is feeling much better. She cannot write at the moment however — but asks me to say that she has read your letter. In reply, she asks me to write as follows: –

"I *have* been going though an intense emotional crisis. One less poignant period was on the evening or night of the 1st, but far more so, & more poignantly on the 2nd. But of this, being private, I cannot speak further. I was, on both occasions (though differently & for different reasons) undergoing tragic feeling. I am at present at a perilous physical & spiritual crisis. I can say no more. The one who shares my life & self is here. It is as crucial for him. I will talk over your letter to us — for to us it is, though you send it to me. Are you sure it was not Will whom you felt or saw? If I, then I must only[38]

P.S. Hurriedly adding this at the PO to say that my friend's neuralgia was too severe to talk any more. The subject too was exciting her. She will show me your letter when I get back.

Note *this* time today. About 3 p.m. today Thursday she went through (& I too) a wave of intense tragic emotion — and last night, between 10 and 12 or later, we nearly lost each other in a very strange way. Something I did by the will was too potent, & for a time severed some unconscious links (we were apart at the time: I thought she was sleeping) — & we both suffered in consequence. But I think the extreme crisis of tragic psychic emotion is over.[39]

God grant it

ACS Yale, printed in Letters to Yeats, I, pp. 36-37

To Grant Richards, May 9, 1898

St Margaret's Bay Hotel | near Dover | Monday 9th May: 98

My dear Richards,

My delay in sending you the first pages of *Wives in Exile* for press has been mainly due to my consideration of the point you addressed. After some hesitation I wrote a supplementary chapter — Then I read the book right through critically, and today reread the opening and this new chapter. The result is that I have destroyed this interpolated new chapter, and am convinced that my own shaping instinct was in the main right. I may add that no single review in America indicated any hesitancy as to the point you alluded to, nor any one over there who wrote to me about the book. My own strong feeling is that I could not now touch the book, by *interpolation*, except to spoil it. It must stand as it is, in this respect. In a story of this kind, so much depends on spontaneity and rapid continuity: I can do nothing to it, I realise, that would not militate against these qualities. From the first, I may add, my instinct was dead against your suggestion — but in courtesy, and also because I believe in the frequent value of outside suggestions, I was willing to put the matter to the test. I have done so. — And so, *Finis*.

I find, however, that I have forgotten to say I think I have very materially improved the opening of the book (& incidentally practically met your point abt making Harry Adoir & his true, merely incidental relationship, obvious at once) — by making it now begin with P16 and then heading on to present beginning, minus first sentence. (The story now starts, too, on absolutely the right "prognostic note.")

Herewith I send you the opening forty six pp., revised and ready for press. (There are 329 pp. of text.) The remainder I shall send you with all possible expedition, for I am as anxious as you can be that there should now be no avoidable delay.

I trust you will not bring out the book in the same small size as the American edition. Here, I am convinced for my part, the public will not purchase small books. The book will have far more chances as an ordinary sized 6/ volume — & I would suggest that it might be printed page for page as here, but bigger type & wider spaced — so as still to be about 330 pp. in length.

I expect to be here till the week-end, but if I make an abrupt move shall let you know.

Yours sincerely, | William Sharp

ALS University of Wisconsin–Milwaukee Library

To Dr. John Goodchild,[40] [mid-May, 1898]

The Outlook Tower, | Edinburgh,

Dear Sir,

I have to thank you very cordially for your book and the long and interesting letter which accompanied it. It must be to you also that I am indebted for an unrevised proof-copy of *The Light of the West*.[41]

Everything connected with the study of the Celtic past has an especial and deep interest for me, and there are few if any periods more significant than that of the era of St. Columba. His personality has charmed me, in the old and right sense of the word "charm": but I have come to it, or it to me, not through books (though of course largely through Adamnan) so much as through a knowledge gained partly by reading, partly by legendary lore and hearsay, and mainly by much brooding on these, and on every known saying and record of Colum, in Iona itself. When I wrote certain of my writings (e.g. "Muime Chriosd" and "The Three Marvels of Iona") I felt, rightly or wrongly, as though I had in some measure become interpretative of the spirit of "Colum the White."

Again, I have long had a conviction — partly an emotion of the imagination, and partly a belief insensibly deduced through a hundred avenues of knowledge and surmise — that out of Iona is again to come a Divine Word, that Iona, the little northern isle, will be as it were the tongue in the mouth of the South.

Believe me, sincerely yours, | Fiona Macleod.

Memoir, pp. 316–17

To Robert M. Gilchrist, [mid-May?, 1898][42]

Rutland House

My Dear Robert,

... After months of sickness, at one time at the gates of death, I am whirled back from the Iron Gates and am in the maelstrom again — fighting with mind and soul and body for that inevitable losing game which we call victory. Well, the hour waits: and for good or ill I put forth that which is in me. The Utmost for the Highest. There is that motto for all faithful failures... .

I am busy of course. And so, too, our friend F. M. — with an elixir of too potent life. The flame is best: and the keener, the less obscured of smoke. So I believe: upon this I build. *Cosmopolis* will era long have "The Wayfarer" of hers — *Good Words* "The Wells of Peace" — *Harper's* something[43] — *Literature* a spiritual ballad[44] — and so forth. But her life thought is in another and stranger thing than she has done yet.[45] ... Your friend W. S. is busy too, with new and deeper and stronger work. The fugitive powers impel. I look eagerly to new works of yours: above all to what you colour with yourself. I care little for anything that is not quick with that volatile part of one which is the effluence of the spirit within. Write to me soon: by return best of all. You can help me — as I, I hope, can help *you*.[46]

It is only the fullest and richest lives that know what the *heart* of loneliness is.

You are my comrade, and have my love, | Will

Memoir, pp. 293–94

To Robert Murray Gilchrist, May 17, 1898[47]

Rutland House | May 17th '98

Dear Mr. Gilchrist

My birthday has been gladdened by your most friendly letter, and made fragrant by the beautiful flowers you sent me. As I write I am conscious of the sweet wild wood scent of the lilies-of-the-valley — my favourite flower. It is indeed good of you to remember me, and it is one of my urgent wishes that before long the opportunity may come for me to know you well, for already I count you among my valued friends. Your photograph stands near one of Will, who asks me to send you his love.

Your word of the moorlands made me long for uplands and wide spaces. There are only indications of spring here, and no real spring — a veil of smoke hangs between us and clear bright sunshine, and makes a sadness of what should be a glorious day. Your mother, Mrs. Murray Gilchrist very kindly has asked me to stay some day with her. We go North to Scotland about the latter end of July, and I think it would be so very nice if we might stay for a day or so with her on our way. This is of course only a suggestion, and wholly depends upon whether or not it would be convenient to Mrs. Gilchrist.

Will has not been very well; tomorrow he goes to Holland for four days. I hope the newness of the surroundings there will send him home well & ready for work.

Are you working I wonder? Are you gathering more of those vivid strong tales to put together in another book? I hope so very much.

With cordial thanks for your friendliness

Very sincerely yours | Elizabeth A. Sharp

ALS Sheffield City Archive

To Editors, Harper's Magazine, May 19, 1898

C/o Miss Rea. | The Columbia Literary Agency |
9. Mill St. Conduit St. | London — W. | 19:May:1898

Dear Sirs,

Thanks for the Draft from Editor of *Harper's Magazine* for £20. (Twenty Pounds) for the Serial rights of my story *"The White Heron"*:

Yours very truly | Fiona Macleod | 19/5/98

ACS University of Texas, Austin

To Elizabeth A. Sharp [late May, 1898]

... We are now in the south Zuyder Zee, with marvellous sky effects, and low lines of land in the distance. Looking back at Eiland Marken[48] one sees six clusters of houses, at wide intervals, dropped casually into the sea.

We had a delightful time in that quaintest of old world places, where the women are grotesque, the men grotesquer, and the children grotesquest — as for the tubby, capped, gorgeous-garbed, blue-eyed, yellow haired, imperturbable babies, they alone are worth coming to see ... .

Memoir, p. 298

To Grant Richards, [*late May, 1898*]

30 Greencroft Gardens | So. Hampstead

My dear Grant Richards

I meant to send you some notices of "Wives in Exile" — but I can't "lay my memory to one o'them" as they say in Ireland.[49] All be somewhere in a package. But by a chance I came across this in one of Lamson's letters, & send it to you. It was quoted from, among others, a good deal in U.S.A.

Very glad of your good news.[50] In a double sense you can now say the lovely Italian words of the Romagna folksong: — "O dolce primavera pien' di olezzo e amor!"[51]

In haste | Sincerely Yours | William Sharp

ALS Stanford University

To Grant Richards [*early June, 1898*]

Dear Mr. Richards

In reply to your note, I send enclosed. I suppose it is the kind of thing you want.

Certainly the two U.S.A. quotations ought to prove stimulant both to the public and the critic — no small consideration.

Please let me know the date when it is intended to publish the book.[52] There ought not to be a day's unnecessary delay now — especially as the yachting season begins at once.

By the way, your traveler shd. try and make a special sale with it in Glasgow (Maclehose, Forester, Hadden, etc.,) and Edinburgh (Andrew Elliot, etc., etc.,) as a Yachting Romance of the Clyde.

In haste, | Yours sincerely, | William Sharp

ALS Pierpont Morgan Library

To William Butler Yeats, June 28, 1898

Temporary 9 Upper Coltbridge Terrace | Murrayfield. |
Midlothian. | Scotland

My dear Mr. Yeats

I am very glad to get the letter duly forwarded to me, and to hear from
you again. As you know, there is no living writer with whom I find
myself so absolutely in rapport as with you. I am eagerly hoping for
more beautiful work from you again in prose and verse, soon. How
often I have meant to write to you about your lovely opening pages of
"The Shadowy Waters", which I do hope you will complete soon, and
about the alas still unpublished lyrics "The Wind in the Reeds".[53] I was
deeply interested in your Folklore articles — but it is new imaginative
work that I most long to see.[54] I dread for you a too great preoccupation
in other interests — and the consequent inevitable dispersal of energy,
and the insatiable avarice of the hours and days of our brief time. I
was glad to hear that you liked "Children of the Dark Star" and "The
Wayfarer".[55]

   I have been told that long ago one of the subtlest and strangest minds
of his time — a man of Celtic ancestry on one side and of Norse on the
other — was so profoundly influenced by the kindred nature and spirit
of a woman whom he loved, a Celt of Celts, that, having in a sense
accidentally discovered[56] the mystery of absolute mental and spiritual
union of two impassioned and kindred natures the flame of anguish that
had been his in a far back day was in him, so that besides a strange and
far reaching ancestral memory, he remembered anew and acutely every
last clue and significance of his boyhood and early life, spent mostly
among the shepherds and fishers of the Hebrides and Gaelic Highlands.
His was the genius, the ancestral memory, the creative power — she was
the flame — she, too, being also a visionary, and with unusual and all
but lost old wisdom of the Gael. Without her, he would have been lost
to the Beauty which was his impassioned quest: with her, as a flame to
his slumbering flame, he became what he was. The outer life of each was
singular, beyond that of any man or woman I have heard of: how much

stranger that of their spiritual union. A profound and resolute silence lay upon the man, save when he knew the flame of the woman "through whom he saw Beauty," and his soul quickened. She gave him[57] all she could, and without her he could not be what he was, and he needed her vision to help his own, and her dream, and her thought, and her life, till hers and his ceased to be hers and his and merged into one, and became ...... a spirit of shaping power born of them both.[58]

How does that strike you as a subject for a tale, a book? It would be a strange one. Does it seem to you impossible? It does not seem so to me.[59]

Your friend and comrade | Fiona Macleod[60]

ALS Yeats Papers, printed in Collected Letters to Letters to Yeats, I, pp. 38-39

To Richard Watson Gilder, July 5, 1898

30 Greencroft Gardens | South Hampstead | 5/July/98

My dear Mr. Gilder,

Herewith I send a couple of short poems: perhaps one or both may appeal to you.

Like our common friends (and near neighbours) the Janviers, I had hoped to see Mrs. Gilder and yourself in London this season: but perhaps next Spring may see you again in a town you both love well. The Janviers, too, are become Londoners!

Recently, Janvier accompanied me in a little trip through Holland, a country with which I am familiar but which was new to him. He enjoyed it greatly.

Later (I have another volume of short stories coming out first) I wish to publish a series of short stories with North-Holland scenery or old Dutch towns as background. Would it be any use my sending you one of these? I am now writing them. The first is already accepted: the others, available soon, are, (this will be the titular story), (2) "The Merchant of Dreams" (with Amsterdam as background) (3) "The Flower of

Oblivion" (Flemish-Dutch, not "Hollandisch" proper, as it is an effort to convey the mysterious charm and fascination of Bruges.) (4) "The Ivory Sculptor" (Delft) (5) "The House in the Wood," (North Holland) (6) "The Scarlet Peacock" (North Holland).[61]

What are you doing yourself just now, apart from your editorial work? 1 hope you are going to publish a volume of poetry soon. You may not have as many but you have as sincere admirers here as oversea. My cordial regards to Mrs. Gilder.

Yours sincerely, | William Sharp

Just finished today a difficult task — that of writing an article on Burne-Jones for two magazines for (I understand) the same month. But that for the "Atlantic" is personal, while that for the "Fortnightly" is critical, an appreciation.[62]

ALS Huntington Library

To William Butler Yeats, July 6, 1898

6th July /98

Dear Mr. Yeats

I hope you duly received the private letter I sent you on the 28th of June. I am a little anxious about it.[63]

Yours most sincerely | Fiona Macleod

ACS New York Public Library, Berg Collection

To Grant Richards, July 11, 1898

30 Greencroft Gardens | South Hampstead | 11 July/98

My dear Grant Richards

What day will you send out review copies of *Wives in Exile*? If you have copies in hand could you let me have two of mine by *Friday*, as wanted for birthdays!

I think it would be advisable if you would send (*as review copies, though not to be so indicated: simply a slip with the author's compliments*) copies to

(1) H. D. *Traill* Esq | Editor *Literature* | Printing House Square | E.C. (this not to interfere with the copy to *Literature* itself, which Mr. T. will give out. If he has a copy himself he may be able to do something for it in two other quarters.)
   For same reason to W. L. *Courtney* Esq[64] | C/o Messrs. Chapman & Hall

(3) James *Knowles* Esq | Queen Anne's Lodge | St. James Park | SW

(4) *Richard Whiteing* Esq | 45 Mecklenburgh Square | W.C.

(5) *Charles Russell* Esq | 12 Buckingham Terrace | Hillhead | Glasgow

(6) The Rev. Donald Macleod D.D.[65] | 1 Woodlands Terrace | Glasgow

(7) Clement K. Shorter Esq[66] | *Sketch* Office etc.

Each of these, I have reason to know, will prove a "well-placed" copy — sent in this way. I would add Coulson Kernahan, but I think he said you had promised him a copy.

Please let me know if you are sending above as indicated.

I think I have already suggested your traveller making a special push of the book in Glasgow & Edinburgh — particularly where a Clyde yachting romance ought to "take".

For my own use, in addition to the Six Authors Copies agreed upon (two by Friday if possible) — please send me (I presume at trade-price, as is usual?) six other copies.

And will you please oblige me by letting me have *by this week-end* the £25 advance, owing to an unexpected sudden emergency — a courtesy for which I will venture to thank you in advance. Will you & Mrs. Richards come & have tea with Mrs. Sharp & myself some afternoon either at her club or at mine?[67] (From the 19th till 25th I expect to be with Murray Gilchrist, & then here for 2 or 3 days again)

Yours Sincerely | William Sharp

ALS New York University, Fales Library

To Grant Richards, [July 15, 1898]

Friday

My dear Richards

Thanks for the copies of our Exiled Dames to hand. The book is very well got up, & I am delighted with the cover, which is at once simple & charming, & the colour effective. I hope the combined efforts of author & publisher will allure the stray "4s/6 cash" from many pockets — notwithstanding a war-spent season and this being "sae waefu' far on i' the year".[68]

Of course the book is heavily handicapped by coming so late in the season — but even now I hope the big booksellers out of town, at Brighton, Cromer etc. etc. may be able to catch some of the holiday public who might care for a book such as this.

If some good reviews appear (I expect "a mixed lot" as the auctioneers say!) the book may take a sudden life — & in any case will I hope have a fresh lease in the Autumn.

Thanks, too, for the cheque for advance £25.

Sorry we are not likely to meet this summer. We shall be away from the 19th till the 25th or 26th — & then back till the 31st, on which day we leave for Scotland.

I presume it is *this* Saty that you go to Cornwall. If not, could you both come here Monday? (Don't bother to answer if it *is* this Saty you go.)[69]

Hoping you will have a happy second honeymoon —

Very sincerely yours, | William Sharp

ALS State University of New York at Buffalo

To Ernest Rhys, July 23, 1898

23rd July, 1898

My Dear Mr. Rhys,[70]

On my coming to Edinburgh for a few days I find the book you have so kindly sent to me.[71] It is none the less welcome because it comes as no new acquaintance: for on its appearance a friend we have in common sent it to me. Alas, that copy lies among the sea-weed in a remote Highland loch; for the book, while still reading in part, slipped overboard the small yacht in which I was sailing, and with it the MS. of a short story of mine appropriately named "Beneath the Shadow of the Wave"! The two may have comforted each other in that solitude: or the tides may have carried them southward, and tossed them now to the Pembroke Stacks, now to the cliffs of Howth. Perhaps a Welsh crab may now be squeaking (they do say that crabs make a whistling squeak!) with a Gaelic accent or the deep-sea congers be reciting Welsh ballads to the young-lady-eels of The Hebrides. Believe me, your book has given me singular pleasure. I find in it the indescribable: and to me that is one of the tests, perhaps the supreme test (for it involves so much) of imaginative literature. A nimble air of the hills is there; the rustle of remote woods; the morning cry, that is so ancient, and that still so thrills us.

I most eagerly hope that you will recreate in beauty the all but lost beauty of the old Cymric singers. There is a true originality in this, as in anything else. The green leaf, the grey wave, the mountain wind — after all, are they not murmurus in the old Celtic poets, whether Alban or Irish or Welsh: and to translate, and recreate anew, from these, is but to bring back into the world again a lost wandering beauty of hill-wind or green leaf or grey wave. There is, I take it, no one living who could interpret Davyth ap Gwilym[72] and other old Welsh singers as you could do. I long to have the Green Book of "the Poet of the Leaves" in English verse, and in English verse such as that into which you could transform it... .

F. M.

Memoir, pp. 298–99

To William Butler Yeats, [c. July 20, 1898]

[This letter, which is in private hands, responded to a letter from Yeats in which he reported that the legal difficulties encountered by the Celtic Theatre were settled and asked F. M. what plays she would have ready for the fall. In this reply, F. M. said she was "very glad indeed to hear about the Celtic Theatre and that she hoped to have "Fand and Cuchulain" finished this autumn and possibly the shorter "The Hour of Beauty." She said she had also "virtually completed 'The King of Ys' and 'Dahut the Red.'"]

To Benjamin Burgess Moore, July 31, 1898

Address during August | Seaview West | Kilcreggan, Dumbartonshire | Scotland | 31:July:98

Dear Mr. Moore

Many thanks for your letter, and all the trouble you have taken. It will be pleasant if Mr. Lamson would take "Peterkin": I have not heard from him. If you are writing to him again you might add that I have a volume of short stories (from the Collective 3-Vol. Edn., and magazine sources) not published in America (Stone & Kimball published *The Sin-Eater* and the *Washer of the Ford*, and Messrs. Harper *Green Fire*) which I would be pleased to issue through him, if he is agreeable to my terms — royalty of 12½% (instead of 15% — as usual), with an advance on publication of £20 ($100), and a dozen copies free on publication — terms which I imagine will commend themselves as moderate, only, I should like to hear soon.

No, it is not quite true that Mr. Yeats and I are collaborating on a drama: but we are each writing a drama, which we hope to see brought out in the new Celtic theater in Dublin next year. Yes — "Ulick Deane" in Mr. Moore's *Evelyn Innes* is an exact (indeed an extraordinarily exact) portraiture of Mr. Yeats.[73] It is a remarkable book, with all its faults — and interested me profoundly. It has not been at all adequately treated, I think.

My recent stories in the *Dome* and *Cosmopolis* were very well received. Among others that might interest you are "The Wells of Peace" coming out soon I believe in *Good Words*: "Enya of the Dark Eyes", coming out in one of the autumn issues of *Literature*: and "The White Heron", with illustrations, in the Christmas number of *Harper's*. (By the way you might mention this latter fact to Mr. Lamson when you write — as I understand that the appearance of a story in the Christmas number is held of great account in U.S.A. as an advertisement — you will be thinking I am becoming very commercial!)

I hope that "Paul Smith's, Franklin County" means that you are to be in some beautiful place for a holiday.

You can think of me in August among the lochs of Eastern Argyll, and in September among the Isles.

As soon as I have finished my new book[74] I shall get on with the two [for three] short plays, "The Hour of Beauty" and "The King of Ys" and "Dahut the Red."[75]

I send you a little spray of Highland heather,

Yours most sincerely | Fiona Macleod

ALS Huntington Library

To Edward Martyn, [early August, 1898][76]

Scalasaig | Isle of Colonsay | (Inner Hebrides)

My dear Martyn

Very many thanks — but it must be some other time: not this summer or autumn now, I fear. I shall be in the isles till September any way.

But sometime I hope very much to see you again, in Ireland.

Ever sincerely yours | William Sharp

ALS Princeton University

To John Macleay, August 8, 1898

Argyll House / Kilcreggan / Scotland

Dear Mr. Macleay,

Your letter found me in the North we both love so well. Yes, I know & love Glenmoriston[?] & Loch Duich & Glengnoich[?]: it is a lovely region, a haunted land.

The Loch Duich neighborhood will, I understand, figure largely in Miss Macleod's historical romance — though I believe she has changed the original plan as I heard it a year or two ago. I expect to see her in September — either in Skye or the Hebrides — unless, as is possible, I may have to go abroad at the beginning of Sept., tho' I hope not. I fear that this romance of hers has been lagging — partly because of her preoccupation with work more after her own heart and (as I believe) more suitable for her. However, the result will be the only proof, one way or the other. Have you seen her recent published stories in the *Dome* and *Cosmopolis*? She tells me that in a few weeks (i.e. either in August or September) there is to be a short story by her in *Literature*, & that Mr. Sterner(?)[77]

ALS National Library of Scotland

To (*Manager for*) *Messrs. Herbert S. Stone & Co.,* [*August 16, 1898*]⁷⁸

30 Greencroft Gardens | South Hampstead | London | NW

Thanks for your Royalty statement of *Vistas* to hand. Please send me one, or two, copies in lieu of the small sum due. Please note not to address Miss Macleod's statements or letters to my care as I very often do not know her address. Her business address is c/o Miss Rea | The Columbia Literary Agency | 9 Mill St. | Conduit St. | London.

I have just had a letter from her to this effect, also ... book as I have done above covering mine.⁷⁹

Yrs very truly | William Sharp

ACS Newberry Library

To Coulson Kernahan, August 24, 1898⁸⁰

Kilcreggan | Argyll

My dear Kernahan

Pray excuse a Postal Card in lieu of note paper — but I am "en route", & have nothing at hand.

Thanks for your kind words my dear fellow. Your notice will, I am sure, help the book;⁸¹ & in any case I thank you for it. For myself, I do not agree with you abt the "personal element" — & that part in your notice I do not like. The "Tirebuck" was an impossible & absurd slip of some stupid compiler, long ago corrected & forgotten: and the Fiona Macleod matter is also one no longer mixt up with my name, Miss M's work standing so unmistakably by itself & she herself now being known to a few at least. The A. Hope matter is persiflage of course. But I am certainly thankful the article was *not* headed "The Mystery of W. S.", as I wd. have had published a protest.⁸² Well, dear old man, I am frank you see. But you know that for your good will & good deed I am grateful.

The book was a mere jiu d'esprit — & has been both over-praised & unduly disparaged.

Our joint love to you both, dear friends. | W. S.

ACS Princeton University

To Benjamin Burgess Moore, September 17, 1898

c/o Miss Rea | The Columbia Literary Agency | 9 Mill Street | Conduit St. | London | 17: Sept: 98

My dear Mr. Moore

Prolonged absence must be my excuse for not writing to you sooner to send you my grateful thanks for all the trouble you have so kindly taken on my behalf. I will write to you again as soon as I hear from Mr. Lamson, to whom I wrote at once. I send you a copy of last week's *Literature*, containing a short story of mine. If you can't get *Good Words* in America (September number) let me know, and I will get a copy and send to you. It contains "The Wells of Peace." The new issue of the *Dome* (Oct.) will also have two short poems by me.[83]

Meanwhile in great haste, | Believe me | Most cordially yours, | Fiona Macleod

ALS Huntington Library

To Edmund Clarence Stedman, [September 28, 1898]

30 Greencroft Gardens | South Hampstead, | London

For the birthday! I have written it to reach you on morning of the 8th!

My everdear Poet & Friend

Illness — followed by heavy work, & latterly a big exigent writing commission in Holland, for "Cosmopolis" etc. — are responsible for much, including a necessarily more brief note now, for I have hours & hours of work to do yet — But however busy I have never yet & I hope never will let the time go past without sending you my deep & true affection, my comradely greetings, & my homage too, to you on the occasion of your birthday. Dear Edmund of the Bays, may your new year be one of better health & more peace & rest than you have had of late — & may in all ways all things go well with you. If the love & loyal devotion of one of your truest friends on this side the Atlantic — & indeed, on my part, I will yield to no one! — can count for anything. Then at least one good influence goes to the making of a happy new year.

I had a very wonderful & happy time this summer with the dear friend of whom you know, & whose writings you admire so much — & I look to another week at least about mid-October. My love to my dear friend Mrs. Stedman. I often think of you both longingly — & "Casa Laura."[84] And Miss Mary Stuart? I wrote her a long letter (and you too!) but neither was ever acknowledged or answered! I hope she is well. She is a dear girl. She was to be married this autumn perhaps: Has it come off! If so, please send me her address. She is a friend of whom I do not wish to lose sight. In another letter I must tell you of my many literary doings — more ambitious now. (In magazine way, see Fortnightly for August, etc. etc. Also Cosmopolis in Nov. — am now writing for *all* the big mags here and U.S.A.).

Lovingly your friend, | Will | (to others, | William Sharp)

ALS Columbia University Library

To Theodore Watts-Dunton [*? Early October, 1898*]

[E. A. S. printed (*Memoir*, pp. 302–3) a letter from Theodore Watts-Dunton to "My Dear Sharp" dated October 19, 1898, which is a response to letter he had recently received from Sharp. That letter has not surfaced, but

Watts-Dunton writes at some length about *Aylwin*, a novel which had been completed for several years and was finally about to be published late in 1898 (by Hurst and Blackett in London, and, in 1899, by Dodd, Mead and Company in New York). Of that novel, which chronicles the passionate and ultimately spiritualistic love of two Romany (Gypsy) men for the girls of their dreams, Watts-Dunton wrote to Sharp: "Although it is of course primarily a love-story, and, as such, will be read by the majority of readers, it is intended to be the pronouncement of something like a new gospel — the gospel of love as the great power which stands up and confronts a materialistic cosmogony." Watts-Dunton sent Sharp with this letter a copy of a book of poems, *The Coming of Love*, which had recently been published by John Lane (London). The title poem of that volume, Watts-Dunton told Sharp, was a sequel to *Aylwin*, though it preceded the publication of the novel, and it more fully expressed his "gospel of love." This idea, deriving from Blake, Shelley, and other romantic poets of the early nineteenth century, was a central theme of the Fiona Macleod writings.]

To Ernest James Oldmeadow [*December, 1898*][85]

c/o Miss Rea

Dear Mr. Oldmeadow[86]

If you can use the enclosed in your January number, I will not only be glad that it would appear in *The Dome* but will in this instance waive the question of payment.[87] *The Dome* is the only periodical where I would care to see this poem, which of necessity must appeal only to the few. It will appear in a book which I hope to issue early in the Spring.

With cordial regards, | Sincerely yours, | Fiona Macleod

ALS National Library of Scotland

To [*Dora Sigerson Shorter,*[88] *December, 1898*]

For you, high hopes — and for you and yours *Bliadha mhath ur!*

Fiona Macleod

P.S. In an article in the forthcoming (Jan 7) number of *The Fortnightly*[89] on what I take to be the true significance of the so-called Celtic movement, and on certain representative writers, I have had great pleasure in saying how much I enjoy your work, tho' unavoidably (when proofs come) with less detail and quotation than what was in my overlong original.

Fiona Macleod

ACS University of Texas, Austin

To Catherine Ann Janvier, December 20, 1898

The House of Dreams[90] | 20th Dec., 1898

... It has been a memorable time here. I have written some of my best work — including two or three of the new things for *The Dominion of Dreams* — viz. "The Rose of Flame", "Honey of the Wild Bees", and "The Secrets of the Night."[91]

What a glorious day it has been. The most beautiful I have ever seen at Pettycur I think. Cloudless blue sky, clear exquisite air tho' cold, with a marvelous golden light in the afternoon. Arthur's Seat, the Crags and the Castle and the 14 ranges of the Pentlands all clear-cut as steel, and the city itself visible in fluent golden light. The whole coast-line purple blue, down to Berwick law and the Bass Rock, and the Isle of May 16 miles out in the north sea.

And now I listen to the gathering of the tidal waters under the stars. There is an infinite solemnity — a hush, something sacred and wonderful. A benediction lies upon the world. Far off I hear the roaming wind. Thoughts and memories crowd in on me. Here I have lived and suffered — here I have touched the heights — here I have done my best. And now, here, I am going through a new birth.

"Sic itur ad astral!"[92]

Memoir, pp. 300–01

Chapter Eighteen

Life: January–June, 1899

Sharp as Fiona Macleod contributed a lengthy article entitled "A Group of Celtic Writers" to the January issue of *The Fortnightly Review*. There was too much looseness of phrase, he thought, among journalists who wrote about "the Celtic spirit, the Celtic movement, and that mysterious entity Celticism." To clarify matters, he offered a definition:

> What is called "the Celtic Renascence" is simply a fresh development of creative energy coloured by nationality and moulded by inherited forces, a development diverted from the common way by accident of race and temperament. The Celtic writer is the writer the temper of whose mind is more ancient, more primitive, and in a sense more natural than that of his compatriot in whom the Teutonic strain prevails.

After some confusing efforts to define the differences between Celtic and Teutonic writers, Sharp settled on a simple definition:

> All that the new generation of Celtic or Anglo-Celtic (for the most part Anglo-Celtic) writers hold in conscious aim, is to interpret anew "the beauty at the heart of things," not along the lines of English tradition but along that of racial instinct, coloured and informed by individual temperament.

The writers he singled out as fitting the definition were Anglo-Irish: W. B. Yeats, George Russell (AE), Nora Hopper, and Katherine Tynan Hinkson. The article was designed to solidify Fiona Macleod's position in the Celtic Renascence and curry favor among the Irish writers, and it was favorably noted in the Irish press.

The article also elicited another less favorable response. The sections reproduced above are enough to show the prose of the article was unlike

 https://doi.org/10.11647/OBP.0196.07

that of Fiona Macleod. Indeed, it resembled the articles William Sharp was writing for London periodicals. Not surprisingly, it precipitated a lengthy article entitled "Who is Fiona Macleod: A Study in Two Styles" in the January 28 volume of the *London Daily Chronicle*. Unsigned, it set passages of prose side by side, and challenged Sharp to deny his authorship (n.p.): "Will Mr. Sharp deny that he is identical with Miss Macleod? That Miss Macleod is Mr. Sharp. I for one, have not a lingering doubt, and I congratulate the latter on the success, the real magic and strength of the work issued under the assumed name." This article stood out among others, as it coupled the assertion that Sharp was Fiona with praise for the pseudonymous writings. The article was also hard to refute. According to Elizabeth, Sharp was worried about its effect, but decided to ignore it. Several months later, at the insistence of his publishers, he published as Fiona a brief denial in *The Literary World* (*Memoir*, p. 305).

Concern about a possible unmasking contributed to the various maladies he suffered during the winter months of 1899, but he managed to finish and prepare two books for publishers. Macleod's *The Dominion of Dreams* was published by Archibald Constable and Co. on May 27, 1899, and Sharp's novel *Silence Farm* was published by Grant Richards on June 13, 1899. The former was a collection of stories and ruminations Sharp considered the deepest and most significant of the Fiona writings to date, and the latter was a realistic novel about a young farmer falling in love with his father's ward and incurring his father's wrath. After talking Richards into publishing the novel, he promoted it among his friends and fellow writers in the hope of favorable reviews that would boost its sales. Unfortunately, trying to read it is like falling into a swamp of words; it disappeared quickly into the silence of its title. Sharp was a skillful and energetic editor and critic, but successful adult fiction eluded him when writing as William Sharp. The fiction he published under the feminine pseudonym is uneven and far from faultless, but adopting the persona of an elusive lady who roamed the western isles of Scotland released his creative and formative powers. As Fiona, he was able to mold stories from start to finish, many based in ancient Gaelic lore and all rooted in the lives of simple rural people, stories that enabled readers to suspend disbelief and identify with the characters. Sharp thought his ability to adopt the Fiona Macleod persona and tell her stories depended on maintaining the fiction of her existence as a real person. That being so, it is unsurprising he was anxious about the truth emerging, and therefore tried hard to preserve the fiction.

In January Sharp began a series of letters to Grant Richards about the publication of *Silence Farm*. On January 18, he told Richards he thought it "will be considered the strongest and best piece of work I have done in fiction." The previous May, Richards married Elisina Palamidessi de Castelvecchio (1878–1959), the great-great-granddaughter of Napoleon's brother Louis. They were planning a delayed honeymoon on the French Riviera, and Sharp put Richards in touch with Thomas Janvier, who had a home in Provence and was currently living in London. If Janvier failed to contact Richards, Sharp offered assistance since he knew the area well. He knew Mistral and Felix Gras and was at that time engaged in "a critical study of modern Provençal literature." Years later, in *Author Hunting by an Old Literary Sportsman* (New York: Coward-McCann, 1934), Richards wrote that William Sharp and Thomas A. Janvier had collaborated in drawing up his itinerary.

The Sharps spent a long weekend in late March with Grant Richards' uncle and aunt, the Grant Allens, in Haslemere, Surrey. Accepting the invitation, Sharp said his insomnia required a separate bed; he would stay at a nearby inn if a room having two beds was not available at the Allen's. He informed the Allens, perhaps to mitigate the request for separate beds, that Elizabeth was about to return from a month-long absence in Scotland and commented: "How fortunate that I am an austere Anchorite — eh?" In a follow-up letter to Nellie Allen, who must have assured him of the desired sleeping arrangement, Sharp hoped "in your fine air to get a surcease from too much nervous headache and from indifferent sleep."

In a late January letter to Richards, Sharp said he understood his friend Mrs. Wingate Rinder had begun to translate Jules Boissiere's *Fumeurs d'Opium*. Referring to the success the previous year of her translation of C. Le Goffic's "Le Crucifié de Keraliès," published as *The Dark Way of Love*, he suggested that Richards commission Mrs. Rinder to translate it for him. Mrs. Rinder had sent Sharp's copy of *Fumeurs d'Opium* to Richards, who either failed to receive it or mislaid it, which caused Sharp to tell Richards in late April he hoped it might still be traced, as copies were not easy to come by. Mrs. Rinder was "naturally put out about it as the translation had to be stopped," and it was not resumed.

On March 25, Fiona thanked Frederick Ernest Green (1867–1922), a prolific writer on agricultural policy, for his letter praising her *Washer of the Ford*, and Green printed Fiona's letter in his "Book of the Week" column in the January 21, 1909 issue of *The New Age* (Vol. 4, No. 13, 266–67). The book that occasioned Green's column was Fiona's *Songs and Poems, Old and New*, published posthumously in 1909 by Eliot Stock. Green recalled sitting next to Richard Whiteing at a dinner in 1899 following the publication of his *No.5 St. John Street*, a popular novel that went through sixteen editions, made Whiteing famous, and became Grant Richards' first commercial success. Green asked Whiteing if he knew William Sharp. It had been rumored, he wrote, that Sharp "was either Fiona Macleod or else a near relation to that personality." Whiteing replied, "Yes, I do. Now, he is my ideal of a Man — magnificent physically as well as intellectually." Green commented, "How I should have liked to see these two Titans among men of letters standing together or walking arm-in-arm down Fleet Street." This is the only instance I can recall of William Sharp being called a "Titan among men of letters." He would have been pleased.

Green recalled having talked with W. B. Yeats, the honored guest and speaker at another dinner which took place on March 1, 1899:

> From telling me how he could cast a spell upon an Irish peasant and make him see a ghost, we got on to talk of crystal-gazing and from thence to Fiona Macleod, whose writings were to me the most beautiful efflorescence of the Celtic Renaissance. I remember asking him point-blank if he knew who Fiona Macleod was. He answered in the affirmative. He spoke about a pilgrimage, too, that she had made to George Meredith, and how in her was wedded beauty and intellect. This inspired me to speak of my wife, who had died a few years anterior to this, and I promised to send him a little book of her poems.
>
> This is the strange reply I received from Mr. Yeats: "My dear Mr. Green, — I thank you very much for your wife's little book. What a beautiful face she must have had. Her photograph is a little like Miss Fiona Macleod's, curiously enough. I have been so busy about "The Irish Literary Theatre" that [I] have put off writing to you from day to day. Again thanking you, I remain, yours sincerely, W. B. Yeats."

After receiving that letter from Yeats, Green decided to write a letter to Fiona Macleod, which produced her reply of March 25. Yeats's letter to Green is of interest for its direct evidence that Sharp showed Yeats a picture of Edith Rinder and identified it as a portrait of the woman who inspired Fiona Macleod. Green commented: "Whether or not Mr. Yeats ever knew the truth and felt obliged to sustain the fiction invented by the author himself I cannot say." Yeats did know a version of the truth. He knew Sharp was the author of the Fiona stories and poems; he had seen a picture of the woman who inspired them, the woman Sharp identified as Fiona Macleod; he was intrigued by the dual personality aspect of the case; and he maintained for many years his pledge of secrecy.

In a letter thanking Yeats for a copy of his "long-awaited" volume of new poems, *The Wind Among the Reeds*, Sharp wrote, "It is beautifully got up — and you know what intimate appeal and constant charm its contents have for me. Some of your loveliest work is here. And the notes (which I must read again and again) have, in their kind, a like charm." He ended the letter, "Either I or Miss M. — or both, separately — will review your beautiful book in one or two places. Miss M. has written to the Express." Fiona's review appeared in the *Dublin Daily Express* on April 22, 1899 under the title "Mr. Yeats' New Book" (3):

> It is not often, I imagine, that titles are as apt as that which Mr. Yeats has chosen for this little book. These fewer than two-score poems, most of them within the boundary of a page, are small and slight as reeds; and the wind which moves them, which whispers or sings from them a delicate music, is as invisible, as mysterious, as elemental as that "strong creature, without flesh, without bone, that neither sees nor is seen," of which long ago Taliesin sang.

Having thus caught the spirit of the poems, Sharp as Fiona proceeded to praise the poet: "Mr. Yeats is assuredly of that small band of poets and dreamers who write from no other impulse than because they see and dream in a reality so vivid that it is called imagination. With him the imagination is in truth the second-sight of the inward life. Thus it is that he lives with symbols, as an unimaginative nature might live with barren facts." Then a caution creeps in: "When the reader, unfamiliar with the signature of symbol, shall read these and kindred lines, will he not feel that this young priest of the Sun should translate to a more human key his too transcendental vision?" The question leads to a discussion of the notes which comprise half of the book: "If all notes afforded reading such as one may read here! Mr. Yeats turns round mentally and shows us the other side, where the roots grow and the fibres fill with sap, and how they grow to that blossom we have already seen, and what the sap is." They are full of learning and "have something of the charm of the poems to which they stand interpreter," but

> one cannot ignore the incongruity which lies in the wedded union of brief lyrical poems with many explicatory pages. It is not their presence, then, that one objects to, but their need. Poetry is an art which is, or should be, as rigorously aloof from the extraneously explicative, as the art of painting is, or as sculpture is, or music. When Mr. Yeats gives us work on a larger scale, with a greater sweep, he will, I trust, remember that every purely esoteric symbol is an idle haze — and haze, as we know, is apt to develop into a blank mist.

From questioning the need for the notes, learned though they might be, and asserting that poetry should stand by itself without explication, Fiona reverted to high praise: "what a lovely gift of music and spiritual intensity and beauty Mr. Yeats delivers in this book" and "no lovelier, more convincingly poetic verse has been given to us of late than these light, yet strenuous, airs of a wind that is forever mysterious, though we hold it more familiar when it blows across the mind of some poet such as Mr. Yeats, whom we know, and to whom we look."

A revised and expanded version of this review appeared as "The Later Work of Mr. W. B. Yeats," *The North American Review*, 175 (October, 1902), 473–85. There, Fiona called the volume the "beginning of a new music" and wrote, "This little book has the remoteness, the melancholy of all poetry inspired by spiritual passion" (475). She repeated her concerns about the obscure symbolism and the copious notes, but praised Yeas' imagination as "the second sight of the mind" and called the book "one of a small company that are pioneers in that intimate return to nature from which we may and do expect so profound and beautiful a revelation." E. A. S. reprinted the article as "The Shadowy Waters" in volume five of the *Collected Works of Fiona Macleod: The Winged Destiny Studies in the Spiritual History of the Gael* (London: Chapman and Hall, Ltd., 1904).

Couched as they are amid words of praise that should have warmed the heart of any young poet, the critical comments in the review (and the subsequent article) contributed to the breach that occurred between Yeats and Sharp/Macleod over the next few years. Coolness had begun to surface during Sharp's visit to the West of Ireland in the fall of 1897. Yeats's Irish friends were not hesitant in sharing their reservations about Sharp's strange behavior and lack of enthusiasm for Irish nationalism. Fiona was not alone among reviewers in questioning the arcane symbolism and lengthy notes in *The Winds Among the Reeds.* Yeats anticipated the criticism when he described the volume to Henry Davray (*Collected Letters II*, p. 306): the notes, he said, had given him "a good deal of trouble & will probably make most of the critics spend half of every review complaining that I have written very long notes about very short poems" (R. F. Foster, *W. B. Yeats, A Life, I* (Oxford: Oxford University Press, 1998), p. 214). When it appeared in the July 1899 *Mercure de France* (pp. 267–68), Davray's review addressed both Yeats's book and, interestingly, Fiona Macleod's *Dominion of Dreams* as the work of the two major exemplars of the Celtic movement in Britain. Though Yeats knew his symbols and notes would invite criticism and though he eliminated the notes in later printings of the poems, he did not expect any critical remarks from Sharp/Macleod, one of his secret confederates in the Celtic Mystical Order and a major force in the Celtic Revival. Sharp, of all people, should have appreciated the symbols, some derived from the Golden Dawn and the Celtic Order, as well as the attempt to enlighten the world about Celtic myth and lore. It was not long until Yeats's reciprocated with a different and more telling critique of Fiona's *Dominion of Dreams.*

In mid-April, having finished *Silence Farm* and with Fiona's *Dominion of Dreams* in galleys, Sharp was set to go to Paris to review the Salons and then on to the country for a period of rest and relaxation. Difficult negotiations with Grant Richards delayed his departure, as he indicated to Richards in a series of letters. On April 16 he was leaving the following week. On April 26 he would leave on the 28th; on the 28th he could not leave until April 30 or May 1. The main cause of these delays was Sharp's need for an advance from Richards to fund the trip. On April 25 he told Richards he was willing to accept fifty pounds instead of his first request for one hundred pounds upon delivery of the manuscript. Two days later, he agreed to accept an advance of twenty-five pounds, returned the manuscript to Richards (who had shipped it back to him), and said he wanted the money now "owing to an unforeseen emergency." Richards had the upper hand, since the sale of Sharp's previous novel, *Wives in Exile*, was disappointing, but it is sad to witness Sharp, who wanted so much to be in his own right a successful writer of fiction, pleading with the young publisher for money.

Once in France, Sharp spent about two weeks reviewing the salons in Paris. While there, he met Moina and Macgregor Mathers who, along with Sharp and Fiona and Maud Gonne, were contributing their psychic abilities to Yeats's Celtic Order. Sharp read aloud several stories from his proof copy of Fiona's *Dominion of Dreams* and the Mathers were deeply impressed. In a letter to Yeats dated May 29, after Sharp's return to London, Moina Mathers wrote: "We have been much delighted to meet William Sharp, who was over here. It is impossible to say how much we liked him — We felt greatly in sympathy — He is a very remarkable being I think — in every respect, & so strangely psychic." After signing the letter "Yours fraternally ever | Vestigia," her name in the Golden Dawn, she added a footnote: "Have just received 'The Dominion of Dreams' — & am much looking forward to it" (*Collected Letters II*, p. 51). Moina was an enthusiastic reader of the Fiona Macleod writings, and this meeting turned her into an enthusiastic admirer of William Sharp, though she did not know he was Fiona.

On May 14, Sharp left Paris to spend a week in the countryside with Edith Rinder. During that week, we learn from later letters, he became ill enough to need two physicians, but he was able to return to London on May 22, where he found an author's copy of *Silence Farm*. The next day, he told Grant Richards he was pleased by the appearance of the book: "the binding, the print, the paper, are just what I would choose." He said he was sorry Richards had postponed publication until June 13, and gave him a list of people who should, along with the weeklies and monthlies, receive complimentary copies so they could write reviews or otherwise spread word about the book.

The year's work began to bear fruit when Fiona's *Dominion of Dreams* was officially published on May 27. On May 29 Sharp sent one of his author's copies to Frank Rinder. He wanted him to have one of the first because the book "is at once the deepest and most intimate that F. M. has written." The letter must be read with the knowledge that Sharp's relationship with Rinder's wife was the disguised subject of many of the book's stories. The book, Sharp told Rinder, was "born out of the incurable heartache, 'the nostalgia for impossible things.'" He hoped "the issues of life have been woven to beauty, for its own sake, and in divers ways to reach and help or enrich other lives." That, he said, is "a clue to the whole book [...] at once my solace, my hope, and my ideal." In future writings of Fiona, he hoped to achieve "a deeper and richer and truer note of inward joy and spiritual hope." One of the book's stories, "The Distant Country," is a direct and compelling portrayal of his relationship with Edith Rinder. It is also the story he mentioned often in his letters. He concluded his letter to Frank Rinder by reproducing a sentence from that story: "Love is more great than we conceive, and Death is the keeper of unknown redemptions.

Sharp began writing "The Distant Country" in the summer of 1898, not long after he invented, in his June 28 letter to Yeats, the metaphor of the match, the flame, and the torch to describe his relationship with Edith Rinder. He concluded that letter, we recall, by saying: "How does that strike you as a subject for a tale, a book? It would be a strange one. Does it seem to you impossible? It does not seem so to me." Fiona's "The Distant Country" is the tale that did not seem impossible to Sharp as it incorporates the imagery of the match and the torch and the flame. Writing in the first person, Fiona began by describing two pairs of great lovers from the Gaelic past; Red Ithel and Pale Bronwen, and Aillinn and Baile. After recalling those lovers, she moved on to a pair of lovers she loved well, who "had their day in this West of rains and rainbows, of tears and hopes," and have now passed on to the "Distant Country." The body of the tale is an effort on the part of Sharp, speaking as Fiona, to understand and describe the powerful love that bound him to Edith Rinder. Before launching that story, he announced its theme by introducing the metaphor of the flame:

> Love is at once so great and so frail that there is perhaps no thought which can at the same time so appall and uplift us. And there is in love, at times, for some an unfathomed mystery. That which can lead to the stars can lead to the abyss. There is a limit set to mortal joy as well as to mortal suffering, and the flame may overleap itself in one as in the other. The most dread mystery of a love that is overwhelming is its death through its own flame.

The woman who is "a flame to his mind as well as to his life" develops a foreboding that as their all-consuming love becomes more powerful it will burn itself out. At first the man rejects that fear and speaks to the woman "of love more enduring than the hills, of passion, of the spirit, of deathless things." She senses the end approaching when the man becomes "strangely disquieted": "'Too many dreams,' he said once, with double meaning, smiling as he looked at her, but with an unexpressed trouble in his eyes." Soon her love for him became "too great a flame" and implodes. She has not ceased to love him, she will continue to give him her entire being, but it has become "an image that has no life." Love had come close, he decides, and looked at them in its "immortal guise," a tameless and fierce thing "more intense than fire," which consumes what death only silences.

Here the story begins to make more sense, as we realize Sharp has ventured into the spiritualist experiments he and Edith were conducting. The "immortal had become mortal." He had not foreseen the result when "by a spiritual force, he accomplished that too intimate, that too close union in which none may endure. I speak of a mystery." Fiona says she believes in the mystery but cannot explain it in words because she knows of it "only through those two who broke (or of whom one broke) some occult but imperious spiritual law." The two lovers continued to love each other, but it was not the same, and the man came to realize he "had not known the innermost flame, that is pure fire." Now that the lovers have gone to "that distant country of Splendour and Terror," Fiona concludes; "Love is more great than we conceive, and Death is the keeper of unknown redemptions." That sentence became fixed in Sharp's mind and in the minds of many Fiona Macleod readers; it is inscribed on his gravestone under a Celtic cross in a remote protestant cemetery in Sicily.

For all its contradictions and excesses of language, this story was Sharp's effort to explain how his love for Edith Rinder and hers for him quickened his imagination and enabled him to write as Fiona Macleod. More significantly, it speculates that their love for each other became too passionate, too intense, augmented by their efforts to contact and join the realm of spirits. They broke, or, more precisely, he broke "some occult but imperious spiritual law" that produced his intense mental conflicts. Either the flame of his love was so intense it burned itself out or, he speculates, perhaps he had not reached the "innermost flame," the flame of pure fire. Either way, the love that was so passionate became unsustainable. It could be fulfilled only in some "distant country of Splendour or Terror," wherever their spirits may live when they die. "Love is more great than we conceive, and Death is the keeper of unknown redemptions." That the story ends with the suggestion that the fire that fed the love affair has burned itself out explains why Sharp sent the book to Frank Rinder and highlighted that story. The sentence he quotes from the story, moreover, is a plea for forgiveness. Deep love is beyond our ability to understand and control. Redemption from the pain it causes others may come only after death. Perhaps that is also why Elizabeth decided to include portions of the letter in the *Memoir*. If the operation of love is a mystery beyond human comprehension, the actions it precipitates are beyond human control and unreconcilable on this side of the shade that separates life and death.

The importance of the story for Sharp is clear in two letters he wrote to Yeats after its appearance in *The Dominion of Dreams*. In late May, he wrote of the book, "Few can guess how personal much of it is. You almost alone will read 'The Distant Country,' for example, with 'other eyes.'" Yeats would recognize the two principle characters are based on the relationship between Sharp and the woman he loved, and he would appreciate the references to the occult activities. In a letter to Yeats dated September 16, 1899, Sharp, this time as Fiona Macleod, had more to say about the story:

> Of one thing only I am convinced, as is my friend (an opinion shared with the rare few whose judgment really means much), that there is nothing in *Dominion of Dreams* or elsewhere in these writings under my name to stand beside "The Distant Country". Nothing else has made so deep and vital an impression both on men and women — and possibly it may be true what a very subtle and powerful mind has written about it, that it is the deepest and most searching utterance on the mystery of passion which has appeared in our time. It is indeed the core of *all* these writings — and will outlast them all.

Nowhere else is Sharp so direct in asserting the autobiographical qualities of the Fiona Macleod writings and the importance therein of love and sexual passion. He continued:

Of course, I am speaking for myself only. As for my friend, his heart is in the ancient world and his mind for ever questing in the domain of the spirit. I think he cares little for anything but through the remembering imagination to recall and interpret, and through the formative and penetrative imagination to discover certain mysteries of psychological and spiritual life. (Apropos, I wish you very much to read, when it appears in *The Fortnightly Review* — probably either in October or in November — the spiritual "essay" called "The Divine Adventure" — an imaginative effort to reach the same vital problems of spiritual life along the separate, yet inevitably interrelated, lines of the Body, the Will (Mind or Intellect), and the Soul.) ["The Divine Adventure" appeared in the November 1 and December 11 issues of *The Fortnightly Review.*]

Here Sharp draws the same distinction he made in "The Distant Country" between the feminine and the masculine approaches to writing and to love. *The Divine Adventure* is "apropos" of her friend's approach to love and life. Her friend was William Sharp, and *The Divine Adventure* was published as the work of Fiona Macleod. Such were the contradictions that often surfaced in Sharp's management of the double identity and the dual authorship.

On May 29 Sharp also wrote letters about *The Dominion of Dreams* to AE (George Russell) and Coulson Kernahan, and drafted Fiona letters to Benjamin Burgess Moore in the United States and to Edith Lyttelton in London. The latter presents a telling instance of Sharp's efforts to ingratiate himself with the London establishment. Edith Sophy Balfour Lyttelton, later Dame Edith Lyttelton, was a writer and an enthusiastic reader of Fiona Macleod. She was also a prominent hostess and the wife of Alfred Lyttelton (1857–1913), a Member of Parliament and, for a time, Secretary of State. In responding as Fiona in early May to a fan letter from Mrs. Lyttelton, Sharp said

I would like to know a little more of you, though more than likely we may never meet. Will you tell me? (Are you Miss or Mrs.?) But just as you like, of course. I ask, partly because of yourself as revealed in your letter: partly because of a keen personal association unwittingly awakened. But it does not matter. I am content that you are a friend, that you bear a name dear to me, and that you have been generous enough to write whole heartedly to a stranger.

Edith Lyttleton's name was dear to Sharp/Macleod, of course, because she shared her given name with Edith Rinder. Fiona continued, "You live in London, and know Mr. Yeats. Do you know his, and my friend and kinsman, Mr. William Sharp? As doubtless you have seen in the papers — for the controversy about myself seems as recurrent as the sea-serpent — he is often supposed to be me, or I to be him, or both of us to be each other, with many other speculative variations! I would like you to meet."

Fig. 18 Dame Edith Sophy Lyttelton (née Balfour) after a picture by Romney; by Lafayette, photogravure by Walker & Boutall, 1897; published 1899. © National Portrait Gallery, London. Some rights reserved.

Sharp did meet Edith Lyttleton at a social gathering shortly after he returned from France. In what must have been a brief conversation she said she had been ill. Sharp invented his passing this news to Fiona as an excuse for her to tell Edith how sorry she was to hear of her illness. She added: "You will, of course, know at once how I have heard of your illness." She continued, "After your second letter I wanted you to meet Mr. William Sharp, and he would have called a month or more ago but that he had to go to France. I am glad you have met: for as I think I told you, he is my most intimate friend, as well as my kinsman. If you like him, you would like me: if you do not like him, you would not like me. There! It is a woman's argument — but perhaps none the less convincing." Silly as those sentences sound, Sharp was not simply having fun with Mrs. Lyttleton. He was angling for another meeting, this time alone. "So you live in an old house in Westminster and have 'a swift and individual mind', and are 'keenly sensitive to impressions,' and 'seem tuned to that finer inward suffering which goes with every nature open to mystery and to beauty.'" That is what Sharp had told her. "Well, I knew that," he continued as Fiona, "and more I have mentally reproached my friend for not being more explicit — though he says frankly 'It is not only that I have no time, but that I am unable to say more. If ever I meet her alone, I will see and know what, in a first visit, in the circumstances and with others present, was of necessity fugitive or uncertain.'" As the letter continued, discussing *The Dominion of Dreams*, Sharp worked hard to build a strong bond of friendship between Fiona and Edith: "We can never meet, but we can always be friends." He was using the Fiona ruse to prepare the way for calling on Edith in hopes of finding her alone and prepared for an in-depth discussion of their dreams and desires. Sharp was especially attracted to women he thought might become confidants, and this one had the added advantage of being highly placed in society.

It did not take Sharp long to call on Mrs. Lyttleton. In Fiona's next letter to her on June 18, she said

> I am very very glad that you can feel to me as to a friend. I hope you will write when so ever you will. I shall always be glad to hear from you. Indeed, I feel that we *are* friends. There are things — but above all there is *something* — in your letter which comes home to me intimately.
>
> As some slight sign of this I sent you the "Kingdom of Silence," and also asked Mr. Sharp to send you from me (I thought he had an extra copy of mine, but he hadn't!) a copy of my most personal or intimate book, "From the Hills of Dream".
>
> Do you not "write" yourself? Your letters (with their eager note, and distinctive touch) make me think you do. If so, I wish you would let me see something.
>
> I am glad you have seen my friend again. I think you and he will become friends. It is my hope. He says you are "the Hon. Mrs. Lyttelton," and wife of one of whose family I know something.
>
> And I am sure I would like you now as much as he does.

Sharp's effort to start through Fiona a friendship with a woman of importance had a limited success mirroring the relationship both Sharps developed — via Yeats — with Lady Gregory.

In late May, Sharp assured Yeats he had read and carefully considered the draft of a Celtic Mystical Order Rite. He thought it needed "something more definite in visionary insight and significance." It needed "spiritual recasting." He was waiting for inspiration, a "resurrection," that would enable him to recast the Rite. He would let Yeats know when the rebirth occurred if it was of "any worth." His "stream of inward thought" was "moving that way." He had been ill and was now better, but his doctor had ordered "hill and sea air" native to him. He and Elizabeth would forego their plans to visit Scandinavia and go instead to Ireland at the end of July, probably to the East coast, as it would be too expensive to go to the West. He hoped Yeats will like *The Dominion of Dreams*, which will appeal to few but hopefully "sink deep." The play Fiona Macleod would soon finish for Yeats's Celtic Theatre would no longer be called "The Tarist," but "The King of Ireland's Son." Sharp also asked whether Yeats be at Gort (with Lady Gregory) or Tillyra (with Edward Martyn) in August? If so, Sharp said, he envied him as his heart was always in the West. Having to stay in hotels would make the West too expensive for their Ireland visit. Yeats surely got the unspoken point that an invitation from Lady Gregory to stay at Coole Park or from Martyn to stay at Tillyra would make the West affordable. In a postscript, Sharp sent his "most cordial remembrances & regards to Lady Gregory"

Through most of June, Sharp remained in London, trying to promote sales of his two books through friends and reviewers. On or around June 5, he wrote again to Yeats. He was still too weak to undertake the psychic effort to comment in detail on the draft copy of the Rite. It needed more work, and he would get to it as soon as he could muster the energy. Again, he asked Yeats what he thought of *The Dominion of Dreams* and wondered if he would be reviewing it. He remained curious on this point through June, and, having heard nothing in response, he was surprised when Yeats's review appeared in the July *Bookman*. That review and its aftermath will be discussed in the "Life" section of Chapter Nineteen. After asking Yeats to do something for *Silence Farm* if he could, he said he and Elizabeth would be leaving their South Hampstead flat (30 Greencroft Gardens) for good around July 20. If Yeats would be in town before then, he hoped to see him. He told Yeats for the second time he and Elizabeth would spend some time on the east coast of Ireland, north of Dublin. Then he explicitly stated his hope that

Edward Martyn or Lady Gregory would invite them to the West. The lines containing that hope are crossed through with a single wavy line. If the line was Sharp's, he must have wanted Yeats to think he had thought better about conveying his hope for an invitation while leaving the hint highly visible. Uncharacteristically, Sharp ended by telling Yeats he was suffering one of his periodic bouts of depression: "I doubt if I'll ever live in London again. It is not likely. I do not know that I am overwhelmingly anxious to live anywhere. I think you know enough of me to know how profoundly I feel the strain of life — the strain of double life. Still, there is much to be done yet. But for that..." The mention of his double life reminds us again that Sharp told Yeats, probably in June 1897, he was responsible for the Fiona Macleod writings and he experienced Fiona as an alternative personality triggered and inspired by a real woman with whom he enjoyed an intimate relationship.

Yeats had also sent a draft copy of his rite to Fiona Macleod asking her to comment. Strange as that sounds, it may have been intended for the woman who inspired Sharp to write as Fiona Macleod, the woman who was helping Sharp with the Celtic Rite whom he knew only as Fiona Macleod. On June 14, Sharp wrote to Yeats as Fiona asking him to be patient about the Rite for a bit longer. Sharp, she said, would be coming to see her in Scotland at the end of the following week (around June 24), and "it is important he and I should talk over, rather than correspond about this."

In late May, Sharp told AE (George Russell) that he would receive a copy of *The Dominion of Dreams* "from Miss Macleod & myself (per the publishers)." When he met with AE in Dublin the previous fall, Sharp claimed authorship of the Fiona writings and asserted she was a separate personality inhabiting his body. He knew Sharp was talking about one aspect of his self when he said the book "comes from deeper depths of life, both of suffering & spiritual exaltation, than any other of F. M.'s books." Preserving the fiction of Fiona's separate existence, AE sent her a letter, which has not surfaced, that mixed praise with criticism. Writing as Fiona, Sharp responded on June 17 to AE's "friendly and sincere letter," echoing AE's heightened prose:

> I am like one in an apparently clear wood which is yet a mysterious maze out of which I cannot escape, or even reach the frontiers so as to discern where I am and what vistas are beyond me: nay, even the stars

themselves become confused often in the darkness of the branches, and the sun's way seems equally to lead west or east, or north or south, so that I fare often bewildered even at full noon.

Perhaps your letter — perhaps your will and thought — can help me. I hope so. I can say neither "yea" nor "nay" to the central part of your letter. But that spiritually I have been furnishing the palaces of the mind with empty shadows is, I fear, true. Well, I *hope* — and *believe*.

The letter ended with a request for a copy of the review AE was writing for the *Dublin Daily Express*. When AE sent the review to Fiona later in the summer, he excused his delay by saying he had said all he wished to say directly to her in the earlier letter: "The review is sincere if critical. But I can judge by no other than an absolute standard." He concluded sadly: "if you hope and believe you are on the path: Faith and hope are companions only met on the straight road and having them you have help I could not give you having lost them awhile" (unpublished letter in private hands).

Sharp did go to Edinburgh on or around June 24. On June 27 he mailed a card to Grant Richards from Sterling on his way to Glasgow and the West. He wanted to assure Richards he would answer the letter sent to him in Edinburgh when he returned there in "about a week." He told Yeats he planned to meet Fiona in Edinburgh and go with her to the western isles. It was his habit to talk about the time he spent with Edith Rinder as time spent with Fiona, who he claimed variously was both his cousin and his beloved. He was constructing and taking part in a drama with multiplying complexities that only he understood, and they were becoming difficult to manage. He told people different and contradictory details about Fiona — who she was and how they were related — and it had become harder to keep his stories straight. Sequencing Fiona's movements with those of Edith Rinder enabled him to preserve some consistency. It is likely that Sharp and Edith were together in the country southwest of Glasgow, in or near the Kyles of Bute, in late June, a respite that may well have lasted longer than a week and one that provided an escape from his financial problems and the nagging doubts of friends and fellow writers about the authenticity of Fiona.

Letters: January–June, 1899

To Clement Shorter, January 2, 1899

30 Greencroft Gardens | South Hampstead | 2nd January 1899

Private

My dear Clement Shorter,[1]

You asked me if I had any "big" fiction on hand. I do not think I need speak to you of *Silence Farm*,[2] as it is probably not suited for serial use. It will be about 60,000 words: & I hope to finish it in a month or so: It is a sombre story, told with as much reserve and concentrated power "as I know how".

But I am anxious to get on at once with (if practicable) a romance of young lives, of their first beginnings, strivings, successes, failures, loves, and vicissitudes, in the world of art and literature.

It is to be called *Bugle Music*, and will be the first of three connected (but independent) romances, each of considerable length: — (alternative title, *The Stars of Fortune*, but I think this wd. be best for the second of the three): — in which I hope to create a living picture of the artistic and literary world in these later Victorian days.[3]

I began the scheme ten years ago, in Paris, but decided to wait, as I wished to make this trilogy a big work in every sense of the word.

But the time has now come when I wish to take it up in earnest. Though my own experiences of the literary & artistic world go back only to 1880 (all but 20 years, alas!) I knew and know well many, now famous or notable, of an earlier date, who "went through the mill" before & during my time.

Bugle Music begins about 1855 — and among those who come into it are Rossetti, Morris, Burton, Swinburne, & Geo. Meredith., & others of marked personality — more or less importantly or incidentally as the case may be.

In the three books (the third of which will be contemporary in the most immediate sense) I hope to give not only a true and living picture, but to write the romance of contemporary life with the utmost keen and romantic and vivid interest. Romances must be vivid, telling, dramatic, first & foremost.

I prefer the name *Bugle Music* as significant not only of the spirit throughout, but as a good name for the new generation at the century-end & the century-beginning!

Do you think there is any likelihood that you could use *Bugle Music*. I need not say how glad I should be, were it so.

With cordial good will for 1899

Sincerely Yours | William Sharp

P.S. Have you seen the allusion to your wife's fine and distinctive work in Miss Macleod's article in the current *Fortnightly*?

ALS University of Leeds, Brotherton Library

To John Macleay, [early January, 1899]

30 Greencroft Gardens | South Hampstead | N.W.[4]

My dear Mr. Macleay

Extreme pressure has made it impossible for me to write to you before this, though I was very glad to hear from you again.

On the whole, Liverpool seems to suit you. I fancy that after London it is one of the best places to live in, in England — i.e. for those whom the Gods punish by compelling to dwell within grimy cities.

I am bound to say that a perusal of "John Splendid," a month or so ago, greatly enhanced my opinion of (as well as my pleasure in) that book.[5] At the same time I found, & still find, the style hangs too continuously to one insistent note. But, at its best, it is most truly delightful, stimulating, and winsome. I hope & believe the new story will be a success: I like the opening apparently better than you do. But, like you, I look to the ensuing book for his masterpiece. When I was in Edinburgh recently I met Neil Munro, and a day or two later we spent an afternoon together. I took a very definite liking to him: he seems to me in every way "a good fellow."

As to your enquiries about Miss Macleod I can say that she is slowly but surely getting along with her historical romance — having canceled all she had written & started afresh. I have, however, seen only the opening chapters. She is so much preoccupied with other work — most of it, I fancy, more akin to her own taste, but some of it, critical & other, in a sense "put upon" her by editors — that her big romance emulates the snail. However, when done, I fancy every one will be surprised by this book.

N. B. don't pass on [?] anything given by Miss M! She seems to change her titles & contents without remorse. A few weeks ago a friend in U.S.A. begged me for some particulars about her next book — which, authorized, I gave. I now hear that the book is to have a different (certainly a much finer) name, with contents which involve a markedly different character for the book regarded as a whole. It is confusing, but at least the changes seem to make for strength & variety.

I suppose you have seen Miss M's article in the current *Fortnightly*[6] — Today I recd., presumably at her request, tho' it was not in her writing, a copy of the "Dublin Express" of Monday, with her letter. She certainly turns the tables on the "Express" reviewer who had rashly echoed the parrot-cry about her "Gaelic."

For myself, I am very busy, & in more ways than I have time to tell or egotism to inflict. Apart from books on hand, & needful ephemeral pen-work in periodicals, I have a good many articles & short stories commissioned.

If he puts it in, there may be something about the less important things (for I have forbidden allusion pro. tem. to the more ambitious) I have on hand in this week's *Ill. London News* (where I have also a short art-paper): at any rate, Clement Shorter wrote me the other day & asked if I had any objection to his "literary lettering" what he had remembered me saying in conversation.

I forgot to say that I strongly agree with you in your opinion about Miss Macleod's Scandinavian & Viking stories. Personally, I consider them her best achievement, or with only casual exception.

With all good will for 1899, & hoping it may bring you luck in all way —

Cordially Yours | William Sharp

ALS National Library of Scotland

To Grant Richards, January 18, 1899

30 Greencroft Gardens | South Hampstead | 18/1/99

My dear Richards,

I haven't yet seen Clement Shorter's notice to which you allude — though as he was specially asking me about my work recently I know of course to what he must be alluding. I have had a letter from two other publishers.

Frankly, I can say nothing definite at the moment. It must be *largely* a matter of £. S. P.[7] with me.

I think "*Silence Farm*" will be considered the strongest and best piece of work I have done in fiction.[8] It is a sombre story — which, therefore, some will like & possibly more won't.

Sister Eunice (or some other title) will either be a shortlist book of 3 or 4 stories of an oriental kind — or be a longer book comprising all the best short fiction I have done or am still engaged on.[9]

Of the two critical volumes — only one will be ready this Spring — namely, that on literary subjects. It will be *the* book of W. S. the critic!

I forwarded your letter to Janvier — a near neighbor (14 Winchester Road, Swiss Cottage, N. W.)

If perchance you don't hear from him, I can give you a good deal of information about Provence — which I know well. I also know Mistral, Felix Gras, etc. (One of the things I am now engaged on is a critical study of modern Provençal literature. It will, I *hope*, be in the book I speak of.)

Hope you & your wife are well.[10]

Cordially Yours | William Sharp

P.S. I suppose you got my note about a review-copy of *Wives in Exile* to Mr. J. Strang?

ALS Stanford University

To Grant Richards, [late January, 1899]

30 Greencroft Gardens | South Hampstead | NW

My dear Richards,

I sent the "Provence Maritime"[11] to your Chelsea address, & have just heard that *Fumeurs d'Opium* was duly sent on to you this morning at Henrietta St., at my request, from my friend Mrs. Wingate Rinder, to whom I had lent it. I gave it to her some time ago with the strong recommendation to translate it (you know her admirable translative work, I expect) — and she has begun to do so. It will, I believe, make a very striking book in English. The tales are powerful. If it strikes you as desirable, I hope you may see your way to commissioning Mrs. Rinder to translate it for you.[12] (Her recent "The Dark Way of Love", a translation of C. Le Goffic's "Le Crucifié de Keraliès", was a success in both senses).

When you have done with the book will you please let me have it again. Mrs. Rinder is anxious to get on with the translation.

The other book will do when you return. I hope you & your wife (what a charming as well as a pretty woman, you unduly lucky devil!) will have a memorably happy & fortunate time. My cordial greetings to you both. Bon voyage!

William Sharp

ALS State University of New York at Buffalo

To Doctor John Goodchild, March 4, 1899

(Edinburgh) | 4th March 1899

My dear Sir

Your letter reached me yesterday from the address of my London agent where for private reasons all my correspondence goes.

Let me say at once that your surmise is wrong: far from not interesting me your second kind letter interested me profoundly, and not only intellectually but because of spiritual coincidence.

I was, however, unable to answer it on account of a feverish chill which ended in Influenza, now fortunately overcome, though it has weakened me somewhat and has also thrown all my correspondence and work into arrears.

I have considered as well as read your letter, and more and more I am impressed by the strangeness of the fundamentally identical spiritual ideas which come to many minds. Race, temperament, and perhaps conditions modify or affect these ideas, but below the accident lies the same spiritual reality. I have long believed in the arising of the Woman Redeemer: and that she will be born in the west, perhaps in Ireland, perhaps in Iona of the Prophecy. The place matters little. Even in my writings you could find traces of this — notably in the last section of *Green Fire* ("The Beauty of the World") — [a book which as a book I care little for and think immature and in almost every way unsatisfactory] —

There is a strange and obscure prophecy in the Hebrides upon which I had meant to write a long study, but this for several reasons I had to relinquish. I have in my mind, however, all but finally thought out (my way of work) a spiritual study called "The Second Coming of St. Bride" which will give utterance to this faith in a new redeeming spiritual force, — a women who will express the old Celtic Bride or Brigit (goddess of fire, song, music), the first modern Saintliness of woman (Bride-nan-Brat etc., St. Brigit of the Mantle; Muime-Chriosda, Christ's Foster-Mother; Mary's Sister etc.): the Virgin Mother of Catholicism: Mary of Motherhood: Mary, the Goddess of the Human Soul: Mary, Destiny, the Star-Kindler, for Destiny is but the name of the starry light hidden in each human soul: Consolatrix: Genetrix: the immortal Sister of Orchil, the Earth Goddess, at once Hêra, Pan, and Demogorgon: the Daughter of God: the Star of Dreams: the Soul of Beauty: the Shepherd of Immortality.[13]

In the short story called "The Washer of the Ford" (in the volume so called, and in *Spiritual Tales*) there is a hint of this in another way — that of the conflict between the Pagan and early Christian ideals of the mysterious Woman, whether a Celtic Fate or a Mary Bride of God: as again, in another way, in a story called "The Woman with the Net" in the pagan section of my forthcoming book, "The Dominion of Dreams."[14]

It may well be that through what you have written to me, or along the indicated lines, I may reach some more direct and more vital view of a great spiritual problem than I have done. I am but a dreamer of dreams.

Let me thank you again for your long and interesting letters and diagrams. I must try and go to Glastonbury. If you feel inclined to write further on this strange problem I hope you will do so.

Believe me, | Sincerely yours, | Fiona Macleod

ALS National Library of Scotland

To Egan Mew, March 20, 1899

c/o Miss Rea | The Columbia Literary Agency |
9. Mill Street. Conduit St. | London |

20: March: 99

My dear Sir[15]

In response to a letter of yours of some date back, I now write to let you know that my new book, *The Dominion of Dreams*, is to be published in the course of the Spring by Mess.rs Archibald Constable & Co. It is in three sections: Tales, with a modern setting; Narratives of a purely psychological kind; and Tales with an old Celtic and pagan background. The greater part of the contents is published for the first time. The book has an epilogue entitled "The Wind, the Shadows, and the Soul." One of the longest stories in it, "By the Yellow Moonrock," is the essential part of a short book once announced as *The Lily Leven*. With this exception" The Dominion of Dreams" is more akin to *The Washer of the Ford* than any other of my books: and so is of a wholly distinct nature from the Jacobite Romance I have on hand. In the one I have been preoccupied with the explicit drama of actual things — events, actions, externals.

I will ask you, however, not to print this item of literary news in any other quarter than Literature before Friday.

Yours very truly | Fiona Macleod

ALS Princeton University

To Egan Mew, March 25, 1899

Private | Edinburgh | 25th March. | 99

Dear Sir

I do not wish to seem ungracious, and am glad that you have announced so fully my new book — but I must again protest (for this is not the first time, that what I complain of has occurred in *Literature,* to my annoyance, and enhanced "botherations" in correspondence) against your giving my name in inverted commas.[16]

How would Mr. Egan Mew, for instance, like it if I alluded to him in print as "Egan Mew"?

I do ask to preserve my own absolute privacy and in my own way, but I have the natural wish, in sacrificing publicity but also to sacrifice my own name.

Believe me | Yours very truly | Fiona Macleod

ALS Princeton University

To Mr. and Mrs. Grant Allen, [*March 25, 1899*]

Rutland House, | Greencroft Gardens, | So. Hampstead | Saty

My dear Grant and Nellie,

Elizabeth has been delayed in Edinburgh but returns tomorrow. Meanwhile I have telegraphed to her — and now I have just sent you a wire to say with what pleasure we accept your kind invitation to come to you on Thursday next. And, considering what kind of day E. Monday is in town we shall very thankfully stay with you over the Monday as you most kindly suggest.[17]

I shall have to work in the mornings (for I am trying to finish a new book, a romance called *Silence Farm*, besides having many proofs, and other writing, etc., etc., etc. to attend to — but I shall be in no one's way, for if fine I can work in the Garden — or in "any corner anywhere.")

But one thing I will ask, if I may: for my insomnia is still troublesome, and by the doctor's orders I must sleep alone. So if you have not a room with two beds in it, or cannot (as may well be) let us have a room each, I will ask you to allow me to take for myself a bedroom at the (?) or somewhere near, if that be feasible. Sorry to be such a confounded bother (pray say it, but out of your affectionate good hearts, smilingly overlook!).

So you have Dick and Julie Le Gallienne now as near neighbours?

I shall be glad to see my truant Spouse again — she has been away a month.

How fortunate that I am an austere Anchorite — eh?

Ever yours | Will

ALS Pierpont Morgan Library

To F. E. Green, March 25, 1899[18]

c/o Miss Rea | The Columbia Literary Agency, |
9. Mill Street, Conduit Street, | London | March 25, 1899

My Dear Sir,

I must ask you to excuse my delay in response, though the fault is not wholly mine, for the address to which you wrote is an old one, and the letter had to be forwarded to my London agent, and thence to me.

I am grateful for your letter. It has been the happiest thing connected with my work that I have been able to appeal strongly to certain natures, particularly to those who have loved deeply and deeply suffered. You say you have read "The Washer of the Ford," and you may have noted that the story called "Muime Chriosd" is inscribed to "a beautiful memory".

The Mrs. Alden was a stranger, an American, of singular beauty of character and life (wife of the editor of "Harper's Magazine"), but she was of those who feel as you are generous enough to tell me you feel; and when she was dying she put away all else from here, and asked her husband to read certain things of mine, and died with the MS. of "Muime Chriosd" in one hand and some white flowers in the other. These are to me the unforgettable things, and your letter is of them, and I thank you.

I wish I had known your wife. In her strong and fine face, to me beautiful, I see, as well as in her verses and heart-inspired prose, that she was a poet, in life, in thought, in spirit.

When it is published, probably in later part of April, I would much like you to read certain things in my new book, "The Dominion of Dreams". Especially, perhaps, in tales (or spiritual narratives) such as "In the Silence of the Hills", or "The Wells of Peace", you may find something of inward appeal. It may be so. I would be glad.

I seem to read much from your wife's face, from her book, from your letter. Let me quote one sentence from part of "The Dominion of Dreams" (from the end of "The Distant Country"): — "Love is more great than we conceive, and Death is the keeper of unknown redemptions."

Believe me, | Most sincerely yours, | Fiona Macleod

Printed Letter, The New Age, 4/13 (January, 1909), 267

To Mrs. Grant Allen, [March 28, 1899]

Tuesday

My dear Nellie

Just a hurried line to say that E. has just returned, and that she is as glad as I am (tho' fortunately without the same need) of so happy a chance and holiday. Very sorry to hear Grant is seedy — but feel sure you are too good a friend to hesitate in asking us if our coming were to burden him or you just now. We shall hope to find him his cheery self again — & you as blithe as usual.

I doubted if I could get away till the late afternoon — but as the Eastertide crowd well be very unpleasant anytime after 2 o'clock on Thursday, we have decided to leave Waterloo by the 1:50 train, due at Haslemere at 3:25 — so I suppose we'll be with you somewhere about 4 or so.[19] For myself I can assure I look forward in every way to this visit — & apart from your and Grant's affectionate comradeship I hope in your fine air to get a surcease from too much nervous headache and from indifferent sleep. Well, till Thursday, Aufwiedersehn,

Will

ALS Pierpont Morgan Library

To T Fisher Unwin, [April 10, 1899][20]

Sunday

Dear Mr. Unwin,

Thanks for your note, and kindly sending the advance copy of Dr. Hyde's book which will doubtless come tomorrow. Of course I'll say nothing about it (except possibly a useful paragraph in one or two places) till on or after the day of publication.

In haste | Yrs very truly | W. S.

APS New York Public Library, Berg Collection

To T Fisher Unwin, [April 12, 1899][21]

Monday Night

Dear Mr. Unwin

Dr. Hyde's book has not come yet — I send this reminder only because in your note of Saty you say "I have today sent you advance copy etc." Perhaps it may come tomorrow — but you will know, of course, if it has been sent.

Yrs very truly | William Sharp

ACS New York Public Library, Berg Collection

To William Butler Yeats, [*April 16, 1899*]

Sunday

My dear Yeats,

A hurried line from the country (Pinnar) where I am for this evening — to thank you for your book.[22] It is beautifully got up — and you know what intimate appeal and constant charm its contents have for me. Some of your loveliest work is here. And the notes (which I must read again and again) have, in their kind, a like charm. In no hypercritical spirit, but a little wonderingly, I wd ask you if you are *sure Sidhe*[23] ever means "Wind." I write away from books of course — but I have never heard of any words for wind except | *Goath* (wind) | Soilbheas (blast) | *Anail* (breeze or breath) | One has to be careful in these matters.

Either I or Miss M. — or both, separately — will review your beautiful book in one or two places. Miss M. has written to the Express — "Literature" is already secured.[24]

Ever yours, | W. S.

ALS Yale University

To Grant Richards, [*April 16, 1899*][25]

(In train from Country) | Sunday

My Dear Richards

I hope to send you "Silence Farm" before this week-end — but for your immediate consideration, as agreed, as not only do two other publishers want it, but I wish to arrange at once, both because for urgent reasons it shd. come out this season — & because next week I have to go abroad for a week or two.

Mrs. Wingate Rinder is for every reason very disappointed about the miscarriage of "Fumeurs D'Opium" — for personal as well as for other reasons — & she hopes, as I do, & as I know you do, that the missing volume may yet be recovered.

You have not written to her — she told me yesterday.

Hoping you are all right now —

Believe me, my Dear Richards | Most Sincerely Yours | William Sharp

P.S. Glad to have been instrumental in several quarters in helping Whiteing's book.[26]

ALS State University of New York at Buffalo

To T. Fisher Unwin, [April 18, 1899][27]

Thanks — but I now have another photo of Douglas Hyde. (I shall be noticing his book in 3 places.)

When is Yeats's reissued "Poems" to be out.[28] If you send me an advance copy I'll do what I can for it.

W. S.

ACS New York Public Library, Berg Collection

To Grant Richards, April 21, 1899

30 Greencroft Gardens | South Hampstead | Friday night 21: Apl:99

My dear Richards,

Herewith I fulfill my promise, and give you first offer of *Silence Farm*, which I think the strongest and in every way best book I have done. (It is about 58,000 words or so; with the 14 sectional forepages equivalent to over 60,000.)

I have already told you what I would like to get for it as an advance against royalties: and I think urged, but may do so again, the advisability of its being brought out with the utmost expedition now — on account of the recent widespread and continued controversy about Miss Macleod and myself. As Miss Macleod is publishing a new book, "The Dominion of Dreams", through A. Constable and Co., about the beginning of May, and as that controversy (in some ways deeply regretted both by her and me) is certain to arise again in consequence, and cannot but materially affect the sales of her book, and, if mine is ready, of mine, you will at once see the urgency of bringing out *Silence Farm* with the least possible delay.[29] Little proof-revision will be called for — only textual errors: for I have already revised in MS and in typed-copy.

For the same reason of urgency, I will ask you to keep to your promise — to let me hear from you within two days: i.e., I shall look to hear from you by Monday evening, or at latest by Tuesday morning. This is the more imperative for me, as I have, if possible, to go to France on Wednesday or Wedny night. If you do not wish the book, I shall thus have time to arrange with one of the two other publishers who are desirous of it.

I reserve American (U. S. A.) rights, and shall myself arrange for publication there and on Wedny shall post my typed duplicate there. This, however, is not to delay issue here.

Cordially yours | William Sharp

ALS Private

To John Macleay, [April 25, 1899]

Tuesday

My dear Mr. Macleay

It is not often coincidences happen as today — for your letter (largely about Miss Macleod's new book) — one from Miss Macleod about the same points — and W. B. Yeats (to whom you allude) in person, came to me practically simultaneously.

I am under great pressure, with my art-work etc., and just before going to Paris and elsewhere in France for two or three weeks — whither I hope to get on Friday. Besides, I have just finished a new book, "*Silence Farm*," which I think is in every way the best thing I have ever done in fiction. One of the chief "readers" in London has just reported on it in a way that has deeply gratified me — speaking of it as one of the most powerful & moving studies he has ever read.

It will (I hope) be out this summer — if so, probably abt end of May: but I don't know for certain yet. It *may* have to wait till autumn on account of the American edn.

I'm not sure when Miss Macleod's "Dominion of Dreams" is to be out. I understood the first week in May — but today she writes simply that final revises etc. are now off her hands. When she first set aside her historical romance to give herself up to this book, I thought she made a mistake. But I do not now think so. I see that it was inevitable. She was right in her instinct that she had to go to her own frontiers before she could step into a new realm. Her new book is the logical outcome of the others: the deeper note, the vox humana, of these.[30] I think it is more than merely likely that *this* is the last book of its kind. "I have had to live my books — and so must follow an inward Law" — that is truth to art as well as to life I think. There is, however, a miscellaneous volume (of "appreciations," and mystical studies) — and then a poetic vol. which I suppose shd be classed with it. I imagine that, thereafter, her development will be on unexpected lines, both in fiction & the drama: judging both from what I know and what I have seen. In every sense I think you are right when you speak of "surprise" as an element in what we may expect from her.

I am glad to hear you are to be married in August. I suppose it would occur to you to try for the new *Morning Herald*?

When I come back — i.e. any time after May 20th or so — I'll be glad to look at your work as you suggest.

Yes, simplicity — severity even is best — but *not* without flexibility, & that can only be got by a fusion of Saxon, English, Latin-English, & all other English, into the one fine instrument of — English.

I hope that you may be able to do something for Miss M's book in the H/News. I'll send you her address.

Sincerely Yours/William Sharp

P. S. Yeats has left me a copy of the *Dublin Express*, and George Russell has sent me one with his article, so I send you one of them with pleasure, as you say you regret having missed it. I don't want it back of course. Have not yet had time to read, but Yeats very pleased. I see there is a para about Miss M in it.

P.S. I suppose some of that confounded controversy about Miss M. & myself will [begin] again — this I hope the Chronicle will not have the bad taste to start as it did Etc.[31]

ALS National Library of Scotland

To Grant Richards, [April 25, 1899]

30 Greencroft Gardens | South Hampstead

My dear Richards

I realise there is a good deal of general truth in what you say — as, I am sure, absolute truth from *your* standpoint: and, believe me, I shall very regretfully publish this book elsewhere, if need be. I have important work on hand (& I believe work likely to appeal widely) & would like to keep it in one publisher's hands if possible — and as I know and trust you as a publisher as well as know & like you as a friend. I am reluctant to go elsewhere for a temporary advantage.

If, therefore, I am willing to accept your point of view financially, so far — perhaps you can meet me. If you can bring it out this season — & this could surely be managed quite well (& this is, I admit, to me a matter of signal importance), I am willing to accept a less royalty — namely 15% instead of 20% — up to first edn. — and an advance of (instead of £100) £50.

I think you will admit that, as I am obviously waiving immediate advantage to myself — though of course I believe to our mutual benefit later, & in several ways — I am showing both my confidence in you & in this book — & my willingness to do as I said when I gave you "Wives in Exile", that I wd. do my utmost to "keep with you".

If, as I hope, we can now meet on ground fair to each, please wire to me *as early in the forenoon* as you can.

Believe me | Cordially Yours | William Sharp

Far from objecting, I wd. very much prefer to see it come out at 3/6 instead of 6/-

ALS Stanford University

To Grant Richards, April 27, 1899

30 Greencroft Gardens | South Hampstead | 27:April:99

My dear Richards

I have been far too "rushed" with the R. A.[32] and much other pressing work either to get off to Paris today or to make other arrangements about "Silence Farm". I have, besides, carefully considered your letter from every point of view, present and prospective, & have come to the conclusion that it's a square enough arrangement as things are — tho' I don't think "Wives in Exile" was a fair test, for several reasons. Again, it seems to me of imperative importance, partly for the reasons already explained, to get the book out this season, and as early as practicable — and I am willing to this end to forfeit the greater immediate advantage elsewhere open to me.

I have, therefore, decided to accept your offer as indicated in your telegram: namely, an advance of £25. I think a fair royalty arrangement would be 15% up to an edition of 1000 — & thereafter, if a successful sale calls for more, at 20%.

So I return the MS. for you to put in hand at once. I hope you will make every effort to have the book struck off as swiftly as practicable:

I on my part will pass the proofs at once, & probably with no other corrigenda than printer's errors: & I hope that it may be publishable by the end of May. A relatively short typed & corrected "copy" such as this should be easily and swiftly printed.

As I have shown my friendly goodwill throughout, I daresay you will be able to oblige me by letting me have the £25 advance on signature of the contract — as that, owing to an unforeseen emergency, would be a very great convenience to me.

As if at all possible I want to get away either tonight or tomorrow morning will you very kindly send me agreement by return.

I shall be in France till the 15th of May at any rate: and shall send you my address or addresses, for proofs.

I was very pleased to hear that you thought so highly of *Silence Farm*. One well-known "reader" who saw it at my house, & begged the loan of it for a night, wrote to me that it was "a very long time indeed since I have read anything so fine, so powerful, so moving. It is the best thing you have done. It will certainly gain wide recognition."

By the way, please have as simple a cover as practicable. Personally, I like smooth dark-red or brown buckram.

In haste, | Sincerely yours, | William Sharp

P.S. Telegram just come from one of the big London dailies, & I may have to go to Paris early this evening. So please, if you can manage it, send up Contract etc. by P.O. Messenger-Boy, with instructions that he will be paid here.

ALS State University of New York at Buffalo

To Grant Richards, [April 28, 1899]

30 Greencroft Gardens | South Hampstead

My dear Richards

I think it is better to have the usual contract, & with the same clause in it as in *"Wives in Exile"* contract (which please consult) as to 7 years duration — a condition I invariably adhere to with everything I publish.

I cannot now get away to Paris till Sunday night or Monday morning.[33]

As I wrote last night, I am obliged to you for your ready courtesy about the cheque: and am sincerely glad that you are to be the publisher of *Silence Farm*: and am also very glad at the expedition you promise.

Unless you hear to the contrary, my address in Paris from Monday evg till the 15th anyway will be

Poste Restante | Bureaux des Posts: Palais du Luxembourg | Rue de Vangirard | Paris

(a district office contiguous to where I shall stay).

I don't know if it will commend itself to you — but I much like the enclosed as a binding.

I am hopeful that unfortunate *Fumeurs d'Opium* may still be traced — the more so as the book is not easy to get now, as it is *épuisé*.[34] Mrs. Wingate Rinder is naturally put out about it, as the translation too is stopped.

Yours Sincerely | William Sharp

ALS State University of New York at Buffalo

To Grant Richards, April [29], 1899

My dear Richards

I think I forgot to enclose the sample binding I alluded to last night. I enclose both — the red being that which I prefer.

This, of course, is only suggestion. You know best — & will I am sure bring out the book at once as severely simply & with as much chic as practicable.

Yours in haste | W. S.

ALS Private

To Edith Lyttelton,[35] [*early May, 1899*]

C/o. Miss Rea. | The Columbia Literary Agency |
9 Mill Street. Conduit Street. | London. W.

My dear Miss Lyttelton,

I am sure that you will not have attributed my delay in reply to your letter of the 6th either to indifference or discourtesy. But partly because it was addressed (not through Mr. Yeats surely? unless he was very forgetful) to an old address, involving roundabout reforwarding, and partly because I have just come to Midlothian from the West, I have only today received it.

If you have had a real and deep pleasure from my writings, or from some things I have written, I also have had some of my rarest pleasure from letters such as yours. Yours itself I have read with genuine pleasure. I get a great many letters from England and Ireland, and many from America, but few of them "come home" to me. But every now and again I find myself in close rapport with some unknown friend, whom all at once I seem to know. And now, dear Miss Lyttelton, comes your own generous and to me welcome letter.

I am glad you know and love the Highlands: and I am glad to think that I have helped you to a fuller and deeper understanding. You, I feel, are of the few who discern that I am not the less a realist because I strive to interpret the Gaelic spirit and nature and inmost mind, rather [than] their familiar and often wholly misleading outward expression, or than the outward ordinary life. To every man, his woman of women; to every woman, her man of men; and to every soul its own flight. So, too, should it be with the creative artist. There is one way: his or hers: and he or she should go that way and no other. Thus it is that I pay no heed to those who would have me be other than I am.

I do not suppose that I can ever have a wide audience, and quite frankly I am indifferent. I am content to do what I can, in my own way, and to leave the rest to other discretionary powers and influences. If, soon or late, my work should appeal to the many, so much the more fortunate for me, or, rather, for those influences in life and art by which I take my stand. If not, I know I shall not any the more have missed my goal. Success in literature is measurable by depth, not by extension. It is perhaps because of outer accident as well as my temperament that I think so very little of, care so next to nothing about, what is commonly called success. Yet I would not have you interpret this as arrogance or affectation. Every writer must be sincerely glad to win appreciation, and must regret apparent failure. But I simply *cannot* care much. All my thought and care is in my work: in the life of thought and dream, emotion and passion: in the ceaseless revelation of the human heart, nature, and that little infinite flame in each of us that we call the spiritual life. In the deepest sense of the words I have *lived* my books. In the truest sense they are profoundly realistic. There is, I need hardly say to *you*, a realism of the imagination, of the spirit, as well as of material vision.

Many, because of the reputation I have fortunate enough to win, such as it is, will read my shortly forthcoming book, "The Dominion of Dreams", (which I venture to hope *you* will read, when published 2 or three weeks hence by Archd Constable & Co.): but how few will care much for it, how fewer still will really understand it, or the most intimate part of it.[36]

Yet, in a sense, if I may say so, it is a profoundly revelative book.[37] Well, if it gains wide and sincere appreciation, I shall be glad: if it should practically be ignored I shall be sorry: but, beyond that, I am indifferent. I know what I have tried to do: I know what I have done: I know the end to which I work: I believe in the sowers who will sow and the reapers who will reap, from some seed of the spirit in this book: and knowing this, I have little heed of other considerations. Beauty, in itself, is my dream: and in some expression of it, in the difficult and subtle art of words, I have a passionate absorption.

I would like to know a little more of you, though more than likely we may never meet. Will you tell me? (Are you Miss or Mrs?) But just as you like, of course. I ask, partly because of yourself as revealed in your letter: partly because of a keen personal association unwittingly awakened. But it does not matter. I am content that you are a friend, that you bear a name dear to me, and that you have been generous enough to write whole heartedly to a stranger.

You live in London, and know Mr. Yeats. Do you know his, and my friend and kinsman, Mr. William Sharp? As doubtless you have seen in the papers — for the controversy about myself seems as recurrent as the sea-serpent — he is often supposed to be me, or I to be him, or both of us to be each other, with many other speculative variations! I would like you to meet.

And now I must apologise for so long a letter. I am constantly reproached for being so bad a correspondent, and for brevity and taciturnity when I *do* write — and lo this "screed" to an unknown friend! But perhaps, dear Miss Lyttelton, you will forgive it, since it is from your *caraid dileas*,

Fiona Macleod

ALS Churchill Archive Center, Churchill College, Cambridge

To Archibald Constable and Co., May 13, 1899

Dear Sirs,[38]

I am much annoyed at this continued identification of myself with this or that man or woman of letters — in one or two instances with people whom I have never seen and do not even know by correspondence. For what seem o myself not only good, but imperative private reasons, I wish to preserve absolutely my privacy. It is not only that temperamentally I shrink from and dislike the publicity of reputation, but that my very writing depends upon this privacy.

But in one respect, to satisfy those who will not be content to take or leave, to read or ignore my writings, I give you authority to say definitely that "Fiona Macleod" is not any of those with whom she has been "identified"; that she writes only under the name Fiona Macleod; that her name is her own; and that all she asks is the courtesy both of good breeding and common sense — a courtesy which is the right of all, and surely imperatively of a woman acting by and for herself.

Believe me sincerely your, | Fiona Macleod

Printed Letter, The Athenaeum, 3733 (May, 1899), 596

To William Butler Yeats, [mid-May, 1899][39]

... pieces are less "personal."

I read to the Macgregors, from Miss Macleod's proofs, "The Woman with the Net," "Dalua," "Book of the Opal". They were deeply impressed they said, and I saw.

I hope very much too that you will be able to write authoritatively about it. We lay more stress on a sympathetic appreciation from you than from any other of course.[40]

Would not Traill let you write a special article?[41]

I send you a cutting which has been circulated throughout the literary Press & chief papers. If you remember, let me have it again.

I think this wise: do you not?

(I think some of the best of F. M. will be found in this book. Few can guess how personal much of it is. You almost alone will read "The Distant Country," for example, with "other eyes".

I think, too, that both in style & thought [& imaginative treatment of imaginative thought][42] the other unpublished book, "The Reddening of the West"[43] — which Miss Macleod intends to dedicate to you — & which will likely be publd... .[44]

From every point of view we are very eager about the plays.

Two will be finished before this summerend — and also if possible the most purely dramatic, "The Tarrist". "Dahut the Red" may only be for book form.

I have been away, as you know, with my friend. It has been an eventful time. Life presses. New and vivid developments await.

Sometime I want you to read something that Miss M. wished kept back from "The Dominion of Dreams." It is called "The Second Mystery of the Incarnation" — and is in great part an actual record of that mysterious union of which I have spoken to you. It will probably be incorporated in the chief section of "The Reddening of the West":

(It preceded "The Distant Country")[45]

I am more glad than I[46]

AL Private

To Grant Richards, [May 23, 1899][47]

Tuesday night

My dear Richards

I am very pleased indeed with the get-up of the book: the binding, the print, the paper, are just what I would choose. It seems to me a very fine "turn-out" for a 3/6 volume. It is a great pleasure to me the way you turn out most of your books: and I am particularly glad "Silence Farm" is just as I would wish it.

I am sorry about the postponement — the season is already so far advanced. But you know best as to what is advisable — & so of course I have no more to say.

Can you let me have my other author's copies soon — three in particular I want for America: the others I wd. hold over till publishing-date.

You say I am sending advance copies to *Daily Chronicle* and *Literature* — but why advance to these two in particular? In any case, would it not be very risky to send copies so much in advance? Would not others object? I sh^d think it well to send at once to the weeklies (*Literature, Academy*, etc., etc., *Sketch*, etc..) — but not to the D/C unless also to the other dailies.

To your provincial list add the *Liverpool Courier*, please: also *Nottingham Guardian*. It would also be well to send advance copies to the following (who will all do what they can):

1. Richard *Whiteing* Esq.

2. Chas. G. D. *Roberts*, 8 Templeton Place, Earl's Court (who is to do a special article)

3. John *Macleay* Esq., 194 Grove Street, Liverpool

4. Coulson Kernahan Esq.

5. Richard *Le Gallienne* Esq., Waggoner's Wells, Haslemere

6. Lionel Johnson Esq., 8 New Square, Lincoln's Inn

7. Ernest Rhys Esq., Hunt Cottage, The Vale, Hampstead N.W.

Let me know if you have sent or will send to these, please. If I remember any others, or hear to that effect, I'll let you know.

In haste, | Cordially yours, | William Sharp

We'll meet at the Omar meeting, I hope.[48]

P.S. I forgot to ask you to be sure to add to your list The *Daily Express, Dublin* and to the other list to add

7. Geo. Russell Esq. 28 Upper Mount Pleasant Avenue, Ranelagh, Dublin

and

8. W. B. Yeats Esq. | c/o Lady Gregory, Coole Park, Gort, Co. Galway, and

9. to Mr. Henry D. Davray,[49] 33 Avenue D'Orleans, Paris, who will write about it in 2 places. Please let me have list of those you send to.

ALS Pierpont Morgan Library

To Frank Rinder, [late May, 1899]

My Dear Frank,

Today I got three or four copies of *The Dominion of Dreams*. I wish you to have one, for this book is at once the deepest and most intimate that F. M. has written.

Too much of it is born out of incurable heartache, "the nostalgia for impossible things".... My hope is that the issues of life have been woven to beauty, for its own sake, and in divers ways to reach and help or enrich other lives.... "The Wells of Peace" must, I think, appeal to many tired souls, spiritually athirst. That is a clue to the whole book — or all but the more impersonal part of it, such as the four opening stories and "The Herdsman"; this is at once my solace, my hope and my ideal. If ever a book (in the deeper portion of it) came out of the depths of a life it is this: and so, I suppose it shall live — for by a mysterious law, only the work of suffering, or great joy, survives, and that in degree to its intensity... .

F. M.'s influence is now steadily deepening and, thank God, along the lines I have hoped and dreamed... . In the writings to come I hope a deeper and richer and truer note of inward joy and spiritual hope will be the living influence. In one of the stories in this book, "The Distant Country", occurs a sentence that is to be inscribed on my gravestone when my time comes.

"Love is more great than we conceive and Death is the keeper of unknown redemptions."

Lovingly, | Will[50]

Memoir, p. 306

To George Russell (AE), [late May, 1899]

30 Greencroft Gardens | South Hampstead | London

My dear George Russell

Today or tomorrow you shd. receive from Miss Macleod & myself (per the publishers) a copy of *"The Dominion of Dreams."* I hope you will find some living beauty in it. It comes from deeper depths of life, both of suffering & spiritual exaltation, than any other of F. M.'s books — particularly the second section of *Ulad*.

It is sent as a gift of friendship & camaraderie; but at the same time I may frankly say that if you can write anything about it I shall be glad — because it is *you*.

My greetings to you & your wife.

W. S.

If by chance Yeats's copy comes to your care, please post it c/o Lady Gregory

ALS Indiana University, Lilly Library

To Benjamin Burgess Moore, May 29, 1899

c/o Miss Rea | The Columbia Literary Agency |
9 Mill Street Conduit St. | London E. C.

Dear Mr. Moore

I know I am in your debt — but you must forgive me.

I have had a good deal of illness, and been abroad, and have been hopelessly preoccupied with work and correspondence since leisure has been approximately mine again. But I bear you ever in friendly remembrance — one of my sincerest friends oversea I know.

Yes — I have been much annoyed at all these personal and often impertinently obtrusive remarks etc about myself. But I think that is all over now — with the result that my privacy will be safeguarded and let useless speculations cease.

Do write to me about my new book, *The Dominion of Dreams*, which I have asked the publishers to send to you. It was published two days ago. It is my deepest, most intimate book.

If, too, you can help it at all, I know you will (though I do not send it for that, but simply as a friend).

Always yours sincerely | Fiona Macleod

29th May 1899

ALS Huntington Library

To Coulson Kernahan, [May, 29, 1899]

30 Greencroft Gardens | South Hampstead

My dear Kernahan

Miss Macleod asked me for your address, as I had told her you wd probably be able to say a good word for her new book, "The Dominion of Dreams," and as in any case she wished you to have it. But I have been in France, and am just back, & my lost letters are coming in upon me many days late!

However I hear that she gave your name to Constables, & that a copy was sent to you. I am sure you will do what you can.

My own new book, *Silence Farm* (a tragic romance), is to be issued by Grant Richards tomorrow fortnight (June 13th).[51]

You, of course, are very busy too — and your dear wife. Our love to you both.

Ever yours, | William Sharp

ALS Princeton University

To Edith Lyttelton, May 29, 1899

C/o. Miss Rea | The Columbia Literary Agency | 9 Mill Street. Conduit Street | London | 29:May:99

My dear Mrs. Lyttelton

I am in Edinburgh for a couple of days, mainly in connection with the publication of my new book — but leave again tomorrow for Loch Fyne.

It is not to tell you about myself, however, that I look up this page to write to you. I write to say that I am so sorry to hear you have been seriously unwell, and are not yet strong: and to express a not conventional but genuine hope that you will soon be in full enjoyment of life. Do you know that any time in the Yellow Month (i.e. from the mid-May day called Yellow-May-Day — *Là buidhe Bealltainn* — till *Là Fheill-Eòin*, St. John's Day) a friend may put "green-life" into the heart of another? Well, I wish "green life" to you — that is, youth, and the living spirit, and inward joy. And so... get well! You will, of course, know at once how I have heard of your illness.

After your second letter I wanted you to meet Mr. William Sharp, and he would have called a month or more ago but that he had to go to France. I am glad you have met: for as I think I told you, he is my most intimate friend, as well as my kinsman. If you like him, you would like me: if you do not like him, you would not like me. There! It is a woman's argument — but perhaps none the less convincing.

So you live in an old house in Westminster and have "a swift and individual mind," and are "keenly sensitive to impressions," and "seem tuned to that finer inward suffering which goes with every nature open to mystery and to beauty." Well, I knew that, and more I have mentally reproached my friend for not being more explicit — though he says frankly "It is not only that I have no time, but that I am unable to say more. If ever I meet her alone, I will see and know what, in a first visit, in the circumstances and with others present, was of necessity fugitive or uncertain." I was glad to hear that you are going to read "The Dominion of Dreams" — and if you care for the book, or feel deeply anything in it, I hope you will tell me: for sympathy and understanding such as shown in your letters, and others akin to them, mean far more to me than the most laudatory reviews. Not that I anticipate more than a somewhat puzzled reception, even at best, for this book: much of it can of necessity appeal only to the few.

We may never meet, but we can always be friends: and in token of that indefinable but real comradeship that means so much I send for your acceptance one of a little private edition of ten copies, made up of a certain intimate section of "The Dominion of Dreams," but here entitled anew "The Kingdom of Silence." All of us who suffer — whether fully known, or in the shadows of insight, of foreknowledge — know how not only we must live, but must alone find symbolic or disguised expression, in this domain of silence.

But I must be wearying you. Forgive so long a letter, and believe me, your unknown and yet not unknown friend

Fiona Macleod

ALS Churchill Archive Center, Churchill College, Cambridge

To William Butler Yeats, [May 29?, 1899][52]

Monday

My dear Yeats

I have read and carefully considered the rite — but I think it calls for something more definite in visionary insight and significance — for spiritual recasting, so to say. And as you well know, all work of this kind — as all imaginative work — is truly alive only when it has died into the mind and been born again. The mystery of dissolution is the common mean of growth. Resurrection is the test of any spiritual idea — as of the spiritual life itself, of art, and of any final expression of the inward life.

I cannot say when this rebirth will be: but when it comes I will write to you, if the result seems to me to be of any worth, any significance: as I hope it will be. The sole stream of inward thought that can help is moving that way.

I have been ill — and seriously — but am now better, though I have to be careful still. All our plans for Scandinavia in the autumn are now over — partly for the now impracticable expense, partly by doctor's order, who says I must have hill & sea air native to me — Scotland or Ireland.

So about the end of July my wife and I intend to go to Ireland. It will probably be to the east coast, Mourne Mountains coast, as we must live cheaply & simply. Will you be eastward at all? Surely Tara-land, Ulidia, must have strong appeal to you?[53] I would be glad go west of course, but we cannot afford it, as it would involve going about & living in hotels. We think of Kilkeel or Annalong or Newcastle.[54]

I hope you like "The Dominion of Dreams." Miss Macleod has received two or three very strange & moving letters from strangers, as well as others. The book of course can appeal to few, — that is, much of it. But, I hope, it will sink deep.

If you are at any time announcing, or speaking of the play by Miss Macleod for acting next year, do not now speak of it as "The Tarrist". Either that name will be relinquished, or used later for another play. Of *course if thought advisable* it can be retained — for the acting play — but in its literary & published form it will be called "The King of Ireland's Son."[55] You will be interested to hear, if Miss Macleod has not already told you, that this play will be finished soon, relatively. I think it will not disappoint you.

Are you to be at Gort (or Tillyra) in August?[56] I hope you are happily at work. What are you doing? I envy you in the West. My heart is always there. And you are amid green and beautiful things. There is no nostalgia like that of the green way.

Yours | W. S.

My most cordial remembrances & regards to Lady Gregory. London is prostratingly hot. You are well out of it.

ALS Yale University, Letters to Yeats,I. pp. 54-55

To John Macleay, May 31, 1899

c/o Miss Lilian Rea | The Columbia Literary Agency |
9 Mill Street. Conduit St. | London

Dear Mr. Macleay

I am indebted to Mr. Sharp for your new address — and I asked Messrs. Constable to send you a copy of my new book. I greatly hope that you, one of my earliest and staunchest friends across the pen will care for "The Dominion of Dreams." To me it stands for my best work, as it is certainly the deepest and most mature: though I can well understand how its appeal must be limited.

After all, I doubt if I really care for any work save that which tells imaginatively of

[page or pages missing here]

Jacobite romance (which will in movement, and, in a sense, in style, recall the Pagan and Scandinavian tales in "The Washer of the Ford" or "The Sad Queen" in the present volume — and to my mind my strongest work is here; though not necessarily my deepest or most intimate) — a book of "spiritual studies" of the Gael, a book after my own heart — and a volume of poems and with them two prose plays. I have also a play of a necessarily rougher mould, for the stage.

If you like "The Dominion of Dreams" I hope you will tell me so.

(Write to me as above: I am at present on Argyll.)

You yourself are busy, of course. I look for your work. I may be wrong, but I *think* Mr. Sharp told me you are about to be married.

If so, my sincere good wishes!

Yours most truly | Fiona Macleod

ALS National Library of Scotland

To Grant Richards, early June, 1899

My dear Richards

On my return I find that I stupidly omitted two names of reviewing friends who will do their best for "S/F," namely

(1) J. Stanley Little Esq | 18 Drakefield Road | Balham | SW

(2) Percy White Esq | 22 Holland St. | Kensington W.

I suppose you are now sending out review copies? Please send above with them.

I hope the book will do well. Our friend Janvier writes me that he has rarely been more moved and more profoundly interested by any book — & says other things which, coming from so exacting a critic, greatly please me.

What a lovely little book you have made of Mr. Lucas' "The Open Road."[57] I will say what I can for it. I am sending a copy to Miss Macleod, who has long meditated a little anthology of lovely and rare things in prose & verse — purely by personal choice of selection — to be called (I believe) "The Hour of beauty." This lovely little book should be a further spur to her intent.

The few who have seen "Silence Farm" concur with me in liking greatly its get up.

Ever yours | William Sharp

ALS State University of New York at Buffalo

To Coulson Kernahan, [June 5, 1899]⁵⁸

30 Greencroft Gardens | South Hampstead

My dear Kernahan

Today or in a day or so Grant Richards should send you a copy of my new book, "*Silence Farm*" — which I hope you will like, and which I (to say nothing of G. R. and his readers) — think the best thing I have done.

If you can say anything about it anywhere, I sh^d be grateful — but in any case I want so good a friend as yourself to have this book from me.

I am now back from France — where I was very ill (2 doctors etc.) — and though better have to be careful).

I hope you two are both well, and happily at work.

We are soon going to leave our flat, and for good: I doubt if we'll ever live in town again. First we go to Ireland for two months.

Shall you be at the Omar dinner? I hope so.

With affectionate greetings to you both | Cordially yours, | William Sharp

ALS Princeton University

To William Butler Yeats, [June 5?, 1899]

30 Greencroft Gardens | South Hampstead | London

My dear Yeats

Serious illness (in France I had to have a doctor) has still left me so down, mentally & bodily, that I find myself unable to do anything just now involving deep concentration & spiritual intensity. Therefore the rite waits. But I feel something moving within me. (I do not think what you sent can stand, i.e. can do more than spiritually indicate a direction. I'll explain later.)

I am very eager to hear what you think of "The Dominion of Dreams." If ever a book was born out of spiritual stress & suffering, out of the *depths*, this book was: as I think Miss Macleod herself has written to you.

Shall you be writing about it anywhere?[59]

It is probable that after "The King of Ireland's Son," Miss M's next play will be a short modern play of a deep & moving human interest, called "Dark Rosaleen" (meaning Ireland mainly).[60]

Today or in a day or so Grant Richards should send you a copy of a new book by myself "Silence Farm". I think you will find it the best & most satisfying thing that has appeared under my name (G. R. & his reader seem to have a very high opinion, & very high hopes of it, indeed.) If, perchance, you sh^d be able to say anything about it anywhere I should be grateful. But this is just as you can, & feel inclined. In any case I want you to have the book. I would send you an advance copy with my inscription — but I find that the last of the very few I have has my inscription to Lady Gregory — but G. R. will have had my instructions by this. I'm sending Lady Gregory's to her.

We leave our flat about 20th July. Shall you be in town before then?[61]

Then we go to Ireland but I don't know where yet, [Possibly Lady Gregory or Martyn may ask us west. Otherwise we'll go straight to the][62] probably to the Mourne Mountains coast.[63]

I doubt if I'll ever live in London again. It is not likely. I do not know that I am overwhelmingly anxious to live anywhere. I think you know enough of me to know how profoundly I feel the strain of life — the strain of double life.[64] Still, there is much to be done yet. But for that… .

Your friend | William Sharp

ALS Yale University, Letters to Yeats I, pp. 51–52

To George Russell (AE), [June 5?, 1899][65]

30 Greencroft Gardens | South Hampstead | London | N.W.

My dear Russell

I know you will be glad to hear that Miss Macleod's book has made a far deeper and more moving impression on at least a few than any other of her writings. It is not to be expected that a book such as this — coming deep out of a life — could be of wide or at any rate of immediately wide appeal: but it will, I hope, help to mould the minds and spiritual temper of many. Already a response has come, and from strangers as well as those in a sense known. The book seems to have not only moved profoundly, but to have revealed much — and that is perhaps one of the ultimate tests.

But if out of much spiritual suffering and joy, and a too great pressure of sorrow and that "unknown grief," the nostalgia for impossible things, this book has been woven, it is easily understandable, at least *you* will understand, that a great and ultra-sensitive weariness may follow. Oftenest the soul best finds refreshment by following its own guidance to the secret Fountain of Youth: sometimes it is through the dreams and visions of others: sometimes through the gates of personal joy, or, oftener, of sorrow and anguish: but sometimes only through the sympathy and comradely help of others of close spiritual kindred. I think it is so with Miss Macleod just now — and *you* are of the few to whom she turns. When you have time, I hope you will write to her about "The Dominion of Dreams." Neither she for herself, nor I for her, would ask this, were there not times when one should not let even just scruples of consideration make one refrain from asking for spiritual help or word of helpful greeting. If some day, when a little of your rare leisure permits, you write to her, do so | c/o Miss Rea | The Columbia Literary Agency

| 9 Mill St. | Conduit St | London W. | which is now her sole address for correspondence.

I hope the book I saw announced sometime ago is soon to be out — that of your and Yeats's reprinted essays. I look for it eagerly. I think our little band is already exercising a deep and far-reaching influence: and that this will steadfastly deepen and widen. I often think of you, & what you are doing — & often keep in touch by a glance into something you have written. Yes: as you wrote once: we go to the same goal, and are never far apart.

My wife and I (I have been seriously unwell, & need rest & sea-air & hill-air of a native kind) give up our flat in London towards the end of July — I mean give it up for good — (& personally I never wish to live in London again, where a terrible devitalisation in all ways forever was) — and to come to Ireland for August & Septr., probably crossing before the end of July. We intend going to the east coast (Mourne Mountains), as we must live cheaply as well as simply: probably to Kilkeel, or Annalong, or Newcastle. If so, I hope greatly we may see you & your wife. Perhaps she does not remember me — but I well remember her. I hope you are both very happy in a true comradeship.

The heat here is very great — prostratively — & so more than ever I long for the unimprisoned life. As I wrote to Yeats recently — there is no nostalgia like that of the green way.

Ever your friend | William Sharp

ALS Indiana University, Lilly Library

To J. Stanley Little, [June 8, 1899]

Thursday

My dear Stanley

I have asked Grant Richards to send you a copy of my new book, *Silence Farm*, which I think the best thing I have done (as others do). Advance copies are to go out this week, and the book nominally to be publd? on Tuesday next.

If you can say a good word for it I shall be grateful: but that is as you find convenient. In any case I want you to have the book from me, in old friendship.

I was very ill recently in France (2 doctors etc.) but am now better tho' I have still to be careful.

We leave our flat for good about mid July.

I hope you are both well — and that things prosper.

Ever yours, | Will

ALS Princeton University

To John Macleay, June 8, [1899][66]

c/o Miss Rea | The Columbia Literary Agency | 9 Mill Street | Conduit St. | London

Dear Mr. Macleay

Thanks for your friendly letter. Yes, I *do* wish you could obtain the control of the "Highland News." Much could be done with that paper.

I daresay there is much truth in what you say — but each of us must seek according to the light that is in us for guidance. Yet on the face of it, there must surely be more likelihood of spiritual beauty where life is attuned to the great natural influences and where simple natures have more depth and scope. There is moral and spiritual beauty in the slums — but not the same degree, I suppose: at any rate, we have overmuch literature pointing out all this in slum-life and the like — a little pharisaically it seems to me.

But I don't "go to the isles" for beauty. The isles — the past — the pagan wonder and mystery — *come to me*! It is what a writer *receives* that makes him or her. All art is from within. It is from what dies into one, and is reborn.

Each to his kind. My cordial good wishes for your wedded life.

In haste | Sincerely yours | Fiona Macleod

ALS National Library of Scotland

To Grant Richards, [*June 9, 1899*]

Friday night

My dear Richards

A hurried line to say that I know Miss Macleod has not (unless quite recently which is wholly unlikely) arranged about "The Hour of Beauty" — as she knew that besides Constables etc. Lane for one would be glad to have it. So the best plan would be for you to write direct — to say what your own preferences are — and to make what proposal you see your way to. Miss M. is at present on Lochfyneside in Argyle — but it is quicker (as well as her invariable rule now) for all save private correspondence to go to her per her London typist and agent

c/o Miss Rea | The Columbia Literary Agency, |
9 Mill St. | Conduit St. | W.

You can (and in circumstances should) of course state that you have heard of this anthology through me. She consulted me sometime ago as to whether to make it entirely from contemporary (i.e. Victorian) literature, including Maeterlinck etc. — or to make it a gleaming at random from all periods of English literature — indeed from all or any source (the Greek anthology — the old Celtic writers — etc. — or to make it purely from Celtic and Anglo-Celtic sources, old and modern. From actual choice she prefers the last.

It would be simplest for you to say what you think best. (I *think* I suggested that she sh^d act on a hint thrown out that Macmillans would like something of the kind from her for the G. Treasury series.) But I am certain she has done nothing since — and indeed is working at her play just now.

I will write to her also, following my dispatch of "The Open Road" — which I know will fascinate her if she thinks she might have a book done like it —

In haste, Yours Ever | W. S.

ALS Yale University

To William Butler Yeats, June 14, [*1899*]

c/o Miss Rea. | 2. Carlyle Square | Chelsea. | London. S.W.

14: June.

Dear Mr. Yeats

I have just come to Midlothian again from the Middle Isles. Will you be patient as to the Rite for a brief while longer?[67] My reason for asking this is that our friend W. S. will be in Scotland (to see me) at the end of next week — and that it is important he and I should talk over, rather than correspond about this.[68]

Then, too, I will write on other matters.

I have work, too, on hand about which I should like to write to you. Do you know German? ... if so, would you care to see, when it appears soon, "a 'Kritik' on Fiona Macleod," dealing largely with the mythopoeic aspects of the work and particularly with what the writer somewhat cumbrously calls in his letter "the newly conceived and newly shaped, howsoever old-world-based idea of the incorporate madness of men, of the madness that is wisdom and of the wisdom that is madness, in your 'Dalua,' the most deeply significant mythopoeic creation in our time."[69] But if you are pressed about the Rite, I could ... but no, that would be inadvisable. You will wait, now, I am sure! Lest I forget, let me add that the "Touch of the Queen" is in May. [It is also fatal on St. Bride's Day i.e. 1st February (am Fheill Bhrighde)].[70]

I cannot say at the moment, but I believe the times to beware of in May are the 1st (and its eve), and the three cold days (17th to 19th or 19th to 21st according to some).

In haste | Sincerely yours | Fiona Macleod

ALS Private

To George Russell (AE), June 17, 1899[71]

c/o. Miss Rea | The Columbia Literary Agency | 9. Mill Street. Conduit St. | London

17: June: 99.

My dear "A. E."

I thank you for your friendly and sincere letter. It has given me, will give me, subject for close thought. I am like one in an apparently clear wood which is yet a mysterious maze out of which I cannot escape, or even reach the frontiers so as to discern where I am and what vistas are beyond me: nay, even the stars themselves become confused often in the darkness of the branches, and the sun's way seems equally to lead west or east, or north or south, so that I fare often bewildered even at full noon.

Perhaps your letter — perhaps your will and thought — can help me. I hope so. I can say neither "yea" nor "nay" to the central part of your letter. But that spiritually I have been furnishing the palaces of the mind with empty shadows is, I fear, true. Well, I *hope* — and *believe*.

I have no doubt you are right in what you say about "The Book of the Opal." I think you are a little off the trail about "The Yellow Moonrock,"[72] which is the essential part of a piper-story called "The Lily Leven,"[73] before W. B. Yeats's "Hanrahan" was written (or appeared).[74] Yet it *may* be that in its later reshaping it has been influenced as you say. I will be on guard.

Will you send me your Express review?[75] Please do.

Always your friend and comrade, | Fiona Macleod

ALS Indiana University, Lilly Library

To Edith Lyttelton, June 18, 1899

C/o. Miss Rea | The Columbia Literary Agency |
9. Mill Street. Conduit St. | London.

18th June | 99

My dear new friend

In this lovely and continuous sunflood I have been too indolent — save when pricked by some unwelcome necessity — to answer letters. But in your case, it is from no forgetfulness. I have had your letter often by me: have read it thrice at least. I am genuinely glad that you like "the Dominion of Dreams" so well — that something in it has deeply appealed to you. It will interest you to hear that two or three of the important reviews which have appeared and I am agreeably surprised at the sympathetic and generous welcome given to this book — and even *The Athenaeum*,[76] usually hostile, gives it this week a most generous criticism (with a foolish objection to certain Gaelic names being anglicised — and I wonder how English readers would like "Sine MacIllcathain" or "Eoghau Mac-an-t'-Saoir" for "Jean Maclean" or "Hugh Macintyre"!) — ah, I've lost my breath, so to say! ... well, I meant to say at once that you would be interested to hear that one you like so well, "In the Shadow of the Hills," is noted as the best or one of the best. I think *The Athenaeum* says so too — and so does another just to hand, the *Daily Telegraph* (Mr. Courtney), of which I send you a copy as it has come to me in duplicate.

And now enough about my book.

I am very very glad that you can feel to me as to a friend. I hope you will write when so ever you will. I shall always be glad to hear from you.

Indeed, I feel that we *are* friends. There are things — but above all there is *something* — in your letter which comes home to me intimately.

As some slight sign of this I sent you the "Kingdom of Silence," and also asked Mr. Sharp to send you from me (I thought he had an extra copy of mine, but he hadn't!) a copy of my most personal or intimate book, "From the Hills of Dream".

Do you not "write" yourself? Your letters (with their eager note, and distinctive touch) make me think you do. If so, I wish you would let me see something.

I am glad you have seen my friend again. I think you and he will become friends. It is my hope. He says you are "the Hon. Mrs. Lyttelton", and wife of one of whose family I know something.

And I am sure I would like you now as much as he does.

I do hope you are now quite strong again. If you could hear the last call of the cuckoo in the woods of Claondiri, and see the brown-sailed herring smacks coming up Loch Fyne, as I do, you would be glad to be here for a while and not in London.

I have not been very well, (life ever wears me too much), but the sunflood heals.

I hope all my work hence will have less of sorrow and regret, and more of strength and joy: not because life is so attuned for me, but because of inward growth. But ... well, one can only hope, and work.

I don't quite know yet what next of things begun, half-done, projected, to go on with. At the actual moment I am finishing a play for the Irish Literary Theatre[77] — and have begun a commissioned article for the *Fortnightly* on Contemporary Breton Poetry. But I will tire you.

Write to *me*, please!

Your friend, | Fiona Macleod

ALS Churchill Archive Center, Churchill College, Cambridge

To The Editor of The Athenaeum, [June 18, 1899][78]

Not wholly as a Personal Matter — and I would be ill to please were I not gratified with the sympathetic and generously worded review of

The Dominion of Dreams in the current *Athenaeum* — I write to say that it is perhaps a little misleading to indicate as careless Gaelic what is obviously anglicised. Surely no one with even an elementary knowledge of Gaelic could think "Sheumais" the proper spelling of "Seumas" or "muirnean" of "mhuirnein": but is it not wiser when foreign words are introduced (and I think this use should be sparing and only when inevitable or at least advisable for emphasis or subtler effect) that they should be given as nearly as possible as they are pronounced. "Seumas" would certainly be mispronounced by the English reader, but "Sheumais" is sufficiently near: in "mhuirnein" there is not only the puzzling aspirate but the (to most English readers) apparently Teutonic "nein"; whereas "muirnean" is unmistakable. It is, I think, out of place to introduce words of an unpronounceable kind: and even personal names must be anglicised (e.g. Domnhuill, Mhic Illeathain, Mac-an-t-davir — Donald, Mclean, Macintyre) or else they will be as obscure and difficult as for example would be my own name if, instead of Fiona Macleod, I signed

Yours truly, | Fionaghal nic Lèoid

ALS National Library of Scotland

To T Fisher Unwin, [June 19, 1899][79]

Rutland House | Greencroft Gardens | South Hampstead

Dear Mr. Unwin,

Will you kindly oblige me with a P/C as to when Yeats's "Complete Poems" will be out. I have to write about him before long. You are to issue the book, if I remember rightly. (You publish no other Celtic work, do you, except the Irish Library?)

Yrs very truly | William Sharp

ACS New York Public Library, Berg Collection

To Grant Richards, June 22, 1899

C/o. Miss Rea. | The Columbia Literary Agency |
9. Mill St. Conduit St. | London

22nd June /99

My dear Sir

Your letter reached me just as I am leaving the west for a short time in Edinburgh.[80] Yes, it is true I have projected a little anthology which I propose to call "The Hour of Beauty." The idea is a severely chosen and severely limited selection of short prose and verse pieces which (1) come up to a high and rare standard of beauty and distinction (2) scrupulously to make my own personal delight and conviction the means of choice, thus, too, giving a greater unity and avoiding all conventionality in selection — and (3) that "The Hour of Beauty" should be a truly indicative title. I, too, on the whole prefer that this "Hour" should not be limited to any one period, country, or literature.

No, I have not yet made any arrangement elsewhere, though I had intended it should go either to Messrs. Constable, John Lane, or Macmillans. It would, however, certainly weigh with me greatly if "The Hour of Beauty" were to come out in the same *format* as the beautiful little book you have just published, with its lovely end-papers.[81] Therefore, I certainly hold myself free to consider any offer you have to make to me. I have, unfortunately, to be biased by other considerations than those of personal preference — but, I admit, "The Open Road" invites me to any proposal of yours. I take it, of course, that the possible coincidence of a few pieces (*probably* only a few, but I cannot tell yet) being also in Mr. Lucas' anthology does not matter.

I have thought of a possible periodic division (dawn, noon, dusk, etc.) but doubt if advisable.

The above is my sole letter-address now, so kindly address to me there.

Believe me | Yours very truly | Fiona Macleod

Grant Richards. Esq.

ALS Stanford University

To Grant Richards [*June 26, 1899*]

South Bantaskine | Falkirk

My dear Grant Richards

Your letter has been forwarded to me as I am en route.[82] When I return to Edinburgh within a week I'll answer it. (Meanwhile let me say that I rec'd Statement of a/c/ & in same slip, without any other note, request for payment, which naturally I took for a request for Balance)

In haste | Yrs very truly | William Sharp

ALS State University of New York at Buffalo

To Ernest Rhys, June 29, 1899[83]

Thursday Night | 29th June 1899

My dear Mr. Rhys

Your letter gave me great pleasure in several ways — first, because you are one of those I most want to hear from: next, because you tell me your wife is going to write to me, at which I am glad, for I am deeply interested in her fine work, and in the strong and controlled personality underlying it.[84] A letter from her will be very welcome indeed. I like to think of you two, and the blending of the Cymric and Gaelic flame into one fine Celtic spirit. You may have much to contend with, but you are both such true artists and do such beautiful work, and are together and work together, that I think life must mean gladness for you both. I am sure your wife has both the need and the power to express herself: and I await her new work, as yours, with keen anticipation. It is very good of you to say you will write to me more fully and soon. I look to it; so do not disappoint me. I much wish to hear from you as to certain things in and problems involved in this book, if possible. To my great and genuine surprise, the "Dominion of Dreams" has been so much sought for that it is already in a second edition — though that does not mean very much, perhaps, as the first edition did not exceed 2000 copies, if that [(possibly only 1,000, alas!).][85]

Perhaps the many influential reviews have brought this unexpected result about. As I know you are so genuinely interested in what I am doing and trying to do, and as you may be far from all papers, I send you an advt. cutting from last week's *Spectator* and also one from yesterday's (no, Wednesday's) *London Daily Chronicle*. For certain reasons, I had expected either to be ignored or unpleasantly treated in the latter: so am very glad. Will you kindly, however, return both these when you (or your wife) write. What a charming address! I wish I could suddenly look in at Carrig Cennen.

Believe me, dear Mr. and Mrs. Rhys,

Most sincerely yours, | Fiona Macleod

ALS National Library of Scotland

To F. E. Green, *[June 30?, 1899]*[86]

c/o Miss Rea | The Columbia Literary Agency, |
9. Mill Street, Conduit Street | London

Dear Mr. Green,

I thank you for your letter, which has reached me in the Highlands.

I am glad you like "The Dominion of Dreams". Some of it I knew (from your letter) would appeal to you. It is my hope that a book which has come out of the depths will be an influence to sink deep in other minds and spirits.

No, I am afraid my books are not in any sense popular; but they are reaching further, and sinking deeper, and that contents me. Of necessity, work like the second part of "The Dominion of Dreams" can appeal only to a few — and perhaps only to those whose imaginative insight is clarified by suffering.

The "Epilogue" has reached some, as well as yourself, I am glad.

I hope you will have in every way a pleasant and encouraging time in Wales.

Sincerely yours, | Fiona Macleod

Perhaps something of what you want from me as a writer will be found in the book of miscellaneous prose "The Reddening of the West," to be published probably in November.

Printed Letter, The New Age, 4/13 (January, 1909), 267

Chapter Nineteen

Life: July–December, 1899

William Sharp asked W. B. Yeats several times in May and June to review the new Fiona Macleod book of stories, *The Dominion of Dreams*. He assumed Yeats would praise the book and thereby boost its sales. On July 3, while he was in the west of Scotland, he received a letter telling him Yeats had reviewed the book negatively. The day before he received the letter, he began a letter to let Yeats know he was ready to write about the Celtic Order and to describe the plays he was writing as Fiona. He was interrupted, and when he resumed on July 3, he was so distraught he could not continue writing about the rite or the plays. Rather he quoted at length from the letter he received that morning from a friend who said he had a conversation with several "literary men" who spoke favorably about Sharp's *Silence Farm*, but then

> the talk drifted to your friend (she is your friend, is she not?) Miss Macleod's new book, and what a notable thing it is for a book of that kind to go into a second edition within three weeks of publication. So, there is a split in the Celtic Camp! I admit it amuses me. I never have believed, never can believe, in the ability of these folk to sink minor matters for a common end. I'm speaking of course of W. B. Yeats's article on Miss M. in *The Bookman*. Mr. _____ laughed & said that it was the worst snub Miss M. had received. Have you seen it? Yeats says she has enough faults to ruin any ordinary writer, and that there's not a story in her book which should not have many words struck out. As he doesn't say a word of praise or welcome about it, but only something about her surely unquestioned mythopoeic faculty — it's obvious he either doesn't find much in the book, or wants to take her down a peg or two.

Sharp had not seen the July issue of *The Bookman*, but he expected it to arrive the next day. "Meanwhile," he continued, "I can hardly credit what my friend writes."

   https://doi.org/10.11647/OBP.0196.08

I hope it is not true. It will greatly distress & dishearten Miss Macleod, who had hoped so much for a cordial & generous word from you about her maturest & most carefully wrought book: but I hope it is not true for the sake of the plays also, for if once deeply discouraged Miss M. may not touch them again for months. And still more, & far more importantly than for any individual concern, I hope it is not so — for the always bitterly opposed idea of unselfish & united action among "our scattered few" will be grievously handicapped by any suggestion that you have "gone for" or even "snubbed" Miss Macleod.

When a copy of *The Bookman* arrived the next day, Sharp found in Yeats's review two paragraphs of praise and only one expressing reservations about Fiona's overly florid style. He decided not to send the letter to Yeats, and it has surfaced only recently in a batch of Sharp's letters to John Macleay which was acquired by the National Library of Scotland. How it came into Macleay's hands is unknown, but it may have been mistakenly included among letters Elizabeth returned to Macleay after using them in the *Memoir*. Instead of sending this letter, Sharp wrote to Yeats as Fiona and asked him "to indicate the passages he took most exception to." According to Elizabeth, Yeats sent "a carefully annotated copy of the book," and "a number of the revisions that differentiate the version in the Collected Edition from the original issue are the outcome of this criticism" (*Memoir*, p. 309).

The person most likely to have decided to stir up trouble between two leading figures of the Celtic Renaissance was Sharp's publisher, Grant Richards, who knew where Sharp was staying in Scotland. He also knew Sharp would be sensitive to any criticism of Fiona's *Dominion of Dreams*, particularly any negative comments by W. B. Yeats. The letter writer's conversation with the "literary men" took place at the Saville Club in London. According to the Club's records, Richards became a member on March 24, 1899. That the men spoke positively about Sharp's *Silence Farm* is not surprising since Grant Richards published it. Nor is it surprising the men were amused by Yeats's criticism of *The Dominion if Dreams* and viewed it as a "split in the Celtic camp." Though not a correct account of Yeats's *Bookman* review, the letter indicates some in the London literary establishment, Richards among them, viewed Fiona Macleod and the Irish contingent of Celtic Revivalists with a mixture of humor and contempt.

The Sharps stored their furniture and vacated their South Hampstead flat on July 20. It was decreed, perhaps by their precarious financial situation or perhaps by their physician, "that we were to live no more in London; so we decided to make the experiment of wintering at Chorleywood," a small town immediately northwest of London, now part of greater London. After vacating their flat, the Sharps stayed briefly with Elizabeth's mother in Bayswater and then went to their "dear West Highlands, to Loch Goil, to Corrie in Arran, and to Iona" (*Memoir*, p. 311). In August they crossed to Belfast and, after a few days in the city, went north to Ballycastle on the Antrim coast. On August 26, they moved south to Newcastle in County Down, stayed there three weeks, and spent ten days in Dublin before returning to London on September 26.

Benjamin Burgess Moore, a Yale undergraduate who fell in love with Fiona, announced he was coming to England and hoped to meet her. In a July 12 letter, Fiona assured him he was one of the few for whom she would break her invariable rule, but she needed complete and prolonged rest and was about to leave Edinburgh for a two- or three-month yachting trip in the far north. She hoped Moore would instead meet her "most intimate friend, Mr. William Sharp," who "asked me to say he hoped you would call next Monday afternoon (17th) about 3 or 3.30." Moore did call on Sharp, and Fiona, in an August 11 letter, said she was glad Moore liked Sharp and continued, surprisingly, "If you had not, you would not like me! Truly: for we are not only close kindred but at one in all things." Mr. Sharp had taken a liking to his "American friend" and, she continued, hoped he would call again on his way back to America from the continent sometime in October. Did Sharp plan to tell Moore in their second meeting he was Fiona? In any case, he was leaving his South Hampstead address at the end of July and it was now decided he would be living from October first at least into November in Chorleywood, just northwest of London and reachable by train. Moore could call on him either there or at his club, the Grosvenor in New Bond Street. He was currently in Ireland, "on the north Antrim coast called Ballycastle (the neighborhood whence Deirdre and the Sons of Usna sailed for Scotland when fleeing from Concobar). Fiona had just received a letter from Sharp in which he described his "titanic swim among rough breakers on a wild coast near the Giant's Causeway, so, after all, his hated London life does not seem to have sapped his vigor!" Later she will go to Ireland to meet him. She already knew "the wild Antrim coast — and the lonely, remote, Gaelic-speaking isle of Ragherry (Rathlin) where the grandson of the great Nial the Victorious went down with all his fleet." Why Sharp wanted to portray himself to Moore as strong and vigorous is not clear, but the mentions of Gaelic mythology were clearly designed to sustain his interested in Fiona.

Having now met Moore and decided he was a sensible young man who might become a useful promoter of Fiona in America, Sharp had Fiona share some details about her work. She planned several revisions of *The Dominion of Dreams*. They were too late for the third edition, but she hoped there would be a fourth so she could insert the changes despite the publisher's opposition. She mentioned an "exceedingly good" review the book received the previous week in *The Publisher's Circular*, and a complimentary notice of the book in, of all papers, *Punch*. Then surprisingly, given the good reviews and Sharp's claims that it was the best Fiona had done, he wrote as Fiona: "I am very dissatisfied with it — and would gladly rearrange and rewrite it all from beginning to end." He was waiting for Yeats to send his specific criticisms of the book, and he may have feared the worst. During the fall, Fiona hoped to finish a volume of spiritual tales that would be called either "the Reddening of the West" or, after its chief essay, "The Divine Adventure." She would delay its publication until the spring of 1900 unless she could finish a piece about Iona. She also hoped to finish before Christmas a volume of three plays: "The King of Ireland's Sons," "The Immortal Hour," and "Queen Ganore." That volume did not materialize, but the first play, retitled "The House of Ushna," was performed in April 1900 and published in July 1900 in *The National and English Review*. The second play, "The Immortal Hour," was published in the *Fortnightly Review* in November 1900. More will be said about them in the next chapter. After sounding more like the masculine William Sharp than the modest lady of the Isles, Sharp revived her coyness in concluding: "Now after all this personal detail see that you write to me from France, or I will not forgive you, nor ever write to you again. | So, conditionally, your friend, Fiona Macleod."

In addition to the Fiona letter to Benjamin Burgess Moore, Sharp wrote several other remarkable letters in Ireland. In late August, he told his new friend, Edith Lyttelton, that Fiona sailed to Iceland but did not stay long before being blown south to the Inner Hebrides by

"a continuous polar wind which almost made sails as swift as steam."
He spent some time with her there before he left for Ireland, and she
might come to Ireland "for a week or so in Connemara, and again in
Antrim." After reading Sharp's *Silence Farm*, Edith Lyttelton had written
to ask about his other writings. Among other books Sharp mentioned
Sospiri di Roma, the lyrics he wrote and published in Italy in 1891. He
promised to give or lend Mrs. Lyttleton a copy of the rare limited edition
and described some of the circumstances of its composition. He might
tell her more in person that "he did not care to write." Was that just
another effort to land a meeting with Mrs. Lyttleton, or did he intend to
tell her about the beautiful young woman who inspired the poems when
they met and fell in love in Rome. Had he done so he would not have
identified the woman as Edith Rinder, but probably as Fiona Macleod.
He sometimes claimed the mysterious and elusive Fiona was his cousin,
and sometimes he went further, implying that they were lovers. Edith
was often conflated in his mind with Fiona, and the fictional Fiona story
was intricately interwoven with the facts of his life.

On September 12, his forty-fourth birthday, Sharp, in a reflective
mood, wrote a letter to Adelaide Elder, Elizabeth's girlhood friend, in
which he recalled that on his twenty-second birthday in 1877 she had
given him "a beautifully bound book by a poet with a strange name
and by me quite unknown — Dante Gabriel Rossetti." Had he not
received that gift, the whole course of his life would have been different.
He mentioned the book to Sir Noel Patton, a Scottish painter, a family
friend, and a friend of Rossetti who dissuaded him from "going
abroad on a career of adventure." Later, in 1881, Patton provided an
introduction which Sharp presented to Rossetti when he knocked on his
door in Cheyne Walk on the Thames Embankment and was invited to
come in for the first of many visits. That event, Sharp wrote, "completely
redirected the whole course of my life." Sharp went on to say he and
Adelaide understood how "in the complex spiritual interrelation of life,"
the "single impulse of a friend" can have "so profound a significance."
As Sharp approached his fiftieth birthday, which would be his last, his
birthdays became occasions for reflecting on his past and mustering
resolve to get on with unfinished projects.

The most interesting letter he drafted in Ireland was copied by his
sister into the Fiona handwriting, dated September 16, and mailed from

Edinburgh to W. B. Yeats. It was an extensive attempt to describe the nature of his relationship with Edith Rinder, who Yeats knew only as Fiona Macleod, and to satisfy Yeats's curiosity about her role in the Fiona Macleod writings. The letter's immediate purpose was to thank Yeats for sending her a copy of *The Dominion of Dreams* marked with his suggested revisions. Fiona said the book had "already been in great part revised by my friend" (Sharp himself) who had "in one notable instance followed [Yeats's] suggestion." Sharp as Fiona did not bother to say why he was revising a Fiona book.

Yeats had asked Fiona which of her tales she liked best, and she responded "Temperamentally, those which appeal to me most are those with the play of mysterious psychic force in them," a preference designed to appeal to Yeats's interest in spiritualism. She was sure of one thing, as was her friend Sharp:

> There is nothing in *Dominion of Dreams* or elsewhere in these writings under my name to stand beside "The Distant Country." Nothing else has made so deep and vital an impression both on men and women — and possibly it may be true what a very subtle and powerful mind has written about it, that it is the deepest and most searching utterance on the mystery of passion which has appeared in our time. It is indeed the core of *all* these writings — and will outlast them all.

This was the second time Sharp drew Yeats's attention to "The Distant Country." In mid-May, he wrote: "I think some of the best of F. M. will be found in this book. Few can guess how personal much of it is." Then, affirming the spiritualist content of the story, he said: "You almost alone will read 'The Distant Country,' for example, with 'other eyes.'" Sharp hoped Yeats would read the story as an honest though coded effort to describe how his love for Edith and hers for him quickened his imagination, enabled him to write as Fiona Macleod, and, by burning too brightly, evolved from hot flames to simmering coals. Whether or not anyone but Sharp had called "The Distant Country" "the deepest and most searching utterance on the mystery of passion which has appeared in our time," the story, as indicated in the previous chapter, is a deeply personal attempt to portray and explain the passion that underlay and defined Sharp's relationship with Edith Rinder. Concurrently, the story articulates Sharp's hope that Yeats would understand how the occult experiments they were conducting, which had paralleled and often propelled both the course of the love affair and the career of Fiona, had dangerously disturbed his mental well-being.

Yeats knew Sharp was the writer of the Fiona stories and poems, but he continued to ask if Fiona was a real person who inspired Sharp to write as Fiona, a secondary personality of Sharp's, a spiritual being inhabiting Sharp's body and using him as an amanuensis, or some combination of the three. In the September 16 Fiona letter, after drawing Yeats's attention to "The Distant Country," Sharp turned to the story's fire metaphor he had introduced to Yeats, in a letter dated June 28, 1898, and transformed it into an elaborate allegory involving the match, the torch, and a new element, the spiritual wind that fans the flame. Writing as Fiona, he said:

> Again, I must tell you that all the formative and expressional as well as nearly all the visionary power is my friend's. In a sense only his is the passive part; but it is the allegory of the match, the wind, and the torch. Everything is in the torch in readiness, and, as you know, there is nothing in itself in the match. But there is the mysterious latency of fire between them: in that latent fire of love — the little touch of silent igneous potency at the end of the match. Well, the match comes to the torch, or the torch to the match — and, in what these symbolize, one adds spiritual affinity as a factor — and all at once flame is born. The torch says all is due to the match. The match knows that the flame is not hers, but lies in that mystery of thitherto awakened love, suddenly brought into being by contact. But beyond both is the wind, the spiritual air. Out of the unseen world it fans the flame. In that mysterious air, both the match and the torch hear strange voices. But the match is now part of the torch, lost in him, lost in that flame. Her small still voice speaks in the mind and spirit of the torch, sometimes guiding, sometimes inspiring, out of the deep mysterious intimacies of love and passion. That which is born of both, the flame, is subject to neither — but is the property of the torch. The air which came at the union of both is sometimes called Memory, sometimes Art, sometimes Genius, sometimes Imagination, sometimes Life, sometimes the Spirit. It is all.

The match is Fiona Macleod, the presumed author of the letter, and the torch is William Sharp. Most people, he continued, admire the flame and wonder only at the torch. A few "look for the match beyond the torch, and, finding her [Edith Rinder], are apt to attribute to her that which is not hers, save as a spiritual dynamic agent." Occasionally the "match may also have *in petto* the qualities of the torch — particularly memory and vision: and so can stimulate and amplify the imaginative life of the torch. But the torch is at once the passive, the formative, the mnemonic and the artistically and imaginatively creative force." And even more explicitly: "he and he alone is the flame, his alone both the visionary, the formative, and the expressional." Here Sharp, writing as Fiona, attributed the Fiona writings entirely to Sharp. Yeats knew Sharp was writing the Fiona letter, and he surely realized Sharp was relegating Fiona, or more precisely the real woman behind her, to the role of a muse. Yeats surely understood the point Sharp was making, especially the role of the newly introduced spiritual wind that made it all possible. Anyone else, with only a limited understanding of the symbolism, would read the letter as Sharp, pretending to be Fiona Macleod, claiming for himself authorship of the Fiona writings. It is no wonder that Sharp asked Yeats to destroy the letter after reading it.

In "The Distant Country," Sharp made the point that the passionate love between Edith and William had changed shape. In this letter he made the point more explicitly: Edith's role as Sharp's muse, as his inspiration for the Fiona Macleod writings, was diminishing. "Of late," he wrote, "the 'match' is more than ever simply a hidden flame in the mind of the 'torch.' When I add that the match never saw or heard a line of "Honey of the Wild Bees" (which you admire so much) till after written, you will understand better." "Honey of the Wild Bees" takes allegory to the realm of mythology and introduces very precisely the equation between Love and Death. Rinn, known as "Honey of the Wild Bees" in ancient Celtic lore, fell in love with Aevgrain, the beautiful daughter of Deirdre and Naois. Having seduced her and caused her to love and follow him, he announced he was the Lord of the Shadow whose name in this world is Death. As in "The Distant Country," passionate love can be perfectly consummated only in death. In drawing Yeats's attention to this story, Sharp wanted him to know that the real woman behind Fiona Macleod had become less essential in enabling Sharp to assume the Fiona persona and less important in producing the writings published as her work. He, the torch, was entirely responsible for "The Honey of the Wild Bees." Beyond claiming sole authorship of the Fiona writings, Sharp was asserting the gradual reintegration of his personality. It is an exceptionally personal — indeed confessional — letter.

In the September 16 letter, Fiona assured Yeats she was speaking only for herself in expressing her preferences for stories in *The Dominion of Dreams*, not for her friend Sharp:

[His] heart is in the ancient world and his mind forever questing in the domain of the spirit. I think he cares little for anything but through the *remembering* imagination to recall and interpret, and through the formative and penetrative imagination to discover certain mysteries of psychological and spiritual life. (Apropos, I wish you very much to read, when it appears in the *Fortnightly Review* — probably either in October or in November — the spiritual 'essay' called "The Divine Adventure" — an imaginative effort to reach the same vital problems of spiritual life along the separate, yet inevitably interrelated, lines of the Body, the Will (Mind or Intellect), and the Soul.)

The forthcoming "Divine Adventure" would be published as the work of Fiona Macleod, but it would be an expression of William Sharp's attempt to discover through "the *remembering*, formative and penetrative imagination certain mysteries of psychological and spiritual life." The gender difference between the voice of Fiona Macleod and that of William Sharp which Sharp had tried so hard to maintain in his fiction and poetry no longer seemed important. Moving forward, the Fiona Macleod writings would be the product of a voice that combined feminine and masculine sensibilities, a voice close to that which William Sharp adopted in his reviews and essays on literature and art.

On the first of October 1899, the Sharps occupied their new residence, rooms overlooking the high common in Chorleywood, Hertfordshire, then a village, now part of Greater London. Ever in need of more money, they hoped to economize by living outside London and avoid having to go abroad to escape London's smoke and smog in the winter. At first, they were pleased by their new abode. On October 8, Sharp began a letter to Richard Garnett: "We are now settled here, at this bracing & delightful place, near Milton's Chalfont St. Giles and Arnold's beloved Chess: & here sometime you may feel inclined to come for a breath of vivid air." On October 19, he thanked Watts-Dunton for a poem and concluded: "How lovely autumn is at this moment. The trees here are divinely lovely." In a letter dated October 20 to John Macleay, Sharp, writing as Fiona, said *The Dominion of Dreams* was now in its fifth edition, but she had still been unable to make any revisions. She hoped to be able to make the revisions in the seventh edition, and it seemed probable that would occur by or shortly after the first of the year. As it turned out, the revisions had to wait until Elizabeth reprinted *The Dominion of Dreams* as Volume III of the Uniform Edition of *The Works of "Fiona Macleod"* in 1910 (London: William Heinemann).

Having returned from Ireland, Sharp promptly wrote on September 28 to Nellie Allen to say he and Elizabeth were infinitely regretful to learn first from a paper and then from friends that her husband, Grant Allen, was still seriously ill. They hoped he would soon get well and "be his old brave buoyant self again." If there was anything they could do, please let them know with a brief card to their new address in Chorleywood. A month later, on October 25, Allen suffered a painful death from what was diagnosed as liver cancer. His family arranged for his body to be cremated on October 27 following a brief ceremony in the Brookwood Crematorium in Woking. Sharp was deeply moved by the death of his friend who shared many of his "advanced" views about the nature of love and the restraints of marriage. His effort to attend the service in Woking was stymied by poor communications and missed connections. After returning to Chorleywood on October 27 he wrote a letter of sympathy to Allen's son. Only in that morning's paper had he learned of Allen's death and the service set for three o'clock that afternoon: "I at once changed my clothes, caught the one available train, & drove straight across — but, in the hurried departure, I had unfortunately read 'Charing Cross' for 'Waterloo' — & so I missed the train after all, to my profound regret everyway." On October 27 he also explained his absence and conveyed his sympathy to Grant Richards, his publisher and Allen's nephew. In a letter to Murray Gilchrist that day, he said he was acutely saddened by the death of his good friend, Grant Allen:

> I loved the man — and admired the brilliant writer and catholic critic and eager student. He was of a most winsome nature. The world seems shrunken a bit more. As yet, I cannot realise I am not to see him again. Our hearts ache for his wife — an ideal loveable woman — a dear friend of us both.

With Allen's death, the world seemed shrunken to Sharp. He also told Gilchrist he had undertaken, for financial reasons, a huge study of art in the nineteenth century that, with his other writing, occupied all his time. Still, he remained pleased with Chorleywood and the beauty of the fall season: "We like this most beautiful and bracing neighborhood greatly [... .] It has been the loveliest October I remember for years. The equinoxial bloom is on every tree. But today, after long drought, the weather has broken, and a heavy rain has begun."

Sharp wrote again to Murray Gilchrist in early November to invite him to come to London for a few days at the end of the month to be his guest at a dinner of the Omar Khayyam Club.

> You know that the Omar Khayyam Club is the "Blue Ribbon" so to speak of Literary Associations, and that its occasional meetings are more sought after than any other. As I think you know I am one of the 49 members — and I much want you to be my guest at the forthcoming meeting on Friday Dec. 1st.

It would be a special occasion. The President of the club had honored Sharp by asking him to write and recite a poem at the dinner. The invitation meant a great deal to Sharp, since it confirmed his presence among London's literary elite. As soon as Elizabeth heard about the invitation, she said Murray Gilchrist must be invited to attend.

An undertow soon diminished the pleasure of life in Chorleywood. As November darkened into December, Sharp had to take the unusual step of asking Watts-Dunton for a loan:

> What with long and disastrous illness at the beginning of the year — having to help others dear to me — and, finally, losses involved through the misdeed of another, I find myself on my beam-ends. By next Spring I hope to have things righted so far, if health holds out — but my pinch is just now, with less than £5 in the world to call my own at this moment!

Since so much of his and Elizabeth's income was dependent on journalistic art criticism, they were feeling the severe effect of the Boer War as all such work had been cut back by two-thirds. The history of Fine Arts in the nineteenth century he was writing would eventually repay the time and effort he was devoting to it. He asked Watts-Dunton if he could lend him fifty pounds. If that was too much, he might be able to manage with twenty-five pounds, which had the buying power then of 2,766 of today's pounds and 3,350 of today's dollars. He would be able to repay that much by February or even sooner. Watts-Dunton was a man of some means and a man of considerable compassion since he and Sharp had grown apart through the years. Watts-Dunton responded by loaning Sharp twenty-five pounds, which Sharp, in February 1900, was still unable to repay. How ironic that a man who was about to be honored by his peers at the Omar Khayyam Club dinner had only five pounds to his name.

"The Divine Adventure," which will be discussed in Chapter Twenty (Volume 3), appeared as the work of Fiona Macleod in the November and December issues of *The Fortnightly Review*. On December 30, Sharp told Gilchrist, who knew Fiona was Sharp, "It was written *de profundis*, partly because of a compelling spirit, partly to help others passionately eager to obtain some light on this most complex and intimate spiritual destiny." On that day, he also wrote to Frank Rinder, his "dear friend and literary comrade" to wish him "health and prosperity in 1900." He wanted him to read the opening pages of the Fiona Macleod essay called "Iona" which would appear in a book with "The Divine Adventure" in 1900: "I have never written anything [...] so spiritually autobiographical. Strange as it may seem it is almost all literal reproduction of actuality with only some dates and names altered." Having asserted his authorship of the essay, he said to Rinder, "But enough of that troublesome F. M!" This assertion — he is, and he is not Fiona Macleod — is a fitting conclusion to a year in which he made some progress in clarifying, for himself if not for others, the complex relationship among William Sharp, Edith Rinder, and Fiona Macleod.

Letters: July–December, 1899

To William Butler Yeats, July 3–4, 1899[1]

Monday

My Dear Yeats

I want to write to you about the rite, and a very strange outcome of inward concentration upon it. Also about the plays — I believe they will appeal to you deeply.

(Tuesday Forenoon)

was interrupted by people last night — & so could not write, & now am not in the mood & cannot.

I have not yet seen your "Bookman" article, but this morning I had a letter from a friend, who incidentally writes as follows: — "and upon that we all pretty well agreed (i.e. abt "Silence Farm," which my friend was discussing with 3 literary men at the Savile,[2] & all spoke of in a way that has deeply gratified &encouraged me) — "Then the talk drifted to your friend (she is your friend, is she not?) Miss Macleod's new book, and what a notable thing it is for a book of that kind to go into a second edition within three weeks of publication. So, there is a split in the Celtic Camp! I admit it amuses me. I never have believed, never can believe, in the ability of these folk to sink minor matters for a common end. I'm speaking of course of W. B. Yeats's article on Miss M. in The Bookman. Mr. _____ laughed, & said that it was the worst snub Miss M. had received. Have you seen it? Yeats says she has enough faults to ruin any ordinary writer, and that there's not a story in her book which should not have many words struck out. As he doesn't say a word of praise or welcome about it, but only something about her surely unquestioned mythopoeic faculty — it's obvious he either doesn't find much in the book, or wants to take her down a peg or two."

(He then adds something I needn't repeat.)

I have sent for "The Bookman," & shall get it by tomorrow, I daresay.

However, I write on the head of that letter only. Tonight or tomorrow I'll see the "Bookman": & so meanwhile hold my opinion in suspense.

I was profoundly disappointed, & in every way, with "Literary Ideals in Ireland."[3] How significantly it proves that there is no literary Ideal in Ireland — but only individual & continuous tendencies, just as everywhere else!

I have been dreaming, dreaming, dreaming, of a great awakening, a great redemption, a small & faithful concert of unselfish & individual aims. I still believe — shall still, and as long as I live, work towards that end. But at times one stands profoundly disheartened.

Yours | W. S.

ALS National Library of Scotland

To Richard Garnett, [early July, 1899][4]

30 Greencroft Gardens | South Hampstead

Reverend Companion of the Bath, (as my brother-in-law told me a Parsee recently addressed an eminent official, as though he were a Sponge!)

Where shall I find the best account or record of your pen-work? I am I believe to do an article on "Richard Garnett."[5]

I have just returned from Scotland — but during my absence I know that you have retired from the Brit. Mus. Are you actually at last at leisure? It must be strange, but on the whole very welcome. You will now give more time to your own work I hope.

Ever cordially yours with kind regards & congratulations to you and yours,

William Sharp

ALS University of Texas, Austin

To Grant Richards, July 10, 1899

Monday | 10th July | 99

My dear Sir,

I thank you for your letter of Friday last agreeing to my amended form of your kind proposal as to my anthology, "The Hour of Beauty."[6]

I am glad, too, to be relieved from the pressure of urgency — particularly as a book of this kind should grow leisurely — however much it has already been nurtured and trimmed. So I will let you have it, as you suggest, by or just before the end of this year.

Thanking you for your consideration of my requests, and for your kind remark about myself,

Believe me | Yours faithfully | Fiona Macleod

P.S. You may care to know that my new book "The Dominion of Dreams" has gone into a second edition within the month of issue. I mention it because publishers are said never to believe that the public will buy books of short stories!!

ALS Stanford University

To Grant Richards, July 11, 1899

Tuesday | July 11th /99

My dear Sir,

I forgot to ask you if Mr. Lucas found it necessary to obtain author's or publisher's consent for fragmentary excerpts (e.g. Mrs. Maynell, Jefferies, etc.). I presume not.

I have just been reading a review of my new book in *The Highland News* (Inverness) and as there is an allusion in it to a book you publish, the *Silence Farm* of my friend and Kinsman Mr. William Sharp, I send it to you, as you are not likely to see *The Highland News* in London. (You need not return it.) I read the book in question with very deep interest, naturally: but admit that I cannot see where any likeness to my own work, either in style or method is shown: certainly I know it would be impossible for me to write "Silence Farm".

Each of us "gangs his own gait," as we say in the Lowlands here.

With kind regards | Yours very truly | Fiona Macleod

ALS Stanford University

To John Macleay, [July 11, 1899][7]

Tuesday

Dear Mr. Macleay

I received simultaneously your note and review, and a letter from Miss Macleod. She says "Do you still take the 'Highland News' — if so you will have seen the generous and also suggestive notice of my book by "Mac," i.e. Mr. John Macleay. I am particularly glad to have a review by so sympathetic and understanding a critic, in the H. N. And on the whole am in agreement with him on one important point: I am sure that my best work, from the standpoint of literature, is in the old tales, and particularly in those like "The Laughter of Scathach," "The Sad Queen," "Enya" etc. — i.e. those wherein there is a Scandinavian as well as a Celtic element, and perhaps one earlier than either. On the other hand I don't think he understands, or, rather, sympathizes with that other vital side which seems so far the more essential to "AE" and those for whom he stands. (There follows some private matter about the second section.) But in any case I am grateful to Mr. Macleay for his steadfast and early and continued friendship — and if you write to him, as I hope you will (for I must, as you know, do no writing just now that I can possibly avoid) please give him my cordial thanks."

She adds, later, "I am very glad about that allusion to 'Silence Farm,' at once so sympathetic & so critical in its discernment."

For myself let me thank you, too. I think your review excellent every way — though I don't agree with either you or AE about the "Moonrock": that is, I don't think AE is right about the frankly human and true opening parts, & I don't think you are right about the imaginative close. But that is doubtless an all round disputable matter.

With Miss Macleod, I am very glad that so good & sympathetic a paper has appeared in the H. News. Than the critical allusion to my own work I could wish nothing better.

Yesterday at my Club I read the review in *The Outlook*. It interested me extremely: and I would like to know the name of the writer. *Who* is the literary editor of the "Outlook." Of course it may not be he — but I shd, be glad if you would kindly let me know. I fancied from the writing that it was W. E. Henley's. Perhaps he is still (as at the start I know he was) litry Editor.

My wife and I go to Ireland shortly. Let me know, later, the exact date of your marriage so that I may wish you well.

Sincerely Yours | William Sharp

P.S. There is, I have just seen, a long article on "Silence Farm" by R. Le Gallienne in Saty's *Star* — good if somewhat patronizing or unconsciously arrogant: & he too notices the divergence between Miss M. & myself.

ALS National Library of Scotland

To Benjamin Burgess Moore, July 12, 1899

c/o Miss Rea. | The Columbia Literary Agency |
9 Mill Street. Conduit St. | London | 12: July: 99

My dear Mr. Moore

I thank you for your long and friendly and generously appreciative letter about "The Dominion of Dreams" — which, you will care to know, is already in a second edition. I am very glad indeed that you like the book so well, and what you say interested me very much. It has been very widely and influentially reviewed — and, all things considered, with surprising sympathy and understanding. The two most recent of any weight are that in the current number of The *Outlook* (8ᵗʰ July) which you may likely come across in London, and the enclosed from T*he Highland News,* which you need not return. It is the more significant as that influential Highland paper (Inverness) has sometimes been hostile to my writings, and to what for good or ill they stand, and are supposed to stand.

I am glad to hear that you are to be in this country, and hope you will have a memorably pleasant visit. It is with genuine regret that I know there is no likelihood of our meeting, as you suggest.

You are one of the very few for whom I might break my otherwise invariable rule — for private reasons, and only so far my own, of a complicated kind — but in any case it can't be this year. I   have   not been strong: and a complete and prolonged rest and bracing is necessary. A day or two hence I leave Edinburgh (where I have just come from the Hebrides) to go on a two or three months yachting voyage in the far north, including Ireland and Scandinavia.

But though we can't meet I would much like you, if practicable, to meet my most intimate friend, Mr. William Sharp (who has seen several of your letters, and knows your friendly interest, and would, I know, be very glad to meet you).

He and his wife, however, are about to relinquish their flat in South Hampstead, and leave London soon. I wrote to him two days ago, and he asked me to say that he hoped you would call next Monday afternoon (17ᵗʰ) about 3 or 3.30 — when he would be in — and perhaps, now, his only free day, as he and Mrs. Sharp leave their flat before the end of that week.

The address is | Rutland House | 30 Greencroft Gardens | South Hampstead — and the neighboring station is "Finchley Road" on the Metropolitan line via Baker St.

I will write you again about literary matters at some later date (to same address?) but now am tired and must write no more.

Cordially yours, | Fiona Macleod

ALS Huntington Library

To Mrs. Grant Allen, [July 24?, 1899][8]

72 Inverness Terrace | Bayswater W.

My dear Nellie,

We have now "moved" and "stored" — and as soon as we possibly can (we hope in a week) intend to go to Wales and Ireland. But I must snatch a moment to write and say how deeply sorry I was to hear that Grant was feeling so far from well. We both realized how much we love him and you when we heard of this unwelcome mischance.

Do not let us add to any weariness by asking you to write a letter — but could you send a Post Card to say if he is now better. I do hope he is — and that this lovely summertide is bringing warmth to his life and bloom to your own bonnie face. With love from us both,

Your friend, | Will.

ALS Pierpont Morgan Library

[*To Catherine Ann Janvier*] *August 6, 1899*[9]

... We are glad to get away from Belfast, tho' very glad to be there, in a nice hotel, after our fatigues and 10 hours' exposure in the damp sea-fog. It was a lovely day in Belfast, and Elizabeth had her first experience of an Irish car.

We are on the shore of a beautiful bay — with the great ram-shaped headland of Fair Head on the right, the Atlantic in front, and also in front but leftward the remote Gaelic island of Rathlin.[10] It is the neighbourhood whence Deirdrê and Naois fled from Concobar, and it is from a haven in this coast that they sailed for Scotland. It is an enchanted land for those who dream the old dreams: though perhaps without magic or even appeal for those who do not.

[William Sharp]

Memoir, p. 311

To W. Lawler Wilson Esq.,[11] August 7, 1899

Ballycastle | Co. Antrim | 7/Aug/99

Dear Sir,

Your letter has been forwarded to me in Ireland.

I meant to have answered your previous letter — but I went abroad, and the address escaped me.

As I am in Ireland, I cannot do as you are good enough to suggest — call on your official photographers, and as you prefer not to use copyright photos, I do not refer you to one or other of the London photographers who have specially taken me — but send you one taken recently of me privately. (Of course it must be understood that your using this does not give you copyright in it.) The photographer is Stanley, of Dublin — the same who did the other photograph reproduced in the current "Bookman."[12]

My bibliographical record is, I think, given most fully and accurately in *Who's Who* (1899) and "Dictionary of English Authors".

A proof made up from either can be revised and if wished augmented — if you desire it.

My best letter-address (as I have just left my South Hampstead address) is 72 Inverness Terrace, Kensington Gardens W.

Believe me, | Yours very truly, | William Sharp

ALS University of Texas, Austin

To Richard Le Gallienne, August 11, 1899[13]

c/o Miss Rea | The Columbia Literary Agency |
9 Mill St. Conduit St. | London |

11th Augt 1899

Dear Mr. Le Gallienne

It was only a day or two ago that I saw your most friendly and sympathetic notice of "The Dominion of Dreams" — for I have been yachting round the extreme north of Scotland: and though I have but a snatched quarter of an hour today to spare, for I[14]

...

article I have seen sent me by our common friend) — and hope that you will publish the second in book form. I also greatly hope for another volume of poetry soon. You are a poet first and foremost.

Hurriedly but with most cordial greetings,

Sincerely yours, | Fiona Macleod

Romantic '90s, pp. 91–92

To Benjamin Burgess Moore, August 11, 1899

c/o Miss Rea | The Columbia Literary Agency |
9 Mill Street. Conduit St. | London

11th Augt. 1899

My dear Mr. Moore,

We have "put in," pro-tem, at a place called Nairn on the North coast of Scotland after a delightful voyage west and north of Cape Wrath.

Your welcome letter gave me great pleasure. I am glad you went to see Mr. William Sharp, and glad that you liked him. If you had not, you would not like me! Truly: for we are not only close kindred but at one in all things. Did you speak of your "beloved France"? You would have found a sympathetic listener, for his love for France is almost a passion — in which I share, though with less knowledge, for he knows it from north to south as few do. After Italy, he knows it better than any other European country. You know Italy too? I have been there three times, and long to go again. Venice in the Summer, Sicily in Winter, Rome always — that is what I advise, with endless interludes of "anywhere everywhere" from Verona in the north to the Umbrian Maremma and from that strange borderland to Messina and Palermo.

 But I must not begin to talk of Italy! Give me Scotland, Ireland, France, and Italy, and I will relinquish the world, from San Francisco to the Gates of Eden!

I hope you will have a delightful time abroad. Be sure you see Mr. Sharp again before you go back to America. He will be greatly disappointed if you do not, for he took a genuine liking to you, and wrote to me appreciatively about "my American friend."

He was sorry he could see so little of you — but (as he wrote) looks to seeing you in October. When he left South Hampstead, his plans were still uncertain: but now he has arranged to be in pleasant upland country not far from there, beyond Harrow — and asked me to let you know that on the 1st of October and for that month and into November anyway his address will be Wharncliff[e] | Chorley Wood | (via Rickmansworth) — and either there, or at his club, the Grosvenor, in New Bond Street, he would be most glad to see you. He is now in Ireland at a place on the north Antrim coast called Ballycastle (the neighbourhood whence Deirdre and the Sons of Usna sailed for Scotland when fleeing from Concobar) — and in a letter I have just received speaks of a titanic swim among rough breakers on a wild coast near the Giant's Causeway, so, after all, his hated London life does not seem to have sapped his vigour! Later, we shall meet in Ireland, for my plans are in part changed. I already know that wild Antrim coast — and the lonely, remote, Gaelic-speaking isle of Ragherry (Rathlin) where the grandson of the great Nial the Victorious went down with all his fleet.

Yes, I have decided to take out "The House of Sand & Foam" from *The Dominion of Dreams*, and to substitute (about the same length) "The Four Winds of the Spirit." There will be other alterations, and a revised text. The piece in question has been much admired, but in the wrong way and by the wrong people — and it was that which made me suspicious, re-read it in cold blood, and decide against its prettiness, a poor quality. The publishers are against any such changes — but I hope to gain my point. After all, the third edition has not got my revisions — for at the last the demand necessitated an immediate reprinting, and so now I have to look to the fourth, if that should be called for, as I hope it will, for I much want to give the book its final form.

I am very dissatisfied with it — and would gladly rearrange and rewrite it all from beginning to end. There was an exceedingly good review of it last week in an important Book-trade weekly, "The Publisher's Circular"[15] and also (what I understand is not only a compliment but an extremely serviceable one) a very favorable notice in *Punch*[16] of all papers!

I hope this autumn to finish the volume of spiritual essays called "The Reddening of the West" (or, after its chief inclusion, "The Divine Adventure") but I shall probably postpone the book till Spring. It depends on whether I can get the "Iona" part done.[17] I also hope to finish and issue before Christmas, the volume of three plays: The King of Ireland's Son | The Immortal Hour | Queen Ganore.[18] (The first, old Celtic, the longest: the second, the same, in blank verse: the third and shortest, a wild Scottish variant of the Guinevere story, in ruder form.) I shall probably add some poems to the volume. By the way, in the current issue of *Literature* (5th August) there is a poem of mine, "The Tryst of Queen Hynde," I would like you to see.

Now after all this personal detail see that you write to me from France, or I will not forgive you, nor ever write to you again.

So, conditionally, your friend, Fiona Macleod

ALS Huntington Library

To [*Edith Lyttelton*], [*August 23?, 1899*]

... Her visit to Iceland was a short one, however: and she came south to the Inner Hebrides before a continuous polar wind which almost made sails as swift as steam. Then we had a short time together. She is still

uncertain whether to go to Venice or not: it means railway-travelling &
much else that is neither good for nor welcome to her — though eager to
see again a place she loves & knows well. If she goes, it will be at once. It
depends on health as well as friends. The chances are that she will come
to Ireland for a week or so in Connemara, and again in Antrim.

I am glad you cared for "Silence Farm" — and in the way you do. I
daresay you are right in your objection that "There is too much dung in
it". It may be. In the artistic instinct of emphasis there is always danger
of excess. It was not done self-consciously, however: that is, the book,
in its minor details as well as its broad development, was written just
as it was quintessentially seen, quintessentially felt — after that final
resurrection in the mind out of which alone any work of art can come.
Strangely, out of this "Silence Farm" another has arisen. But it must
remain unwritten — though its lesson may mould & strengthen other
work. Someday I will tell you of this — & of what lies behind "Silence
Farm" and how it came to be written just as it is.

If you ever see "The Speaker" I would be glad if you read a review
of it in that weekly for last week (Augt. 19th).[19] A friend who saw it has
just sent it to me: but what especially pleases me, apart from [...],[20] is
the intimate artistic understanding of the book & what may be called
its artistic *motif*. I was just about to add, "Enough about myself," when I
recalled your request about which of my books I like best myself — apart
from "Silence Farm" and "Ecce Puella".

I can hardly say: the law of association has so much to do with one's
partialities. I think that which I could in later life take up with most
pleasure, or least dissatisfaction, as the occasion might rule — would
be my book of unrhymed irregular verse, "*Sospiri di Roma,*" written
when I lived in Rome some nine or ten years ago (though reminiscent
also of Rome when I first knew it, in 1882) — and printed under my
supervision at a rude printing press in the Sabine Hills, worked by
"Horace's Fall" at Tivoli, & nominally published by the Società Laziale
of Rome. The edition of (I think) 400 was mostly taken up at once, &
soon the book became difficult to get, & is now very rare. There has been
no later English edition — though it was reprinted in America, along
with an earlier volume of poems called "Romantic Ballads and Poems of
Phantasy." It is probable that next Spring I may (it is my wife's urgency,
for I am not eager) bring out a selection of these *Sospiri* with a few other

published & unpublished poems, all I care to preserve. But I think (I dare not promise for certain) that I have a spare copy: if, on my return, I find that this is so, you shall have it. In any case, you can have one to read, if you care — as I think you will the more when I may perhaps tell you something about it which I do not care to write.[21]

The "Sospiri" and the volume of imaginative dramatic psychological studies called "*Vistas*" are the two most intimate of my books. The latter is best read in the 3ʳᵈ American edition, which has a preface, & this I know I can let you have later.

In fiction I don't care for my two early efforts: my more recent comedy, "Wives in Exile" (Grant Richards) had a success in both countries, as also a vol. of short stories called "Madge o' the Pool" (Constables). Among my critical writings, I care most for "*Heine*" (Walter Scott). Even in Germany itself it is, I understand, accepted as (short as it is) the most vivid monograph on Heine.

And now — enough! I write at this length only because you are a friend whom I value — for frankly I am not of those authors who find their own work in the mass a subject of profound interest! I care only for the little that is best, or what really touches some spiritual or other vital problem, or (in an intimate way) for what has some vivid personal association. My interest indeed lies in what is to be done: not in the tentative little I h*ave* done. And above all, I am interested in life: in men and women: in every phase of art and literature — & hope to win therefrom, later, a little honey, perhaps bittersweet, to give to others. Do you write at all? *That* would interest me. I would like to talk over with you a phrase in your letter, when you say, apropos of the dramatic intensity of "Silence Farm," "that you long for this same intensity for a moment on something beautiful".

Yes: I too. But perhaps there is an undue limitation in your "something beautiful." In any case, we can talk it over — & this letter is already too long & may have wearied you. Forgive it for the friendly intent. I hope, too, you will write again, and that we shall meet again & become friends.

Sincerely yours, | William Sharp

ALS Churchill Archive Center, Churchill College, Cambridge

To Grant Richards, August 26, 1899

"Post Office House" | Newcastle | Co. Down | Ireland | 26/8/99

My dear Richards

Herewith payment for the two copies of "Wives in Exile" sent me.

I hope "Silence Farm" has gone fairly well. I have seen it little advtd·
but then of late I have not seen many papers. In the main the reviews
have been good. I was glad to see such a splendid one in *The Speaker* of
last week (19th Aug). Surely such a review should have some effect. I
would be glad to know how the book is faring. As I gave away my own
copy received at special request for a review copy, I shd· be glad if you
will kindly send me one in its place.

I hope you & your wife are well, & having a pleasant autumn. My
wife & I came to Ireland at the end of July, & have had glorious weather
& a pleasant time (with partial holiday for me). We have just come to
Newcastle, Co. Down, & shall be here till mid-September.

I may take this opportunity of saying that (my South Hampstead
address being cancelled) from 1st October my address will be
Wharncliff | Chorleywood | Herts (it is a pleasant place not far beyond
Harrow & Rickmansworth).

Best regards | Sincerely Yours | William Sharp

ALS State University of New York at Buffalo

To Adelaide Elder, [September 12, 1899][22]

Dear Adelaide,

Do you know why I thought of you to-day particularly, it being my
birthday? For it was you who some two and twenty years ago sent me on
the 12th of September a copy of a beautifully bound book by a poet with
a strange name and by me quite unknown — Dante Gabriel Rossetti.

To that event it is impossible to trace all I owe, but what is fairly
certain is that, without it, the whole course of my life might have
been very different. For the book not only influenced and directed me

mentally at a crucial period, but made me speak of it to an elderly friend (Sir Noel Paton) through whom I was dissuaded from going abroad on a career of adventure (I was going to Turkey or as I vaguely put it, Asia) and through whom, later, I came to know Rossetti himself — an event which completely redirected the whole course of my life.

It would be strange to think how a single impulse of a friend may thus have so profound a significance were it not that to you and me there is nothing strange (in the sense of incredible) in the complex spiritual interrelation of life. Looking back through all those years I daresay we can now both see a strange and in much inscrutable, but still recognisable, direction.

[William Sharp]

Memoir, pp. 35–36

To William Butler Yeats, September 16, 1899[23]

16 September 1899

P.S. As this is such a long letter I have typed it.

My dear Mr. Yeats

I am at present like one of these equinoctial leaves which are whirling before me as I write, now this way and now that: for I am, just now, addressless, and drift between East and West, with round-the-compass eddies, including a flying visit of a day or two in a yacht from Cantyre to the north Antrim coast.[24]

Thus it is that your welcome note of the 3rd was delayed in reaching me. You, I suppose, are still at your friend's in Galway.

I am very interested in what you write about the "Dominion of Dreams," and shall examine with closest attention all your suggestions.[25] The book has already been in great part revised by my friend.[26] In a few textual changes in "Dalua" he has in one notable instance followed your suggestion, that about the too literary "lamentable elder voices." The order is slightly changed, too: for "The House of Sand and Foam" is to be withdrawn, and a piece called "The Winds of the Spirit" substituted: and "Lost" is to come after "Dalua" and precede "The Yellow Moonrock."[27]

You will like to know what I most care for myself. From a standpoint of literary art *per se* I think the best work is that wherein the barbaric (the old Gaelic or Celto-Scandinavian) note occurs. My three favorite tales in this kind are "The Sad Queen" in the *Dominion of Dreams*, "The Laughter of Scathach" in *The Washer of the Ford*, and "The Harping of Cravetheen" in *The Sin-Eater*. In art, I think "Dalua," and "The Sad Queen," and "Enya of the Dark Eyes," the best [in] the *Dominion of Dreams*.

Temperamentally, those which appeal to me most are those with the play of mysterious psychic force in them — as in "Alasdair the Proud," "Children of the Dark Star," "Enya of the Dark Eyes," and, in earlier tales, "Cravetheen" and "The Dan-nan-Ron" and the Iona tales. Those others which are full of the individual note of suffering and other emotion I find it very difficult to judge. Of one thing only I am convinced, as is my friend (an opinion shared with the rare few whose judgment really means much), that there is nothing in *Dominion of Dreams* or elsewhere in these writings under my name to stand beside "The Distant Country."[28] Nothing else has made so deep and vital an impression both on men and women — and possibly it may be true what a very subtle and powerful mind has written about it, that it is the deepest and most searching utterance on the mystery of passion which has appeared in our time. It is indeed the core of *all* these writings — and will outlast them all.

Of course I am speaking for myself only. As for my friend, his heart is in the ancient world and his mind for ever questing in the domain of the spirit. I think he cares little for anything but through the *remembering* imagination to recall and interpret, and through the formative and penetrative imagination to discover certain mysteries of psychological and spiritual life. (Apropos, I wish you very much to read, when it appears in the *Fortnightly Review* — probably either in October or in November — the spiritual "essay" called "The Divine Adventure" — an imaginative effort to reach the same vital problems of spiritual life along the separate, yet inevitably interrelated, lines of the Body, the Will (Mind or Intellect), and the Soul.)[29]

And this brings me to a point about which I must again write to you — I say "again", for once last summer I wrote to you, trying so far as practicable in a strange and complex matter to be explicit. Let me add that I write to you, as before, trusting to you honourably to destroy this letter.

You are both right and wrong in your diagnosis of the passive and expressional factors. (As a *generalisation,* I think what you say is right: but here, as so often elsewhere, the puzzling exception invalidates the ides of invariability.)

Again I must tell you that all the formative and expressional as well as nearly all the visionary power is my friend's. In a sense only his is the passive part; but it is the allegory of the match, the wind, and the torch. Everything is in the torch in readiness, and, as you know, there is nothing in itself in the match. But there is the mysterious latency of fire between them: in that latent fire of love — the little touch of silent igneous potency at the end of the match. Well, the match comes to the torch, or the torch to the match — and, in what these symbolize, one adds spiritual affinity as a factor — and all at once flame is born. The torch says all is due to the match. The match knows that the flame is not hers, but lies in that mystery of thitherto unawakened love, suddenly brought into being by contact. But beyond both is the wind, the spiritual air. Out of the unseen world it fans the flame. In that mysterious air, both the match and the torch hear strange voices. But the match is now part of the torch, lost in him, lost in that flame. Her small still voice speaks in the mind and spirit of the torch, sometimes guiding, sometimes inspiring, out of the deep mysterious intimacies of love and passion. That which is born of both, the flame, is subject to neither — but is the property of the torch. The air which came at the union of both is sometimes called Memory, sometimes Art, sometimes Genius, sometimes Imagination, sometimes Life, sometimes the Spirit. It is all.

But, before that flame, people wonder and admire. Most wonder only at the torch. A few look for the match beyond the torch, and, finding her, are apt to attribute to her that which is not her's, save as a spiritual dynamic agent. Now and then that match may also have *in petto* the qualities of the torch — particularly memory and vision: and so can stimulate and amplify the imaginative life of the torch. But the torch is at once the passive, the formative, the mnemonic and the artistically and imaginatively creative force. He knows that in one sense he would be flameless — or at least without that ideal blend of the white flame and the red — without the match: and he knows that the flame is the offspring of both, and that the wind has many airs in it, and that one of the most potent of these under-airs is that which blows from the life and mind and soul of the "match" — but in his heart he knows that, to all others, he and he alone is the flame, his alone both the visionary, the formative, and the expressional.

Do you understand? Read — copy what you will, as apart from me — and destroy this.

Of late the "match" is more than ever simply a hidden flame in the mind of the "torch". When I add that the match never saw or heard a line of "Honey of the Wild Bees" (which you admire so much) till after written, you will understand better.[30]

Please send me a note by return to say that you have received this — and destroyed it — and if you understand: but as my address is uncertain, send it in an *outer envelope* addressed simply, William Sharp Esq, Murrayfield, Midlothian. When [for Where] it will safely reach me.

I have no time now to write you about the plays. Two are typed: the third, and chief, is not yet finished. When all are revised and ready, you can see them. "The Immortal Hour" (the shortest — practically a 1 act play in time,) is in verse.[31]

Sincerely yours | Fiona Macleod

P.S. I think you could have a proof-set of "The Divine Adventure" in your case.

TLS Yale University, Letters to Yeats I, 61–64, and partially in Memoir, pp. 309–10

To Henry Mills Alden, September 18, [1899]

72 Inverness Terrace | London | W. | 18th September

Dear Mr. Alden

As I have never had any word, nor even mem. [for memo?] of acknowledgment, of my letter to you with enclosures, & notably of my long sea-ballad, *The Admiral of the Sea* — which I sent to you from

London about mid-*June* — three months ago — I am afraid that some mishap has occurred.

I now send you my duplicate copy of "The Admiral of the Sea" — hoping very much that you may care for it for H*arper's Monthly.*

As I said in my June letter with it — it would lend itself to picturesque illustration (if so, the ship should be very archaic, with the crossbow-men in little turrets on the mast, etc.).

The theme itself is a stirring one, apart from its interest as the first naval battle between England & Scotland: & as what led on to Flodden.

I send with it also a copy of the other short poem which accompanied it — "Cap'n Goldsack."

I hope all goes well with you & yours?

Did you get the copy of "The Dominion of Dreams" which Miss Macleod sent to you at Metuchen (I *think* — tho' she may have sent it to C/o Messrs. Harper's) — for she tells me she has not heard from you.

I hope this long silence has meant that you have had a long holiday — not that you have been unwell?

Ever sincerely yours | William Sharp

ALS Stanford University

To Edmund Clarence Stedman, September 27, 1899

72 Inverness Terrace | London. W. | 27th Sept /99 | For the 8th Oct?

Dear Poet, Comrade, and E. C. S.

For "a good few" years now I have not forgotten to write to you for year birthday — & I certainly am not going to stop now! From my heart, cher ami, I wish all good to you and yours — & hope most eagerly that your new year will be one of greater health, leisure, & congenial work than any you have had for long. You have few friends in America, & I am sure none here, who love you & are more proud of you than your friend W. S.

I won't upbraid you for leaving both my long birthday letter of last year, and that at Xmas, unanswered. You have not been strong, &

always been overworked, &, with Charamard, old friends like ourselves can say "Love is Enough." I don't suppose either you've had time to read my latest book, "Silence Farm," which has had so marked a literary reception — which I sent you last summer.

I saw the Janviers the other day. Tom has been very seedy, but is now slowly getting stronger. Ned Dodd, too, has been *very* ill — but is convalescing satisfactorily, and Nan Dodd is to come over to England for a short visit next week. She is a dear.

Is Miss Stuart married yet? I would like to hear of her.

Could not you or my good friend Mrs. Stedman (to whom my love) send me a Postal Card, just to say how things are with you. D*o*. A card will do: don't think of writing.

> Ever, Dear Stedman, Affectionately, William Sharp

Again (& now my wife joins — & so does Chas. G. D. Roberts, who has just looked in) all loving good wishes for your new year.

ALS Princeton University

To Mrs. Grant Allen, September 28, 1899

> Wharncliffe | Chorleywood, Herts | 9/28/99

Dear Nellie

We are only a day or two back from Irish wilds — and learned with infinite regret, first from a paper and then from friends, that Grant was not up and about again as we had hoped (having been unaware of what has happened the past 6 or 8 weeks) but is still seriously ill. We are so sorry, dear Nellie, and send you our loving sympathy — and our most eager hopes that dear Grant will soon get well and be his old brave buoyant self again. It must have been, must still be, a horribly anxious time for you. Is there anything I can do for Grant. Please ask him. And Elizabeth will so gladly do anything for *you*.

Don't trouble to write a note, but do send a postcard. The above is our new address (not far beyond Harrow) — a kind of small Hindhead!

Our love to you and poor dear Grant, and all eager good wishes.

Ever dear Nellie, for Elizabeth and myself | Your friend, | Will

ALS Pierpont Morgan Library

To Anatole Le Braz,[32] [October] 1899

Dear M. Le Braz,

Your letter was a great pleasure to me. It was the more welcome as coming from one who is not only an author whose writings have a constant charm for me, but as from a Celtic comrade and spiritual brother who is also the foremost living exponent of the Breton genius. It may interest you to know that I am preparing an *etude* on Contemporary Breton (i.e. Franco-Breton) Literature;[33] which, however, will be largely occupied with consideration of your own high achievement in prose and verse.

It gives me sincere pleasure to send to you by this post a copy of the "popular" edition of Adamnan's *Life of St. Colum*[34] — which please me by accepting. You will find, below these primitive and often credulous legends of Iona, a beauty of thought and a certain poignant exquisiteness of sentiment that cannot but appeal to you, a Breton of the Bretons... .

It seems to me that in writing the spiritual history of Iona I am writing the spiritual history of the Gael, of all our Celtic race.[35] The lovely wonderful little island sometimes appears to me as a wistful mortal, in his eyes the pathos of infinite desires and inalienable ideals — sometimes as a woman, beautiful, wild, sacred, inviolate, clad in rags, but aureoled with the Rainbows of the west.

"Tell the story of Iona, and you go back to God, and end in God." (The first words of my "spiritual history")... .

But you will have already wearied of so long a letter. My excuse is ... that you are Anatole Le Braz, and I am your far-away but true comrade,

Fiona Macleod

Memoir, p. 315

To Richard Garnett, October 8, 1899

Wharncliffe | *Chorleywood* | Herts

My dear Garnett

We are now settled here, at this bracing & delightful place, near Milton's Chalfont St. Giles and Arnold's beloved Ches: & here sometime you may feel inclined to come for a breath of vivid air.

If in this new undertaking of yours you have some part you could depute to me, I should be glad to be associated with it & with you. But that of course is just as suits your no doubt already matured plan of operations.

I thought at first the Library was to be a reprint of the Amer. Library of World's Best Literature to which I contributed several essays ("Kalevala", "Icelandic Sagas", "Celtic Lit", "Villemarqué & Burzaz Breiz" etc. etc.)[36] — but I see it is not.

I hope Mrs. Garnett is better of the change, & that you & yours are well. My wife would join in cordial regards & remembrances, but she is at Tunbridge Wells.

Ever sincerely yours | William Sharp

ALS University of Texas, Austin

To Theodore Watts-Dunton, [October 19, 1899][37]

Wharncliffe | *Chorleywood* | Herts

Dear Aylwin

This is only a brief line to say that I have read your beautiful poem with singular pleasure. There is no mistaking its authorship — & how great a thing that is in these mocking-bird days none can know better than yourself. To its flawless metrical beauty is added a floating atmosphere of essential poetry: it is as impossible not to feel the one as not to be charmed by the other. I look forward greatly to "The Luck of Vesprie Towers" when it is published complete.[38] (By the way, the phenomenon of the mirrored rainbow is not so rare as you imagine. I have myself seen it, & in a note I had from Miss Macleod the other day — who, I may add, greatly admires your poem — she says that she has seen it in Aora Water & elsewhere in the West Highlands, and adds that if you will visit Benbecula[39] you may on rare occasion from a certain standpoint see the lovely effect known as the Rainbow Chain — the innumerable fiord-lets, pools, inlets, tarns, etc. of any part of that "Isle of the Thousand Lakes," within immediate vision, linked by the mirrored rainbow). She has a description of it in one of her uncollected stories.

How lovely Autumn is at this moment. The trees here are divinely lovely. I am so glad of having "Vesprie Towers" to look forward to.

Ever affectly yrs. | William Sharp

ALS University of Leeds, Brotherton Library

To John Macleay, October 20, 1899[40]

Friday, / 20th October 1899

Dear Mr. Macleay

It is very kind of you to send to me that appreciative and gratifying notice from the "Liverpool Courier" — which, I take it, is from your own pen, and, if so, is the more welcome.

I was interested to hear recently of your marriage, and wish happiness and well-being to you and your wife. But I wish you could be in Inverness instead of Liverpool! Yes, you may be sure, if ever I can direct any work or influence your way, that it will give me pleasure to do so.

Thank you, I am now in much better health: but a brief return to Edinburgh is convincing me that I shall never be well in any town. And that reminds me, that I would have answered your letter earlier, but that it followed me about from Kyleakin to Oban and then to Islay, and ultimately arrived in Edinburgh just as I did I suppose.

You have always been so friendly and so interested in my work that I know you will be pleased to hear that "The Dominion of Dreams" is now in a fifth edition (though it is not yet quite five months since first issue). Had I foreseen so unlikely a success, I would have had this fifth edition my "definitive" one as to revisions and alterations — but, now, this "definitive" edition is to be the Seventh — if, as seems probable, that is called for by or soon after the end of the year. I am very dissatisfied with much of the book: but I shall cancel only one piece, the weak because merely pretty "House of Sand and Foam." Strangely, the story which will take its place is also so-called — indeed its title was "lifted" for the other — but I may rename it. What brought me to do this was the glowing praise of it in an ill-written adulatory article: whereat I at once became suspicious, re-read the story, and promptly canceled it. I may alter the arrangement a little — and there are few pages except in "The Herdsman" which will not have at least an emendatory touch. I am uncertain what to do about the first part of "The Yellow Moon Rock." Mr. Yeats and Mr. George Russell write to me begging me to cancel it as "unworthy of me": Mr. Sharp and others do not concur: a few others highly esteem these condemned pages: and I am myself on the back of the blind wind, as we say in the isles.

There is a sudden departure from fiction ancient or modern in something of mine that is coming out in the November and December issues of "The Fortnightly Review." I hope you will read "The Divine Adventure," as it is called — though this spiritual essay is more "remote,'" i.e. unconventional, and in a sense more "mystical," than anything I have done. But it is out of my inward life. It is an essential part of a forthcoming book of spiritual and critical essays or studies in the spiritual history of the Gael, called "The Reddening of the West."

I have much else on hand — some of which you know about already, but of this I need not speak even to one so interested as you have always shown yourself, and to whom I am indebted. No, I have not yet read Mr. Munro's book. I took it up, but I admit that the greater virility and power of Mr. Maurice Hewlett's new Italian stories prevailed with me. Of course though, I shall read it later. I liked the opening, but did not care much for what I said [for "saw"] "dippingly."

A book I look forward to with singular interest is Mr. Arthur Symons's announced "Symbolist Movement in Literature."[41]

This is the longest letter I have written for — well, I know not when. But, then, you are a good friend.

Believe me, | Yours most sincerely, | Fiona Macleod

TLS National Library of Scotland

To Jerrard Grant Allen, October 27, 1899

Wharncliffe | Chorleywood, Herts | 27/Oct/99

My dear Allen[42]

It was a grief to me (as explained in enclosed copy of telegram sent) not to be able to be present in person at Woking, in evidence both of my deep affection and high regard for my dear friend your father.

I send this to you now only lest my telegram never reached Grant Richards. (I sent it to him, as I thought you would have heavy enough a burden to bear without my adding to it at such a moment.) It was only by chance that I saw in a morning paper today that the service was to take place at Woking at 3 — & I at once changed my clothes, caught the one available train, & drove straight across — but, in the hurried departure, I had unfortunately read "Charing Cross" for "Waterloo" — & so I missed the train after all, to my profound regret everyway.

You have my deepest sympathy, as has your bereaved mother to whom I wrote two days ago. Your friend, | William Sharp

ALS Pierpont Morgan Library

To Grant Richards, [*October 27, 1899*]

Wharncliffe | Chorleywood, Herts

My dear Richards,

I hope you got my telegram. It was a deep regret to me not to be present. It was only at the last moment I saw in a morning paper that the funeral was to be today, at 3, at Woking — and I had time only to change my clothes and catch the one available train. I drove straight across — but in my hurry I had taken a wrong memory with me, and so went to Charing Cross instead of to Waterloo — and only too late discovered my mistake. It is a very deep regret to me, every way. He was a dear and loved friend.

As the one thing I could do, then, I telegraphed to you as per enclosed, and hope you received it.

Perhaps you will not grudge the time to let me know, and add how poor Nellie is.

(Did you not say that your sister lived at Chorleywood? Is she a married sister?)

Ever yours, my dear Richards, with deep sympathy for you in the loss of one so near and dear to you —

William Sharp

ALS Pierpont Morgan Library

To R. Murray Gilchrist, [*October 25, 1899*][43]

My Dear Robert,

It is a disappointment to us both that you are not coming south immediately. Yes.; the war-news saddens one, and in many ways.[44] Yet, the war was inevitable: of that I am convinced, apart from political engineering or financial interests. There are strifes as recurrent and inevitable as tidal waves. Today I am acutely saddened by the loss of a very dear friend, Grant Allen. I loved the man — and admired the brilliant writer and catholic critic and eager student. He was of a most winsome nature. The world seems shrunken a bit more. As yet, I cannot realise I am not to see him again. Our hearts ache for his wife — an ideal loveable woman — a dear friend of us both.

We are both very busy. Elizabeth has now the artwork to do for a London paper as well as *The Glasgow Herald*. For myself, in addition to a great complication of work on hand I have undertaken (for financial reasons) to do a big book on the Fine Arts in the Nineteenth Century.[45] I hope to begin on it Monday next. It is to be about 125,000 words, (over 400 close-printed pp.), and if possible is to be done by December-end! ...

You see I am not so idle as you think me. It is likely that our friend Miss Macleod will have a new book out in January or thereabouts — but not fiction.[46] It is a volume of "Spiritual Essays" etc. — studies in the spiritual history of the Gael.

We like this most beautiful and bracing neighbourhood greatly: and as we have pleasant artist-friends near, and are so quickly and easily reached from London, we are as little isolated as at So. Hampstead — personally, I wish we were more! It has been the loveliest October I remember for years. The equinoxial bloom is on every tree. But today, after long drought, the weather has broken, and a heavy rain has begun.

Yours, | Will

Memoir, pp. 311–12

To William Blackwood, October 31, 1899

Wharncliff | Chorleywood | Herts | 31/Oct/99

Dear Sir,

I send herewith for your consideration a poem — a sea-ballad called "The Admiral of the Sea" — for which I hope you may care.

Indeed this is the reason why I do not send it to *Harpers*, where I have promised to send something of the kind — for I am anxious that a poem of so patriotic a nature should appear in an English magazine, and, among these, preferably in "Blackwood's".

Believe me | Yours very brief | William Sharp

William Blackwood Esq.

P. S. I find I have to send you the rather untidy first-typed copy, as the duplicate has been accidentally destroyed.

ALS National Library of Scotland

To Theodore Watts-Dunton, [November 6, 1899][47]

Chorleywood | Monday Night

My dear Watts-Dunton

Excuse a delayed acknowledgment. I have been away for five days, & returned only tonight. I hope soon now to send you the MS.[48] but it cannot be for about a week yet. I expect — on account of exceptional pressure both of literary & private affairs (& as Dalton's series in Literature[49] is arranged in advance some 3 weeks). But there shall be no avoidable delay. Meanwhile my thanks, not only for "Astrophel"[50] (& at this moment, I see, C. Kernahan's book)[51] but the other Material, which shall go safely back to you in due course.

Part of my absence was spent on a brief visit to George Meredith. He told me you had been down, & spoke cordially of you. I had a very happy visit, loving him as I do.

Have just left Eugene Lee Hamilton & his wife. He too spoke of you. In haste for the last train (by which I shall send this in)

Yours ever | William Sharp

ALS University of Leeds, Brotherton Library

To Grant Richards, [early November, 1899]

Wharncliffe | Chorleywood

My dear Richards

Thank you for your letter. I am indeed glad to hear that our dear friend Nellie is behaving with so much heroism of good sense and courage and loving fealty. I am glad you have written to the *Athenaeum* (which by an accident I have not seen). If ever there was an unembittered and generous nature it was Grant Allen. I never knew a sweeter and finer. It is either gross heedlessness or culpable malice that could call him bitter.

No time for more (post just going). I have already met your sister.

Yours cordially, | W. S.

P. S. Could you send me kindly a P/C to say if G. A. was a member of the Omar K. Club. I ask because I want to make a special allusion to his death, and our loss, in the Presidential verses for the 1st Omar dinner, which Sir Geo. Robertson[52] has asked me to write. (This is between ourselves meanwhile.)

ALS Pierpont Morgan Library

To R. Murray Gilchrist, [early] November, 1899

Chorleywood, | Nov., 1899.

My Dear Robert,

The reason for another note so soon is to ask if you cannot arrange to come here for a few days about November-end, and for this reason. You know that the Omar Khayyam Club is the "Blue Ribbon" so to speak of Literary Associations, and that its occasional meetings are more sought after than any other. As I think you know I am one of the 49 members — and I much want you to be my guest at the forthcoming meeting on Friday Dec. 1st, the first of the new year.

The new President is Sir George Robertson ("Robertson of Chitral") — and he has asked me to write (and recite) the poem which, annually or biennially, someone is honored by the club request to write. The moment she heard of it, Elizabeth declared that it must be the occasion of your coming here — so don't disappoint her as well as myself! ...

Ever affectly yours, | Will.

Memoir, pp. 312–13

To Theodore Watts-Dunton, [*November 1899*]

Wharncliffe | *Chorleywood* | Herts

My Dear Aylwin

I am not writing to you this time about literary doings, but about a personal matter. I want to know if you can help me with a loan.

What with long and disastrous illness at the beginning of the year — having to help others dear to me — and, finally, losses involved through the misdeeds of another, I find myself on my beam-ends. By next Spring I hope to have things righted so far, if health holds out — but my pinch is just now, with less than £5 in the world to call my own at this moment!

If, therefore, you could lend me £50 — no, that will only be the harder to repay, & I m*ay* be able to manage all right with less — if, then, you can lend me £25, repayable as early next year as I can manage (probably February, if not, as possible, much sooner) you would be doing an old friend a vital service in a time of great difficulty.[53] (So much of our small income being dependent on journalistic art-work, we are feeling severely the pinch of the war, as all work of the kind is curtailed by two-thirds.)

Meanwhile I have undertaken to do a big History of the Fine Arts in the Nineteenth Century, which, eventually, should repay the heavy outlay of time & labor I must give to it (I have 100,000 words of it to write before the end of the year!).

Fortunately I need to go to town very seldom just now — so both health & pocket benefit, as well as sorely needed time.

My wife is away today, or would join with me in cordial greetings.

Ever affectly Yours | William Sharp

ALS British Library

To Frank Rinder, [December 30, 1899]

... Just a line, dear Frank, both as a dear friend and literary comrade, to greet you on New Year's morning, and to wish you health and prosperity in 1900. I would like you very much to read some of this new Fiona work, especially the opening pages of "Iona," for they contain a very deep and potent spiritual faith and hope, that has been with me ever since, as there told, as a child of seven, old Seumas Macleod (who taught me so much — was indeed the *father* of Fiona) — took me on his knees one sundown on the island of Eigg, and made me pray to "Her." I have never written anything mentally so spiritually autobiographical. Strange as it may seem it is almost all literal reproduction of actuality with only some dates and names altered.

But enough about that troublesome F. M.! ...

William Sharp

Memoir, pp. 315–16

To R. Murray Gilchrist, [December 30, 1900]

... It was written *de profundis*, partly because of a compelling spirit, partly to help others passionately eager to obtain some light on this most complex and intimate spiritual destiny.[54]

William Sharp

Memoir, p. 316

Endnotes

Introduction

1   This Introduction is a slightly revised version of the Introduction to Volume 1 of *The Life and Letters*.

Chapter 12

1   Preceding this letter in the *Memoir*, Elizabeth Sharp wrote: "At the New Year, 1895, he wrote to a friend." Following the excerpt, she said, "The strain of the two kinds of work he was attempting to do. The immediate pressure of the imaginative work [by which she meant the work of Fiona Macleod] became unbearable."

2   Robert Fergusson (1750–1774) was a Scottish poet who, after studying at the University of St Andrews, led a bohemian life in Edinburgh, the city of his birth, at the height of intellectual and cultural ferment of the Scottish enlightenment. Many of his extant poems were printed from 1771 onwards in Walter Ruddiman's *Weekly Magazine*, and a collected works was first published early in 1773. Despite his short life, his career was highly influential, especially through its impact on Robert Burns. He wrote both in Scottish English and the Scots language, and it is his vivid and masterly writing in the latter for which he is principally acclaimed. The brutal circumstances of the poet's early death prompted the young doctor Andrew Duncan (1744–1828) to pioneer better institutional practices for the treatment of mental health problems through the creation of what is today the Royal Edinburgh Hospital. Wikipedia contributors, "Robert Fergusson," *Wikipedia*, 10 January 2020, https://en.wikipedia.org/wiki/Robert_Fergusson

3   Known as the "Weaver Poet," Robert Tannahill (1774–1810) wrote poetry in English and lyrics in Scots in the wake of Robert Burns. Working as a weaver in Paisley, his interest in poetry and music blossomed after

becoming acquainted with the composer Robert Archibald Smith, who set some of his songs in the Scots language to music. While taking part in the literary life of the town, he helped found the Paisley Burns Club and became its secretary. His work began to appear in periodicals such as *The Scots Magazine* and in 1807 he published a small collection of poems and songs in an edition of 900 copies which sold out in a few weeks. In 1810, following the rejection of an augmented collection of his work by publishers in Greenock and Edinburgh, he fell into a depression aggravated by fears for his own health, burned all his manuscripts, and drowned himself in a culverted stream under the Paisley Canal. Wikipedia contributors, "Robert Tannahill," *Wikipedia*, 15 November 2019, https://en.wikipedia.org/wiki/Robert_Tannahill

4   Horace Scudder, *Childhood in Literature and Art* (Boston and New York: Houghton, Mifflin and Company, 1894).

5   William Sharp, "Some Reminiscences of Christina Rossetti," *The Atlantic Monthly*, 75 (June, 1895), 736–48.

6   *The Germ*, a Pre-Raphaelite periodical devoted to literature and art, was edited by William M. Rossetti. Four numbers appeared in 1850 during January, February, March, and April. The second two of the four issues were renamed *Art* and *Poetry*.

7   This hope was not realized.

8   Thomas A. Janvier, Catherine's husband.

9   The beginning portion of this letter is missing. Patrick Geddes (1854–1932) was a Scottish philosopher, sociologist, biologist, and city-planner. He had been Senior Demonstrator of Practical Physiology at University College, London (1877–1878) and Demonstrator of Botany and Lecturer on Zoology at the University of Edinburgh (1880–1889). From 1889–1919, he was Professor of Botany at University College, Dundee. Geddes organized the first student hostel in Scotland at University Hall, Edinburgh in 1887. During the same year, he established a summer school of arts, letters, and science in Edinburgh which continued until 1899 and attracted students and scholars from Great Britain and the continent. In 1894, he transformed a town mansion known as "Laird of Cockpen," located near the Castle on the Edinburgh High Street, into the Outlook Tower, the first sociological laboratory in the world. Best known for the camera obscura in its tower in which one can view a panorama of the city of Edinburgh, the building is now a museum and library for studying Geddes and his associates. Following its opening in 1894, the building became the locus of the Scottish version of the Celtic Revival. Geddes fostered this movement as

a means of furthering his ambition to restore Edinburgh as a major center of learning in Europe. He served as Professor of Sociology and Civics at the University of Bombay from 1919–1924 and Director of Scots College at Montpelier University from 1924–1932. He contributed in lectures and writings to the theory of sociology and the practice of civics, and devoted nearly twenty years of his life (1894–1914) to planning towns for India. He was also instrumental in designing the Mt. Scopus campus of the Hebrew University in Jerusalem. In 1911, with his life-long friend, Victor Branford, Geddes outlined a series of books called "The Making of the Future" wherein they would explain to English-speaking people the causes and the nature of the disastrous war he thought would break out by 1915. Among Geddes works are *Evolution of Sex* with J. Arthur Thomson (1889), *Cities in Evolution* (1915), and *Ideas at War* (1917). The Sharps met the Geddes in the fall of 1894, and they became close friends. Geddes employed Sharp variously in his publishing firm, which Sharp used as a vehicle for the publication of his books and those of his friends. Wikipedia contributors, "Patrick Geddes," *Wikipedia*, 9 February 2020, https://en.wikipedia.org/wiki/Patrick_Geddes

10   Amyl Nitrate dilates blood vessels and was used to relieve the pain of angina by expanding the vessels in the heart. Since suffering rheumatic fever as a young man, Sharp's heart was weak and subject to periodic angina attacks. Geddes must have given Sharp some amyl nitrate capsules to use when he felt an angina attack coming on.

11   The Sharps went to Ventnor on Sunday January 6 and returned to London on Friday January 18. This letter was written on Tuesday January 15.

12   Geddes wrote "21/1/5-" at the top of this letter and made many notes on the pages as he read them. Sharp's "Monday" establishes the letter's date.

13   The publishing firm of P. G. Geddes and Colleagues was established in 1895. As this letter makes clear, it was designed as a medium for the expression and dissemination of Celtic-oriented poems and stories and of scientific works that would help to restore Edinburgh's reputation as a center of learning. William Sharp served briefly as Manager of the firm and then became its Literary Adviser. He saw the firm as a vehicle for his writings, and under his guidance, it published beautifully designed editions of Fiona Macleod's *The Sin-Eater* (1895), *The Washer of the Ford* (1896), and *From the Hills of Dream* (1896). These were followed by Fiona's *Songs and Tales of St. Columba and His Age* (1897), and *The Shorter Stories of Fiona Macleod* (1897), a rearrangement and reissue in three inexpensive paper-covered volumes of the stories published in The Sin-Eater and The Washer of the Ford. The firm's most successful publication, a book that went through several editions, was an anthology of Celtic poetry called

Lyra Celtica (1896) which Elizabeth Sharp compiled and edited and for which William Sharp wrote a lengthy introduction and copious notes.

14   *The Chap-Book.*

15   J. Arthur Thomson (1858–1935) was Professor of Human Anatomy at Oxford (1893), Lecturer on Anatomy in Relation to Art at the Royal College of Art in South Kensington, and Professor of Anatomy at the Royal Academy (1900–1934). He also served as Representative of the University of Oxford on the General Medical Council (1904–1929). Besides co-authoring *The Evolution of Sex* (1889) with P. G. Geddes, Thomson wrote *Biology for Everyman* (1935), *The Biology of the Seasons* (1911), *Darwinism and Human Life* (1909), and *Heredity* (1911).

16   Edinburgh.

17   William Angus Knight (1836–1916) was a Scotsman and professor of moral philosophy at the University of St. Andrews from 1867–1902. His many publications include *Poems from the Dawn of English Literature to the Year 1699* (1863), *Studies in Philosophy and Literature* (1879), *Wordsworth's Prose* (1893), and *Some Nineteenth Century Scotsmen* (1902).

18   This was published in November 1895 by Stone and Kimball in Chicago, and by Patrick Geddes and Colleagues in Edinburgh. It was advertised in *The Chap-Book*, 3 (November 1, 1895).

19   Sharp became dissatisfied with *Greenfire*, which he published as the work of Fiona Macleod and dedicated to Edith Rinder. He rewrote the "Highland" portion of the book, "named it 'The Herdsman,' and included it in Fiona Macleod's *The Dominion of Dreams* in 1899" (*Memoir*, p. 276).

20   Fiona Macleod's "From the Hebrid Isles" appeared in *Harper's New Monthly Magazine*, 92 (December, 1895), 45–60.

21   There is no evidence that Sharp completed this article.

22   George Santayana, *Sonnets* (Chicago and Cambridge: Stone & Kimball, 1894); probably Gilbert Parker, *A Lover's Diary: Songs in Sequence* (Chicago and Cambridge: Stone & Kimball; 1894); probably Hamlin Garland, *Prairie Folks* (Chicago: F. J. Schulte and Company, 1893).

23   Joseph Pennell (1857–1926) was an American artist and writer who lived in England. Among his publications are *A Canterbury Pilgrimage* (1885), *Modern Illustration* (1895), *The Life of James McNeill Whistler* (1907), and *The Graphic Arts* (1922).

24 "Some Personal Reminiscences of Walter Pater," *The Atlantic Monthly*, 74 (December, 1894), 801–14.

25 William Sharp, "John Addington Symonds," *The Atlantic Monthly*, 47 (February, 1895), 95–6.

26 Sharp, "Some Reminiscences of Christina Rossetti."

27 Here, Sharp indicates that the editor of the *Academy* has agreed to accept an article by him on Scudder's *Childhood in Literature and Art*. This article did not materialize.

28 Sharp, "John Addington Symonds."

29 Frederick Shields.

30 Paul Verlaine, *The Poems of Paul Verlaine*, trans. by Gertrude Hall (Chicago: Stone & Kimball, 1895). This was actually the fourth title issued in the *Green Tree Library* Series.

31 This volume did not appear.

32 See letter *To Herbert Stuart Stone, December 31, 1894* (Volume 1) for contents and final ordering of *The Gypsy Christ*.

33 Sharp was working on the Fiona Macleod stories that appeared in *The Sin-Eater and Other Tales*.

34 This quarterly materialized not as "The Celtic World," as proposed here by Sharp, but as *The Evergreen: A Northern Seasonal*. As Sharp suggested, there is no editor given on the title page. It reads simply: "Published in the Lawnmarket of Edinburgh by Patrick Geddes and Colleagues | in London by T. Fisher Unwin, and | in America by J. B. Lippincott Co." The first of four projected parts simply called Spring was published in the spring of 1895 with a "proem" by William Macdonald and J. Arthur Thomson. Part II (Autumn) appeared in the fall of 1895, and Part III (Summer) and Part IV (Winter) in 1896. See note 13 above to Sharp's letter to Patrick Geddes dated April 27, 1895.

35 J. Stanley Little recently married the Viscomtess Fanny Maude Therese de la Blache. For more information on J. Stanley Little, see Endnote 49, Chapter 3 (Volume 1).

36 Mrs. Alden was very ill, and this letter, the first part of which is missing, was an effort to lift her spirits and provide some comfort. Her son-in-law, Joyce Kilmer, dedicated his famous poem "Trees" to her.

37   Henry Mills Alden, *God in His World: An Interpretation* (New York: Harper & Brothers, 1890).

38   The frustration expressed by Sharp in this letter at the lack of communication from Stone is an early indication the Stone and Kimball firm was having difficulties. Stone's father, whose money helped start the firm, was not pleased that expenses continued to outweigh revenues, and Stone himself was beginning to tire of the endless details of running a business. Furthermore, stresses had begun to develop between the two young partners.

39   Sir Thomas Barclay (1853–1941), a journalist who became a barrister, moved to Paris in 1888 to join a small group of British lawyers practicing there. An advocate of arbitration and conciliation, he became an expert in international law. He served as President of the British Chamber of Commerce in Paris in 1899–1900 and as an Honorary President of the Institute of International Law in 1919. For the 1911 edition of the *Encyclopedia Britannica*, he wrote the sections on International Law, Neutrality, Peace and several related subjects. One of Patrick Geddes's aims was to reestablish close ties between Scotland and France as a means of reasserting Edinburgh's prominence as a center of learning. Geddes asked Sharp to explore with Barclay in Paris the possibility of his assisting in the establishment of a Franco-Scottish College to jump start closer ties between France and Scotland. Not one to abandon a cause, Geddes persisted until, in 1924, he helped establish Scots College, a residence hall for Scottish and other foreign students, at Montpelier University in France, for which he subsequently served as Director for eight years. Wikipedia contributors, "Thomas Barclay (economic writer)," *Wikipedia*, 8 June 2019, https://en.wikipedia.org/wiki/Thomas_Barclay_(economic_writer)

40   Phoebe Anna Traquair was married to Ramsay Heatley Traquair (1840–1912), a friend of Geddes and a Scottish naturalist and paleontologist who served for thirty-three years as Keeper of the Natural History Collections at the Royal Scottish Museum in Edinburgh. Wikipedia contributors, "Ramsay Traquair," *Wikipedia*, 25 September 2019, https://en.wikipedia.org/wiki/Ramsay_Heatley_Traquair

41   William Macdonald was an aspiring poet who Geddes asked to assemble and oversee the publication the first volume of *The Evergreen*, the journal which Sharp proposed to Geddes in his letter of March 3, 1895. Macdonald and J. Arthur Thomson, a biologist friend of Geddes, signed the seven-page "Proem," or introduction, to that volume, but Geddes's influence is apparent throughout, as evidenced in its concluding sentence: "The music of the coming Renascence is heard so far only in 'broken snatches,' but in these snatches four chords are sounded, which we would fain carry

in our hearts – That faith may be had still in the friendliness of fellows; that the love of country is not a lost cause; that the love of women is the way of life; and that in the eternal newness of every Child is an undying promise for the Race." Macdonald contributed two poems to the first volume of *The Evergreen* and one poem to each of the succeeding three volumes. Sharp's opinion of this first *Evergreen* is contained in his letter to Patrick Geddes, May 15, 1895. Wikipedia contributors, "Arthur Thomson (naturalist)," *Wikipedia*, 8 July 2019, https://en.wikipedia.org/wiki/John_Arthur_Thomson

42   James Campbell Irons (1840–1910) was the author of *The Burgh Police Act* (1893), *The Autobiographical Sketch of James Croll* (1896), *Leigh and Its Antiquities* (1893), and *The Law and Practice in Scotland Relative to Judicial Factors* (1908). Wikipedia contributors, "James Campbell Irons," *Wikipedia*, 16 November 2019, https://en.wikipedia.org/wiki/James_Campbell_Irons

43   Sir Thomas Barclay. See Endnote 39.

44   For Irons, see Endnote 42. Victor Branford (1864–1931), a London banker, sociologist, and historian, was a life-long friend of Patrick Geddes, and he co-authored with him a series of books on the problems of war and peace under the general title "The Making of the Future." The three main books of the series are *The Coming Polity* (1917), *Ideas at War* (1917), and *Our Social Inheritance* (1919). He also wrote *The Life of Frederic Le Play* (1931), *An Atlas of Chemistry* (1889), and *The Coal Crisis and the Future* (1926). The latter was co-authored with P. Abercrombie, C. Desch, P. Geddes, C. W. Salerby, and E. Kilburn Scott.

45   Geddes has written on the letter: "Press for July – Agreed 23/5/5 for the Autumn." This indicates that Sharp and Geddes were together on 23 May, and that Sharp agreed to place Fiona Macleod's *The Sin-Eater* with Patrick Geddes and Colleagues.

46   *The Sin-Eater and Other Tales* was published in the fall of 1895 by Stone and Kimball in Chicago, and by Patrick Geddes and Colleagues in Edinburgh.

47   The first edition of *Lyra Celtica*, with a long introductory essay by W. S. and edited by E. A. S., was published in the fall of 1895 by Patrick Geddes and Colleagues in Edinburgh. I have found no record of *Musa Catholica*.

48   Here Geddes wrote: "Not now." Sharp had proposed as the firm's first publication a book either by or about Robert Louis Stevenson who died in 1894, but that proposal did not materialize. Sharp habitually looked upon the death of a writer as an opportunity to write about the author or publish the author's work. This trait prompted Oscar Wilde, following the

publication of books about Daniel Gabriel Rossetti by both Sharp and Hall Caine in the year following Rossetti's death, to remark, "When a great man dies, Sharp and Caine go in with the undertaker."

49   The references here are to James Campbell Irons' *Autobiographical Sketch of James Croll* and J. Arthur Thomson's *Heredity*. The former was published in 1896 by Edward Stanford University (London), and *Heredity* was published by John Murray (London) in 1909.

50   Here Geddes wrote: "Discuss in August." This book did not materialize. Sharp may have intended it be the series of lectures he was scheduled to present at Geddes's summer school in August 1895. If so, Geddes wanted to hear them before agreeing to publish them as a book. Sharp collapsed during his first lecture with what E. A. S. said was a heart attack and did not complete the others.

51   Here Geddes wrote: "Mrs. Mona Caird – Agreed 23/5/5." Sharp suggested yet another close friend to produce a book for the publishing firm when he and Geddes met in May. Mona Caird was a popular spokesperson for the rights of women, especially for granting women the right to vote and equal legal rights within the marriage contract.

52   Neither series materialized.

53   Jonas Lie (1833–1908) was a Norwegian novelist. Among his works are *Den Fremsynte* (1870), *Tremasteren Fremtideneller, eller Liv nordpå* (1872), *Lodsen og hans Hustru* (1879), *Rutland* (1881). Ola Hansson (1860–1925) was a Swedish poet, narrative writer, and essayist. Among his works are a collection of poems, *Dikter* (1884), a novella collection, *Sensitiva amorosa* (1887), and the novels *Resan hem* (1894), *Vägen till livet* (1896), and *Rustgården* (1910). Gabriele d'Annunzio (1863–1938) was an Italian poet, playwright, novelist, propagandist, military leader, and eccentric. Among his works are the novels *The Triumph of Death* (1896), *The Maiden of the Rocks* (1898), *The Flame of Life* (1900), and the plays *The Dead City* (1902), *La Gioconda* (1902), and *The Honeysuckle* (1915). Antonio Fogazzaro (1842–1911) was an Italian novelist and poet who wrote *The Patriot* (1907), *The Saint* (1907), *The Woman* (1907), *The Politician* (1908), *Leila* (1901). Matilde Serao (1856–1927) was an Italian novelist whose works include *La conquista di Roma: Romanzo* (1885), *Addio, amore!* (1897), and *La Bellerina: Romanzo* (1901). José Eschegaray y Eizaguirre (1832–1916) was a Spanish dramatist who wrote *La Esposa del Vengador* (1874), *El Estigma* (1876), and *El Loco Dios* (1908). Hermann Sudermann (1857–1928) was a well-known German author who wrote *Heimat* (1893), *Morituri* (1897), *Frau Sorge* (1888), *Die Drei reiherfedern* (1898), *Drei Reden Gehalten* (1900), *Die Ehre* (1900), *Das Hohe Lied* (1908), *Die entgötterte Welt* (1916). Anatole France

(1844–1924) was a French novelist and critic whose books include *L'Etui de Nacre* (1892), *La Rotisserie de la Reine Pedauque* (1893), *Le Jardin d'Epicure* (1895), *Thais* (1909). Between 1886 and 1891, he was the literary critic for *Le Temps*, producing a mass of highly subjective criticism which appeared in book form as *La Vie Litteraire Sur La Vole Glorieuse* (1914). *The Human Tragedy* (1917), *The Mummer's Tale* (1921), and *Latin Genius* (1924) are some of his better-known works. J. H. Rosny (pseudonym of the brothers Joseph-Henri (1856–1940) and Seraphin Justin (1859–1948) Boex) wrote the novels *Nell Horn, de l'Armée du Salut* (1886), *Le Bilatéral* (1887), *La Termite* (1890), and *La Fauve* (1899). Georges Eekhoud (1854–1927) was a Belgian poet and novelist whose publications include *Kees Doorik*; *Les Dermesses* (1884); *La Nouvelle Carthage* (1888); and *La Faneuse d'Amour*. His novels treat social issues of the urban working class and peasants. In the 1880s he worked with the publication *La Jeune Belgique* in an effort to breathe life into Belgian literature. Camille Lemonnier (1845–1913) was a Belgian novelist and art critic who wrote in French and was connected with the review *La Jeune Belgique*. Among his writings are *Contes flamands et wallons* (1873), *Happe-chair* (1886), *Un Mâle* (1892), *Au cœur frais de la forêt* (1899), *Le Vent dans les Moulins* (1900), and *Le Petit Homme de Dieu* (1903). Hamlin Garland (1860–1940) was an American novelist and essayist who wrote *Main Travelled Roads* (1890), *Crumbling Idols* (1894), *The Life of Ulysses S. Grant* (1898), *A Son of the Middle Border* (1917), *Roadside Meetings* (1930), and *Forty Years of Psychic Research* (1936).

54   Date from postmark.

55   Deò-grein translates as "ray of sunshine," and refers to Anna Geddes.

56   George Cotterell (1839–1898) was an English poet, who edited the *Yorkshire Herald*, and reviewed poetry and fiction for *The Academy*. He published *Constantia, and Other Poems* (London: Provost, 1870), *The Banquet: A Political Satire* (London: W. Blackwood, 1885), and *Poems: Old and New* (London: D. Nutt, 1894).

57   John Duncan (1866–1931) was a Scots artist who became a central figure in the revival of interest in Celtic art. He was a protégé of Geddes and with him founded the Edinburgh School of Art, which flourished between 1892 and 1900. He and Geddes executed a number of panels and murals depicting Celtic figures of legend and history for the dining and common rooms of Ramsey Lodge and St. Giles House, a student hostel near the Castle in Edinburgh. In the Spring number of *The Evergreen*, Duncan contributed, in addition to Celtic designs, several plates in black and white that were influenced by Aubrey Beardsley's drawings for *The Yellow Book*.

58   James Cadenhead (1858–1927) was employed by Geddes to paint the Edinburgh Room of Ramsey Lodge with friezes portraying the main features of the city. He also contributed black-and-white head and tail pieces to *The Evergreen*.

59   Unable to identify.

60   Robert Burns (1869–1941) was a Scottish landscape and figure painter, illustrator and designer. He was the Director of Painting at the Edinburgh College of Art.

61   Aubrey Beardsley (1874–1898) is best known for the illustrations he contributed to various periodicals of the fin de siècle, among them the *Yellow Book* and the *Savoy*, and for the drawings he executed for *Le Morte d'Arthur* (1893), *Salome* (1894), and *The Rape of the Lock* (1896).

62   *The Yellow Book* was a periodical published in book form. It offered a comprehensive view of the literary movements of the 1890s and provided the best examples of fin de siècle art. It was named for its brilliant yellow cover. The first number was published in April 1894 with Henry Harland as literary editor and Aubrey Beardsley as art editor.

63   T. & A. Constable, Ltd. (London) served as a secondary publisher and distributor of *The Evergreen*.

64   Sharp is referring to himself as "Porporsia Celtica."

65   Sharp wrote this letter from London shortly before he went to York on Saturday May 18 and on to Dundee on Monday May 20 to stay with the Geddes.

66   Cartledge Hall was the Gilchrist's family home in Holmesfield, where his mother and sisters lived. In the summer of 1895, Gilchrist and his companion George Garfitt moved from their house – Highcliffe in Eyam – to Cartledge Hall where they lived with Gilchrist's sisters until he died in 1917. Sharp's approval of his "going over to Cartledge," refers to that move, since a reference in his next letter to Gilchrist suggests that Cartledge is now, or will shortly be, his home. For more information about Gilchrist, see the "Life" section of Chapter 9 (Volume 1) for more information.

67   This letter from E. A. S is included to demonstrate the intense concern she felt about the physical and mental state of her husband, and as an indication of the generosity Patrick Geddes and his wife demonstrated to the Sharps. E. A. S. and the Geddes shared a hope that providing Sharp a salaried position with the fledgling publishing company would provide sufficient income to enable him to reduce the amount of time he had to

spend writing articles and reviews. After Sharp left the Geddes's home in Dundee on May 22 for the west of Scotland, Geddes wrote to E. A. S. to express his concern about Sharp's health and to offer to alleviate his need to write for money by providing a stipend from the publishing firm. He mentioned that Sharp was suffering from back pain, and here Elizabeth says she will put him in a doctor's hands to treat the back problem when he returns. When he did return, Sharp told Geddes in a letter of 4 June: "I am sorry you wrote exigently about my health – & particularly about my back." He did not want to worry Elizabeth about this particular ailment.

68   Geddes invited Sharp to give a series of twelve lectures in August at his Summer School in Edinburgh. According to E. A. S., Sharp "was seized with a severe heart attack" during his first lecture ("Life & Art: Art & Nature: Nature"). He finished that lecture with great difficulty, canceled the remaining lectures, and repaired to the Pettycur Inn across the Firth of Forth to recover while his wife stayed on in the flat they had taken for the month of August in Ramsay Gardens "to keep open house for the entertainment of the students." See letter *To J. Stanley Little, [early August, 1895]* (Volume 2) and its accompanying endnote.

69   Rutland House | Greencroft Gardens | So. Hampstead is printed on the stationery. Sharp told Gilchrist in the previous letter that he would be going back to London "somewhere about Whitsuntide," or a few days after May 26. The return addresses of that letter indicated he would be staying with the Geddes at Dundee on the nights of May 20–22 and leaving on May 23. This letter indicates that Sharp came to Edinburgh overnight, after spending a few days in the west of Scotland near Loch Fyne. He returned to London on Wednesday May 29, and told Geddes on June 4 that he had spent four glorious days (May 17–20) at a remote place on Loch Fyne. His description of his experience in the west – "the dream is over," etc. – suggests that he may have been joined by Edith Rinder for this brief interlude. That suggestion is supported by the ecstatic "Paganism" and promise "to be good" in the letter to Geddes.

70   Unable to identify.

71   *The Washer of the Ford: Legendary Moralities and Barbaric Tales* was published by Stone and Kimball in early 1896.

Chapter 13

1   The Allens lived in a house called "The Croft," in Hindhead, Haslemere, Surrey. A free thinker and a prolific writer, he had many friends in the London literary establishment. He became famous in 1895 with the publication of *The Woman Who Did*, a novel about a woman who refused to marry her lover because of the unfairness of the marriage laws. The novel was both widely attacked and satirized, and widely praised by advocates of women's rights. For more information about Grant Allen, see Sharp's letter *To Richard Le Gallienne, [May 22, 1888]* (Volume 1).

2   The lectures for Patrick Geddes's Summer School in Edinburgh in August 1895.

3   Date from postmark.

4   Recently married to the Viscomtess Fanny Maude Therese de la Blache, Little had apparently suffered a loss with financial implications, perhaps the loss of his job as a reporter/columnist on the *West Sussex Gazette*.

5   The first portion of this letter is missing. Its approximate date is established by Sharp's statement that he hears *The Mountain Lovers* has been published but has not seen a copy. It was published by John Lane (London) on 9 July 1895.

6   Sharp's *Ecce Puella and Other Prose Imaginings* was published on November 1, 1895 by Elkin Matthews in London and simultaneously by Stone and Kimball in Chicago. See Sharp's letter *To Edward Clodd, November 2, 1895* (Volume 2). At least some copies of the edition carry the date 1896.

7   "Fragments from the Lost Journal of Piero di Cosimo," *The Scottish Art Review* (June, 1890).

8   Sharp wrote "Fair Women in Painting and Prose" for P. G. Hamerton's *Portfolio of Artistic Monographs* (London: Seeley and Company, 1894).

9   "Love in a Mist," *Good Words*, 34 (December, 1893), 845–50.

10   Copeland and Day Publishing Company in Boston.

11   Sharp signed the English and American rights for *Ecce Puella* with Elkin Matthews on the condition that Matthews give first offer for American publication to Stone and Kimball.

12   *The Gypsy Christ and other Tales* (Chicago: Stone & Kimball, 1895).

13   *The Mountain Lovers*.

14   *The Massacre of the Innocents and Other Tales by Belgian Writers* (Chicago: Stone and Kimball, 1895) was a collection of Belgian stories translated and introduced by Edith Wingate Rinder.

15   *The Mountain Lovers.*

16   Meredith replied to this letter on July 13. He apologized to Fiona for not having acknowledged *Pharais* ("a gift to our literature") the previous year due to the press of his work. The "book on the Mountains" promises "as richly." And he added "Be sure that I am among those readers of yours whom you kindle."

17   Sharp's *Vistas* (1894) and *The Gypsy Christ* (1895).

18   Edward Clodd (1840–1930) worked for the London Joint Stock Bank from 1870–1915. A prolific writer, a friend of Charles Darwin, a folklorist, and chair of the Rationalist Press Association from 1906–1913, he was a close friend of Grant Allen. He published *Grant Allen: A Memoir* in 1900, the year after Allen died. Among his other books are *The Childhood of the World* (1873), *The Childhood Religions* (1875), *Jesus of Nazareth* (1886), *A Primer of Evolution* (1895), *Tom Tit Tot: An Essay on Savage Philosophies in Folk Tale* (1898), *The Story of the Alphabet* (1900), and *Animism: Seed of Religion* (1905).

19   This individual is yet to be identified.

20   Sharp must have mentioned a rumor about Grant Allen and "a literary Parisian" that upset Mrs. Allen and proved to be untrue.

21   Marie Adelaide (Belloc) Lowndes (1868–1947) was a translator and prolific author. Besides translating *The de Goncourt Journals* in 1895, she wrote many novels, among them *Another Man's Wife* (1934), *And Call It An Accident* (1936), *After the Storm* (1941).

22   James Sutherland Cotton, editor of *The Atheneum.*

23   Henry Mills Alden, editor of *Harper's Magazine* in New York, was a friend of Sharp's. Sharp had recommended Allen's stories or novels for American publication by Stone and Alden.

24   The reference must be to the manuscript of Grant Allen's *The Woman Who Did* which Lane published later in 1895. Perhaps Allen originally intended to publish it pseudonymously, and Lane had inadvertently made that difficult by telling someone Allen was the author.

25   Many well-known writers were members of the Omar Khayyam Club which was dedicated, as its name suggests, to good food and wine and

convivial companionship. This dinner was held at Burford Bridge, an historic hotel in the village of Mickleham south of Box Hill in Surrey. Edward Clodd, President of the Omar Khayyam Club, had enticed his friend George Meredith, who lived on Box Hill, to attend. Meredith was famously reticent about appearing and speaking in public. He did not arrive until the dessert course was being served whereupon Clodd welcomed him in a "charming and eloquent speech." Realizing he was the guest of honor, Meredith expressed his appreciation in a witty talk. For more about Clodd see note Sharp letter *To Mrs. Grant Allen, July 11, 1895* (Volume 2). Sharp became a member of the Omar Khayyam Club in the fall of 1895 upon Clodd's recommendation (*Memoir*, p. 246). See Sharp's letter *To Edward Clodd, November 2, 1895* (Volume 2), in which he expressed his appreciation for Clodd's recommendation.

26   Le Gallienne was staying with Grant Allen in Surrey in early summer 1894 when a copy of *Pharais* arrived for Allen to read and review. Le Gallienne recognized in the work an image that had appeared in a Sharp poem and said to Allen "I'll bet you anything that 'Fiona Macleod' is no one else but — William Sharp." Though somewhat suspicious, Allen accepted Fiona at face value and praised the book in the *Westminster Gazette*. Le Gallienne, however, said in his review of *Pharais* in *The Star*, "Either Miss Macleod is plagiarizing or William Sharp is masquerading as Fiona Macleod." When he saw the review Sharp sent Le Gallienne a telegram saying, "For God's Sake, shut your mouth" and then a letter promising an explanation when they next met (*Romantic 90's*). When Le Gallienne reviewed Fiona's *Mountain Lovers* in *The Star* in early July 1895, he again hinted that Fiona Macleod was a pseudonym and again Sharp asked him not to raise that suspicion. Sharp was trying to arrange a meeting with Le Gallienne to "explain" about Fiona Macleod, but his letter *To Richard le Gallienne, July 15, 1895* (Volume 2) indicates the meeting would probably have to wait until later in the year when Le Gallienne returned from America.

27   A "retouched" version of the first English edition of *Pharais* (Derby: Frank Murray, 1894) was published by Stone and Kimball in 1895. By making slight changes in the text, it was possible to obtain a separate U.S. copyright. Simultaneous publication of Fiona Macleod's collection of tales (*The Sin-Eater*) in November 1895 by Patrick Geddes and Colleagues in Edinburgh and Stone and Kimball in Chicago assured copyright in both countries. Stone had gone from London to Paris where, presumably, he planned to stay for a time.

28   This copy is in the Mark Samuels Lasner Collection in the University of Delaware Library. Mr. Lasner has kindly sent me the inscription, which

reads: "Dear Mrs. Gilchrist, Give me pleasure by accepting this new book by my most intimate friend & closest comrade, Fiona Macleod — whose acquaintance you have already made in *Pharais*. She does not forget your kind letter, and wants to meet you, and her unknown friend Robert Murray Gilchrist, in good time. Her salutations and my cordial regard to you both. William Sharp 1895."

29   Meredith was the guest of honor at this dinner. He may have been the "leading genius" in attendance, but he did not preside. See note to Sharp's letter *To Richard Le Gallienne, July 11, 1895* (Volume 2).

30   Printing this letter in her *Memoir* (pp. 230–31), Elizabeth omitted the second paragraph.

31   *The Mountain Lovers.*

32   These words of praise by Meredith are in a letter dated July 13, 1895 which is reproduced in the *Memoir* (pp. 245–46).

33   Sharp will be in Scotland alone but not in Edinburgh the last week of July before Elizabeth joins him in Edinburgh for the Summer Session in Ramsay Gardens. The likelihood is that he was not alone but in St. Andrews — about an hour north of Edinburgh — accompanied by Edith Rinder.

34   William Strang (1859–1921), painter and sculptor, was President of the International Society of Sculptors, Painters, and Gravers from 1918 to 1921. He won the Silver Medal for Etching at the Paris International Exhibition in 1889 and the First Class Gold Medal for Painting at the Dresden International Exhibition in 1897. A copy of Strang's fine etching of William Sharp (1896) is the frontispiece for E. A. S.'s *Memoir*.

35   *The Sin-Eater* was printed in Edinburgh by W. H. White and Company, The Riverside Press.

36   This ambitious list of the lectures Sharp planned to deliver in Edinburgh is copied from *Memoir*, p. 251. Since it is doubtful that Sharp had more than rough notes on any of them, his collapse during the first, as reported by E. A. S., may have been a fortunate act of avoidance.

37   These three poems appeared in Le Gallienne's *Robert Louis Stevenson and Other Poems* (Boston: Copeland and Day, 1895).

38   *Ecce Puella and Other Prose Imaginings* which was published on 1 November 1895.

39   Henry Alden's wife and Miss Alden's mother had recently died following a long and debilitating illness.

40   This story was "Mary of the Gael," which appeared first in *The Evergreen: A Northern Seasonal, The Book of Autumn* (Edinburgh: Patrick Geddes and Colleagues, 1895) and then in *The Washer of the Ford* (Edinburgh: Patrick Geddes and Colleagues, 1896) where it was called "Muime Chriosd," or "Foster-Mother of Christ". Sharp had sent the story to Mrs. Alden as his own work, but it appeared both in *The Evergreen* and in *The Washer of the Ford* as the work of Fiona Macleod. It is evident that Sharp had told Alden and his family that Fiona Macleod was William Sharp.

41   A book by Henry Mills Alden published in 1890.

42   Alden's *A Study of Death* (New York: Harper Bros.) was published in December, 1895.

43   Allen's review of *The Mountain Lovers* appeared in the *Westminster Gazette* in late July. Sharp had Mary copy this letter when he passed through Edinburgh and mailed it from St Andrews. The ALS in the Pierpont Morgan Library Library is in the Fiona handwriting.

44   *The Sin-Eater and Other Tales.*

45   This review appeared in *The Bookman*, 8 (August, 1895), 146–67.

46   *Athenaeum*, 106/3536 (August 3, 1895), 156.

47   This loss was clearly more serious than that mentioned in Sharp's letter To *J. Stanley Little, July 9, 1895* (Volume 2). It may have been the death of one of his parents.

48   According to E. A. S. (*Memoir*, p. 251), Sharp collapsed during his first lecture, barely finished it, and was unable to present the others.

49   In the following letter Sharp has Fiona staying with him in Ramsey Gardens for easy communication between the two regarding Stone and Kimball's publication of *Pharais* and *The Sin-Eater*. Sharp had continued easy access to the Fiona handwriting for further Fiona letters to Stone, since his sister Mary was nearby in Edinburgh, and she then traveled with the Sharps and Fiona in the West. The return address of this letter and others suggests that Sharp returned to Ramsay Gardens at least once in August. If Elizabeth is accurate in her recollection that Sharp collapsed after his first lecture, retired across the Firth of Forth to the Pettycur Inn, and delivered no more, then he would not have delivered a lecture on "The Celtic Renascence" as he claims in the next letter.

50   Although this letter is undated, internal evidence implies it was sent at the same time as the previous letter (the Fiona letter of August 12, 1895).

51   This article appeared as "A Note on the Belgian Renaissance," *The Chap-Book* (December, 1895), 149–57. It was intended to promote not Fiona's *The Sin Eater*, but Edith Rinder's *The Massacre of the Innocents and Other Tales*.

52   The remainder of the manuscript is missing.

53   Three British publishers.

54   *The Gypsy Christ* (1895).

55   Sharp had returned briefly from the Pettycur Inn to the flat the Sharps had taken for the month of August in Edinburgh. They left the next day for the cottage they had let in the Kyles of Bute.

56   *The Massacre of the Innocents and Other Tales.*

57   The Canadian poet Bliss Carman was a mutual friend. Stone had been in London and Paris earlier in the summer.

58   When he was in London, Stone must have met Theodore Watts, as he was then known, and arranged to publish a volume of his poems. Apparently Sharp was to receive a proof copy of the volume so he could promote the book by writing an article in Stone and Kimball's *Chap-Book*. Plans for the volume fell through, and Sharp did not write the article. He did write a note on the Belgian literary renascence for the December 1895 edition of *The Chap-Book*, in which he lavishly praised Edith Rinder's "Belgium book." Watts-Dunton's first volume of poems was *The Coming of Love | Rhona Boswell's Story | And Other Poems* which was published by John Lane at the Bodley Head (London and New York) in 1897. It was a sequel to his prose *Aylwin*, which appeared a year later (London: Hurst and Blackett, 1898). Both volumes went through many editions and established Watts-Dunton's reputation as a writer. Watts appended Dunton, his mother's maiden name, to his surname when he published *The Coming of Love*. That addition caused many of his friends, including William Sharp, to wonder what they should call him. James MacNeil Whistler is reported to have written to him as "Theodore" and asked "What's Dunton?"

59   Here, amazingly, Sharp tells Stone not only that Edith Rinder is Fiona's most intimate woman friend, but that Edith and Fiona have been "staying together recently." Since Sharp claimed to become Fiona Macleod when he and Edith were alone together, the statement lends support to the probability that Sharp and Edith were "staying together," probably in St. Andrews, during the last week of July. This passage is also interesting for its broaching — and then discounting — the possibility of some collaboration between Sharp and Edith Rinder on both the Fiona Macleod writings, and the writing Edith was doing on continental literature. The Rinders, both

of whom had deep roots in Scotland, were staying somewhere in Fifeshire in August. Edith probably helped Sharp recuperate at the Pettycur Inn following his angina attack in Edinburgh. She also seems to have visited the Sharps at Ramsay Gardens in Edinburgh briefly in late August on her way to Brittany "to work up Breton legends and folklore." Those tales formed the basis of her *The Shadows of Arvor*, which Patrick Geddes and Colleagues published in 1896 upon the recommendation of the firm's Literary Editor, William Sharp.

60   *The Gypsy Christ* was not published in England until 1897 (Westminster: Archibald Constable & Co.), when it bore the title *Madge o' the Pool: The Gypsy Christ and other Tales*.

61   *The Sin-Eater and Other Tales*.

62   This letter is written on *The Evergreen* letterhead, but that name and the printed return address (Patrick Geddes & Colleagues | Riddles Court Lawnmarket | Edinburgh) are crossed through. Sharp initially thought Stone's letters should go to him in Edinburgh. Then he decided they should go to his London address. Perhaps his use of the letter-head stationary was meant to assure Stone that he was closely associated with the firm and able to act for the firm regarding the publication of Fiona Macleod's *The Sin-Eater*.

63   *The Massacre of the Innocents and Other Tales*.

64   Sharp's *Wives in Exile* was printed by the University Press in Cambridge, and published by Stone and Kimball in 1896 after Kimball purchased Stone's holdings and moved the firm to New York. It was entered into copyright on June 20, 1896; copies (in boards) were deposited on September 11; and it appeared in the firms List of New Books for November, 1896. Shortly after the book was published, Ignalls Kimball sold the copyright and the unbound sheets to Lamson, Wolffe and Co. of Boston, which issued them with another title page and cover prior to the end of 1896. Publication of the English edition by Grant Richards in London was delayed until 1898.

65   For the Watt's article, see Endnote 60, Chapter 13 (Volume 2). Sharp sent for possible publication in *The Chap-Book* his translation of Charles Van Lerberghe's "dramalet" which was to appear in *The Evergreen: A Northern Seasonal, The Book of Autumn*, 61–71. Van Lerberghe (1861–1907) was a Belgian poet whose works include *Pan* (1906); *Entrevisions* (1898); and *La Chanson d'Ève* (1904).

66   Maurice Maeterlinck (1862–1949) was a Belgian essayist and dramatist who won the Nobel Prize for literature in 1911. *The Massacre of the Innocents*

was his first and only published prose essay (1886). He was best known for his symbolist dramas, among them "La Princesse Maliene (1889), "Pelleas et Melisande" (1892), and "Moons Vanna" (1902).

67 "Laclosely Belgique" was the first name of the literary movement with which Maeterlinck was affiliated. Subsequently, the movement was renamed "Le Coq Rouge."

68 Sharp's mother and sisters and Elizabeth's mother were staying with them in Tigh-Na-Bruaich.

69 Patrick Geddes had asked Sharp to review the "Prefatory Note" he had written for *The Evergreen: A Northern Seasonal, The Book of Autumn*, which would be published in mid-October. It may be that Sharp was responsible for the concluding sentences of that short note:

"Yet if man be one with Nature, her evolution is also his and this not only through the ages and the generations, but through the year and its Seasons. Here then are some of the ideas of 'The Evergreen.' It makes no promise of perpetual life, but seeks only to link the Autumn of our own age with an approaching Spring, and pass, through Decadence, towards a Renascence."

Geddes and Sharp shared the hope of renewal, but the personification of Nature and the cadence are Sharpian. Sharp served for a time as Literary Editor of Patrick Geddes and Colleagues, but his status was changed to Colleague, perhaps in August after his health prevented him from delivering the promised lectures in Geddes's Summer School. In Sharp's letter *To Edmund Clarence Stedman, September 27, 1895* (Volume 2), Sharp asserted that he was the "chief literary partner" of the firm.

70 In his letter *To Edmund Clarence Stedman, September 27, 1895* (Volume 2), Sharp told Stedman that he, Mrs. Sharp, and her mother were leaving the Kyles of Bute for Edinburgh that day. In this letter to Gilchrist, he tells Gilchrist they will leave "tomorrow." That establishes the letter's date as September 26.

71 Gilchrist must have worried that Sharp's failure to visit him on his way north, and the lack of correspondence from Sharp in the meantime, portended a breach in their friendship.

72 The three figures in the sketch entitled "Summersleep" are Sharp, Gilchrist, and Gilchrist's house mate/companion/lover George Garfitt. The latter two visited Sharp at Phenice Croft in July 1893. Near the end of "Summersleep," the shadow of Gilchrist says "in his heart": "There is something of awe, of terror, about that house; nay, the whole land here is under a tragic gloom. I should die here, stifled. I am glad I go on the

morrow." The shadow of William Sharp then says "in his heart: "It may be that the gate of hell is hidden there among the grass, or beneath the foundations of my house. Would God I were free! Oh my God, madness and death!" At Phenice Croft, Sharp had invented the persona of Fiona Macleod, and, according to E. A. S., "His imagination was in a perpetual ferment" (*Memoir*, p. 221). He was engaged there with psychic experiments, possibly drug induced. It was at Phenice Croft in 1893–1894 that he began to feel the presence of a second female personality, which led at times to a troublesome psychic splitting that that seemed to threaten his mental stability. Of this phenomenon, E. A. S. said, "During those two years at Phenice Croft, to which he always looked back with deep thankfulness, he was the dreamer — he was testing his new powers, living his new life, and delighting in the opportunity for psychic experimentation. And for such experimentation the place seemed to him peculiarly suited. To me it seemed 'uncanny,' and to have a haunted atmosphere — created unquestionably by him — that I found difficult to live in, unless the sun was shining. This uncanny effect was felt by more than one friend; by Mr. Murray Gilchrist, for instance, whose impressions were described by his host in one of the short 'Tragic Landscapes'" (*Memoir*, p. 223).

73 Sharp turned forty on 12 September 1895.

74 *The Massacre of the Innocents and Other Tales.*

75 "Les Flaireurs."

76 This sentence was taken from a letter Sharp sent to Catherine Janvier in the autumn of 1895.

77 In his 26 September letter to Gilchrist, Sharp said he would be back in his London residence on Tuesday, 1 October.

78 *Ecce Puella* was published on November 1, 1895. See Sharp's letter *To Edward Clodd, November 2, 1895* (Volume 2). Those dates and the dates of Sharp's trip to Scotland establish the date of this letter.

79 *Old World Japan: Legends of the Land of the Gods* (London: Grant Allen, 1895).

80 Originally scheduled for publication on October 15, delays by Stone and Kimball pushed back the publication date of *The Sin-Eater and Other Tales* to early November.

81 Date from postmark.

82 William Edward Garrett Fisher wrote *The Transvaal and the Boers* (1896). This letter accompanied the following letter from Garrett Fisher to Richard Garnett:

Savoy Mansions | Strand, W. C. | Oct:26, 1895

Richard Garnett, Esq., LL. D.

Dear Sir,

Mr. William Sharp has done me the honour to give me the enclosed letter of introduction to you. I am very happy to have this opportunity of forwarding it to you and of saying how much pleasure it would give me to make your acquaintance, and realize the personality that as yet I only know from books.

I shall do myself the honour of calling upon you at the British Museum next Wednesday at 3 o'clock, and trust that I may be fortunate enough to find you at home and disengaged. And in the meantime I am,

Dear Sir,

Your obedient servant | W. E. Garrett Fisher

83   *The Sin-Eater* was published in October, 1895. Thus the approximate date.

84   He refers to *The Sin-Eater, and Other Tales* and asks Gilchrist for a more detailed and thoughtful response to the book. The "one other than myself" who can know must be Edith Rinder.

85   For a discussion of this letter and the need expressed herein, see the "Life" section of this chapter.

86   See note to Sharp letter *To Mrs. Grant Allen, July 11, 1895* (Volume 2).

87   "Fragments from the Lost Journal of Piero di Cosimo" appeared first in *The Scottish Art Review* (June, 1890).

88   Hannibal Ingalls Kimball (1874–1933) began his publishing career in 1893, while an undergraduate at Harvard where, with Herbert Stuart Stone, he founded a company and issued among other works, a bibliography of American first editions and the first copies of *The Chap-Book*, a literary and artistic magazine designed to publicize books published by their company. In 1894, Kimball and Stone moved the firm to Chicago. In March of 1896, a New York sales office was opened and Kimball moved to New York to take charge. A month later, in April, the firm's principal financial backer, Melville E. Stone, Sr., Herbert Stone's father and owner/editor of the *Chicago Daily News*, insisted the firm release capital through liquidation of investments. Kimball did not wish to comply and offered to buy out Stone's interest. Stone accepted and soon started his own publishing firm, Herbert S. Stone and Company. Kimball continued to operate Stone

and Kimball Company in New York, shortly changing its name to reflect his sole ownership, and published thirty-six additional titles between May 8 1896 and July 3 1897. By October 1897, debts were such that the firm had to be liquidated, and Kimball turned to the printing business. He started Cheltenham Press, wherein he could apply his experimental typographical designs to printed advertising. In addition to designing and printing advertisements, Cheltenham issued privately several pamphlets by Stone and Kimball authors, among them Bliss Carman and Robert Louis Stevenson. Kimball left the printing business in 1917 to become President of the National Thrift Bond Corporation. While working in the investment field, Kimball invented the "baby bond" as an investment mechanism for low income groups. In 1921, he joined the Metropolitan Life Insurance Company as first Director of Group Annuities. At the time of his death in 1933, he was a recognized authority on industrial pension plans.

89   *The Gypsy Christ and Other Tales* (Chicago: Stone & Kimball, 1895) appeared in England as *Madge o' the Pool: The Gipsy Christ and Other Tales* (Westminster: Archibald Constable & Co., 1897).

90   This is the "formal receipt" mentioned in Fiona's letter *To [Hannibal Ingalls Kimball], November 25, 1895* (Volume 2), above.

91   The letter to a publisher, of which this note is a continuation, has not surfaced.

92   Sir George Brisbane Douglas (1856–1935) was described by E. A. S. (*Memoir*, pp. 253–54) as a "poet, scholar, and keen critic" who "had followed the literary career of William Sharp with careful interest, and gave the same heed to the writings of 'Fiona Macleod.'" After reading *The Sin-Eater*, Douglas concluded on the basis of internal evidence that Fiona Macleod was William Sharp and wrote to tell him his conclusion. Douglas edited for the Canterbury Poet series, of which Sharp was the general editor, *Poems of the Scottish Minor Poets, from the Age of Ramsay to David Gray* (London: Walter Scott, 1891), *Contemporary Scottish Verse* (London: Walter Scott, 1893), and *Scottish Fairy and Folk Tales* (London: Walter Scott, 1901). A series of lectures he gave at Glasgow University was published as *Scottish Poetry; Drummond of Hawthornden to Fergusson* (Glasgow: J. Maclehose and Sons, 1911).

93   The eight preceding lines in the manuscript have been heavily crossed through. The fourth line contains the name Edith Rinder, but the other words are impossible to make out. Presumably, Sharp decided to tell Douglas the role Edith Rinder played in the genesis of Fiona Macleod and then thought better of it. Sharp's characterization here of Fiona Macleod as a "puzzling literary entity" is an apt description of what she was for Sharp

during his lifetime and for Elizabeth as long as she lived. There were many efforts to explain that puzzle while Sharp was alive, and there have been many more in the century following his death in 1905.

94   See Sharp's letter *To Richard Garnett, October 25, 1895* (Volume 2).

95   The reference is to Fiona Macleod's "Mary of the Gael," which appeared in *The Evergreen: A Northern Seasonal, The Book of Autumn* in the fall of 1895. See Endnote 40, above. Douglas would have seen it in the autumn *Evergreen* because his tale, "Cobweb Hall", also appeared in that volume.

96   Fiona Macleod, "From the Hebrid Isles," *Harper's New Monthly Magazine*, 92 (December, 1895), 45–60.

97   See *Memoir*, pp. 245–46.

98   E. A. S. (*Memoir*, pp. 253–54) printed Douglas's response to this letter from Sharp, in which he maintained the fiction of Fiona Macleod's separate identity. It reads, in part, "I am very glad to find that you think I have understood Miss Macleod's work, and I think it very good of her to have taken my out-spoken criticisms in such good part. Certainly if she thinks I can be of any use to her in reading over the proofs of 'The Washer of the Ford,' it will be a great pleasure to me."

99   John Lane, the publisher.

100 See Endnote 65.

101 The firm was having managerial and financial problems. See Endnote 88.

102 As in his letter *To Robert Murray Gilchrist, November 1, 1895* (Volume 2), Sharp confided in Gilchrist regarding his depression and asked for help. The two struggling souls are Sharp's and Edith Rinder's, or Sharp's and Fiona Macleod's, or both, in the sense that Sharp identified Fiona with Edith.

103 John S. Stuart-Glennie was the son of the daughter of John Stuart of Inchbreck FRSE, Professor of Greek in the University of Aberdeen; his father was Alexander Glennie of Maybank Aberdeen. He was educated in law at the University of Aberdeen and became a barrister, called to the bar at the Middle Temple in 1853. He later undertook a series of journeys of historical exploration across Europe and Asia to collect folklore. This letter concerns a book — probably of folklore — by Stuart-Glennie. To my knowledge, it was not issued by the Geddes firm.

104 Alexander Carmichael's "The Land of Lorne and the Satirists of Taynuilt" appeared in *The Evergreen: A Northern Seasonal, The Book of Spring* (Edinburgh: Patrick Geddes and Colleagues, 1895), 110–15.

105   This brief note accompanied a copy of the above letter to Stuart Glennie, dated December 26, 1895.

106   As it turned out, Sharp accompanied his wife as far as Paris on January 4 and could not have visited Le Gallienne on Sunday, January 5. See his letter *To Richard Le Gallienne, [January 6, 1896]* (Volume 2).

107   *The Washer of the Ford: Legendary Moralities and Barbaric Tales* (Chicago: Stone and Kimball, 1896) and (Edinburgh: P. G. Geddes and Colleagues, 1896). The month of the Edinburgh publication was May, and its arrangement of tales differed from the one here.

108   A second edition of *The Mountain Lovers* was not published by Lane until February, 1906.

109   "Bliadhue mhath ur duit!" translates as "Happy New Year!"

Chapter 14

1   The Dr. Tebb who collected Arnold's books must have been W. Scott Tebb, a physician who wrote *A Century of Vaccination and What it Teaches* (London: Swan Sonnenschein & Co, 1898). Sharp's Canterbury Poets edition of Matthew Arnold's poems containing his critical introduction was published by Walter Scott in spring 1896.

2   Richard Garnett (1835–1906) was a scholar, librarian, biographer and poet. He rose to become Keeper of Printed Books in the British Museum in 1890 and served in that position until his retirement in 1899. His literary works include numerous translations from the Greek, German, Italian, Spanish, and Portuguese; several books of verse; a book of short stories *The Twilight of the Gods* (1888); and biographies of Thomas Carlyle, John Milton, and William Blake. His *The Age of Dryden* was published by Bell in December, 1895.

3   Sharp probably wrote this letter during his brief trip to Edinburgh in January, 1896. He was in Edinburgh from Sunday January 12 to Thursday, January 16. The letter is written on the stationery of Patrick Geddes and Colleagues, and Geddes was at home in Dundee. In addition to copies of the letters from Belgian novelists, Sharp enclosed a typed digest of excerpts from reviews of Fiona Macleod, mainly of *The Sin Eater*, which the Geddes firm published in November 1895.

4   Eugene Demolder (1850–1919) was the author of *La Route d'Emeraude* (1899), *Roman* (1899), *L'Agonie d'Albion* (1901), and *Constantin Meunier*

(1901). Louis Delattre (b. 1870) was the author of *Bonne Chère; Bon Remde* (1938); and *Pain de Mon Blé* (1938). For previous mention of Georges Eekhoud by Sharp, see Sharp's letter *To Patrick Geddes, April 29, 1895* (Volume 2). The letters thank Edith Rinder for the copies of her translations of Belgian stories which were published as *The Massacre of the Innocents and Other Tales* by Stone and Kimball (1895) in their Green Tree Library series.

5   No writings by Eekhoud, Demolder, or Delattre appeared in *The Evergreen*.

6   Sharp's brackets.

7   In his January 10 letter to Nellie Allen, Sharp said he would be glad to see more of Mrs. Bird and her husband. Friends of the Allens, the Birds lived in London.

8   Edith Wingate Rinder's *The Shadow of Arvor* was published by Patrick Geddes and Colleagues in the Celtic Library series in the fall of 1896.

9   The bottom of the page is cut off. It may have contained something about the nature of his strain and anxiety.

10   Ernest Percival Rhys (1859–1946) was a literary critic, poet, editor. He and Sharp became close friends when editing publications for the Walter Scott publishing company in the 1880s (Rhys the Camelot Prose Series, and Sharp the Canterbury Poets Series). He is best known for his long editorship of "Everyman's Library" (1906–1946). In *Everyman Remembers* (London: J. M. Dent and Sons Limited, 1931), a literary reminiscence of London from the 1880s through the 1920s, he described William Sharp as "a veritable literary chameleon, taking on the colours of the regions and people he visited." His master stroke of magic, Rhys wrote, was "the discovery of the mysterious 'Fiona Macleod.' Sharp kept current an imaginary biography of her, which in some moods he fully believed to be fact, the lines between fact and fantasy being very carelessly drawn, or not drawn at all, in his cosmogony" (*Everyman Remembers*, p. 79). His *Fiddler of Carne* was published by Patrick Geddes and Colleagues later in 1896. Sharp wanted Stone and Kimball to publish an American edition, which Sharp accepted for the Geddes firm. His other publications include *Welsh Ballads* (1898), *Rhymes for Everyman* (1933), and *Letters from Limbo* (1936).

11   This paragraph and the next are written in red ink.

12   Louise Chandler Moulton.

13   The following annotation signed P. G. (Patrick Geddes) is inserted here: "Yes £75 due to W. S. as manager in two installments before May." In the lower left-hand corner of the letter appears the following: "1896. | Feb. 1. Pd. £25. | Apr. 11. Pd. £50."

14   This William Sharp letter, and the Fiona Macleod letter that follows, are among several solicited by John Macleay and published in issues of *The Highland News* dated February 1 and February 8, 1896. In the previous issue (January 25), Macleay called on fellow Highlanders to follow the lead of Fiona Macleod, to "come forward and give the benefit of their ideas and experiences." It is to be hoped, he said, that "Miss Macleod is but the first in a movement which shall bring the Highlands into line with the great band of young Irish writers who are at present attracting so much attention in the literary world." The January 25 issue also contained the first of two articles about Fiona Macleod: "A Highland Novelist." The second article, in the February 1 issue, praises the Irish writers and calls for Highland writers to try their best to emulate their "wide culture" and "commanding knowledge of the laws of their art." Although the Highlands "do not show well" in this Celtic revival, he continued, they have "one writer of great worth and greater promise," and that writer is Fiona Macleod, whose first three books — *Pharais, The Mountain Lovers,* and *The Sin-Eater* — are discussed in some detail and lavishly praised. The Sharp and Macleod letters reproduced here appear with others in a section of the February 1 issue called "The Highlands in Literature: A Symposium." Macleay continued the symposium the following week (February 8) with letters from, among others, Katherine Tynan Hinkson, who wrote, "What can I say except that I am fully in sympathy with your desire to see the Highlands in line with a Celtic revival, and to wish you God-speed in your endeavors to promote it? You have begun well with Miss Fiona Macleod. She is worth many lesser and less Celtic writers."

15   E. A. S. asserts (*Memoir*, p. 260) that this letter was written in mid-February, but the two articles on Fiona Macleod by John Macleay which Sharp says *The Highland News* "is printing" appeared in the issues of January 25 and February 1. That suggests a late January date for the letter, which is confirmed by the fact that the *Academy* review Sharp mentions — a favorable review of *The Sin-Eater* by Ernest Rhys which appeared "last week" — was in the issue number 1238, dated January 25, 1896 (72 –73).

16   *Ecce Puella: And Other Prose Imaginings* was published (London: Elkin Mathews) in November 1895, though its title page carried the date 1896. Gilchrist knew Sharp was the author of the Fiona Macleod writings.

17   *The Gypsy Christ and Other Tales* (Chicago: Stone & Kimball, 1895). This book was listed in Stone and Kimball's *Chap-Book* of November 1, 1895 as "now ready." Its British published was delayed until January 1897 when it appeared (by Constable's) under the title of another of its tales, *Madge o' the Pool.*

18   Having received a summary and several chapters of *Wives in Exile* for review, Herbert Stone accepted it for publication and promised one-hundred pounds on receipt of the manuscript. Sharp continued writing it during February and submitted the final manuscript in mid-March. Sharp counted on receiving that money, but it was not forthcoming.

19   E. A. S. stated that Sharp went north to the Pettycur Inn on February 1. In this letter, he tells Nellie Allen he is writing on a Sunday. February 2 was a Sunday, which dates the letter. E. A. S. (*Memoir*, p. 260) reproduced diary entries of what he wrote at the Pettycur Inn between February 3 and 10.

20   The Allens are to assume the friend is Fiona Macleod. Although Allen suspected Fiona Macleod was Sharp when he read *Pharais*, he did not dwell on the matter and accepted her as a real person in accord with what Sharp wanted him to believe. Edith Rinder was probably the friend who joined him at the Pettycur Inn. They stayed there often in these years for its relative privacy and easy access to Edinburgh. Sharp found it conducive to writing as Fiona Macleod.

21   See Endnote 14. Macleay has just sent Sharp copies of the weekly paper — probably the January 25 issue, which contained the first of his two pieces on Fiona Macelod, and the February 1 issue, which contained his second article on Fiona, along with the Sharp and Macleod letters dated January 28. The "Symposium" was continued in the February 8 issue. Uncertainty about the letter's date derives from uncertainty about whether Macleay sent Sharp all three issues, or only the first two.

22   John Macleay contributed a brief reflective essay called "The Breath of the Snow" to the second volume of *The Evergreen: A Northern Seasonal, The Book of Autumn* (113–17), which appeared in the fall of 1895. The reference here is to Macleay's second and last contribution to *The Evergreen*, a story called "Nannack" which appeared in the Summer 1896 issue (129–34). Sharp seems to have been more involved in editing this issue, and there is a marked improvement in the quality of its contents. It contains a poem by Sharp, a poem and a tale signed Fiona Macleod, and a sketch by Edith Wingate Rinder based on a recent work by the Breton writer Anatole La Braz. The latter also appeared in Mrs. Rinder's collection entitled *The Shadow of Arvor*, which the Geddes firm published in the fall of 1896.

23   Here, Sharp likely had Edith Rinder on account of her beauty.

24   The manuscript contains a note that the letter was posted on February 7, 1896.

25   Richard Le Gallienne.

26   Sharp sent Allen the February 1 issue which contained the letters from Sharp and Fiona Macleod and Macleay's second article on Fiona Macleod. A letter from Grant Allen, whose name may have been suggested by Sharp, appeared in the "Symposium" in *The Highland News* of February 8: "Dear Sir: I have every sympathy with the movement you are trying to inaugurate, but I hardly know how I can personally be of any service to it. I have welcomed and will continue to welcome (so far as opportunity is afforded me) all good work of Celtic writers which comes under my notice. More than this, I fear, I have no means of doing. Yours, very faithfully, Grant Allen."

27   James Barrie (1860–1937), playwright, biographer, and novelist, wrote *Peter Pan* (1916). Among his many other works are *The Admirable Crichton* (1914), *Dear Brutus* (1922), *Farewell, Miss Julie Logan* (1932), *Quality Street* (1934) and *The Boy David* (1938). Samuel Crockett (1860–1914) was the author of many tales, poems, and novels. Among his publications are *The Silver Skull* (1898), *The Loves of Miss Anne* (1904), and *Rogues Island* (1926).

28   Robert Farquharson Sharp, who worked with Garnett in the Department of Printed Books at the British Museum and later succeeded Garnett as Keeper, was Elizabeth Sharp's brother as well as William Sharp's cousin.

29   Fiona Macleod's *Green Fire: A Romance* was published in the fall of 1896 by Archibald Constable Ltd.

30   "Feb 18 '96" is written in pencil at the top of the letter. We can identify this day as a Tuesday.

31   *An Etymological Dictionary of the Gaelic Language* by Alexander MacBain was published in Glasgow in 1896.

32   *Lyra Celtica: An Anthology of Representative Celtic Poetry*, edited by Elizabeth Sharp, with an introduction and notes by William Sharp, was published in Edinburgh by the Geddes firm on February 21, 1896.

33   The body of the letter is typed, but the postscript is in Sharp's hand.

34   An article on Fiona Macleod appeared in the issues of January 25 and February 1. The letters from W. S. and F. M. appeared in the February 1 issue. See Endnote 14.

35   "Introduction," *The Poems of Matthew Arnold*, ed. by William Sharp, Canterbury Series (London: Walter Scott, 1896).

36   "Morag of the Glen" was published in *The Savoy Magazine* in November, 1896, in *The Shorter Stories of Fiona Macleod*, Vol. III, *Tragic Romances*

(Edinburgh: P. G. Geddes and Colleagues, 1897); and in the Tauchintz volume *The Sunset of Old Tales* in 1905. E. A. S. placed it in *The Dominion of Dreams* volume of the *Collected Works*.

37   E. A. S.'s friend, Mona Caird, was with her when she left Sienna for Rome. She must have joined Elizabeth in Florence.

38   "The Three Marvels of Hy" appeared in *The Washer of the Ford and Other Legendary Moralities* (Edinburgh: P. G. Geddes & Colleagues, 1896).

39   The "Prologue" to *The Washer of the Ford* was written "To Kathia," who was Catherine Janvier, the American painter and folklorist. She and her husband, Thomas Janvier, a popular fiction writer, lived during the winter months in Provence and in Greenwich Village in NYC the rest of the year. They were very close friends with the Sharps.

40   In his letter *To Elizabeth A. Sharp, February 21, 1896* (Volume 2), Sharp said he hoped to finish "Morag of the Glen" that night. In F. M.'s letter *To the Editor, Blackwood's Magazine, March 21, 1896* (Volume 2), Sharp asked the editor to make a decision about the story. Thus, this letter was written in late February or early March. *Blackwood's* did not accept "Morag of the Glen." See Endnote 36.

41   Robert McClure was the representative in England of *McClure's Magazine*, which was founded in America by his brother, S. S. McClure. In 1895, Stone and Kimball appointed Robert McClure as the firm's London "buying agent."

42   In his letter *To Edmund Clarence Stedman, January 25, 1897* (Volume 2), Sharp described Lillian Rea as "an American girl who after much residence abroad and fairly wide experience came to London first to assist me secretarially, and afterwards succeeded to a responsible position in the firm of Patrick Geddes & Colleagues." By that date, Miss Rea had left the Geddes firm and settled in London as a literary agent. Sharp was responsible for having her hired by the Geddes firm, and he continued to think of her as his assistant. He was annoyed with Geddes for delaying her departure to assist him in London. He needed secretarial help, and he needed her as a companion. His doctor had ordered he not be left alone which suggests a companion helped him ward off the demons of depression. Of the two women who usually performed that function, Elizabeth was in Italy, and Edith Rinder was ill.

43   E. A. S. edited the anthology *Lyra Celtica*, which was published by the Geddes firm on February 21. Her regular work was writing art reviews for the *Glasgow Herald*.

44   L/C is *Lyra Celtica*; Rhys is Ernest Rhys's *The Fiddler of Carne*.

45   His sister, Mary Sharp.

46   Date from postmark.

47   Irving Bacheller (1859–1950), a popular American novelist, established in 1884 the Bacheller Newspaper Syndicate, which supplied fiction and feature stories to major newspapers and periodicals. Bacheller's syndicate introduced the American reading public to Stephen Crane's *The Red Badge of Courage*, Joseph Conrad, Rudyard Kipling, and Sir Arthur Conan Doyle. More than 3.5 million copies of his own novels were sold during his lifetime.

48   By which, Sharp likely meant restoring/renewing his health.

49   In his letter *To Herbert Stuart Stone, March 11, 1896* (Volume 1), Sharp proposed an article on Le Gallienne for Stone and Kimball's *Chap-Book*, but the proposal was not accepted. Le Gallienne's *Prose Fancies* was published by Stone and Kimball on June 25, 1896 and concurrently in London by John Lane. It was advertised in the June 15 issue of *The Chap-Book*.

50   The first two sentences of the Prologue read as follows: "To you, in your far — away home in Provence, I send these tales out of the remote North you love so well, and so well understand. The same blood is in our veins, a deep current somewhere beneath the tide that sustains us."

51   Mrs. Janvier continued: "I refer to this because a little later Mr. Sharp gave me the original draft of this Prologue, written partly with pen and partly with pencil. For the student of Fiona Macleod, it is instructive to compare draft and printed page; to note the precise choice of word, the careful ordering of phrase and placing of paragraph. This same painstaking precision is shown in some other manuscripts and corrected proof in my possession. Never was there a more careful writer than Fiona Macleod, while of her creator this cannot be said." Shortly after the bound "Prologue" reached the Janviers on May 1, Sharp himself arrived, en route to the Riviera.

52   *The Washer of the Ford* was published by the Geddes firm on May 12 and by Stone and Kimball on June 12, 1896.

53   This transcription is from Sharp's draft for Mary to copy into the F. M. hand. James Ashcroft Noble (1844–1896) was a well-known critic and editor. See Sharp's letter *To James Ashcroft Noble, November 11, 1885* (Volume 1).

54   The remaining text from here to the end of the paragraph is crossed out in the manuscript.

55   The text from this point to "you and your daughters" is crossed out on the manuscript.

56   Good Friday was April 3 in 1896.

57   John Ross was hired by Geddes to manage the finances of the publishing company. Several letters in the Geddes Collection (NLS) provide context for this letter. An April 4 letter from Ross to Sharp precipitated this letter from Sharp to Geddes. On April 10, Geddes assured Sharp he would receive a check and wrote a short note to Elizabeth (to be forwarded to her in Italy by Lillian Rea) assuring her that Sharp's financial concerns would soon be alleviated. Lillian Rea returned that note to Geddes, stating that Sharp wished to keep knowledge of his ill health and concern over money matters from his wife.

58   Town and Gown Association, Ltd. was a stock-holding company formed in May, 1896, by Martin White, a long-time friend of P. G. Geddes, to place the various enterprises of Geddes on a strictly business basis. The association would support projects for civic betterment and provide a common meeting ground for men of affairs and men of learning so they might work together on such projects as the eradication of slum areas in the cities and the elimination of specializations in the universities.

59   Thomas Barclay. See Endnote 39, Chapter 23 (Volume 2).

60   *Wives in Exile* was published in London by Grant Richards in 1898.

61   Stone must have told Sharp to go ahead with an article on Le Gallienne, but Sharp seems not to have produced it.

62   Le Gallienne's *The Quest of the Golden Girl* was published by John Lane in the fall of 1896 in London and New York.

63   The surviving fragment begins here. Its handwriting is probably that of Lillian Rea who was serving as Sharp's secretary. Its signature and postscript are in Sharp's handwriting.

64   John Stuart Glennie who was the author of *Arthurian Localities: Their Historical Origin, Chief Country, and Fengalian Relations* (1869), *King Arthur: Or, the Drama of the Revolution* (1867–1870), *Christ and Osiris* (1876), *Merlin* (1899), and *Sociological Studies* (1906). He seems not to have published a book from the Geddes firm.

65   "Introductory Note," *The Poems of Ossian*, trans. by James Macpherson (Edinburgh: P. G. Geddes and Colleagues, 1896).

66   Edith Wingate-Rinder contributed "Telen Rumengal" to *The Evergreen: A Northern Seasonal, The Book of Summer* (1896, pp. 90–97) and "Sant Efflamm and King Arthur," to *The Book of Winter* (1896–1897, p. 69). Nora Hopper's "Swan White" appeared in *The Book of Summer* (41–42), and her "All Soul's Day" in *The Book of Winter* (75).

67   George Eyre-Todd's "Night in Arran" appeared in *The Book of Summer* (137–41).

68   Date from postmark. Sharp joined his wife in Venice on May 16, and they returned to England via the Italian Lakes. Sharp told Geddes in his letter of 9 April that it would be at least a week or ten days after he left Paris before he would meet his wife "as I am told [presumably by his doctor] to go by the Riviera, & stay somewhere 3 or 4 days on the way, at least — This for the head." That seems strangely specific advice from a physician and makes one wonder if Sharp wanted an interlude with his friends Thomas and Catherine Janvier in Provence. They may have accompanied him when he went on to Monte Carlo on the Riviera where he made more money in one night than he received from any of the books over which he had been laboring. The problems alluded to in this letter were probably the break-up of Stone and Kimball. Janvier would have had the latest U.S. publishing gossip, and Sharp was very concerned about whether Kimball, having established a successor firm in New York, could save Stone and Kimball's publishing list and continue to market his books. Sharp may have been trying to interest the firm in the American publication of one of Gilchrist's books.

69   The publication date of *The Washer of the Ford* (May 12, 1896) approximately dates this letter.

70   William Maxse Meredith, a son of George Meredith, had recently become an editor at Archibald Constable and Co. Perhaps on the strength of his father's enthusiasm for Fiona Macleod, he had agreed to publish a Fiona Macleod novel. Her *Green Fire: A Romance* was published by Constable in November, 1896. It was not well received, and Sharp decreed that only one section of it, "The Herdsman," be preserved in the Fiona Macleod canon.

71   Date from postmark. As always, Sharp was eager to have Gilchrist's opinion of his work.

72   Mrs. Gilchrist was Murray's mother.

73 Sharp is responding to someone who asked him about "The Three Miracles of Hy," which he wrote in February 1896 (see letter to *To Elizabeth A. Sharp, February 21, 1896* (Volume 2)), and included in Fiona Macleod's *Washer of the Ford* which was published in May. Thus the approximate date of the letter.

74 The American edition of *The Washer of the Ford* was finally published by Stone and Kimball on June 12, 1896 in New York. Having first opened a sales office for Stone and Kimball in New York, Kimball bought out Stone in early April, 1896, moved the firm to New York, and continued to publish for a while under the name Stone and Kimball, and then just Kimball. Herbert Stone retained *The Chap-Book* and started the H. S. Stone Publishing Company in Chicago. Later in 1896, when Kimball had to dissolve his firm, the *Washer of the Ford* sheets were acquired by Lamson, Wolffe and Co. in Boston. The delays in publication dates and payments which so annoyed and inconvenienced Sharp, who needed the money, were caused by the firm's financial difficulties and Stone's gradual loss of interest in its fate.

75 Sharp finally learned from Kimball the reason for the delays he had been experiencing. Melville Stone, Herbert's father, decided he could no longer cover the losses of the publishing firm whereupon Ingalls Kimball's father provided funds for his son to purchase Herbert Stone's share of the firm and move it to New York.

76 *Wives in Exile, A Comedy in Romance* was entered for copyright on June 20, 1896 by Stone and Kimball, New York, and copies were deposited on September 11. Shortly after its publication date, Kimball sold the remaining sheets to Lamson, Wolffe and Co. of Boston which reissued them with its imprint and a different cover. Herbert Stone had promised Sharp one-hundred pounds upon receipt of his manuscript, but Kimball was unable or unwilling to fulfill that promise. The first English edition was published by Grant Richards, in June 1898.

77 Since this letter was written on a Sunday, and since Sharp tells Garnett he spent a few days in Dover and reached London a week later than his wife, he must have returned to London on June 11 and written this letter to Garnett on June 14, a Sunday.

78 *Dante, Petrarch, and Camoens: CXXIV Sonnets* (London: John Lane, 1896).

79 Luis de Camoëns (also Camoës) (1524–1580) was a Portuguese poet and adventurer of Galician descent. During an eventful life which included losing an eye while fighting the Moors and being shipwrecked off the coast of China, he wrote lyric poetry, sonnets, and drama. He is most

remembered as the author of the *The Lusiads*, an epic poem that was widely read in nineteenth-century Britain after it was translated by Sir Richard Burton.

80   In his note to Gilchrist from Belagio, Sharp said he and his wife would return to England on 4 June, with Elizabeth going directly to London and William following a few days later. In the June 14 letter to Garnett he said he had spent a week in Dover on the way to London, which means that he arrived there on Thursday, June 11. In this letter, Elizabeth tells Geddes she called a doctor to see to her husband upon his return. That would probably have been during the week of June 14. Since she is forwarding Geddes's note to Fiona to the Pettycur Inn, Sharp must have left London for Edinburgh shortly before E. A. S. wrote to Geddes. We know Sharp stayed at the Pettycur Inn from about June 20 until June 30. The probable date of this letter is, therefore, June 20, a Saturday.

81   Elizabeth had taken over from her husband the job of writing of art reviews for the *Glasgow Herald*.

82   Arthur Allhallow Geddes was born on Allhallows Day in the fall of 1895; the Sharps were his godparents.

83   The Pettycur Inn, which is where Sharp was headed, was across the Forth from Edinburgh. Although Elizabeth asked Geddes in this letter not to discuss business matters with her husband "for any length of time at any one sitting" since he is so weak, subsequent letters indicate he was significantly involved with publishing firm business while he was there.

84   This letter was typed by Lillian Rea on Patrick Geddes and Colleagues stationery. "WILLIAM SHARP. per L. H. R." is also typed. Sharp did not sign the letter. Geddes was teaching in Dundee.

85   James Campbell Irons's *Autobiographical Sketch of James Croll* was published privately in 1896.

86   June 30 was a Tuesday, which means Sharp left Edinburgh for London on July 2 or 3. The first two typed pages are on blank sheets, and *Copy* is written at the top of page one. The last three pages are typed on Geddes and Colleagues stationery. Again, Sharp's signature is typed, and below it L. H. R. is written in Lillian Rea's hand.

87   Catherine Janvier's anthropological essay, "A Devolution of Terror" appeared in the fourth and final volume of *The Evergreen: A Northern Seasonal, The Book of Winter*, 106–11.

88   To my knowledge, none of these works by Thomson materialized.

89 Marion Isabel Newbigin (1869–1934) was a biologist, geographer, and editor of the *Scottish Geographical Magazine* from 1902 to 1934. She has been called one of the founders of modern British Geography. Her works include *Life by the Sea Shore* (1901), *Animal Geography* (1913), and *Geographical Aspects of Balkan Problems* (1915).

90 Sharp's critical biographies of Heinrich Heine (1888) and Robert Browning (1890) were published in the Walter Scott firm's Great Writer's Series.

91 This project never materialized.

Chapter 15

1 On this passage, E. A. S. wrote the following: "During the writing of *Pharais* the author began to realize how much the feminine element dominated in the book, that it grew out of the subjective or feminine side of his nature. He, therefore, decided to issue the book under the name of Fiona Macleod, that 'flashed ready-made' into his mind" (*Memoir*, p. 227).

2 Date from postmark.

3 Eugene Lee Hamilton sent this letter to Louise Chandler Moulton with the following note:

Prince of Wales Hotel | DeVere Gardens, W. | July 17 | Dear Mrs. Moulton | Our friend William Sharp has given me this note of introduction for you, in case you should not remember that I was once introduced to you at Florence in the days when I was still an invalid. Would you let me call on you? And in that case would you tell me when I should be likely to find you at home. | very truly yours | Eugene Lee Hamilton

4 This statement dates the letter as Sunday, July 19, 1896.

5 The fourth and last number of *The Evergreen: A Northern Seasonal, The Book of Winter* (published 1896–1897) contains no contributions from Macleay. This letter was written sometime during the week of July 27 when the Sharps were staying in Bamborough before proceeding on August 1 to spend a fortnight on "the little Holy Isle off the Eastern Shores, Lindisfarne, Iona's daughter" and do some "sea bathing" (*Memoir*, p. 266).

6 Neil Munro (1863–1930) was a Scottish journalist, newspaper editor, author and literary critic. He worked as a journalist on the *Greenock Advertiser*, the *Glasgow News*, the *Falkirk Herald* and the *Glasgow Evening News*, and he became editor of the *Glasgow Evening News* in 1918. A key figure in Scottish

literary circles, he was a friend of many writers and an early promoter of the works of Joseph Conrad and Rudyard Kipling. Efforts to identify Dr. Robertson Nieal have been unsuccessful.

7   *Green Fire: A Romance* was published by Archibald Constable and Co. in London, and Harpers & Brothers in New York in November 1896.

8   In a letter dated March 21, 1896, F. M. offered the editor of *Blackwood's* the British serial rights for her story "Morag of the Glen." *The Washer of the Ford* was published by Patrick Geddes and Colleagues in Edinburgh in May, 1896, and by Stone and Kimball in New York on 12 June 1896.

9   Date from postmark.

10   Kernahan must have made a proposal through Sharp to prepare an edition of a writer's work, perhaps an edition of poetry in the Canterbury Series, for which Sharp was a general editor.

11   With no more than a brief stop in Edinburgh, the Sharps went from Lindisfarne to Dunoon on the western shore of the upper Firth of Clyde west of Glasgow. In Edinburgh, Sharp found a letter from Macleay saying he had begun to arrange for Sharp to give a lecture on "The Celtic Spirit," which Sharp mentioned in his letter *To John Macleay [July 28?, 1896]* (Volume 2) as a possibility for early October in Inverness. After the debacle of his first lecture at Geddes's Edinburgh Summer School in August 1895, Sharp was afraid to commit himself to giving a lecture, much as he wanted to be a public spokesman for the Scottish Celtic cause. The letter was probably written in Edinburgh at the office of Patrick Geddes and Colleagues.

12   "1896" is written in pencil at the top right of the first page. Having welcomed Macleay's praise for the Fiona Macleod writings and his support for the cause of Scottish Celticism, Sharp reacted with alarm when the August 15 issue of *The Highland News* reached him in Dunoon. It contained Macleay's article entitled "Mystery! Mystery! All in a Celtic Haze," which quoted speculation by others about the true identity of Fiona Macleod. In this letter, Sharp reacts angrily to counter the speculation and chastises Macleay for repeating slanders against the poor defenseless woman. In succeeding letters to Macleay during the week, it began to occur to Sharp that the publicity generated by Macleay might well improve sales of the Fiona books.

13   At the close of Sharp's letter *To John Macleay [July 28?, 1896]* (Volume 2), he gave Macleay permission to reprint a statement he had made to the *Glasgow Evening News*: "Miss Fiona Macleod is not Mr. William Sharp; Miss

Fiona Macleod is <u>not</u> Mrs. William Sharp; and [...] Miss Fiona Macleod is — Miss Fiona Macleod."

14 Sharp's letter of "Tuesday night," August 18, must have been enclosed with this letter written on "Wednesday forenoon."

15 The Sharps returned briefly to Edinburgh on Saturday August 22.

16 After receiving Sharp's August 19 letter, Macleay must have responded with apologies for his actions. Since the Sharps went to Edinburgh on Saturday, August 22, this letter was written on Friday, August 21.

17 In his August 19 letter, Sharp said he expected to be in Inverness on September 4 or 5.

18 Sharp told Macleay on Friday August 21 he had forwarded his letter of apology to F. M. Here he has Fiona acknowledge receipt of Macleay's letter. Sharp probably dictated this letter or gave a draft to Mary for transcription when he reached Edinburgh on August 22.

19 Elizabeth, William, and Mary Sharp left Edinburgh for the Kyles of Bute on Monday, August 24.

20 *From the Hills of Dream: Mountain Songs and Island Runes* was published in Edinburgh by Patrick Geddes and Colleagues in November, 1896.

21 Henry Chandler Bowen (1813–1896) was the founder and an occasional editor of the *New York Independent*.

22 In the *Memoir* (pp. 266–68), E. A. S. printed this fragment, which she said was sent from the Tighnabruaich Hotel, after those dated 9/23 and 9/26. The Sharps and his sister Mary went to Tignabruaich in the Kyles of Bute on August 24 to join his mother and his other sisters. In mid-September, E. A. S. returned to London "to recommence [her] work on *The Glasgow Herald*" (*Memoir*, p. 266). This letter was written after she left and before Sharp and Mary left to stay near the Rinders in Tarbert. The next two fragments of letters to EAS, which she published in the *Memoir* (pp. 266–67) and dated September 23 and 26, were written at Tarbert. The letters to Yeats, Gilchrist, and Stedman that follow have Strath-Na-Mara, Tarbert of Loch Fynne, Argyll as their return address.

23 "The Awakening of Angus Ogue" appeared in *The Evergreen: A Northern Seasonal, The Book of Winter*, 118–23.

24 "The Rune of the Passion of Women" first appeared in Fiona Macleod's *From the Hills of Dream*. Arthur Symons, editor of *The Savoy*, accepted not "The Archer" but a second story Sharp submitted, "Morag of the Glen,"

which appeared in *The Savoy*, 7 (November, 1896), 227–48. "The Archer" appeared first in *The Shorter Stories of Fiona Macleod*, Vol. III, *Tragic Romances* (Edinburgh: P. G. Geddes & Colleagues, 1897). "Ahez the Pale" appeared in Vol. II of *The Shorter Stories: Barbaric Tales*, also 1897. "The Lily Leven" was a book Sharp intended to publish under the feminine pseudonym, but was never finished. A Fiona Macleod letter *To William Meredith, October 17, 1896* (Volume 2) indicates Sharp intended to send the book to him for publication by Constables.

25   Mona Caird, Edith Wingate Rinder.

26   This letter is unique in that two manuscript copies survive. The draft in Sharp's hand is in the National Library of Scotland, and Mary Sharp's copy in the Fiona Macleod handwriting is in the Yale Library. Sharp and Mary were staying in a hotel in Tarbert. Mary's copy in the Fiona Macleod hand, which was sent to Yeats, contains a few revisions in Sharp's hand. One is of special interest. He has Fiona tell Yeats her soon to be published volume of poetry will be called *From the Hills of Dream*. In the draft, Sharp first wrote "our" when referring to the volume, and then crossed out the "our" and wrote "my [Fiona's] own book of verse". Mary copied "my own book of verse," but in the manuscript there is a carat after "my," and "(our)" is written above the line in Sharp's hand and then lightly crossed through. Sharp was trying to decide whether or not to signal to Yeats that he shared responsibility for the poems in the Fiona volume. He remained conflicted in his dealings with Yeats in the matter of Fiona Macleod. Yeats was interested in the writings of Fiona Macleod, not those of William Sharp. Sharp wanted Yeats to accept him as a colleague in the Celtic Revival, but that desire was frustrated as long as he could not take credit for the writings he was contributing to the movement. The complex relationship between Sharp and Yeats is a fascinating story I have recounted partially in numbers 13 and 14 of the *Yeats Annual* (edited by Warwick Gould, 1998 (Macmillan Press) and 2001 (Palgrave)). For comments on the circumstances and significance of the visions mentioned in the letter, see my "W. B. Yeats and William Sharp: The Archer Vision," *English Language Notes*, 6/4 (1969), 273–80.

27   The reference here is to Sharp, her "dear friend and confrere." In the next paragraph, the friend has been with her during "much sailing about and faring in remote places," and he has participated in the "work we are doing, and putting together the volume of verse." Sharp wanted Yeats to believe not only that he figured somehow in the writings of Fiona Macleod, but also that the two were traveling companions.

28   *From the Hills of Dream*.

29   In his recent letter to Fiona, Yeats commented on her *The Washer of the Ford and Other Legendary Moralities* which had been published by the Geddes firm in May, 1896. "Annir Choille," mentioned in the next paragraph, is one of the stories in that volume.

30   This poem was first published in *The Savoy*, 5 (September, 1896), 52. When it next appeared in April, 1897 (*The Secret Rose* (London: Laurence and Bullen, Ltd.), pp. ix–x), it became "To the Secret Rose," and contained one revision in accord with the advice Sharp offers in this paragraph: "heavy" in line 7 became not "slumbrous," but "great."

31   Yeats's Blake paper — "William Blake and his Illustrations to *The Divine Comedy*" — was published in three parts in the July, August, and September issues of *The Savoy*. A reproduction of a Blake illustration of *The Divine Comedy* which accompanied the essay caused Messrs. W. H. Smith & Son to ban the magazine from newsstands. See Holbrook Jackson, *The Eighteen Nineties* (New York: Alfred A. Knopf, 1927), p. 50.

32   *John Sherman and Dhoya* (London: T. Fisher Unwin, 1891).

33   *The Celtic Twilight, Men and Women, Dhouls and Faeries* (London: Laurence and Bullen, 1893).

34   The promised volume was Yeats's next volume of poems, *The Wind Among the Reeds* (London: Elkin Matthews, 1899).

35   See Endnote 24.

36   In transcribing this letter (*Memoir*, pp. 270–72), E. A. S. read this word as "bare." In Mary's final copy it is clearly "wan," but it could easily be read as "bare" in Sharp's draft. E. A. S must have transcribed the letter from the draft, even though Yeats loaned her his letters from Sharp for the *Memoir*.

37   The Rinders probably rented the house in Tarbert for the month of September. On Saturday September 26, Sharp wrote to E. A. S from Tarbert. Thus he left for Glasgow on Friday, October 2 and spent that night in Glasgow before going on to Edinburgh the next day. That dates this letter as about September 28 and the following letter to Stedman ("In a day or two now I leave the West Highlands.") as about September 30.

38   "Edmund-mo-ghraidh" translates as "Edmund, my friend"; and "Stedman mo-caraid" translates as "Stedman, my dear one."

39   Sharp adopted a masculine, comradely and slightly risqué persona in writing to Stedman. It reflected what he perceived to be the prevailing pagan spirit, derived from the powerful influence of Whitman, among

the literary men he knew in the United States. Several letters suggest they shared confidences about their free-spirited extra-marital affairs, real or imagined, when they were together.

40   Edith Wingate Rinder's *The Shadow of Arvor* was published by the Geddes firm in the fall of 1896.

41   Mrs. Clothilde Balfour's essay "The Black Month," appeared in *The Evergreen: A Northern Seasonal, The Book of Winter*, 132–37.

42   J. H. Pearce's story "Fantasies" appeared in *The Evergreen: A Northern Seasonal, The Book of Winter*, 35–42.

43   William Cuthbertson, who contributed the poem "Grierson of Lag" to *The Evergreen's* winter volume, had a supervisory position in the Geddes firm.

44   This letter is in Lillian Rea's handwriting and is signed by William Sharp.

45   William Meredith (1865–1937) was George Meredith's son. He was a director and partner at Archibald Constable Publishing Company and was responsible for issuing reprints of his father's books as well as for the posthumous publishing of works left unfinished by Meredith at his death. He also edited *The Letters of George Meredith*.

46   This book was never finished. After publishing Fiona Macleod's *Green Fire* in November 1896, Archibald Constable and Co. next published her *The Laughter of Peterkin: A Retelling of Old Tales of the Celtic Wonderland* in October, 1897. *The Laughter of Peterkin* contains retellings of Celtic tales with the following titles: "Prologue: The Laughter of Peterkin," "The Four White Swans," "The Gate of the Sons of Turenn," and "Darthool and the Sons of Usna." Since Fiona Macleod in the above letter refers to a "Chapter" of "The Lily Leven," this work was probably the proposed novel and not one of the tales published as *The Laughter of Peterkin*.

47   Sharp went to Southhampton on October 22, and sailed from there on October 23.

48   I have been unable to identify this individual.

49   Date from postmark. Sharp inadvertently wrote "October 3" for "October 30" as his arrival date.

50   Henry Mills Alden, the editor of *Harper's Magazine*.

51   Immediately preceding this fragment in the *Memoir* (p. 222), E. A. S. described the effect upon her husband's work of his friendship with Edith Wingate Rinder: "And though this newer phase of his work was at no

time the result of collaboration, as certain of his critics have suggested, he was deeply conscious of his indebtedness to this friend, for as he stated to me in a letter of instructions, written before he went to America in 1896, concerning his wishes in the event of his death — he realised that it was 'to her, etc.'" Following that fragment from his letter of instructions, E. A. S. went on to say why Edith Rinder had such a profound effect on her husband.

52 In a letter of October 14, Sharp told Arthur Stedman his departure date would be October 23.

53 Louise Chandler Moulton.

54 Writing from Henry Alden's home in Metuchen where he stayed upon his arrival in New York on October 30, Sharp described the frenzied lead-up to the 1896 presidential election on Tuesday, November 3, in which William McKinley defeated William Jennings Bryan. The huge parade in New York occurred on Saturday, October 31, which was Halloween.

55 Fiona Macleod's *Green Fire* was published while Sharp was in New York, and this letter to E. A. S was written from New York (*Memoir*, p. 275).

56 This letter is pasted into the front of a first edition of *From the Hills of Dream*. Though undated, "Received Nov 7 / 96" is written at the top of the letter. The letter itself is in the Fiona handwriting.

57 Following this sentence, "C. & D." appears in Sharp's or another's hand. Sharp had asked Carman, who was an editor at Copeland and Day, to enquire about the possibility of that firm publishing an American edition of *From the Hills of Dream*.

58 Perhaps Fiona Macleod's *Washer of the Ford and Other Legendary Moralities* which appeared in May 1896.

59 Sharp's steamer left Hoboken on November 14 (Saturday) which dates this letter November 13 (Friday).

60 Ingalls Kimball sent a "ship reporter" to interview Sharp after he landed in New York to placate him before conducting business. The reporter was John D. Barry who wrote a favorable piece about Sharp in *The Daily Tatler*, a short -lived literary magazine which was edited by Kimball (also its publisher) and Carolyn Wells. Sidney Kramer, in his *History of Stone and Kimball and Herbert S. Stone and Company* (Chicago: Norman W. Forgue, 1940), said of the publication: "Kimball was granted time [from bankruptcy] to publish between November 7 and 21, 1896, *The Daily Tatler*,[...] the only daily paper published for profit in the United States

devoted exclusively to literary and artistic topics." Kramer quoted Carolyn Wells saying the paper did not die of "inanition." Rather it proved "too great a strain on the time and energies of the staff, who discovered that to rise at six o'clock every morning is a sad grind and without its due reward in fun. So the thirteenth day saw the final edition of what was doubtless the only daily literary paper ever attempted." In his November 13 letter Sharp expressed his thanks for the notice in *The Daily Tatler* and his hope that the publication would become more influential (greater shadow) and survive as a daily.

61   This book never appeared.

62   Sharp did not publish a story under this title.

63   Sharp's signature has been cut out of the letter.

64   This sentence was omitted from E. A. S.'s transcription of the letter (*Memoir*, p. 279), but Ernest Rhys retained it in the excerpt of the letter he included in his *Letters from Limbo* (London: J. M. Dent and Sons, 1936).

65   Sharp arranged for Lamson, Wolffe, and Company to take the plates and printed sheets of *Wives in Exile* from Stone and Kimball in 1896 and issue the volume. See Endnote 68.

66   Two Fiona Macleod books were published while Sharp was in America: *Green Fire* and *From the Hills of Dream*. The books intended for the three Americans were probably copies of the latter.

67   In switching to a new sheet of paper, Sharp repeated #4.

68   In his descriptive bibliography of the published books of Stone and Kimball (*History of Stone and Kimball and Herbert S. Stone and Company*, p. 242), Sidney Kramer described *Wives in Exile* as published by Stone and Kimball, and gave the following information:

Entered for copyright June 20, 1896; copies (in boards) deposited September 11. Included in *A New List of the Books of Stone & Kimball*, November 1896. Price $1.25. Copyright assigned shortly after publication to Lamson, Wolffe & Co. of Boston; who issued the same sheets, with cancel title and binding of blue buckram, before the end of the year. English edition not published until July 1898, by Grant Richards.

Having negotiated with Kimball to obtain the rights for the book, Sharp arranged for the transfer of sheets and plates from Kimball to Lamson, Wolffe, and Company and assigned his rights to that firm for the sum of £150. He next tried unsuccessfully to recover from Herbert Stuart Stone the £150 difference between what he received from Lamson and what Stone had originally offered. In New York, he met with Herbert Stone's father,

Melville Stone, who was founder and editor of the *Chicago Daily News* and a man of considerable means. Melville Stone agreed his son had a moral obligation and suggested the matter go to E. C. Stedman for arbitration. Sharp agreed.

69   This letter to Ross is in Patrick Geddes's handwriting and signed by William Sharp. It represents Geddes's effort to enlist Ross's help in retrieving the £100 Sharp had invested in Geddes's Town and Gown Association. Geddes added a separate note to Ross which reads, "Dear Ross | The accompanying copy of receipt in addition to the preceding note from W. S. explains itself. | Yours, | Pat Geddes." With the uncertain outcome of his efforts in the United States to recover the £300, Sharp was desperately seeking money.

70   Messrs. White and Wilson were connected with the Riverside Press of Edinburgh, which printed material for P. G. Geddes and Colleagues.

71   Arshag Chobanian (1872–1954), author of *Chants Populaires Arméniens* (1903), *The People of Armenia* (1914), *La Femme Arménienne* (1918), and *La Roseraie d'Arménie* (1918).

72   For the final ordering of the contents of *The Shorter Stories of Fiona Macleod*, see Elizabeth Sharp's bibliography in the second volume of the two-volume edition of her *Memoir* (pp. 390–92).

Chapter 16

1   Although undated, this card was written when Sharp stopped in Paris on his way to England from the South of France in early January, 1897. The last Fiona Macleod book mentioned, *From the Hills of Dream*, was published by Geddes in November, 1896. This card pinpoints where Sharp was staying when he stopped in Paris to see Yeats, who is the "important writer" for whom the books are being ordered. Yeats owned copies of all four books, but they were in London. The additional copies were probably intended for Macgregor Mathers, his wife Moina Mathers, or Maud Gonne, friends with whom Yeats was interacting closely during his time in Paris. Yeats described his activities in Paris, including his remarkable interactions with William Sharp, in his *Autobiographies* (London: Macmillan, 1955, pp. 329–40). I have recounted it in a section called "A Plunge in the Seine" in my article on "W. B. Yeats, William Sharp, and Fiona Macleod: A Celtic Drama, 1897," in *Yeats Annual No. 14, Yeats and the Nineties*, ed. Warwick Gould (Basingstoke: Palgrave, 2001), pp. 62–109.

2   Although undated, this short letter was written when Sharp passed through London briefly on his way from Paris to the Pettycur Inn in Fife, where he stayed for the rest of the month.

3   This section is written in Sharp's hand at the top left of the typed first page of the signed letter. Four words following the last word — friend — are crossed out and are illegible, and above them are the initials "FM." From Paris, Sharp stopped briefly in London, went straight on to Edinburgh, and crossed the Forth to stay at the Pettycur Inn. He arranged for Edith Rinder to meet him there so they could discuss Yeats's request that Sharp and Fiona Macleod assist him in his psychic search for the rituals of his Celtic Mystical Order. Sharp must have convinced Edith to function as his partner, thus standing in for Fiona Macleod, in this endeavor, which went on for several years.

4   Sharp had led Stedman to believe he was having an extramarital affair with Fiona Macleod. Here he implies that he has been surreptitiously with Fiona and that Stedman had or was having similar rendezvous. This theme recurs in Sharp's letters to Stedman.

5   The remainder of the letter is hand-written.

6   This reissue of the Fiona Macleod stories in three soft-covered and relatively inexpensive volumes was published by Patrick Geddes and Colleagues in March, 1897.

7   Neither of these proposed American editions materialized.

8   George Cotterell (?1865–1939), a poet, critic, and good friend of Sharp's, was the editor of *The Yorkshire Herald*. His works include *The Banquiet: A Political Satire in Verse* (1885) and *Poems: Old and New* (1894). Stedman included two of his poems in his exhaustive *Victorian Anthology, 1837–1895* (Cambridge: Riverside Press, 1895).

9   "Century Club | New York" is crossed through. Evidence for dating this and the previous letter to Gilchrist is the likelihood that Sharp was using stationery he had brought home from New York in November 1896 when he stayed as a guest at the Century Club. The mention in this letter of the possibility of Gilchrist coming to London in March suggests the February date for this and the previous letter to Gilchrist.

10   Sharp's mid-March letter to Coulson Kernahan indicates that Gilchrist was in London about that time.

11   Born and educated in Scotland, Andrew Lang (1844–1912) took a first in classics at Balliol College, Oxford, held a fellowship there, and went on

to become a popular poet, journalist, critic and collector of folk and fairy tales. George Gissing (1857–1903) was a British novelist who wrote, among other works, *New Grub Street* (1891); *The Whirlpool* (1897); and *The Town Traveler* (1901). Austin Dobson, a well-known poet, critic, and biographer, was employed as a civil servant at the Board of Trade from 1856 until 1901. Garnet Joseph Wolseley (1833–1913) was an Irish soldier and historian who wrote *Narrative of the War in China* (1862); *Life of Marlborough* (1894); *The Decline and Fall of Napoleon* (1895); and *The Story of a Soldier's Life* (1903).

12 E. C. Stedman described the Stoddard dinner in two letters to Sharp, portions of which Elizabeth Sharp included in the *Memoir* (pp. 272–73). The first of these is dated February 17: "The most important social matter here this winter relating to our Guild will be a large important dinner to be given on March 25th by the Author's Club and his other friends, to Richard Henry Stoddard. We are going to try to make an exception to the rule that New York is not good to her own, and to render a tribute somewhat commensurate with Stoddard's lifelong services, and his quality as poet and man... . Of course I do not expect that you will come over here, and I am quite sure you will write a letter which can be read at the dinner, for I have in mind your personal friendship with Stoddard and affectionate comprehension of his genius and career." The second, dated April 13, describes the occasion: "Your letter to the Stoddard Banquet was by far the best and most inclusive of the various ones received, and it was read out to the 150 diners and met with high favour... . It proved to be the most notable literary occasion yet known in this city — was brilliant, magnetic, enthusiastic throughout. I felt a pride in my office as Chairman. The Stoddards were deeply gratified by your letter."

13 The letter from Patrick Geddes jointly to William Cuthbertson and William Sharp made the points Sharp took up in this letter. Born in Constantinople, Arshag Tchobanian (1872–1954) was a teacher and writer who contributed poems, fairy tales, literary studies and criticisms to various periodicals. In 1895, he fled the Turks and settled in Paris, where he devoted himself to making the Armenians better known in Europe. He published a number of volumes containing French translations of Armenian literature, ancient and modern, and founded and edited *Anahit*, a literary and critical magazine.

14 The exuberance and specificity of this paragraph suggest Sharp had enjoyed a few days with Edith Rinder after not having been with her for three weeks and three days. The intimacy of their relationship is suggested by asserting the privacy of the postscript and asking that the letter be destroyed. Since he had been with Fiona/Edith just three days ago "by

the sea," they may have been, as on other occasions, in the St. Margaret's Bay Hotel near Dover. Sharp repeatedly confided in Stedman about his relationship with Edith disguised as Fiona. He also conflated Fiona and Edith in his dealings with Yeats and others. The two women — one real and the other imagined — were inextricably bound in his own mind, since Edith's presence, as he said and may have believed, enabled him to write as Fiona. In June, three months hence, he took Edith to meet George Meredith and introduced her as Fiona.

15   E. R. Lamson. This letter to Stedman and that of 5 March indicate the Lamson, Wolffe firm, which was established in 1895, was in financial difficulty. The following item in *The Publisher's Weekly*, 1414 (4 March, 1899), p. 391, sheds light on the matter: "Lamson, Wolffe & Co., Publishers, have failed. Liabilities are reported to be $73,105.90 and assets, $26,748.72. The firm was organized by E. R. Lamson and Mr. Wolffe, then a student in Harvard. The latter was obliged to withdraw, owing to a college rule which prohibits students from engaging in business. Besides the office here, the firm also had an office in New York." It is interesting to note that Stone and Kimball were undergraduates at Harvard when they planned their publishing firm. Sharp had the bad luck of associating himself sequentially with two firms started by Harvard students that failed after a few unprofitable years.

16   "The Red Rider: A Romance of the Garibaldian Campaign in the Two Sicilies" was issued serially in the *Weekly Budget* (London: James Henderson and Sons, Ltd., 1892).

17   Sharp did not proceed with this work.

18   On March 5, Sharp told Stedman he had been with Fiona Macleod at the shore "two days ago." "In mind and body," he said, "I am ten years younger, with that joy and delight." Here on March 10, he tells Catherine Janvier, he had a "mental and physical set-back the last three days." Apparently, his sound physical and mental health lasted only a few days — from March 3 to March 7. In order to be well in mind and body — at least in the winter — Sharp needed to be away from the smoke and fog of London. When he and Edith Rinder were alone together, he, at least, was attempting to communicate with the realm of spirits to obtain rituals for Yeats's Celtic Mystical Order. Edith may have encouraged Sharp in this endeavor, but the extent to which she actively participated is unknown. The project provided an additional reason to be alone with Edith. Correspondence in May, 1898 casts some light on their contributions to Yeats's project.

19   The Greco-Turkish War of 1897 was the result of Greece's attempted annexation of Crete. Greece lost the war.

20   Four members of the European Concert — Great Britain, France, Italy, and Russia — were instrumental in bringing an end to the Greco-Turkish War.

21   Born at Ilfracombe, Devonshire, Coulson Kernahan (1858–1943) contributed to many periodicals, wrote humorous verse, and gained wide popularity for his fiction. Among his many books are: *A Dead Man's Diary* (1890), *A Book of Strange Sins* (1893), *The Child, the Wise Man, and the Devil* (1896), *Scoundrels and Co.* (1899), *A World without a Child* (1905), *The Dumpling* (1906), and *The Duel* (1906).

22   A. Harvey Moore was a popular British painter of the Victorian period who died in 1905.

23   Stone and Kimball published an edition of Sharp's *Vistas* in Chicago in 1894 (*The Green Tree Library*), which contains a Foreword and an additional piece entitled "The Whisper."

24   *Flower o' the Vine: Romantic Ballads and Sospiri di Roma* (New York: Charles L. Webster and Company, 1892). This volume contained all the poems in *Romantic Ballads and Poems of Phantasy*, and "The Last Voyage of Keir the Monk." It also contained all of the poems in the 1891 edition of Sharp's *Sospiri di Roma* and a new "Epilogue."

25   Kernahan's *The Child, the Wise Man, and the Devil* (London: J. Bowden and Co.,1896).

26   An American Journalist and critic. Hamilton Wright Mabie (1845–1916), was Associate Editor of *The Outlook* from 1884 until his death. There is no evidence to support Sharp's claim to have been in France, but the references to Fiona's *Shorter Tales* and Elizabeth's being in bed with rheumatism seem to date the letter mid-March, about the same time as the letter to Kernahan. France may have been invented to explain Sharp's delay in acknowledging Mabie's books, the praise for which — from Fiona — is intended to encourage Mabie to print a favorable review of her reissued *Shorter Tales* in *The Outlook*.

27   Probably Mabie's *Books and Culture* (New York: Dodd and Meade, 1896), and *Essays on Nature and Culture* (New York: Dodd and Meade, 1896).

28   *Madge o' the Pool: The Gypsy Christ and Other Tales* was published by Archibald Constable and Co. late in 1896 or early January 1897. It was first published in Chicago by Stone and Kimball in 1895 under the title *The Gipsy Christ and Other Tales*. Since some found that title offensive, the British publisher decided to use another story, "Madge o' the Pool," as the primary title. The book was reviewed, among other places, in the *Academy* of March 6 (280).

29   The defeat of Greece in the Greco-Turkish War.

30   Elizabeth noted here: "The letter ends abruptly." She does not elaborate, but the hyperbolic assertions about the "spiral flames of the spirit" and the West reddening in a new light for the forlorn people of Ireland reflects the language he was hearing from Yeats and AE as they laid the groundwork for a Celtic-inspired revolution. The passage takes on new meaning when we realize the manic state of mind it reveals was enhanced by the psychic experiments he was conducting to discover rituals for Yeats's Celtic Mystical Order.

31   Hinkson reprinted this letter in its entirety with only minor changes in *Middle Years* (pp. 130–33).

32   *The Speaker: A Review of Politics, Letters, Science and the Arts* (1890–1907) was a weekly paper which published articles on politics, science and the arts, as well as verse, foreign correspondence, letters to the editor and reviews of books. Its title became *The Speaker, The Liberal Review* in October 1899.

33   This article did not appear.

34   Charles O'Conor (1838–1906) was a Roman Catholic politician. As a liberal for Roscommon County from 1860–1880, he frequently spoke on Irish education and land tenure. He held an honorary LL. D. from the Royal University of Ireland and was mainly responsible for the Irish Sunday Closing Act of 1879. He was President of the Royal Irish Academy and the Irish Language society.

35   Norman MacLeod (1812–1872) was a distinguished minister of the Scottish Church. He studied at Glasgow and Edinburgh and was ordained in 1838. He was made one of the Royal Chaplains in Scotland in 1857, and became a trusted friend of Queen Victoria. He was the first editor of *Good Words*, to which he contributed many articles and stories.

36   Maud Gonne (1866–1953) was the daughter of Colonel Gonne who had been on the staff of the Irish command. She was an ardent Irish Nationalist and a close friend of W. B. Yeats. His devotion to her, along with their association in the cause of Irish independence and in the Irish Theatre Movement during the nineties and the early years of the twentieth century, inspired some of his finest lyric poems. In 1903, she married John MacBride, who had recruited and led the Irish Brigade in the Boer War and who was executed following the Easter insurrection in Dublin in 1916. Their son, Sean MacBride, would become Irish Minister for External Affairs (1948–1951).

37 Annie MacDonald's article "Fiona Macleod" appeared in *The Bookman*, 2 (October, 1895), 135–36.

38 After reproducing this letter in *Middle Years* (p. 132), Hinkson stated: "With regard to this last letter Mrs. Sharp writes that 'the autobiographical details given in it are fictitious details, which were used in order to prevent the assumption by the recipient of the letter that the writer was William Sharp: that it was his imperative desire from the outset of that phase of his work that the secret of the authorship should be preserved till his death; that through the loyalty of the few friends who knew that he and he alone was Fiona Macleod, and by means of efforts of his own, the wish was fulfilled.'"

39 See Endnote 28. The location of Little's review of *Madge o' the Pool* is unknown, but it may have appeared in the *West Sussex Gazette* for which he sometimes wrote reviews.

40 Little was planning to go to Paris with a press pass to review the annual Salons. William or Elizabeth Sharp attended the Salons each year and reviewed them for the Glasgow Herald. Sharp was planning to go elsewhere for two or three weeks at the beginning of April, he did not go abroad, but to St. Margaret's Bay near Dover in Kent. See Sharp's letter *To Elizabeth Sharp [April 18, 1897]* (Volume 2). E. A. S. did attend the two 1897 Salons and then went south to spend time with the Janviers in St. Remy

41 Sharp took a woman, almost certainly Edith Rinder, pretending to be Fiona Macleod to meet Meredith at Box Hill on June 10, 1897. In a letter to Alice Meynell dated June 13, 1897, Meredith described her as "a handsome woman, who would not give me her eyes for awhile." In a letter to Maud Gonne dated January 14, 1907, Yeats recalled Meredith saying "she was the most beautiful woman he ever saw." To my knowledge, this is the only time Sharp was able to convince Edith to meet one of his friends as Fiona (see *Yeats Annual, No. 14*, p. 182 and note, and *The Gonne-Yeats Letters*, ed. Anna MacBride White and A. Norman Jeffares, London: Hutchinson, 1992, p. 234).

42 The photograph he sent with this letter is reproduced in the "Life" section of this chapter. Ms. Moulton wrote on the side of the card "This letter reached me on April 10 — just the other day."

43 This letter is transcribed from a draft in Sharp's handwriting with W. E. Henley's name and address in the upper left corner. The draft was for Mary Sharp to copy in the Fiona Macleod hand. W. E. Henley (1849–1903) was a well-known poet, editor, arbiter of taste, and man of letters. He edited *London* (1877–1882) and the *Magazine of Art* (1882–1886). In 1889,

he became editor of the *Scots Observer* and continued in that position when the magazine was transferred to London and retitled the *National Observer* in 1891. He resigned his editorship in 1894. As an editor, he was a leading opponent of 1890's "decadence." It is not surprising he encouraged Fiona to simplify her style. His best-known poem, "Invictus" was written in 1875 and published in his first volume of poems, *Book of Verses* (1888). It is best known for its concluding stanza: "It matters not how strait the gate,| How charged with punishments the scroll,| I am the master of my fate: | I am the captain of my soul." The stanza alludes to Matthew 7:14 in the King James Bible: "Because strait is the gate, and narrow is the way, which leadeth unto life, and few there be that find it."

44   An area in the far northwest of Scotland.

45   This article did not appear. "Fiona Macleod," an article which appeared in *The Critic*, 48 (May, 1906), 460–63, is the only piece by Miss Rea that has been located.

46   Benjamin Burgess Moore was an undergraduate at Yale University who wrote an article about the Fiona Macleod writings that appeared in the *Yale Literary Magazine.*

47   Introducing this fragment, E. A. S. said, "Towards the end of April I went to Paris to write upon the two 'Salons,' and my husband, still very unwell, went to St. Margaret's Bay." Sharp told Little in his letter of March 24 the "Old Salon" would open on April 14 and the "New Salon" on April 20. Elizabeth was in Paris on those dates for the press previews which would date this letter Sunday, April 18.

48   These essays appeared in Maeterlinck's *The Treasure of the Humble,* tr. by Alfred Surto (London: Grant Allen, 1897).

49   The final sentence ending in an ellipsis (either reflecting the original or cut off by E. A. S.) refers to his relationship with E. W. R. who was with him at least part of the time in St. Margaret's Bay. The marriage metaphor to define the relationship between the two sides of his nature takes on a deeper significance when we know he was, at this time, frequently conflating Edith Rinder with Fiona Macleod, the female "second self" he had within. He asserted that he needed to be with Edith in order to think and write as Fiona. Identifying with her, adopting her perspective, facilitated, he thought, his ability to write as a woman. Elizabeth said of Sharp's use of the name "Wilfion:"

In surveying the dual life as a whole I have seen how, from the early partially realised twin-ship, "W. S." was the first to go adventuring and find himself, while his twin, "F. M.," remained passive, or a separate self. When "she" awoke to active consciousness "she" became the deeper, the more impelling, the more essential factor. By reason of this severance, and of the acute conflict that at times resulted therefrom, the flaming of the dual life became so fierce that "Wilfion" — as I named the inner and third Self that lay behind that dual expression — realised the imperativeness of gaining control over his two separated selves and of bringing them into some kind of conscious harmony (*Memoir,* p. 423).

50   *The Laughter of Peterkin: A Retelling of Old Tales of the Celtic Wonderland* (London: Archibald Constable & Co., 1897).

51   Felix Gras (1844–1901) was a poet, novelist, and prominent member of the Félibrige, becoming its president in 1891. His works include *Li Carbounié*; *Toloza*; *The Reds of the Midi*; and *The White Terror* (1899).

52   Marie Josephine (Girard) Gasquet (1872–1960) was the author of *Une fille de Saint François* (1922), *Une enfance provençale* (1926–1941), *Sainte Jeanne d'Arc* (1929), and *La Fête-Dieu* (1932). E. A. S is referring to a title Gasquet received at the Floral Games, an event the Félibrige held every seven years. At the Games a poet laureate was crowned, after which he would choose a queen. Gasquet must have been the reigning queen in 1897. For more on the Félibrige, see Endnote 53.

53   Frédéric Mistral (1830–1914) was a poet who led the nineteenth-century revival of Provençal language and literature. He was co-winner of the Nobel Prize for literature in 1904 for his contributions to literature and philology. In 1854 he and several friends founded the Félibrige, which was dedicated to maintaining Provençal culture. His works include *Miréio* (1859), *Lou Pouémo dóu Rose* (1897), and his memoirs, *Moun Espelido* (1906), which was his most popular work.

54   This and another letter from Elizabeth Sharp are included here to demonstrate her acute intelligence, and the range of her literary and cultural interests. Her entry to the Félibrige was provided by Catherine and Thomas Janvier. The remainder of the letter is missing.

55   The card is postmarked May 7, 1897. Its content indicates its likely date is May 6.

56   Interestingly, these are the three most important women in Sharp's life at this time: E. A. S, E. W. R., and Catherine Ann Janvier. Grant R. is Grant Richards, a mutual friend. The paragraph casts light on Gilchrist's personality, and suggests a predisposition for gossip. It also illuminates the relationship between Sharp and Gilchrist, who was ten years Sharp's junior.

57   Sharp left London on Friday, May 14 for St. Remy, where he surprised
      Elizabeth on Sunday morning, celebrated her birthday on Monday, May
      17, and left again for London on May 18, arriving there on the evening of
      Wednesday, May 19. On Thursday, May 20, he wrote to Elizabeth that he
      was not sure a week ago if he would be able to make the "flying visit."

58   E. A. S. had received Gilchrist's photograph, as had Sharp, who asked
      Gilchrist to send one to Edith Rinder. *The Stone Dragon* was a collection of
      Gilchrist's short stories published in 1894.

59   Cartledge is a hamlet in Derbyshire which grew around Cartledge Hall,
      where Murray Gilchrist lived with his partner, mother, and sisters. The
      content of the important letter Sharp received during his brief visit remains
      a mystery. Built in the late fifteenth century, Cartledge Hall is a Grade II
      listed building.

60   This post card was intended as a post script to a letter (now missing) Sharp
      sent to Stedman in the preceding mail.

61   "L" refers here to the publisher Lamson, who owed Sharp money which
      Stedman was trying to collect for him.

62   For date, see Endnote 60.

63   I have been unable to locate the essay on Maurice Maeterlinck or the
      monograph on Sir William Quiller Orchardson RA (1832–1910), a Scottish
      portraitist and painter of domestic and historical subjects who was
      knighted in June 1907. Sharp may not have completed either one.

64   Thomas Wentworth Higginson (1823–1911), a Unitarian minister, was
      active in the American Abolitionist movement during the 1840s and 1850s.
      From 1862–1864, he served as colonel of the 1st South Carolina Volunteer
      Infantry Regiment the first federally authorized black regiment. Following
      the war, he devoted his life to fighting for the rights of freed people,
      women and other disfranchised peoples. A prolific author long associated
      with *The Atlantic Monthly*, he was an early supporter of Emily Dickinson,
      and following her death he collaborated with Mabel Loomis Todd in
      publishing several volumes of her poetry.

65   May 24 was a Monday in 1897. After returning from France on Wednesday,
      May 19, Sharp went to Edinburgh for the weekend, returning to London
      on Monday, May 24. On the weekend (May 28–29), he went north again
      to spend a week with Murray Gilchrist at his home, Cartledge Hall, in
      Derbyshire.

66   "William Sharp, May. 1897." has been typed onto the letter just below
      where Sharp had written "Monday," and May 24 was a Monday in 1897.

67 Fiona Macleod's "The Wayfarer," was published in *Cosmopolis* (June, 1898), pp. 613–26. A revised version was included in Fiona Macleod's *The Winged Destiny* (London: Chapman and Hall, 1904). In 1906, it was published by Thomas Mosher as a separate volume, prefaced by a sonnet, "In Memoriam," by Alfred Noyes.

68 These two stories were in *The Washer of the Ford and Other Legendary Moralities* (Edinburgh: P. G. Geddes and Colleagues, 1896).

69 Richard Alexander Streatfeild (1866–1919) was a musicologist and critic. He was educated at Pembroke College, Cambridge, and worked in the Department of Printed Books in the British Museum from 1889, until his death at the age of fifty-three.

70 George Darley (1795–1846) was an Irish poet, novelist, literary critic, and author of mathematical texts. In 1820, he received a B.A. from Trinity College Dublin in mathematics and classics. In 1821, he went to London to pursue a literary career and began publishing poetry and fiction. In 1827, he joined *The Athenaeum* as a critic. In 1897, R. A. Streatfeild published Darley's unfinished lyrical epic *Nepenthe: A Poem in Two Cantos* (1835), which was distinguished by its dream imagery, use of symbolism to reveal inner consciousness, and tumultuous metrical organization.

71 Robert Laurence Binyon (1869–1943) was an English poet, dramatist and art scholar. A colleague of R. A. Streatfeild at the British Museum, he designed the woodcut that was the frontispiece of Streatfeild's edition of *Nepenthe*, a design Sharp thought Blakean.

72 Gilchrist's *A Peakland Faggot: Tales Told of Milton Folk* was published in 1897 by Grant Richards, in London. It is a collection of stories set in his native Peak district near Sheffield in Derbyshire. The village called Milton was based on the village of Eyam and many of the stories contain characters based on people who lived in and near Eyam. Long after Gilchrist died in 1917, a selection of his stories with a memoir by his friend Eden Phillpotts (1862–1960) was published under the title *A Peakland Faggot* (Faber & Gwyer: London, 1926).

73 A handwritten letter from Gilchrist.

74 See Endnote 72. The Jubilee was a year-long celebration in 1897 of Queen Victoria's ascension to the throne in 1847.

75 *The Laughter of Peterkin: A Retelling of Old Tales of the Celtic Wonderland* (London: Archibald Constable & Co.) was published in November 1897.

76 This sentence references the drug he and W. B. Yeats were occasionally using to facilitate the visions they hoped would produce the rites and

talismans for Yeats's projected Celtic Mystical Order. He and Gilchrist must have discussed the drug and its effects or, perhaps, smoked some together.

77   This birthday letter from Fiona Macleod to William Sharp is undated, but the date is established by the publication of F. M.'s *The Laughter of Peterkin* in November 1897 and by the date of Sharp's birthday, September 12. The letter is in Sharp's hand, not the Fiona Macleod hand provided by Mary Sharp. It must have been written when W. S. and E. A. S. were staying with friends at Good Rest | Parkstone | Dorset. He reminds himself that he must become more productive in the "new year," but the letter is also an attempt to reaffirm and strengthen his sense of being two separate people. There is also, of course, a note of whimsy.

78   *The Daughters of Danaeus* was published by Bliss, Sands and Co. (London) in 1894. *The Pathway of the Gods* was published in 1898 by Skeffington and Son (London).

79   His father was Sharp's friend, the novelist and poet George Meredith.

80   In his letter to Meredith, Sharp said he would be leaving London on September 15 or 16. If that expectation materialized, his destination is unknown. He was back in London when he wrote to Martyn which, from its description of his plans, must have been on September 22, for he tells Martyn that he will leave for Dublin tomorrow (Thursday, September 23), see George Russell there (Friday, September 24), leave Dublin on Saturday morning, and be at the Royal Hotel in Greenore, a port village on the East coast north of Dublin, on Sunday and Monday mornings, September 26 and 27. His plans after that, he tells Martyn, are uncertain, but he implies he will be travelling in Ireland until Saturday, October 2. The letters that follow indicate that, on the contrary, he made his way on Monday, September 27 to the Isle of Arran off the west coast of Scotland, where he stayed four or five nights, before returning to Ireland and taking the train to Galway on Saturday, October 2. The letter he wrote to E. C. Stedman from Iona says he is staying there with Fiona Macleod. The Arran interlude in his visit to Ireland may have been pre-planned to enable him to spend time with Edith Rinder, who was spending the month of September, as usual, in a rented house on the mainland near Tarbert, just north of Arran.

81   Edward Martyn (1859–1923) inherited money, properties, and an impressive establishment (Tillyra Castle) near the town of Gort in the west of Ireland. British by heritage, he nonetheless considered himself an Irishman. He wrote plays and supported the Irish Dramatic Movement in the 1890s. He entertained his guests by playing the harmonium in the great hall of his castle. He founded the Palestrina Choir of Men and

Boys in Dublin in 1899, and served as President of Sinn Fein from 1904 to 1908. In 1914, he founded in Dublin the Irish Theatre for the production of native non-peasant plays in the Irish language, and translations of continental master dramas. He was a promoter of the Gaelic league and other educational improvements for Ireland. Among his publications are *Morgan Libraryte the Lesser* (1890) and *Preface to Robert Elliot's Art and Ireland*. His best-known plays include *The Heather Field, Maeve,* and *The Dream Physician.*

82 George Russell (AE) (1867–1935) was an Irish writer and painter, a close friend of W. B. Yeats, and, most significantly, a fellow member of the coterie Yeats had put together to find in the spirit world the elements of his projected Celtic Mystical Order. Russell had praised the writings of Fiona Macleod, and there is reason to believe Sharp, when he met Russell in Dublin, stated or implied strongly that he was producing the writings of Fiona Macleod. This confession seems not to have endeared Sharp to Russell, who before long began to attack Sharp's ideas, as expressed through the F. M. writings, about Pan-Celticism. Russell remained fervently Irish and wanted to keep the Celtic Revival largely, if not exclusively, an Irish movement in order that it might further the Irish cause against the British. Among his publications are *Homeward* (1894), *The Earth Breath* (1897), *The Divine Vision* (1904), and *Deirdre* (1907).

83 *The Laughter of Peterkin.*

84 This may be a preliminary title for Fiona Macleod's *The Dominion of Dreams,* which Archibald Constable and Co. published in May, 1899.

85 In the letter's last paragraph, Sharp tells Stedman that he and F. M. will leave Arran the next day. In all likelihood, F. M., here and as in other letters to Stedman, was a stand-in for Edith Rinder, his "beautiful friend and comrade."

86 Stedman was about to lose Mary Stewart, a good friend who did secretarial work, to marriage. The quotation marks suggest she may have had another name. Perhaps Sharp was implying Stedman had a romantic relationship with her and the "other friend" in the next sentence.

87 For a description of the Celtic gathering Sharp mentions in this letter, see my article, "W. B. Yeats, William Sharp, and Fiona Macleod."

88 Sharp is referring here to Martin Morris (1867–1925), son of Baron Michael Morris. Martin Morris was an aspiring writer, whose article, "The Philosophy of Poetry," had just appeared in *The Nineteenth Century*, 46 (September, 1897), 504–13. Martin succeeded to the title, Baron Morris of Killanin, when his father died in 1901.

89   A member of the English landed gentry in Ireland, Lady Augusta Gregory (1859–1932) played a crucial role in the Irish literary revival. Best known for welcoming W. B. Yeats every summer to stay at Coole Park, her estate in Galway, she collected and published stories gathered among the people who lived in the area. She also wrote plays and served for many years as a Director of the Abbey Theatre in Dublin. Among her publications are *Poets and Dreamers* (1903), *Gods and Fighting Men* (1904), and *Our Irish Theatre* (1913). Her plays include *The Image* (1910), *The Full Moon* (1911), *The Golden Apple* (1916), and *Three Last Plays* (1928). Douglas Hyde and Standish O'Grady were crucial figures in the artistic, intellectual, social, and political movements that led eventually to Irish independence.

90   Sir William Nevill Geary (1859–1944), a well-known lawyer and diplomat, was a friend and neighbor of Lady Gregory and Edward Martyn.

91   E. A. S. said of this plan: "But the pressure of health, of the needs of daily livelihood, and of the more dominating ambitions of F. M. prevented the fulfilment of this scheme. Many times he talked of it, drafted out portions of it — but it remained unaccomplished, and all that exists of it is the beginning chapters of the first book written in Paris ten years before, and then called *Caesar of France*" (*Memoir*, p. 290).

92   Allen's *The Evolution of the Idea of God: An Enquiry into the Origin of Religions* was published in 1897 by Grant Richards in London and Henry Holt in New York.

93   Le Gallienne's *If I Were God: A Conversation* was published in 1897 by James Bowden in London. This booklet was an effort to reconcile the loss of his first wife in 1894 with his faith in God. "The best and finest thing he has done" may be Le Gallienne's translation of *The Rubaiyat of Omar Khayyam*, subtitled "a paraphrase from several literal translations," which was published, also in 1897, by Grant Richards.

94   In 1897, Le Gallienne married Julie Nørregaard, a Danish journalist. Their daughter, Eva le Gallienne, went on to become a famous actress.

95   E. A. S. said of this letter: "London proved to be impossible to him owing to the excitable condition of his brain. Therefore he took rooms in Hastings whence he wrote to me."

96   Sharp is withdrawing, at Lady Gregory's request, from serving as Chair at a meeting of the Irish Literary Society in London on December 4, where Yeats was scheduled to give a lecture on the Celtic movement. Yeats had written to Sharp on November 20 asking him to withdraw in favor of Edward Martyn, but Sharp had refused. A. P. Graves, Secretary of the

Society, had asked Sharp to assume the Chair for the occasion without asking Yeats's approval of his choice. Yeats thought that having Sharp, a Scotsman and with minimal public credentials as a Celtic writer, in the Chair would undermine the seriousness of the meeting and cast a bad light on what Yeats wanted to say to fellow members of the Society. Sharp was offended by Yeats's request. When Lady Gregory spoke to Sharp, he was resistant. She promptly invited him to dinner, and when he accepted on the condition he could bring his wife, she knew her objective had been accomplished. See *Collected Letters II*, p. 148; and Augusta Gregory, *Lady Gregory's Diaries: 1892–1902*, ed. James Pethica (Oxford: Oxford University Press, 1996), 156–57.

97   Stedman's *Poems Now First Collected* (Boston and New York: Houghton, Mifflin & Co., 1897).

98   Date from postmark.

Chapter 17

1   Elizabeth Sharp dated this letter May 1898, but it was probably written in February. St. Margaret's Bay was one of the places he stayed during his absences from London in January and February. In writing to his wife, Sharp frequently omitted a return address and the date. Since Elizabeth assigned a month but no day to the letter, it was probably written without a date on the stationery of the St. Margaret's Bay Hotel which contained a drawing of the establishment. Its content reflects his state of mind in February, not in April. When he arrived in St. Margaret's Bay on April 29, he was not "serenely at peace with the world." Rather, he was in a state of near panic at having to abort his plan to take Edith Rinder to Paris as Fiona Macleod to meet W. B. Yeats and his friends. This is the first of two letters E. A. S. received from her husband in the spring of 1898 and used in the *Memoir* to reflect his thinking (pp. 294–98). This letter, she said, "gives an insight into the primitive and elemental soul that so often swayed him, and his work." The "Life" section of this chapter contains more about the two letters and their context.

2   See letter *To Elizabeth A. Sharp, [October 4, 1897]* (Volume 2) and the statement in his letter To Edmund Clarence Stedman, March 1, 1898 (Volume 2) that he is working on "a romance of the destinies of France."

3   E. A. S. implied this letter "to a friend" was written shortly after the preceding letter (*Memoir*, p. 298). She was meticulous in identifying the

recipients of her husband's letters except those he wrote to a "friend." Edith Rinder probably allowed Elizabeth to use some of the letters she received from Sharp with the understanding that she would not be identified as the recipient.

4   E. A. S. said that this letter was written in St. Margaret's Bay at the end of April. However, its content suggests that it was written in mid-February, since Sharp speaks of recovering from influenza and its side effects. Also, the publication of Fiona Macleod's *Dominion of Dreams* "this Spring" remained a possibility when the letter was written. By February 25, according to the following letter to Benjamin Burgess Moore, that volume had been postponed for a least a year.

5   At this point, E. A. S. inserted in brackets: "published in the following year under the title of *The Dominion of Dreams*." The volume was published by Archibald Constable and Co. in June 1899.

6   June, 1898, 614–26.

7   September, 1898, 595–98.

8   An etcher and art teacher, Charles Frederick William Mielatz (1860–1919) was born in Germany and immigrated at age six with his family to America. He married Mary Stuart McKinney on February 25, 1903 and resided thereafter in New York City.

9   *An American Anthology 1787–1900* (Cambridge, Massachusetts: Riverside Press, 1900).

10   Edith Rinder had visited Sharp frequently during the past two months. This sentence implies Sharp had shown a photograph of her to Stedman (probably during his trip to New York in November 1896) as he showed it to Yeats and Rhys and Le Gallienne in June 1897.

11   *Poems Now First Collected* (New York: Houghton, Mifflin, and Co., 1897).

12   This sentence suggests Edith Rinder was temporarily in Brussels, perhaps for further study of the Belgian writers she had translated and published in 1895 in *The Massacre of the Innocents*. In this letter, Sharp conveys a cavalier attitude toward his relationship with Edith Rinder, which he assumes Stedman will find compatible. The robust male camaraderie Sharp projected in his letters to Stedman reflected their in-person relationship. It is diametrically opposed to the manner in which Sharp was portraying his deep and overpowering love for Edith in the Fiona Macleod stories that made their way later into *The Dominion of Dreams* (1899). Sharp's assuring Stedman that his "Queen" approved of his being "a very bad boy with a very dear & delightful 'friend'" supports Elizabeth's statement in

the *Memoir* that she welcomed Edith's cooperation in the effort to restore Sharp's mental and physical health.

13   Sharp described this ambitious, unrealized project in his letter *To Elizabeth A. Sharp*, [*October 4, 1897*] (Volume 2) from Tillyra Castle. There, the first volume of *The Epic of Youth* was to be called "The Hunter of Wisdom." None were completed.

14   The first half of this brief paragraph has been heavily crossed out and is illegible. The lines reproduced here have also been struck through but remain legible. Sharp was trying to raise Stedman's spirits by referring to his relationship with a young woman and expressing his hope the relationship is ongoing.

15   The references to his own and Stedman's relationships with women led Sharp to ask Stedman to burn the letter.

16   Macleay had left *The Highland News* in Inverness and was working for a Liverpool paper.

17   After including portions of this letter in the *Memoir* (pp. 294–6), E. A. S. destroyed the manuscript. The portions she printed in the *Memoir*, transcribed here, present important insights into the nature of their relationship with each other and their relationship with Edith Rinder. Elizabeth said this letter "relates to views we held in common," opinions about love and the harmful effects of conventional restrictions. The letter is discussed in the "Life" section of this chapter.

18   Sharp left London on Friday, April 29 for Paris, but made it only to Dover, where he spent a fortnight at the St Margaret's Bay Hotel. His intent had been that both he and Edith Rinder would go to Paris to meet Yeats and his friends, but that plan did not materialize, probably because Edith in the end refused to play the role of Fiona Macleod. Rather, she seems to have joined Sharp at the St. Margaret's Bay Hotel on April 30 and stayed for at least a week.

19   The reference is to William Sharp's *Wives in Exile*, a "yachting romance" that was published first in America and then, in July 1898, by Grant Richards (1872–1948) in England. The nephew of Sharp's friend Grant Allen, Richards left his London boarding school in 1888 at the age of sixteen to become a writer. A menial job in a London wholesale bookstore sustained him for several months whereupon he was hired by W. T. Stead as a staff writer on the *Review of Reviews*. In that position he met many writers and became an active participant in the London literary scene of the early 1890s. On January 1, 1897, with backing from his uncle and others, he opened his own publishing firm in Henrietta Street, Covent Garden which through many ups and downs published many of the important

British writers of the late nineties and the early twentieth century. Grant described his life before becoming a publisher in *Memories of a Misspent Youth, 1872–1896* (London: William Heinemann, 1932) and his life as a publisher in *Author Hunting by an Old Literary Sportsman, Memories of Years Spent Mainly in Publishing* (London: Unicorn, 1934; with a revised edition with a preface by Alec Waugh and a postscript by Martin Secker published in 1960).

20   Richard Vynne Harold's *Love Letters: A Romance in Correspondence* (New York: Zimmerman's, 1898), which Grant Richards was considering for publication in England.

21   This postcard is postmarked April 30, '98 from Dover and addressed to Yeats at Chez M. Macgregor Mathers, 87 Rue Mozart, Paris. On April 25, 1898, Yeats had written to Lady Gregory: "I have been here in Paris for a couple of days.... I am buried in Celtic mythology and shall be for a couple of weeks or so. Miss Gonne has been ill with bronchitis.... She comes here to-morrow to see visions. Fiona Macleod (this is private as she is curiously secret about her movements) talks of coming here too, so we will have a great Celtic gathering." In a postscript to this letter, Yeats added: "My host is a Celtic enthusiast who spends most of his day in highland costume to the wonder of the neighbours." His host was Macgregor Mathers (*Collected Letters II*, pp. 214–15).

22   This sentence reinforces the point that Sharp had by this time told Yeats that Fiona Macleod was a second self or a spiritual presence whose appearance was dependent on the presence of the woman he loved. In an article entitled "William Sharp and Fiona Macleod," *The Century Magazine*, 74 (May, 1907), 111–17, Ernest Rhys said Sharp arranged to meet him and Yeats sometime before May, 1900, to make a "confession" concerning the Fiona Macleod stories and romances. Rhys says that what Sharp told them on this occasion "entirely corroborated what he had told me casually at other times, and I see no reason to doubt that, while the account was colored, it represented a genuine mental experience, and was psychologically true. Its effect was this: that he, wishing to interpret nature and the supernatural, and all their occult human contingencies had never been able to attain what he called 'vision,' until after an illness and some fever he found himself newly sensitized, and made the vehicle of a woman's vision — one far exceeding his own. Then, and not till then, he became the instrument of that creative work which, actually written down by himself, was yet the positive result of a dual state of consciousness, new, he thought, to human experience." I believe the "confession" meeting occurred in June 1897, about the time he took Edith to Box Hill to play Fiona Macleod for George Meredith.

23 The Plain of Moytura, located in County Mayo, was the site of two great battles in Irish mythical history, the first between the Danaans and the Firbolgs and the second between the Danaans and the Fomorians. Here, Sharp refers to a modern abridged translation by Whitley Stokes from a fifteenth-century manuscript in the British Museum describing "The Second Battle of Moytura," *Revue Celtique*, 12 (1891), 52–130, with corrections and notes 306–08.

24 Marie Henri d'Arbois de Jubainville (1827–1910) was a Celtic scholar, the first to head the Department of Celtic Language and Literature at the College de France. In 1885 he assumed direction of the *Revue Celtique* (1870–1934). His most important book was *The Irish Mythological Cycle and Celtic Mythology* translated into English in 1903. Yeats knew him, or of him, as early as 1890, and he is cited by Virginia Moore as being the "best equipped and most esteemed Celtic scholar" of the late nineteenth and early twentieth centuries (*The Unicorn: W. B. Yeats Search for Reality* (New York: The Macmillan Co., 1954), p. 50).

25 A prominent figure in the Irish Literary Revival and the Irish Nationalist movement, Hyde (1860–1949) championed the revival of the Irish language and served from 1938–1945 as the first President of Ireland.

26 Richard Vynne Harold's *Love Letter.*

27 The letter's approximate date is "a few days" after Sharp arrived in Lanzardle on April 29. It is likely that Edith joined him there on April 30 and quite possible that she had become ill since Sharp described Fiona as ill on April 30 and again on May 5. He may well have thought he might be leaving the next day, but it appears that Edith left on the weekend (May 7) and Sharp stayed for another week.

28 Charles Le Goffic (1863–1932) was a Breton poet, novelist and historian whose influence was especially strong in his native Brittany. A translation of his *Le Crucifié de Kéraliès* (1892) by Edith Wingate Rinder was published in April 1898 under the title *The Dark Way of Love* by Archibald Constable and Co. As Sharp indicates, a favorable notice of the book appeared in *The Scotsman* of May 2, 1898.

29 *The Laughter of Peterkin* (1897) was not published in America.

30 Vol. 79 (November 27, 1897), 774.

31 "Children of the Dark Star," *The Dome* (May, 1898), 39–58.

32 April, 1898, 245–6.

33   June, 1898, 614–26.

34   September, 1898, 595–98

35   Sharp probably composed this letter shortly after arriving in St. Margaret's
      Bay and sent it to his sister in Edinburgh for transcription.

36   This strange letter responds to two letters from Yeats — one to Sharp and
      a second to Fiona — asking about visions he and Macgregor Mathers had
      in Paris involving Sharp and Fiona. The content of the letter is described in
      the "Life" section of this chapter. This sentence implies that Edith Rinder
      left St. Margaret's Bay after a week, though Sharp stayed on till mid-month.

37   The May 1898 issue of *The Dome* contained, in addition to Fiona Macleod's
      "Children of the Dark Star" (39–58), Yeats's "Aedh to Doctora: Three
      Songs" (37–38). The three songs were: "Aedh hears the cry of the Sedge,"
      "Aedh Laments the Loss of Love," and "Aedh thinks of those who have
      spoken Evil of his Beloved."

38   After "only" there is a space in the MS letter where one or two lines have
      been erased. Sharp must have had second thought about what he had
      written. In the next postscript he attributes the mid-sentence break to
      Fiona's neuralgia.

39   Yeats's response to this letter, both in a May 7 letter to Sharp and many
      years later in writing his autobiography, is discussed in the "Life" section
      of this chapter.

40   John Arthur Goodchild (1851–1914) was a medical doctor who cared for
      his British patients in Italy during the six darker months of the year and
      in England for the remainder. He was also a serious student of the early
      civilizations of Ireland, England, and Scotland and had a special affection
      for the Celts and early converts to Christianity. He responded favorably to
      the writings of Fiona Macleod and valued Sharp's knowledge the Celtic
      past. The book Fiona thanked him for was a collection of his poetry called
      The Book of Telphi (1897). His best-known publication was *The Light of the
      West* (1898), and Fiona also thanked him for a proof copy of that work.
      Fiona Macleod's *The Winged Destiny* (London: Chapman and Hall, 1904)
      contained a "Dedicatory Introduction to J. A. G."

41   The mid-May date of this letter is based on the assumption that Fiona
      received the proof copy of *The Light of the West* shortly after it was
      published.

42   According to E. A. S. (*Memoir*, p. 293), this letter was written after Sharp
      returned to London from St. Margaret's Bay. He returned at the start of the
      third week of May, or about May 15, and, after spending May 17 with his

wife on her birthday, he left with Thomas Janvier on May 18 for a four-day walking tour in Holland.

43   "The White Heron," *Harper's Magazine* (December, 1898), 71–8.

44   "Enya of the Dark Eyes," *Literature*, 47 (September, 1898).

45   This reference, according to Mrs. Sharp, is to *The Divine Adventure: Iona: By Sundown Shores: Studies in Spiritual History* (London: Chapman and Hall, 1900).

46   Although Sharp claimed at the start of the letter to have regained his health, the letter suggests his mental state remained precarious.

47   This letter from Elizabeth to Gilchrist is included for its demonstration of her patience, good will, and genuine concern for the state of her husband's physical and mental health, despite the fact that he had been separated from her for most of the previous five months as she worked in London to earn money to support them.

48   Marken Island of the coast of Holland.

49   Richards had asked Sharp for some favorable notices of the American publication of *Wives in Exile* he could use to promote the book which was scheduled for publication in July.

50   Richards's good news is explained in a sentence from his memoir *Author Hunting* (p. 116): "Some time in the early spring of 1898, I became engaged to a young Italian lady; in May of the same year we were married."

51   "O sweet Spring filled with fragrance and love."

52   Sharp had found some favorable notices of the American edition of *Wives in Exile* for Richards to use promoting the English edition which he published in July.

53   Yeats had given Sharp typescripts of some of the poems that would appear in *The Wind Among the Reeds* (London: Elkin Mathews, 1899) with the hope he would carry through on his promise to mention the book as forthcoming. A review of *Wind Among the Reeds* appeared over the signature of Fiona Macleod in the Dublin *Daily Express* on April 22, 1899, shortly after the volume appeared. *The Shadowy Waters* and *The Wind Among the Reeds* are discussed in "The Later Work of Mr. Yeats," also by Fiona Macleod, in *The North American Review* of September, 1902.

54   Sharp as Fiona Macleod was referring to Yeats's recent critical work in prose: "Le Mouvement Celtique" (which focuses on Fiona Macleod) in *L'Irlande Libre* (April, 1898), "Irish Fairy Land" in *The Outlook* (April,

1898), "The Broken Gates of Death" in the *Fortnightly Review* (April, 1898), and "The Celtic Element in Literature" in *Cosmopolis* (June, 1898) which also contained "The Wayfarer" by Fiona Macleod.

55   At this point, thirteen lines have been blotted out, probably by Yeats or perhaps by Mrs. Sharp if Yeats loaned the letter to her when she was writing the *Memoir*. The lines are not decipherable.

56   From this point through to "early life," lines have been blotted out but are decipherable.

57   From this point through to "one," the lines have been blotted out but are decipherable.

58   The ellipsis is in the MS letter.

59   It was not impossible for Sharp as he used the subject as the basis for a story called "The Distant Country" which was included in Fiona Macleod's *The Dominion of Dreams* in 1899.

60   There is an eight-line postscript to the letter which has been crossed through line-by-line and is not decipherable. It probably asks Yeats to destroy the letter because of its very personal nature. Again as Fiona, Sharp wrote a brief note to Yeats on July 6 asking if he received her letter of June 28 and saying she was anxious about it. That is understandable because here Sharp described metaphorically how he wanted Yeats to understand his relationship with Edith Rinder which enabled him to write as Fiona Macleod. He distanced himself only slightly — by the "long ago" — from the man, half Celt and half Norse as was Sharp, who possessed "one of the subtlest and strangest minds of his time." To his "genius, ancestral memory, creative power," she brought her Beauty, her vision, her dreams, her thought, and her life. Their love for each other brought them together in a spiritual union. A mystical melding of the two produced the shaping power that enabled Sharp to write the stories and poems of Fiona Macleod.

61   Among these projected titles, the only story to appear was "The Merchant of Dreams," which can be found in Volume V of *The Selected Writings of William Sharp* (London: William Heinemann, 1912).

62   "Sir Edward Burne-Jones," *The Atlantic Monthly*, 82 (September, 1898), 375–83. "Edward Burne-Jones," *The Fortnightly Review*, 70 (August, 1898), 289–306.

63   The anxiety is due to the fact that the Fiona Macleod letter *To William Butler Yeats, June 28, 1898* (Volume 2) describes as material for a story the relationship between William Sharp and Edith Rinder that produced the Fiona Macleod writings. This relationship and its effects were known to only a few, and their general discovery would have had disastrous effects

on Sharp's personal and creative life. This explains his concern about what may have happened to the June 28 Fiona Macleod letter to Yeats.

64   William Leonard Courtney (1850–1928) was a philosopher, journalist, and editor who became the editor of the influential *Fortnightly Review* in 1894 and remained in that position until 1928. His books include *The Metaphysics of John Stuart Mill* (1879), *The Development of Maeterlinck* (1904), and *The Soul of a Suffragette* (1913).

65   The Reverend Donald Macleod (d. 1911) served as Minister of the Parish of the Park in Glasgow and edited *Good Words* from 1872–1905. His publications include *Christ and Society* (1893) and *Memoir of Norman Macleod* (1876)

66   Clement King Shorter (1857–1926) was a journalist and author who, after working as editor on various London news and periodical publications, founded *The Sphere* in 1900 which he edited until his death. He also founded *The Tatler* in 1901 and, much earlier, he had helped establish the Omar Khayyam Club, of which Sharp was a member. His publications include *Charlotte Brontë and Her Circle* (1896), *Napoleon's Fellow Travelers* (1909), and *George Borrow and his Circle* (1913).

67   E. A. S. was a member of the Sesame Club and W. S. of the Grosvenor Club.

68   So woefully far on in the year.

69   If the Richards left for Cornwall on Saturday July 23, they might have had tea with the Sharps on Monday, July 18. In any case, Sharp had met the new Mrs. Richards when he next wrote to her husband early in 1899.

70   Mrs. Sharp printed (*Memoir*, pp. 299–300) Rhys' reply to this letter:

Dear "Fiona Macleod,"

I believe I never wrote to thank you for your story in the *Dome*, which I read eventually in an old Welsh tower. It was the right place to read such a fantasy of the dark and bright blindness of the Celt: and I found it, if not of your very best, yet full of imaginative stimulus.

Not many weeks ago, in very different surroundings, Mr. Sharp read me a poem — two poems — of yours. So I feel that I have the sense, at least, of your continued journeys thro' the divine and earthly regions of the Gael, and how life looks to you, and what colours it wears. What should we do were it not for that sense of the little group of simple and faithful souls, who love the clay of earth because heaven is wrapt in it, and stand by and support their lonely fellows in the struggle against them? I trust at some time it may be my great good fortune to see you and talk of these things, and hear more of your doings. Ernest Rhys.

71   Rhys's *Welsh Ballads and Other Poems* (London: David Nutt, 1898).

72   A fourteenth-century Welsh poet.

73   George Moore's *Evelyn Innes* (New York: Appleton & Co., 1898).

74   *The Dominion of Dreams* (1899).

75   "The Hour of Beauty" became "The Immortal Hour" and was published in the *Fortnightly Review* in November 1900. "The King of Ys" and "Dahut the Red" were intended by Sharp to form part of a series of plays to be published collectively as *The Theatre of the Soul* or *The Psychic Drama*. Neither the plays nor the series materialized. See "Bibliographical Note" in *Poems and Dramas*, Vol. VII of *The Works of Fiona Macleod*, Unified Edition arranged by Mrs. William Sharp (London: William Heinemann, 1910), p. 448.

76   The Isle of Colonsay in Argyll is not far off-shore from Kilcreggan where Sharp seem to have spent most of his time for the first three weeks of August. In a July 4 letter, Yeats told Sharp that Martyn was too upset by his mother's death (on May 12) to invite anyone to Tillyra, but might change his mind. He also promised to speak to Martyn about inviting Sharp if the occasion arose. Apparently, Martyn did invite Sharp, but the formality and cool tone of Sharp's response suggest Martyn's invitation was less cordial and welcoming than it might have been.

77   The remaining page or pages of this letter are missing.

78   Date from postmark; postcard addressed to Eldridge Court | Chicago.

79   The concluding sentence was written vertically on the left side of the postcard and the writing is difficult to make out. The sense seems to be that Fiona Macleod would also like copies of the books she published with Stone and Kimball — *Pharais* (1895); *The Sin-Eater* (1896); and *The Washer of the Ford* (1896) — in lieu of royalty payments.

80   The card is postmarked Glasgow, Aug 24,'98. Since Sharp says he is "en route," he must have been returning to London from Kilcreggan, Argyll.

81   *Wives in Exile* (1898).

82   Sir Anthony Hope Hawkins (1863–1933) was a novelist and playwright who used the pseudonym Anthony Hope. Someone must have speculated in print that Hawkins was Hope. Sharp was pleased the article wasn't speculating about him and Fiona. As Anthony Hope, Hawkins published, among other works, *The Prisoner of Zenda* (1894) and *The Great Miss Driver* (1908).

83   "Enya of the Dark Eyes" appeared in *Literature*; "The Last Night of Artan the Culdee" and "The Monody of Isle the Singer" appeared in *The Dome*, 1 [New Series] (October, 1898), 75–76.

84   The Stedman's house was named for the Stedmans's daughter, Laura.

85   The manuscript letter is in William Sharp's hand for copying by Mary Sharp into the Fiona Macleod hand.

86   Ernest James Oldmeadow (1867–1949) was the editor of *The Dome* (1897–1900), music critic of *The Outlook* (1900–1904), editor of the *Tablet* (1923–1936), and the author of *Chopin* (1905), *Aunt Maud* (1908), *A Babe Unborn* (1911), and *Miss Watts, an Old Fashioned Romance* (1923).

87   "The Secrets of the Night" appeared in *The Dome* in January 1899, 68–69.

88   The addressee is probably Dora (Sigerson) Shorter (1866–1918), a novelist and poet from Ireland who married Clement Shorter in 1896. Her works include *Ballads and Poems* (1899), *The Woman Who Went to Hell* (1902), and *Love of Ireland: Poems and Ballads* (1916). See postscript to letter to Clement Shorter dated January 2, 1899.

89   "A Group of Celtic Writers," *The Fortnightly Review* (January, 1899), 34–53, wherein Fiona Macleod said "The most notable new addition to this group of young writers is Miss Dora Sigerson (Mrs. Clement Shorter)."

90   The Pettycur Inn, Kinghorn, Fife (*Memoir*, p. 300).

91   Of these three titles, only one, "Honey of the Wild Bees," appeared in *The Dominion of Dreams*.

92   "Thus onward to the stars!"

Chapter 18

1   Clement Shorter (1857–1926) was editor of the *Illustrated London News*. His wife was the Irish poet Dora Sigerson (1866–1918) who, after her marriage in 1895, wrote as Dora Sigerson Shorter. Born in Dublin, she contributed significantly to the Irish Literary Revival. Her work was mentioned in Fiona Macleod, "A Group of Celtic Writers", *The Fortnightly Review* (January, 1899), 34–53. See Fiona's letter *To [Dora Sigerson Shorter, December, 1898]* (Volume 2).

2   *Silence Farm* was published by Grant Richards (London) on June 13, 1899.

3   Like many of Sharp's ambitious projects, this one failed to materialize. In a letter to E. A. S. in the fall of 1897, Sharp described a work of epic proportions that would contain and transmit all he had learned about life. At that time, it was to be six books under the general title "The Epic of Youth" (*Memoir*, p. 289).

4   Written on Grosvenor Club mourning stationery with that address crossed out and this address written over it.

5   Neil Munro (1863–1930) was an influential Scottish journalist and novelist. After serialization in *Blackwood's Magazine*, his first novel *John Splendid, The Tale of a Poor Gentleman, and the Little Wars of Lorn*, was published in 1898 by William Blackwood And Sons (Edinburgh and London). It deals with the sack of Inverary by Montrose and his subsequent victory at the battle of Inverlochy in 1645.

6   "A Group of Celtic Writers."

7   Pounds, shillings, pence.

8   This is the first of several letters Sharp addressed to Richards about the realistic novel he was writing. After much back and forth about royalties and other business matters, Richards accepted the book and published it on June 13, 1899.

9   This book never materialized.

10   In a memoir, *Author Hunting by an Old Literary Sportsman: Memories of Years Spent Mainly in Publishing, 1897–1925* (New York: Coward-McCann, 1934), Grant Richards wrote "Sometime in the early spring of 1898, I became engaged to a young Italian lady; in May of the same year we were married. I shall have, I think, no need to mention that marriage again, so I will confine myself to saying that my wife bore me children [three boys and a girl] and that the union was dissolved" (p. 135). The young lady he married was Elisina Palamidessi de Castelvecchio (1878–1959), the great-great-granddaughter of Napoleon's brother Louis. In 1909, Elisina left her family to live with Royall Tyler, with whom she had a child in 1910. After her divorce from Richards in 1914, she married Tyler, and in 1915 Richards married a young Hungarian widow named Maria Magdalena de Csanády. Elisina was the first editor of *Englishwoman* which the Richards firm published from 1909–1921. Later, as Elisina Tyler, she became a close friend of the novelist Edith Wharton, and assisted with her charities during the First World War, becoming vice president of the American Hostels for Belgian Refugees and the Children of Flanders Rescue Committee. She was also chairman of the Franco-American Committee of the Viennese

Children's Fund. She was co-awarded (with Edith Wharton) the Médaille de la Reine Elisabeth by the Belgian government in 1918 for their work with refugees. Later, she was made a chevalier of the French Legion of Honor. She and her husband acquired Antigny-le-Château, near Arnay-le-Duc, in 1923. Elisina became the executor of the French will and estate of Edith Wharton, and she inherited Wharton's Sainte-Claire du Château, her property at Hyères, where she died in 1959. See https://www.doaks.org/research/library-archives for more information.

11   Grant Richards first visited the French Riviera in February 1899. In *Author Hunting*, he wrote: "William Sharp and Thomas A. Janvier collaborated in drawing up my itinerary" (p. 145). It was a delayed honeymoon trip with Elisina Palamidessi de Castelvecchio whom he married in May, 1898. Some years later, Richards wrote *The Coast of Pleasure: An Unconventional Guide to the French Riviera*.

12   Jules Bossière (1863–1897), poet, traveler, Chinese scholar, and opium addict, was a disciple of Mallarmé and the Symbolists. He wrote seven books in his short life, the two on opium usage his finest. *Fumeurs d'opium*, a collection of stories, was first published in 1896 and went through four editions. The autobiographical *Propos d'un intoxiqué* first appeared in 1911. He was one of the first French writers to study the action of opium on the intelligence and sensibilities (Arnould de Liedekerke, *La Belle Epoque de l'Opium* (Paris: Le Sphinx, 1984), p. 197). The suggestion that Edith Rinder translate *Fumeurs d'opium* for publication by Grant Richards did not materialize. Her translation of *Le Crucifié de Keraliès* by Charles Henri Le Goffic was published in 1898 under the title, *The Dark Way of Love* (Westminster: Archibald Constable & Co., 1898).

13   The concept of a female redeemer, especially the St. Bride story, appears frequently in the Fiona writings.

14   This was published by Archibald Constable and Co. on May 27, 1899.

15   Egan Mew, who wrote for *Literature*, was living in Gray's Inn Place, London. He wrote *A London Comedy and Other Vanities* (1897) and *Historical Books of the World*. He also wrote six books on porcelain — Japanese, Chinese, and British.

16   Although Egan Mew had written an announcement of Fiona Macleod's forthcoming *The Dominion of Dreams* in Literature, she was nonetheless annoyed by his continued assumption that Fiona Macleod was a pseudonym.

17   Easter Monday, April 3.

18   This letter appeared in "Book of the Week," a column by F. E. Green, in the January 21, 1909 issue of *The New Age*. The book that occasioned Green's column was an edition of Fiona Macleod's works called *Songs and Poems, Old and New* published posthumously that year by Eliot Stock. Frederick Ernest Green (1867–1922) was a prolific writer on agricultural policy. The circumstances that led to Fiona's letter to Green, as recalled in Green's column, are described in the "Life" section of this chapter.

19   Elizabeth Sharp recalled visiting Mr. and Mrs. Grant Allen in Surrey "at their charming house, The Croft, built among the heather and the pines on the hill-top just by the edge of the chasm called 'The Devil's Punch Bowl'" (*Memoir*, p. 317).

20   This card is postmarked April 10, 1899. Douglas Hyde's *A Literary History* was published by Unwin in late April, 1899. Accompanying this card is a manuscript note which reads: "Hyde's Literary History / Sent to Sharp per Pickford on the 8th. Signed for, / on behalf of Pickford, by A. Smith."

21   Postcard postmarked April 12, 1899.

22   *The Wind Among the Reeds* (London: Elkin Matthews, 1899) was published on April 15, 1899. Pinar is a village northwest of London in Middlesex.

23   In his note to "The Hosting of the Sidhe," the first poem in *The Wind Among the Reeds*, Yeats indicated that the gods of ancient Ireland were known among the poor as the Sidhe and stated: "Sidhe is also Gaelic for wind" (p. 65).

24   A review of *The Wind Among the Reeds* signed Fiona Macleod appeared in the *Dublin Daily Express* on April 22, 1899. Sharp wrote about the volume again as Fiona Macleod in "The Later Work of Mr. W. B. Yeats," *The North American Review*, 175 (October, 1902), 473–85. Sharp thought H. D. Traill's weekly *Literature* would publish a review under his signature, but I have been unable to find this. Sharp's opinions of the volume in the context of his ongoing relationship with Yeats are discussed in the "Life" section of this chapter.

25   Sharp wrote this letter on the train returning to London from Pinner where he had been for the evening.

26   The reference is to *No. 5 St. John Street* by Richard Whiteing (1840–1928), which Grant Richards had recently published. The book went through many editions and became Grant Richards' first successful book.

27   Date from postmark.

28 Originally published by T. Fisher Unwin in 1895, a revised edition of Yeats' *Poems* was published by Unwin on May 8, 1899.

29 The book's official date of publication was May 27, 1899.

30 E. A. S. printed this sentence and the rest of the paragraph (*Memoir*, p. 307).

31 A journalist and aspiring novelist from Scotland, Macleay began his career as a writer for *The Highland News* in Inverness. Though he continued to write occasional pieces for that paper, he had recently moved to Liverpool to join the staff of the *Liverpool Chronicle*. He suspected that Fiona Macleod might be William Sharp and speculated on that point in both papers, usually quoting unnamed sources. Sharp was pulled between the need to keep Macleay at a distance from the truth while also encouraging him to write about Fiona in order to boost sales of her books.

32 Sharp was reviewing the annual exhibit at the Royal Academy of Art for either the *Glasgow Herald* or the *Art Review*.

33 Sharp finally left for France on Sunday April 30 or Monday May 1.

34 See Sharp's letter *To Grant Richards, [late January, 1899]* (Volume 2).

35 Edith Sophy Balfour Lyttelton (1865–1948), later Dame Edith Lyttelton, was a playwright and author. Her works include *Warp and Woof* (1904); *Peter's Chance* (1912); *The Faculty of Communion* (1925); and *Our Superconscious Mind* (1931). A prominent society hostess, she was the wife and biographer of Alfred Lyttelton (1857–1913), a Member of Parliament and, for a time, Secretary of State.

36 *The Dominion of Dreams* was published by Archibald Constable and Co. (Westminster) on May 27, 1899.

37 The remainder of this paragraph was reproduced separately by E. A. S. in the *Memoir* (306–07) where it is introduced by "to another correspondent he wrote" with the implication it was an extract from a William Sharp letter.

38 This letter was sent to Archibald Constable at the request of the publishers, who were worried that speculation about the identity of Fiona Macleod would interfere with sales of *The Dominion of Dreams*. It was sent to several publications. This transcription is from *The Athenaeum*, 3733 (May, 1899), 596. I am indebted to Michael Shaw for bringing this letter to my attention.

39 What follows are fragments of two or three letters Sharp wrote to Yeats. They were owned by Yeats' son, Michael B. Yeats, who gave me copies. The

paper and script of the fragments are similar, but how they fit together, if they do, is unclear. It is likely all three fragments were written when Sharp was in or near Paris in early May 1899. The fragment placed first here (ending at "special article") was certainly written while Sharp was in Paris. The introduction to this section of the letters comments on his reading to the Mathers. The next fragment, which begins with "I send you a cutting" and ends with the first "Reddening of the West," also deals with *The Dominion of Dreams*. In the final fragment, Sharp addresses the plays he will write as Fiona before the end of the summer for Yeats' theatre in Dublin. It seems also to have been written in France since Sharp wrote two letters to Yeats after he returned to England both of which said he was seriously ill in France. It was surely written before May 29, when he cautioned Yeats against referring to "The Tarist" since he intended to name it "The King of Ireland's Son."

40   This is the first of several times Sharp expressed his desire for Yeats' opinion of *The Dominion of Dreams* and his hope that Yeats would review the book. Without responding to Sharp about the book, Yeats reviewed it in the July 1899 issue of *The Bookman*. He praised the book, but also criticized its wordiness and overblown style. Sharp was greatly distressed at first by the criticism, but came to recognize Yeats' comments were at least partially justified (*Memoir*, p. 308).

41   This sentence is written in the left margin of the page. Henry Duff Traill (1842–1900) had become the first editor of the weekly *Literature* in October 1897, and he directed its fortunes until his death. The subject of the "cutting" in the next line and the advice it must have contained are unknown.

42   The words in brackets are inserted above the line.

43   This book became *The Divine Adventure: Iona: By Sundown Shores* when it was published in early summer 1900 by Chapman and Hall (London). By then, Sharp's relationship with Yeats had cooled, and the volume was not dedicated to him, but to EALASAIDH, which is Elizabeth (or E. A. S.) in Gaelic. In the spring and fall of 1899, he expected to finish and publish the book in November 1899.

44   This is the end of two pages that fit together. The next excerpt is from the beginning of two pages written side-by-side on a single sheet. Although we cannot be certain, these pages are likely part of the same letter as the two pages above.

45   This line is written in the left margin.

46   The page ends here, and the next page is missing.

47 Sharp probably returned from France on Monday May 22 and found waiting him an author's copy of *Silence Farm*. See his letter *To John Macleay, [April 25, 1899]* (Volume 2). Richards had decided to delay official publication until June 13.

48 The Omar Khayyam Club was a group of literary men who met periodically for dinners, listened to each other deliver speeches, and inducted new members.

49 Henry D. Davray (1873–1944) wrote and translated for the *Mercure de France*. He was the author of *Chez les Anglais pendant la Grande Guerre* (1916), *Through French Eyes: Britain's Effort* (1916), and *Lord Kitchener: His Work and His Prestige* (1917).

50 Frank Rinder was the husband of Edith Rinder, the woman Sharp loved, and their love is the subject of many stories in the book. In "The Distant Country," for example, the female narrator describes a love affair that is so intense it threatens to burn itself out. His mention of this story may have been an indirect means of suggesting to Rinder that his affair with Edith was beginning to wane. The sentence Sharp quoted suggests he believed Rinder would concur that intense love between two human beings cannot be denied and whatever redemption might be required for the harm that love causes others comes only after death. This is one of very few letters from Sharp to the Rinders that Elizabeth used partially in the *Memoir*. Since she knew the facts of Sharp's relationship with Edith would one day emerge, she must have wanted future readers to know that both she and Edith's husband knew about and tolerated the love affair between their two spouses.

51 This statement dates the letter as Monday, May 29.

52 Yeats had asked Sharp to comment on or add to a draft of a ritual he had constructed for his Celtic Mystical order. A note in *Collected Notes II* (p. 422) says of this draft: "Probably an early version of 'The Initiation of the Spear,' which he [Yeats] had repeatedly experienced since 17 Dec 1898. By January 1899 WBY had also worked out a structure for the rituals based on cauldron, stone, sword, and spear related to the four seasons ('Visions Notebook')."

53 The area around Tara in County Meath in the east of Ireland. The ancient kings of Ireland were said to have their seat and hold their assemblies in Tara until 563. Ulidia or Uladlh (Ulla, i.e., Ulster), an original kingdom of ancient Ireland, became the northern province of Ulster composed of nine counties, six of which are now in Northern Ireland.

54   Kilkeel and Newcastle are seaport towns in County Down. Annalong is a fishing village five miles north of Kilkeel.

55   Sharp finished and published two plays under the Fiona Macleod pseudonym: "The House of Usna," *National Review*, 35 (July, 1900), 733ff; and "The Immortal Hour," *The Fortnightly Review*, 68 (November, 1900), 867–96. "The Tarist" and "The King of Ireland's Son" were rejected titles for "The House of Usna." "The King of Ireland's Son" was probably rejected because it was the title of a poem by Nora Hopper which was quoted in "Dalvan," a story in *Ballads in Prose*, 1894 (*Collected Letters I*, p. 54). In his letter *To William Butler Yeats, September 16, 1899* (Volume 2), Sharp told Yeats "The House of Usna" and "The Immortal Hour" were the two finished plays (*Memoir*, p. 310). "The House of Usna" was performed "under the auspices of The Stage Society, of which William Sharp was the first Chairman" at the Fifth Meeting of the Society at the Globe Theatre, April 29, 1900. It was directed by Granville Barker, and Y. M. Capel wrote the music that accompanied it (*Memoir*, pp. 317–18). Two short plays by Maeterlinck were also performed that evening.

56   Gort is in County Galway near Coole Park, the residence of Lady Gregory, and not far from Edward Martyn's Tillyra Castle.

57   Edward Verrall Lucas (1868–1938) was a versatile and popular English writer of nearly one hundred books. *The Open Road* went through many editions both in England and in America, where it was published by Henry Holt. Born in Kent, educated at Friends' school in Saffron Walden, without university education he joined the staff at *Punch* in 1904 and wrote prolifically for the magazine. In 1924, he became chairman of the London publishers Methuen and Company. According to R. G. G. Price's *A History of Punch* (London: Collins, 1957), his polished and gentlemanly essayist's persona concealed "a cynical clubman ... very bitter about men and politics ... [with] the finest pornographic library in London" (194).

58   In his Thursday, June 8 letter to Little, Sharp said review copies were going out that week, the week preceding publication on June 13. This letter and the letter to Yeats, both of which are undated, similar in handwriting and some wording and written on the same stationery, were probably written early in the week of June 5, a Monday. I have therefore chosen that as the probable date of both letters.

59   Sharp asked Yeats several times in late May and June what he thought about *The Dominion of Dreams* and wondered if he would review the book. Having heard nothing on the subject from Yeats by the end of June, he was surprised, and more than a little annoyed, when he learned in early July

that Yeats' review had appeared in that month's *Bookman*. This matter will be described in more detail in the "Life" section of Chapter Nineteen.

60 "The King of Ireland's Son" became "The House of Usna." Sharp is telling Yeats indirectly he is capable of writing contemporary "Irish" plays, which might be suitable for an Irish Literary Theater in addition to the Pan-Celtic dramas set in the mythic past. Political considerations had caused Yeats in late 1897 to shift the name of the theater he and others were developing in Dublin from "Celtic" to "Irish."

61 E. A. S. combined this line and the last paragraph of this letter with passages from a letter to Yeats (which I have dated May 29) into what appears as a single letter in the *Memoir*. She omitted from both letters references to the possibility that Lady Gregory or Edward Martyn would invite them as guests to the West, references to their financial difficulties, references to the plays Sharp was writing as Fiona for Yeats' Irish theater, and, most significantly, all references to the Rite for the Celtic Mystical Order

62 The bracketed words are crossed through in the manuscript letter, probably by Sharp since the inserted words "probably to the" appear to be in his hand. Presumably he wanted Yeats to think he had thought better about conveying his hope for an invitation while leaving enough to plant the idea.

63 The east coast north of Dublin in County Down.

64 Sharp had told Yeats, probably in June 1897, that he was responsible for the Fiona Macleod writings and that he experienced her as an alternative personality triggered and inspired by a real woman with whom he enjoyed an intimate relationship. Sharp was suffering one of his periodic bouts of depression.

65 This strange letter to Russell, which assumes a closer relationship between the two men than in fact existed, was written about the same time as the previous letter to Yeats, thus the probable date of June 5. It conveyed the same note of depression and disdain for city life in London that Sharp expressed to Yeats in his May 29 letter and again on June 5. Somewhat plaintively, Sharp asked AE to provide Fiona some "sympathy and comradely help" which she needed to refresh her soul. He must have done so right away since Fiona, in a letter dated June 17, thanked AE for his "friendly and sincere letter."

66 In her letter *To John Macleay, May 31, 1899* (Volume 2), Fiona asked if she was correct in thinking that Macleay was soon to be married. Macleay

answered that question affirmatively, and here Fiona sent good wishes for "his wedded life." That fixes the date as 1899.

67   Sharp was stalling, through Fiona, for more time to comment substantively on the Rite as he had in his May 29 and June 5 letters to Yeats. Yeats sent separate copies of the Rite to Fiona and to Sharp for comment. Since he knew Sharp was writing the Fiona Macleod works under the influence of a woman he loved and since that woman was cooperating with Sharp in divining the rites for Yeats' Celtic Order, the intended recipient of the second copy of the Rite must have been Edith Rinder. Following Sharp's lead and because he did not know who she was, Yeats addressed her as Fiona Macleod.

68   Sharp stated that Fiona was in Midlothian from the "Middle Isles" in order to explain the Edinburgh postmark. Sharp drafted the letter in London and sent it to his sister in Edinburgh to copy and send. Yeats is to presume that Fiona will remain in Edinburgh for a week and Sharp will join her there on or about June 23. Subsequent letters confirm this supposed meeting and imply they went together back to the "Middle Isles" south and west of Glasgow where they remained until early July. It is likely that he was with Edith Rinder in the West.

69   The "Kritik" which was to appear soon, and its author, are unknown to me. "Dalua" is the first story in the first section of *The Dominion of Dreams*.

70   These square brackets appear in the original letter, and are not my own addition. am Fheill Bhrighde can be roughly translated into English as St. Bridgit or St. Bride.

71   Sharp's handwritten draft of this letter is in the National Library of Scotland. Mary Sharp's transcription, used here, is in the Lilly Library at Indiana University.

72   "The Book of the Opal" and "The Yellow Moonrock" appeared in *The Dominion of Dreams* (1899). AE's letter to F. M. about the book contained some advice and some criticism as did his review in the *Dublin Daily Express*.

73   Sharp began "The Lily Leven" in 1896, but it was not published. See Endnote 24, Chapter 15 (Volume 2).

74   Yeats's stories about Hanrahan the Red first appeared in *The Secret Rose: A Collection of Stories* (London: Lawrence and Bullen, 1897). They were published later as *The Stories of Hanrahan the Red* (Dundrum: The Dun Emer Press, 1904).

75 AE's review of *The Dominion of Dreams* appeared in the *Dublin Daily Express* in June 1899.

76 *The Athenaeum*, 3738 (June, 1899), p. 751: "in some respects the most considerable work yet issued by the writer who has been for several years the protagonist of the Scottish Gael."

77 Probably *The House of Usna*.

78 The letter is transcribed from Sharp's draft for Mary to copy. It was written in response to the review of *The Dominion of Dreams* in the June 17 issue of *The Athenaeum* (see Endnote 75). I do not know if it was published.

79 Unwin published a revised edition of Yeats's *Poems* in May, 1899. The postmark on this card is "Ju 19 9_." The numeral after the second 9 is unclear. 20/6/98 has been written in pencil above the salutation. "Send," appears in another hand in pencil above the message with a line going to "Complete Poems" in the body of the note. Since Sharp asked Unwin on April 18, 1899 when Yeats' reissued *Poems* would be out and offered to do what he could for the book, June 19, 1899 is the probable date of the card.

80 The idea here is that Sharp would join Fiona in Edinburgh on the June 23 or 24, and they would go to the West together. Sharp's mother's house in Edinburgh was, before Miss Rea entered the picture, Fiona's return address since Sharp's sister Mary who provided the Fiona handwriting lived there with their mother. That was where Sharp stayed when he was in Edinburgh and where Fiona supposedly stayed with her aunt and cousins when she was in Edinburgh. Sharp could place her there only for brief time slots for fear someone would knock on the door looking for her.

81 Edward Verrall Lucas, *The Open Road* (1899). See Endnote 57.

82 This card was written and mailed on June 26 in Falkirk, near Stirling, when Sharp was traveling on the main line from Edinburgh to Glasgow and on to the west. He probably received Richard's letter during his brief stop in Edinburgh.

83 This letter is transcribed from the draft in Sharp's hand intended for Mary to copy into the Fiona hand. Sharp found the letter to Fiona from Rhys in Edinburgh when he stopped there on June 24/5. He must have drafted this response in the west and sent it to Mary from there. Letters in the Fiona hand usually carry the date of Sharp's drafts.

84 Grace Rhys (*née* Little, 1865–1929) was an Irish writer raised in Boyle, County Roscommon. She met her husband at a garden party given by Yeats, and they married in 1891. Her first novel, *Mary Dominic*, was

published in 1898. Her other work includes *The Wooing of Sheila* (1901), *The Bride* (1909), and *Five Beads on a String* (1907), a book of essays. She died in Washington, D. C. while accompanying her husband on an American lecture tour.

85   The phrase in brackets was crossed out.

86   F. E. Green included this letter in his column — "Book of the Week" — in *The New Age*, 4/13 (January, 1909). He concluded the article: "I may say that I was not actuated by mere literary curiosity in writing to Fiona Macleod; but by a genuine desire to find out more of the philosophy and religion underlying the spiritual romances which emanated from that wonderful pen" (267). I have dated the letter about June 30 because it places Fiona in the Highlands, where Sharp was located in late June and early July. Also in late June, *The Dominion of Dreams* had appeared recently, and Sharp still thought "The Reddening of the West" (which became *The Divine Adventure*) might be published in November 1899.

Chapter 19

1   Yeats's review of Fiona Macleod's *The Dominion of Dreams* appeared in the July issue of *The Bookman*. Sharp was in the west of Scotland when he received word from a "friend" about Yeats's review so he had to wait a day for a copy of the July *Bookman*. He probably started this letter to Yeats on Monday, July 3, finished it on July 4, and held it until he received and read the *Bookman* review on July 5. He then decided not to send the letter because the review turned out to be less negative than he was led to believe. The ALS was recently acquired by the National Library of Scotland with a group of letters to John Macleay from William Sharp and Fiona Macleod. How the letter came into the group of Sharp letters to Macleay remains unknown. The most likely explanation is that it was preserved among Sharp's own papers and E. A. S. sent it to Macleay by mistake when she returned the letters he received from Sharp/Macleod after using some in the *Memoir*. It certainly went to someone since it escaped Elizabeth's burning of most of her husband's papers before she died, and it was not among the few that were saved by E. A. S's brother, Robert Farquharson Sharp, and donated to the National Library of Scotland by Robert's son, Noel Farquharson Sharp.

2   The Saville Club was founded in 1868 by a group of like-minded young men who deplored the suffocating traditions of the traditional Victorian men's clubs. In the 1870s, it established itself at 107 Piccadilly and

eventually attracted many important literary figures, among them Robert Louis Stevenson, Thomas Hardy, H. G. Wells, Rudyard Kipling, Compton Mackenzie, Max Beerbohm and W. B. Yeats. The club outgrew its Piccadilly quarters in 1927 and moved to its current location, 69 Brook Street. The person most likely to have contacted Sharp about the Yeats review was Sharp's publisher Grant Richards who knew his whereabouts and who knew he would be sensitive to any criticism of Fiona Macleod. Richards became a member of the Saville Club on March 24, 1899.

3   This article by AE (George Russell) appeared in the Dublin *Daily Express* on November 12, 1898. The paper had published an exchange of letters between John Eglinton and Yeats which AE had encouraged in order to draw attention to the Celtic cause. In this article, AE supported Yeats position that ancient legends can and should be used by contemporary writers. "Arguing that WBY sought to ennoble literature 'by making it religious,' he thought Eglinton simply unfamiliar with the symbolist tradition, and pointed out that since WBY's aesthetic was governed by the mystical temper and his art 'inspired by the Holy Breath,' he was using his art for the 'revelation of another world' rather than 'to depict this one'" (*Collected Letters II*, 293n). AE's nationalistic linking of Celtic literature with Irish literature and his disavowal of "Pan-Celticism," which emerged in this article and others, was offensive to Sharp because he saw it as devaluing the Scottish contributions, particularly those of Fiona Macleod, to the broader Celtic movement. The disagreement between AE and Sharp on this issue became more pronounced and more public in the months ahead.

4   This letter is not dated, but Richard Garnett retired from his position as Keeper of Printed Books at the British Museum in 1899 and it was written when Sharp had just returned from Scotland. The Sharps permanently left their flat at 30 Greencroft Gardens on July 20, 1899.

5   I have not located an article by Sharp on Garnett.

6   This anthology never materialized. "The Hour of Beauty" is the title of a section of poems in the 1907 edition of Fiona Macleod's *From the Hills of Dream* (Portland, Maine: Thomas Mosher).

7   Ireland/1899 is written in the top left corner in pencil not in Sharp's hand. Internal evidence confirms that the letter was written on Tuesday July 11, 1899 when the Sharps were in London preparing to vacate their South Hampstead flat and go, via Scotland, to the east coast of Ireland for August and September. The two reviews of *The Dominion of Dreams* mentioned in the letter appeared in early July: *The Outlook* review, titled "Priestess

of Beauty," appeared in the issue of July 8 and Macleay's review in *The Highland News* appeared the previous week.

8   This letter was written shortly before or after the Sharp's left their South Hampstead flat on July 20, 1899 since its return address is that of Elizabeth Sharp's mother where they spent some time before leaving London.

9   Printing this excerpt in the *Memoir*, E. A. S. identified Mrs. Janvier as the recipient.

10   Fairhead is a promontory on the North Coast of County Antrim in Northern Ireland, five miles from Balleycastle.

11   W. Lawler Wilson was best known as the author of *The Menace of Socialism* which Grant Richards published in 1909. Sharp's letter suggests Wilson asked for Sharp's portrait and biographical information for his *The Imperial Gallery of Portraiture: and Biographical Encyclopedia* which was published in 1902. He also wrote *The Lords and Liberty* (1910) and co-authored with C. P. Yates *The Will of the People* (1910).

12   A photograph of Sharp appeared along with a review of *Silence Farm* in *The Bookman* (London: August, 1899).

13   This letter is reproduced from Le Gallienne's *The Romantic '90s*, where it is used as an example of the Fiona Macleod handwriting.

14   The middle portion of the letter is missing.

15   This review of F. M.'s book of stories, improbably titled "A Beautiful Novel," appeared in *The Publisher's Circular*, 1727 (August, 1899), 120.

16   This review by Baron De B.-W. appeared in *Punch* (August 2, 1899), 53.

17   *The Divine Adventure* was published in May, 1900.

18   According to E. A. S., this volume of plays, which did not materialize, was to be called *The Theatre of the Soul* or *The Psychic Drama*. "The King of Ireland's Son" had become "The House of Usna" when it was performed "under the auspices of The Stage Society, of which William Sharp was the first Chairman" at the Fifth Meeting of the Society at the Globe Theatre, April 29, 1900 (*Memoir*, p. 317). "The House of Usna," appeared in *The National and English Review* in July, 1900 (733ff) and as a separate publication by Thomas Mosher of Portland Maine, in 1903. "The Immortal Hour" appeared first in the *Fortnightly Review* of November 1900 (867–96). It was published as a book in the United States by Thomas Mosher (1907) and in England by T. N. Foulis (1908). The two plays are included in *Poems*

and Dramas, Vol. VII of *The Works of Fiona Macleod*. "Queen Ganore" was not completed.

19 This reference indicates the letter was written from Ballycastle in County Antrim after August 20 and before August 26 when the Sharps had moved on to Newcastle in County Down.

20 Several words are impossible to decipher here.

21 This sentence suggests Sharp was intending to tell Edith Lyttelton about the crucial role his love affair with a beautiful young woman, perhaps calling her Fiona Macleod, played in his composition of the poems in *Sospiri di Roma* in the winter of 1891–1892.

22 Elizabeth Sharp said (*Memoir*, p. 35) this letter was written in 1899. Sharp's birthday was September 12.

23 In a letter to Yeats dated 19 September, 1899, George Russell (AE) wrote in a postscript: "I saw Sharp last night on his way to England. No particular news of him. Mrs. Sharp with him." Sharp must have drafted this letter while he and Elizabeth were in Ireland and sent it to Edinburgh for his sister to type, date, and send.

24 Cantyre is a peninsula at the southern part of Argyllshire between the Firth of Clyde and the Atlantic across the ocean from County Antrim in Northern Ireland.

25 After Sharp read Yeats's review of Fiona's *Dominion of Dreams* in the July *Bookman*, which contained a paragraph critical of the book, he (as Fiona) asked Yeats "to indicate the passages he took most exception to, and Mr. Yeats sent a carefully annotated copy of the book under discussion (*Memoir*, p. 309; see also Endnote 1). Yeats's "welcome note of the third" must have accompanied the annotated copy of Fiona's *Dominion of Dreams*.

26 This sentence exemplifies the conundrum Sharp created. In a letter to Yeats, William Sharp, writing as Fiona Macleod, said her friend William Sharp had made some revisions in a book he wrote and published as the work of Fiona Macleod.

27 *The Dominion of Dreams* went through several reprintings, but there was no new edition until 1910, when it appeared in Vol. III of the Uniform Edition of *The Works of "Fiona Macleod,"* arranged by Mrs. William Sharp. There, according to E. A. S., it contained revisions a number of which were the outcome of Yeats's suggestions. E. A. S. also moved stories in and out of the volume, "in accordance with the instructions and wishes of the author," as she described in a "Biographical Note" (pp. 427–28).

28   This story appeared in *The Dominion of Dreams* and is discussed at some length in the introduction to this section of the letters as it relates to the elaborate metaphor Sharp constructed later in this letter to Yeats.

29   Here Sharp, as Fiona, suggests "The Divine Adventure" was written by "her" friend William Sharp, whose "heart is in the ancient world and his mind for ever questing in the domain of the spirit." When the essay appeared in the November and December 1899 issues of the *Fortnightly Review*, it was the work of Fiona Macleod, and it became the titular essay of Fiona Macleod's *The Divine Adventure: Iona: By Sundown Shores: Studies in Spiritual History* which was published by Chapman and Hall in May 1900.

30   "Honey of the Wild Bees" appeared in *The Dominion of Dreams*. Drawing on the elaborate allegory in this letter of the match, torch, and flame — which is discussed in the "Life" section of this chapter — this sentence assigns principal responsibility to Sharp rather than Fiona for the stories in *The Dominion of Dreams*.

31   Regarding the plays, see Endnote 18.

32   Le Braz (1859–1926), often called the Bard of Brittany, was a was a Breton poet, folklore collector and translator. He was highly regarded amongst both European and American scholars, and known for his warmth and charm. His publications include *Au pays des pardons* (1894), *Le Gardien du feu* (1900), *Essai sur l'histoire du Théatre Celtique* (1904), *Ames d'Occident* (1911), and *La Bretagne* (1925).

33   Not completed.

34   St. Adamnan, Abbot of Hy (c. 624–704), wrote a *Life of Saint Columba* (*Columb-Kille*). A popular edition of Adamnan's work entitled *The Light of the West* and edited by Dr. John Goodchild appeared in April, 1898. See letter to *Dr. John Goodchild, [mid-May, 1898]* (Volume 2).

35   The essay entitled "Iona" appeared first in the *Fortnightly Review* of March (507–23) and April (692–709) 1900. Later that year it was included in *The Divine Adventure*.

36   *Library of Best Literature: Ancient and Modern* (New York: R. S. Peele and J. A. Hill, 1898), edited by Charles Dudley Warner. Sharp contributed entries on the following topics: Celtic literature (with Ernest Rhys) to Vol. V; Maurice Maeterlinck to Vol. XVI; Henri Conscience to Vol. VII; Icelandic literature to Vol. XIV; Maarten Maartens to Vol. XVI; myths and folklore of Aryan People (with Ernest Rhys) to Vol. XVIII; Ossian (with Ernest Rhys) to Vol. XIX; and Hersart de la Villemarqué to vol. XXVI. The *Kalevala* is an

epic poem compiled from Finnish and Karelian folklore by Elias Lönnrot in the nineteenth century.

37   Although added to the manuscript in pencil, presumably by the letter's recipient or his secretary, the date is supported by internal evidence. Also added in pencil at the top of the first page in the same hand is the following statement: "T W. D rep Wm Sharp Letter — referring to The Luck of Vesprie Towers."

38   The novel *The Luck of Vesprie Towers* did not appear until 1909 (London: John Lane). The *New York Times* review of the book, which appeared in the issue of May 20, 1909, begins as follows: "Amazement is perhaps the predominating sensation of the reader who turns the pages of the story 'Vesprie Towers,' the posthumous novel by Swinburne's old friend and faithful comrade, Watts-Dunton. It seems incredible that such a book could be published in our day and hour. Nothing like it has seen the light since 1870 or thereabout, we feel sure. It is entirely of mid — or later (very little later) — Victorian times, the sort of tale our grandmothers would have read in *Godey's Lady's Book* with the most genteel approval and many maidenly thrills." The poem Sharp praises is unknown, but it may have been intended for inclusion in the novel.

39   Benbecula is an island of the Outer Hebrides.

40   Elizabeth included a portion of this letter in the *Memoir*, p. 314.

41   Prior to this point the letter is typed. The rest is in the Fiona Macleod hand.

42   Grant Allen died on October 25, 1899, and his body was cremated at Woking two days later: "On Friday, 27 October, in pouring rain, the body was taken in a coffin of papier-mâché covered with white cloth to the Brookwood Crematorium, Woking. At the railway station it was met by Jerrard Allen, Grant Richards, Frank Whelan, J. S. Cotton, Rayner Storr, the Le Galliennes, and others. The only ceremony was a moving, simple and short memorial address by the positivist Frederic Harrison. It would, Harrison said rightly, be 'an outrage on the life and last wishes of Grant Allen that any theological hopes or invocations should be uttered over his helpless body now resting in the sublime stillness of death'. Accordingly, none was offered. There was no music, the only sound coming from the roaring of the furnace nearby. His ashes were scattered in the garden of The Croft, his home in Hindhead" (Peter Morton, *The Busiest Man in England: Grant Allen and the Writing Trade, 1875–1900* (New York: Palgrave Macmillan, 2005), https://sites.google.com/site/petermortonswebsite/home/grant-allen-homepage/busiest-temp).

43   This letter was written on October 27, the day Grant Allen's body was cremated.

44   The Boer War.

45   *The Progress of Art in the Nineteenth Century* (London and Edinburgh: W. & R. Chambers, Ltd., 1902). This book also appeared in *The Nineteenth Century Series* edited by Justin McCarthy, et al. (Toronto and Philadelphia: The Linscott Publishing Co., 1902).

46   Sharp had in mind the book that would become *The Divine Adventure: Iona; By Sundown Shores: Studies in Spiritual History*, which was published by Chapman and Hall in May 1900.

47   This letter is postmarked November 7, which was a Tuesday.

48   Watts-Dunton, who was poetry editor of *The Athenaeum*, must have sent Sharp several books to review. That would explain his promise to get them safely back in due course, presumably after he wrote the reviews. I have found no record of Sharp publishing anything in *The Athenaeum* in late 1899 or 1900, though he might have a written one or more reviews published anonymously.

49   *Literature*, a weekly paper established in 1897 by *The Times*, was edited by Henry Duff Traill (1842–1900). Dalton must have edited a series, perhaps reviews of poetry, in the paper. Sharp was writing something for the series. He had published in *Literature* in July a poem, "The Ballad of the Ram," and a story, "The Cafe of the Blind."

50   Perhaps an edition of Sir Philip Sidney's sonnet sequence "Astrophel and Stella," first published in 1591.

51   Probably Coulson Kernahan's *Scoundrels & Co.* (1899), which Watts-Dunton sent Sharp to review.

52   George Scott Robertson (1852–1916) was a British physician, government agent, and author. He entered the Indian Medical service in 1898 and served through the Afghan campaign of 1879–1880. He was the British agent of Gilgit in Kashmir in 1888 and 1889. From 1890 to 1891 he lived amongst wild hill men in Kafiristan. He conducted a political mission to Chitral in 1893. During this mission, Chitral was besieged, and Robertson was severely wounded. He survived his wounds and was installed as ruler of Chitral in September of 1895. Among his publications are *The Kafirs of the Hindu Kush* (1896) and *Chitral: The Story of a Minor Siege* (1898).

53 We know Watts-Dunton loaned twenty-five pounds because on February 9, 1900 Sharp wrote a long letter to Watts-Dunton explaining ill health had intervened and made it impossible to repay the loan. He promised to repay it whenever he could get the money together.

54 The reference is to "The Divine Adventure," which appeared in the *Fortnightly Review* in November and December.

List of Illustrations

Appendix

Letter location	Recipients of letters
The Athenaeum	Archibald Constable and Co., May 13, 1899
British Library	Theodore Watts-Dunton, [November 1899]
Churchill Archive Center, Churchill College, Cambridge	Edith Lyttelton, [early May, 1899]
	Edith Lyttelton, May 29, 1899
	Edith Lyttelton, June 18, 1899
	[Edith Lyttelton], [August 23?, 1899]
Columbia University Library Rare Book and Manuscript Library, Kenneth Lohf Papers	Edmund Clarence Stedman, [September 30?, 1896]
	Arthur Stedman, October 14, 1896
	Edmund Clarence Stedman, [October 21, 1896]
	Edmund Clarence Stedman, November 25, 1896
	Edmund Clarence Stedman, November 28, 1896
	Edmund Clarence Stedman, December 5, 1896
	Edmund Clarence Stedman, December 16, [1896]

Edmund Clarence Stedman, January 25, 1897

Edmund Clarence Stedman, January 30, 1897

Edmund Clarence Stedman, March 3, 1897

Edmund Clarence Stedman, March 5, 1897

Edmund Clarence Stedman, March 9, 1897

Edmund Clarence Stedman, May 12, 1897

Mary Stuart, March 1, 1898

Edmund Clarence Stedman, March 1, 1898

Edmund Clarence Stedman, [September 28, 1898]

The Highland News

Editor, *The Highland News*, January 28, 1896

Editor, *The Highland News*, January 28, 1896

Harper's Magazine

Editors, *Harper's Magazine*, May 19, 1898

Harvard University, Houghton Library

Herbert Stuart Stone, February 1, 1895

Herbert Stuart Scudder, January 2, 1895

Horace Stuart Scudder, February 2, 1895

Herbert Stuart Stone, [July 9?, 1895]

Thomas Wentworth Higginson,
[May 22?, 1897]

Huntington Library, San Marino,
California

Herbert Stuart Stone, February 1,
1895

Stone and Kimball, [early
February, 1895]

Herbert Stuart Stone, February 13,
1895

Herbert Stuart Stone, [July 12?,
1895]

Herbert S. Stone, [August 12,
1895]

Herbert S. Stone, [August 25?,
1895]

Herbert S. Stone, [early
September, 1895]

Herbert Stuart Stone, September
6, [1895]

Stone and Kimball, [mid-
September 1895]

Herbert Stuart Stone, September
18, 1895

Herbert Stuart Stone, September
28, 1895

Hannibal Ingalls Kimball,
November 8, 1895

[Hannibal Ingalls Kimball],
November 23, 1895

[Hannibal Ingalls Kimball],
November 25, 1895

[Stone and Kimball], November
25, 1895

Herbert S. Stone December 30, 1895

Herbert Stuart Stone, February 8, 1896

Herbert Stuart Stone, February 28, [1896]

Herbert Stuart Stone, March 4, [1896]

Herbert Stuart Stone, March 11, 1896

Herbert Stuart Stone, March 14, 1896

Herbert Stuart Stone, [mid-March, 1896]

Herbert Stuart Stone, [mid-March, 1896]

Herbert Stuart Stone, April 4, 1896

Herbert Stuart Stone, April 11, 1896

Herbert Stuart Stone June 9, 1896

Herbert Stuart Stone, June 24, 1896

Stone and Kimball, October 16, 1896

Stone and Kimball, October 21, 1896

Hannibal Ingalls Kimball, [November 13, 1896]

Hannibal Ingalls Kimball, January 28, 1897

Benjamin Burgess Moore, April 9, 1897

Edmund Clarence Stedman,
September 28, [1897]

Edmund Clarence Stedman,
December 3, 1897

Benjamin Burgess Moore,
February 25, 1898

Benjamin Burgess Moore, May 3,
1898

Richard Watson Gilder, July 5,
1898

Benjamin Burgess Moore, July 31,
1898

Benjamin Burgess Moore,
September 17, 1898

Benjamin Burgess Moore, July 12,
1899

Benjamin Burgess Moore, May 29,
1899

Benjamin Burgess Moore, August
11, 1899

Indiana University, Lilly Library   George Russell (AE), [late May,
1899]

George Russell (AE), [June 5?,
1899]

George Russell (AE), June 17,
1899

Library of Congress,   Louise Chandler Moulton, July
Louise Chandler Moulton Collection   17, 1896

Hamilton W. Mabie, [mid-March,
1897]

Manx Museum, Isle of Man   Hall Caine, February 20, 1896

National Library of Ireland   Edward Martyn, [September 22?, 1897]

National Library of Scotland   Patrick Geddes, [January 10, 1895]

Anna Geddes, January 10, 1895

Patrick Geddes, [January 15, 1895]

Patrick Geddes, [January 21, 1895]

Patrick Geddes, March 3, 1895

Patrick Geddes, April 27, 1895

Patrick Geddes, May 15, 1895

Patrick Geddes, [late May, 1895]

Patrick Geddes, June 4, 1895

Patrick Geddes, July 15, 1895

Patrick Geddes, [mid-September,1895]

Blackwood's Magazine, [late Fall, 1895]

Patrick Geddes, December 27, 1895

John S. Stuart-Glennie, December 26, 1895

Patrick Geddes, [January 14?, 1896]

John Ross, January 27, 1896

John Macleay, [February 5?, 1896]

John Macleay, [Feb 18, 1896]

Blackwood's Magazine, [late February, 1896]

Patrick Geddes, [early March, 1896]

Blackwood's Magazine, March 21, 1896

Mrs. James Ashcroft Noble, [April 8?, 1896]

Patrick Geddes, [April 9, 1896]

[John Ross], [April 27, 1896]

Patrick Geddes, [June 20?, 1896]

Patrick Geddes June 22, 1896

Patrick Geddes, June 30, 1896

John Macleay [July 28?, 1896]

Blackwood's Magazine, August 6, 1896

John Macleay, [August 10, 1896]

John Macleay, [August 17, 1896]

John Macleay, [August 18, 1896]

John Macleay, [August 19, 1896]

John Macleay, [August 21, 1896]

John Macleay, [August 22, 1896]

Patrick Geddes [August 23, 1896]

John Macleay, [August 24, 1896]

William Butler Yeats, [late September, 1896]

John Ross, October 9, 1896

John Macleay, October 13, 1896

John Ross, December 6, 1896

John Ross, December 9, 1896

[John Ross], December 16, 1896

[John Ross], December 16, 1896

John Ross, December 16, 1896

Patrick Geddes, [late December, 1896]

Patrick Geddes and Colleagues, [early January, 1897]

P. G. Geddes and Colleagues, January 28, 1897

Mr. Cuthbertson, March 5, 1897

John Macleay, March 16, 1997

W. E. Henley, April 1, 1897

Patrick Geddes, [May 24, 1897]

John Macleay, [September 29, 1897]

John Macleay, [mid-December?, 1897]

John Macleay, [mid-March?, 1898]

John Macleay, [May 3?, 1898]

John Macleay, August 8, 1898

Ernest James Oldmeadow [December, 1898]

John Macleay, [early January, 1899]

Doctor John Goodchild, March 4, 1899

T Fisher Unwin, [April 10, 18991

T Fisher Unwin, [April 12, 1899]

John Macleay, [April 25,1899]

John Macleay, May 31, 1899

John Macleay, June 8, [1899]

The Editor of *The Athenaeum*,
[June 18, 1899]

Ernest Rhys, June 29, 1899

William Butler Yeats, July 3–4,
1899

John Macleay, [July 11, 1899]

John Macleay, October 20, 1899

William Blackwood, October 31,
1899

The New Age   F. E. Green, March 25, 1899

F. E. Green, [June 30?, 1899]

Newberry Library, Chicago   Herbert Stuart Stone, August 12,
1895

Herbert Stone, January 24, 1896

Messrs. Herbert S. Stone & Co.,
[August 16, 1898]

New York Public Library,   Herbert S. Stone, April 6, 1895
Berg Collection
Herbert S. Stone, August 30, 1895

Herbert S. Stone, [mid-September,
1895]

Messrs. Stone and Kimball,
December 21, 1895

Herbert Stuart Stone, May 4, 1896

Hannibal Ingalls Kimball June 10,
1896

Hannibal Ingalls Kimball,
February 20, 1897

R. A. Streatfield, [June 4?, 1897]

	Lady Augusta Gregory, [November 27?, 1997]
	William Butler Yeats, July 6, 1898
	T Fisher Unwin, [April 10, 18991
	T Fisher Unwin, [April 12, 1899]
	T. Fisher Unwin, [April 18, 1899]
	T Fisher Unwin, [June 19, 1899]
New York University, Fales Library	Bliss Carman, February 24, 1897
	Grant Richards, July 11, 1898
Pierpont Morgan Library, New York	Professor William Knight, January 30, 1895
	Herbert Stuart Stone, [late June, 1895]
	Mrs. Grant Allen, July 11, 1895
	Grant Allen, [July 15? 1895]
	Grant Allen, [?, 1895]
	Mrs. Grant Allen, January 10, 1896
	Mrs. Grant Allen, [January 17, 1896]
	Mrs. Grant Allen, [January 21 or 22, 1896]
	Mrs. Grant Allen, [February 2, 1896]
	Mrs. Grant Allen, [February 7, 1896
	Bliss Carman, [November 9, 1896]
	[Richard Le Gallienne?], February 19, 1897

Mr. and Mrs. Grant Allen, November 5, 1897

Grant Richards [early June, 1898]

Mr. and Mrs. Grant Allen, [March 25, 1899]

Mrs. Grant Allen, [March 28, 1899]

Grant Richards, [May 23, 1899

Mrs. Grant Allen, [July 24?, 1899]

Mrs. Grant Allen, September 28, 1899

Jerrard Grant Allen, October 27, 1899

Grant Richards, [October 27, 1899]

Grant Richards [early November, 1899]

Princeton University, Firestone Library, Rare Books and Special Collections

Dr. Ward, January 1, 1895

J. Stanley Little, March 21, 1895

Edmund Clarence Stedman, March 30, 1895

J. Stanley Little, May 10, 1895

J. Stanley Little, July 5, 1895

J. Stanley Little, July 9, 1895

J. Stanley Little, [early August, 1895]

J. Stanley Little, [October 11?, 1895]

Richard Le Gallienne, [December] 28, [1895]

Coulson Kernahan, August 15, 1896

Henry Chandler Bowen, August 26, 1896

Coulson Kernahan, [October 22, 1896]

Coulson Kernahan [mid-March, 1897]

Louise Chandler Moulton, March 31, 1897

J. Stanley Little, [May 24, 1897]

Mrs. Coulson Kernahan [August 4, 1897]

Coulson Kernahan, [December 28, 1897]

Edward Martyn, [early August, 1898]

Coulson Kernahan, August 24, 1898

Egan Mew, March 20, 1899

Egan Mew, March 25, 1899

Coulson Kernahan, [May, 29, 1899]

Coulson Kernahan, [June 5, 1899]

J. Stanley Little, [June 8, 1899]

Edmund Clarence Stedman, September 27, 1899

Sheffield City Archives

Robert Murray Gilchrist, April 30, 1895

Robert Murray Gilchrist, [May 16?, 1895]

Robert Murray Gilchrist, [May 28, 1895]

Robert Murray Gilchrist, July 13, 1895

Robert Murray Gilchrist, July 18, [1895]

Robert Murray Gilchrist, [September 26, 1895]

Robert Murray Gilchrist, [October 1?, 1895]

Robert Murray Gilchrist, [October 14, 1895]

Robert Murray Gilchrist, [October 16, 1895]

Robert Murray Gilchrist, November 1, 1895

Robert Murray Gilchrist, [December 22?, 1895]

Robert Murray Gilchrist, [May 6, 1896]

Robert Murray Gilchrist, [May 28, 1896]

Robert Murray Gilchrist, [July 19, 1896]

Robert Murray Gilchrist, [September 28?, 1896]

Robert Murray Gilchrist, October 18, 1896

Robert Murray Gilchrist, [Early December, 1896]

Robert Murray Gilchrist, [January 15?, 1897]

Robert Murray Gilchrist, [mid-February, 1897]

Robert Murray Gilchrist, [mid-February, 1897]

Robert Murray Gilchrist, [May 3, 1897]

Robert Murray Gilchrist, [May 4, 1897]

Robert Murray Gilchrist, [May 6, 1897]

Robert Murray Gilchrist, [May 10, 1897]

Robert Murray Gilchrist, May 24, [1897]

Robert Murray Gilchrist, June 14, 1897

Robert Murray Gilchrist, [mid-August, 1897]

Robert M. Gilchrist, [mid-February, 1898]

Robert Murray Gilchrist, [April 22, 1898]

Robert M. Gilchrist, [mid-May?, 1898]

Robert Murray Gilchrist, May 17, 1898

Stanford University

Herbert S. Stone, January 31, [1895]

Richard Le Gallienne, March 16, 1897

Grant Richards, April 26, 1898

Grant Richards, [late May, 1898]

Grant Richards, January 18, 1899

Grant Richards, [April 25, 1899]

Grant Richards, June 22, 1899

Grant Richards, July 10, 1899

Grant Richards, July 11, 1899

Henry Mills Alden, September 18, [1899]

State University of New York at Buffalo Library

Grant Richards, May 2, 1898

Grant Richards, [July 15, 1898]

Grant Richards, [late January, 1899]

Grant Richards, [April 16, 1899]

Grant Richards, April 27, 1899

Grant Richards, [April 28, 1899]

Grant Richards, April [29], 1899

Grant Richards, early June, 1899

Grant Richards [June 26, 1899]

Grant Richards, August 26, 1899

University of British Columbia Library, Special Collections

Edmund Clarence Stedman, September 27, 1895

J. Stanley Little, [March 15?, 1897]

J. Stanley Little, [March 24?, 1897]

University of California, Berkeley, University Research Library, Bancroft Collection

William Meredith, September 14, 1897

William Meredith, September 24, [1897]

University of Delaware Library, Newark	Mrs. Henry Mills Alden, [April, 1895]
	Miss Anne Alden, July 20, [1895]
	Henry Mills Alden, [December, 1895]
	Elkin Mathews, January 6, 1896
University of Kentucky, W. Hugh Pearl Collection	?, December 11, 1895
University of Leeds, Brotherton Library	Clement Shorter, January 2, 1899
	Theodore Watts-Dunton, [October 19, 1899]
	Theodore Watts-Dunton, [November 6, 1899]
University of Texas, Austin, Ransom Humanities Research Center	Richard Le Gallienne, July 11, 1895
	Richard Le Gallienne, July 15, 1895
	Richard Garnett, October 25, 1895
	Richard Le Gallienne, [January 6, 1896]
	Richard Garnett, [January 6, 1896]
	Richard Garnett, [February 7?, 1896]
	[Dora Sigerson Shorter, December, 1898]
	Richard Garnett, [early July, 1899]
	W. Lawler Wilson Esq., August 7, 1899
	Richard Garnett, October 8, 1899

University of Toronto Library, *Thomas Fisher Rare Book Library*	Katherine Tynan Hinkson, March 24, 1897
University of Washington Libraries, *Walter Beals Autograph Collection*	[E. C. Stedman], [November 12, 1896]
University of Wisconsin–Milwaukee, *Golda Meir Library*	Dr. Tebb, [January 6, 1896]
	William Meredith, [May 15?, 1896]
	Grant Richards, May 9, 1898
Yale University, Beinecke Library	Frederick Shields, June 24, 1895
	Sir George Douglas, December 21, 1895
	William Butler Yeats, [late September, 1896]
	William Butler Yeats, April 30, 1898
	William Butler Yeats, May 5, 1998
	William Butler Yeats, [April 16, 1899]
	William Butler Yeats, [May 29?, 1899]
	William Butler Yeats, [June 5?, 1899]
	Grant Richards, [June 9, 1899]
	William Butler Yeats, September 16, 1899

About the team

Alessandra Tosi was the managing editor for this book.

Adèle Kreager performed the copy-editing and proofreading.

Anna Gatti designed the cover using InDesign. The cover was produced in InDesign using Fontin (titles) and Calibri (text body) fonts.

Luca Baffa typeset the book in InDesign. The text font is Tex Gyre Pagella; the heading font is Californian FB. Luca created all of the editions — paperback, hardback, EPUB, MOBI, PDF, HTML, and XML — the conversion is performed with open source software freely available on our GitHub page (https://github.com/OpenBookPublishers).

This book need not end here...

Share

All our books — including the one you have just read — are free to access online so that students, researchers and members of the public who can't afford a printed edition will have access to the same ideas. This title will be accessed online by hundreds of readers each month across the globe: why not share the link so that someone you know is one of them?

This book and additional content is available at:

https://doi.org/10.11647/OBP.0196

Customise

Personalise your copy of this book or design new books using OBP and third-party material. Take chapters or whole books from our published list and make a special edition, a new anthology or an illuminating coursepack. Each customised edition will be produced as a paperback and a downloadable PDF.

Find out more at:

https://www.openbookpublishers.com/section/59/1

Like Open Book Publishers

Follow @OpenBookPublish

Read more at the Open Book Publishers BLOG

You may also be interested in:

The Life and Letters of William Sharp and "Fiona Macleod"
Volume 1: 1855–1894
By William F. Halloran

https://doi.org/10.11647/OBP.0142

A Fleet Street in Every Town
The Provincial Press in England, 1855–1900
By Andrew Hobbs

https://doi.org/10.11647/OBP.0152

Verdi in Victorian London
By Massimo Zicari

https://doi.org/10.11647/OBP.0090

www.ingramcontent.com/pod-product-compliance
Lightning Source LLC
Chambersburg PA
CBHW070043130726
47907CB00018B/1522